FUNDAMENTALS OF MEASUREMENT IN APPLIED RESEARCH

FUNDAMENTALS OF MEASUREMENT IN APPLIED RESEARCH

THERESA A. THORKILDSEN

University of Illinois at Chicago

Boston ▪ New York ▪ San Francisco
Mexico City ▪ Montreal ▪ Toronto ▪ London ▪ Madrid ▪ Munich ▪ Paris
Hong Kong ▪ Singapore ▪ Tokyo ▪ Cape Town ▪ Sydney

Senior Editor: *Arnis E. Burvikovs*
Editorial Assistant: *Kelly Hopkins*
Marketing Manager: *Tara Whorf*
Editorial Production Service: *Chestnut Hill Enterprises, Inc.*
Manufacturing Buyer: *Andrew Turso*
Cover Administrator: *Kristina Mose-Libon*
Electronic Composition: *Omegatype Typography, Inc.*

For related titles and support materials, visit our online catalog at www.ablongman.com.

Between the time Website information is gathered and then published, some sites may have closed. Also, the transcription of URLs can result in typographical errors. The publisher would appreciate being notified of any problems with URLs so that they may be corrected in subsequent editions.

Library of Congress Cataloging-in-Publication Data

Thorkildsen, Theresa A.
    Fundamentals of measurement in applied research / Theresa A. Thorkildsen.
        p. cm.
    Includes bibliographical references and index.
    ISBN 0-205-38066-2 (alk. paper)
    1. Education—Research—Methodology. I. Title.

    LB1028.T449   2005
    370'.7'2—dc22

                                                              2004017934

Printed in the United States of America

10 9 8 7 6 5 4 3 2 1   09 08 07 06 05 04

To all the doctoral students,
too numerous to name, who were thoughtful enough
to point out which of the many assigned measurement
handouts and activities actually helped with their dissertations

CONTENTS

■ ■ ■ ■ ■

CHAPTER 4   Measuring Attitudes   96

CHAPTER 5   Measuring Personality   129

CHAPTER 6   Measuring Intelligence and Abilities   160

CHAPTER 15   Measuring Group Structures and Functioning   444

Most social scientists assume their work is grounded in science rather than politics, religion, or philosophy and place great weight on reliable and valid evidence. Despite this commonality, investigators hold vastly different views on whether science is a quest for truth. Most investigators accept the contingent nature of knowledge and assume research is about inventing meaningful and useful languages for representing human experience. For many, however, truth is at best limited to particular topics or questions, and, more commonly, elusive.

Fundamentals of Measurement in Applied Research was formulated by accepting the contingent nature of knowledge and the belief that conversations about human functioning require a starting place. Our point of entry concerns what to measure and how best to obtain evidence in applied research. Conversations about measurement are highly influenced by existing languages for conveying what is known and questions about the unknown, rendering all measurement decisions inherently controversial.

Concepts of *objectivity, individuality,* and *solidarity* are central to understanding measurement controversies in the social sciences, although discourse communities hold different definitions and values about these concerns. Decisions on whether evidence can be objective affect whether investigators are willing to design standardized tools. Questions of individuality and solidarity reflect the nature of the discourse community for which results are being generated and with whom they are being communicated.

Diverse measurement goals can be represented using somewhat decontextualized vocabulary as well as theory-driven languages. Decontextualized language makes salient differences in how investigators come to conclusions while coordinating objectivity, individuality, and solidarity. Yet, readers are frequently reminded that measurement is valid only in light of a *theoretical framework*. This framework is assumed to contain *concepts, constructs, dimensions,* and *indicants* measurable only in relation to guiding assumptions about their structure and functioning. Inferences about levels of organization, levels of operation, relations, relationships, and change mechanisms are also salient features of theories, but are rarely measured directly. All measurement plans, regardless of the larger goals leading to their design, contain these general ideas, yet most investigators rely on specific theory-driven language to represent their plans.

Several very different approaches to measurement are reviewed in this book, but these distinctive features do not reflect competing paradigms. As will be apparent in the first chapter, *paradigms* are integrated sets of theoretical propositions that guide researchers' interests. They cannot be in competition because they reflect different metaphysical ontologies or assumptions about the nature of being. Measurement techniques are not paradigmatic even though theorists differ in how much emphasis they place on direct experience. It is reasonable, for example, to assert that all social scientists work within the same paradigm and that their paradigm differs from that of philosophers, theologians, or politicians. Nevertheless, social scientists often use different tools and techniques to accomplish their goals. Investigators may change their interests, but it is nearly impossible to falsify an "old" paradigm because old and new typically coexist.

Before delving into the details of different measurement approaches, it may be helpful to learn that mistakes in perspective-taking can emerge when investigators try to integrate social sciences such as psychology, sociology, and anthropology without considering the unique underlying assumptions about the nature of evidence. When experimental results have been used to support purified generalizations, valuable information about individual differences has sometimes been obfuscated. Generalizations from empirically generated sociological facts have sometimes fostered faulty typologies, misused to sort people. Conclusions from case studies have misrepresented cultural norms, principles, and ideologies. For these and other similar reasons, there is strong support for a skeptical stance toward measuring human functioning and a critical need for generating greater awareness of how different measurement procedures have actually been used.

Experienced investigators have learned to avoid some common pitfalls by giving up the simplistic language of *proof* and *confirmation;* they focus more directly on the implications of their findings and consider possible sociopolitical implications of their research. Drawing comparisons across disciplines may offer a richer picture of the overarching systems that dominate human functioning, but remembering that *to validate is to investigate* allows investigators to use caution when developing new languages.

ORGANIZATION OF THIS BOOK

In the spirit of caution, this book is organized using a *toolbox metaphor* that is introduced in Chapter 1 and explored from an ethical perspective in Chapter 2. The toolbox metaphor also guided decisions about what to describe in the remaining chapters.

Chapters 3–8 offer tools that are designed using *psychometric measurement theory.* Tenets of *classical measurement theory* and *item-response theory* are adapted for use in the study of human functioning. These approaches rely heavily on *random sampling theory* in which *observed scores* are assumed to reflect a sample of responses selected from a population of possible indicants, and *true scores* reflect a theoretical ideal for all possible indicants in a population.

There are two common approaches to *random sampling theory. Classical measurement theory,* revised to account for uncontrollable systematic error when measuring human functioning, continues to dominate research. This adaptation in which individuals' obtained scores are compared to a normative standard offers a common means of comparing indicants and drawing inferences about measurement error. Early forms of *psychometric measurement theory* are also contrasted with newer versions of *item-response theory* to illustrate that new tools facilitate estimates of error variance with greater precision.

Generalizability theory is a second type of random sampling theory and is best represented as a more general case of psychometric measurement theory rather than an alternative approach. Distinguishing different types of measurement variance, generalizability theory allows investigators to partition measurement error and estimate its contribution to the distribution of indicants in a sample. A brief introduction is included in Chapter 14, but methods rely heavily on analysis of variance and regression techniques that are beyond the scope of this book.

The middle of the book (Chapters 9–12) focuses on the measurement of change. Such *developmental measurement theory* offers a segue into more interpretive forms of measurement because not all tenets of random sampling theory can be accepted. Change can occur in the structure of concepts to be measured or in daily functioning, and although the causes of change are complex, change is rarely random. Developmentalists endeavor to explain the dynamic nature of human functioning by theorizing about change mechanisms. Measurement chapters emphasize change in the representation of human functioning as it occurs over time, or as an indication of individual differences. As will become apparent in these chapters, most developmentalists remember that useful claims about change mechanisms require variation in research designs as well as measurement.

The final approach to measurement is labeled here as *interpretive measurement theory* (Chapters 13–16). Like developmentalists, interpretive theorists cannot assume that indicants are likely to be randomly distributed in their samples, and they recognize that stability may not be apparent in how tools function. Many interpretive theorists also assume that mechanical scoring and evaluation procedures cannot yield an accurate account of human functioning. They may use mechanical techniques for counting the frequency of indicants, but endeavor to understand the intangible features of how individuals make meaning out of their experiences. These investigators commonly compare representations of human functioning, but treat the evidence as a metaphorical account of experience.

The book is subdivided into *psychometric, developmental,* and *interpretive* sections to highlight central measurement dilemmas while assuming that readers will select those techniques that offer the most cogent means of achieving their goals. All measurement routines are grounded in examples of their use, but this and the natural limitations of each measurement technique pose challenges for generating hard boundaries between sections. Applied researchers who are concerned with finding the best techniques for exploring a particular problem are encouraged to use these examples to refine their theoretical framework and creatively use those measurement techniques that best align with particular theoretical goals.

Ideally, readers will acquire a richer understanding of why investigators often assume there are no firm standards for reliable and valid measurement. Instead, validity and reliability take different forms and functions guided by theoretical assumptions, the nature of variance in how indicants function, and the discourse communities with whom researchers are trying to communicate.

Linking measurement themes to more global research concepts, most *psychometric approaches* weigh objectivity more heavily than individuality or solidarity. These tools are especially useful when investigators have a clear sense of what they hope to measure and can identify a concrete standard or a set of probabilistic norms to which indicants, dimensions, constructs, and concepts might be compared. *Developmental methods* are more useful to researchers interested in how people evolve over time and in describing the developmental systems in which that evolution takes place. Individuality tends to be weighed most heavily because it cannot be assumed that structures or functioning are stable, yet generalizations are contingent on achieving some level of objectivity and solidarity. *Interpretive methods* are most useful when researchers concern themselves with questions of power, authority, and the principles that guide cultures. Questions of solidarity may be the first language of these investigators, but they may also explore less communal themes of objectivity and individuality to defend their assertions. Despite differences in theoretical leanings and assumptions about variance, all measurement processes aim to help investigators find better languages for explaining their own and others' experience.

AUDIENCES FOR THIS BOOK

This book is written for an audience of researchers working in professional schools. The graduate students whose perspectives have informed the design of this book have typically come from education, psychology, nursing, or social work. Learning the skills necessary for thesis research, they found themselves reexamining their experience as practitioners. Like other students who enter professional practice before thinking about conducting research, professionals may need to review or learn basic research skills along with more sophisticated research methods. Those graduate students who have conducted research throughout their career are likely to benefit from the review of basic ideas as well as feel challenged by new directions sampled here.

Pedagogical Features

Sections called *Making Connections,* placed throughout each chapter, are intended to encourage readers to look for evidence of measurement practices in their area of research. Questions offer guidance on how to analyze the existing research readers are hopefully reviewing as they study measurement.

■ ■ ■ ■ ■ ▬▬▬▬▬

LEARNING BY DOING

Learning by Doing activities, designed for each chapter, are posted on the Web, http://www.uic.edu/educ/measure. These activities can be done in classes or as independent projects. In classes, students have included one another as sample participants or otherwise worked in teams to practice central measurement skills. Comparing their own work to published reports, individuals who prefer to work independently have also used some of these activities to strengthen their data collection and reporting skills. Some activities can be linked directly to an answer key or to published reports of articles from which the tools were extracted. Dr. Thorkildsen would also appreciate any feedback or sample projects that might be posted.

ACKNOWLEDGMENTS

The intellectual struggles of many doctoral students with a wide range of agendas have informed the design of this book. Over a decade of teaching measurement, I met many students who engaged in honest inquiry, retaining an open-minded approach to learning material that was both challenging and sometimes antithetical to their deeply held values. Each of those students has confirmed or challenged central measurement concepts in the course of thesis work. I am especially grateful to Becky Greenberg, Fred Klonsky, John Lapham, and Paula Smith who challenged their professor to think out of the box without forgetting to engage in their own diligent learning. Jim Houston has also provided a wide range of helpful suggestions and thoughtfully labeled many ideas students are likely to find confusing. Sharon Manjack and Sandy Schwartz offered helpful editorial feedback when I was too bleary-eyed to see the gibberish left in my writing.

I am also thankful for the many informal conversations and thoughtful responses by individuals who had no incentive to offer their time. Veronica Manning, Ed Flores, and the staff at Jamoch's Caffe offered indispensable clerical support, kept my printers well-stocked with ink and paper, and drew forth my sense of humor through the tedious parts of the writing process. Informal conversations with Ivor Pritchard, Chris Pappas, Bill Schubert, and Steve Tozer focused on common struggles with ethics in research. Mavis Donahue, Dan Hart, Karl Hennig, Ruth Pearl, and Larry Walker offered helpful suggestions for differentiating the measurement of personality, development, discourse, and groups when the overlap among tools produced incomprehensibly dense writing. Valuable editorial advice came from Arnis Burvikovs and Christine Lyons at Allyn and Bacon as well as Sandra Graham, and Fred Erickson. I want to thank the following reviewers for their helpful suggestions: Linlin Irene Chen, University of Houston, Downtown; Marie Kraska, Auburn University; Todd Little, University of Kansas; Larry C. Loesch, University of Florida; and Mary Katherine Mastruserio Reynolds, University of Wisconsin Eau Claire. E-mail or lunchtime conversations with Mavis Donahue, Larry Loesch, Martin Tangora, and Harry Wolcott improved the pedagogical features of the book. Tom Berndt, George Karabatsos, Carol Myford, and Ev Smith provided useful suggestions for additional readings and Web sites.

It has been a pleasure to engage in so many rich measurement discussions with these and other supportive colleagues. I am continually reminded of the centrality of trust and honesty to the measurement enterprise and feel lucky to have found colleagues who take seriously these virtues.

CHAPTER ONE

THE ROLE OF MEASUREMENT IN RESEARCH

Most individuals have more experience with measurement than they are willing to acknowledge when beginning their first research courses. If you have any doubt about your vast knowledge, think about your role in the following situations.

- To enroll in a university, students are required to take at least one formal exam to reveal their qualifications for particular programs or placement within a program.
- Application materials involve a portfolio of evidence that students have the necessary prerequisites for admission.
- While walking on campus, students look at those around them to determine if they are appropriately dressed and if they are heading toward the right class.
- When searching for a study group, students interview their classmates to identify who is and is not confident about mastering the material.

Somewhere in your educational history, you have probably participated in these types of events and recognize that different forms of measurement facilitated decision making. You may have assessed others' qualifications or had your own abilities evaluated to determine a personal course of action. To make such judgments, general standards or criteria for success were used in the design of assessment tools. Thoughts, actions, and reactions of individuals were compared to relevant standards regardless of whether numbers were used to record such decisions.

Despite your skill at informally measuring everyday events, it would not be surprising if you were uncomfortable equating these forms of measurement with those commonly used in research. In assessment situations, individuals' performance is compared to a predetermined standard. Hopefully, those who select assessment tools match particular standards to available measurement techniques, choosing the most appropriate methods for making classifications. Regardless of an individual's performance, standards or evaluation criteria usually remain stable. Because assessment tools are calibrated against a known set of standards, the value of these tools is constrained by existing theoretical frameworks. The goal of such measurement is to determine if an individual's performance adheres to known criteria.

Measurement in research situations does not always involve known standards. To support new theories, researchers endeavor to invent new knowledge and classification criteria. Their generalizations invariably alter existing standards and ideas about how to organize particular types of information. Assessment tools may be used to verify what is known, but new tools are also designed to challenge existing theories. Consider some of the following ideas that were once assumed to be facts, but have been soundly refuted with evidence to the contrary.

- Babies are born with their eyes closed because their eyes are not fully developed.
- Telling low-achieving students to work harder will improve their motivation.
- Children are unable to think about the fairness of institutional practices because they do not yet know the difference between right and wrong.
- Eskimos have 32 different words for snow.

Each of these ideas has been promoted by researchers who were unaware of reliable and valid evidence to the contrary. When most babies were born with their eyes closed, for example, mothers were also given drugs during childbirth that passed into the infant's bloodstream. It often took several days for the effects of these drugs to fully wear off and for the infant to become fully awakened to the outside world. Studies in infant vision confirmed that babies' eyes were very well developed at birth, and as mothers avoided drugs or were given less invasive therapies, infants' eyes quickly opened to see the new world they had entered. Measurement was used both to generate the initial false belief and to identify the misconceptions underlying such beliefs, but the existence of a predetermined standard had to be questioned in the process. Had researchers been constrained in their use of measurement tools, they could not have generated new knowledge about infant vision and the effects of drug use in childbirth.

Although researchers typically question common beliefs and the standards used to support those beliefs, measurement is nevertheless rule-governed. Rules used in research may be similar to those used in assessment, but notable differences are also apparent. In this book, I will introduce measurement assumptions common to research and assessment, relentlessly calling attention to the challenges of designing tools for generating new knowledge. Reports of the virtues of particular measurement techniques will be balanced with talk of their limitations. When evaluating the technologies of measurement, the elegance and beauty of particular tools as well as some of their inadequacies and biases usually become evident. When theoretical positions are considered, the resulting information, thought experiments, and measurement tools lead to multiple conceptions of when evidence is strong enough to support theoretical assertions.

Chapters are organized in the same way as a toolbox. Each tool has its intended purpose, but researchers who understand fundamental measurement concepts are able to see other uses. Screwdrivers and hammers have an intended purpose, but are also used in novel ways. Similarly, when used in research, most measurement techniques are rarely standardized to such a degree that they inhibit the generation of new knowledge. Researchers are as excited about known sources of variance as they are about stability in how particular instruments function. This is apparent in Slosson's statement about his IQ test, "We should not ask a pint to fill a quart, but we should ask that a quart give its full measure." Like most researchers, Slosson could see value in identifying variance and designing new tools that are sensitive to the characteristics being measured.

Determining the quality of evidence hinges on the degree to which investigators establish a clear measurement purpose and an overall sense of what they would like to accomplish with their project. Obvious as this might sound, a great source of measurement error in social science research can be attributed to a lack of planning and goal setting. Individuals are not always aware of the degree to which they expect a proverbial screwdriver to do the work of a hammer. Measuring individual differences in people and the social forces that influence their behavior is intangible, making it easy to assume that a tool designed for one purpose can be creatively applied to another purpose without recalibration.

UNDERSTANDING THE STRUCTURE OF RESEARCH

Before launching into details of how particular tools are typically designed and their use validated, some essential distinctions between questions of measurement and other aspects of the research process are important to acknowledge. In a typical piece of research, investigators distinguish five levels of decision making:

- Theories and questions in need of investigation
- The organization of a study
- The tools used to record ideas
- Approaches to testing research questions
- Conclusions about the viability of particular assumptions

To understand differences in these levels, researchers usually differentiate the processes of *theory construction, design, measurement, analysis,* and *drawing conclusions* (Figure 1.1). In this chapter, I will outline some of the common similarities and differences associated with these levels of inquiry to illustrate where measurement falls within the

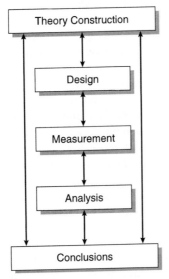

FIGURE 1.1 Levels of Organization in a Research Study.

structure of research. To maximize clarity, these representations are simplified to highlight various levels of decision making without going into too much detail on the intricacies of each one. Once these differences are available, fundamental measurement questions should seem more obvious.

■ ■ ■ ■ ■

MAKING CONNECTIONS

Find a research study in your area of interest and identify all five components. How did the authors represent the theoretical framework? Is the design clearly distinguished? Identify information on the qualities of each measurement tool. How was the evidence summarized and interpreted? Were the conclusions supported with adequate evidence?

Distinguishing Philosophical, Theoretical, and Measurement Assumptions

Regardless of whether investigators identify the philosophical traditions from which their questions emerge, all research is comprised of at least one set of philosophical beliefs about the nature of research and the purpose of scientific investigation. Investigators who participated in debates about the value of qualitative and quantitative research, for example, have become more aware of multiple philosophies of science and definitions of theory. The debates highlighted variability in philosophical assumptions about the nature of "reality" and which levels of analysis are most highly valued (see Burman, 1997; Eisner, 1992, 1997; Erickson, 1992; Kuhn, 1992; Popkewitz, 1992; Rabinowitz & Weseen, 1997; Schrag, 1992a, 1992b). These debates helped new researchers understand that all forms of science are value-laden and that choosing a discourse community is an important step in scholarship.

Unfortunately, these debates also generated confusion when generalizations about the validity of theories were associated with data. Issues of philosophy and measurement were confounded in sometimes overly simplistic ways. Investigators who focused on *hermeneutic* or *qualitative research* were inclined to emphasize philosophical differences in their approach, but also rejected the use of numbers. Contrary to these beliefs, "qualitative" data often involve the translation of ideas into numbers. That is, even if numbers do not represent magnitude, they often serve as symbolic representations of categories or as indicators for how often events are observed. In contrast, self-proclaimed *positivists* who defended *quantitative research* tended to focus too much on numerical representations of evidence without considering the multiple levels of inference that invariably occur in measurement. Preoccupied with defending the value of statistics, they failed to acknowledge that all numerical representations involve interpretation. Investigators who use numbers still decide which indicants are measurable and in doing so draw inferences about the phenomenon to be evaluated. Given this overlap, why do such debates persist?

Common Definitions.   One reason debates about the nature of evidence persist is that philosophical, theoretical, and measurement issues are easily confused once investigators develop a high degree of proficiency; many investigators can accurately move in and out of these forms of thought without taking time to label their assumptions. Even experts benefit from occasional reminders of the basic distinctions between these levels of inquiry. The Oxford English Dictionary defines **philosophy** as *"the use of reason and argument in seeking truth and knowledge of reality, especially of the causes and nature of things* and the principles governing existence, the material universe, perception of physical phenomenon, and *human behavior* (1990, p. 894; italics added). Social scientists are primarily interested in human functioning. They regularly dispute the existence of "reality," and differ in which levels of generality they emphasize when representing target concepts. Regardless of disciplinary norms, however, most social scientists accept multiple forms of evidence and logic in the quest for new knowledge. Table 1.1 samples common philosophical approaches to social science research that are sometimes used in combination as well as in isolation.

At another level, *theory* is defined as "a supposition or system of ideas explaining something, esp. one based on general principles independent of the particular things to be explained" (1990, p. 1266). Social scientists strive to explain common patterns in how humans function in the world, but rarely devote energy to defining universal laws. Their system of ideas regularly undergoes revision, and can serve as temporally valid explanations for everyday events. Whereas philosophy is a quest, theory involves explanation. Table 1.2 contains the common theoretical frameworks used to explore human functioning.

Measurement becomes important when investigators imagine which features of a problem are included in the explanatory process. More specifically, **measurement** is "the act or instance of measuring" with the verb taking on multiple meanings. The simplest definition of *measuring* is to "ascertain the extent or quantity of (a thing) by comparison with a fixed unit or with an object of known size" (1990, p. 736). Researchers in the social sciences dispute the nature of "fixed units or objects of known size" because there is rarely an absolute absence of the constructs being measured. It is impossible, for example, to find an absence of intelligence in human life. Understanding an abstract construct like intelligence involves imagining its concrete features, and measurement involves the comparison of such concrete features with other known entities.

To solve measurement dilemmas, social scientists often rely on a rather restricted set of measurement rules when identifying the correspondence between actual observations or responses and symbolic representations. Measurement tools are calibrated by clearly defining concrete features of the constructs to be measured and aligning those definitions with an appropriate scale. Scales are reliable if they offer an accurate and stable means of assessing variability in the measured characteristics. If data are to be considered evidence for later use in theory construction or to exemplify philosophical claims, each variable or construct should be clearly represented.

Variability in Rules of Evidence. Obviously, the definitions of philosophy and theory are much broader in scope than is the definition of *measurement,* yet all of these definitions contain rules of evidence. At the *philosophical level,* researchers usually identify abstract relationships among theories, evidence, and inferences. At the *theoretical level,* they offer concrete representations of the same kinds of information. At the *measurement level,* investigators further narrow their focus to imagine the characteristics of each form of evidence. Some measurement tools offer better evidence than others for certain kinds of philosophical analyses, and some forms of philosophy cannot be measured at all. With

TABLE 1.1   Sample Philosophical Approaches Underlying Research

PHILOSOPHICAL APPROACH	DEFINITION
Constructive-empiricism	Science is divided into observation statements and theory statements. Observations can be evaluated for truth, but should be treated with skepticism and coordinated with other kinds of evidence.
Contextualism	Knowledge is seen as relative to the historical and cultural contexts in which it is generated.
Deconstructionism	There is no starting point from which external reality can be confirmed, but there are limitless opportunities for fresh perspectives on experience.
Determinism	Every event is assumed to have a cause that is likely to be associated with antecedent states.
Empiricism	Knowledge is tied directly to sensory contents of consciousness or to other expressed classes of experience. Other forms of knowledge are assumed to be nonexistent.
Functionalism	Mental states can be defined by knowing their causes and their effects on other mental states or behavior.
Humanism	Emphasis is placed on human dignity, welfare, and ability to acquire understanding without help.
Phenomenology	The object of study is the basis for generating constructs. Human functioning reflects the structure and essence of experience with particular entities.
Positivism	The highest form of knowledge is assumed to be a description of sensory phenomena. Truth about reality serves as a regulative ideal to strive for, but is unlikely to be identified.
Postmodernism	A playful acceptance of transient surface characteristics, superficial styles, and irony in reaction against commitments to objectivity and scientific truth.
Pragmatism	The meaning of ideas is assumed to be the same as the practical effects of adopting those ideas and putting them into practice.
Rationalism	Unaided reason can lead to the acquisition and justification of knowledge and is preferred over sensory experience.
Relativism	Truth is assumed to be in the eye of the beholder and there can be no universal understanding of reality.
Utilitarianism	A vision of the good precedes any determination of what is right. When the goal is to maximize human functioning, happiness often represents the good.

Note: Philosophers are likely to dispute the inclusion of some of these categories, but selected categories reflect common assumptions embedded in various theoretical research traditions. These categories are not mutually exclusive or exhaustive.

TABLE 1.2   Common Theoretical Agendas in Social Science Research

AGENDA	DESCRIPTION
Behaviorism	Study behavior and its causes.
Deconstructionist theories	Question the validity of all foundational assumptions.
Chaos theories	Find order in seemingly random events.
Critical theories	Label the effects of power hierarchies and subjective experience during particular historical periods.
Ecological theories	Study how individuals accomplish goals through specific behaviors in particular environments.
Ethnographic theories	Study cultures and how individuals' behavior is regulated by their environments.
Hermeneutic theories	Construct theories such that one element can only be understood in terms of the meaning of others or of the whole.
Heuristics	Study an individual's intense experience of a phenomenon.
Interpretive analytic theories	Explore how forces of history and power offer positive direction to human functioning.
Linguistic theories	Study language and its role in communication.
Personality theories	Explore individuals' characteristics and the phenomena of personhood.
Social cognitive theories	Study psychological functioning in social contexts.
Symbolic interactionism	Question how symbols and understandings give meaning to human interactions.
Systems theories	Identify how people and contexts reflect different levels of a common system.

these relationships in mind, questions about the value of evidence hinge on the relevance of data to the process of theory-building as well as on the qualities of the data itself.

Inferential Processes.   To make matters even more challenging, theory-building differs depending on one's philosophical assumptions about research, and measurement decisions are influenced by these agendas. Researchers who rely on experimental techniques often adhere to rationalist assumptions that human feelings, thoughts, and actions follow predictable patterns (see, for example, Kuhn, 1970; Popper, 1999). Those who rely on hermeneutic methods often adhere to *phenomenological, ethnographic, critical theory, interpretive analytic,* or *deconstructionist* assumptions about how knowledge is a meaning-making enterprise (see Cherryholmes, 1988). Although more elaborate representations of the differences in these systems of thought will be introduced along with common measurement tools, it is helpful to be consistently reminded of the different purposes associated with experimental and nonexperimental research.

Use of *experimental techniques* is common when investigators are striving to predict and control variance and construct universalistic theories of human behavior; they are not useful for determining the meaning individuals make of their experience. *Hermeneutic methods* of comparing and contrasting ideas are commonly used to describe events and generate highly contextual theories; they are not useful for validating universal laws. Philosophical assumptions about which forms of knowledge are of most worth lead individuals to value different kinds of evidence and conclusions. Not surprisingly, investigators' choices of measurement techniques vary to accommodate these differences. Imagine the topic of understanding student achievement and how philosophical and theoretical assumptions call attention to different facets of this issue (Table 1.3). A seemingly straightforward issue becomes quickly complex when considered from multiple perspectives.

Despite their different reasons for seeking knowledge, investigators rely on similar approaches to theory-building when defining relationships between philosophical assumptions and evidence. Theories differ in the phenomenon to be explained and the degree of specificity accepted as adequate, but researchers usually rely on relatively few forms of logic to build their arguments (see, for example, Burisch, 1984). Theorists construct a framework for their ideas externally, deductively, inductively, or using a combination of these logical approaches (Table 1.4). It is probably easier to rely consistently on one form of logic, but respect for evidence inevitably thwarts even the best-laid plans; different forms of evidence lead most social scientists to move between systems of logic when striving to describe or explain human functioning.

TABLE 1.3   Questions Reflecting a Sample of Theoretical Agendas

AGENDA	QUESTION
TOPIC: UNDERSTANDING SCHOOL ACHIEVEMENT	
Behaviorism	How can achievement test scores be increased?
Critical theory	Who has power in achievement settings and who is oppressed?
Ecological theory	What environmental structures can maximize students' achievement?
Ethnographic theory	What do the cultures of school look like and how does achievement vary across contexts?
Hermeneutic theory	In school, how do teachers and students make meaning out of the curriculum?
Linguistic theory	How does the language on achievement tests affect the scores students attain?
Personality theory	What are the characteristics of the students who score well on tests?
Social–cognitive theory	How does students' engagement in school affect their performance?
Symbolic interactionism	What do the scores on an achievement test symbolize and how do people interpret them?
Systems theory	How does the combination of a person's physiology, personality, social–cognitive abilities, and intelligence affect performance in school?

TABLE 1.4 Types of Logic Used in Theory Construction

LOGIC	DESCRIPTION
External logic	Start with characteristics outside the realm of the research problem and identify the distinguishing features of persons with that characteristic, using evidence.
Deductive logic	Start with an explanatory law or theoretical framework and generate predictions about specific relationships among dimensions of the framework.
Inductive logic	Start with patterns in evidence and particular instances of a phenomenon and use that information to generate a more general explanatory law or theoretical model.
Interactionist logic	Combine two or more of the procedures associated with external, deductive, and inductive logic.

As different kinds of tools are introduced in the following chapters, I will elaborate on some of the distinctions between philosophical, theoretical, and measurement concerns. By the end of this book, you should have a richer sense of how the calibration of similar tools is adjusted to fulfill different philosophical purposes. Measurement tools are independent of theoretical and philosophical paradigms, yet all tools are evaluated in light of these concerns. To illustrate diversity in how investigators coordinate the quest, explanation, and verification of knowledge, this book is organized into three sections. Sections highlight how *psychometric, developmental,* and *interpretive* measurement agendas involve similar principles of measurement, yet the rules generated from these principles reflect different philosophical assumptions about the nature of inquiry.

MAKING CONNECTIONS

Find a theoretical paper in your field. Try determining which philosophical traditions are associated with the theory you selected. After identifying the variables that were measured, try to imagine how investigators came to their framework. Does the theoretical paper rely on external, deductive, inductive, or interactionist forms of logic? Did investigators assume that findings would eventually reveal stable truths or general laws? Did investigators assume that theories are pragmatic networks of statements about current evidence? Did the theory emphasize discourse between researchers and participants?

Distinguishing Research Design and Measurement

How do researchers go about finding an answer once they have defined a question and reasons for exploring that question? Regardless of their philosophical and theoretical assumptions, most investigators construct a *research design* to draw relationships between theoretical ideas, particular forms of evidence, and conclusions. Some investigators rely on *ex post facto designs* when they are uninterested in replicating findings or cannot manipulate variables. Most researchers, however, spend a great deal of time planning their research, imagining the strengths of their plans, and looking for better ways to accomplish their goals before collecting data. The product of these deliberations is the research design. Sample categories of designs can be found in Table 1.5.

TABLE 1.5   Common Types of Research Design in Social Science Research

DESIGN	DESCRIPTION
USING PSYCHOMETRIC TOOLS	
Experimental designs	A design for determining the influence of a treatment on randomly selected participants who are randomly assigned to groups.
Quasi-experimental designs	A design for determining the influence of a treatment on participants who could not be randomly selected from a population.
Correlational designs	Designs for exploring the associations between two or more variables.
Survey designs	Designs for sampling attitudes, personality characteristics, or behavior using questionnaires or other recording devices.
USING DEVELOPMENTAL TOOLS	
Structural-evaluation designs	Designs used to identify common physical, psychological, and behavioral components and how they are coordinated to direct human functioning.
Time-series designs	Designs used to identify common intrapersonal components and how they are coordinated with one another.
Diversity-focused designs	Designs typically integrating correlational and survey information to draw conclusions about diversity in human functioning.
USING INTERPRETIVE TOOLS	
Grounded theory designs	Designs for identifying processes, actions, or interactions at a broad, conceptual level.
Ethnographic designs	Designs for exploring shared patterns of behavior, thoughts, and feelings in a particular cultural context.
Narrative designs	Designs for offering a thick description of individual lives.
Action research designs	Designs used by practitioners to gather and analyze data to inform daily practice.
USING A COMBINATION OF TOOLS	
Mixed method designs	Designs for combining a wide variety of measurement techniques to draw logically consistent conclusions.
Ex post facto designs	Designs generated after data have been collected.

Confusing issues of design and measurement is easy because both involve similar kinds of research dilemmas. Design consists of a research plan and structure for whatever investigation is conceived to answer a research question (see Kerlinger & Lee, 2000). The *research plan* consists of the overall process by which theoretical assumptions are related to conclusions, and may involve multiple studies. The *structure of the research problem* is the framework used to relate parts of the plan to the conclusions of a particular study. Similarly, measurement consists of a *plan* for each variable and a *structure* for how the components of each variable are related to one another.

Identifying a Design and Its Constraints. After articulating theoretical assumptions, most investigators construct designs by generating a series of predictions, questions, or hypotheses. They determine how many studies to conduct, how many participants are required for each study, and who should participate. Investigators also determine which variables will be measured, techniques for measurement, and predicted relationships among variables. In the planning phase of a project, investigators often imagine how adequately the structure of a study facilitates the generation of evidence necessary for supporting theoretical claims. They typically look for known threats to the validity of a study and try to minimize those that are likely to undermine the quality of evidence.

Despite the seemingly simple rule of eliminating threats to validity, this is rarely easy to accomplish, partly because one researcher's theoretical confound may be another's topic of inquiry. Furthermore, threats to validity are more and less well-defined depending on researchers' philosophical and theoretical agendas. When conducting experimental research to predict and control human functioning, for example, investigators try to eliminate as many confounding sources of variance as possible to maximize the strength of their causal assertions. Table 1.6 outlines many of the common threats that investigators think about when evaluating the quality of experimental designs, but, as you can imagine, it would be impossible to design one study that eliminates all the included threats.

You may notice that some of the categories listed as threats in Table 1.6 actually form the foundation for disciplines within the social sciences. Maturation, for example, is a primary topic of inquiry for investigators interested in human development. History is central to strong ethnography. What one investigator might see as a form of selection bias in the identification of participants, another might assume reflects the identification of expert informants.

Some Qualities of a Strong Design. Regardless of a researcher's agenda, strong designs involve the maximization of objectivity, accuracy, and economy by offering theoretically rational structures for exploring relationships among variables. Most complex studies also yield unpredictable findings, sometimes necessitating revisions in a theoretical framework. In addition to finding support for a theory, investigators usually try to rule out alternative explanations for particular findings. The more well-developed a theoretical framework, the easier it becomes to construct a strong design. Strong designs facilitate direct comparisons between predicted and alternative theories with greater accuracy when information gleaned early in the research process informs later decisions.

In constructing a research design, most investigators articulate a plan for finding answers to their research questions while prohibiting other forms of variance from intruding

TABLE 1.6   **Factors Jeopardizing the Validity of an Experimental Study**

CATEGORY	SAMPLE QUESTIONS
THREATS TO INTERNAL VALIDITY	
History	Were the data collected at an unusual point in history? Is it possible that some world or local event occurred between when pretest and posttest data were collected that might influence posttest scores?
Maturation	Could the findings be attributed to internal changes within the individual that are unrelated to the research question?
Selection bias	Is there a bias in how participants are selected for the study or in how they are assigned to groups?
Statistical regression	Is it possible that findings are caused by the fact that extreme scores are likely to regress toward the mean by chance rather than experimental factors?
Testing	Has participants' experience with the measure resulted in improvements that are unrelated to the research questions?
Instrumentation	Is the calibration of the measurement tool likely to change over the course of the data collection process?
Selection-maturation interaction	Is it possible that the findings are attributable to an interaction of selection and factors such as maturation rather than to the treatment variables?
Resentful demoralization	Did the respondents feel so demoralized about the treatment they received that the results were influenced?
Experimental mortality	Does attrition in the sample influence the results? Are these rates different for treatment and control groups in ways that affect the findings? Are there known characteristics that caused attrition differences?
THREATS TO EXTERNAL VALIDITY	
Selection-treatment interaction	Is there a selection bias that favors the treatment group over the control group or vice versa?
Diffusion of treatments, compensatory equalization of treatments, or compensatory rivalry	Is it possible that the different groups were not treated as differently as the investigators imagined, that members of the control group were exposed to the treatment, or that members of the control group applied more effort because they knew they were in a study?
Multiple treatment interaction	Is it possible that there are multiple treatments occurring simultaneously that affect the outcome?
Ambiguity about the direction of the causal inference	Is it possible that the dependent variables were likely to cause variation in the independent variables rather than the other way around?

Note: The basic question used to establish this set of questions concerns the degree to which findings can be attributed to the intended variables or whether there are methodological confounds that influence the results. Campbell and Stanley (1963, pp. 5–6) offered this list in another form.

on the results. They compare experimental or nonexperimental designs, manipulating variables in the former case and relying on intact classifications in the latter. Most investigators hope to *explain anticipated variance* relevant to their theoretical claims. They label different levels of inference such as that apparent between indicants of each variable or between measures of multiple variables.

Investigators also try to *control extraneous variance* attributable to factors unrelated to the question at hand, minimizing error variance in the design as well as in measurement tools. Unknown variance is often controlled by taking advantage of all opportunities to randomly select or assign participants to conditions. *Random selection* of participants can lead to unequal groups, but the resulting error is assumed to be unrelated to the question under consideration; ideally, uncontrolled error would be randomly distributed across individuals. *Random assignment* of individuals to groups in experimental research is sometimes used to ensure that a study begins with uncontrolled error that is randomly distributed across groups. Known sources of variance are assumed to be equally distributed across groups at the beginning of a study. If that is evident and unequal variance is found at the end of an experiment, it seems reasonable to assume that the experimental manipulation caused the difference in outcome. When groups are unequal at the onset, investigators interested in the effects of a particular treatment often manipulate features of their design to account for the initial inequality.

In nonexperimental research, variables are not manipulated and investigators do not draw causal inferences to explain patterns. Investigators are interested in general descriptions of normative patterns or thick descriptions of lives in progress and living cultures. If participants could be randomly selected from a larger population of qualified individuals, some sources of extraneous variance might be minimized even when experimental designs are theoretically and ethically problematic.

Parallels in Measurement.　　These approaches to strengthening a design are parallel to methods for calibrating a measurement tool. Minimizing uncontrollable error and extraneous variance is a goal of both design and measurement phases of a study, and researchers usually understand that they are unable to entirely prevent such problems. At the design level, most investigators are preoccupied with how multiple variables are related to one another and strive to constrain the effects of variables that might pose confounds in their explanations. For example, when a design includes participants from two age groups, but the participants from each group are selected from different educational tracks, an ability by age group confound is present. Investigators will not be able to determine if the difference between the two groups is attributable to age or academic ability.

At the measurement level, investigators are preoccupied with representing each variable as accurately as possible and strive to exclude characteristics of a variable that involve overlapping components. The term *reliability* is used to reflect this concern with stability and accuracy in how a tool functions. *Validity* involves the extent to which a tool measures what it purports to measure. Tools can be reliable without being valid, but all valid tools are generally reliable. Levels of inference enter the measurement enterprise when investigators combine indicants to form scales or aggregate scales to represent a set of constructs. At the top of Figure 1.2, for example, similarly worded items are combined to show an internal

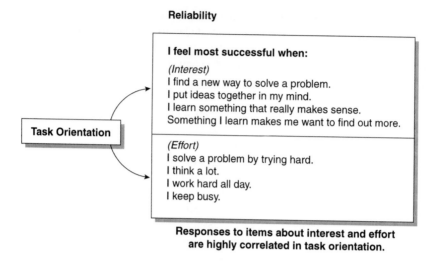

FIGURE 1.2   Exploring Reliability and Validity within a Single Measure.

consistency in two aspects of task orientation. The bottom of the figure illustrates how comparisons among related scales can reflect internal validity between two distinct scales of a larger construct.

When measurement is the focus of an investigator's attention, there is a preoccupation with the calibration of particular tools, but, as with design, it is impossible to obtain error-free measurement. Some forms of error cannot be identified and investigators usually rely on estimates calculated from simulation studies to anticipate such error. Other forms of error become known to investigators when tools are calibrated against known standards or once analyses are shared with others. Identifiable error is apparent when investigators inadvertently include items or scales with confounds that they could not anticipate prior to using the measure.

In one of my studies on students' motivation, for example, the item "I feel most successful when my work is chosen as an example for others," contained a confound we had not anticipated (Figure 1.3). Some adolescents placed an emphasis on the information that might be acquired from examples whereas others focused on the degree to which students might seem superior to their peers. This item did not help us discriminate a disposition toward task mastery from a disposition toward ego-enhancement. Had I retained the item in my measurement tools, I would have introduced a known source of error that would eventually distort my findings.

For each variable, establishing the *stability* in how data points are combined and *accuracy* in the interpretation of each data point is necessary for measuring anticipated variance and minimizing error. Using theoretical and empirical information, investigators can identify forms of error that can be minimized, even though other forms of uncontrollable error typically remain in all tools. At the design phase, investigators sometimes use multiple measures of each variable to maximize the validity of conclusions and control unpredictable forms of error. Similarly, investigators may use multiple indicants of the same construct on a single tool to estimate and eliminate as many sources of error as they can identify.

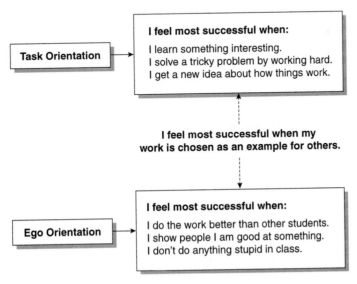

FIGURE 1.3 Comparison of a Problematic Item to Theoretical Constructs.

In summary, it is not surprising to find confusion among the measurement and design aspects of a study because the two levels of thought often involve parallel goals. In one case, investigators are concerned with relationships among variables and in the other they are concerned with relationships among observations or responses to items for measuring each variable. When extraneous variance and error intrude on both design and measurement, the integrity of the study as a whole is called into question. Logically, however, if the accuracy, stability, and validity of measurement tools are called into question, even the strongest design is unlikely to yield theoretically valuable information.

MAKING CONNECTIONS

Find an empirical study in your field of interest. Identify the research plan and structure. (This information can be in the introduction and/or methods sections of a paper.) Also try to identify each variable in the design and determine how it was measured. Was the study experimental or nonexperimental? How many variables were in the design? How many times was each variable measured? Did the authors write a section on the design of the study or did you have to find it by looking at the results section of the paper? Did the authors report information on the measurement properties of each variable?

Distinguishing Methods of Analysis, Interpretation, and Measurement

The design stage of an investigation involves planning, and measurement carries that planning to the collection of data, but how do investigators draw inferences to answer their research questions? Moving to the analysis phase of an investigation, most researchers look for opportunities to reduce the number of data points or *indicants* collected during the measurement phase. They look for methods of classifying, ordering, manipulating, and summarizing findings into a form that can be linked to features of the research question. Whereas the measurement phase involves verifying the accuracy and stability of tools for recording and combining indicants, the analysis phase involves combining variables in the search for theoretical meaning. Different forms of measurement involve levels of inference that associate indicants with the concepts being measured. In the analysis phase, investigators usually draw another layer of inferences about how the resulting variables can be combined. Researchers may use statistical tools or rely on logical comparisons, but analyses are predicated on the assumption that variables are measured with adequate precision.

It is easy to confuse those features of measurement and analysis that involve the manipulation of numbers. In measurement, investigators look for patterns in data to determine if they align with definitions of each variable and if participants responded in relatively consistent ways. Investigators often begin with a blueprint or set of assumptions about the variable to be measured. Using data, they verify that each tool functions with a maximum degree of reliability. Those variables measured with accuracy and stability are typically carried forth to the analysis phase and used to explore research questions. Ideally, investigators also confirm that measurement tools offer a balanced and fair representation of the concepts being explored before combining them to test theoretical claims.

In the analysis phase, investigators rely on a number of devices for combining variables. They often use inferential statistics to compare obtained patterns among variables to the probability that results could be simply attributed to chance. This allows investigators to determine if the variance in their evidence deviates from a generic distribution significantly enough to warrant interpretation. Some investigators also rely on categorical analysis, looking for patterns in the proportions or frequency with which responses occur. In such analyses, comparisons between obtained findings and probability estimates are typically used to verify the significance of particular patterns. Significant patterns may differ across groups or over time, but comparing one set of ideas with another is essential for generating new knowledge. A small number of researchers avoid labeling patterns in their data and rely on anecdotes to represent their evidence. In such work, levels of inference may be labeled, but only a few illustrative examples are recorded.

Challenges.   The nature of the research questions posed and designs utilized raise different kinds of dilemmas when investigators are analyzing their findings. For research designs that depend on discourse between participants and researchers, for example, the verification of accuracy and stability may involve a subset of data points selected from a larger pool of responses. *Ex post facto* designs are commonly used in such work and the researcher's perceptions and beliefs serve as an important tool for prioritizing events. Features of the argument being proposed are used to help investigators decide how to classify and summarize particular events. Some investigators using such descriptive designs reject the idea that they are working with data at all and may avoid thinking carefully about measurement. More often, investigators who want findings to adequately support generalizations report stable patterns that can be identified by others. They assume that accurate reporting is a feature of qualitative judgments as well as quantitative judgments and may offer both kinds of evidence to support their theoretical claims.

Regardless of the theoretical paradigms being adopted, measurement and design issues are tightly coordinated in the analysis phase of a study. When the intended structure of a research design accounts for a significant percentage of variance in the analysis, researchers draw theoretically relevant inferences with confidence. If a relatively small percentage of variance is accounted for, confounding variables and error variance may offer a better explanation for the findings. To maximize the potential for a study to yield theoretically useful results, investigators strive for precision in how the study is conducted and how particular variables are measured. They usually strive to maximize the reliability of each measurement tool while accepting the inevitability of error. Many investigators also explore the degree to which measured indicants validly represent constructs under consideration.

Poor planning invariably has a snowball effect in any study. It can be frustrating to learn that error grows progressively greater throughout the analysis and interpretation phases. This occurs because, when two variables are measured independently (a requirement for most statistical tools), each contains two forms of error. You may remember that one form is likely to be known to investigators and the other is unknown. Neither type of error, whether large or small, can be completely eliminated. When the two variables are later compared to one another, a third level of uncontrollable error (known and unknown) is also introduced. As additional variables are added, error is also added exponentially. When investigators strive to maximize accuracy and stability in how each tool is calibrated, they can find the best possible evidence for verifying theoretical claims.

■ ■ ■ ■ ■

MAKING CONNECTIONS

After finding a data-based study in your area of interest, try distinguishing information on measurement and analysis. How were the parts of the research question measured? How were relationships among the variables tested? What did investigators do to minimize error variance? Do you see any confounding variables or alternative explanations? Were the inferences supported by the findings?

Disseminating Findings

Although at this point it seems reasonable to assume that you are not ready to disseminate research findings, planning ahead can save time later in the process. Knowing some of the steps authors consider at the publishing stage before designing a new study may raise key questions about why new research is conducted and how investigators find like-minded scholars with whom to share information. As will become fully apparent by the end of this book, the process of drawing inferences about human functioning differs considerably depending on the philosophical, theoretical, design, and measurement assumptions prevalent within each discourse community. Levels of generality and inference differ across the social sciences and the means by which ideas are defended reflects that variability. Learning to write about the findings of research is quite challenging in the face of such diversity. Nevertheless, a few general tips for writing can be generated and are outlined in Table 1.7.

IS A NEW STUDY ALWAYS NECESSARY?

Seasoned investigators try to remember that they are part of a discourse community when designing their research. Becoming a producer of new knowledge inevitably requires effortful attempts to identify a target audience and the salient assumptions that draw community members together. Investigators identify key people to talk with, even if such talk occurs only in the context of published papers. Where do new scholars acquire this information?

The importance of reading existing research and looking for seminal assumptions cannot be overemphasized and is no doubt central to the courses that are part of your academic studies. Discovering new ideas is pleasurable in its own right, but researchers who take shortcuts when reviewing existing research can easily fall into the trap of rediscovering ideas that are already taken for granted in their field. It can be very frustrating to go to the trouble of conducting new research, only to find a series of similar papers already available. Reading widely and deeply within an area can save inordinate amounts of time and energy. As literature is mastered through critical evaluation of the strengths and limitations of existing research, gaps begin to emerge in the questions raised, designs utilized, and findings disseminated. It is at this point that investigators begin to ask whether new studies are necessary and to identify or design appropriate tools for conducting research.

The remainder of this book assumes that investigators have identified an important question that has not been adequately addressed in the literature. Working with practice re-

TABLE 1.7   Tips for the Writing Process

Identify a publishing outlet and read existing work to identify common norms for that outlet.

■ Are books or journals more appropriate for your project?

■ Who is most likely to be interested in your findings?

■ Which publishing outlets focus on work related to your topic?

■ Is the style of a selected outlet consistent with the theoretical agenda of your project?

(Note: Individual authors are unlikely to change the publication policies of a particular journal or publishing house.)

Diagram the style used by the publishing outlet by reading articles or books, regardless of the topic.

■ How are research questions represented in each article or book?

■ How detailed is the review of research? Is there balance in how authors represent others' findings?

■ What methods are used to represent data?

■ How are the design, methods, and results reported?

■ How well do conclusions follow from the evidence?

■ How can your work be organized to match the style of the publishing outlet you selected?

■ Which style manual was used for organizing the text?

(Note: It is a good idea to read the style manual before beginning to write and to have a copy nearby while writing.)

Determine balance in your own writing.

■ What story can your data tell readers? What question can you address with the data you have? What questions can't be answered?

■ Why is the question addressed by your data important? What new knowledge will be introduced?

■ Should the original questions or predictions be modified to account for your findings?

■ How well did you measure the target variables?

■ How well did your design allow for the exploration of your research question?

■ Have you reported your methods and results well enough so that someone can replicate your study?

■ Have you avoided walking readers through all your mistakes?

■ Do the conclusions follow directly from your evidence?

■ Have you considered the limitations of your project when writing conclusions?

(Note: It is very difficult for writers to see the flaws in their own logic. It might be helpful to have someone other than yourself read the final product before you send it out for review.)

search questions can also be helpful until knowledge of existing research is more firmly available. New investigators often compare their impressions of published work with the contents of books on design and measurement to both test their understanding of research concepts and develop a more elaborate understanding of research in their field. Even if this process results in the selection of an existing tool, investigators who are familiar with available research can write with greater clarity and design stronger studies if they know the fundamentals of how measurement tools are developed.

■ ■ ■ ■ ■ ■

MAKING CONNECTIONS

What have you started doing to become an expert on the existing research in your field? Have you started to collect studies that are related to your areas of interest? Have you found databases like the Web of Science, www.isi5.isiknowledge.com/portal.cgi? Are you a member of the Community of Science, http://cos.com? What are the common ways in which researchers in your field find existing research? How will you organize the research you are reading so that you can find key ideas when you start to write a review? Have you found a gap in existing research that might lead to the design of an important study?

DEFINING A MEASUREMENT PURPOSE

After distinguishing the structure of research, it will be a bit easier to imagine the importance of careful measurement, regardless of your theoretical or philosophical agenda. In most research, measurement involves the assignment of numerals to objects or events according to rules. The numerals may reflect place holders of nominal indicants (e.g., differentiating gender or occupation) or take on different forms of quantitative meaning, forming ordinal, interval, or ratio scales. It is easy to think of variables as tangible objects, but this connotes a level of concreteness that is rarely apparent in the study of human functioning. Investigators typically define and defend abstract constructs by identifying a measurement purpose that corresponds to their theoretical reasons for conducting a study. With that purpose in mind, the next step involves the selection of an appropriate measurement scale for each variable in the research design.

Measurement Scales

Regardless of how a construct is defined, most forms of measurement rely on one of four different scales and the logic of these scales is often applied even by investigators who do not represent their evidence with numbers (Table 1.8). When numerals simply reflect place holders, the measurement scale is *nominal*. Categories have no particular order and the assignment of numbers simply serves as a classification tool. Classifying all males as 1 and females as 2, for example, could be reversed with no measurement consequences. Nominal scales do not lend themselves to the use of addition, subtraction, multiplication, or division because numbers have no correspondence with quantity. Nevertheless, investigators can draw comparisons among the frequency or proportion of indicants within each category.

Numerals can also form an order in which the distance between numbers has no value, but the placement of categories is hierarchical. In such an *ordinal* scale, objects can be ranked because numbers reflect more and less advanced positions, but there is no clear 0 point. To use an ordinal scale, investigators identify a natural or beginning point and a degree to which higher or lower numbers reflect movement from that origin. Numbers reflect an order such that position $a > b > c$ and so forth, but investigators are careful to avoid assuming that numbers have quantitative meaning.

TABLE 1.8 Measurement Scales

SCALE	DESCRIPTION
Nominal	Numbers are used only to represent place holders and do not have quantitative value.
Ordinal	Numbers can be put in a hierarchical order, but the distance between numbers has no quantitative meaning.
Interval	Numbers can be placed in a meaningful order and the distance between numbers is equal.
Ratio	Numbers can be placed in a meaningful order with equal distance between numbers and an absolute 0 point on the scale.

Responses to items on an intelligence test correspond to an ordinal scale when points are assigned for correct answers but not for incorrect answers. Items on this ordinal scale vary in difficulty and content. For example, one individual may get all but three easy items correct and another might get all but the three most difficult items correct. Both individuals would receive the same rank in the hierarchy of test-takers, but would reveal different types of knowledge. Similar assumptions are relevant for Likert and other rating scales in which the origin is at the midpoint rather than an endpoint of the scale; scores below the point of origin are lower in rank than scores above that point. It is possible to rank answers, but the distance between numbers does not remain sufficiently equal to warrant the use of mathematical operations.

Interval scales are formed when the *distance between numbers* has value as well as the numbers themselves. These scales contain most of the properties of nominal and ordinal scales, but the distance between numbers is assumed to be equal. The assumption of equal distance allows investigators to add and subtract numbers, and to compare the distance between points anywhere on a distribution. Investigators can create a scale in which a score of 1 is considered highest or where larger numbers reflect a stronger presence of an indicant. Whatever the decision, it is usually applied consistently across indicants in a single tool.

Most tools used in social science are constructed using nominal or ordinal scales, but investigators often transform measures to approximate an interval scale. The most common techniques for such approximation involve combining items intended to measure the same construct either by using simple addition or an arithmetic mean. Variance in the resulting scores reflects an interval measurement scale and investigators typically use that variance to estimate the distance between points on the scale. Investigators sometimes use transformations to formulate interval scales using ordinal data by grouping indicants to estimate the magnitude of an entity. They may also transform each indicant and rely on estimates such as the *probability log odds* commonly used with Rasch techniques to transform ordinal data into something approximating equal intervals (see Wright, 1999).

A *ratio* scale contains most of the properties of nominal, ordinal, and interval scales with the added benefit of including a natural 0 in which the object being measured has none of the properties being measured. Here the scaling of numbers is rarely reversed because 0 indicates the absence of an entity and higher numbers reflect magnitude. With ratio scales, all arithmetic operations are possible, including addition, subtraction, multiplication, division, and ratio computations. Scales can be interpreted without transforming the data or comparing it to a probability distribution. Put another way, a ratio scale is usually isomorphic to the objects it measures.

Unfortunately, most social science variables cannot be measured using a ratio scale because there is rarely a complete absence of the phenomenon being measured or a deterministic standard for comparison. Instead, investigators usually identify and defend an origin for their scale. Most statistical techniques for combining variables were designed for data collected using a ratio scale, but researchers generally violate this assumption, transforming their scales to offer the closest possible approximation.

Selecting a Scale.   Scales are determined by establishing a rule of correspondence for mapping symbolic representations of an object (e.g., numbers) and the object itself (e.g., attitudes, knowledge). If measurement could be error-free, one set of objects would correspond perfectly to another set of objects; the two sets would be identical in form. Although error is a feature of measurement, researchers still use numerical or symbolic sets to represent the objects to be measured and describe the rules of assignment.

Before ascribing rules of correspondence for each variable, how do investigators determine which measurement scale is appropriate? The first thing social scientists typically do is determine the purpose of their design and for measuring each variable within a design. If the purpose of the design is to *predict or control* human responses, some variables are manipulated while others remain fixed. Variables also may be classified rather than manipulated if the purpose is to *make descriptive generalizations* about themes as broad as historical events, current contexts, or personal characteristics. Furthermore, if the purpose is to *offer a thick description* of a person, context, or set of objects, the same set of materials may be examined by different individuals while avoiding systematic attempts at classification or prediction. Put simply, most social scientists try to decide if the purpose of their design is to predict and control human functioning, describe general patterns in human functioning, or offer a thick description of highly contextual events and responses before designing measurement tools. That decision places restrictions on what is to be measured and how measurement occurs.

Linking an Agenda with Tools

In the remaining portion of this chapter, a few examples of how investigators might coordinate theoretical and measurement issues are outlined. The designs represented in these examples are relatively simple so that differences in theoretical agendas are kept salient.

Prediction and Control.   If investigators are interested in prediction or control, they typically use an experimental design. Variables to be predicted are manipulated across groups of participants, and variables that are readily understood are kept stable. Consider the question of whether telling low-achieving children that they should work harder improves their motivation. (It does not.) An experiment could be conducted in which motivation is the outcome variable, instructions to work harder would be manipulated, and the selection of low-achieving students would be controlled. Investigators would predict an increase in motivation for those low-achieving students who are told to work harder and relatively stable levels of motivation for low-achieving students who are not given such instructions. Any possible extraneous causes for a change in motivation could be controlled by randomly assigning low-achieving students to the feedback and no-feedback conditions, but investigators would also look for other threats to the validity of this design. Investigators would strive to minimize error in how they identify low-achieving students, how feedback is provided, and in how motivation is measured. Conclusions would be supported with confidence by maximizing variance in how some variables are measured (e.g., motivation), minimizing variance in how other variables are measured (e.g., low achievement, feedback), and controlling extraneous and error variance. Measurement scales when used appropriately usually assist investigators in representing which features of their design are controlled and which features are not. Ideally, interval or ratio scales would be used to measure motivation, and nominal scales would be adequate for labeling whether students received feedback. The selection of low-achieving students might require complex measurement scales prior to the investigation to verify their achievement, but a nominal scale would be sufficient once the label is assigned.

The assumptions associated with random sampling theory would be appropriate for this type of investigation because stability and predictability would be essential for validating conclusions. This tradition strives to accurately measure an individual's "true score" by exploring the relationship between an obtained score and estimates of error. Probability theory is used to generate measurement conclusions about the stability with which scores are obtained from groups of participants and comparing the obtained distribution with a corresponding error distribution to predict accuracy. Such logic is appropriate when the variables being measured are assumed to be stable across samples (or over time). For experimental designs in which individuals take the measurement of variables for granted, such stability is ideal even if it is rarely available.

If investigators are interested in describing typical forms of human functioning, they may use nonexperimental designs as often as experimental designs. They may rely on experimental designs to verify assumptions about the mechanisms that cause relationships among variables, but it may be premature to start at this point in a research plan. Investigators who identify explanatory mechanisms are usually certain that participants will define central constructs in similar ways and confident about the accuracy with which abstract ideas are measured. Measurement tools are accurate if participants and investigators hold a similar understanding of the rules of the game. Experimental research does not usually involve the exploration of individual differences in how the problems under investigation are defined.

Describing General Patterns. Most investigators who choose to describe general patterns in human functioning do so because they are aware of pluralistic interpretations of seemingly identical events. Pluralism can emerge as a function of individual differences in the expression of psychological skills, values, or experiences. It can also emerge as a function of systematic personal characteristics such as age or gender. Investigators interested in describing these general patterns may do so to facilitate knowledge that is valuable in its own right or to improve their understanding of constructs that will later be included in experimental designs. Understanding human diversity may facilitate improved communication and tolerance, but to do so will probably require a combination of experimental and nonexperimental research designs.

Consider the belief that children cannot evaluate the fairness of institutional practices because they do not yet understand right from wrong. (Another claim that is false.) Investigators striving to describe these patterns might want to conduct at least three descriptive studies. In one, they would describe patterns in children's conceptions of the fairness of institutional practices. In a second, they would describe patterns in children's conceptions of right and wrong. In a third study, they might use an experimental design to compare children's knowledge of fairness and conduct, to determine if children can simultaneously consider both forms of moral functioning, or if the two types of moral knowledge follow different developmental pathways. Manipulations in the kinds of problems children solve can be used to determine whether one type of reasoning develops before another or if the two types of moral thought co-occur across childhood. Investigators could rely on a nominal scale to classify individual differences in children's reasoning or an ordinal scale to indicate that some children offer more complex solutions to fairness and conduct problems than others. Age could be measured with an interval or ratio scale serving as a ruler to indicate development. This combination of research designs can facilitate a description of general patterns in children's development but does not offer an explanation for those patterns. Investigators might be able to make strong predictions about how children reason about particular moral dilemmas, but these findings do not offer insight into how children act in social situations or which aspects of an actual situation would capture a child's attention.

This kind of descriptive research is common in the study of human development. Investigators are interested in measuring change (e.g., over time or across situations) and determining the sources associated with such change. They may also be interested in explanations for change but cannot adequately address that concern until they can accurately determine what is changing and whether such change is associated with individual differences in personality or with age-related sources of development.

Exploring Lives in Context.   Investigators who are interested in describing highly contextual forms of human functioning raise a third set of questions. They are typically interested in understanding a particular person, situation, environment, or culture. They may draw conclusions about their observations and those conclusions may be instructive to others working outside the context under investigation, but the broader implications of such findings are inevitably limited in scope.

Consider the claim that Eskimos have 32 words for snow because their understanding of snow is more complex than the knowledge apparent in other cultures. (This myth apparently has numerous iterations.) Investigators who explore this idea enter the research enterprise with a set of beliefs about the relationship between language and culture. Ideally, they would explore their assumptions, label their beliefs, find evidence for their beliefs, and discuss those beliefs with members of the Inuit culture. Investigators would identify members of the Inuit culture who would challenge their misconceptions and offer alternative interpretations of the same events. The resulting conversations could continue until both the participants and the investigators agree with the research findings and conclusions, or are willing to label their reasons for supporting different conclusions. As part of these deliberations, evidence would be collected and critiqued by everyone involved. Nominal scales might be used to classify the features of a culture. Terms for snow, for example, could be placed into a single category or classified into independent categories along with the details of the context in which they are commonly used. A list of terms and their use could be generated as a cultural artifact that might later be compared with artifacts from other cultures, but this is not the purpose of a thick description. Instead, investigators and participants are usually more interested in understanding how cultural norms evolved or remained static and whether particular events and artifacts are more or less common. They may look for cultural boundaries by debating where one context ends and another begins.

This kind of descriptive research is common in ethnographic investigations of living cultures and historical investigations of static cultures. The boundaries between living and static cultures are as murky as the measurement tools used to verify such boundaries. Nevertheless, such thick descriptions can serve as informative models of successful and shameful events. They can facilitate future decisions about how individuals may think, feel, and act if similar cycles of human events recur. Ethnographies can also serve as mirrors into which readers might gaze to determine the effects of their own and others' behavior on the individuals around them.

Blending Agendas.   Investigators sometimes blend agendas within an overall research plan. In doing so, they can look for convergence in the conclusions generated from very different tools to strengthen claims about the validity of theoretical assertions and avoid mono-method bias in a research plan. Nevertheless, it is less prudent to mix measurement approaches in the structure of a particular research problem. Tools constructed to fulfill vastly different measurement purposes are rarely strong enough to warrant direct comparison in a single problem. Levels of inference and relations between indicants and constructs are often too incompatible to yield meaningful results.

MAKING CONNECTIONS

To what extent does the research in your field suffer from a mono-method bias? In answering this question, see if you can identify an experimental study that uses psychometric measurement tools, a developmental study that includes measures of change, and an interpretive study that relies on thick description of human functioning. How difficult was it to find studies in your field that relied on these diverse approaches to research?

DIFFERENTIATING MEASUREMENT CONCERNS

Exploring relationships among issues of theory, design, measurement, and analysis reveals how the research enterprise is permeated with questions about the quality of evidence. Identifying reasons for conducting new research is usually a multifaceted process in which existing work is compared with an investigator's theoretical questions. Investigators may try to validate a theoretical framework by conducting new studies, but the nature of that framework is influenced by their philosophical assumptions. Similarly, the design of a study, the measurement of variables, and the analysis of relationships are also rule-governed processes that correspond to more general assumptions about what knowledge is of most worth. Before finding volunteers to participate in a new study, investigators are likely to share their plans with others to obtain feedback and suggestions for improvement.

The next chapter introduces some of the ethical considerations associated with conducting research. Once these preliminary considerations are fully addressed, the remainder of the book will focus on the details of particular kinds of measurement tools. Although this collection is divided into three sections, the corresponding assumptions about the purpose of measurement can also be combined into a single, complex research design. Investigators usually make decisions about which assumptions to emphasize by considering the norms of those discourse communities with whom they would like to converse.

SUGGESTED READINGS

Best, J. W., & Kahn, J. V. (2003). *Research in education* (9th ed.). Boston: Allyn & Bacon.

Braun, H. I., Jackson, D. N., & Wiley, D. E. (2002). *The role of constructs in psychological and educational measurement.* Mahwah, NJ: Erlbaum.

Creswell, J. W. (2002). *Educational research: Planning, conducting and evaluating qualitative and quantitative research.* Upper Saddle River, NJ: Merrill-Prentice-Hall.

Hoyle, R. H., Harris, M. J., & Judd, C. M. (2002). *Research methods in social relations* (7th ed.). Stamford, CT: Wadsworth.

Kerlinger, F. N. & Lee, H. B. (2000). *Foundations of behavioral research* (4th ed.). Stamford, CT: Wadsworth.

McMillan, J. H., & Schumacher, S. (2001). *Research in education: A conceptual introduction* (5th ed.). Boston: Allyn & Bacon.

Mertens, D. M. (1998). *Research methods in education and psychology: Integrating diversity with quantitative and qualitative approaches.* Thousand Oaks, CA: Sage.

Miller, S. A. (1998). *Developmental research methods* (2nd ed.). Upper Saddle River, NJ: Prentice-Hall.

SUGGESTED WEB SITES

Most universities have library databases that can be searched for journals and books.

American Philosophical Association: http://www.apa.udel.edu/apa
Community of Science: http://cos.com
Stanford Encyclopedia of Philosophy: http://plato.stanford.edu
Web of Science: http://www.isi5.isiknowledge.com/portal.cgi

CHAPTER TWO

INTEGRITY IN
THE RESEARCH ENTERPRISE

In addition to learning about the structure of research, most investigators explore their own personalities and qualifications before conducting new studies. Because social scientists are interested in explaining human functioning, investigators who understand their own responsibilities and abilities are much better able to regulate their behavior when accomplishing research goals. To improve self-awareness, new investigators often seek out mentorship opportunities and learn research ethics from scholars in their field. They also study the ethical standards and codes of conduct used to regulate their profession. Some of the resulting moral questions associated with measuring human functioning are reviewed in this chapter along with a sample of the most common ethical practices.

New investigators who have worked as practitioners have already learned about ethical practices in their profession. They sometimes find it difficult to distinguish the integrity a practitioner shows when enhancing others' well-being from the integrity associated with conducting research. Nevertheless, there are marked differences in these two kinds of professional responsibilities. In research, interactions with humans (or animals) are often a means to the end of generating new knowledge whereas in practice they are valuable ends in their own right. Researchers interact with other humans to explore questions, test predictions, and draw conclusions about relationships among variables. Even though investigators are committed to constructing general statements of relationships, theories, or principles, they are ideally self-conscious about how they treat the people who help them accomplish these goals.

As may have been apparent when looking at the theoretical lenses in Chapter 1, some researchers also try to blend the challenges of ethical practice and research. A major obligation of all researchers is to acquire the necessary moral attitudes, knowledge, and problem-solving abilities for consistently treating research participants with dignity and respect. To maximize integrity and minimize the potential for harm, seasoned investigators have constructed procedures and practices that draw thoughtful attention to how they interact with the volunteers in their studies. Ordinarily new research plans are scrutinized by ethical review boards and investigators elicit feedback on how to coordinate research agendas with plans for the ethical treatment of human subjects.

Why do researchers require such reminders? Historically, some very inhumane activities were initiated in the name of science as researchers became so preoccupied with their own generalizations that they forgot to think about the dignity of those with whom they interacted. To minimize the potential for future harm, a National Commission for the Protection of Human Subjects of Biomedical and Behavioral Research wrote *The Belmont Report,* which outlines principles and rules for conducting research.[1] Prior to conducting research, you may find it worthwhile to study the contents of *The Belmont Report.* Specialized clinical or practical training prove to be a bonus in research because the same principles apply to both kinds of work. Yet, additional procedures have been established for researchers, acknowledging the sometimes conflicting agendas of minimizing harm and acquiring new knowledge. The complex dilemmas that arise when coordinating these concerns lead most investigators to regularly solicit critical feedback on how well they simultaneously preserve the dignity of their participants and maintain integrity when making generalizations.

ETHICAL PRINCIPLES

The Belmont Report reminds investigators of three basic ethical principles: respect for persons, beneficence, and justice. Because each study and corresponding combination of measurement tools raises different ethical concerns, many investigators remain skeptical of simple procedural rules for addressing these principles. Instead, work is normally reviewed by governing boards who evaluate the ratio of benefits to harm and offer advice on minimizing possible aversive effects. Most investigators learn procedural norms from case studies and examples of how other researchers have solved similar problems. Taking a little time to study the formalities of ethical decision making is also helpful in research training. Although investigators generally coordinate all three principles when making decisions, each will be considered in isolation to facilitate a clearer understanding of differences among them.

Respect for Persons

When considering *respect for persons,* most of the same rules used to regulate clinical practice also apply to research. Individuals are assumed to be autonomous agents and respect is typically maintained by maximizing personal autonomy. As autonomous agents, people strive to maintain dignity and are capable of making choices when they understand all the information necessary for doing so. Typically, only participants who freely volunteer for research are included in a study and investigators avoid using coercion or undue influence to recruit volunteers.

Unfortunately, some people are incapable of the self-determination necessary for making informed choices. They are protected from activities and experiences that might cause them harm by an intermediary who makes decisions on their behalf. Children or individuals who suffer from physical or mental illness, for example, are usually permitted to make as many choices as possible, but may not be able to fully understand the potential for harm in particular situations. These people fall into protected classes whose involvement in research is monitored closely by ethical review boards. Investigators adopt special procedures for obtaining assent from such people and formal consent from appropriate intermediary agents. All parties do their best to ensure that everyone understands the potential risks and benefits as well as the nature of the research activities while realizing that not everyone will have the same understanding of these implications.

Consider, for example, a plan to interview children. Parents are usually informed of the nature and purpose of the study and offer formal consent. Children are usually given instructions that maximize their ability to assent to the interview and are asked to indicate their willingness to participate. Investigators are also obligated to monitor children's reactions during an interview, eliminating questions that foster discomfort or aborting the interview if a child wishes to stop. The nature of the interview as well as the age and abilities of the children play key roles in procedural decisions about obtaining consent and assent.

Existing mechanisms of ethical review and the monitoring of research activities can minimize the potential for harm to volunteers. By making participants aware of their rights, such mechanisms can also preserve a person's ability to refuse unwanted requests. In balancing the pressures for autonomous decision making and the protection of participants from harm, reviewers and investigators identify those practices that embody respect for persons.

At the measurement stage, respect for persons holds at least two kinds of implications. The most obvious implication concerns the selection and design of tools that maximize feelings of autonomy and minimize harm. It is problematic, for example, to create such levels of anxiety in standardized test situations that children soil themselves or cry, adults punish curious students, or normal learning opportunities are undermined. When such testing is necessary, investigators think carefully about the conditions under which tests are implemented and devices for accommodating the perspectives and concerns of participants. Investigators may alter the presentation of tasks, break tasks into smaller, more manageable components, or completely alter their techniques for acquiring necessary information.

Asking participants to critique their research experiences serves as another device for learning how to better convey respect for persons. Some investigators use the information gleaned from such sessions in the reporting of their results. They may also advocate for the needs and agendas of target populations. Studies that include homeless persons, for example, raise a risk that researchers might exert undue influence when requesting information. Homeless people need access to resources and may assume, rightly or wrongly, that researchers can provide such things. Nevertheless, if such risks are minimized, important knowledge on how homeless persons are and are not like others in their environment can be very useful. Measuring participants' opinions gives voice to members of society who might otherwise be overlooked, subtly maximizing individuals' sense of autonomy.

Beneficence

The principle of respect for persons overlaps with *beneficence,* but holds somewhat different implications. Whereas the emphasis is on maximizing autonomy when investigators show respect for persons, making efforts to secure participants' well-being is central to the principle of beneficence. Both principles require researchers to protect people from harm.

Investigators typically focus on two levels of beneficence. At one level, they demonstrate the benefits of their research for the actual participants in a study; if participants benefit and harm is minimized, the welfare of the individual is preserved. At a second level, investigators demonstrate the benefits of their work to society at large; if society benefits and harm to participants is minimized, the research may also adhere to the beneficence principle even if there are no direct benefits to volunteers. Work that neither offers direct benefit to participants nor causes them harm may result in socially valuable knowledge.

The principle of beneficence sounds relatively easy to adhere to until we begin thinking carefully about why much of our research is conducted. Sometimes, for example, harm would be a likely occurrence despite participants' involvement in research. Consider situations in which participants are injured or ill and would benefit from a new kind of treatment. In such cases, investigators may not know enough to fully determine the harm caused by treatments even if participants require immediate care. Most investigators are expected to maximize possible benefits and minimize the potential for harm, even if they do not have the knowledge necessary for anticipating all the consequences of their work. Participants are typically informed about known ambiguities when investigators describe the potential risks of a study. As the research progresses, participants are also informed of any potentially harmful knowledge that is acquired.

Of course, research that knowingly causes harm to participants without offering benefits to their overall well-being is usually judged inappropriate. Even if a study seems to be of benefit to society, if it is harmful to participants, researchers are expected to look for better methods of balancing the interests of the participants and those of society. In rare cases, investigators cannot minimize the harm they would inflict on participants and a line of research is aborted or abandoned.

Sticking with the theme of standardized achievement testing in schools, forms of harm and social benefits are apparent in current practices. At the societal level, economists and government officials are looking for ways to maximize the cost-effectiveness of schooling and may treat test scores like products to be evaluated for quality. Schools are assumed to be businesses turning out comparable products that can be evaluated against a common standard. Researchers working within this framework have a vested interest in finding progressively better standardized tests, administering them to students, and comparing the aggregate results to evaluate school quality. Ideally, teachers and students are assumed to benefit from feedback on individual and collective achievement.

Such a vision might work well if people were randomly distributed in society and students were randomly assigned to schools and classrooms. Unfortunately, such designs are not possible when beneficence and respect for persons are added to the equation. People are free to move about in society and tend to cluster in communities with others like themselves. School funding is typically tied to the taxes of particular communities, and students either attend neighborhood schools or compete for placement in schools drawing from multiple neighborhoods. These geographical constraints suggest that social class differences are likely to be salient when schools are compared because economic inequalities typically translate into inequalities in educational opportunity. It may not be in the best interests of less privileged members of society to be consistently labeled intellectually "inferior" using a seemingly "objective" tool that is derived from the assumption that everyone has equal access to core knowledge.

In designing studies to maximize achievement, investigators can be blinded to social class differences when preoccupied with benefits for students who have a chance of improving their test scores. Investigators may overlook the fact that standardized testing programs will not necessarily benefit all participants or all segments of society. Using test scores to pressure schools already stressed by inadequate resources, to fire teachers who are willing to work with the most at-risk students, or to punish students whose performance does not match that of their peers may introduce levels of harm. Rather than abort the quest for improving achievement levels, most investigators accept responsibility for minimizing potential risks while maximizing individual and societal benefits. Investigators who are overly preoccupied with a global vision of improving education may need forceful reminders that change often yields unforeseen dilemmas and can even cause more harm than good.

Justice

The least well-understood of the principles for research is *justice,* but it also overlaps with the principles of beneficence and respect for persons. The definition of *justice* described in *The Belmont Report* is rather thin in that it focuses primarily on issues of distributive justice while overlooking issues of corrective, procedural, and commutative justice.[2] Nevertheless, *The Belmont Report* raises questions of who ought to receive the benefits of research and bear its burdens.

Historically, most of the harm induced by researchers has involved serious forms of injustice. Consider, for example, the exploitation of unwilling prisoners who were used as research subjects in Nazi concentration camps; or the rural Black men whose syphilis remained untreated in the 1940s so that investigators could study the natural course of the disease; or the participants in Milgram's studies of obedience whose trust in the research enterprise was seriously compromised when they were led to believe they had administered electric shocks to an unseen person. Today we see no ambiguity in labeling the injustice of these activities, but the individuals who executed these studies were so preoccupied with the social benefits of new knowledge, they seemed unaware of their ethical transgressions.[3]

The Belmont Report's emphasis on distributive justice was no doubt prompted by the degree to which individuals were treated unequally when the costs and benefits of research transgressions were evaluated. Members of some groups experienced an overabundance of the burdens associated with new discoveries and other groups experienced an overabundance of the benefits. To establish greater balance between the benefits and burdens of research, decisions about who should be invited to participate in a study and what characteristics those persons should hold are most salient in current practice. Formulations such as those based on simple equality (to each person an equal share), need (to each person according to his or her indigence), effort (to each person according to his or her contribution), equity (to each person according to his or her merit), or social utility (to each person according to his or her value in society) are commonly used to make decisions.

Ideally, the people who are most likely to benefit from research are expected to bear the burden of involvement. As with the principles of respect for persons and beneficence, the consequences of these decisions are not so easily anticipated. Imagine research in which only participants who are likely to benefit from a new practice are invited to participate; not only would the study fail to offer an equitable distribution of opportunities, the scientific merit of the findings would be questionable. Similarly, suppose a risky study only included the most vulnerable of participants, but the findings would benefit everyone; vulnerable populations would bear a greater burden in the research process than is ethically warranted. Such decisions seem easy to imagine when the outcomes of a study are already determined, but when new knowledge is generated, identifying benefits and burdens may not be so straightforward.

Let's again look at standardized testing to think about how measurement plays a role in justice concerns. Suppose economists wanted to determine if it would be better for society to close all the schools whose aggregate achievement levels fell below students' grade level. Politicians who wish to see better schools are likely to find this a laudable goal and to campaign for the idea that all students should perform at grade level. Unfortunately, understanding the moral dilemma embedded in this campaign requires more knowledge about measurement and how tests are designed than politicians are likely to bother acquiring.

As you will discover in subsequent chapters, grade level is usually another name for the statistical mean of scores obtained either from a current group of test-takers or respondents who were considered to be part of a normative comparison group. Theoretically, standardized tests are designed so that half the participants will perform below grade level. Norms are adjusted when samples deviate too far from this standard. If students are randomly assigned to schools, by definition, half the population of students at each grade level should perform below the school quality standard.

To more fully understand the moral implications of these facts, think about how students are currently distributed across schools. Is the distribution random? How do curricular agendas differ across schools? Is it reasonable to assume that even half the students in every school will be performing at or above a national mean?

Educators know that students are not randomly assigned to schools and family income plays a central role in who attends each school. Students from low-income families often attend neighborhood schools and have fewer educational resources than those from middle- or high-income families. Even when choice is introduced, families in economic distress have difficulty finding better schools or academic enrichment programs that might compensate for a lack of household resources. Norm-referenced comparison of test scores is not particularly problematic when determining the relative standing of individual students. Most standardized tests, however, are not designed for use in measuring the vagaries of school quality. Such tests depend heavily on probability theory and comparisons between obtained samples and theoretical populations. Standards invariably fluctuate and the mathematical assumptions that underlie normative comparisons are not available for policymakers and politicians.

The justice principle suggests that, if all students are evaluated using the same tool to determine if schools should remain open, those attending schools in low-income neighborhoods might bear a greater burden for the school-closing policy than students in other communities. With fewer educational opportunities at their disposal, it seems reasonable to assume that poor communities will not contain students with a normative range of academic skill; knowledge is not equally available to those students. Therefore, students from low-income families would be more likely than others to face the displacement dilemmas associated with eliminating neighborhood schools and the community deprivation of missing educational resources. Relying on aggregated standardized test scores may not be the fairest way of achieving an otherwise worthy school improvement goal.

Continuing Moral Tensions

New questions are emerging in every one of the social sciences. Institutions are also exploring whom to hold accountable when research practices begin to fall out of sync with ethical norms, how particular procedures ought to be regulated, and the role of research in society. Since *The Belmont Report* was written, these questions have led investigators to explore new ground in how they conduct research. New investigators may want to listen to national conversations about ethics in their field before jumping into the measurement enterprise. It is assumed that investigators will accept responsibility for conversing about research ethics, the surprising outcomes of their investigations, and the degree to which they encounter new ethical dilemmas. Occasionally, these conversations also make their way into general media discussions about scientific research.

Despite ongoing conversations, some ethical practices are likely to remain central to the research enterprise. Investigators will continue to determine if their studies are worth doing, how to select and approach participants, and which measurement tools will yield the most appropriate results. They will also determine if their studies are implemented correctly, how findings will be disseminated, and ethical issues associated with reporting results.

The remainder of this chapter should help you see that ethical investigators remain highly self-conscious about the soundness of their own judgments and the ethics of their work. They regularly question their knowledge of the moral principles and facts relevant to each research dilemma. Such investigators also rely on wisdom and collective experience when designing new research, implementing agendas, summarizing findings, and sharing results.

MAKING CONNECTIONS

Many investigators who are just learning about the principles of ethical research conduct confuse specific rules with more general ethical principles. List common procedural rules used by researchers in your university. You may find these general rules on a Web site, but it is also a good topic to discuss with professors and research mentors. After generating a list of local rules, align each rule with the principles of respect for persons, beneficence, and justice. How well do the rules reflect the concerns embodied in the principle? Should rules be rigidly enforced? Is it possible that some rules could actually cause harm to participants if enforced without thinking about their implications in particular contexts?

IS A STUDY WARRANTED?

One fundamental ethical question involves the social utility of research. If findings have no social value, investigators may not find the necessary support to conduct new studies. In addition, some conclusions can be drawn using logic and are unlikely to require systematic inquiry. Decisions to avoid jumping off a bridge or locking children in closets, for example, probably do not require empirical support.

More subtly, investigators usually take time to ask if they should implement a research plan and weigh the likely contributions in comparison to time constraints, risks, discomfort, or inconvenience for themselves and research participants. If a study offers few significant contributions, it may not be necessary to bother participants. If a study poses too much risk or discomfort to participants, it may be unethical to proceed. And, as is the case for many nonresearch-related activities, if a study is inconvenient to participants and offers little in the way of a contribution, investigators may have grounds for aborting their efforts.

Review Existing Research.   How do investigators know if their research is worthwhile? As you may remember from the previous chapter, investigators often begin by reviewing existing research. They explore the social value of the ideas they want to test and look for ways in which new knowledge might be beneficial. Practical issues related to funding and the availability of participants also foster relevant pressures. Table 2.1 offers suggestions for reviewing research to determine if new studies are necessary.

Use Common Sense.   New investigators are sometimes surprised to learn that researchers often rely on common sense to help them coordinate ethical and theoretical issues and determine the value of a new research plan. It is rare for an investigator to introduce a brand-new theory or explain a problem that has not been previously identified. More often, research findings extend existing knowledge and investigators imagine how their work aligns with current notions of common sense. Most investigators study common sense beliefs about how the world works and how humans function within it.

New research with adolescents, for example, offers an explanation for common sense notions about their daily functioning. Most parents can attest to the fact that something strange happens to their children once they enter puberty. Teenagers' sense of logic can become confusing to follow; they may be inclined to show erratic behavior; or they may withdraw from interactions with others. The availability of functional magnetic resonance

TABLE 2.1   Suggestions for Reviewing Research

- Have you learned how to navigate the library? What databases are most informative in your field?
- What is your research question? How can you restrict your literature search to focus on issues related to your question?
- What kinds of research will you review? Will you look at articles, abstracts, monographs, reviews, books, dissertations, technical reports, or electronic media sources?
- What keywords will help you find the research most relevant to your topic?
- How will you evaluate the quality of the research you find? Will the *Social Science Citation Index* help you find the most important studies on your topic?
- What methods have been used to explore your question? Are they appropriate?
- What measurement techniques have been used? Are they reliable and valid?
- How will you summarize essential details for each source? Avoid plagiarism—always mark direct quotes or avoid copying the things you read.
- What work has already been done on your topic? What work still needs to be done?

imagining (fMRI) has fostered new knowledge about this period of development that helps explain some of this erratic behavior.[4] The brain apparently shows signs of new growth that had not otherwise been detected. Common sense understanding of behavior change was partially explained once investigators developed noninvasive techniques for measuring brain functioning.

At the simplest level, common sense involves at least three levels of interpretation. It involves (1) fundamental assumptions about human functioning and how the world works, (2) beliefs about the role of culture and context in human functioning, and (3) expectations for the dynamic processes of thinking and generating knowledge. Much of common sense is assumed to be tacit, but researchers strive to make such knowledge explicit.

Conduct Thought Experiments. Investigators usually begin to verify common sense by conducting thought experiments to imagine the short- and long-term consequences of their efforts. Despite opinions to the contrary, today's "common sense" values were often yesterday's "new research findings." Beliefs about human functioning may sometimes be more valid if situated in utilitarian notions of adaptation, historical time, and regional contexts, but occasionally those beliefs are thwarted with new evidence (see, for example, Bruner, 1990; Clifford, 1988; Fletcher, 1984; Geertz, 1973, 1983).

Combining findings from two studies with parallel conclusions, for example, can be done using matters of logic or by repeating both studies using the same participants. Depending on the importance of the new knowledge, investigators may or may not take time to measure all dimensions of a construct well enough to make direct comparisons. Considering the risks-to-benefits ratio associated with a new study may be one part of this decision-making process. Using reason to work through the problem may offer sufficient information to allow investigators to move on to new questions. Thought experiments are most likely to be valuable (1) when a particular course of events presents an important dilemma, (2) when a great deal of relevant knowledge is already available, and (3) when new knowledge can be generated by looking at an old problem in a new way.[5]

Many investigators consider formal logic before becoming preoccupied with issues of research design and measurement.[6] Yet, designing imaginary studies can help investigators identify and organize related research problems that have already been tested

Coordinate Research Plans. Once investigators determine that a study is warranted, they may use common sense to imagine how that study fits into a more general research plan and if that plan shows an adequate level of integrity. In addition to determining if particular studies conform to the principles of respect for persons, beneficence, and justice, investigators hold themselves accountable to the people who might use findings from an entire program of research. Each time investigators design a new study they keep in mind their responsibilities to groups of possible participants, to their chosen profession, to the public institutions in which they conduct their inquiries, and to society at large. They also look for opportunities to foster helpful conversations among the members of these various constituencies and sometimes play an advocacy role in enhancing the status of participants in their communities. In short, investigators also serve as ambassadors who assist others in understanding the research process and facilitate communication with one another. If they cannot fulfill these responsibilities, investigators may decide that new research is unwarranted.

■ ■ ■ ■ ■

MAKING CONNECTIONS

Define a set of issues in your field. Have those issues been explored systematically? What evidence is available to support theoretical conclusions? How would you go about determining if a new study is warranted? What information would tell you that the available evidence is sufficient for verifying a theory? What evidence is necessary for determining if a particular theory is harmful or helpful?

INTERACTING WITH PARTICIPANTS

After determining that a study is necessary, investigators often think carefully about who should participate in such events. Ethical concerns at three decision-making steps are relevant. Investigators imagine the perspectives of participants at the (1) design stage of planning, (2) when actually recruiting participants, and (3) once participants become involved in research activities. At each level, similar questions are revisited (Table 2.2), and researchers invariably face conflicts concerning the ethical treatment of human subjects while maximizing the scientific merit of their investigations.

If the conflicts are resolved adequately, researchers can come away from an investigation with greater awareness of the meaning of their data, more willing participants, and samples that are more representative of the populations to which research findings are generalized.[7] For example, if investigators select volunteers rather than entice participants through the use of inducements, they may find individuals willing to offer thoughtful responses to research activities. Similarly, when investigators maximize confidentiality in reporting sensitive information, they could obtain more honest responses to their tasks. And, when investigators take time to debrief participants on the nature and purpose of their research, participants might come away from a research experience with greater levels of trust and a sense of civic responsibility.

Planning a Design

The simplest rule of thumb for the design process is to imagine how it might feel to be a participant in the study and the skills that individuals are likely to bring to the research enterprise. As part of the design process, investigators select performance sites by imagining which kinds of people to include, how many participants will be necessary, and exclusion criteria. The result of these decisions affects the selection of measurement tools for accurately testing theoretical claims. When selecting appropriate age groups and identifying any necessary characteristics for their target population, investigators also consider the skills participants will need to complete particular research activities. They look for ways to select a representative sample from the target population, including those people in protected classes. To include all selected volunteers, measurement tasks may have to be modified to account for participants' abilities.

TABLE 2.2 Common Questions When Interacting with Human Subjects

DESIGN QUESTIONS

- What is the anticipated scientific benefit of the project?
- Who would benefit from participating in this study?
- What human characteristics are likely to influence the outcome? How will that be tested?
- What human characteristics are likely to be unrelated to theoretical claims? How will random variation of participants be maximized along these dimensions?
- How many participants will be necessary for conducting the study? How many participants would you like to include?
- Who will you exclude from the study? Why?
- Will it be necessary to record identifiers for each participant (e.g., through videotaping or recording names and contact information)? If so, how will confidentiality be preserved? If not, how can you preserve anonymity?
- What skills are all participants likely to have available for research activities? Are the measurement procedures appropriately matched with these abilities?
- What are participants likely to think and/or feel about the experiences they have in your study?
- How long are the activities likely to take? Are your requests reasonable? Have you tested your assumptions with someone from the target population?
- What are the potential risks of the study? Label the degree of severity, likely frequency, and potential reversibility of any harmful effects.
- Will any of the following risks be possible in your study? Will investigators use private records, invade the privacy of participants or their family members, use physiological deprivation, manipulate psychological or social aspects of human functioning, collect sensitive information in surveys or interviews, present threatening or offensive materials, change diet or exercise regimens?
- What precautions will be taken to minimize each type of risk?
- What can be done to minimize any possible aversive effects of a measurement plan?
- Why is each type of risk necessary?
- Is deception absolutely necessary? What other options might there be to achieve the research goals? If no options exist, what can be done to minimize the harmful effects?
- Will the data for each participant be treated with appropriate balance so as not to distort the contribution of each person to the study as a whole?

RECRUITMENT QUESTIONS

- How will participants be identified?
- What information will they be told at the recruitment phase?
- Who will make initial contact with possible volunteers? How will such contact be made? Will persons making contact have access to private records?
- Are there finders' fees to recruiters that might lead them to exert undue influence on potential participants?
- What inclusion criteria will be used to select participants?
- What exclusion criteria will be used?
- Who will determine if the inclusion/exclusion criteria are adhered to? How will this decision be made?
- Will there be inducements that might pressure individuals to participate?
- Will participants be charged for their participation? Does this exert pressure on those who need clinical services?

(continued)

TABLE 2.2   Continued

CONSENT QUESTIONS

- Do participants have the capacity to give informed consent? If not, who will give consent on their behalf and why is that person qualified?
- Exactly what will investigators tell participants when explaining the research?
- Will there be written consent/assent forms that verify participants' rights? Will signatures be obtained? How will the confidentiality of those signatures be preserved?
- How will participants' understanding of their rights be assessed?
- How will participants' understanding of the study be assessed?
- When will the consent process take place? Will it occur prior to data collection? How far ahead of time?
- Will investigators secure consent? If so, do they have other relationships with participants that might foster coercion or undue influence in the consent process?

PARTICIPATION QUESTIONS

- How will investigators make sure that participants feel equally good about themselves after completing a task as they did before?
- What direction will participants be given when completing research tasks?
- Will there be contingent rewards given to participants at the completion of a study that might exert undue influence on their participation?
- What benefits will participants acquire from their involvement in the study?
- Are participants likely to feel pressured into completing activities they find uncomfortable?
- How will participants' confidence in research be maintained? How will it be restored if deception is used?

DATA STORAGE QUESTIONS

- Who will have access to the data collected for each participant? How will issues of privacy be influenced?
- How will data be shared? How will participants be informed of these decisions?
- Will it be possible to identify participants when data are reported? How will participants be informed of this possibility?
- How long will the raw data be stored? How will it be stored?
- When audio- and videotapes are no longer needed, how will they be destroyed?
- Will individuals other than researchers have access to raw data sources? If so, how will participants be informed of their refusal rights for this occurrence?
- Will data be part of participants' permanent records? If so, how will participants be informed of this possibility?
- Will institutional representatives receive data with identifying information attached? If so, how will participants learn of this possibility?

Note: These questions are apparent in many of the forms used for proposals to the institutional review boards that regulate the protection of human subjects.

In addition to imagining whether potential participants can adequately complete each activity, investigators also determine how long the activities are likely to take. When their imaginations offer insufficient information, researchers may approach individuals in the target groups to elicit advice. Naturally, researchers consider which individuals might benefit or be harmed by involvement with particular activities. Researchers also evaluate the amount of effort that might be appropriately exerted by participants and strategize about minimizing any discomfort or inconvenience. In addition, they evaluate the process of collecting information and how acquired information might affect the social and emotional welfare of each volunteer. Planning how to arrange activities and where participants are situated in an environment is easy to overlook, but is essential for evaluating the ethics of a design.

Investigators are naturally wary of using *deception* in research and many have decided that deception is always unethical.[8] Deception is apparent whenever investigators knowingly withhold information from participants. The most common form of deception occurs when investigators fail to fully disclose the purpose of their study or knowingly withhold details about possible long- or short-term risks. An inevitable consequence of deception is that participants are likely to feel betrayed, cease to trust in the research enterprise, or see researchers as dishonest. On occasions when deception cannot be avoided, as soon as it is practical to do so participants are usually told about the nature and rationale for the trickery. Investigators typically plan debriefing exercises to rectify any harm, informing participants of their role in generating findings and how the findings will be used.

Once planning is complete and approved by appropriate review committees, investigators can proceed to the recruitment phase. Before moving on, some investigators take time to pilot-test their activities using individuals with characteristics similar to those of the target population.

Recruiting Participants and Obtaining Consent

The process of identifying participants usually contains more steps than is obvious from reading typical research reports. Investigators usually face constraints that are imposed by their geographical location and the availability of performance sites for their research. When working within existing institutions, investigators are also regulated by the policies and practices that are features of those institutions. Some institutions may have their own review policies that are independent of those regulated by the national Office for Human Research Protections (OHRP) from which most universities' Institutional Review Boards (IRBs) are derived.[9] Investigators are obligated to coordinate the standards of all governing boards when conducting research.

One step in the recruitment process involves identifying participants and evaluating the qualities of the resulting sample. In many cases, investigators would prefer to randomly select participants from a clearly defined population. Unfortunately, randomization is nearly impossible when voluntary participation is a requirement of research because it is rare for everyone approached about a study to agree to participate. Randomization may also be inappropriate for some studies. It is commonly preferred when using psychometric tools and may be useful when studying development. Nevertheless, randomization may be inappropriate for ethnographic studies in which participants are recruited for their cultural expertise or role within a community. Investigators may also find it necessary to include persons they would not otherwise select to balance the needs of particular research sites and their own interests. These and other related dilemmas have led investigators to distinguish various sampling techniques for coordinating design and practical concerns, some of which are defined in Table 2.3.

TABLE 2.3   Sampling Techniques

TECHNIQUE	DEFINITION
Random sampling	A target population is identified and participants are randomly selected from all possible persons in that population.
Stratified random sampling	A target population is identified and participants are selected to reflect a balance along planned dimensions (e.g., gender, ethnicity).
Representative or proportional sampling	A research site is identified and participants are recruited until a sample contains the same range of characteristics as is evident in the population of individuals at the performance site.
Nonprobability or convenience sampling	All who volunteer from target performance sites are included in the study.
Expertise-based sampling	Participants are identified because they hold levels of expertise that are essential for understanding the phenomenon under investigation.

Ordinarily, investigators think of recruitment and consent processes as two steps in the research enterprise, even if both activities are completed simultaneously. Recruitment procedures are established to ensure the resulting data will offer a balanced representation of how humans function, and that no one feels unnecessarily pressured into volunteering or unjustly excluded. Individuals may be approached in the recruitment phase of a study, but excluded if they fail to offer consent or meet investigators' sampling needs.

In clinical settings, to avoid misunderstandings about the availability of necessary services, the recruitment step is sometimes kept separate from the consent process. This minimizes the pressure on clients to volunteer. Investigators may send out notices requesting that volunteers contact them about the study or ask permission to continue with the consent process after offering assurances about client's rights.

Scrutinizing the practices associated with obtaining informed consent is important for ensuring that interactions with participants are as fair as possible. Sometimes resulting practices limit researchers' ability to obtain all the research information they would like; participants may be willing to cooperate with only some activities. Obtaining consent may also require the modification of research practices to better accommodate participants' needs.

Ideally, participants are fully informed of their rights and of people to contact if they find themselves mistreated. In addition to the information in Table 2.4, investigators also consider participants' potential for anxiety. Investigators who feel compelled to use inducements, for example, ensure that those inducements are not so extravagant or coercive that participants feel unduly influenced to volunteer for a study.

Another highly important feature of the consent process involves the treatment of data that are generated by and on behalf of each participant. Sometimes investigators keep absolutely no record of who did and did not participate in a study. In that case, the information remains *anonymous*. In other cases, researchers may ask participants to sign consent forms, provide contact information, or reveal unusual features of their identity that would ensure they stand out in a research report. When some facet of a person's identity is detectable, investigators are obligated to maximize *confidentiality* when storing data and reporting their findings. There are times when neither anonymity nor confidentiality can be sustained. Prior to such investigations, investigators submit their work for careful review in which their procedures for adhering to the principles of respect for persons, beneficence, and justice are scrutinized. Regardless of how much privacy will be provided, volunteers are told of any known risks associated with their role in a study and how the data they help generate will be used.

When most adults are given as much information as commonly occurs during the consent process, they are able to make informed choices about whether to participate in a study. If anonymity is not preserved, investigators often take time to put various agreements in writing and ask participants to sign a copy after clearly indicating an understanding of the information. If anonymity is preserved, participants may be given oral instructions and/or a written outline of the agreement, but would not be asked to give researchers a signed copy to indicate consent or assent. During this process, volunteers may be asked to summarize the ideas they hear and are free to ask questions as investigators monitor their knowledge of particular rights.

As was noted earlier, there are people who are unqualified to offer consent without assistance. Members of some protected groups may be unable to fully understand research details or the long- and short-term consequences of their involvement. Others may reside in institutions where *coercion* (an overt threat of harm) or *undue influence* (an offer of excessive, unwarranted, or inappropriate rewards) could be used to obtain compliance. Special protections are put in place for these individuals to ensure their well-being takes precedence over research goals.

Consider once again the special protections in place for research including children and adolescents. Special guidelines were established in 1990 by a Committee for Ethical Conduct in Child Development Research, sponsored by the Society for Research in Child Development. For most studies, children and adolescents are not qualified to offer informed consent. Research on normal educational practices is usually exempt from this rule because

---

TABLE 2.4   A Participant's Bill of Rights

Participants have the right to know:

- Why the study is being conducted.
- Why they are being recruited.
- What procedures are involved in the investigation.
- What possible risks or discomforts they might face.
- Any benefits from participating in research.
- Emerging information that might affect their willingness to participate.
- How investigators will preserve privacy (confidentiality or anonymity).
- Any costs or reimbursements for participation.
- Their right to withdraw at any time during a study.
- Investigators' right to remove individuals from a study.
- Relationships with participating institutions will not be affected.
- Who to contact about particular rights.
- Who to contact for information about the study.

the topic of inquiry would undergo scrutiny without being included as research. Ideally, everyone involved with young people as well as the young people themselves accept some level of responsibility for their welfare. Whenever possible, young people are asked to assent before participating in research activities. More formal kinds of consent are obtained from young people's parents or guardians as well as any other adults who are responsible for their care.

These guidelines also extend to the design phase of a study. Research involving children and adolescents cannot knowingly be harmful. Deception and excessive incentives are studiously avoided. Investigators, caregivers, and young people are expected to avoid miscommunication about the research project, label any surprising events that could place children at risk, and search for unforeseen consequences. Before reporting any research results, investigators agree to carefully consider the long- and short-term implications of their design and possible findings. They also adhere to all confidentiality or anonymity agreements with research participants and their families.

These guidelines may seem familiar to investigators who work with other protected classes of persons, and the rules were generated using the three principles of respect for persons, beneficence, and justice. When working with special populations, procedures for spelling out these rights during the consent process tend to be more elaborate than is the case with adults; adults are assumed to be strong enough to convey their reactions as they occur whereas protected classes of individuals are seen as more vulnerable. Not surprisingly, these recruitment and consent procedures have a profound effect on who participates in studies of human functioning.

Interactions during a Study

Just because participants have given their formal consent prior to encountering research activities does not absolve investigators of responsibilities when collecting data. This is an especially important reminder for situations in which the principal investigator or senior researcher does not directly work with participants. It is easy for individuals who are not particularly invested in the outcome of a project to take shortcuts and otherwise fail to take seriously their responsibilities for ensuring participants' rights. Research assistants benefit from special reminders of their obligation to help participants leave research situations feeling as good about themselves as they did on entering.

As a new investigator, you may find yourself working as a research assistant and are likely to benefit from such on-the-job training. It might be helpful to know that, for major studies, participants are sometimes interviewed about the qualities of their interactions with investigators. More commonly, it is up to investigators to monitor their skill at conducting research by eliciting feedback from participants and those who work with them.

Opportunities to collect data can offer rich insights into individuals' perspectives. Establishing working relationships with participants while watching senior scholars produce a strong product can be quite pleasurable as well as instructive. Talking about these experiences with mentors and peers can offer rich perspectives on the subtlety of research on human functioning. Joining several different projects can reveal the versatility of many measurement tools as they are used for different theoretical purposes. Volunteering for such experience, even if it is not part of a paid job, can teach as much or more than formal coursework.

The actual processes of measuring human functioning may seem easy when observed from a distance, but most investigators require training and practice before obtaining strong data. Even the administration of a simple survey can be complex if researchers have not thought carefully enough about the range of responses to (1) research situations, (2) the role of the investigator, and (3) the task at hand. When investigators understand tasks well enough to automatically implement them, they are likely to have sufficient mental resources to imagine the perspectives of each volunteer. This level of proficiency helps investigators monitor the progress of each participant and evaluate comfort levels. When confident about their responsibilities, most investigators are also better able to work with a sense of humor and positive demeanor.

Putting Planning into Action

Before approaching potential research participants, investigators generate solutions to several dilemmas. In designing a study, investigators verify that the data obtained from each volunteer will be treated with appropriate balance so as not to distort the contributions of each individual to the study as a whole. They usually ensure that participants are adequately informed about the research enterprise and determine if incentives are likely to instigate undue influence or coercion. Investigators also plan methods for assuring confidentiality or anonymity when findings are reported. At the core of these activities is pressure to help volunteers feel confident about their research efforts and to ensure this sense of dignity remains while results are shared. Investigators also verify that volunteers remain confident in the value of research, even if deception is used. Unforeseen consequences cannot be prevented, but researchers can anticipate many of the benefits and burdens instigated by the structure of a research problem.

MAKING CONNECTIONS

Suppose you decide to conduct a study. How would you approach individuals about participating? Will members of protected classes be included? If so, how will you obtain consent and assent? Will it be important to preserve anonymity? If so, how will you inform participants of their rights without recording their names or the names of any designated guardians? How will you avoid labeling individuals who do not volunteer? What will you say to help participants realize that their involvement is voluntary? What will you tell participants about your plans for the data? What will you say about the risks associated with your study?

IDENTIFYING APPROPRIATE MEASUREMENT TOOLS

Even if participants are well-treated, there are still ethical decisions that can affect the integrity of a study. One of those decisions concerns the selection or design of appropriate measurement tools. Investigators who take time to explore existing measures can sometimes save themselves the frustration of designing and validating new measures. One means for doing this is to explore the *Buros Mental Measurements Yearbook* and the corresponding *Tests in Print* catalogue.[10] This contains reviews of the strengths and limitations of many existing measures. Different disciplines also offer databases of available measures.

If so many tests are already available, why do investigators need to design new ones? One reason is that, when constructing new knowledge, investigators often do not fully understand the standards they will need for measuring each variable. Investigators may use a combination of existing and newly developed tools to tap into new directions. Using well-developed tools for purposes other than that for which they were intended can undermine an investigator's ability to collect necessary information for drawing sound conclusions. Not surprisingly, the most straightforward guidelines for identifying measurement standards emerge from well-developed theoretical frameworks, but such frameworks are not always readily available.

Across disciplines, measurement techniques have become quite specialized, yet a few ethical concerns seem to permeate most investigations. In choosing an appropriate measurement tool, most investigators try to imagine how data will be utilized, acknowledge limitations by considering fair use and measurement bias, and admit that measurement always contains error. They also consider respondents' attitudes and elicit feedback from respondents. The following sections elaborate on each of these themes, yet theory construction in each discipline invariably introduces additional issues.

How Will Data Be Utilized?

To construct or identify an appropriate form of measurement, investigators determine a plan for using the information they gather from participants. When measuring competence, for example, investigators look for ways to distinguish what participants can and cannot do; responses are evaluated as correct or incorrect. Attitudes are typically measured using scales designed to accentuate individual differences in beliefs. When measuring behavior and physical characteristics, investigators are now able to evaluate and code many once fleeting types of action. To measure change, investigators consider a host of additional measurement dilemmas that are solved differently, depending on the kind of change being explored. Techniques are invented for recording interactions to explore dynamic relationships among participants or between investigators and the participants of a study. Sometimes investigators also use a combination of tools in a single study. Regardless of how elaborate their measurement plan, most investigators try to match the information obtained from each tool to the components of the theoretical framework being measured.

Are the Limitations of Each Tool Acknowledged?

All tools contain some form of bias and offer only limited information on the phenomena being measured. Investigators commonly struggle to identify bias and determine if it reflects something that is *in a test* or something associated with *the way a test is used*.[11] Questioning the distortion in a test reflects *balance*, while the use of a test reflects *fairness*.

Distinguishing these two levels of consideration has made it easier to recognize how both concerns are important when selecting or designing measurement tools.

Consider a complicated tale reported by Frederikson (1984) that raises issues of bias and fairness. During World War II, the U.S. Navy initially relied on multiple-choice tests of technical manuals for maintaining, adjusting, and repairing guns to verify that gunner's mates could fulfill their responsibilities. The test alone, according to this story, ultimately led to the training of incompetent gunner's mates. Recruits could pass the written tests with high scores, but apparently could not perform essential skills in the field. Once the Navy initiated a testing plan that required recruits to actually manipulate guns, students spent their time practicing necessary job skills. The content of the curriculum remained the same, but a change in the measurement tool led to a change in students' knowledge and the abilities they developed to pass the exams.

Although the article in which this story was published was called "The Real Test Bias," the story of the gunner's mate also illustrates fairness. Bias was relatively easy to detect because the ideal skills were observable and the test did not offer a balanced representation of those skills. Nevertheless, the wrong style of measurement was being used, which inadvertently affected the skills that students acquired. Frederikson noted that bias was introduced into the measurement tool because a complex concept was tailored to a particular measurement scale. In focusing on test bias, he raised questions about the limitations of multiple-choice item formats and cogently argued that items included on the test did not reflect the skills to be assessed. Others might see this as an argument about fair use; multiple-choice tests do not offer a fair assessment of the skills that gunner's mates were expected to perform. To see the difference, let's untangle these issues a bit more clearly.

Fair Use. Investigators learn to live with the fact that all measurement tools are imperfect, but they are also careful to be fair when formulating generalizations about their data. Gunner's mates who could not perform well in the field were labeled incompetent even though they could competently pass multiple-choice training tests. To maximize fair use, examiners probably matched the blueprint for the training measure to the skills required by the training. They could also have determined if the combination of tools in a study adequately addressed the range of issues embedded in the more general theoretical framework; behavior was as important as knowledge in the training of gunners' mates, yet the test only measured the latter. Comparing measurement tools and desired outcomes inevitably led to the selection of new tools.

Fair use ultimately involves the selection of measurement techniques and requires knowledge of the researcher's measurement purpose. Ethics are violated when the two knowingly do not match. This was also evident in the earlier discussion of achievement tests. It might be unfair, for example, to use tests designed to evaluate individual differences in achievement for evaluating the overall quality of schools. To make this case, investigators require knowledge of how particular instruments are designed and strengths and limitations of data generated by such tools.

Balance. Ideally, investigators remember that even the fairest choice of tools introduces bias because abstract or complex constructs are represented using limited measurement scales. As was evident for gunner's mates, the presentation of items and their format directs attention to particular features of a problem and cues participants to the nature of the task at hand. The ability of gunner's mates to actually perform maintenance tasks remained unmeasured. Similarly, the economists' evaluation of school quality using achievement test scores does not explore the curriculum available to students; comparing test scores without sufficient information on the details of students' daily school experience offers an incomplete assessment of school quality. The incompleteness in both measures fostered bias that disrupted the balance of the measurement plan and the overall structure of the research problem. Preoccupation with efficiency in measurement can leave important dimensions unmeasured, leading to false conclusions about the data.

To minimize the effects of bias, some investigators use multiple measures of the same construct or of related constructs. They also look at how the structure of particular measurement activities aligns with the skills and abilities of respondents. Investigators may avoid creating such lengthy tools that participants' attention wanders during a test. They may minimize distortion by ensuring that respondents fully understand all the points on scales they utilize and can use such scales consistently. Similar examples emerge out of the particulars of how different tools function. Exploring the content of items to determine if they offer an adequate representation of each dimension for relevant constructs is also an essential aspect of balance.

Integrating Fairness and Balance Concerns.   The fair use of a test requires thoughtful consideration of a theoretical framework and the kinds of conclusions to be explored. Balance is determined by imagining all aspects of the phenomenon to be measured. If investigators are striving to predict or control behavior, they will imagine different criteria for evaluating the limitations of a tool than if they are trying to describe general patterns of human functioning or offer a thick description of an isolated phenomenon. When completed ethically, both fairness and balance issues are integrated in all measurement plans.

What Types of Error Can Be Minimized?

A third generalization related to measurement bias is the recognition that all tools contain an error score that cannot be accurately represented. Many statistical tools are used to estimate this kind of unknown error, but investigators also learn to interpret obtained scores with caution. Investigators usually distinguish sources of variance in scores to better isolate undetected random error from controllable error that emerges over the course of a study.

The safest way to estimate controllable error is to adhere to the technical skills established for inventing tools using different measurement scales. In coming up with guidelines that form the core of this book, measurement experts carefully conducted computer simulations in which new suggestions for designing tools were tested for a wide range of contingencies. They also monitored the application of different styles of measurement to particular kinds of research questions and identified which administration procedures are more and less likely to result in accurate judgments. Identifying and minimizing controllable forms of error can strengthen the accuracy of each tool, even if all measures inevitably contain undetectable random error.

How Will Respondents' Attitudes Influence the Performance of a Tool?

A fourth generalization involves understanding the perspectives of individuals who are likely to use each measurement instrument. Recall that the ethical treatment of human subjects usually leads participants to maintain their dignity in a research setting. This implies that the measurement of participants' thoughts, feelings, and behavior should not induce long-lasting forms of discomfort. Investigators cannot control participants' attitudes and beliefs, but they can try to anticipate the range of perspectives that are likely to emerge. With these ideas in mind, some methods for responding to problems or correcting misinformation can be devised prior to situations in which they are likely to occur.

Toward this end, many investigators decide if particular tools are likely to make participants feel denigrated, embarrassed, or ashamed. They also look for pressures embedded in research situations that could entice participants into unethical behavior such as tattling, lying, cheating, or stealing. Considering the tone of particular measurement tools, it is also helpful to ask if participants are likely to feel accused, coerced, deceived, or cheated. Similarly, honest responses are unlikely if participants feel manipulated or overworked to such an extent that they feel their abilities and ideas are being distorted. Finding ways to minimize these possibilities can maintain dignity while facilitating accuracy in the representation of participants' functioning.

How Will Respondents Be Informed about the Use of Their Responses?

Measurement can also be more accurate if participants are able to anticipate their own role in a study as well as researchers' interests. Volunteers are more likely to be comfortable about responding to particular tasks and tend to exhibit more honesty and signs of commitment. Investigators typically assure participants that their responses will remain confidential or anonymous unless otherwise negotiated. Nevertheless, participants are naturally curious about how their interests will be represented during the study and once the findings are reported. They wonder if anyone might benefit or be harmed by the information collected and are naturally critical about the measurement tools. Participants also wonder if investigators will be accurately listening to and recording their views or behavior.

As part of this scrutiny, many participants can be naturally critical of requests for personal information and may think about whether their answers would stand out. Investigators who want personal information from participants are often aware of a natural tendency for individuals to hide their vices and celebrate their virtues. Adults may exhibit extra concern with privacy when asked to report on their family background, personal history, interests and values, financial management skills, and social adjustment (Rosenbaum, 1973). Some young people are also highly self-conscious about responding to measures of their competence. When investigators take time to let participants know what they plan to do with personal information, some of this anxiety can be alleviated.

Debriefing as a Source of Information

Taking time to talk with participants at the end of a study can often teach investigators about the strengths and limitations of their choice of measurement tools. When conducting surveys on adolescent's ability to notice exclusion, for example, participants were ready to respond to the items we offered, but also suggested that more in-depth interviews might help us understand the complexities they faced. They also asked questions while responding to the survey that helped us imagine which items might be confusing and whether we had offered a comprehensive representation of behavior they noticed. Although this information did not change the measurement tool itself, it offered new information on the limits of our assessment that we otherwise might have missed. Participants' advice has even spawned new directions for our research program.

MAKING CONNECTIONS

How will you identify the measures for your study? Looking at *Tests in Print* or similar databases, are there tools already available for your agenda or will you have to design new tools? What theoretical concerns are most important to measure? What kinds of information will you require? How will you combine information from your measurement tools? What are the limitations of the tools you selected? How will you ensure that you adhere to fairness and minimize bias in your measurement plan? How will you ensure that you do not make participants inordinately uncomfortable? What can you do to minimize error? What are respondents likely to think about your plan? How will you find out about their experience in your study?

IMPLEMENTING A STUDY WITH ACCURACY

Once a study has been designed, measurement tools selected, and participants recruited, investigators confront additional ethical dilemmas associated with procedural justice (Baumrind, 1964). Regardless of how data are collected, the implementation of any study is inevitably fraught with error caused by the unpredictability of human functioning and current events. Responses to particular dilemmas differ considerably across disciplines. Here, I will illustrate some dilemmas from my research with children, but encourage you to discuss the pragmatics of collecting data with others in your area.

Working in established institutions such as public schools, I have been confronted with the four primary dilemmas: (1) minimizing invasiveness, (2) accommodating a design to include all volunteers, (3) comparing an accommodated design to a theoretical framework, and (4) isolating valid conclusions. Working with a small team of assistants, I collect my own research data rather than send teams of research assistants into schools. This is unusual and investigators who work with data-collection teams are likely to face more extreme versions of the dilemmas than I have uncovered as well as dilemmas I have not anticipated. Being readily available to consider situational challenges, I have minimized misapplied effort and maximized strong communication. Nevertheless, the scope of each study tends to be narrower than would be possible with a larger team of investigators. Regardless of the scope, some generalizations can still be useful.

Minimizing Invasiveness

Probably the most difficult dilemma in the implementation phase involves minimizing disruption while knowingly intruding on normal routines. Thoughtful investigators remain sensitive to the potential invasiveness of their study for individuals who have little or no concern for research. When gaining permission from performance sites, researchers typically justify why their work is important enough to interrupt individuals' normal routines and alter daily institutional practices. You may remember that, when the design of a study is reviewed, investigators try to eliminate potential risks to participants. At the implementation stage, they revisit this question and may become fixated on limiting adversity associated with any unpreventable risks. Although participants are usually told about potential risks, opportunities to minimize them are explored while studies are underway. Many investigators also go out of their way to graciously thank participants for their time and efforts, but are careful not to rely too heavily on inducements.

Accommodating the Design to Volunteers

The selection of participants and performance sites inevitably leads to modifications in preplanned research designs. Investigators often explore whether the interests of volunteers can be better coordinated with the needs of researchers. Sampling issues and contingencies that occur at the research site commonly pose threats to the implementation of even the best-laid research plans, but flexibility in decision making can sometimes foster more valid conclusions than would otherwise have been possible.

Sampling Dilemmas. Invariably, researchers face dilemmas concerning the representativeness of samples in relation to the population to which conclusions will be generalized. Sometimes the necessity of voluntary participation prohibits investigators from achieving the goals of a particular piece of research, but the resulting sample can still yield interesting and useful findings. Although investigators realize that bias in the selection of a sample can limit the integrity of research findings, they often make field-based decisions on how to stratify samples along unanticipated dimensions. Remembering that investigators use different sampling techniques to recruit participants (Table 2.3), the initial plans for one kind of sample are sometimes adjusted using another, more practical technique.

Unplanned Events. Despite the best of intentions, investigators usually face unplanned events that undermine their ability to accurately execute a study. Cooperation of performance sites sometimes wavers, space that should have been available ceases to exist, or people who intended to be cooperative sometimes change their minds. Most investigators respond to these contingencies by engaging in on-the-spot problem solving, preserving the integrity of their relationships with participants and of their research design. Knowing why each activity in a design was planned, each tool was selected, and each participant was included can help investigators remain flexible during frustrating events.

Compare an Accommodated Design to Theoretical Concerns

When designs are changed out of necessity, most investigators are careful to reevaluate the relationship of a new design to the theory it reflects. Using external logic, for example, investigators sometimes select participants with predetermined characteristics and identify how these participants differ from others. Consider research on children with learning disabilities. Investigators have learned a great deal about the learning process by identifying children who exhibit academic difficulties and describing their characteristics. In so doing, investigators cannot fully identify the population to be sampled. Instead, they label the characteristics that comprise learning disabilities and select participants with those characteristics. Research would lose integrity if investigators mislabeled the characteristics of learning disabilities or if they included participants without the required characteristics. Such a study might not lose integrity, however, if characteristics like gender were irrelevant to the theoretical framework and a sample contained more boys than girls.

Using inferential logic, either deductively or inductively, random assignment is often necessary for initial investigations, but the definition of the populations under investigation may vary across studies. Working deductively, investigators typically identify a theoretical framework and look for validation of that framework. Working inductively, investigators typically identify a set of relationships among variables and look for a means of explaining those relationships. Exploring individual differences among participants may be a central component for accurate tests of a theory, but other details of a design may be malleable. Constant comparison between obtained evidence and theoretical claims can ensure that investigators do their best to offer valid evidence.

Isolating Valid Conclusions

All the frustrations associated with actually conducting a study can lead investigators to mistakes as well as successes in the research enterprise. This awareness keeps investigators concerned with separating valid and invalid forms of influence on the outcome of a study. Invariably, samples are imperfectly selected, participants behave in unpredictable ways, and the qualities of the data collected do not always conform to expectations. Some forms of error are unlikely to influence the value of the information collected, but other sources ultimately undermine a study's validity. A major part of implementing a study is to collect the information necessary for drawing conclusions about the viability of particular findings.

In settings where participants are assumed to be representative of a population, investigators sometimes look for equitable distributions of scores across various samples and acknowledge apparent flaws when distributions are unbalanced. The more experience investigators have with a particular field or tool, the better they are able to determine which unpredictable events are likely to influence the findings of a study and which are superfluous. Similar questions take different forms when the design of a study is nonexperimental. Investigators look at how findings converge to draw conclusions about the strengths of their evidence. In questioning the accuracy with which their plans are executed, most investigators identify those constraints that are likely to limit the value of their research. To avoid this step for each stage of an investigation is to raise serious ethical dilemmas about the integrity of a research program.

MAKING CONNECTIONS

Imagine implementing a study. What procedures will you use to make sure your study is conducted accurately? How will you cross-check your work? What converging evidence will you use to verify that your sample is appropriate? How will you determine that any manipulations in your design were apparent in the results? Should this manipulation also be apparent to participants? What problems are likely to emerge as you collect evidence? How will you distinguish valid and invalid evidence? Find senior scholars in your field who are willing to tell you about their trials and tribulations with research.

REPORTING RESULTS

Given that most studies acquire imperfections at the implementation stage, investigators typically realize that an uncritical analysis of their findings would result in unethical levels of distortion. The process of reporting results typically involves levels of critique that may not be shared when findings are disseminated. The critiques reflect a careful cross-checking of relationships between indicants on measurement tools, dimensions of a construct, relationships between constructs, and relationships between evidence and theoretical claims. Some ethical rules of thumb are evident for each of these steps, keeping in mind that the outcome of earlier steps tends to influence the outcome of later steps.

Promote Parsimony in Analysis

Parsimony in research is a norm that governs all fields. Investigators combine indicants into scales, scales into variables, and variables into evidence for theoretical assertions. To take deliberate shortcuts at any of these points is to introduce problematic forms of distortion. This simple norm is obviously very complex and one field's definition of a shortcut may be another's definition of parsimony. Nevertheless, if investigators label the strengths and limitations of their work, they realize that all forms of measurement are merely indicators of a more elaborate phenomenon. Labeling the points at which indicants fall short while striving for parsimony can minimize the potential to make exaggerated claims.

To treat motivation as if it were a switch that can be turned on or off, for example, is to radically oversimplify existing knowledge of motivation. Simple behavioral indicators may be sufficient for some kinds of analysis, but not for others. Investigators' theoretical agendas offer key guidelines for deciding what does and does not constitute adequate levels of parsimony.

Evaluate the Balance and Fairness
of Each Measurement Outcome

While implementing a study, investigators often make decisions to modify a measurement tool or plan, accommodating any beneficial interests of volunteers. They also find that volunteers may not behave as planned. An important step in constructing results, therefore, is to evaluate the performance of each tool.

Looking at particular indicants, investigators tend to explore the variability in responses. They also identify methods for combining indicants that do not misrepresent the dimensions measured and verify the stability and accuracy of these decisions. Looking at the resulting instruments, investigators reconsider the balance with which each dimension is measured. They also compare the details of their final measure with its purpose in the design to determine if the outcome fairly represents each construct. Skipping these steps can introduce a form of distortion that might otherwise be avoided, and knowingly reporting distorted findings is unethical. When distortion cannot be minimized, investigators often replicate a study before disseminating its findings.

Acknowledge the Limitations
of Each Measurement Technique

Investigators are also obligated to remember the limitations of each measurement technique when analyzing their results. This is essential for determining how to combine variables; differences in analytical techniques account for variability in the types of data available. Distinguishing statistical techniques for data involving psychometric measurement is relatively straightforward compared to the complexities associated with analyzing dynamic forms of development or the levels of inference in ethnography. Nevertheless, misalignment can occur for all forms of analysis.

Investigators sometimes use available analytical tools to help them chunk variables in the analysis phase. Considering the interview example again, analysis of variance techniques may be used to compare average ratings across groups and may be included in the same paper as a content analysis of justifications. However, the measurement scales for these two types of data do not lend themselves to direct comparison. Both types of information may help validate theoretical assertions, but investigators who remember the limitations of each technique will use caution when combining them into a single set of analyses.

Compare the Design and Final Measures

Balance and fairness can be considered at the design level as well as at the measurement level of an investigation. When some tools do not show the reliability, validity, or generalizability that investigators had anticipated, design changes may be necessary. Frustrating as it can be, when a design becomes so imbalanced that theoretical claims can no longer be evaluated, most investigators abort a project or repeat the study rather than offer problematic results.

Determine Authorship

Research is often a collaborative enterprise and investigators generally find it necessary to negotiate intellectual credit for the final product. Ethical dilemmas invariably arise in this process.[12] Generally speaking, investigators take on credit and authorship only for work to which they have introduced intellectual contributions.[13] Credit is usually assigned to reflect the scientific contributions of the individuals involved and does not include clerical or other support staff. In many fields, papers generated from masters' or doctoral theses typically list the student as a primary author even if the student required enough assistance to warrant multiple authors.

It might seem easy to make such determinations, but authorship can involve quite a bit of negotiation when teams of researchers are inventing new knowledge. Senior or more knowledgeable researchers do not often convey how much coaching they instigate while trying to maximize feelings of autonomy among team members. Preoccupation with credit is also a means of undermining the intellectual value of research because egos rather than ideas tend to be the central focus of collaboration. To facilitate negotiations, guidelines for determining authorship are usually published by the professional organizations of most disciplines.

Credit Sources

You may recall that most studies reflect an extension of existing lines of work that is usually grounded in common sense. Scholarly writing, therefore, requires a judicious use of citations linking current findings to previous work (Madigan, Johnson, & Linton, 1995). Citations establish authors' credibility as an expert in the field and offer background information. Writers use citations to label members of a discourse community, contrast positions, or otherwise indicate the background of a study. Unlike writing in the humanities, social scientists summarize findings rather than offer quotes and are less burdened with making transitions between different rhetorical styles.

This combination of factors can sometimes challenge investigators' ability to accurately identify the sources for their ideas. The game of telephone comes to mind: As individuals pass information from one person to another, that information can become distorted. Seasoned investigators maximize the likelihood of fully crediting their sources by constructing their own database of articles they have read, informal conversations that were instructive, or the sharing of unpublished papers. Developing rituals for citing research while designing new studies, reporting new findings, or reviewing existing research are highly valuable resources for a career researcher.

A hard lesson for most new investigators comes from the adage, "imitation is the sincerest form of flattery." Investigators who assume they have invented truly original ideas usually fail to understand how the mind stores and retrieves information and that most topics emerge from common sense. Some individuals may think at such a concrete level that they are unconscious of just how often they borrow ideas from others around them. Others are overly attuned to commonalities in key words but may not take time to discriminate different theoretical perspectives. Investigators who capriciously offer discrepant accounts of their research eventually undermine their own credibility and the credibility of their field as a whole. Attempts at fraud, either through the fabrication of data or data collected with an identifiable conflict of interest, may be difficult to replicate. Clever cheaters may take a longer time to be identified, but ideas that have limited credibility ultimately lose their potency in more general conversations.

Seasoned scholars remember that research is a conversational enterprise in which ideas are usually compared in open and honest ways. More often than not, historical times and local contexts tend to direct the attention of multiple researchers to the same topic of inquiry. Plagiarism—the deliberate copying of ideas or words without citing the source—certainly exists and can be relatively easy to detect by experts in a field. Remembering the role of common sense in research, the importance of evidence to support ideas, and the value of converging evidence from multiple research communities can help investigators sustain a level of humility about their own contributions to a field. In many fields, quality research is more valuable than personal popularity and quality is determined, in part, through replication. Staying grounded in the details of a particular project can maximize investigators' ability to label creative contributions while remembering the role of common sense when defining interesting research problems.

Coordinating Issues

Knowing the imperfections in human memories and in how a study is conducted, most investigators are cautious about summarizing their findings. Looking for limitations as well as strengths in each study, investigators learn to understand the fallibility of individual products and the value of aggregate forms of evidence. Over time, meaningful evidence often becomes more salient and rare findings lose their potency. Staying productive is more likely if investigators approach science with some level of humility and a willingness to converse with other researchers. Sales people may emphasize only the positive or unique features of their products, but researchers learn as much from exploring the limitations of their work as from exploring its strengths.

- - - - - ▬▬▬▬▬▬▬▬▬▬▬▬▬▬▬▬▬▬▬▬▬▬▬▬▬▬

MAKING CONNECTIONS

Have you ever found a study in which the results were reported in a biased manner? What helped you see the bias? When the investigators reported their results, did they label the limitations of their study? Have you seen examples of plagiarism? How should the work have been cited? What penalties could be enforced for such cases?

QUESTIONING PERSONAL JUDGMENT

At this point, it is probably obvious that investigators learn to scrutinize every aspect of their work and to openly criticize its strengths and limitations. They also scrutinize their own motives and judgment, and at least two institutional structures are in place for helping investigators do so. One set of structures is associated with membership in national and international professional organizations. Investigators remain affiliated with such organizations to keep their knowledge of a field current and most of these organizations offer some means of evaluating investigators' qualifications. Professional organizations may offer licensing procedures, some type of formal test of investigators' qualifications, or publishing opportunities for disseminating new knowledge. Regardless of how they do so, these organizations offer an external assessment of investigators' training and competence.

A second set of institutional structures is associated with funding for research. Before receiving research funds, universities cooperate with federal agencies and foundations in the support of ethical review boards that recommend procedures for the treatment of human subjects and animals in research. Investigators submit research proposals to institutional review boards as well as federal grant agencies for peer review. In those two kinds of review, investigators receive feedback on the quality of their project as well as on their qualifications for implementing a project. This feedback helps investigators decide which avenues to pursue in their work and which avenues to avoid.

Investigators participate in such different kinds of work that it is impractical to establish a single set of criteria for evaluating their professional judgment, but some key questions are asked of anyone who conducts research. The most basic questions involve evaluating the qualifications of each investigator. Investigators can assist in this process by participating in the following activities.

Update Training

Before receiving institutional support for research, investigators are asked to verify the adequacy of their professional training and competence. They do so by acquiring degrees, licenses, and skills that confirm their abilities. The training process may also involve opportunities for direct experience in an apprentice role wherein future investigators learn from experts. Trainees may leave with knowledge about the research process, but until they demonstrate competence by collaborating with other qualified researchers, they will continue to be supervised while conducting research.

Develop Professional Relationships

Once actively involved in research, investigators are also expected to maintain professional relationships to function in their field. This kind of competence reflects the acquisition of new skills that emerge in informal contexts. Investigators learn from the materials that are published in their fields and from their experience with data, but they also learn from professional colleagues who show integrity when sharing their discoveries. Ideally, investigators develop professional relationships with people who are and are not researchers and maintain integrity in all of those relationships. As with any kind of relationship, investigators are aware that if they make decisions when overtired or otherwise unfit, their diminished competence can undermine important professional relationships.

Seek Feedback

Even when investigators are well-qualified and working at an optimal level of competence, there is convincing evidence that their clinical judgments are usually less consistent than those generated using systematic methods.[14] Some types of decisions are unavoidably generated using clinical judgments but to ensure balance, most investigators rely on actuarial methods of validating their conclusions. They realize that humans usually overattend to ideas that support their hypotheses and overlook contradictory evidence. This propensity can be constrained by finding tools to facilitate the consistent scoring and recording of research findings. Such actuarial procedures can minimize investigators' propensity for overconfidence in their professional judgments because the resulting tools offer a means for comparing personal preferences and those based on systematic inquiry.

Evaluate Measurement Skills

In one study of the common qualifications necessary for using tests effectively, investigators also found evidence of poor test use (Moreland, Eyde, Robertson, Primoff, & Most, 1995). This clinical study allowed investigators to identify some of the essential competencies relevant for research. Investigators with strong measurement skills can be seen:

- ensuring that their measurement plans are comprehensive enough to achieve the goals of their investigations;
- refraining from helping respondents during an investigation;
- accepting responsibility for the competent use of each measurement technique;
- interpreting observations and test scores using current knowledge about the limitations of the measure;
- maintaining the reliability, validity, and accuracy of scoring when classifying results;
- establishing new norms for each type of measurement;
- offering participants the interpretive feedback necessary for understanding their scores and the use of those scores.

Not all investigators rely on formal testing, but these guidelines can be adapted to many different kinds of measurement settings. As new information about the constructs or phenomena under investigation become apparent, investigators are obligated to remain knowledgeable about existing technologies. They ideally cross-check their assumptions with sources in their discourse community and look for opportunities to learn new ways of conducting research. Finding reliable critics can be quite challenging in the highly competitive world of research, yet finding such persons becomes essential for learning the limitations of personal judgments.

MAKING CONNECTIONS

What kinds of feedback do you elicit on your work? To what extent are you looking for ways to improve your work? What sources of information do you rely on? How do you elicit peer reviews? How do you evaluate your measurement skills? What do you do with evaluative information?

LEARNING ETHICS

Every discipline has ethical principles and guidelines for ethical conduct.[15] The guidelines are regularly critiqued and revised as the knowledge within a particular field evolves.[16] Conversations typically include members of the ethical review committees that are local arms of a federal governing body, leaders of national and international professional organizations, and national commissions formed to solve particular ethical dilemmas. Over time ethical guidelines have become progressively more elaborate, and investigators are expected to follow the ethical codes of their respective disciplines. In doing so, they adhere to moral as well as legal standards.

New researchers learn appropriate attitudes, facts, and behaviors by participating in conversations that stimulate collegial debate. Voluntary compliance is hopefully accomplished through moral persuasion rather than legalistic means. Evaluating the features of case studies is one means for stimulating such conversations.[17] Investigators can coordinate the details of specific cases with the features of the standards in their discipline and make judgments on various courses of action. Questions such as those in Table 2.5 can be useful when engaging in this process.

In the process of analyzing the decisions of others, investigators can learn to question their own personal judgment. Even seasoned investigators participate in ethical conversations with professionals who offer helpful critiques of such judgment. When investigators disagree, they ideally probe the disagreement to determine if everyone is considering the same set of contextual assumptions. When critiquing particular situations, it is helpful to label differences in interpretation and evaluate which assumptions can be changed to facilitate a common definition of the dilemma at hand. Investigators also imagine how particular

---

TABLE 2.5   Questions Associated with Ethical Decision Making

After identifying the details of a case study, investigators can ask themselves the following:

- What are the features of the problem to be solved in this case?
- Are there paradigmatic considerations that should affect the judgments?
- Are there features of the problem that conform directly to particular standards?
- Are there features that seem relevant to a set of standards but are obfuscated by the choice of words?
- Is the intent of a standard accurately represented in the case being evaluated?
- Are there features of a standard that are vague or ambiguous? How can the clarity of a standard be improved?
- Identify the relevant facts that seem important for consideration when making judgments? How should these be prioritized?
- How can facts be used to justify judgments about ethical considerations?
- How does the rendering of a judgment alter the perceptions of the dilemma? Would the case look differently if the judgments were changed?

Note: These guidelines are adapted from those found in Strike, Anderson, Curren, van Geel, Pritchard, & Robertson (2002, p. xiv).

decisions might be changed for variations in facts and/or imagined contexts. Once investigators agree on the facts of a situation, it is usually easy to make wise moral judgments. Most investigators would like to maximize respect for persons, beneficence, and justice in the research enterprise. Seasoned investigators realize that no one is qualified to determine the validity of their own judgment; everyone's human interests lead to somewhat distorted perspectives of themselves as well as others. They learn to be wise and moral in their treatment of others' research and hope their colleagues will do likewise.

SUGGESTED READINGS

American Bar Association. (1990). *Model code of professional responsibility and code of judicial conduct.* Chicago, IL: Author.

Rawls, J. (1972). *A theory of justice.* Cambridge, MA: Harvard University Press.

Sales, B. D., & Folkman, S. (Eds.). (2000). *Ethics in research with human subjects.* Washington, DC: American Psychological Association.

Strike, K. A., Anderson, M. S., Curren, R., van Geel, T., Pritchard, I., & Robertson, E. (2002). *Ethical standards of the American Educational Research Association: Cases and commentary.* Washington, DC: AERA.

Walzer, M. (1983). *Spheres of justice: A defense of pluralism and equality.* New York: Basic Books.

SUGGESTED WEB SITES

American Anthropological Association: http://www.aaanet.org/committees/ethics/ethics.htm
American Bar Association: http://www.abanet.org/
American Counseling Association: http://www.counseling.org/site/PageServer
American Educational Research Association: http://www.aera.net
American Political Science Association: http://www.apsanet.org/
American Psychological Association: http://www.apa.org/science/faq-findtests.html
American Sociological Association: http://www.asanet.org/members/ecostand.html
Buros Center for Testing: http://www.unl.edu/buros
National Association of Social Workers: http://www.socialworkers.org/
Office for Human Research Protections: http://ohrp.osophs.dhhs.gov/
Society for Research in Child Development: http://www.srcd.org/about.html#standards
The Belmont Report: http://ohrp.osophs.dhhs.gov/humansubjects/guidance/belmont.htm

ENDNOTES

1. One Web site where *The Belmont Report* can be found is http://ohrp.osophs.dhhs.gov/humansubjects/guidance/belmont.htm..

2. Ordinarily, distributive justice involves the distribution of goods and resources, corrective justice involves decisions about regulating conduct, procedural justice involves evaluations of the steps by which individuals attain goals, and commutative justice involves consideration of the greater good or the welfare of society.

3. See, for example, a once controversial paper by Baumrind (1964) that no longer seems controversial.

4. Luciana & Nelson (2002) and Nelson, Monk, Lin, Carver, Thomas, & Truwit (2000) offer examples of such research.

5. See an example of the process and a product in Kuhn (1968).

6. Kuhn (1992) has done systematic investigations of how individuals learn to rely on thinking as a form of argument.

7. See Blanck, Bellack, Rosnow, Rotheram-Borus, & Schooler (1992) for an outline of how these benefits seem to emerge over time. See Ellickson & Hawes (1989) for a

study on the effects of different forms of parental consent on the selection of a sample that has not been incorporated into accepted practice.

8. Baumrind (1964, 1985) offers fairly obvious accounts of this process. Sieber (1992) reviews some subtle forms of deception and their effects.

9. The Office for Human Research Protections, http://ohrp.osophs.dhhs.gov/, currently regulates most universities.

10. University libraries generally hold these books, but the Buros Center for Testing can also be found on-line at http://www.unl.edu/buros.

11. See Shepard (1982) for an elaboration of both test bias and fairness issues.

12. American Psychological Association (2001, 2002). See also Strike, Anderson, Curren, van Geel, Pritchard, & Robertson (2002) for guidelines established for the American Educational Research Association, and interesting case study material designed to facilitate ethical thought about implementing such standards. Fisher et al. (2002) raise ethical dilemmas about conducting research with minority youth.

13. Fine & Kurdek (1993) offer case studies that can be compared while negotiating authorship.

14. Meehl (1986) and Dawes, Faust, & Meehl (1989), among the most outspoken scholars who have investigated this issue, have outlined the benefits of relying on actuarial methods of decision making.

15. For example, the National Commission for the Protection of Human Subjects of Biomedical and Behavioral Research published *The Belmont Report* (1979). The American Psychological Association has published several iterations of their Ethical Principles of Psychologists and Codes of Conduct (1992); the most current version is available on their Web site and in the style manual, while ethical deliberations are regularly published in *American Psychologist*. The Ethical Standards of the American Educational Research Association (1992) were published in the *Educational Researcher.* The Society for Research in Child Development (1990) typically relies on the guidelines established by APA, but contributes information on the ethical treatment of young people to national conversations. Web sites for most major organizations have or will have their ethical standards posted.

16. Critiques and guidelines are available in books (e.g., Canter, Bennett, Jones, & Nagy, 1994; Hoagwood, Jensen, & Fisher, 1996; Sieber, 1992; Strike et al., 2002) and journals (e.g., Pritchard, 1993, 2002).

17. These guidelines are adapted from those found in Strike et al. (2002, p. xiv).

CHAPTER THREE

ASSUMPTIONS OF PSYCHOMETRIC MEASUREMENT

The remaining portions of this book are divided into three sections focusing on psychometric, developmental, and interpretive measurement techniques. You may remember from reading the Preface that concepts like stability, accuracy, validity, and generalizability change in meaning across measurement styles but remain central to the challenge of properly calibrating a tool and ensuring that tools measure the entities they purport to measure. One major challenge in this enterprise is that some dimensions of a measurement plan are inferred rather than measured directly and different techniques reflect variation in decisions about what constitutes appropriate forms of inference.

Although this book highlights three different approaches to actual and inferential forms of measurement, the approaches are neither mutually exclusive nor mutually exhaustive. There are also times when the material is somewhat arbitrarily subdivided or placed near other information to facilitate sufficient topical balance while maintaining readability. Similarly, external, inductive, deductive, and interactionist logic can be used when designing measurement plans. Remembering the toolbox metaphor and the value of identifying norms within particular discourse communities may help you see that metaphorical wrenches or screwdrivers come in many different shapes and sizes without losing their constitutive purpose. Investigators commonly borrow assumptions from more than one research paradigm, yet the psychometric, developmental, and interpretive measurement approaches introduced here are sufficiently distinct that differences among them are likely to become apparent.

For each section, an outline of common assumptions is offered to emphasize theoretical differences in measurement. This first section begins with psychometric assumptions and distinguishes measurement concerns based on *random sampling theory* from those common to the physical sciences. Psychometricians try to account for forms of systematic error that are rarely evident in the measurement of physical entities. The developmental section adds questions about the measurement of change. Tools for measuring development are often used in combination with psychometric tools, but new techniques are also necessary for measuring unpredictably dynamic phenomena. The interpretive section introduces questions of how communal agendas and cultural norms are interesting in their own right and affect measures of individual variation. These cultural influences raise yet another level of uncertainty that cannot be adequately measured by relying only on psychometric or developmental assumptions. Interpretive theorists typically request that research participants play a role in designing and evaluating instruments; they assume tools based solely on deductive or interactionist logic offer an inaccurate sense of human functioning. Taking inductive logic to an extreme, for example, ethnographers consistently question their assumptions and alter those assumptions throughout the project; very little remains stable in their measurement approaches, but accuracy takes on many levels of meaning.

In theory construction, regardless of a theorists' measurement paradigm, concepts are usually seen as dynamic entities. To reify a theory or set of ideas is to misunderstand the nature of social science even if that theory offers the best current explanation for the phenomena under investigation. Similarly, the measurement enterprise can involve several different levels of inference. Investigators may try to evaluate:

- *Indicants*—actual entities that can be recorded using the senses or equipment that simulates direct observations
- *Dimensions*—combinations of indicants or theoretical components of a more general construct
- *Latent variables*—entities that cannot be recorded but reflect second-order inferences about particular dimensions or constructs
- *Constructs*—combinations of dimensions that reflect abstract or theoretical entities embedded within a more general concept
- *Concepts*—combinations of latent and observed constructs used to explain particular theoretical claims

Figure 3.1 offers two schematic representations that combine indicants, dimensions, latent variables, and constructs. Those entities that can be directly measured are represented using boxes and those entities that reflect inferences are represented with ovals.

Figure 3.2 contains one schematic representation of academic engagement, used to explore motivation. Combining latent variables and indicants, the concept brings forth several kinds of interpretations. Generally speaking, individuals' dispositions toward demonstrating competence affect their beliefs about the purposes of school, which in turn affect their participation in classroom activities. A strong task orientation leads individuals to see school as teaching them to contribute to society and understand the world, driving classroom participation. An ego orientation calls attention to understanding the world and gaining wealth and status, with classroom participation a means to the end of fulfilling such agendas. Work avoidance is associated with the belief that school should facilitate wealth and status, but not with participation. Despite the seemingly permanent nature of this measurement plan, this theoretical concept remains open to variability in use and definition.

The fact that concepts cannot be directly observed constrains investigators' ability to measure them. Nevertheless, investigators try to identify all known parameters or observable dimensions of a theory and explore possible relations.

Deductive Model

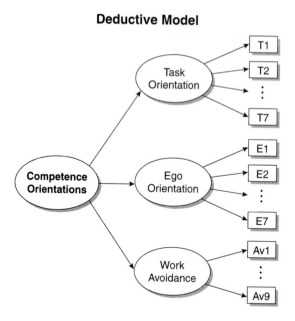

Inductive Model

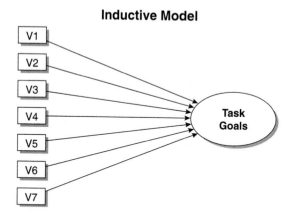

FIGURE 3.1   Representations of Indicants, Dimensions, and Constructs

COORDINATING THEORY AND MEASUREMENT

Some levels of analysis apparent in psychometric measurement can be elaborated and exemplified by comparing the models in Figures 3.1 and 3.2 with several key terms. Recall that *indicants* are items, observation points, or codes that represent ideas being measured

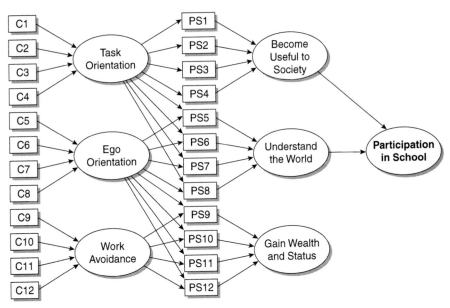

FIGURE 3.2   The Theoretical Concept of Academic Engagement (PS = Purposes of School, C = Competence Orientations)

and are represented with boxes. *Dimensions* are levels of a construct that ensure a comprehensive representation of theoretical ideas and are usually inferred from the measurement of indicants. In the example, task orientation, ego orientation, and work avoidance are dimensions of individuals' competence orientations and reflect parts of a larger personality theory. Table 3.1 contains sample items from competence orientation measures designed for use with adolescents. Ordinarily, indicants are selected to offer fair and balanced representations of each dimension, but this final measure admittedly contained error. Notice, for example, that the inferiority dimension of ego orientation contains only two items. Many individuals express these feelings by also demeaning the work they are expected to accomplish, a tendency that made it difficult to distinguish ego orientation's inferiority dimension from work avoidance.

Constructs reflect abstract entities or the estimated latent variables and may contain one or more dimensions. In the deductive model of Figure 3.1, *competence orientation* reflects a latent construct that is superordinate to task, ego, and work avoidance orientations, but these dimensions reflect inferences about what makes individuals feel successful in school. Indicants offer information about corresponding latent variables, but rarely reflect a complete representation of each dimension. In the inductive model, a *task goal* is inferred from particular indicants to represent a future-oriented construct that focuses on what an individual would like to accomplish. Task orientation is a personality dimension linked to someone's definition of competence, but a task goal refers to the agenda someone sets for a

TABLE 3.1   Communalities for Indicants of Competence Orientations

IN SCHOOL, I FEEL MOST SUCCESSFUL WHEN . . .	COMMUNALITIES
TASK ORIENTATION	
Something I learned makes me want to find out more.	.54
I get a new idea about how things work.	.52
I learned something interesting.	.54
I solve a tricky problem by working hard.	.60
I finally understand a really complicated idea.	.58
Something I learned really makes sense to me.	.59
A class makes me think about things.	.40
EGO ORIENTATION AS SHOWING SUPERIORITY	
I do the work better than other students.	.63
I show people I am good at something.	.61
I show people I'm smart.	.64
I score higher than other students.	.69
I am the only one who can answer the teachers' questions.	.48
EGO ORIENTATION AS AVOIDING INFERIORITY	
I don't do anything stupid in class.	.78
People don't think I'm dumb.	.75
ACADEMIC ALIENATION	
I get out of some work.	.47
I do almost no work and get away with it.	.60
I put one over on the teacher.	.57
I fool around and get away with it.	.61
I don't have to do any homework.	.59
I didn't have to work hard.	.64
All the work was easy.	.54
The teacher didn't ask any hard questions.	.60
I didn't have any tough tests.	.56

Note: This report involves secondary data analysis of multiple samples, $n = 951$, ages 13 to 20.

particular situation. Decisions about how terms are defined and used typically hinge on what investigators want to accomplish in a measurement plan and how that agenda corresponds to more general theoretical claims.

Constructs are also combined to form *concepts* or sets of relations between latent variables and their corresponding estimates. The concept of academic engagement represented in Figure 3.2 reflects an explanation that can be verified alone or used in combination with other concepts in a larger theoretical framework. Competence orientations, beliefs about the purpose of school, and class participation reflect three constructs in this more general engagement concept.

These features of a measurement model represent a hierarchy of inference that can be relatively stable when psychometricians draw conclusions about their data, but some levels are not acknowledged as often or as clearly as new investigators might like. Investigators design tools to empirically verify levels of abstraction in as concrete, bounded, and exact a ways as possible.[1] They begin with assumptions about a concept and identify relevant constructs and corresponding dimensions. Task orientation, for example, is assumed to involve commitments to interest and effort whereas ego orientation is assumed to reflect a preoccupation with the self and identity issues. Searching for methods to verify the existence of task and ego orientation, investigators identified entities in the world around them. To represent those entities, investigators may attach numbers to their observations while realizing that each empirical indicant represents only a small subset of the possible range for a particular dimension. When evaluating a tool, constructs are combined using iterative procedures to form theoretical concepts that may eventually be simplified or measured more directly. Ego orientation, for example, was initially conceived as involving several different components, but the dimensions of showing superiority and avoiding inferiority have proven to be stable across samples while interests in social approval or conformity have not been consistently detected.

Explanations, in this approach, represent the final associations between abstract concepts and empirical indicants. In Figures 3.1 and 3.2, explanatory connections are designated by arrows to indicate relationships between constructs. When investigators rely on two-way arrows, they are making weak empirical claims about relationships. One-way arrows reflect stronger claims concerning relationships between indicants and dimensions, dimensions and constructs, or constructs and concepts. Gaps in the logic of associations between indicants and concepts reveal theoretical directions in need of improvement, either by strengthening a measurement plan or by revising theoretical claims.

To verify the existence of a concept, psychometricians typically compare new concepts to previously measured, theoretically related concepts. They explore variance and verify possible relationships among dimensions to estimate the predictability of particular entities. These investigators struggle to identify guidelines for such decisions before designing an actuarial instrument that actually measures their assumptions. Guidelines emerge from comparisons of new dimensions, constructs, or concepts with those already assumed to exist, but some researchers also associate previously unexplained ideas with physical entities. The resulting tools, regardless of established guidelines, are usually calibrated against probabilistic rather than deterministic standards.[2] This differs significantly from the physical sciences because scores are interpreted using *means, estimates of variance,* and *probabilities.* Numbers rarely have quantitative value in their own right.

DIFFERENCES IN PHYSICAL AND PSYCHOLOGICAL MEASUREMENT

In the physical sciences there are relatively few measurement controversies once a unit of measurement is agreed on because latent variables and inferences occur at later stages of the research process. Physical scientists can find deterministic parameters such as inches, quarts, or pressure for use in comparing new indicants against a standard. Social scientists, on the other hand, consider many levels of controversy when designing a measurement plan. There is controversy over how a concept is defined, how it is measured, and its general meaning in relation to other concepts.[3] Psychometricians debate the value of every new concept, establish a wide range of parameters for defining it, and offer diverse forms of evidence for its existence. Not only is the identification of a comparative standard highly controversial, in some cases it may not be possible.

Let's compare, for example, the similarities and differences in measurement for social and computer sciences. Measuring human characteristics and programming a computer each involves the translation of abstract ideas into concrete indicants. Like variables in the social sciences, one kind of computer program is usually constrained by the operating system used to run that program. Dimensions of a single program like *Picture It!* or *Word* are obligated to correspond to the larger operating system in which it must function.

Unlike social scientists, computer scientists can rely on the stable features of computer hardware when making assumptions about relationships among the indicants of programs and operating systems. The hardware for which operating systems and corresponding software is calibrated is deterministic in that hardware offers a stable set of constraints that software designers have no choice but to consider. Even well-designed software cannot work if it is incompatible with existing hardware or if there is a hardware failure. Social scientists, in contrast, rarely find such tangible entities for anchoring their measurement tools. They rely on the abstract assumptions of probability theory and use somewhat arbitrary guidelines when testing assumptions about the existence of a construct. Indicants form a sample of entities used to estimate a particular dimension, but nothing in the design of social science research functions with the certainty that is possible when abstract concepts can be calibrated in relation to tangible entities.

MAKING CONNECTIONS

Define the components of a theory in your field of study. Does the theory contain more than one concept? Are there different constructs in this theory? How are constructs related to the concept under investigation? Does each construct contain more than one dimension? Can any of the constructs be compared with a known physical entity? How are the dimensions related to one another? What are some of the common indicants of each dimension to be measured?

STRATEGIES FOR LINKING INDICANTS AND CONSTRUCTS

To design an effective measurement tool and include that tool in a larger research design, psychometricians address several questions:

- What is the empirical meaning of each concept?
- Are there underlying latent variables necessary for exploring a concept?
- What constructs and dimensions will be measured?
- What measurement scale is appropriate for each dimension?
- How important is replication for theory construction?
- What kinds of stability are required for adequate tool performance?
- How adequate is the concrete representation of abstract ideas?

Starting at the theoretical level, investigators endeavor to formulate concrete definitions of their concepts and identify measurable features. By looking for relationships among new constructs and existing concepts, they try to subdivide abstract ideas into manageable constructs and corresponding dimensions. If a theory offers a strong enough explanation for ideas, investigators are able to directly explore relationships by measuring each dimension of all relevant constructs. Once relevant dimensions are labeled, indicants are associated with constructs. Ideally, all dimensions are represented with concrete items, observations, or other measurable entities.

MAKING CONNECTIONS

It is often difficult to link concepts and indicants. To do so, investigators endeavor to record known, measurable information and estimate unknown features of a measurement plan. By verifying known dimensions and estimating predicted dimensions, new knowledge becomes possible through an iterative process. Investigators learn as much from their failures as from their successes. Identify a concept in your field, and develop a plan to connect indicants to that concept. Will the process of designing a new tool involve one study or many?

MEASUREMENT LANGUAGE

Reliability and *validity* are devices used to evaluate every use of a measurement tool and all research designs. These devices, in combination, enable investigators to translate abstract, indirectly observable constructs into the concrete representations associated with sensory experience. As was evident in Chapter 1, reliability involves relations between indicants and is often verified using *correlations*. Validity is often explored by comparing patterns between variables that have been measured with different tools. Details on these processes will be introduced later, but the remaining portion of this chapter will focus on the logic underlying these central and related concepts.

The most commonly used formula for computing correlations is the Pearson product moment correlation (r_{XY}). This coefficient estimates the degree to which two sets of scores show a linear relationship when one is compared with the other and is typically used with interval or ratio data. The formula for the Pearson r is:

PEARSON PRODUCT MOMENT FORMULA

$$r_{XY} = \frac{n \sum XY - (\sum X)(\sum Y)}{\sqrt{\left[n \sum X^2 - (\sum X)^2 \right]} \cdot \sqrt{\left[n \sum Y^2 - (\sum Y)^2 \right]}}$$

In this formula, $\sum XY$ is the sum of the cross products of X and Y (calculated by multiplying, for each participant, their obtained X and Y scores). $\sum X$ is the sum of the X scores and $\sum Y$ is the sum of the Y scores. $\sum X^2$ and $\sum X^2$ involve squaring each score and then adding the squared numbers together. Finally, n refers to the number of paired scores and often reflects the number of participants in a measurement sample.[4] As will become apparent in later chapters, the normal range of a correlation coefficient is from -1 to $+1$, but in reliability evaluations all relations are assumed to be positive.

As is the case for theorizing about physical relationships, *classical test theory* remains a dominant statistical approach to defining indicants. Psychometricians have revised this theory to acknowledge a type of error related to the probability assumptions that underlie measurement. Psychometricians accept that:

- all measurement in the social sciences contains error;
- some forms of error are random;
- some forms of error are not random;
- systematic error remains an uncontrollable component of any score.

This revision accounts for two important limitations of classical measurement theory.[5] First, classical measurement theorists assume that all obtained scores are comprised of a *true score* and an *error score* and that all measurement error is random. The assumption that all error is random is untenable in the social sciences where there is no deterministic point of certainty. Therefore, *systematic error* is an uncontrollable feature of each tool.

In graphic illustrations of how collections of obtained scores are typically related in comparison to an ideal true score distribution, the overall variability of actual scores is usually larger than that of the true score distribution: the area under the obtained score distributions is often wider and the curve is flatter than the theoretical distribution. Patterns of error lead to different types of distributions across samples. Figure 3.3 reflects the theoretical true score distribution. Repeated administrations of the same tool would typically result in different curves, but if the measure could be administered an infinite number of times, those curves are expected to aggregate around a "true" midpoint. Differences in how well obtained and theoretical distributions are aligned reflect systematic error in how the

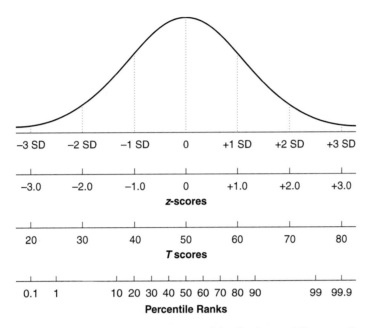

FIGURE 3.3   The Theoretical Normal Distribution and Common Standard Scores

tool functions. Investigators try to estimate that error by comparing results from repeated use of the tool.

Reliability and Measurement Error

Given these calibration issues, *reliability* is the calculation of whether any expected relationships between true and obtained scores are consistent with the data collected. At a conceptual level, reliability can be seen as the variance of true scores divided by that of obtained scores to estimate the proportion of nonrandom variance captured by a measure. Reliability can be calculated whenever at least two indicants of the same dimension are available. Ideally, indicants of the same dimension are correlated with one another and do not fluctuate wildly as a result of random error. The theoretical formula is as follows:

RELIABILITY

$$r_{XT} = \frac{\sigma^2(T)}{\sigma^2(X)}$$

In this formula $\sigma^2(T)$ represents the variance of the true scores and $\sigma^2(X)$ represents the variance of the obtained scores. The index r_{XT} refers to the reliability estimate where X refers to obtained scores and T refers to theoretical true scores. Not surprisingly, the variance of true scores is typically based on probability estimates that are derived from the number of indicants on the measure and the number of participants in a sample; true scores cannot be directly measured.

Another way of looking at reliability coefficients is to think of them as aggregate indices of whether indicants on a scale are intercorrelated. If scores can be estimated using parallel items, items will contain similar variance in their respective true and error scores. Introducing systematic or random error would undermine the strength of the association between such scores.[6] If all observed variance is contaminated by error, the reliability across indicants will be 0. If all observed variance is error-free, the reliability will be 1.

Table 3.2 contains both an overall reliability coefficient for the items measuring task orientation and the change that would take place if an item were deleted from the scale. Comparing these two kinds of indices allows investigators to evaluate the quality of items on a scale as well as the overall consistency in item functioning. As measurement scales differ across tools, different mathematical procedures are required to estimate reliability, but the logic of this process remains the same.

Psychometricians' decision to introduce *unknown systematic error* terms into representations of true scores is not trivial. If all error were random, it would be safe to assume that on repeated use of a tool, the *expected mean* or average of all error estimates is 0. The correlation between *theoretical true scores* and *error scores* would also be 0 because error terms would be treated as the constant 0. Without a systematic error term, it could also be assumed that the correlation between the error score on one measurement and the true score on a second administration of the same tool is 0. Similarly, the correlation between the error scores on distinct measurements using the same tool would be 0. Variability across distributions of obtained scores would not be detected. In essence, an error term would be left out

TABLE 3.2 Reliability and Item Analysis Information for Task Orientation

TASK ORIENTATION	RELIABILITY COEFFICIENTS (α)
Overall alpha coefficient	.85
Alpha if the designated item is deleted from the scale	
I feel successful if . . .	
Something I learned makes me want to find out more.	.83
I get a new idea about how things work.	.83
I learned something interesting.	.83
I solve a tricky problem by working hard.	.82
I finally understand a really complicated idea.	.82
Something I learned really makes sense to me.	.82
A class makes me think about things.	.85

Note: Cronbach's alpha (α) was used to estimate reliability for participants ranging in age from 13 to 20, $n = 951$. All the items offer a meaningful contribution to the scale; alpha coefficients do not become larger if an item is deleted.

when interpreting obtained scores and there would be no accounting for the fact that instruments are rarely calibrated the same across repeated use.

Even though some forms of error in social science research are systematic rather than random, investigators do not always know the source of such error. Ignoring systematic error has mistakenly led many investigators to assume that the *expected mean of a true score* equals the *expected mean of an obtained score* and to overlook the necessity of estimating the amount of error in their tools. Because of the untenable assumption that all error is random, a systematic error term is introduced to acknowledge the inevitable error in a tool's performance.

Differentiating Reliability and Validity

The second limitation of classical measurement theory noticed by psychometricians concerns the relationship between *reliability* and *validity*. Before explaining this limitation, let's think about how the two measurement criteria differ from one another. You may remember that reliability estimates the error in how one tool functions. *Validity* estimates how well constructs are measured by a particular set of indicants.[7] Items may cluster together nicely on a scale, but have nothing to do with the dimension or construct being measured. Whereas reliability is the correlation between two or more indicants of *X,* validity involves relations between measurements from tools *X* and *Y. Y* is usually a known measure of a construct and *X* is a new measure of theoretically related or contrasting variables. When two measures are parallel, the proportion of shared variance evident in obtained scores can be estimated.

Figure 3.4 offers a graphic depiction of task orientation and task goals, two measures that are assumed to be highly associated. Notice that the distribution of scores on each measure differs, but the overall pattern of scores seems to follow the trend line. This suggests that when the same people respond to both measures, higher scores on one measure are likely to be associated with higher scores on the other. Investigators might predict that individuals with a task-oriented definition of competence also set task-focused goals for themselves and that the high degree of association between both measures indicates validity.

Next, consider the assumption that individuals who support a task-oriented definition of competence may not support an ego-oriented definition of competence. This is also a validity question, but involves the determination of dimensions within a tool. Although some samples show low correlations, task orientation and ego orientation are not typically correlated; correlations that are near 0 indicate discriminant validity. Look at how many scores in this distribution fall away from the trend line. Both graphs depict validity, but one compares highly related measures and the other compares unrelated dimensions on a single competence orientation tool.

There is a mathematical constraint for evaluating the validity of a tool. Comparisons cannot be greater than the square root of a tool's reliability.[8] Reliability constrains validity. There may be systematic error between two indicants of the same construct, and the relationship between constructs and indicants is also likely to contain unknown forms of systematic error. Investigators do their best to identify all forms of systematic error using existing knowledge, reasonable assumptions, and informed guesses about the nature of the concept underlying a set of indicants. Despite everyone's best efforts, systematic error is

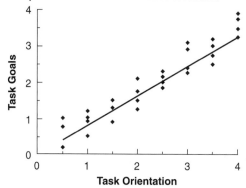

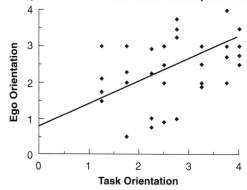

FIGURE 3.4 Examples of Reliability and Validity Associations

still likely to be a feature of the measurement process and estimates of validity are affected by this error. As is apparent in Figure 3.4, validity estimates sometimes involve predictable contrasting as well as converging evidence. Correlations between tools can be negative.

Turning back to the shortcomings of traditional classical measurement theory, the distinction between reliability and validity had been eliminated when all error terms were treated as random. It became impossible to estimate error in the variability of scores from two different measures because error terms dropped out of mathematical calculations. Put another way, if all correlations involving error terms are 0 across multiple measures, error is eliminated from validity formulas, rendering reliability and parallel estimates of validity equivalent. Such equivalence would not accurately reveal the relationship between theoretical entities (be they concepts, constructs, or dimensions) and corresponding indicants because the resulting model excludes the reasonable assumption that two different tools will not be identically calibrated. Among other things, to eliminate the error term is to ignore the fact that indicants offer only a small sense of the abstract dimensions they represent.

Adjusted True Score Theory

In short, psychometricians assume that their tools contain uncontrollable systematic error that is not accounted for in the classical representation of *true score theory.* Systematic error can include features like personal characteristics (e.g., health, concentration, recent life events), features of the situation (e.g., comfort of the room), examiner characteristics (e.g., examiner's race, idiosyncrasies or subjectivity in ratings or observations), and characteristics of instruments (e.g., equipment issues, sample items, appropriateness of item format). For stronger theories, investigators are able to identify many of these potential constraints, but it is safe to assume that the dynamic nature of human functioning will render it impossible to rule out all forms of error. While remaining aware of error constraints, most investigators admit to an inability to discern which features are operating at any given point in time.

Psychometricians have proposed an *adjusted true score theory* that accounts for systematic error and the lack of randomization in error distributions. They break down the error term into component parts and accept that an observed score is equal to the sum of a *true score* (T), *systematic error* (s), and *random error* (r).

ADJUSTED TRUE SCORE THEORY

$$X = T + s + r$$

Random error may drop out of estimations, but systematic error is accounted for when calibrating a tool. Rather than try to add up known and unknown components of an obtained score, psychometricians usually apportion the obtained variance by determining which portions are attributable to a true score, systematic error, and random error. Some theorists go so far as to differentiate *shared variance among indicants* from the *variance exclusively attributable to each indicant* when imagining the true score, *T.* They assume that the variance of any obtained score X is the covariance *TS,* accepting that systematic error is such a notable feature of any score that this common variance should be acknowledged. *Obtained variance* and *random variance* may be estimated, but most methods of analysis cannot accurately differentiate estimates of the *unique true score variance* associated with each indicant, the *systematic error variance,* or the common covariance, *TS.* Even sophisticated formulas have their limitations.

Summary

Psychometricians recognize that relationships between reliability and validity depend largely on the degree of systematic error generated by each tool. Although validity cannot be stronger than reliability, validity and reliability can be equal when two sets of related indicants contain no systematic error; indicants would show only the random fluctuation estimated by reliability coefficients. Validity is significantly lower than reliability when there is a high degree of systematic error in one or both tools. Furthermore, tools may show perfect reliability, but have no validity; the measurement may be repeatable but have no correspondence with theoretical concepts. Well-designed theories typically support tools developed with less systematic error and greater levels of validity than newly emerging theories. Investigators can use relevant evidence to support their decisions about which indicants do and do not belong in a model. As investigators become better able to understand systematic error, modify measures to account for this knowledge, and alter their measurement tools to accommodate new questions, they are better able to limit but not eliminate systematic error from their measurement plans.

■ ■ ■ ■ ■

MAKING CONNECTIONS

Choose one dimension of a construct in the theory you identified earlier. What issues would you consider while defining indicants for that dimension? What questions would you ask before confidently assuming that your choice of indicants is adequate? What sources of error would you anticipate?

NUMERICAL REPRESENTATIONS

Before interpreting sets of indicants, several statistical methods are used to compute scores and explore relationships among them. This section offers a general sense of how investigators represent abstract ideas using numbers. Fundamental assumptions are introduced along with methods for generating numerical representations of those assumptions. All of these concepts will be discussed in greater detail in the remainder of the book.

Connecting Indicants to Numbers

Numbers sometimes represent *discrete categories* that are independent of one another. They may also represent *continuous scales* in that numbers represent real differences between points on a scale that can be combined in a variety of ways. To determine which tools to use, investigators explore whether their tool has representational or nonrepresentational measurement properties. *Representational* measurement is evident when numbers correspond to positions on a continuous scale that offers quantitative meaning.[9] With such systems, investigators are free to use mathematical functions to combine indicants because quantitative relationships between the indicants can be deduced from the assigned numbers. This facilitates the use of a wide range of parametric statistical tools to analyze data. In the social sciences, representational measurement is possible if scales achieve interval or ratio properties. Variables like age, weight, or height conform to this structure.

Some ordinal scales may also lend themselves to the parametric statistical analyses associated with representational measurement. Achievement test scores tend to consist of ordinal scales, but approximate an interval scale. Investigators can learn that someone with a high score may understand the material better than someone with a low score, but the details of how "knowledge" is quantified remain confusing. Items may contain different levels of difficulty even if performance scores do not reflect those differences. Such scales could be continuous if investigators were able to show monotonically increasing functions with sufficient correspondence to the latent variable of achievement.

The social sciences also rely heavily on *nonrepresentational scales.* Numbers are used to represent groups, but the number itself has no inherent meaning. Ordinarily, investigators compare the frequencies of indicants or persons within each category to formulate representational information. Consider a study in which students were asked to determine how much testing is fair in school. One group of children reported the belief that "testing is learning," a second group reported that "tests offer helpful feedback," a third group reported that "tests interfere with learning," and a final group reported a desire to "avoid all evaluations." These four categories of beliefs could not be meaningfully ranked. Investigators used chi-square (χ^2) statistics to determine if students' beliefs differed as a function of the schools they attended (Thorkildsen, 2000). The formula for chi-square is:

CHI-SQUARE FORMULA

$$X^2 = \sum n \frac{(P_{obs} - P_{exp})^2}{P_{exp}}$$

In that formula, P_{obs} represents the proportion of observed frequencies in each cell of a matrix of scores, P_{exp} represents the expected proportion for each row of scores, and n is the total number of observations in each column.

When variables do not lend themselves directly to analysis using mathematical operations, investigators also sometimes use transformations to modify the parameters of a scale before using parametric statistical techniques (see Dawes, 1972; Dawes & Smith, 1985). Consider the competence orientation measures once again. Respondents indicated their relative agreement or disagreement with each item, and numbers were assigned from one to five, approximating an order that could ideally elicit a normal distribution of scale scores. When responding to parallel items, each individual is assumed to use the measurement scale in the same way. Investigators who add or average items to form a scale make this assumption by approximating comparable intervals. It is problematic, however, to assume that all respondents use the five-point scale in the same way; individuals may not imagine the same interval between points on the scale. Some respondents, for example, may respond using superlatives that offer strong opinions whereas others may offer a similar opinion using more moderate language. Differences in their mean scores would not necessarily reflect differences in the magnitude of their judgment. This is further confounded by the fact that the middle of the scale is treated as the origin and the average of extreme scores could lead to the same conclusion as would be found if everyone indicated they had no opinion. Relations between responses have meaning, but means and other representational indices may not offer an accurate account of the findings.

When categories form an ordered scale, *monotonic transformations* can preserve the order of indicants whereas *linear transformations* can preserve the distance as well as the order between indicants. These types of transformations offer one means of accommodating different uses in scales when comparisons across individuals are necessary. *Multiplicative transformations* are possible only with ratio scales, but because of the absence of an absolute 0, such scales and transformations are rarely evident in social science research.

The scale of measurement—the degree to which numbers reflect ordinal, interval, or ratio scales—is considered in computing total scores for representing indicants.

Some measurable dimensions have no meaningful order and investigators represent them as discrete categories or *nominal scales.* Relying on nonparametric statistics to compare the frequency of classifications in each category, investigators can still compare quantities. Nevertheless, these numbers do not reflect a magnitude of the measured dimension. Pregnancy is one example of a nominal scale that cannot be quantified. Numbers used to represent yes and no symbolize nonoverlapping categories. Despite political trends toward violating this biological norm, it is rarely assumed that a woman can both be pregnant and not pregnant. To explore such nominal categories, investigators typically look at how characteristics are distributed across a sample and compare that distribution to probabilistic frequencies embedded within their statistical tool.

Ordinal scales are also discrete in that the distance between numbers is unknown. Investigators may look at frequency distributions and rely on nonparametric statistical tools for ordinal as well as nominal data. As noted earlier, they may also combine items to form continuous scales and remain cautious about interpreting magnitudes. As was the case for creating a task orientation scale, investigators may average the ordinal numbers themselves. As is the case for most achievement tests, they may also identify and count the number of "correct" responses across items. In either case, equal intervals between numbers are approximated with an allowance for systematic error, but interpreting the magnitude of an entity remains challenging.

With an *interval scale,* it is possible to use addition and subtraction to explore relationships among particular scores and parametric statistical tools to explore the variance in and between particular variables. When investigators use variables like age or time as a ruler for measuring change, they are acknowledging the importance of interval scales. Because *ratio scales* are rarely if ever found in the social sciences, little will be said about them, yet interval scales like time or pressure are sometimes modified to include an absolute 0 point using equipment that can be turned on or off.

Once a measurement scale is identified and scores are calculated, investigators sort and tally those scores by looking at the overall distribution or at how many respondents obtained each score (Figure 3.5). When data are categorical, investigators rely primarily on histograms to represent the distribution of scores. When data form continuous scales, investigators usually construct frequency polygons or scattergrams to account for the equal intervals between numbers. They can also construct categories for histograms by classifying representational scores into groups.[10]

Characteristics of a Distribution

There are several important features of each distribution. First, an ideal distribution of scores forms a bell-shaped curve that is used as the probabilistic norm to which all obtained distributions are compared. This *normal distribution* of scores and any *obtained distribution* each have *measures of central tendency* that indicate the distribution's midpoint (Figure 3.3).[11] The *mean* reflects the average score, calculated by adding all scores and dividing by the total number of scores. The mean takes into account the actual value of every number in the distribution, but is affected by the placement of extreme scores. The *median* is the

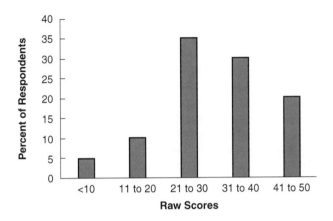

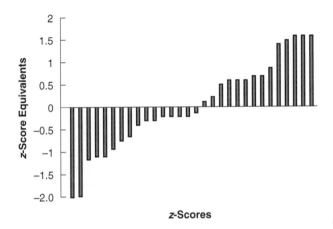

FIGURE 3.5   A Sample Distribution of Raw Scores and Corresponding *z*-score Equivalents

middle score, calculated by ranking all scores from highest to lowest and finding the score that is exactly in the middle. When there is an even number of data points, this middle score can fall between two actual scores. Because only the middle score is selected, the median is not affected by extremely high or low scores. The *mode* is the most frequent score in a distribution, calculated by identifying the common score or scores regardless of their placement in relation to other scores. Ideally, a distribution has only one mode, but in practice bimodal and multimodal distributions are sometimes apparent. In a perfectly normal distribution, such as that represented in Figure 3.3, the mean, median, and mode are all the same: Exactly half the scores fall above the measures of central tendency and half fall below with the most frequent score falling exactly in the middle.

Investigators tend to prefer different measures of central tendency depending on the properties of the scales they are using. The *mean* is generally preferred when scales have *interval* or *ratio qualities* because the scales contain equal intervals between points that permit investigators to calculate an arithmetic average. *Medians* are most often used to represent the results of *ordinal scales* because a mean cannot be calculated and the mode may or may not offer information about the center of the distribution. *Modes* are commonly calculated for *nominal scales* because there is no arithmetic relationship between indicants and investigators are simply looking at those categories that occur most frequently.

When arithmetic relations are possible, most investigators are interested in the degree to which individual scores deviate from the measures of central tendency. They explore the *variance* in scores to rule in explanations for relationships and rule out error. To calculate variance in a single distribution, each *raw score (X)* is subtracted from the *obtained mean* $(\overline{X})$ and that number is squared. Then, all the squared scores are added and divided by the total *number of respondents (N)*. In graphs of the distribution of scores, variance is represented by the space under the curve.

VARIANCE

$$\sigma^2 = \frac{\sum (X - \overline{X})^2}{N - 1}$$

The square root of the variance indicates the *standard deviation* or the spread of scores away from the mean. The standard deviation indicates how far along the *x*-axis scores deviate from the mean to fall within particular probability ranges. For the normal distribution, approximately two thirds or 68 percent of the scores fall within one standard deviation above or below the mean. About 95 percent of the scores are within two standard deviations of the mean. Standard deviations can be computed for obtained distributions that are then compared to the parameters of a normal distribution to estimate the characteristics of a group of scores.

STANDARD DEVIATION

$$\sigma = \sqrt{\frac{\sum (X - \overline{X})^2}{N - 1}}$$

Although investigators would ideally like to obtain a distribution that is parallel to the normal distribution, most distributions are less than optimal. Comparing the obtained range of scores with an optimal range offers insight into how different the two distributions might be (Figure 3.6). When a distribution is *negatively skewed,* there is a concentration of high scores and fewer low scores. When a distribution is *positively skewed,* there is a concentration of low scores and fewer high scores. Some distributions are *flat* or *rectangular* in shape, indicating that most scores are about equally represented. And, *bimodal* or *multimodal* distributions will have more than one peak. The degree to which distributions deviate from the norm offers insight into whether measures are too narrowly or broadly defined for measurement to be accurate. When scores are highly concentrated along an extreme point of a distribution, the range may be so narrow that comparison among variables will be

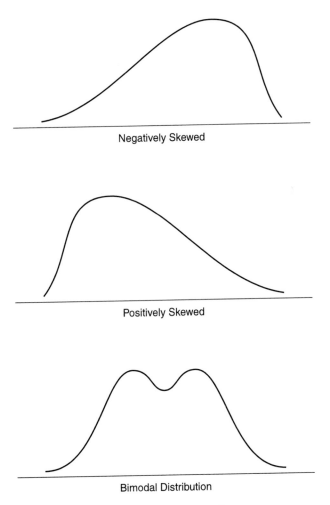

FIGURE 3.6   **Types of Skewed Distributions**

impossible. Scores with a *restricted range* have insufficient variance for inclusion in most forms of statistical analyses. When scores are widely spread out, the range may be so broad that variance is likely to be caused by systematic error as much as by diversity on the characteristic being measured. Bimodal distributions also suggest a high degree of measurement error in relation to a true score.

Reliability as Stability and Accuracy

Once investigators have explored the shape of an obtained distribution, they begin to look at how indicants are related to one another. Exploring the reliability of a measure involves exploring *stability,* the degree to which each tool works the same way in repeated use, and *accuracy,* the degree to which equivalent indicants function in the same way. Several different methods for calculating reliability have been established and will be outlined along with the corresponding item structures for which they are used. Each method differs in the degree to which it represents stability and/or accuracy. Different methods also reflect alternative assumptions about the measurement scales used in item construction. Methods for calculating reliability do share some common limitations.

Estimates of reliability require variance in responses to each item. If a distribution of scores is sufficiently homogeneous that most respondents receive the same score, most formulas for calculating reliability will be untenable. There would be inadequate levels of the variance necessary for parsing measurement error. If all or most parties were to receive the same score, investigators might examine their measurement purpose to see if they were getting the information they intended, but nominal scales typically show such restricted ranges and verifying commonalities in a sample may be worthwhile. At a basic level, the variance required may not seem like such a major challenge, but as will become apparent in later chapters, this limitation can have major consequences for some forms of criterion-referenced or standards-based tools.

A second limitation involves the need for repeated use of a tool to fully estimate stability in performance. Most investigators rely on sample sizes to address this issue, assuming that when samples are sufficiently large and representative of a population, stability can be inferred from indices of accuracy. Depending on the type of tool, this assumption may or may not be reasonable even though sample sizes do affect reliability coefficients.

Interpreting Raw Scores

To interpret an individual score in light of the reliability of a tool, investigators have come to rely on the *standard error of measurement.* The standard error of measurement offers a concrete estimate of how much each score could fluctuate if a respondent took the same test over time. This type of standard deviation is calculated using the reliability coefficient (r_{TX}) obtained for a particular sample and the standard deviation of the obtained distribution (SD_X).

STANDARD ERROR OF MEASUREMENT

$$SD_m = SD_x\sqrt{(1 - r_{TX})}$$

Using the number obtained from this formula, investigators are able to construct confidence intervals for use in interpreting an individual's score. Suppose on a 50-item test, the standard error of measurement was 3; investigators could estimate the probability with which a true score would fall within one, two, or three standard deviations of the obtained score, using 3 as the appropriate deviation measure. They can comfortably assume that on retesting, an individual's score could have easily been three points higher or lower than the obtained score (one standard error above and below the score) and may have been off by as much as six or nine points in either direction (deviating by two or three standard error units). This might lead decision makers to create a range for representing individual scores, especially when performance evaluations have serious consequences. A score of 45 on a 50-item test, for example, could easily fall in the range of 42 to 48; the low end may reflect

B-quality work whereas the high end might reflect A-quality work. Evaluating the abilities of a brain surgeon may require stronger evidence of mastery than this test would provide.

Valid Alignment with Theory

Once investigators are certain their tools have measured concepts with an acceptable degree of stability and accuracy, they begin to determine if the indicants are appropriately aligned with theoretical concepts. This process of exploring validity is multifaceted and has been subdivided into many different steps that are selected to match the obtainable information.[12] All steps cannot be explored with a single set of data, but investigators typically consider more than one set of concerns in a single study. The most basic feature of validity hinges on the assumption that knowledge is gained by comparing sets of indicants. As was evident for comparisons between task orientation (t) and task goals (g), comparisons between parallel indicants ideally yield similar or equivalent patterns ($r_{tg} = .89$). Hopefully, comparisons between conceptually opposite indicants yield negative relationships and are sometimes apparent for task orientation and work avoidance *(a)* ($r_{ta} = -.37$), and comparisons between unrelated indicants yield no identifiable patterns as was evident for some comparisons between task and ego *(e)* orientations ($r_{te} = .09$).

Investigators typically graph these relationships and/or rely on correlation coefficients to help them determine *criterion validity*—the degree of correspondence between related dimensions and constructs. For this kind of analysis, investigators require scores on each measure for every respondent. Plotting one score on the *x*-axis and another on the *y*-axis facilitates comparisons of the distribution of scores (Figure 3.7).

Correlations between two variables offer a summative assessment of how well the two are related to one another. As you will see in subsequent chapters, *Pearson product moment formulas* (r_{XY}) are commonly used to correlate scores for interval or ratio scales and *Spearman's rho* (ρ or r_S) is commonly used for ordinal scales.

SPEARMAN'S RHO

$$r_s = 1 - \frac{6 \sum d^2}{n(n^2 - 1)}$$

Computing this formula, *d* represents the difference between two sets of ranks. That number for each participant is squared and then added for all participants and multiplied by six. The number of participants or pairs of scores is designated as *n*.

In addition to determining the relationships between dimensions and constructs, investigators also look for evidence that the tool has *content validity,* assessing the necessary indicants for measuring a concept. Looking carefully at the definitions of task, ego, and work avoidance orientations, for example, investigators were able to eliminate items that did not permit a clear discrimination between these dimensions. They also confirmed that each item offered a clear representation of the dimension to which it was assigned. Contrasting these dimensions with measures focusing on the purposes of school and other related constructs offered evidence that the variable made scientific and conceptual sense. Once we established this form of *construct validity,* it was possible to explore relationships between constructs

Uncorrelated

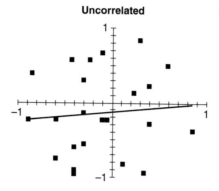

Positive Association

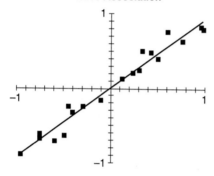

Negative Association

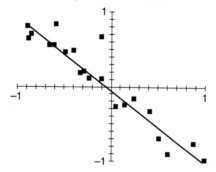

FIGURE 3.7   Sample Correlation Distributions

and establish *theoretical validity.* Looking back at Figure 3.2, the constructs of competence orientations (task, ego, and work avoidance orientations), beliefs about the purposes of school (useful to society, understand the world, wealth and status), and school participation were combined with explanatory arrows in the concept of academic engagement.

■ ■ ■ ■ ■

MAKING CONNECTIONS

There are many different issues associated with translating indicants into numerical systems that can be used to formulate generalizations about respondents and measurement outcomes. Take the dimension you identified earlier and determine which numerical concerns are most relevant for your measurement purpose. Explain your decisions.

EXPLORING RELATIONSHIPS AMONG INDICANTS

Investigators have devised many different means for exploring relationships among indicants. This book includes some of the most basic techniques, but new derivatives of these continue to proliferate as investigators discover new measurement dilemmas. Probably the most frequently used approaches for exploring relationships among indicants involve correlational techniques, and factor analysis is perhaps the most versatile. Investigators use factor analysis to explore the qualities of indicants, the contribution of items to the overall reliability of a scale, and the validity of one scale in relation to others. Factor analysis is often used to establish parsimony by verifying which indicants measure the same dimensions, how many dimensions are evident for a particular construct, and how well different tools are related to one another. Like all techniques, factor analysis has its limitations. Investigators can find meaningful results with nonsensical data or fail to find convergence in concepts that are clearly related but may have a restricted range of variance. Nevertheless, factor analysis remains the strongest tool for determining how well indicants cluster together and for comparing indicants and latent variables.

Before describing the use of factor analysis in solving different measurement problems, some conceptual language will be introduced in this chapter.[13] I will rely on the competence orientation measures to exemplify this, in part to illustrate the fact that imperfections in a tool may not prove fatal to conceptual work. The theory that underlies the development of these scales is strong and has been well articulated using a wide variety of research designs and theoretical positions. That wealth of evidence as well as empirical details from particular data sets facilitated decisions about how to treat particular indicants and which dimensions to include and exclude from conceptual assessments of academic engagement. In making these assertions, I can look back on almost 30 years of research, frequent arguments among scholars, and multiple lines of converging evidence. I can also turn to several different data sets collected for many different purposes by those in my research group.

New investigators may initially feel intimidated by such theoretical strength, but with patience it is possible to learn that consistent theoretical patterns tend to be retained over time even if they are sometimes assigned different names. Failed directions end up being discarded, but learning from others' blind alleys can save investigators an inordinate amount of time and resources. Like the early theorists interested in competence-related themes, I can also expect that others will eventually reinvent this theory using new language.

What Is Factor Analysis?

In the measurement phase of a study, factor analysis involves the process of parsing the total variance evident among a group of indicants into meaningful components. Investigators ask how many latent variables or factors are evident in a collection of indicants, what indicants are located on each factor, and whether the factor structure is reliable. A factor is a hypothetical entity—*a latent variable*—that is assumed to underlie a collection of indicants, scales, or tools. Different forms of factor analysis facilitate the identification of dimensions, constructs, and concepts.

You may remember from Figure 3.2 that task, ego, and work-avoidant orientations are each latent variables. These latent variables are represented by assigning names to significant factors. In this process, investigators identify the significant indicants for each factor, look for their common characteristics, and give that pattern a name. Hopefully, the obtained pattern confirms theoretical assertions, but when investigators begin a new area of inquiry, they may require the use of *exploratory factor analysis* to identify significant relationships in loosely connected indicants. With *confirmatory factor analysis,* investigators have enough theoretical and empirical information to offer a priori determinations of how many factors will be interpreted and which indicants will be associated with each factor. A careful comparison across tables in this chapter will reveal my choice to report confirmatory rather than exploratory results and to ignore statistically significant factors that were not practically significant or theoretically meaningful.

Do All Indicants Belong on the Same Measure?

For a particular scale, factor analysis can sort indicants related to a theoretical concept by verifying (1) whether indicants are sufficiently associated with one another to form a construct, and (2) which indicants correspond to each dimension. Interpreting factor analysis involves two steps, but both steps can be interpreted using the same computer output.

First, the initial factor solution verifies that all the items are associated with the same construct. It offers a sense of the *common factor* variance among a total collection of indicants, but does not verify the existence of meaningful dimensions within the collection. In designing the competence orientation measures, we used communalities to determine if items intended to represent task, ego, and work-avoidant orientations shared enough variance to be associated with the more general construct of competence orientations. You may remember that items intended to represent a social or conformity orientation did not meet these criteria and were dropped from later studies.[14] Table 3.1 offers evidence that indeed all items belong on one measure and we labeled that measure *competence orientations.*

Mathematically, when two or more indicants are highly correlated, they share variance and this common factor variance is used as evidence to support the construct. The shared variance accounted for by a cluster of items (or scales) can be estimated by squaring and adding the loadings of that cluster across factors (across rows of a factor matrix). This *communality index* is always less than or equal to the reliability of the cluster of items, which for all competence orientation items was $\alpha = .79$. Comparison of communalities helps investigators see which clusters of items share variance. The communalities in Table 3.1 are all greater than .40, indicating enough shared variance between each item and the total group of items to proceed with the second interpretive step.

How were these communalities computed? Table 3.3 contains the unrotated *component matrix* or initial solution that emerged when the computer determined whether all indicants were correlated with one another. Communalities were computed by squaring the loadings in each row of the matrix and adding them together. Using the information in Table 3.3 can you determine how each communality in Table 3.1 was computed?

TABLE 3.3   Initial Component Matrix Comparing Items for Competence Orientations

IN SCHOOL, I FEEL MOST SUCCESSFUL WHEN ...	FACTOR LOADINGS			
TASK ORIENTATION				
Something I learned makes me want to find out more.	−.59	.35	.25	.09
I get a new idea about how things work.	−.48	.39	.36	.01
I learned something interesting.	−.49	.40	.38	.00
I solve a tricky problem by working hard.	−.60	.35	.33	−.09
I finally understand a really complicated idea.	−.55	.36	.38	−.06
Something I learned really makes sense to me.	−.54	.37	.40	.01
A class makes me think about things.	−.44	.25	.37	.05
EGO ORIENTATION AS SHOWING SUPERIORITY				
I do the work better than other students.	−.05	.68	−.30	−.27
I show people I am good at something.	−.10	.68	−.36	−.08
I show people I'm smart.	−.07	.66	−.44	−.08
I score higher than other students.	−.07	.69	−.39	−.24
I am the only one who can answer the teachers' questions.	−.01	.63	−.22	−.19
EGO ORIENTATION AS AVOIDING INFERIORITY				
I don't do anything stupid in class.	.06	.38	−.08	.79
People don't think I'm dumb.	.06	.50	−.25	.66
ACADEMIC ALIENATION				
I get out of some work.	.62	.24	.16	.01
I do almost no work and get away with it.	.73	.18	.17	−.06
I put one over on the teacher.	.72	.22	.08	−.03
I fool around and get away with it.	.75	.20	.11	−.05
I don't have to do any homework.	.68	.19	.30	−.06
I didn't have to work hard.	.71	.27	.25	.00
All the work was easy.	.63	.26	.28	−.05
The teacher didn't ask any hard questions.	.68	.31	.22	.03
I didn't have any tough tests.	.65	.30	.20	.01

Note: This report involves secondary data analysis of multiple samples, $n = 951$, ages 13 to 20.

What Does a Factor Look Like?

Once investigators are satisfied with the theoretical and statistical coherence of the communalities, they try to identify dimensions or the latent variables represented by each factor. This second step involves a process of *statistical rotation* that is used to determine how many dimensions are evident in the structure of a particular construct. The rotation process involves a search for the best position for the axes used to represent relationships among indicants in *n*-dimensional space. It involves a search for the most parsimonious way of representing patterns in the *covariance* or shared variance of indicants. When factors are sufficiently clear and strong, the existence of valid dimensions or latent variables for a construct can be inferred, but is often examined further using techniques for estimating reliability.

Figure 3.8 contains a graph for a one-dimensional factor. If all the competence orientation items were significant on the same dimension, this kind of depiction would be warranted. Notice that factor loadings on the graph (designated with boxes) were calculated in relation to a wanted dimension (the *y*-axis) and an unwanted dimension (the *x*-axis). Indicants that clustered close to zero on the unwanted dimension, but showed significant load-

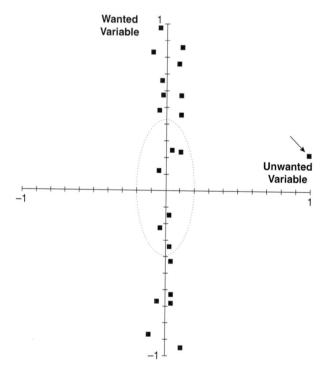

FIGURE 3.8   A Graphic Comparison of Two Hypothetical Variables

ings (e.g., greater than .40 or less than –.40) on the wanted dimension would be seen as reliable measures of the concept. In Figure 3.8, those items were placed at least four tickmarks above or below the 0 point, and the six items circled did not meet this criterion. Indicants that showed a reverse pattern, along the unwanted variable axis, would be inappropriate for inclusion on the unidimensional construct because they are not correlated with the wanted dimension, but are correlated with the unwanted dimension. (See the arrow in Figure 3.8.).

How Many Dimensions Are Evident?

For a measure that is "pure" enough to attain factor unity, all the indicants load on the same factor and are saturated with that factor; little variance is attributable to other factors or to systematic and random error. More commonly, measures are complex and clusters of items may load together such that each cluster reflects a different dimension of the construct being measured. The resulting patterns identified may only account for some of the variance across items. Such complexity keeps investigators dependent on computers to generate results. Findings are generally reported as matrices rather than graphs because items rarely fall along one dimension or even two.

Generalizing from the outcome represented in Figure 3.8, let's think again about how factor analysis permits the identification of task, ego, and work-avoidant orientations. In looking at Tables 3.3 and 3.4, two different kinds of *factor matrices* are evident. Table 3.3 contains the initial solution used to explore communalities and Table 3.4 contains the structure matrix used to identify the dimensions within a construct. Despite these differences, each table contains coefficients expressing the relationship between indicants and the underlying factors. Factor matrices are estimated from covariance matrices where each indicant is correlated with every other indicant. It is this shared variance that is being explored when investigators ask computers to conduct a statistical rotation of the initial solution to identify dimensions.

To read *factor loadings,* imagine interpreting a correlation of each indicant with the total factor. In this analysis, because the factor is a latent or hypothetical variable, a linear combination of all the indicants on the measure is used to estimate each factor. Factor loadings can range from -1.00 to 1.00. Those loadings that deviate significantly from 0 are assumed to represent the latent dimension expressed by the significant assigned factor. Factors and their corresponding loadings can be evaluated for statistical significance, but are practically significant only if they adequately represent theoretical dimensions.[15]

Looking at Table 3.4, the structure matrix for factor analysis of the competence orientations is represented. Notice that there are four columns of numbers, each representing a factor. Numbers in bold type are both statistically and practically significant loadings on the factor to which they are assigned. Why are the loadings in Table 3.3 different from those in Table 3.4? Table 3.4 represents the results of a statistical rotation process that permits investigators to identify how many dimensions are evident in the collection of 23 indicants of competence orientations. This rotation reflects the second-order analysis of variance to determine which patterns best represent the obtained responses.

TABLE 3.4 A Sample Structure Matrix Comparing Items on a Measure of Competence Orientations

IN SCHOOL, I FEEL MOST SUCCESSFUL WHEN . . .	FACTOR LOADINGS			
TASK ORIENTATION ($\alpha = .85$)				
Something I learned makes me want to find out more.	**.71**	.21	.16	−.35
I get a new idea about how things work.	**.72**	.20	.09	−.20
I learned something interesting.	**.73**	.21	.08	−.20
I solve a tricky problem by working hard.	**.76**	.22	−.01	−.33
I finally understand a really complicated idea.	**.76**	.19	.01	−.27
Something I learned really makes sense to me.	**.77**	.17	.07	−.26
A class makes me think about things.	**.62**	.07	.06	−.22
EGO ORIENTATION AS SHOWING SUPERIORITY ($\alpha = .83$)				
I do the work better than other students.	.21	**.79**	.14	.10
I show people I am good at something.	.22	**.77**	.31	.03
I show people I'm smart.	.14	**.79**	.31	.02
I score higher than other students.	.19	**.83**	.19	.06
I am the only one who can answer the teachers' questions.	.20	**.68**	.17	.14
EGO ORIENTATION AS AVOIDING INFERIORITY ($\alpha = .68$)				
I don't do anything stupid in class.	.09	.17	**.88**	.13
People don't think I'm dumb.	.07	.38	**.85**	.12
ACADEMIC ALIENATION ($\alpha = .92$)				
I get out of some work.	−.24	.08	.12	**.68**
I do almost no work and get away with it.	−.35	.04	.03	**.77**
I put one over on the teacher.	−.36	.10	.10	**.74**
I fool around and get away with it.	−.38	.07	.07	**.77**
I don't have to do any homework.	−.24	−.01	.02	**.76**
I didn't have to work hard.	−.25	.06	.11	**.80**
All the work was easy.	−.17	.07	.05	**.73**
The teacher didn't ask any hard questions.	−.22	.11	.16	**.77**
I didn't have any tough tests.	−.22	.12	.15	**.74**

Note: This report involves secondary data analysis of multiple samples, $n = 951$, ages 13 to 20.

There are several methods of rotation available for identifying the most meaningful patterns of responses. These reflect different theoretical assumptions about the degree to which dimensions of a construct are independent or moderately correlated with one another. When dimensions are assumed to be independent, the axes along which factor loadings are rotated starts in an *orthogonal* position, at a 90-degree angle. When dimensions are assumed to be moderately correlated, an *oblique* rotation is used in which the angles between the axes are acute or obtuse. Many investigators compare results using both kinds of assumptions, but sometimes there is a strong theoretical reason for choosing one rotation over another.

When analyzing the competence orientations, for example, I used an oblique rotation because I was aware of the fact that work avoidance is often negatively associated with task orientation, indicting some degree of correlation that could theoretically be acknowledged. This is consistent with early theories of motivation where a two-dimensional model of approach and avoidance was used to represent the construct. Although participants responding to the competence orientation measure were asked to think about what makes them feel successful rather than unsuccessful in school, avoiding schoolwork seemed to be a meaningful dimension in its own right.

What Makes a Factor Reliable?

Investigators begin the process of interpreting the rotated factor matrix by asking which factors in the final solution are significant. Tests of significance involve factors with *eigenvalues* greater than 1 because they account for a significant percentage of variance. What is an eigenvalue? Using the component matrix from the initial solution, separate eigenvalues are calculated for each factor by summing the squared factor loadings vertically (for each column) in the component matrix. For the competence orientation measures, for example, there were four practically significant factors with eigenvalues of 6.23, 4.06, 1.96, and 1.27. Using the information in Table 3.3, try determining which factors correspond with each of the dimensions identified. This collection of factors accounts for 59 percent of the variance in individuals' responses, a moderate amount of shared variance with a reasonable amount of unexplained variance.

It is the investigator, not the computer, who assigns names to each significant factor in the rotated matrix. Looking at items with significant loadings, investigators identify theoretical ideas they have in common. Before becoming committed to the dimensions extracted from factor analysis, investigators typically replicate their findings using multiple samples.

It would be unrealistic to assume that all results obtained with factor analysis were interpretable. Indicants that are and are not expected to be associated are compared and only those dimensions showing evidence of reliability are retained in the final measures. Investigators look for reasons why some indicants do not perform as well as they might before dropping them from a measure or altering their theoretical definitions. Deciding when to ignore or keep a factor that is statistically significant, investigators have generated some simple guidelines that can be helpful. Dimensions can be kept as reliable if they:

- contain four or more indicants with loadings that are each greater than the absolute value of $|.60|$, regardless of the sample size;

- contain three or more indicants with loadings that are each greater than $|.80|$, regardless of the sample size;
- contain ten or more indicants with low loadings (near +/−.40) for sample sizes greater than 150.

These are only rules of thumb, but they can be helpful to investigators who are trying to evaluate the significance of their work. Looking at the four factors in Table 3.4, can you see strengths and limitations in the tool?

Ordinarily, investigators look for several attributes when deciding if the results are sufficiently coherent to warrant further consideration.[16] Ideally, each row of a matrix will have at least one loading that is close to zero. In each column, findings are ideal if there are usually at least as many indicants with near-zero loadings as there are factors.[17] Each factor typically has several significant loadings that are unique to that factor. Strong factors do not contain *cross-loaded items,* those loading significantly on more than one factor. Many of the nonsignificant loadings also commonly approach zero. Finally, the degree to which the content of the indicants on each factor conforms to theoretically meaningful ideas is taken into consideration when determining which of the statistically significant factors warrant interpretation. Confirming these decisions using reliability procedures like those reported in Table 3.2, investigators isolate only those indicants for each dimension when calculating coefficients. Exploring the change in reliability coefficients that result from deleting an item from the scale also facilitates an evaluation of each item's contribution to the total.

The next step is to combine items for each dimension to form a scale (or subscale of a larger construct). Investigators do this either by summing or averaging responses to each item separately for each respondent. Before combining indicants to form a scale, investigators look at the sign of the significant loadings. When one set of loadings contains both positive and negative loadings, the scoring of some items is reversed to ensure that the signs match. The direction of the sign offers information about how indicants are correlated, and within a scale the correlations among items is expected to be positive. To ensure positive inter-item correlations, investigators sometimes imagine external criteria like favorability or, in this case "successful," to help them determine which items to reverse.

Put another way, the numbers assigned to participants' responses have no arithmetic properties and serve only to preserve order. Investigators could assign high numbers to the strongly agree end of a scale or to the strongly disagree end of the scale, but their decision should be consistent when data are initially scored. Later, when factor analysis reveals the direction of relation between indicants, investigators can make sure that all indicants on the same dimension are scored in the same direction. Investigators could, for example, use high numbers to indicate strong agreement with the item, "I feel most successful if I get out of some work." If they did so, high scores would indicate work avoidance. On the other hand, they could see work avoidance as a sign of low motivation and assign low numbers to strong agreement. Once this decision is made, it should be applied consistently across all items that are assumed to represent the work avoidance dimension.

When the reliability of a measure is strong, investigators may not always take time to explore how indicants are associated. For theory development, they do so at their peril. Measures may contain more items than are necessary for a particular purpose or may not

ENDNOTES

1. Some of the language used in this chapter was borrowed from Zeiler & Caraines (1980). Although many other authors describe the same features of the measurement process, these authors drew relationships between measurement techniques and theory construction in ways that have been helpful to new scholars.

2. Grimmett & Stirzaker (2002) offer a strong review of probability theory and Howe (2002) offers a history of controversies associated with this process.

3. See Green (1981) for an example of how the concept of intelligence generates all three forms of controversy.

4. This formula is so versatile that investigators also use it to combine pairs of data points from two different samples, but when used in measurement studies it is common for the number of participants to also equal the number of pairs.

5. Lord & Novick (1968) offer a commonly cited elaboration of classical measurement theory. Zeiler & Caraines (1980) offered a strong comparison of how psychometric assumptions differ from those associated with classical measurement theory.

6. Scores can also be tau-equivalent, wherein true scores are assumed to differ pairwise by no more than an additive constant.

7. Messick (1993) offers a very thorough review of validity.

8. At best, the association $r_{xy} = r_{x\infty y\infty}\sqrt{r_{xx}r_{yy}}$. Knowing the correlation between true predictor and criterion scores ($r_{x\infty y\infty}$), it is possible to see that as the reliability of the predictor (r_{xx}) and the reliability of the criterion (r_{yy}) change, the validity coefficient r_{xy} is affected. When the reliability of one set of scores is extremely low, the validity will be zero. Investigators sometimes correct for this attenuation, but the reliability coefficients used in such corrections are appropriately robust if this is to be effective.

9. See Dawes & Smith (1985), Krantz, Luce, Suppes, & Tversky (1971), or Suppes & Zinnes (1963) for more information on this logic.

10. Nicol & Pexman (2003) offers one of several new guidebooks available to assist investigators in thinking about how to represent their findings.

11. Standard scores noted in Figure 3.3 and other scaling techniques are reviewed in Angoff (1971, 1984), and McCall (1939) first introduced the T-score transformation with a mean of 50 and a standard deviation of 10. Stanines are rarely used in research, but practitioners seem to use them and they have a distribution with a mean of 5 and a standard deviation of 2.

12. Messick (1993) offers the most comprehensive account of these different concerns.

13. Kerlinger & Lee (2000) offered a strong conceptual synthesis of the basic features of factor analysis.

14. Contrast the findings from Nicholls, Patashnick, & Nolen (1985) and Thorkildsen (1988).

15. Stevens (2001) offers a review of debates regarding the value of looking at statistical significance when interpreting a factor loading or whether a rule of thumb such as that provided here offers a more practical approach at this point. I rely on rules of thumb mostly because I am interested in replicating my findings on repeated use of a tool and the rule of thumb tends to be the more conservative assessment. Thurstone (1947) is typically credited for establishing this criterion.

16. Thurstone (1947) is typically credited for establishing this criterion.

17. Notice that this is not the case for Table 3.4. That pattern occurred because I asked the computer to generate a 4-factor solution when the data were better suited to a 3-factor solution to illustrate points about less than ideal outcomes obtained with ego orientation items.

18. Not surprisingly, this method results in controversial findings. Support for the use of the bogus pipeline has been obtained by Arkin, Appelman, & Burger (1980) and Quigley-Fernandez & Tedeschi (1978), but these raise ambiguous conclusions (Arkin & Lake, 1983).

19. Papers by Feldman & Lynch (1988), Schuman & Ludwig (1983), Schuman & Presser (1981), and Schwartz & Strack (1991) outline some of these studies.

20. Cronbach (1946, 1950) and Guilford (1954) have written about such biases.

CHAPTER FOUR

MEASURING ATTITUDES

Considering the issues of distortion raised in the previous chapter, it may not be surprising to discover that measuring attitudes has been one of the most challenging forms of psychometric measurement. Investigators study attitudes when they want to understand judgments about actions or ideas. By identifying groups of social responses that share a family resemblance, researchers document individuals' tendencies toward particular responses in specific situations. Attitudes are assumed to reflect common cultural patterns that are conditioned through life experience rather than ontological dispositions. They ordinarily reflect a range of responses that individuals bring forth out of habit or in response to cultural pressures.[1] Knowledge of such responses is helpful for understanding human functioning, but people are also good at misrepresenting their attitudes or deceiving themselves about which cultural norms they internalize.

Measuring attitudes offers only one dimension of human functioning, but has been explored in a number of ways. Those methods reported here were selected to show that indicants come in many different forms even if they are designed to measure similar constructs. Before offering details on the range of measurement approaches, let's look more closely at how a new attitude scale is typically developed.

SCALE DEVELOPMENT PROCEDURES

In the previous chapter, you saw examples of the measurement properties of three competence orientation scales assumed to reflect personality characteristics. Those measures were incorporated into the more complex concept of academic engagement by linking them to beliefs about the purposes of school, an attitude measure. Looking at how the purposes of school measures were designed offers a concrete sense of the iterative steps in designing a new tool. The details of item format may differ across tools, but the procedures used to design new measures are fairly similar.

In designing the Purposes of School scales, a team of researchers used the details of their theoretical framework to determine what they would like to measure.[2] They used existing research to verify that such measures were not already available and to understand how other researchers measured similar constructs. In many schools, assumptions about the purposes of school form a hidden curriculum that many students come to understand. Investigators looked at research on educational policy, psychology, political science, and economics to label common features of that discourse. Because designers were interested in understanding adolescents' beliefs about the role of school in society, hidden or overt, they organized informal focus group discussions with adolescents. The discussions elicited informal beliefs and allowed investigators to identify linguistic habits of speech in the population they planned to sample.

Finding that many teens were rather inarticulate when asked to describe why they attend school, the designers of this tool decided that a Likert-type scale, similar to that used to measure competence orientations, would offer useful information.[3] Such measures could assess adolescents' beliefs about ideas that were apparent in the educational literature, even if they could not generate each idea on their own. Focusing on fluency, investigators generated as many statements that reflected reasons for attending school as they could imagine. After generating a large collection of statements, the tool's designers selected and edited statements for inclusion on the first draft of the measure. Investigators considered the following criteria:

- Items should allow for variability across respondents.
- Items should reflect beliefs that might be desired or rejected.
- Language should match the abilities of those who will be asked to respond.
- Language should consider cultural norms or conventions that might affect the interpretation of each item.
- Language should be clear, concise, and straightforward.
- Reading levels should be kept relatively low.
- Items should be worded so that the modal response is usually near the midpoint of the scale.
- Items should allow respondents to offer only one response.
- Items should not reflect factual knowledge.
- Items should not foster the evaluation of double negatives.
- Items should not foster socially desirable or threatening emotions.
- Items should not contain more than one idea.

In the end, 58 items met these criteria and seemed to represent the full range of purposes that could be identified at the time. On the final measure, respondents were asked, "In your opinion what are the main things school should do?" Each item was linked to the statement, "A VERY IMPORTANT thing school should do is . . . " This was followed by unnumbered statements, all of which were worded to reflect socially valued reasons for attending school. Investigators asked respondents to indicate whether they strongly disagreed, disagreed, felt neutral, agreed, or strongly agreed with each item. Adolescents offered negative evaluations of the items by disagreeing with these seemingly prosocial options. The initial measure contained more items than appeared on the final measures. Items were pilot-tested using both graduate students and adolescents as respondents, and item functioning was evaluated. A total of 51 items were of sufficient quality for inclusion in the first published version of this scale. Later iterations of the scale, generated after repeated use of the measure on more than one sample, resulted in a shorter scale with adequate reliability (Table 4.1).

As part of this process, the team of researchers who used this measure learned how to select those statements that offer the greatest versatility in responses. We considered the cultural background of respondents when selecting items for this and other related versions of the scale. Validity was explored by adding extra dimensions to the model and selecting only those dimensions that were directly relevant to the concept of academic engagement. Redundant or uninformative information was eliminated to preserve parsimony in the final report.

TABLE 4.1   Likert-Type Scale for Measuring Beliefs about the Purpose of School

ITEM	RESPONSE OPTIONS				
School should . . .	Strongly Disagree	Disagree	Uncertain	Strongly Agree	Agree
BECOME USEFUL TO SOCIETY (13 ITEMS, α = .87 FOR AGES 13 TO 18)					
Prepare us to be useful to others.	SD	D	U	A	SA
Prepare us to be active in the community.	SD	D	U	A	SA
Teach us to do our duty to society.	SD	D	U	A	SA
Teach us to respect authority.	SD	D	U	A	SA
UNDERSTAND THE WORLD (9 ITEMS, α = .83 FOR AGES 13 TO 18)					
Prepare us to understand the importance of new scientific discoveries.	SD	D	U	A	SA
Help us understand nature and how it works.	SD	D	U	A	SA
Prepare us to evaluate critically what experts say.	SD	D	U	A	SA
Help us understand enough to vote wisely in elections.	SD	D	U	A	SA
ATTAIN WEALTH AND STATUS (9 ITEMS, α = .84 FOR AGES 13 TO 18)					
Prepare us to reach the top in our jobs.	SD	D	U	A	SA
Help us get into the best colleges.	SD	D	U	A	SA
Prepare us for jobs that will give us money for luxuries.	SD	D	U	A	SA
Prepare us for jobs that will give us plenty of free time.	SD	D	U	A	SA

Note: This reflects a sample of items from the measure. Items can be clustered to ease the cognitive processing load for participants.

■ ■ ■ ■ ■ ▬▬▬▬▬▬▬▬▬▬▬▬▬▬▬▬▬▬▬▬▬▬▬▬▬▬▬▬▬▬▬

MAKING CONNECTIONS

Design an attitude scale. What type of attitude did you try to measure? Where did you get the content for your items? What items format did you use? How did you determine if an item was appropriate for your measure? Did you pilot-test your items with qualified critics? As you work through this chapter, try imagining how your measure might be changed to accommodate different item styles. Would the measure have to change in meaning?

TYPES OF SCALES

Many researchers consider attitudes and attitude change, but their reasons for doing so may vary. Fields differ in the degree to which they isolate cognitive, affective, and behavioral features or global responses. Nevertheless, it is easy to find agreement that attitudes are forms of opinion that influence individuals' goals, perceptions, reactions, and actions. Also embedded in this research is the assumption that attitudes are normally distributed within a population.

In writing about the measurement of attitudes, Himmelfarb (1993) classified scales into one of three general categories.[4] There are alternative schemes for comparing measures, but Himmelfarb's system is well justified. It illustrates how theoretical concepts and empirical indicants are coordinated as well as how values and beliefs are elicited from respondents.

In this system, *person scaling* techniques locate persons on an attribute by looking directly at their responses. *Stimulus, then person scaling* involves a two-step process in which stimuli such as statements of beliefs, affects, and behaviors are judged by experts and scaled to determine the location of the stimulus along a favorable or unfavorable dimension. Then, respondents whose attitudes will be classified are located on the same dimension, classifying their endorsements of one or more scales. *Simultaneous stimulus and person scaling* is used to locate persons and stimuli on the same scale using an interlocking approach to calibrate one dimension against the other. Understanding the differences among these scaling techniques is helpful for exploring attitudes, but it is also useful for understanding some of the different approaches represented later in this book.

PERSON SCALING

Techniques classified as *person scaling* treat items as direct indicators of a common latent variable. Investigators assume that scales measure only the content of the items and do not try to read between the lines to determine ulterior motives or agendas. Dimensions are often identified a priori, but at the very least items are selected for respondents rather than generated by them. Respondents' answers are classified according to the total number of items with which they agree or disagree. For some person scales, simple "yes" and "no" responses are appropriate, but for others the relative degree of agreement is measured.

Person scales are common in journalistic surveys or telemarketing ploys such as those generated to measure political beliefs. In those surveys, individuals are typically asked to report their opinions of external entities. Attitude surveys are also used to measure beliefs about direct experience such as why something is important, what feelings are elicited by particular events, or what behaviors are observed. Ordinarily, individuals are asked to offer some sort of value judgment and not to simply evaluate the factual accuracy of a statement.

Methods of Summated Ratings

Methods of summated ratings, like those associated with measuring beliefs about the purposes of school, involve adding or averaging related items. Combining items can strengthen estimates of accuracy and stability, calculated as the internal consistency of a collection of responses. In summative measures, multiple indicants of a single concept are constructed. When accurate responses are made to each indicant, those indicants assessing the same dimension are usually highly correlated. *Likert-type* and *semantic differential scales* are the two most commonly used summative measures, but investigators have also modified these approaches to suit their needs.

Likert-Type Scales.   Rensis Likert (1932) developed what is probably the most commonly used *multiple-item person scale.* In the original use of the scale, respondents were given a series of statements and asked to indicate whether they (1) strongly approved, (2) approved, (3) were undecided, (4) disapproved, or (5) strongly disapproved of each statement. Later, the terms related to approval were changed to agreement so the choices ranged from strongly agree to strongly disagree (Likert, Roslow, & Murphy, 1934).

One controversial issue associated with the use of such five-point scales of this type concerns the presentation order of options. Some investigators assume that measures are more easily understood if positive judgments are placed first in the list of choices; individuals decide to strongly agree, agree, stay undecided, disagree, or strongly disagree with each item. Others find the scaling more salient and logical if individuals start with strong disapproval of an item and work their way up the scale to imagine strong approval. As was possible for our adolescent participants, placing "strongly agree" at the far end of the scale can minimize internal pressures to acquiesce, and strongly agree or agree with most items. In his classic paper on this technique, Likert asserted:

> It is quite immaterial what extremes of an attitude continuum are called; the important fact is that persons do differ quantitatively in their attitudes, some being more toward one extreme, some toward the other (1932, p. 48).

Whether strong agreement is rated high or low, indicants consistently correspond to options so that numbers hold the same meaning across items. Similarly, the logic of the task, the cultural norms of communities in which the task is to be completed, and the skills of respondents may influence whether positive options are presented first or last. Most investigators make a decision about order once, applying their decision consistently to all items on the same tool. Inaccuracies are likely to proliferate if investigators present response options in different orders across items.

Before adding scores, continuity in meaning may be adjusted after respondents make their decisions as investigators ensure that scales are used the same way across items. The purposes of school measures contain only positively worded assertions, but some scales may contain statements that hold opposite forms of meaning. Imagine a group of respondents who were asked to evaluate the statements, "I hate school" and "School is interesting to me." If the measure is internally consistent, individuals who agree with one statement would disagree with the other. To combine these items into a single scale, the numerical scoring of one response would ideally be reversed to match the meaning of the other. If the scale was intended to measure students' commitment to school, scoring of the negatively worded "I hate school" might be reversed, but if the scale was intended to measure students' academic alienation, the positively worded statement might be adjusted. As long as there is parallel meaning across items, the determination of whether high scores represent positive attitudes and low scores represent negative attitudes is arbitrary.

Although I prefer to use high scores to represent stronger commitments to a measured attitude, there is no mathematical reason for that decision. If a scoring decision is consistently applied and remembered when interpreting relationships, investigators are able to offer a meaningful interpretation of individual and group scores.

Since Likert validated his scaling method, other investigators have modified the scale with only moderate degrees of success. Some investigators have dropped the middle option that indicates uncertainty, creating a four-point scale.[5] This is done to elicit a clear opinion, but can lead to higher quantities of missing data if respondents feel annoyed by an inability to respond. Error can also be added if respondents distort their uncertainties.[6] The error associated with missing responses cannot be estimated because it is difficult to determine why responses are missing. Distortion in responses is difficult to estimate because most respondents will justify even false beliefs once they assert them.

Other investigators have altered the scale to three points, seven points, or nine points while retaining the midpoint opportunity to express uncertainty. In making these decisions, investigators usually consider how well respondents are able to imagine and consistently use the full range of a scale. Children who have difficulty understanding quantity, for example, may not be able to consistently use complex scales. They may also benefit from other indicators of points on a scale. Finding one solution, measures have been used successfully with children as young as second grade by translating strongly agree into "YES," agree into "yes," undecided into "?," disagree into "no," and strongly disagree into "NO." Emoticons are also helpful for nonreaders, although most young children have difficulty answering surveys.

Altering the range of possible responses places constraints on how much or how little information can be obtained with a given scale. It is always possible to recode responses and reduce the range of a scale. A five-point scale, for example, can be reduced to a three-point scale by placing people who agree and strongly agree in one category and people who disagree and strongly disagree in another category while retaining the middle option. It is not possible to expand the information obtained from a narrow scale; a three-point scale cannot be converted into a five-point scale. To determine which scale to use, most investigators try to anticipate the kinds of information they need, but across studies the five-point scale seems to offer the most parsimonious and practical way of representing beliefs.

Investigators have also altered the meaning assigned to particular numbers. For example, responses such as "always," "sometimes," "unsure," "rarely," and "never" have been used to indicate beliefs about frequency with a high degree of success. Other common anchors have included important—unimportant, like me—not like me, and effective—ineffective. When selecting particular anchors, the meaning is expected to be theoretically relevant and clear to respondents. Presenting examples along with directions is helpful for thwarting confusion about how to use a scale. Ideally, no matter what language represents the option, the range of responses will form a normal distribution with most respondents offering moderate beliefs rather than extremes.

In evaluating item performance, researchers have identified some common reasons why statements fail to adequately differentiate attitudes across persons. These reasons include:

- The item represents a statement of fact that most can evaluate for correctness.
- The statement is written in an unclear manner.
- Most people in a sampled culture share the same opinion.
- The content of the item is different from the content apparent in the rest of the collection.

Like most measures, Likert-type scales have limitations. One limitation is that items are often written intuitively to reflect the investigators' sense of the constructs being measured. Magnitudes remain unknown because such scales contain no internal checks for anchoring the measurement properties. That is, it is difficult to check whether the resulting scales are interval or ordinal; probabilities rather than deterministic standards form the basis for comparing dimensions. New statistical tools assist investigators in offering better estimates of the distance between numbers, but when such information is required, other scales such as those generated using *stimulus, then person* or *simultaneous stimulus and person* methods may offer more precise measurement.

Semantic Differential Scales.   The *semantic differential* is a second type of summative scale that is commonly used by psychologists and anyone interested in learning more about the content of attitudes. Charles Osgood and his colleagues (Osgood, Suci, & Tannenbaum, 1957) found a way to combine controlled associations between an attitude object and adjectives. The attitude object is the concept to be differentiated and adjectives are presented using bipolar scales (e.g., *happy–sad*). A seven-point scale is placed between the poles of an adjective set. (In later work, the spread has been altered to range between five points and 11 points.) Respondents place a mark along the continuum between adjectives to indicate the degree to which particular adjectives offer a better description of the object or if both adjectives are irrelevant.

Table 4.2 offers a sample measure evaluating the idea of academic achievement. The tool illustrates how a semantic differential might be used to explore attitudes about intellectualism. Respondents' marks indicate the direction of the association between adjectives and attitude objects as well as the intensity of that association.

TABLE 4.2   Semantic Differential for Measuring Achievement Attitudes

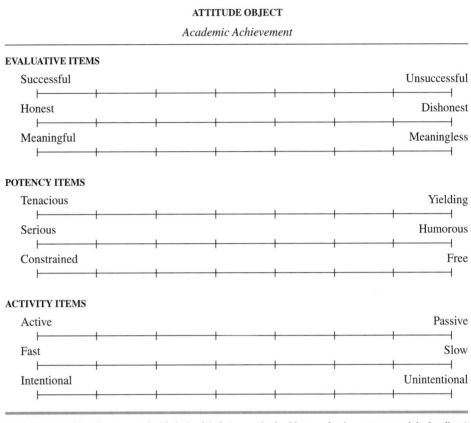

ATTITUDE OBJECT

Academic Achievement

EVALUATIVE ITEMS

Successful / Unsuccessful

Honest / Dishonest

Meaningful / Meaningless

POTENCY ITEMS

Tenacious / Yielding

Serious / Humorous

Constrained / Free

ACTIVITY ITEMS

Active / Passive

Fast / Slow

Intentional / Unintentional

Note: Items would not be presented with design labels (e.g., attitude object, evaluative, potency, activity headings) and may be presented in different orders.

Researchers identify the attitudes embedded in individuals' responses using classification rules. Factor analysis of items on early semantic differential measures typically yielded three factors that were labeled evaluation, potency, and activity, respectively. The evaluative factor usually accounts for the greatest amount of variance and has been defined as the expression of attitude. Potency and activity items offer more detailed representations of the general evaluation. Bipolar items related to a theoretical concept that load on the evaluation dimension are added or averaged to indicate more general positive or negative attitudes.

Semantic differential scales are most useful when abstract ideas can be represented in a concrete, verbal or visual form. Different attitude objects can be rated using the same adjectives if adjectives are carefully selected to extract relevant information. This method can convey more information about values than is possible with other kinds of rating scales because adjectives are highly saturated with evaluative meaning. Yet, this strength may also be a limitation. Not all attitude objects can be evaluated with adjectives; concepts as complex as those associated with the purposes of school, for example, cannot be easily represented in concrete form. Where an attitude object is available, respondents may also have difficulty classifying their beliefs using the adjectives provided.

When attitude objects and relevant adjectives are identifiable, the semantic differential offers a powerful evaluation, but less information on how individuals define the attitude object. It is assumed that respondents hold similar definitions of the attitude object and only their evaluations differ. One virtue of the semantic differential that sustains its popularity is the fact that the same scale can be applied across different attitude objects. This facilitates direct comparison of the meaning inherent in conceptually diverse objects.

As is the case with Likert scales, the semantic differential scales have measurement properties that are difficult to classify. Because there is no way to know if individuals respond to the scale in similar increments, it is difficult to determine if the levels of measurement involve ordinal or interval scales. Intervals between response points can be estimated using methods generated from *item-response theory* or *Rasch techniques*, but those estimates can be calibrated only in relationship to a predefined probability distribution.[7]

Advantages and Disadvantages of Person Scaling

The most advantageous feature of person scaling is the fact that people whose attitudes are being classified offer a direct expression of those attitudes. When investigators are able to identify the theoretical dimensions of a particular concept, they can construct items to represent those dimensions without worrying about whether each dimension conforms to an empirical scale; only people's responses are scaled. Rather than classify stimuli to constrain the classification of persons, responses are seen as indicators of a latent variable that represents the construct being measured.

Person scales are limited by the fact that they can only measure what investigators ask and respondents are willing or able to communicate. Investigators may not have a complete grasp of the theoretical concepts they hope to measure or be able to write the necessary items for measuring a construct. In turn, respondents may choose to misrepresent their views by offering the socially desirable answer, opposing answers, or exaggerated responses. Respondents may also be unaware of their views on the topics being measured or lack the abilities required to answer the questions asked.

■ ■ ■ ■ ■

MAKING CONNECTIONS

Look through studies in your field and identify an attitude measure that you think relies on person scaling. How does that scale compare to the one you designed earlier? What are the characteristics of that scale that led you to this conclusion? What types of responses are called for? Are there limitations in the measure you identified that were not noted in this chapter? What are they? Explain.

STIMULUS, THEN PERSON SCALING

Early social scientists calibrated their measurement tools in relation to physical scales, comparing perceptions of two stimuli to determine which were brighter, louder, more colorful, and so forth. Louis L. Thurstone developed a *theory of judgment and choice* from which it has become possible to measure human attributes that do not have an underlying physical dimension. Thurstone and his colleagues devised three methods for extending the logic of comparing physical and abstract concepts to comparisons of probability distributions; the methods of paired-comparison, equal-appearing intervals, and successive intervals each address a different kind of measurement dilemma associated with calibrating people's attitudes against a predefined stimulus scale (Saffir, 1937; Thurstone, 1927a, 1927b, 1928; Thurstone & Chave, 1929). In all three methods, statements about an attitude object are written to reflect varying degrees of favorability toward the designated object and the object is believed to represent a latent construct. Each stimulus can produce a normal distribution on the dimension of judgment and an item's scale value is the measure of central tendency (e.g., either means or medians) for the evaluative dimension. These methods are most commonly used when investigators are interested in working with a well-defined interval scale.

Imagine giving respondents a deck of cards, each containing a statement about common educational practices. Table 4.3 offers examples of such cards that have been validated

TABLE 4.3 Sample Cards Used in a Q-Sort Study

EDUCATIONAL PRACTICES	PERCENT AGREEMENT AMONG RATERS
TEST SITUATION	
Students earn a grade.	91%
Students get answers right.	90%
Students' knowledge is rated.	90%
CONTEST SITUATION	
Students strive to earn a title.	93%
Students win debates.	94%
Students compete on teams.	95%
LEARNING SITUATION	
Students explore a topic in depth.	98%
Students look for help when they need it.	98%
Students discover how things work.	98%
Students explain things to one another.	97%

Note: A sample of $n = 126$ adults determined which type of situation the practice represented. These reflect a subset of a deck of 30 cards.

in a study of how individuals prioritize learning, tests, and contests. Respondents selected the four ideas they found most important for a fair classroom and justified their decisions. Next, they selected the four cards they found least important, continuing this process until all cards were sorted. To design the cards, investigators identified stimuli and asked experts to rate stimuli on how well they represent particular educational situations. Then, the most representative stimuli were put on cards for individuals to sort. These ratings were then compared to determine an attitude.

Method of Paired-Comparison

In the *method of paired-comparison,* each stimulus is compared with every other stimulus and, using predetermined criteria, experts rank the two. Across judges, the proportion of times one stimulus is favored over another is calculated. These proportions are then used to calculate distances between the values used to scale items, positioning each item on an attitude dimension. Once these calculations are made and items are assigned scale values, it becomes possible to generate predicted proportions to which individual scores can later be compared. It is also possible to calculate a *goodness-of-fit index* for verifying the accuracy of scaling.[8]

After the scaling is established, respondents are asked to check all the statements they find acceptable. The scale scores for the items checked are then averaged to determine a person's attitude score.

The most obvious limitation of this paired-comparison technique concerns the number of pairs generated when each stimulus is compared with every other stimulus. The rate at which the number of comparisons increases is not linear. Five stimuli result in ten pairs, but ten stimuli result in 45 pairs and 15 stimuli result in 105 pairs. Although the precision of scaling and interval assumptions can be assessed more accurately with the rigorous comparison criteria, most investigators are interested in scaling too many items for the method of paired-comparison to be practical.

Method of Equal-Appearing Intervals

Researchers use the *method of equal-appearing intervals* to rank stimuli by asking experts to place them in categories reflecting stronger and weaker versions of a desired characteristic. Judges are told to rate the overall favorableness expressed by the items rather than to offer their opinions of the items. Judges may be told that intervals are equal, but this need not be made explicit for the classification to work appropriately. Classifications are given consecutive numbers from one to the number of categories. Then, the median of the judges' ratings is assigned as the scale value for that item.

Once all the pilot tested items are scaled, investigators select a subset of those items to administer to the participants whose attitudes are being measured. Investigators select items that collectively represent a range of possible scale values from favorable to unfavorable. They then scramble those items on a survey and ask respondents to indicate whether they agree with each item. The scale scores of the items selected are then averaged to reveal an *attitude index.*

The method of equal-appearing intervals requires a two-step process that ideally results in the selection of items representing even gradations. Unfortunately, judging the degree to which items represent a concept in favorable or unfavorable ways often results in a skewed distribution because raters are being asked for factual judgments rather than opinions. To approximate the normal distribution, fewer items ideally fall at the extreme ends of the distribution and the majority of items will fall in the middle intervals. With this method, items seem to bunch together at extreme ends of the scale, creating a bipolar distribution. Identifying appropriate items for the second phase of the study can often prove too challenging or time-consuming for the method of equal-appearing intervals to be practical. Nevertheless, there are times when this method offers the most reasonable means of designing an accurate measurement tool.

Method of Successive Intervals

When investigators compared the scales that emerged from paired-comparison and equal-appearing interval techniques, they found that the relationships were not perfectly linear. This pattern led Thurstone and his colleagues to design the *method of successive intervals,* a technique that accounts for inequality in the width of each interval. For successive intervals, as with the other methods, it is assumed that judgments of an item are normally distributed. Converting *raw scores* to *z-scores* offers a common metric for use in comparing theoretical and obtained distributions. (Figure 3.3 includes the theoretical z-distribution; Figure 4.1 labels the intervals.) When a five-point scale is used, for example, 2.14 percent of the scores would show a z-score that is ≤ -2 and be placed in interval 1; 2.14 percent would show a z-score that is ≥ 2 2 and be placed in interval 5. For interval 2, 13.59 percent of the items would show a z-score that is between –1 and –2. For interval 4, 13.59 percent of the items would show a z-score that is between 1 and 2. The remaining 68.26 percent of the scores would fall within one standard deviation of the mean so that z-scores would be greater than –1 and less than 1 and be classified in interval 3.

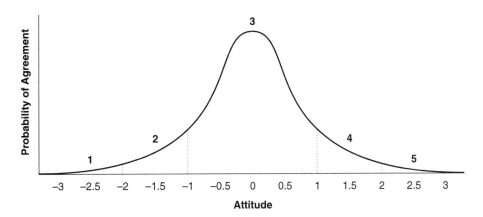

FIGURE 4.1   Theoretical z-Score Distribution Used to Explore Successive Intervals

In actuality, z-scores are calculated for each interval by subtracting an item's score from the mean and dividing it by the standard deviation.

FORMULA FOR STANDARDIZING RAW SCORES

$$z = \frac{(x - M)}{sd}$$

Transforming raw scores into z-scores makes it possible to estimate the widths of intervals and the location of the interval boundaries relative to an item's scale value. Computing these boundaries for each item facilitates comparisons among items by deriving scale locations from actual judgment data. Scale values for each item are calculated by looking at the cumulative proportions for each category of judges' placement decisions. (See Table 4.4 for an example.) Statistical tables that give z-scores for different proportions (areas under the normal curve) are used to assign z-scores to these proportions. (Table 4.5 outlines the z-scores for proportions reported in Table 4.4. Appendix A contains a table for identifying such proportions.)

Investigators typically assume that the standard deviation of these judgments is equal to 1 for all items. Because z-scores can be compared across intervals and/or items, this facilitates direct comparisons among category boundaries and interval widths. Comparing widths and category boundaries need not be done at the item level because the mean of differences are the same as the differences between means once scores have been standardized into z-scores. Investigators typically look at the means of each distribution rather than at relationships between particular items. The mean z-score obtained across intervals reflects the average estimated difference between scale values for a single item; z-scores are averaged across intervals and within items. (See rows in Table 4.5.) The mean z-score obtained across items reflects the average of the estimated differences between interval boundaries; z-scores are averaged across items and within intervals. (See columns in Table 4.5.)

The final scale values for each item are set by establishing a zero point for the distribution that serves as an anchor. Typically, the mean of z-scores for a group of items is cal-

TABLE 4.4   Cumulative Proportion of Items Placed in Each Interval

ITEM	INTERVAL					
	1	*2*	*3*	*4*	*5*	*6*
1	.380	.732	.958	.986	1.000	1.000
2	.190	.514	.810	.937	.979	1.000
3	.049	.155	.472	.824	.979	1.000
4	.056	.254	.690	.873	.972	1.000
5	.007	.035	.099	.239	.606	1.000
6	.014	.042	.099	.324	.746	1.000

TABLE 4.5 *z*-Scores for the Cumulative Proportions of Successive Intervals, Scale Values, and Interval Boundaries

| | INTERVALS | | | | | | SCALE |
ITEMS	*1*	*2*	*3*	*4*	*5*	*M*	VALUES
1	−.31	.62	1.73	2.20	0	.85	−.81
2	−.88	−.03	.88	1.53	2.03	.71	−.67
3	−1.65	−1.01	−.07	.93	2.03	.05	−.01
4	−1.59	−.66	.49	1.13	1.90	.25	−.21
5	−2.33	−1.81	−1.29	−.71	.27	−.60	.64
6	−2.20	−1.72	−1.29	−.45	.66	−1.00	1.04
Interval boundary (*Mean*)	−1.49	−.77	.08	.77	1.15	**.04**	

Note: The number in bold type represents the 0 point of the obtained *z*-distribution.

culated by averaging the *z*-scores across intervals for each item and averaging those numbers across items. (See the number in bold type in Table 4.5. Each value *M* for items 1–6 was added and that total was divided by 6.) Then, the scale value for each item is calculated by subtracting the mean of *z*-scores across intervals from this anchor. (See the far column in Table 4.5. Each value *M* was subtracted from .04.)

The final category boundaries for the measure are calculated by averaging the interval *z*-scores across items. That is, the z-scores for interval 1 are averaged across items to calculate the boundary for that interval. This process is repeated for other intervals to establish the remaining boundaries. (See bottom row of Table 4.5.)

The consistency of the resulting scale can be checked by comparing the cumulative proportion of responses in each interval against the interval boundaries across items. Ideally, a linear pattern emerges. It is also possible to work backward, calculating the cumulative proportions from the scale values of items and category boundaries. Average errors are usually relatively small when investigators have explored these discrepancies.

After scaling items, investigators ask respondents to indicate whether they agree or disagree with each item. As with the other Thurstone techniques, items are selected to collectively represent a gradation of possible scale values. Items are typically placed in a random order and the respondent's score is the mean or median of the scale values they endorse.

Advantages and Disadvantages of Stimulus, Then Person Scales

The *stimulus, then person scales* can be calibrated with greater precision than is possible with scales for which items are generated intuitively and not scaled. The same kinds of item-writing and response biases evident for person scales are also possible for this type of scale, but estimates can be made for both types of error. By calibrating stimuli as well as persons, it is possible to compare stimuli and estimate error variance across indicants with confidence. Suppose, for example, an investigator wanted to measure cognitive, affective, and behavioral indicators of motivation and to be sure that motivation is defined in the same way for each measure. Knowing that the stimulus for one measure is empirically parallel to the stimulus for another measure, precise estimates of the true and error components of each score as well as comparisons among the resulting scales can be calculated.

This strength can also be a drawback because the process of designing such measures is quite time-consuming. Furthermore, it is not always clear why stimuli should be calibrated along with the scores of individual respondents. In comparison studies, Likert and Thurstone scales seem to offer the same kinds of information and to correlate with other variables to a similar degree. Nevertheless, *stimulus, then person* methods may be helpful when investigators are uncertain about how to explore an abstract topic. By classifying stimuli as well as persons, investigators may learn more about the concept to be measured than by simply classifying persons.

MAKING CONNECTIONS

Identify a stimulus, then person measure in your field. What are the characteristics of that measure? What types of responses are called for? Can the information be logically ranked? Are there strengths and limitations in this measure that were not described in this chapter? What are they? Explain.

DILEMMAS FOR SINGLE-ITEM SCALES

The use of *single-item scales* poses a special set of problems for person scales and stimulus, then person scales. Scales with one item are most often used when investigators are interested in the attitudes of an unusually large group of people. In such surveys, more than one single-item scale may be included, but each item represents a different theoretical dimension or concept. Ordinarily the response of one individual to a single item lacks sufficient reliability for use in research. For large scales, a carefully selected item can offer a parsimonious means of representing a construct or dimension, but the sample must be large enough to minimize the effects of extreme scores. Ideally, response error tends to average out over the group and the effects of extreme scores are tempered.

Although most opinion polls contain single-item scales, there are important measurement limitations. It is not possible to estimate the internal consistency of a single-item scale because there are no parallel items for use in intra-item correlations. This means that investigators cannot accurately estimate the degree of relation among variables because the error terms are excluded from analysis.

Typically, investigators explore the skewness and kurtosis of a distribution of answers to determine how far that distribution deviates from the theoretical normal distribution (Figure 3.3). Considering the area under the curve, *skewness* offers an index that is interpreted like a *z*-score, indicating how far away an obtained distribution falls from the theoretical 0 point of a normal distribution. *Kurtosis* offers a sense of the shape of the curve in an obtained distribution. Items with skewed distributions will look less accurate because options seen as implausible will have a marked influence on the deviation estimates.

Investigators can also estimate the error in each proportion of responses, an index that offers an estimate of variability in responses across persons, but contains no information about how indicants are associated with dimensions or constructs. For example, if a single item had five response options, the *standard error of measurement* could be calculated by considering the proportion of responses that fall in each of the five categories rather than estimating the internal consistency of parallel indicants.

Other limitations of single-item scales include a lack of control for bias in how the items are written and/or the degree to which respondents misunderstand the content of the item when responding.[9] The connotations of particular items can exert an unintended influence on individual responses, which in turn introduces an undetectable form of measurement error that would be evident if there were parallel items on the measure. Items written with compound clauses also introduce error because it is impossible to determine which part of the item was considered when respondents made their decision. Those biases can occur for any item because it is difficult to anticipate subtle differences in how individuals interpret particular words. In scales with more than one indicant, such biases are more easily detected; correlations among indicants would be expected and error could be assumed in the absence of such relations. This type of calibration cannot be established for single-item scales.

With no estimate of reliability, it also becomes difficult to estimate validity when constructs are compared. For example, investigators who measured cognition, emotion, and behavior using different items could not determine which feature of reasoning offered a greater contribution to the variance in their design because they would not be able to verify the independence of their measurements of each concept. These limitations have led most researchers to rely on scales with more than one item representing each theoretical dimension.

■ ■ ■ ■ ■

MAKING CONNECTIONS

Try writing a single-item survey and administer it to a group of friends. Then, enter the data into a computer program and calculate the frequency of responses in each category. If you use a statistical package, ask the computer to generate skewness and kurtosis indices. Graph the distribution of scores and look at how far it deviates from the ideal normal distribution. What would you do to construct an item that would result in a better fit?

SIMULTANEOUS STIMULUS AND PERSON SCALING

The *simultaneous stimulus and person techniques* offer scaling of items and persons in one administration. They are most useful when the concept to be measured is unidimensional and responses form an ordinal scale. There is no need to recruit judges for classifying items prior to assessing individuals' attitudes. Items are ranked based on the degree to which individuals agree with the characteristics of all or some of the items in a response set. For respondents to attain the highest score, they typically agree with all the items in a set. For respondents to attain a middle-range score, they agree with an item in the middle range and all items ranked below that point. For respondents to attain a low score, they agree with an item at the bottom of a distribution and none of the items above that point. The resulting cumulative properties of items and responses enable stimuli and persons to be ordered on a single dimension.

Guttman Scales

Louis Guttman designed an interlocking technique in which a scale reflects a joint product of stimuli and people's responses (Guttman 1941, 1944). When persons and items are simultaneously ordered into a matrix that has cumulative properties, the resulting *scalogram* undergoes *scalogram analysis* to determine if people who agree with one item also agree with items of lesser rank and if the resulting order is reproducible. (See Table 4.6 for a sample measure and Table 4.7 for a sample matrix.) This method is appropriate when items can be ranked in a hierarchical order such that sets represented by higher numbers indicate the inclusion of all items classified with lower numbers.

    Items often incorporate details requiring agreement with an item of particular rank to imply agreement with all the features of a lesser rank. Each item has implications for the others. In a social distance scale, for example, someone who would admit members of a given race to close kinship by marriage is also likely to admit that person to their social clubs, neighborhood, area of employment, citizenship in their country, and visit their country. Those who agree to admit individuals only as visitors to their country are unlikely to agree to more intimate forms of social contact. Not surprisingly, only dimensions, constructs, or concepts that form clear progressions are suitable for Guttman scaling.

    Reproducibility across samples of responses to the same sequence of items is essential for valid scalogram analysis. If the scale offers sufficient interlocking assessment of persons and items to indicate the direct measurement of a concept, the conceptual order of items is

TABLE 4.6 Sample Items for a Guttman Scale Addressing Feelings of Success in Science Class

ITEM	SCALE VALUE
■ I feel successful passing a science final.	5
■ I feel successful solving a science problem.	4
■ I feel successful understanding directions in science class.	3
■ I feel successful if I get to science class.	2
■ I feel successful if I arrive at school.	1

TABLE 4.7   **Ideal Scalogram for Hypothetical Persons and Stimuli**

PERSONS	STIMULI					SCALE VALUES
	A	B	C	D	E	
1	1	1	1	1	1	5
2	0	1	1	1	1	4
3	0	0	1	1	1	3
4	0	0	0	1	1	2
5	0	0	0	0	1	1
6	0	0	0	0	0	0

preserved across samples.[10] When hierarchies can be attributed to concepts other than the one being measured, items may be ranked differently across person samples; the systematic error variance would be explored, and Guttman scales could be found unsuitable.

The Guttman scale is ordinal and requires no established zero point to be interpreted. To distinguish between favorable and unfavorable attitudes, investigators look for the point at which the intensity of feeling about an issue is lowest.[11] If, for example, respondents are asked to indicate the strength of their beliefs as well as their relative agreement, responses at the extreme ends of the scale are often highly associated with more intense beliefs. The point of indifference falls at the lowest point of the resulting U-shaped distribution of intensity scores.

The difficulty of finding concepts that can be broken into hierarchically ordered dimensions poses a major limitation for Guttman scales. Scales exceeding six to ten items rarely meet reproducibility criteria, yet short scales do not always provide the necessary information for adequately discriminating individuals' attitudes. Investigators who have used Guttman scales to validate whether responses form a unidimensional content universe, as was Guttman's intention, realize that the process of discarding and rewriting items becomes inappropriate. Generally, it is inappropriate to test a hypothesis by discarding data until the analysis of the remaining data fits a desired outcome. Likewise, when investigators determine whether items are features of a larger, unidimensional content universe, it is inappropriate to discard items until a unidimensional scale is formed.

Most researchers who use Guttman scales today are interested in verifying that a set of items and responses interlock; they are not necessarily interested in theorizing about the unidimensionality of the concept being measured because person scaling offers a more direct approach for such tasks. In time, Guttman himself spent more of his time exploring techniques for multidimensional scaling and most investigators continue to rely on similar assumptions (Guttman, 1959, 1968).

Advantages and Disadvantages of Simultaneous Stimulus and Person Scaling

The most obvious advantage of *simultaneous stimulus and person scaling* is the degree of precision in locating persons on scales when investigators find ordinal data useful. As with all attitude measures, these measures are vulnerable to item-writing and response biases. Nevertheless, gaps between the measurement and analysis of responses are kept to a minimum and intermediate judges are unnecessary for ranking items.

The major limitation of this approach is the fact that most attitudes cannot be parsed into hierarchical dimensions. Ordinal scales also place restrictions on available statistical tools for including these measures in more complex forms of hypothesis testing. The theoretical assumption that constructs must be unidimensional further complicates the use of interlocking techniques. When investigators are interested in obtaining an ordinal scale, simultaneous scaling offers a useful technique for assessing the strength of such scales.

■ ■ ■ ■ ■ ■

MAKING CONNECTIONS

Can you find simultaneous stimulus and person scales in your field? Why is that likely to be difficult? What are the characteristics of such measures? Are there strengths and limitations that are not mentioned in this chapter? What are they? Explain.

EVALUATING THE QUALITIES OF INDICANTS: ITEM ANALYSIS

Item analysis focuses on whether indicants are sufficiently parallel to warrant inclusion on the same scale. Theoretically, if two items are parallel, they are assumed to have similar properties: the expected means are equal, observed score variance of parallel measures are equal, intercorrelations among parallel measurements are equal from pair to pair, and correlations of parallel measures with other variables are equal. As with all aspects of this process, the obtained responses are compared to these theoretical assumptions to estimate the degree to which assumptions are supported. When exploring the relationship between different indicants to determine if those indicants belong on the same measure, investigators are careful to consider whether they reflect nominal, ordinal, interval, or ratio scales. They also look at how the responses were collected and whether there is a predefined scale for classifying scores. These comparisons allow investigators to determine if items belong on a tool, which items might require revision, and which dimensions of a concept are poorly represented.

Person Scales

For person scales, investigators typically pilot-test an initial pool of items by asking a group of respondents to complete the tasks. In evaluating the qualities of Likert-style items, investigators determine if similar items show parallel measurement qualities. In evaluating the qualities of semantic differential items, investigators explore the concept–scale interaction to determine if adjectives have similar connotations when used for more than one attitude object or if the relationship between the object and the adjectives introduces a specialized connotation that was not anticipated.

To eliminate ambiguous or nondiscriminating items, investigators often look at the *item-total correlations*. This number indicates how well a person's score for a given item correlates with a total score consisting of the sum or average of all item scores on the tool. When the item-total correlation is positive, the item contributes to the total and the higher the correlation, the better the contribution. Items with low or no correlation are discarded because they are either irrelevant or overly ambiguous. The scale of items with a negative correlation is usually reversed before further analyses are conducted.

To determine if items adequately discriminate persons with different attitudes, investigators graph the *operating characteristic curve* for each item. This offers a visual representation of the relationship between item scores and the total scale score. Figure 4.2 indicates the ideal operating characteristic curve for most kinds of person scales. As attitudes become more positive, the probability of agreement also increases in a monotonic function. The slope of the function usually reveals a marked difference in item scores. Flat slopes indicate that an item is irrelevant or ambiguous; it is being endorsed by persons with different attitudes and does not enable the investigator to discriminate between positive and negative attitudes.

To verify that items on a scale measure the intended theoretical dimensions, investigators typically use factor analysis. As outlined in Chapter 3, this method explores the intercorrelations among indicants (or items) to determine if a smaller number of patterns reflect dimensions that underlie the structure of a given item-correlations matrix. This procedure identifies clusters of items that are highly correlated with one another, but not with items in other clusters. The resulting factors can be seen as indicators that a given theoretical construct is comprised of more than one dimension. The loading of items on each scale reveals those items that are significantly associated with each theoretical dimension; items that are highly correlated with a particular factor belong on a measure of the corresponding conceptual dimension. The number of factors apparent in this analysis reflects the number of conceptual dimensions—features of a true score and corresponding systematic error—apparent in the measurement tool. As you may remember from thinking about competence

FIGURE 4.2   A Theoretically Ideal Operating Characteristic Curve for Person Scales

orientations, the items on each factor that are significantly correlated with one another can be seen as components of a particular dimension.

Confirmatory factor analysis offers tests of the degree to which items that should load on each dimension actually behave as intended.[12] Goodness-of-fit indices evaluate whether observed relationships among items actually conform to the hypothesized model. Investigators can also determine if all items on a scale have a single-factor structure. Comparing the strength of the single-factor structure with tests of a multidimensional structure can help investigators decide which theoretical approach best explains their data.

Stimulus, Then Person Scales

For Thurstone techniques, researchers also try to detect ambiguous and irrelevant items. For ambiguous items, judges would differ in their evaluations of the favorability of the same item. Highly ambiguous items would be classified across a wide range of intervals whereas more accurate items would be classified in one or two closely connected intervals. The interquartile range offers a useful index of the spread in responses (Thurstone & Chave, 1929). This index explores the variability of scores within a part of the total distribution. When items are not skewed, the standard deviation for an item also offers an appropriate estimate (Guilford, 1954). Investigators select items with the least amount of spread when able to choose between two parallel indicants.

Irrelevant items are those that do not differentiate between people with different attitudes. These items may meet the classification requirements for the first phase of scale construction, but are also rated the same way by all respondents. The item becomes irrelevant because it does not help investigators discriminate between people with favorable and unfavorable beliefs.

To evaluate the operating characteristics of each item, a large number of respondents are grouped according to their attitude scores on the sale (e.g., classified according to the interval reflected by their attitudes). For each group, the proportion of respondents who agreed with an item is calculated and those proportions are plotted against the range of obtained attitude scores. This inevitably results in an upside-down parabola.

Figure 4.3 shows an ideal curve for an attitude that has a scale score of 4. Item responses that fall in the middle of the distribution will be more highly associated with this item because it is close in value to the attitude scale score. Deviations reflect item variance within the attitude group. Graphs of most items result in nonmonotonic curves and contain a single peak that falls somewhere close to the location of the item being scaled. Items with extreme scale values show monotonic trends that reflect the restricted range available to those points. When distributions are flat or contain multiple peaks, the items are dropped because they do not have the necessary discriminating power.

Simultaneous Stimulus and Person Scales

As with all scales, the operating characteristics of a Guttman scale involve relationships between actual responses and the probability that respondents will agree with an item. Because of the hierarchical nature of the scale, the normal curve does not represent the

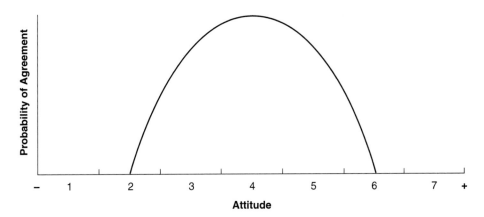

FIGURE 4.3   A Theoretically Ideal Operating Characteristic Curve for Stimulus, Then Person Scales

scalogram's probabilistic ideal. Instead, a step function is estimated. For each item, agreement would be 0 up to the point where the acceptable item is located on the scale. All items beyond an item's placement would be equally positive because respondents who agree with a given item will be agreeing with one another and everyone who has more positive beliefs about the attitude object.

Figure 4.4 shows the ideal distribution for the social distance item introduced earlier. If a person is willing to admit someone of another race to their area of employment, they would also be willing to admit that person to attain citizenship and visit their country. Respondents in this group are unlikely to admit such persons to their neighborhood, social clubs, or family, indicating a detectable form of prejudice.

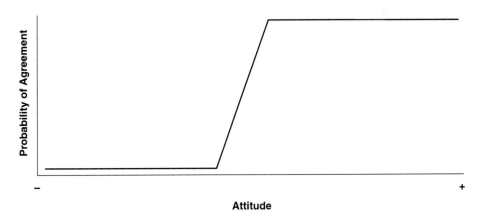

FIGURE 4.4   A Theoretically Ideal Operating Characteristic Curve for a Simultaneous Stimulus and Person Scale

Evaluating Indicants

Item analysis is one step in the process of establishing reliability that enables investigators to evaluate the performance of individual items. When all items are performing at an optimal level, reliability coefficients are likely to be near 1.00. As items reveal imperfections in their clarity and discrimination power, the reliability coefficients begin to decline. Indicants usually contain variance and that variance corresponds to the kinds of individual differences being measured by a particular scale. When indicants fail to perform as expected, investigators can discard that item from their analyses, except when this failure is directly linked to predictions of a scale's unidimensional correspondence with a theoretical construct. When many items fail to perform as expected, investigators usually design and test new measures before proceeding with their research.

MAKING CONNECTIONS

Find a common attitude measure in your field. What methods would be appropriate for exploring the quality of each indicant on that measure? If you can obtain responses to that measure, try exploring the qualities of the items. Are all the items equally strong?

EVALUATING RELATIONSHIPS AMONG INDICANTS: RELIABILITY

Earlier in the book, the idea that reliability involves issues of stability and accuracy was introduced along with some of the most general assumptions about the relationships between reliability and different forms of variance. Reliability coefficients estimate the degree to which a measure is error-free. Typically, it is assumed that errors in the observed scores of one person are independent of errors in the scores of another and that true scores are independent of error scores both within and between persons. This means that the *variance of observed scores* conforms to the following:

OBTAINED SCORE VARIANCE

$$\sigma_x^2 = \sigma_T^2 + (\sigma_S^2 + \sigma_R^2)$$

To estimate reliability, the fact that true score variance is equal to observed score variance minus error variance is accepted. Then, both sides of the equation are divided by σ_x^2 to give the following theoretical definition:

RELIABILITY

$$r_{TX} = \frac{\sigma_T^2}{\sigma_x^2} = 1 - \left(\frac{\sigma_S^2 + \sigma_R^2}{\sigma_x^2} \right)$$

To translate this theoretical definition into forms that account for the levels of measurement inherent in each kind of scale, statisticians have found a way to compute different kinds of item correlations. They have also found ways to apply this definition to estimate stability as well as accuracy in measurement. There are many ways to demonstrate the reliability of a measure, but in the interest of space only the most commonly used tools are introduced here.[13]

Person Scales

Cronbach's α remains the most appropriate method for estimating the reliability of Likert and semantic differential scales.[14] For these summative techniques, it is assumed that items are parallel because they are sampled from the same dimensions of an attitude. An α coefficient is a measure of *internal consistency* that shows the degree to which equivalence or homogeneity is evident among items on a scale. Using a computer to compare variance from each item with every other item, alpha is calculated from the formula:

CRONBACH'S ALPHA

$$\alpha = \left(\frac{n}{n-1}\right)\left(\frac{\sigma_x^2 - \sum \sigma_{x_f}^2}{\sigma_x^2}\right)$$

The number of indicants (or items) of a measure is represented by n, the variance of the respondents' total scores is represented by σ_x^2, and the sum of the item variances is represented by $\sum \sigma_{x_f}^2$. The resulting coefficient is highly dependent on intercorrelations among items. Alpha coefficients are typically computed as part of the item-analysis techniques used for person scales.

You may remember some forms of item analysis involve the calculation of internal consistency by deleting each item in turn (Table 3.2). Comparing the resulting coefficient to the total α, it is possible to determine if the item improves, lowers, or simply contributes to the scale's reliability. Investigators also use factor-analysis procedures to verify clusters of items in meaningful dimensions.

When an alpha coefficient is inordinately low, investigators can do one of two things to adjust the reliability. They can increase the number of participants in a sample, reducing the possibility that extreme scores will influence the outcome. Using the Spearman-Brown prophecy formula, investigators can also determine if increasing the number of items will sufficiently improve the reliability.

SPEARMAN-BROWN PROPHECY FORMULA

$$r_{pp} = \frac{k r_{xx}}{1 + (k-1)r_{xx}}$$

In this formula r_{pp} is the estimate of internal consistency, k is the ratio of a longer to a shorter test (e.g., double, triple), and r_{xx} is the reliability of the shorter test. So, if the reliability of a five-item test was .40 and the investigator increased the length of the test to ten items, the reliability may improve to become as high as:

$$\frac{.80}{1 + .40} = = .57$$

Measures of internal consistency estimate the accuracy of a scale but do not estimate stability for repeated use. To demonstrate that a tool will remain consistently calibrated over time, investigators can complete a *test-retest* analysis. In such analysis, respondents complete a measure twice and the two sets of responses are correlated. Researchers limit the time interval between two administrations to restrict variance attributable to change.

Stimulus, Then Person Scales

Measures of internal consistency are inappropriate for use with the Thurstone scaling techniques and any other measure in which items are assumed to represent points along a continuum. In the case of the paired-comparison, equal-appearing intervals, and simultaneous interval techniques, relations between persons and items are calculated as part of the scale development. Inter-rater reliability formulas can be used to calculate differences in how judges rate items (Chapter 5). More commonly, investigators evaluate how the obtained cumulative proportions of responses are aligned with the proportions estimated for the normal distribution. This comparison involves the calculation of *discriminable dispersions* from which it is possible to estimate error. The deviation of obtained interval boundaries from standard *z*-score boundaries also reveals information about the role of error in Thurstone scales.

Simultaneous Stimulus and Person Scales

Guttman scales, like the Thurstone measures, involve items that represent different points along a continuum. Correlations between items are inappropriate indices of reliability because items are not assumed to be parallel. Guttman proposed a *coefficient of reproducibility* to assess the frequency of item deviations from the ideal pattern of a perfect scale. The coefficient is equal to 1 minus the proportion of responses that must be changed to produce a perfect scale. Coefficients of at least .90 are seen as adequate indications that stimuli and persons are accurately scaled along a single dimension.

Unfortunately, this coefficient is less informative than was initially thought. The value of the coefficient depends so much on the proportion of respondents who endorse items that mathematical algorithms can easily explain the results.[15] Several complex solutions have been proposed for investigators who are dependent on such scaling (see, for example, Dawes & Smith, 1985, or McIver & Carmines, 1981).

Relationships among Indicants

To identify relationships among indicants, internal consistency and factor-analysis techniques are used most commonly. They offer the most detailed representation of whether items are sufficiently parallel to warrant inclusion on a single scale. When items are deliberately constructed to reflect different points along a continuum, it is not appropriate to ask whether items are parallel. Instead, investigators look for reproducible matches between items and their distribution along a scale. The measure as a whole is also evaluated to determine if the proportion of responses reflects those expected by chance alone. These techniques allow investigators to verify how each indicant is measured and that those indicants adequately reflect theoretical claims about theoretical dimensions.

MAKING CONNECTIONS

Looking at the measure you selected earlier, what approach to exploring reliability would be appropriate? How do you know? Would more than one method work for the same measure?

EVALUATING RELATIONSHIPS BETWEEN INDICANTS AND CONCEPTS: VALIDITY

The challenge of establishing validity in the use of a measure is more complex than it may seem from the simple definitions presented earlier. It can be difficult to remember that validity is a property of a data set, not a property of a tool. Every time a tool is used, validity is explored by comparing patterns of association between measures of a theoretical concept, measures assumed to be related to that concept, measures assumed to be different from that concept, and measures that are assumed to be irrelevant to that concept. The same logic applies to establishing the validity of constructs and dimensions. In other words, validity is usually explored using a hierarchy of steps, but changes at one step can seriously alter the evaluations of all other steps.

The form of validity that is most closely linked with reliability involves distinctions among the dimensions of a theoretical construct. Constructs may have one dimension or more than one and investigators are interested in verifying the degree to which a tool measures all the necessary features of each dimension. Once investigators are comfortable that each theoretical construct is adequately measured, they compare the results obtained with their new scale to those obtained with existing scales; the two usually offer similar kinds of information. When a new scale is constructed because there are no existing scales, investigators face the challenge of comparing similar but nonequivalent measures to determine if the two offer compatible conclusions. Investigators also compare tools with contrasting evidence to confirm the relative uniqueness of independent features. If conceptual comparisons are not supported, investigators reevaluate their theoretical assumptions as well as the quality of the tool used to measure each concept.

Content Validity

Exploring *content validity* is one of the earliest steps in this hierarchical process, but is revisited whenever investigators find evidence that a tool is not functioning well. There are no empirical techniques for establishing content validity. Investigators determine the balance of items in relation to the dimensions or constructs being measured. They evaluate the language of each item and determine if the wording of items is sufficiently clear and if the overall scale includes items that represent all necessary dimensions. Careful scrutiny of an item's poor performance can often reveal unanticipated ambiguity. For most person scales, this involves an intuitive process. Measures intended to evaluate beliefs about the purposes of school, for example, involved the omission of redundant or ambiguous ideas. Later, an entire dimension was eliminated because it offered redundant information that was represented more clearly for another part of academic engagement.

The degree to which items fall in the intended position can be empirically validated in the *stimulus, then person* scales and *simultaneous stimulus and person* scales, but even here investigators usually evaluate whether the items reflect the attitude to be measured. When the intended order of indicants is not preserved, investigators question both item quality and the logic of their placement on a scale.

Criterion Validity

The next level of inference involves the comparison of dimensions to a construct. *Criterion validity* involves questions about how the dimensions of a particular theoretical concept are related to one another. Across disciplines, names vary for such progressively more abstract judgments. When establishing criterion validity, investigators look for evidence of concurrent and discriminant validity. They establish *concurrent validity* by determining if two similar dimensions within a scale are associated with one another. They establish *discriminant validity* by determining if two distinct dimensions are uncorrelated.

Criterion validity is typically explored by asking respondents to complete a battery of measures at the same point in time. Looking at the Likert scales of beliefs about the purpose of school, for example, all indicants are assumed to address purposes and to therefore show some correlation with one another ($\alpha = .89$ for the total measure). The dimensions reported in Table 4.1 are explored to determine whether they show signs of concurrent and discriminant validity. The ideas that school should help students attain wealth and status was assumed to be moderately related to the dimensions of "understand the world" and "become socially useful." The beliefs that school should facilitate an understanding of the world and help students become useful to society were predicted to be more highly related to one another. The absence of correlations between the dimensions supports claims of discriminant validity. Relatively high correlations offer evidence for concurrent validity.[16] Table 4.8 contains the correlations between the three purposes of school dimensions. Looking at the correlations, were the predictions upheld? Which correlations might have been stronger? Was the wealth and status scale significantly different from the other two dimensions? Squaring each correlation to identify the percent of variance accounted for by the designated relation offers a simple means of comparing correlations.[17]

Construct Validity

Once relationships between dimensions and constructs are verified, investigators are ready to determine if constructs are related to a more general concept. *Construct validity* involves

TABLE 4.8   A Study of Discriminant and Concurrent Validity: Comparing Purposes of School Dimensions

	BE USEFUL TO SOCIETY	UNDERSTAND THE WORLD	ATTAIN WEALTH AND STATUS
Be useful to society	1.00		
Understand the world	.47	1.00	
Attain wealth and status	.28	.26	1.00

Note: All correlations differed significantly from 0, $p < .01$; $n = 852$ adolescents, ages 13 to 18, from multiple samples.

the determination of how the dimensions of a scale are associated with other scales and with an intended theoretical concept. In establishing construct validity, investigators look for evidence of convergent, divergent, and predictive validity.

Convergent and *divergent validity* involve concerns that are parallel to those associated with *concurrent* and *discriminant validity.* The former represent relationships among theoretical constructs as expressed by different measures, the latter involve relationships among the dimensions of each theoretical construct. In establishing *convergent validity* it is assumed that multiple measures of a single construct function in identical ways; when such concordance is absent, investigators typically question the validity of the scale or of their theoretical assumptions. In establishing *divergent validity,* it is assumed that marked differences are apparent in unrelated constructs; if concordance is evident, investigators look for systematic error and question the discriminating power of their measure.

Comparing beliefs about the purposes of school and competence orientations illustrates such complexities. Table 4.9 reports the correlation between the task, ego, work-avoidant orientations and beliefs that school should promote usefulness to society,

TABLE 4.9   A Study of Convergent and Divergent Validity: Comparing Beliefs about the Purposes of School and Competence Orientations

PURPOSES OF SCHOOL	COMPETENCE ORIENTATIONS		
	Task Orientation	*Ego Orientation*	*Work Avoidance*
Become useful to society	.38	.26	−.19
Understand the world	.41	.22	−.17
Attain wealth and status	.15	.40	.16

Note: All correlations are significantly different from 0, $p < .01$; $n = 852$ adolescents, ages 13 to 18, from multiple samples.

understanding of the world, and wealth and status. Exploring convergent and divergent validity, dimensions for each construct were assumed to reflect their designated construct; three purposes and three orientations reflect beliefs and dispositions, respectively. All the correlations reached statistical significance ($p < .01$) for a sample of $n = 852$. Which competence orientations were most highly associated with each dimension of the purposes of school measures? What does a negative association suggest? Does it seem reasonable to accept the validity of each construct in a more general concept of academic engagement?

Predictive validity involves evidence that scores on one scale predict additional scores in a theoretically relevant manner. Such techniques verify that indicants of an attitude predict a dimension, but relationships between constructs are more commonly explored. The most common predictive validity question asked in attitude research involves the degree to which attitudes predict behavior. This prediction is important to anyone interested in applying research on human functioning to solve social dilemmas because it enables policymakers and practitioners to anticipate particular events. When a prediction does not hold, two outcomes are possible. The measurement of a concept may be inappropriate or the concept itself may not be appropriate for making the intended decisions. Although theoretically interesting, stability in the predictive power of a variable is unnecessary for establishing the measurement properties of a tool. Investigators need only verify that the relationships between dimensions or constructs are consistent with theoretical claims.

In research on attitudes, investigators commonly use at least two techniques for exploring construct validity. In one approach, attitudes are compared to preexisting group differences. When individuals can be classified along a relevant dimension prior to completing an attitude measure, a new tool can validly reveal these group differences.

Consider the possibility of sex differences in competence orientations. If, as some activists have claimed, males are more ego-oriented or work-avoidant and females are more task-oriented, sex differences should be predictable using competence orientations.[18] As is apparent in Table 4.10, task and work-avoidant orientations were significant discriminators between males and females. Looking at means, males reported more work avoidance and less task orientation than females. Males were assigned a score of 1 and females a score of

TABLE 4.10   A Study of Predictive Validity: Using Competence Orientations to Discriminate Gender

COMPETENCE ORIENTATION	DISCRIMINANT FUNCTION	MEANS COMPARISONS		
		Males	*Females*	$F_{(1, 954)}$
Task orientation	.86	4.15 (.56)	4.35 (.53)	31.01***
Ego orientation	.10	3.71 (.62)	3.74 (.69)	.44
Work avoidance	−.79	2.57 (.83)	2.31 (.73)	25.22***

Note: For the discriminant function, $\chi^2(3) = 40.72$, $p < .000$, and the canonical correlation is .21, $n = 477$ males and $n = 479$ females. Standard deviations are reported in parentheses.

***$p < .001$.

2, so the signs of the discriminant function (read like correlation coefficients) indicate the same conclusion.

A second approach to exploring predictive validity involves the comparison of constructs within a concept to examine theoretical relations. This is most commonly accomplished using regression techniques. For example, a blocked regression was computed to determine if competence orientations and beliefs about the purposes of school were sufficiently associated with class participation to warrant inclusion in an academic engagement concept. To predict class participation, competence orientations and beliefs about the purposes of school were entered in a regression equation as two different blocks. Competence orientations alone accounted for 40 percent of the variance in self-reported class participation, $F_{(3, 848)} = 191.86, p < .000$. The purposes of school beliefs accounted for an additional 2 percent of variance, $F_{(3, 845)} = 7,03, p < .000$. Beta coefficients and t-tests are reported in Table 4.11. These indicate that the inclusion of some dimensions were unnecessary predictors of class participation because they are used in more than one way.

Theoretical Validity

Investigators also take the exploration of constructs one step further to explore *theoretical validity*. This often involves the comparison of concepts and/or constructs. Theoretical constructs have been evaluated with a *multiattitude–multimethod matrix* of different attitudes, each measured using different methods.[19] Complex statistical techniques are used to explore *theoretical concepts*.

Suppose adolescents' attitudes about exclusion, fairness, and motivation were measured using cognitive, affective, and behavioral scales. A matrix similar to that presented in

TABLE 4.11 A Study of Predictive Validity: Prediction of Class Participation Using Competence Orientations and Beliefs about the Purposes of School

PREDICTORS	β	t
(Constant)		14.76***
Task orientation	.17	5.24***
Ego orientation	.004	.15
Work avoidance	−.53	−17.53***
Useful to society	.04	1.41
Understand the world	.08	2.43*
Attain wealth and status	.07	2.29*

Note: For this model, the adjusted $R^2 = .42$ and is significantly better than predictions made with competence orientations alone, $F_{(3, 845)} = 7.03, p < .000$.

*p < .05, **p < .01, ***p < .001.

TABLE 4.12   Hypothetical Multiattitude–Multimethod Matrix

	COGNITIVE			AFFECTIVE			BEHAVIORAL		
	Exclusion	*Fairness*	*Motivation*	*Exclusion*	*Fairness*	*Motivation*	*Exclusion*	*Fairness*	*Motivation*
COGNITIVE									
Exclusion	r								
Fairness	m	r							
Motivation	m	m	r						
AFFECTIVE									
Exclusion	v	h	h	r					
Fairness	h	v	h	m	r				
Motivation	h	h	v	m	m	r			
BEHAVIORAL									
Exclusion	v	h	h	v	h	h	r		
Fairness	h	v	h	h	v	h	m	r	
Motivation	h	h	v	h	h	v	m	m	r

Note: r = reliability coefficients, *v* = convergent validity correlations, *m* = same method, different attitude, *h* = different attitude, different method.

Table 4.12 could be constructed to compare the various measures. Scores represented on the diagonal would be the reliability coefficients for each measure, the correlation of the measure with itself. The remaining scores would differ depending on whether the attitude, the method of measurement, or both varied. When the same attitude is measured using a different method, the correlation between the two scores is consistent with typical measures of convergent validity. When independent attitudes are measured using the same method, a low correlation would be expected. Similarly, if both attitudes and methods differ from a target scale, low correlations would be predicted.

The multiattitude–multimethod matrix is limited by the fact that investigators do not have a single statistical criterion for evaluating the strength of relationships in the matrix. Such validity judgments are often difficult to support empirically. Reliability coefficients offer a ceiling for possible inter-scale correlations; measures cannot be more valid than they are reliable. Tests of divergent validity would yield correlations that fall near 0, but this would also be likely if measures have low reliability.

Dilemmas identified for the multiattitude–multimethod approaches are currently being solved as investigators find new tools for testing the goodness-of-fit of factor structures. *Confirmatory factor analysis* can help verify the dimensions that are apparent in a collection of related indicants or relationships between multiple measures of the same constructs. *Path analysis* can be used to compare complex relationships between collections of indicants. General *structural equation modeling* (SEM) can also be used to explore relationships between indicants and latent variables. *Hierarchical linear modeling* (HML) can account for the nested features of variables in a matrix. This collection of tools relies on mathematical knowledge that has been available for quite some time. Advances in computer technology and improvements in software packages like *EQS* and *Lisrel* make it more practical to use this statistical knowledge.[20]

- - - - -

MAKING CONNECTIONS

What evidence supports the validity of the attitude measure you found? Have all forms of validity been explored? What studies would offer a more complete sense of a tool's validity? Name some strengths and limitations of available research.

ATTITUDES AS BELIEFS, OPINIONS, OR VALUES

Research on scaling techniques for measuring attitudes eventually led investigators to conclude that Thurstone, Guttman, Likert, and semantic differential scaling techniques typically correlate well with one another. None of these measures seems to have a particular advantage over the other although they differ in the relative ease of construction. Scales often differ in the depth of processing required to complete them, the degree to which they encourage respondents to worry about self-presentation, and the availability of attitude-relevant cues that affect responses. New developments focus on minimizing distortion in the recording of attitudes, accounting for the fact that attitudes change, and distinguishing attitudes from other types of human functioning. Techniques for demonstrating the stability, accuracy, and validity of new measures proliferate while investigators remain sensitive to immediate pressures to evaluate attitudes associated with current events. Computers also make procedures that were once arduous and impractical much more easily accessible. For these reasons, the measurement of attitudes has become a stable feature of many research designs. At the very least, after completing a study, participants may be asked to evaluate their experiences.

SUGGESTED READINGS

Bond, T. G., & Fox, C. M. (2001). *Applying the Rasch model: Fundamental measurement in the human sciences.* Mahwah, NJ: Erlbaum.

Byrne, B. M. (2001). *Structural equation modeling with AMOS: Basic concepts, applications and programming.* Mahwah, NJ: Erlbaum.

DeVellis, R. F. (2003). *Scale development: Theory and applications* (2nd ed.). Thousand Oaks, CA: Sage.

Dillman, D. A. (2000). *Mail and Internet surveys: The tailored design method.* New York: Wiley.

Eagly, A., & Chaiken, S. (1993). *The psychology of attitudes.* New York: Harcourt Brace.

Netemeyer, R. G., Bearsen, W. O., & Sharma, S. (2003). *Scaling procedures: Issues and applications.* Thousand Oaks, CA: Sage.

Raykov, T., & Marcoulides, G. A. (2000). *A first course in structural equation modeling.* Mahwah, NJ: Erlbaum.

SUGGESTED WEB SITES

Institute of Objective Measurement for *Rasch:* http://www.rasch.org

Muthén & Muthén for *Mplus*: http://www.statmodel.com

Multivariate Software, Inc. for *EQS*: http://www.mvsoft.com

Scientific Software for *Lisrel*: http://www.ssicentral.com

SmallWaters Corporation for *AMOS*: http://www.smallwaters.com

WINSTEPS, Facets Rasch Measurement Software: http://www.winsteps.com

ENDNOTES

1. Likert (1932) offered this definition after conducting a measurement study of attitudes and their stability. These assertions have been refined over time, but not substantially altered.

2. This measure was designed formally by Nicholls, Patashnick, & Nolen (1985) although many groups of adolescents, faculty, and graduate students were involved in the item-writing and scale construction process.

3. Likert (1932) offers many of these guidelines that have since been refined, but not seriously altered.

4. Himmelfarb (1993) outlined the common scales for measuring attitudes in Eagly & Chaiken's (1993) book on the psychology of attitudes.

5. See work by Bishop (1990), Kalton, Roberts, & Holt (1980), Krosnick & Schuman (1988), and Schuman & Presser (1981) for studies of response effects associated with eliminating the option to express uncertainty. Basically, these studies suggest that the overall favorability of an attitude is not evaluated, but people with weaker attitudes are more likely to use this option.

6. Kalton, Roberts, & Holt (1980) offer one study of the effects of including a middle option.

7. Web sites for more information on the emerging technologies for these techniques can be found at the Institute for Objective Measurement (http://www.rasch.org) and Winsteps (http://www.winsteps.com).

8. See Mosteller (1951) for details on this calculation.

9. See Kalton, Collins, & Brook (1978) for a study of item-writing. There are also many available books offering guidelines for item writing.

10. See Dawes & Smith (1985) for a more complete analysis of this issue.

11. See Guttman (1947) and Suchman (1950) for more information on this process.

12. Web sites listed at the end of the chapter offer a range of statistical software packages for computing these indices.

13. See Feldt & Brennan (1993) for a comprehensive summary of reliability that includes formulas adjusted for solving different measurement dilemmas.

14. See Cronbach (1951) for more details.

15. See Nunnally & Bernstein (1994) for an example.

16. These findings were supported in studies by Nicholls, Patashnick, & Nolen (1985) and Thorkildsen (1988).

17. Tests for the significance of differences between correlations are available (Steiger, 1980).

18. It is surprising to find this difference because gender has not been a significant discriminator in the original samples that were combined for this analysis.

19. Himmelfarb (1993) offers a strong adaptation of the multitrait–multimethod approach outlined by Campbell & Fiske (1959).

20. Web sites listed at the end of the chapter offer information on how to find this technology.

CHAPTER FIVE

MEASURING PERSONALITY

When psychometricians measure personality, they try to offer a psychological account of the whole person (McCrae & Costa, 1990). Whereas attitudes reflect judgments in relation to an attitude object, personality is the study of individuals' basic natures, temperaments, and attachments. Personality theorists working from a psychometric tradition have answered "no" to the question of whether an intrapersonal unfolding or changing circumstances can reshape existing personalities, but, as with all theories, there are dissenters. Before introducing the challenging enterprise of measuring personality, a bit more detail on the language of personality theory is in order.

One of the most controversial, but theoretically important distinctions made in personality research concerns relationships between the *self, identity,* and *personality.* Investigators differ in how they theorize about the concept of "the whole person" and their measurement plans reflect these differences. Personality may be the whole of someone's experience, with the self as the core of that theoretical entity and identity as an individual's awareness of how the self and other dimensions of personality are coordinated. Personality can also be seen as a dimension within the self that involves a collection of traits within a larger self-system. Identity would retain its status as the facets of the system that are conscious to particular individuals, but plays a larger role in the measurement enterprise.

Recognizing that psychometricians place heavy emphasis on stability, this chapter will outline how investigators measure personality dimensions that are evident across situations and time. In other parts of the book, additional techniques will reflect the measurement of identities and changes in personality. Developmentalists tend to measure change as an evolution toward greater unity and wisdom in human functioning, distinguishing aspects of personality that show evidence of growth. Methods for measuring change without growth, such as that associated with evaluating *states* and *identity,* are classified with other techniques commonly associated with interpretive measurement. Despite differences in the use of numbers to represent indicants, the underlying assumptions about detectable change are comparable for the different interpretive techniques. To consider the whole person investigators usually rely on a full battery of measurement tools. The classification here serves only to accentuate their differences.

This purely stylistic decision obfuscates one important debate in personality research that has a profound effect on measurement procedures. Investigators differ in the emphasis they place on nomothetic, idiographic, or idiothetic theoretical concerns. *Nomothetic research* emphasizes dispositional *traits* or the general processes through which personality concepts emerge, change, and function over time. Investigators studying nomothetic constructs are likely to use the tools described in this chapter. *Idiographic research* involves a search for the uniqueness of a person without renouncing the search for regularities among groups of persons. Exploring the dynamic features of personality, researchers identify *states* that are assumed to be highly variable across situations, but relatively predictable within repeated examples of the same type of situation. Investigators often use tools classified in the developmental or interpretive sections of this book to measure this type of change. Finally, *idiothetic research* involves the attempt to combine traits and states into a single explanatory model of human functioning. Investigators are likely to use tools classified as interpretive , but can include tools for nomothetic research in their measurement plan. If this logic becomes confusing, imagine our working metaphor of a tool box; tools can take similar forms and still retain different purposes.

In the nomothetic approach to personality, studies of individual differences reveal patterns of thoughts, feelings, and actions that show cross-cultural, cross-situational, and temporal stability.[1] In such work, researchers define *traits* as dimensions along which people can be ranked by their *tendencies* toward behaving in patterned ways. The term tendencies is carefully included in this definition to account for the fact that traits are not deterministic and explain a relatively small percentage of variance in human functioning. Unlike habits, traits find expression in a myriad of different ways, and people can systematically ignore their natural tendencies. Nevertheless, traits are apparent in individuals' emotional, interpersonal, motivational, experiential, and attitudinal styles. They also seem to be detectable across generations, despite a wide range of diversity in life experiences (McCrae & Costa, 1988).

Investigators sometimes measure the *structure* of individuals' characteristics to determine which traits are present or absent. They also measure the *intensity* of a trait or how much of a trait is expressed. Regardless of whether investigators focus on its structure or magnitude, the measurement of a trait is assumed to show high levels of test-retest reliability.

At this point, a theoretically viable five-factor model has been proposed to account for the full range of personality traits.[2] As you may notice in the schematic representation of this theory, the model relies heavily on five major or *cardinal traits* (Figure 5.1). For each trait, a variety of *central traits* have been identified because they tend to converge around a more general construct.

A more specific representation of the relations between the *cardinal trait* of openness to experience, relevant *central traits,* and particular indicants for each trait are apparent in Figure 5.2. A third layer of secondary traits may also be apparent, but are less distinctive because they would not be apparent in most individuals (Caprara & Cervone, 2000; Cattell, 1973). The concept of academic engagement represented in Figure 3.2 reflects a combination of secondary traits, beliefs, and self-reported actions.[3] In contrast, Figure 5.2 represents the dimensions of the openness construct, a cardinal trait. Personality theorists measure constructs or concepts to verify the existence of traits depending on their interest in describing the structure of a trait or explaining its function. Some theorists may also measure the valence of a trait, looking for some way to estimate its intensity.

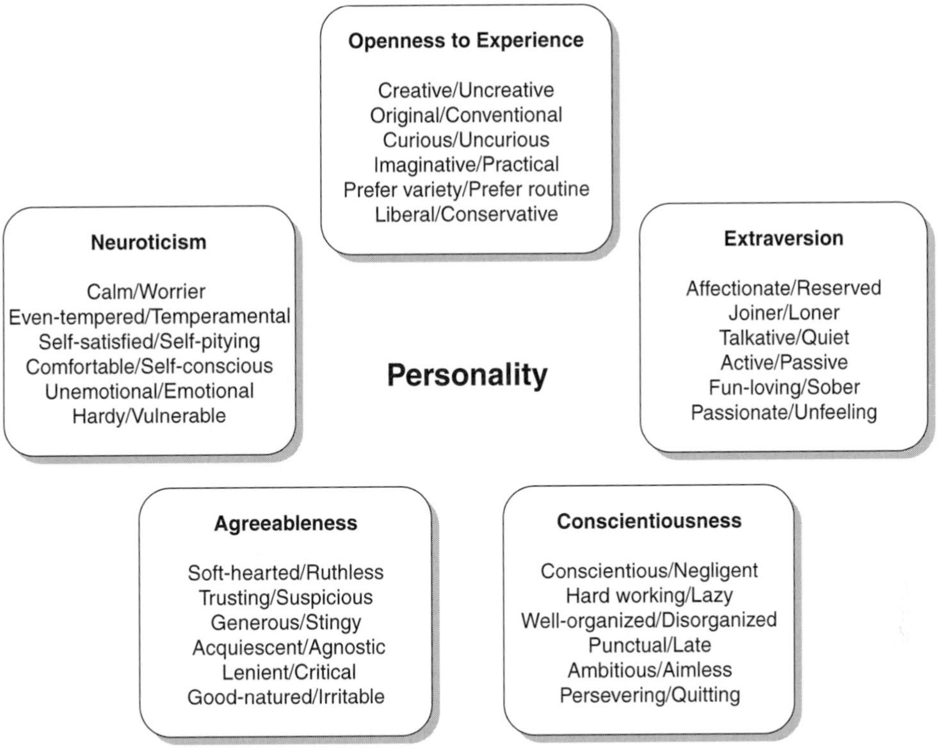

FIGURE 5.1   The Five-Factor Model of Personality[25]

MAKING CONNECTIONS

Using a broad approach to exploring personality, what measures of personality traits or states have you found? Do investigators use other terms for these ideas (e.g., *characteristics, orientations, drives, forms of involvement*). What other labels can you find to represent the features of an individual? Which of those labels offer the most precise term for personality and/or individual differences?

TYPES OF PERSONALITY MEASURES

Regardless of whether investigators are interested in nomothetic or idiographic evidence, they usually search for convergence among more than one type of data. To highlight different types of evidence, the terms *Q-data* (self-reports of one's personality), *L-data* (reports

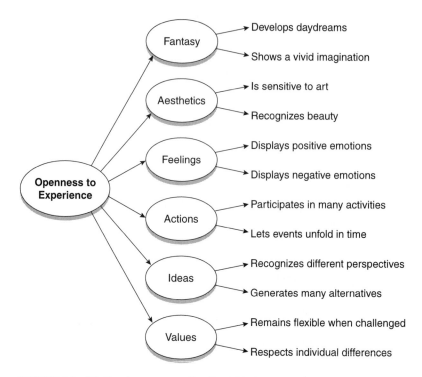

FIGURE 5.2   Distinctions among Cardinal Traits, Central Traits, and Indicants

generated by an observer), and *T-data* (performance on a standardized test) have been distinguished to help new investigators see the subtleties in each measurement technique.[4]

Categories of Measurement

The terms *Q-data, L-data,* and *T-data* reflect labels that no longer appear in published reports of research, but are resurrected here to highlight some of the measurement concerns associated with measuring the "whole person" using a nomothetic approach to personality theory. Chapter 13 offers more information on idiographic and idiothetic measurement.

Q-Data.   Q-data is collected by asking respondents to observe and report their own thoughts, feelings, and behavior. Self-reports often involve introspection and may or may not be highly structured. Investigators can use the methods described in Chapter 4 by placing the self or identity-related entities as an attitude object. Other forms of Q-data include projective measures whereby individuals are asked to talk about their lives in interviews, on surveys, by writing, or by drawing images of their experience. Investigators can take the results of such self-reports at face value or draw inferences about the relationships between those reports and other more general concepts.[5]

To explore the cross-cultural validity of the five-factor model, investigators from countries all over the world asked respondents to complete translated versions of the NEO-PI-R

(McCrae & Allik, 2002). Participants completed this Likert-type measure in which all five cardinal traits and their corresponding central traits were assessed. Stereotypical assumptions about how cultures differ were also explored by combining the results of this and other personality measures.

L-Data. When investigators collect L-data, trained observers often assess an individual's characteristics by evaluating functioning in everyday life. Investigators can use behavioral checklists, rating scales, or other recording devices to facilitate reliable and valid judgments (see Chapter 8). Such evidence can be scored holistically to offer a general rating or quantitatively by counting the frequency of particular behaviors.

Consider a series of studies on children's aggression.[6] In addition to asking participants to rate their own behavior, investigators also asked parents, teachers, and peers to rate the behavior of each target child. The recording instruments differed for each class of raters to ensure that evaluators had the necessary skills for effectively using the tool. Investigators looked for convergence in these ratings although they also suggest that readers should be cautious about assuming the necessity of such convergence.

T-Data. Investigators who collect T-data measure an individual's behavior in a contrived laboratory or testing situation. In such situations there is little ambiguity in whether respondents are being evaluated and a predetermined set of standards is often used for classifying persons and responses.

Perhaps the most famous standardized personality measure is the *Minnesota Multiphasic Personality Inventory* (MMPI), a measure used to diagnose personality disorders as well as typical personality characteristics. The NEO-PI-R is coming to replace other widely used tools like the *Myers-Briggs Personality Inventory* and the *Personality Research Form.*[7] Each of these standardized tests have been used to evaluate personality disorders as well as normal functioning by recording normative responses and comparing deviations from that norm.

Individuals' responses are often compared to those of a normative sample selected from the same population or to a predetermined set of criteria. Standardized measures seem to offer stability in a research plan and allow investigators to make reasonable predictions about how groups of individuals are likely to respond. Comparing standardized data with findings from new measures allows investigators to verify the calibration of new tools and validate emerging generalizations.

Combining Evidence. Although the emphasis of this chapter will be on nomothetic measurement, investigators can look for convergence among states and traits as well as among measures of the same theoretical dimension. They look for patterns in multiple forms of similarly conceptualized tools (e.g., either Q-, L-, or T-data). Patterns reflect convergence when indicants belong on the same dimension and divergence when entities are unrelated.

Investigators have learned to be cautious about assuming that self-report and external evaluations will always converge. Raters are rarely as aware of others' personality characteristics as they might think and there are marked individual differences in people's self-awareness.[8] Despite differing measurement purposes, generalizations about how indicants are related to constructs and constructs are related to general concepts may be more valid if predictable evidence is obtained from different types of data.

■ ■ ■ ■ ■ ■ ▬▬▬▬▬▬▬▬▬▬▬▬▬▬▬▬▬▬▬▬▬▬▬▬▬▬▬▬▬▬▬▬▬

MAKING CONNECTIONS

Find a paper in your area of interest that contains more than one type of data. How did investigators measure each variable? How did they calibrate each tool? How did they coordinate the different kinds of evidence? Could conclusions about personality be supported?

NOMOTHETIC MEASUREMENT

Personality theorists interested in nomothetic measurement are typically involved in the search for *source traits* that exist independently of particular measurement tools (Cattell, 1973). Interested in measuring the structure of these personality concepts, investigators ask if the trait is most accurately measured using a unipolar scale, a bipolar scale, or a multidimensional set of scales. If a trait is multidimensional, investigators endeavor to label any underlying hierarchical structures apparent in each dimension.

Investigators can make inferences about source traits by measuring *surface traits*. Surface traits are those visible indicators of patterned, traitlike thoughts, feelings, and/or actions. Measuring whether a person seeks excitement, is assertive, and exudes warmth, for example, allows investigators to draw inferences about the latent source trait of extraversion. The last two columns of Figure 5.2 reflect generalizations from surface traits as measured by particular indicants to source traits of openness to experience.

Generalizations about personality are strengthened by remaining concrete about the conditions under which a source trait is measured. A source trait will be apparent in different situations and cultural contexts. When error is minimized, measuring surface traits usually allows for accurate inferences about the latent source trait. Variation in measurement techniques introduces methodological error that nomothetic theorists are careful to consider before dismissing the validity of findings. Some of the techniques for estimating and minimizing the effects of such error will be highlighted in the remainder of this chapter.

Self-Report Data

Because psychometricians are interested in stability across cultures, situations, and time, they usually design tools that offer context-free information about personality characteristics. Most investigators are not especially interested in details that foster particular judgments, but plan to aggregate decisions across persons. They often rely on highly structured scales to facilitate comparisons with a set of normative assumptions. Let's look at a few examples to illustrate a range of self-report measures.

Survey Data.   When collecting Q-data, investigators interested in nomothetic measurement rely on many of the methods used to measure attitudes (see Chapter 4 for details on these methods). Relying on survey information, investigators differentiate aspects of personality and write corresponding items. Respondents are usually asked to evaluate the consistency with which characteristics match their identity. Likert-type scales may contain items focused on the self. More didactic measures may use a scale ranging from "very much like me" to "not at all like me." Comparing the dimensions within a tool or how dimensions from one tool are associated with those from others helps investigators determine if their theory sustains integrity.

Projective Techniques.   Because most individuals respond to stimuli by projecting their naïve perspectives onto the tasks placed before them, investigators have designed projective techniques to elicit information about individuals' commitments. In projective techniques, respondents commonly participate in some form of storytelling about a set of stimuli. Themes in the details of individual stories are identified to draw conclusions about interests, intentions, and agendas. The purpose of these methods, when constructing a nomothetic theory, is to discover the enduring features of how individuals represent their experiences. Comparisons across individuals are essential for labeling universal traits, the dimensions that form their structure, and the surface features likely to be apparent to observers.

To explore the construct of agreeableness, for example, an investigator might show participants a picture in which one person has bumped into another. The instructions for such a task might be something like, "Tell me what you would do if you were in this situation." The resulting story would be recorded and/or scored to determine if the person mentioned issues of trust, straightforwardness, altruism, compliance, modesty, or tender-mindedness. These issues are assumed to reflect the central traits associated with agreeableness.

Interviews.   Investigators also collect self-report data by interviewing participants to elicit their reactions to the central dimensions of a source trait. This is accomplished with questions designed to elicit information about surface traits and looking for patterns in individuals' responses. Patterns may be identified by making a broad judgment about the whole of an interview protocol or by evaluating each statement and aggregating those judgments.

In an interview, investigators usually tap each dimension by asking direct questions. When discussing neuroticism, for example, interviewers might ask participants to talk about their worries, temper, tendency to feel glum, comfort in social situations, emotional fluctuations, or feelings of vulnerability. Tactful questions can elicit unnecessarily elaborate explanations, but the presence or absence of particular characteristics can be detected.

Design Procedures.   In addition to the survey design techniques outlined in Chapter 4, projective techniques are sometimes used. Investigators carefully select stimuli to elicit personal references and provide a rationale for the activities. Only forced-choice methods like the semantic differential appear to be inappropriate for measuring self-reports of experience. These methods restrict the need for introspection, encourage respondents to passively accept alternatives, and limit opportunities for fully representing their beliefs.

Observational Data

Self-reports often isolate themes of cognition, affect, or action, and the degree to which construct validity requires the coordination of all three psychological dimensions is highly controversial. Nevertheless, personality theorists want to know if and when these three psychological processes are coordinated. They may strengthen their conclusions by using

L-data to measure what others see when they look at or make judgments about a target person. External ratings also allow investigators to draw conclusions about the prevalence of particular traits in multiple contexts. Measures of behavior in naturalistic settings offer one means of speculating about human functioning. When that is not possible, survey-style ratings by others may be adequate.

Regardless of the methods they use, investigators can evaluate behavior holistically by drawing general conclusions about a collection of events or by counting the number of times they notice particular entities. The degree to which behavior is evaluated at micro- and macrolevels usually corresponds to theoretical claims about behavior rather than conformity to arbitrary rules. Investigators interested in verifying that aggression is common among groups, for example, may simply record the frequency with which they notice such behavior. Those who want to understand the components of aggression will carefully evaluate the dimensions that comprise such behavior.

Behavioral Observations.   Evaluations of behavior in everyday contexts can be independent of other measures. Such techniques require at least one outside observer, but typically two or more raters will observe the same events. There are at least three ways in which such behavioral data are collected.

- Using current advances in technology, investigators sometimes record behavior and evaluate the characteristics of that behavior at a later point in time.
- Using rating scales, observers evaluate behavior while it is occurring, classifying their judgments as the situation unfolds.
- After an observation period, investigators may construct summative reports of their observations.

Expert Rating Scales.   Investigators sometimes convert self-report measures into rating scales. Evaluators with different types of expertise then use the scales to rate target participants. Parents may be asked to rate the typical behavior of their children, teachers of students, or clinicians of clients. Such judgments are prompted by items on the rating scale, but respondents are typically asked to imagine the person they are rating. As with other observational techniques, the nature of the judgment may be global or reflect decisions about a specific collection of indicants.

Designing Observational Tools.   Although Chapter 8 offers more detail, there are important considerations when designing observational measures for validating personality traits. Rating scales used to record observations sometimes involve a simple conversion of self-report measures into observation checklists for use by an external observer. Adaptations may also be necessary. If behavioral and self-report measures are structurally identical, comparisons between the two can minimize the systematic error associated with instrumentation. Evaluators are typically asked to record the frequency of behavior, but may offer global judgments about the appearance of a surface trait. If the two differ, it may be necessary to calibrate each tool against a common scale to draw comparisons.

Some investigators also train evaluators on the definitions of traits and ask them to identify which traits most closely match specific patterns of behavior. Once raters have become proficient, they simply record which traits are and are not evident. This technique was designed to minimize the levels of inference between surface traits and the decisions of each rater. It is also commonly used when evaluators rate characteristics without directly observing behavior.

In designing each tool, investigators anticipate the necessary evidence for defending propositions about source traits. While it may be easy to cluster a wide range of data points, one broadly defined category cannot be expanded into more specific categories. Suppose an investigator wanted to evaluate moral traits. Determining if moral behavior consists of concerns related to justice, care, and character would be possible only if all three dimensions were measured separately. Global judgments about the morality of behavior offer no information about the dimensions of such behavior. Advanced planning and thoughtful critiques of recording methods can ensure that essential information is available for later analysis.

Standardized Test Data

Personality inventories used to obtain T-data have many qualities. Some look very much like attitude surveys in which individuals are asked to rate themselves. Respondents may also complete matching or sorting tasks from which interests, personal styles, and habits are later inferred. Projective tests can involve systematic exploration of how individuals draw inferences about stimuli. Furthermore, patterns in generated attributes can offer insight into how traits are defined. Multiple scales are often compared to identify how personal interests and traits align with a normative sample. Some of the most common techniques for collecting T-data are outlined in the next two chapters, but as is the case for observational measures, personality researchers have noticed several challenging dilemmas

Clinical Assessment Tools.   There are numerous existing tools available to clinicians for use in evaluating personality (see the Web sites provided at the end of this chapter). Several organizations design, norm, and make available particular tests using procedures similar to those outlined in this book. These corporations have resources for obtaining very large samples and can conduct elaborate reliability and validity studies that would be prohibitive for most researchers. Therefore, if investigators can purchase an appropriate tool, they may benefit from the corporate efforts and resources.

Mechanical Tests.   Investigators may design mechanical tools that can be easily standardized over the course of a research program. Such methods require initiative and are usually grounded in thick contextual details.

Working in an infant vision laboratory, for example, I noticed opportunities to study individual differences in temperament. Eye exams were conducted by holding infants in front of stimuli placed in different locations. To explore peripheral vision, stimuli would be placed just beyond the infant's normal viewing range. To study color, a variety of stimuli of different colors would be offered. The stimuli would then move in an interesting way and the infant's looking behavior would be monitored and recorded. Not surprisingly, babies differed in their willingness to cooperate with such procedures. Some readily enjoyed the novelty and pace of the activities whereas others found it startling or even distressing. Over time, investigators developed a sense of typical infant behavior on these activities and might well have been able to draw inferences about temperament if they had decided to do so.

Designing Standardized Measures. To determine the typicality of a trait, investigators sometimes establish a set of *norms* for use when there are no clear criteria for evaluating responses. Beginning with a set of expected outcomes, derived either inductively, deductively, or using an interactionist approach, investigators design a theoretical blueprint.[9] They design items or activities to align with the blueprint. The measure is then pilot-tested and edited until investigators are satisfied with the content. Then the tool is administered to a representative sample of individuals whose responses will serve as a norm to which other responses will be compared.

Investigators use *norm groups* to compare samples, or evaluate the performance of an individual. Norms are sometimes verified by simultaneously administering new and existing personality inventories and comparing the two sets of findings. Investigators may also, somewhat arbitrarily, set a criterion for evaluating the presence or absence of surface traits. In addition, newer *Item Response Theory* (IRT) or *Rasch* techniques work from probabilistic standards that replace answers from a comparison group of actual people. Regardless of how the standard is set, the logic of comparing individual scores to a standard is central to drawing normative conclusions.[10]

Summary

The primary purpose of nomothetic measurement is to identify the more enduring features of personality. Investigators look for convergence among self-report, observational, and testing data to draw conclusions about relationships among source and surface traits. Each type of data draws on assumptions from other research traditions. Self-report tools are similar to those used for measuring attitudes. Observations reflect judgments made by those with an external vantage point, and formal testing is used to draw normative comparisons. Dependable patterns in how surface traits are consolidated into enduring factors strengthen generalizations about the structure of source traits.

■ ■ ■ ■ ■ ▬▬▬

MAKING CONNECTIONS

Identify examples of nomothetic assumptions about people. What typologies are used to classify individuals? What evidence suggests that such categories are valid, useful, and ethical? Do studies contain Q-data, L-data, and/or T-data?

IDEAL QUALITIES OF INDICANTS

All of the empirical techniques introduced thus far are also used to explore items on personality measures. Because decisions evolve from a theory-building process, several caveats and warnings have become apparent in personality research that can be translated into guiding questions.

What Do Indicants Measure?

An essential theoretical question concerns the anticipated relationships between source traits (sometimes called theoretical concepts, constructs, latent variables, or factors), surface traits (sometimes called dimensions, concrete variables, factors, or observables), and the indicants of surface traits (sometimes called items or intra-item correlations). Parallel relationships can also be established for states such that comparisons among states and traits become a feature of theory building.

Knowing the vulnerabilities of each measure, investigators often rely on multiple tools containing different item formats to improve the strength of their evidence. They may ask individuals to list their likes and dislikes as well as the general details of their life and more particular details of different spheres of their experience (e.g., family, education, recreation). Investigators may also ask respondents to evaluate statements about others, to describe what they would like others to think of them, and their perceptions of what their life should be like.

On all these measures, it is important to offer precise instructions and avoid including more than one idea or action in each indicant. When stimuli consist of verbal statements, they typically contain only the vocabulary necessary for effective communication. Investigators who want an honest account commonly avoid objectionable language and unnecessary invasions of privacy.

Which Item Formats Work Best?

As personality theorists have designed methods for assessing traits and states, several issues about item format have been tested. Investigators have asked whether it is better to present survey items as questions or as statements and found that this is a matter of theoretical discretion; ensuring an adequate reading level is more important than the style of inquiry. Similarly, questions of whether items should emphasize the self (e.g., I think I am) or others' opinions of the self (e.g., people say I am) may vary, but the latter calls attention to social comparison more readily than the former.

Questions about the value of projective tests have also proliferated. When investigators measure dynamic states, projective and self-report measures both seem to work well. When focusing on temperament, however, researchers distinguish between true projection and naïve projection. *True projection* involves valid attempts to measure dynamic, interest-based traits that are stable features of someone's personality; individuals are encouraged to define the question as well as the answers. *Naïve projection* is common distortion caused by limitations in someone's experience; individuals typically introduce experience-based distortion when interpreting ambiguous tasks and events.

Another set of cautions are associated with the use of forced-choice methods to assess personality. Investigators have asked whether the poles of a semantic differential should be equally attractive to respondents. In doing so, they discovered that forced-choice designs are inappropriate for measuring personality. The most important limitation of forced-choice methods concerns the constraints placed on the expression of identity-salient information. Not only is it impossible to balance issues of desirability across response fields, the idea of forcing respondents to choose between poles tends to beget resentment. Respondents cannot indicate whether they consider the entire dichotomy to be problematic except by refusing to offer answers. Forced-choice methods also limit the need for introspection because respondents are typically asked to evaluate abstract trait lists rather than concrete forms of behavior. Placing content-laden items at each pole avoids rather than solves the dilemma of establishing parallel response fields. When the result is a pair of opposite statements, one item in a Likert-style survey offers the same information more directly. The clumsiness of extracting ideas is not offset by the quality of information acquired.

When Are Indicants Associated?

When oriented with the same valence, indicants of a single construct are usually highly correlated because they are ideally influenced by the same underlying theoretical concepts. Investigators typically look for such unity by examining the results of factor analysis. For unitary constructs, the rotated factor solution will be the same as the initial solution and essential indicants will all load significantly on each measure.[11] More realistically, indicants will reflect different dimensions of the construct being measured and will cluster along some dimensions and not others. For homogeneous collections of indicants, items perform optimally when they load significantly on one and only one factor. When indicants *cross-load*—load significantly on more than one factor—they are usually edited or deleted. When indicants do not load significantly on any factors, they also add unnecessary error.

What Makes a Strong Indicant?

Methods of item analysis are important for looking at whether each indicant contributes to the overall index. You may remember that factor loadings help investigators eliminate items that are redundant or misclassified. Investigators also consider changes in reliability coefficients when particular items are deleted. When deciding how to edit a scale, investigators look at the item content and not simply at patterns of loading to verify their commonalities. Strong indicants correspond to one and only one dimension in a measurement plan.

In coordinating stability and accuracy, items with similar content are often combined into scales, but reliability and validity are usually distinguished. If items on two different measures include essentially the same content, conclusions about the relative independence of the measures become invalid.[12] For example, a self-concept measure that contains the item, "I have lots of friends," would not be compared to another self-concept measure with the same item because the correlation between the measures would contain spurious associations. Overlapping content in two instruments that are predicted to measure different constructs can also render the evidence inconclusive or invalid because they facilitate exaggerated conclusions about the similarity of the constructs.

Indicants may also have no predictable relationship with one another, but remain highly correlated with a more general theoretical construct. Such independence could be a theoretical strength rather than a limitation. A measure listing the causes of anxiety, for example, may contain very different issues that seemingly have no relationship with one another. Individuals could report anxiety associated with a move, with their schoolwork, or over the quality of a friendship. Although the cluster of issues may be linked with anxiety, an individual may endorse all or none of these causes and still experience this state. A more general tendency to be anxious may also be associated with the more general trait of conscientiousness. Unity would not be appropriate for such a measure regardless of whether it is used to assess states or traits because people are anxious for many different, seemingly unrelated reasons. To offer respondents a plausible range of causes to choose from, indicants could be appropriate if they reflect diverse rather than homogeneous causes of anxiety.

How Can Diverse Items Be Evaluated?

When investigators rely on a heterogeneous collection of items, they compare the relationships between wanted and unwanted variance. Recalling Figure 3.8, wanted variance would reflect the known parameters of a dimension. If investigators learn enough about a source trait to plan for variability in responses, unwanted variance can be minimized by labeling forms of systematic error. Exploratory studies in which problematic items are revised or eliminated can further reduce error and may be repeated until investigators can clarify the dimensions and structure of each characteristic. Given that error can never fully be eliminated, unwanted factor variance often reflects unknown systematic error.

When a factor is bidimensional or multidimensional, it is difficult to detect unwanted variance. Investigators may evaluate the appropriateness of unrelated indicants by constructing a *relational circumplex*. Two related dimensions along which the set of indicants are likely to differ reflect latent variables. Measuring independent features of anxiety, for example, may be compared to a scale of positive versus negative life events, and pleasant versus unpleasant affect (Figure 5.3). In such a graph, investigators are likely to prefer items to be distributed across the four quadrants, essentially forming a circular rather than a linear distribution.

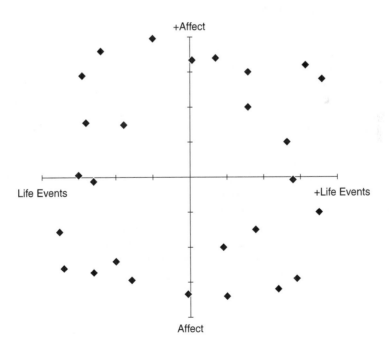

FIGURE 5.3   A Theoretical Circumplex Used to Explore the Expression of Two Traits

Variance in some measures can be attributed to an unwanted, but identifiable personality factor. Despite careful planning, investigators sometimes discover that responses reflect the convergence of more than one dimension. When an unintended personality dimension can be identified, investigators label the resulting systematic error, but such possibilities are not always readily apparent.

How Can Measures of Function Be Evaluated?

Some investigators are interested in how traits function rather than the structure of the trait. They measure the waxing and waning of valence. In doing so, researchers look for linear or curvilinear patterns in how indicants function and compare the performance of indicants serving similar and different purposes across time, situations, and cultures. These investigators are likely to search for the *origin of psychological activation,* the events that triggered the expression of a trait. They also identify the *minimum point at which a construct can be detected.* This preoccupation requires measurement of the magnitude of a trait and renders the *maximum level of activation* and the *total score* more informative than the mean or correlations among indicants. These investigators also search for knowledge of *hydraulic tensions between modes of expression* and the *inherent competition* in related concepts. Evaluating the qualities of indicants in each of these contexts typically requires information about the dynamic features of states and how they relate to more stable trait profiles. Again, knowledge is generated through comparison, but comparison entails the functioning of states and traits.

How Can Indicants Be Linked to Source Traits?

To assess something as complex as a source trait or state, investigators distinguish the psychological parameters of an indicant from item format. Psychological parameters are addressed by looking for the best sampling of a behavioral field. A general personality measure, for example, may focus on home, work, hobbies, physical behavior, social interactions, and any other common feature of someone's life. Comparing the details of a measure to the theorized construct may include forms of thought, feelings, and action. If the content of items is concrete, minimizing the degree of abstraction, spurious, semantic commonalities may also be restricted.

Common sense as often as empirical procedures is used to evaluate psychological parameters. When research participants respond to a list of abstract traits, for example, knowledge of their personality may not be apparent; individual differences in how participants define each term would not be explored. Similarly, meaning-making across cultures becomes especially difficult to assess if a lack of linguistic proficiency interferes with communication. Even with shared assumptions, general items are vulnerable to deception. Traits are often seen as desirable when considered in the abstract, but less so when translated to particular actions. An act judged as courageous in one person, for example, may be seen as aggressive in another.

Summary

Ideally, all relevant indicants are correlated with an intended source trait or state. Yet, depending on researchers' theoretical assumptions, indicants may or may not be expected to correlate. When unity is a defining feature of a factor, items will be correlated. When heterogeneity is a defining feature, items reflect the widest range of issues available for each dimension. Investigators strive to minimize systematic and random error variance for both surface and source levels of analysis by designing indicants that correspond to assumptions about such surface dimensions. When indicants are expected to correspond to a unitary surface state or trait, item quality is reflected in the correlation. When indicants are expected to reflect a heterogeneous array of surface states and traits, predictable relations with source traits or states is an index of quality. Investigators start with inclusion criteria that are sensitive to such theoretical purposes.

MAKING CONNECTIONS

Using guidelines from the previous chapter and suggestions for modification introduced here, design a small personality measure. What is your construct? What are the relevant dimensions of that construct? How could the dimensions be weighted? How many indicants will you write for each dimension? What formats will you use? What predictions would you make about the quality of each indicant?

DIMENSIONS OF RELIABILITY

Before a set of indicants can be seen as representative of a particular trait, investigators verify whether their measure is adequately calibrated to offer a dependable account of someone's characteristics. As with all questions of reliability, issues of accuracy and stability differ, depending on whether investigators are considering traits or states and whether personality characteristics are unidimensional, bidimensional or multidimensional (see Chapter 13 for details on measuring states). Factor-analysis techniques are central to judgments of accuracy, but the dynamic nature of states requires the use of a greater variety of factor-analytic techniques than is commonly used for traits. Stability over time is important in the profile of traits with ideal graphic representations retaining consistent high and low orders of magnitude. Variation across time is a defining feature of states with graphic representations showing relatively volatile distributions.

Establishing Inter-Rater Reliability

Before determining how indicants are related to one another, many investigators verify that indicants are correctly classified. On standardized measures, scores match the dimensions of an instrument. More complex steps are required if measures involve the interpretation of experiences. For example, translating interviews or projective measures into numerical indicants involves inferences on the part of raters. Similarly, most forms of L-data require raters to make inferences. These judgments are usually scrutinized for accuracy by exploring the reproducibility of ratings across raters. A well-defined coding plan is designed and multiple judges evaluate the same responses. *Inter-rater reliability* involves estimates of the agreement among raters after they have independently classified indicants using the same set of categories. When more than one judge can reproduce the same ratings, accuracy is inferred.

Investigators sometimes ask multiple individuals to classify indicants and calculate the percentage of planned classifications. They may also correlate responses between two sets of raters. Both of these methods offer rather crude approximations of inter-rater agreement because they do not offer information about the nature of errors in classification.[13] To consider error variance, Cohen's *kappa coefficient* was designed to estimate inter-rater agreement.[14]

UNWEIGHTED KAPPA COEFFICIENT

$$\kappa = \frac{P_{obs} - P_{exp}}{1 - P_{exp}}$$

Here, P_{obs} is the proportion of agreements in the two total scores and P_{exp} is the proportion expected by chance. Table 5.1 contains a sample distribution of ratings from two observers. P_{obs} is calculated by adding the numbers in matching cells (along the diagonal) and dividing that by the total number of decisions $P_{obs} = [(10 + 15 + 35 + 20 + 25)/120]$. P_{exp} is computed by multiplying the column and row totals for matching traits and adding those totals. Then the obtained total is divided by the square of the grand total.

$$P_{exp} = \frac{[(12 \times 13) + (19 \times 19) + (39 \times 39) + (24 \times 23) + (30 \times 28)]}{120 \times 120}$$

Finally, κ can be computed by including each component in the formula (with rounding error).

$$\kappa = \frac{.875 - .245}{1 - .245} = .83$$

The *weighted kappa* takes into account the degree of inconsistency in misclassifications. Instead of relying only on observed (P_{obs}) and expected frequencies (P_{exp}), a third $k \times k$ matrix of weights is also included. Typically, 0 is on the diagonal to indicate agreement, and 1 is used off the diagonal to represent each position of disagreement, but investigators can also classify some differences as more serious than others. Table 5.2 contains a sample weight matrix that treats each disagreement equally.

Imagine combining the information in both Tables 5.1 and 5.2 to compute a weighted κ. In this formula, x_{ij} reflects the observed matrix (diagonals), and m_{ij} reflects the expected matrix (the sum of column X row totals for each category), and w_{ij} reflects the weights. The weights are added both to the observed and expected frequencies so that κ_{wt} accounts for the magnitude of disagreements as well as the degree of agreement.

WEIGHTED KAPPA COEFFICIENT

$$\kappa_{wt} = 1 - \frac{\sum_{i=1}^{k}\sum_{j=1}^{k} w_{ij} x_{ij}}{\sum_{i=1}^{k}\sum_{j=1}^{k} w_{ij} m_{ij}}$$

TABLE 5.1   Hypothetical Decisions by Two Raters for Use in Computing a Kappa Coefficient

| | RATER 1 | | | | | |
RATER 2	*Neuroticism*	*Extraversion*	*Openness*	*Agreeableness*	*Conscientiousness*	**TOTAL**
Neuroticism	10	1			2	13
Extraversion		15	4			19
Openness		3	35	1		39
Agreeableness				20	3	23
Conscientiousness	2			3	25	28
Total	12	19	39	24	30	$N = 120$

Note: This represents completely fictitious data, and could involve 120 ratings of one person over time, 120 participants, or some combination of ratings.

TABLE 5.2   Suggested Weightings Used to Correct for the Amount of Error

| | RATER 1 | | | | |
RATER 2	*Neuroticism*	*Extraversion*	*Openness*	*Agreeableness*	*Conscientiousness*
Neuroticism	0	1	1	1	1
Extraversion	1	0	1	1	1
Openness	1	1	0	1	1
Agreeableness	1	1	1	0	1
Conscientiousness	1	1	1	1	0

Note: The five traits cannot be ranked in a very meaningful way, so weights are equal. If a hierarchical order could be supported, weights would reflect the degree of miscalculation. These can also be used to rank one reviewer over another.

Regardless of whether investigators use an uncorrected total percentage of agreement, correlation coefficients, or more elaborate approaches to comparing two sets of ratings, this process is often completed before making more complex comparisons among indicants. Inter-rater comparisons are especially helpful when investigators plan to compare data collected using more than one tool because it offers evidence that several raters agree on the intended performance of indicants.

Calibrating Nomothetic Instruments

When calibrating the measurement of traits, investigators distinguish *factor-homogeneous, test-homogeneous,* and *test-heterogeneous* item sets. Factor-homogeneous sets represent source traits and involve estimates of inter-item correlations. Items usually load together in factor analysis, but may not show strong levels of internal consistency (e.g., the magnitude of loadings could easily vary across items); items may show test-homogeneous or test-heterogeneous patterns. Measures of internal consistency, such as Cronbach's α, may be inappropriate for verifying source traits because, although items are typically associated with the factor, they may not be associated with one another (see Chapter 4).

Remembering the Normal Distribution.   Investigators looking for accuracy in how source traits are measured are most likely to keep the *pan-normalization principle* in mind (Cattell, 1973). Human traits are assumed to be influenced by a relatively large number of independent genetic and environmental factors and any distribution of true scores usually approaches normality. This principle underlies many of the statistical techniques used to evaluate constructs and concepts. In conducting factor analysis, for example, investigators typically include items from multiple measures by first standardizing raw scores (e.g., calculating z-scores) and working with correlations among them (see Chapter 3 and 4). The standardization process involves transforming distributions of raw scores to approximate normality.[15]

It is also common for responses to be skewed. Investigators have found methods for transforming raw scores to approximate normality using log transformations or other means of accounting for the fact that not all levels of a scale were used adequately. To ensure that the mathematical transformation does not distort the overall findings, all items on a given scale are transformed using the same method. These devices are used to maximize the comparability of different scales.

Accuracy for Factor-Homogeneous Scales.   You may remember that a factor is a latent variable that is not directly measured. On factor-homogeneous scales, indicants from multiple measures ideally cluster in ways that reflect wanted variance rather than unwanted variance (see Figure 3.8). Multiple factors may be apparent in a complex data set, but items reflecting the same dimension or construct ideally converge. As with items, investigators can rescale intercorrelating scales for different traits to approximate a measure containing equal intervals, constructing *a relational simplex* using scale scores. In doing so, they treat correlations like indicants.[16] A series of experimental raw-score transformations are usually completed to determine which transformations maximize the value of the mean correlation coefficient in a matrix of correlations. Maximizing the aggregate *coefficient of determination* facilitates inferences about the accuracy with which multiple surface traits can be said to correspond to a source trait. For example, Figure 5.2 shows how six surface traits are associated with the source trait of openness.

Investigators may also look for the median correlation in a collection of loadings to represent accuracy. Suppose the characteristic "trustworthy" is measured using several different indicants. Ranking all the loadings of parallel indicants and selecting the median score offers an estimate that accounts for chance variation in responses. Although these techniques require more knowledge of statistics than is covered in this book, it is helpful to remember that measurement theorists have developed several solid methods of consolidating information reflecting different levels of inference.[17]

Accuracy for Test-Homogeneous Scales.   *Test-homogeneous* item sets are common in studies of surface traits, and may be the most commonly identified personality dimensions.

Only items that are included on the same measure are included in a factor analysis. As was the case for the competence orientations, those items reflecting the same surface traits would cluster together and show a high degree of internal consistency when investigators calculate reliability coefficients (see Chapter 4). More than one factor may emerge in the factor analysis, but each factor represents a different surface trait. Ideally, items that are characteristic of one source trait are also characteristic of other source traits in the same measure. When only one or two items are loaded on more than one factor, careful evaluation of such items often suggests a high degree of ambiguity in meaning. When the overlap involves many items, investigators are wise to reconsider the structure of the surface traits being measured.

Two types of test-homogeneous assumptions appear in personality research: univocal and unitractic measures. *Univocal scales* measure a single dimension with corresponding indicants; unwanted factors are assumed to be nonexistent. In such cases, investigators look for "factor purity" in selecting items that are saturated on a single factor such that there is little remaining variance. (Figure 3.8 could represent such a scale if items in the circle and by the arrow were deleted and the remaining items accounted for a large percent of variance.) *Unitractic scales* assess a single unitary trait and all items are expected to show the highest loading on the same uniquely rotated source trait. Factors may be unitary, but fail to account for all the variance in a collection of items. Items may have low or opposite loadings on other common factors. Alternative loadings are suppressed in the rotation process so that investigators can measure the intended source trait while exerting a suppressor action to control for unwanted variance. (The competence orientation scales tend to work this way.)

Accuracy for Test-Heterogeneous Scales. When investigators are interested in a diverse range of trait characteristics, they look for a latent variable to explain the commonalities of indicants. Indicants are *test-heterogeneous* in that they represent a diverse range of experiences. In such cases, it would be illogical to assume that items would show high levels of internal consistency. Instead, investigators look for the degree to which items represent the positive as well as negative features of a trait. A *relational circumplex* like that in Figure 5.3 offers the clearest means of summarizing reliability. If the comparison traits are appropriately selected and the attributes adequately represent the full range of trait characteristics, items will be distributed in all four cells of the circumplex. The angles between items (θ) will also be approximately equal if the measures all belong on the same scale. Comparing angles is a procedure commonly used to verify the "trueness" of a factor, estimating the degree to which the circumplex is not contaminated by other factors. The logic of this analysis hinges on the fact that responses on one pole of a dimension such as "positive life events" also tend to correspond with other positive dimensions like "pleasant affect," but such parallels need not occur for all persons. Balanced scales allow for the expression of all possibilities and not just those that occur by chance alone or reflect common sense.

Stability. For traits, investigators also verify that a tool is calibrated to show stability in the scores obtained over time. That is, if traits represent dispositional features of a personality, their expression would be slow to change and a well-calibrated tool will measure such stability. *Test-retest reliability* is most commonly used to verify that a person's relative position on a particular characteristic remains the same in repeated experiences with the same conditions. Investigators usually use *Pearson product moment formulas* (r_{XY}) for continuous data, *Spearman's rho* (ρ) or r_S for discrete ranked data, and χ^2 derivatives for nominal evaluations (see Chapter 3 for these formulas). Strong test-retest reliability is evident if high correlations between two sets of scores are obtained when the same instrument is administered twice.

When investigators draw inferences about the dispositional features of a trait, respondents may retain their relative position in the distribution of scores and/or receive identical scores when the same measure is completed twice. It may be easier to establish that individuals retain their position in the distribution of respondents than to demonstrate that scores remain the same over time. Retaining position in a distribution is acceptable when precision is less important than theoretical continuity. If everyone's position in a distribution and their obtained scores remain consistent, measurements are especially precise.

Test-retest studies require controlled time segments between administrations to minimize possible outside influences on performance. Investigators also try to minimize the availability of memory cues and implicit pressure to give the same responses although these are but two types of systematic error that may not be adequately controlled.

Balancing Accuracy and Stability.   Theoretical continuity in the definition of a trait is central to calibrating nomothetic tools. High emphasis is placed on stability because traits are assumed to be deeply integrated in someone's personality. Such integration would mean that, even if surface characteristics change, source traits would remain detectable. This assumption is untenable for the measurement of states and is one reason why traits are often validated in comparison to states.

Transferability across Subpopulations

For traits to adhere to nomothetic assumptions, investigators usually verify that the calibration of their tool remains the same across different groups. They are looking for cross-situational and cross-cultural consistency in a tool's performance. Similarly, idiographic assumptions reflect the belief that the structure of states is likely to remain constant over time, but their expression is likely to differ across situations. Investigators address questions of transferability by considering theoretical differences between traits and states, but replicate their findings using different groups regardless of their primary interests.

The most straightforward way to explore transferability is by administering the instrument to a diverse range of respondents and altering the conditions under which it is administered. Comparing the performance of items in each administration verifies the degree to which a tool's calibration remains consistent across groups. Details differ for traits and states, but the basic elaboration procedures can be useful for both classes of measurement.

Summary

Investigators conducting nomothetic and idiographic research estimate accuracy and stability with similar techniques, but different kinds of data. Inter-rater reliability is used to verify the accuracy with which raters and coding schemes represent information that involves interpretation (e.g., personal narratives, observations of behavior). Factor analysis is used to identify patterns among indicants and in relationships between indicants and latent variables. Measures of internal consistency can verify assumptions about test-homogeneity in items, but are inappropriate when test-heterogeneity is warranted. Test-retest reliability offers important information about the stability of the structures or functioning of traits and states. It can also be useful for establishing stability in the magnitude of traits.

Maximizing the reliability of each measure and ensuring a consistent range of reliability coefficients is more important than many investigators realize. In multiple regression analyses, for example, when one variable is significantly more reliable than the others, there may be an overestimation of the importance of that variable. Reliability alone can affect the power of a variable to predict an outcome. Similarly, in the analysis of *multitrait–multimethod matrices* used to assess validity, reliability differences can foster mistaken conclusions. Representing ideas graphically can help investigators understand how to interpret correlations and other aggregate indices of reliability. Examining the angles between items as well as the placement of items in a relational circumplex offers information on relations among indicants with different properties.

MAKING CONNECTIONS

Which of the various reliability concerns are most helpful for determining if your newly designed personality measure is appropriately calibrated? What do you learn about your measure from correlating individual item responses with a total scale score? Are you expecting indicants to be factor-homogeneous, test-homogeneous, or test-heterogeneous? What information do you gain by conducting a test-retest study?

VALIDITY CONSIDERATIONS

As with all forms of measurement, *validity* is a property of interpretations and not an inherent property of the instrument itself. The interpretive quality of this process may become clearer by comparing reliability and validity techniques. Investigators extend the logic of verifying relationships among indicants to include the fact that the meaning of each indicant should match theoretical dimensions, yet theoretical knowledge is constrained by available evidence and is subject to change as new information is acquired. In this respect, quantitative indices offer an insufficient estimate of validity because abstract ideas are invariably translated with uncontrollable forms of distortion.

In personality research, these general facts encourage investigators to carefully consider relations among theoretical constructs and more general trait or state concepts. Many investigators interested in exploring nomothetic relations assume they are labeling and testing the features of a larger *nomological net*.[18] A nomological net contains the whole of a theoretical framework. While acknowledging the measurement scale, investigators imagine how observable properties or indicants of a construct are related to one another. They ask how indicants are related to constructs or dimensions of a latent traitlike variable, how constructs are related to theoretical concepts, and how theoretical concepts are related to one another.

Content Validity

Graphic representations of a factor raise several questions about content validity. After confirming inter-rater agreement for the content of each indicant, the range of ideas represented can be compared with the theoretical dimension. Given that well-defined theories make it easier to critique indicants, investigators may find some facets of a theory to be underrepresented. Other facets may be overrepresented in relation to others, resulting in a *bloated specific factor*. There may also be content-irrelevant dimensions apparent in the measure.

On the original competence orientation measures, the avoid inferiority aspect of ego orientation was underrepresented because only two items functioned well.[19] Academic alienation and work avoidance formed a somewhat bloated scale because there were many items representing similar ideas, and items did not form clearly independent scales. The initial measures also contained social items that focused on feeling liked by teachers and peers. Emphasizing affiliation issues more than achievement, the social items formed reliable scales, but did not offer a valid representation of students' competence orientations. Numbers alone could not clarify the initial levels of confusion.

Criterion Validity

Once content validity has been adequately considered, investigators explore the "trueness" of relationships between variables assumed to be related to the same constructs, and validity in how well indicants are correlated with theoretical concepts.[20] To explore factor trueness, investigators usually determine if measurements of the predicted traits were uncontaminated by other factors. The trueness of a test is represented by the angle θ when indicants are compared to one another.

Criterion validity is represented by the correlation of scales and theoretical factors. In a unidimensional measure, this involves a comparison between wanted and unwanted factors (see Figure 3.8). Like the relations between indicants and dimensions, multiple measures of the same dimensions are usually correlated with the wanted construct, but not with unwanted constructs. In practice, wanted and unwanted factors are rarely independent and graphs tend to reflect oblique rather than orthogonal relations. The oblique relation accounts for systematic variance attributable to interscale correlations of the dimensions that make up a construct.

When constructs are multidimensional, investigators explore criterion validity by comparing one set of dimensions directly to another. When parallel dimensions of theoretical constructs are adequately correlated, the two sets show *concurrent validity*. When opposing dimensions are inversely correlated or irrelevant dimensions are uncorrelated, the two sets show *discriminant validity*. Table 5.3 contains the patterns of results obtained when an initial set of competence orientation scales were correlated. Notice that task and effort orientations were inversely correlated with work avoidance and academic alienation, but ego orientation was positively correlated with the alienation measures. This may seem surprising given that ego and task orientations were also moderately correlated. This pattern

TABLE 5.3   Pearson Correlations between Scales on Competence Orientation Measure

COMPETENCE ORIENTATIONS	COMPETENCE ORIENTATIONS						
	1	*2*	*3*	*4*	*5*	*6*	*7*
1. Task orientation (7 items, $\alpha = .85$)	1.00						
2. Effort orientation (2 items, $\alpha = .74$)	.40	1.00					
3. Ego orientation-superiority (5 items, $\alpha = .83$)	.26	.11	1.00				
4. Ego orientation-inferiority (2 items, $\alpha = .68$)	.10	.07	.33	1.00			
5. Work avoidance (5 items, $\alpha = .87$)	−.31	−.33	.09	.14	1.00		
6. Academic alienation (4 items, $\alpha = .87$)	−.37	−.34	.08	.12	.65	1.00	
7. Affiliation with peers (4 items, $\alpha = .71$)	.26	.05	.20	.28	.20	.12	1.00
8. Affiliation with teachers (4 items, $\alpha = .84$)	.46	.40	.11	.33	−.14	−.22	.26

Note: Multiple samples of adolescents, ages 13 to 20, were combined for this analysis ($n = 908$). The large sample size rendered all correlations statistically significant, $p < .01$.

offers evidence for treating task, ego, and work avoidance separately while accepting an oblique relation. Correlations between competence orientations and affiliation with teachers were also high, even though they represent theoretically different aspects of motivation. Theoretical knowledge was as essential as calculations for this validation step.

Investigators could take this analysis one step further and use regression techniques to compare the relationships among these dimensions, but *predictive validity* is more often used to compare a set of variables with another outcome. You may remember that in the previous chapter a self-report measure of classroom participation was used for this step of the analysis (Table 4.11). Task, ego, and work-avoidant orientations explained roughly 40 percent of the variance in adolescents' participation scores. This could indicate that knowledge about competence orientations can facilitate predictions about academic participation or that the two dimensions are features of academic engagement.

Construct Validity

Personality theorists sometimes distinguish two types of validity that are ordinarily subsumed within the notion of *construct validity* (Cattell, 1973). Because they are interested in defining valid, transferable, and often behaviorally based constructs, they minimize classifications that are based solely on semantic similarities. Exploring *conceptual validity* involves the detection of broad, temperamental traits that are useful for labeling characteristics within a population and establishing standards or norms for use when classifying personalities. The first two columns of Figure 5.2 exemplify conceptual validity concerns. *Concrete validity* involves the comparison of indicants to other specific measures of action. Investigators are primarily interested in concrete validity when they try to match particular persons with situations, goals, and opportunities. The last two columns of Figure 5.2 illustrate this type of validity. Although conceptual validity typically corresponds to theoretical concerns and concrete validity reflects application, a strong theory would address both aspects of construct validity.

When investigators strive for conceptual validity to verify the existence of a single construct, they are interested in convergence among Q-, L-, and T-data. This type of convergence is less important for establishing concrete validity because investigators may have practical interest only in self-evaluations, external evaluations, experimental regularities, or a more restricted combination of these features.

To explore construct validity, responses from one scale can be compared to responses from another or to latent constructs. The fact that the reliability of the scales constrains correlations between scales when establishing validity bears repeating. Correlations between measures cannot be higher than correlations within a measure. Taking the validity test from Chapter 4 to another level, competence orientation measures can be compared to the theoretical traits of agreeableness and conscientiousness. A relational circumplex could be constructed by placing the latent agreeableness trait along the x-axis and the latent conscientiousness trait on the y-axis. Factor analysis revealed two significant factors accounting for variance in the different scales and multidimensional scaling procedures revealed patterns in factor loadings (Figure 5.4). Each quadrant of the circumplex contained at least one scale. Most of the scales fell within the high agreeable/low conscientious quadrant, but most conscientiousness scores were not all that far away from the x-axis. This seems to suggest that agreeableness is more dominant than conscientiousness. Two scales,

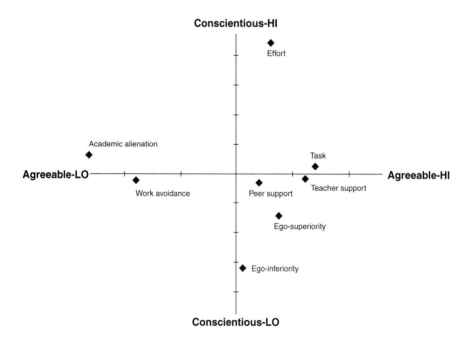

FIGURE 5.4   Relational Circumplex Comparing Competence Orientations to Agreeableness and Conscientiousness

effort and ego orientation as inferiority, showed contrasting kinds of conscientiousness. Although these competence orientation scales were not designed to be compared to these personality traits, perhaps the collection of scales could be improved by thinking more carefully about issues of conscientious attention to schoolwork.

Investigators interested in labeling common traits across persons and cultures tend to be most interested in conceptual validity. They prefer evidence that reflects the enduring qualities of groups of persons and draw comparisons between groups. These investigators are usually committed to describing common human characteristics and understanding their role in daily functioning.

In contrast, investigators who classify particular persons may be more preoccupied with concrete validity. To accurately classify persons, the details of participants' thoughts, feelings, and actions would be consolidated in representations of traits. Individual differences in those traits could be explored for a range of theoretical and practical purposes. In clinical work, for example, individual norms would be more highly valued than group norms, yet comparison of individuals within a group is essential for validating traits and making normative comparisons. Regardless of the long-term reasons for identifying traits, investigators rely on multiple forms of data when drawing conclusions.

Theoretical Validity

After investigators accept the validity of their measurements, they can begin a more systematic exploration of concept validity by looking at how research methods, traits, and states interact. In personality research, investigators are searching for the most parsimonious representation of information about the characteristics of individuals. Over time, knowledge of a nomological net is expected to improve the descriptive power and accuracy of a theory because investigators discover new information about how concepts can be identified, measured, and compared to one another. Investigators also try to rule out competing interpretations of their findings and struggle to design the best representation of how concepts are related to one another. Verification alone is insufficient for establishing validity.

Factor Validity.   In an attempt to refine existing theories, investigators have come to distinguish several questions of theoretical validity. Many of these questions have emerged out of attempts to demonstrate *factor validity* or the validity of a latent variable. Using factor analysis techniques for a wide range of purposes, investigators find ways to classify people and indicants. Hierarchical cluster analysis, for example, is used to consolidate self-views across interpersonal relationships, creating clusters of self-representations within measures of other-representations.[21] Investigators look for convergence in patterns that are apparent in spontaneous descriptions and in more structured tasks. They label the commonalities and contrast these patterns with alternative perspectives.

You may be able to anticipate limitations of factor analysis by thinking about the material already explored. Most obviously, it is difficult to interpret a large number of moderate correlations that are inevitably affected by the reliability of each tool and theoretical convergence in dimensions. Such correlations are but one step in a more elaborate theory-testing plan, but that feature has important implications for at least two additional levels of interpretation.

Comparisons Within a Multitrait–Multimethod Matrix.   A second step may involve comparing the features of a *multitrait–multimethod matrix* to differentiate trait-related and method-related components of a theory.[22] Ideally, correlations of different methods for measuring the same trait are significant and of the same magnitude. Each coefficient representing convergent validity would be higher than the correlations reflecting divergent validity. Similarly, the correlations of different methods for measuring the same trait would also be higher than the same method of measuring different traits. Thinking about blocks of relationships, patterns of low relationships typically hold for different-trait/different-method blocks and different-trait/same-method blocks.

Over the years, investigators have found limitations with the multitrait–multimethod approach to construct validation. Ordinarily, measures are assumed to have equal reliabilities and to result in a normal distribution of scores. In many data sets, both reliability and score distributions are less than optimal. Investigators also have tried to use this method without using a theory to interpret their findings. This undermines predictions of which traits will converge and which will diverge; the numbers may be interpreted, but the meaning of the resulting model would not result in a parsimonious theory. In addition, as theories become more complex and the number of correlations to be interpreted becomes larger, it can become difficult to identify and interpret nonindependent correlations.

In the multitrait–multimethod approach, traits and methods are assumed to be uncorrelated, but in practice they often interact. Not only are interactions among traits and methods common, traits differ in the degree to which they are influenced by particular methods. The assumption that traits will be equally influenced by methodological features is rarely tenable in practice, yet such comparisons may offer some useful information.

Exploring Inferences and Abstractions.   Because of these and other limitations of multitrait–multimethod matrices, many new methods continue to emerge for establishing the theoretical validity of traits. As new methods are introduced, investigators ask whether these techniques are useful for validating the abstractness, naturalness, and directness of traits.[23] To validate *abstractness,* investigators remain relentlessly preoccupied with defining and redefining theoretical concepts in light of new evidence. They are making generalizations from actual evidence rather than from intuition or intention. In this process, investigators evaluate how well concrete indicants reflect the particular characteristics that are to be measured.

To validate *naturalness,* investigators ask whether the measurement process is genuine or artificial. They explore whether theorized concepts are evident in the world to non-experts, and whether respondents are asked to think about themes that are common in their experience.

Directness involves questions of correspondence and inference. Investigators question whether correlations correspond to an adequately diverse set of referents and look for correlations between sets of correlations to strengthen claims about convergence. Knowing that theories often begin with circumstantial evidence, investigators look for more concrete representations of each concept. When evidence is tangible, scales are correlated with a measurable criterion. Circumstantial evidence involves inferences about the latent variables that emerge in a series of correlations. The more abstract, natural, and direct a measurement plan, the more likely the identified source states and traits will find a useful place in practice.

Summary

Validity is a dynamic quest for understanding the abstractness, naturalness, and directness with which theoretical traits and states correspond to concrete indicants. The process of exploring validity is significantly more complex for measuring personality than for attitudes. This complexity is caused, in part, by theoretical assumptions about states and traits and the number of inferences made in the measurement process. The importance of multiple methods for addressing these theoretical constructs poses many challenging dilemmas because the qualities of indicants differ across scales. Comparing indicants to theoretical constructs requires the evaluation of whether content is adequately sampled, indicants yield the planned concurrent and discriminating functions, and findings from multiple measures of personality characteristics adequately converge and diverge according to theoretical predictions. Direct forms of experimentation are used to manipulate states, but other methods for exploring predictive validity are often used to verify traits.

■ ■ ■ ■ ■ ▬▬▬▬▬▬▬▬▬▬▬▬▬▬▬▬▬▬▬▬▬▬▬▬▬▬▬▬▬▬▬

MAKING CONNECTIONS

What approaches to validity are important for verifying the appropriateness of your personality measure? Would all available approaches be relevant? Which ones would be the most/least practical? How would you explore each of the validity techniques you selected?

▬▬▬▬▬▬▬▬▬▬▬▬▬▬▬▬▬▬▬▬▬▬▬▬▬▬▬▬▬▬▬▬

IMPEDIMENTS TO MEASURING PERSONALITY

Although there is little dispute over the existence of individual differences in personality, the measurement of this phenomenon is challenging for a number of reasons. Here, only a few of the most general impediments are mentioned but with each new discovery come additional dilemmas.

Participant-Generated Distortion

Many personality measures require information from participants. This invariably makes it difficult for investigators to control the validity of the information they obtain because participants may not hold the same goals as researchers. Consider the game of *Monopoly*. If everyone agrees to play by the same rules, the game can be fun and strategic planning can be effective, but players must agree to play by the same rules. Personality measurement is constrained by the same parameters. Three kinds of distortion have been detected, indicating that not all investigators and participants may agree to play the same game.

Motivational Distortion.　You may remember that deviations from true scores can occur because of systematic and random error. Over the years, investigators have labeled common forms of systematic error. One pattern has been labeled *motivational distortion* and two forms of such distortion have been proposed. Investigators have proposed that some participants anticipate the *social desirability* of a response and offer those responses rather than their own impressions. Researchers have also noticed that some individuals tend to *acquiesce* by offering positive responses to all items rather than different beliefs.

Attempts to construct measures for estimating these propensities have typically failed across different kinds of tasks, although investigators have had some success. Today, successful attempts to estimate motivational distortion typically involve comparisons among multiple measures of similar constructs rather than the inclusion of more transparent lie scales in a measurement plan. Rather than try to guess the honesty of respondents, investigators look for comfortable, tactful ways of gaining personal information.

Sabotage.   Investigators would also be foolish not to anticipate how some respondents can strive to *sabotage* the success of a study. There are no direct controls for such possibilities, but recognizing and evaluating participants' willingness to comply with requests are acquired skills. Issues of sabotage are likely to occur in all kinds of research, but when measuring personality it is especially important to explore individuals' reasons for resistance. Emotional issues of trust, affection, and embarrassment can arise in personality assessment more often than in less personally revealing kinds of research.

Minimal Self-Awareness.   A *lack of self-understanding* can cause a third type of unintentional distortion in personality measures. Respondents may be largely ignorant of the features of their identity and how others understand who they are and how they function in the world. They may not be deliberately withholding information, but the knowledge may be unavailable. Individuals who admit to a lack of self-awareness may become involved in counseling and less formal kinds of group activities, but personal exploration belongs outside the research setting. Adding counseling components that are not part of a research design can undermine the validity of conclusions.

Investigators typically respond to low levels of self-understanding by using indirect rather than direct approaches to measurement. Research involving children is often conducted this way because children rarely have all the reflective skills needed for a full self-evaluation. When researchers use multiple measures, for example, it becomes possible to discern gaps or inconsistencies in an individual's responses. Rather than assume respondents are engaged in motivational distortion or sabotage, inferring a lack of self-understanding can ensure that investigators continue to treat participants with dignity and respect. Using methods for probing someone's responses can also help investigators gain necessary information and learn about the limitation of their tools.

Estimating Participant-Generated Impediments.   Two methods for estimating impediments to measuring personality have been distinguished. The *trait–view theory* estimates perturbation across responses by comparing the findings from self-report and observational data. *Vulnerability coefficients* estimate the susceptibility of distortion for each scale and a distortion force for individual respondents. Responses to two similar scales that differ in the induction of vulnerability are compared to identify points of discordance.

Investigator-Generated Distortion

Investigators can also be responsible for distortion in the findings of a personality study (see Chapter 2). Everyone's perceptual biases affect what they notice and how they interpret new information. Keeping observers blind to the point of an investigation is one method for constraining such distortion, but more often investigators are trained on how to anticipate their own distorted assumptions. The effects of investigator bias can be constrained by including multiple raters as well as multiple measures of each concept and encouraging others to simultaneously monitor the research process. It is also worth remembering that all research is constrained by existing knowledge.

MAKING CONNECTIONS

Investigators are cautious about describing the personality of one individual. Why is such caution wise? What ethical issues should you consider before measuring personality attributes? What limitations should be acknowledged for nomothetic assumptions? How about for idiographic assumptions?

CHARACTERISTICS OF PERSONALITY

Knowledge of personality has practical as well as theoretical implications.[24] In most applied fields, investigators are as interested in theorizing about the characteristics of individuals as in the attitudes found among groups because they use this information to classify people. Toward this end, investigators may seek information about someone's experiential background (e.g., demographics; family, school, and work experience; talents and accomplishments), affects (internal feelings), interests (pleasurable agendas), motives (forces that impel action), and temperament (dispositions that influence behavior). They may also be interested in an individual's social sensitivity (empathy, interpersonal participation, modeling, social adroitness, leadership, tolerance, persuasiveness), coping strategies (ways of meeting the requirements of an environment), cognitive styles (e.g., attitudes, habits, stable preferences or information-processing patterns), and creativity (fluency, flexibility, and originality in thought and deed). Classifying persons along relevant dimensions is essential for responding to individual as well as group differences in needs and expectations. Similarly, self-understanding requires an awareness of how one stands in relation to others.

When determining the properties of a scale, investigators compare concrete and conceptual information for both traits and states. Theoretical claims are central to the design and selection of tools. Investigators evaluate the qualities of indicants, compare relationships among indicants, and compare relationships between indicants, dimensions, constructs, and concepts. Researchers look for convergence in the performance of a scale when compared to other similar scales. They also compare obtained findings against hypothesized predictions to evaluate relations among concepts. Careful to match definitions of indicants in multiple measures, investigators also assess the dependability of scales over time, across subsamples, and for different situations. They look for the minimum number of indicants required to accurately measure each dimension, and identify the surface characteristics of items as well as their strength for assessing source concepts. Investigators also look for methods of suppressing unwanted error. Such error is often caused by the interference of uncontrolled systematic error such as that related to person, situation, examiner, or instrument characteristics. Integrating tools to measure attitudes, abilities, behavior, and physical characteristics, personality theorists endeavor to integrate the unique and common qualities of people.

SUGGESTED READINGS

Bobko, P. (2001). *Correlation and regression: Applications for industrial/organizational psychology and management* (2nd ed.). Thousand Oaks, CA: Sage.

Caprara, G. V., & Cervone, D. (2000). *Personality: Determinants, dynamics, and potentials.* New York: Cambridge University Press.

Chatterjee, S., Hadi, A. S., & Price, B. (1999). *Regression analysis by example* (3rd ed.). New York: Wiley.

Dana, R. H. (Ed.). (2000). *Handbook of cross-cultural and multicultural personality assessment.* Mahwah, NJ: Erlbaum.

Hogan, R., Johnson, J., & Briggs, S. (Eds.). (1997). *Handbook of personality psychology.* New York: Academic Press.

McCrae, R. R., & Allik, J. (2002). *The five-factor model of personality across cultures.* New York: Kluwer Academic.

McCrae, R. R., & Costa, P. T., Jr. (1990). *Personality in adulthood.* New York: Guilford.

Montgomery, D. C., Peck, E. A., & Vining, G. G. (2001). *Introduction to linear regression analysis* (3rd ed.). New York: Wiley.

SUGGESTED WEB SITES

American Psychological Association: http://www.apa.org/science/faq-findtests.html

Educational Testing Service: http://www.ets.org

ERIC Clearinghouse on Assessment and Evaluation: http://www.ericae.net

Measurement Research Associates: http://www.measurementresearch.com

SAS Institute: http://www.sas.com

Statistical Packages for the Social Sciences: http://www.spss.com

SYSTAT Software, Inc.: http://www.systat.com

ENDNOTES

1. This definition reflects convergence in the work of Cattell (1973) and McCrae & Costa (1990). Caprara & Cervone (2000) also offer an overview of personality research.

2. McCrae & Costa (1990) offer a readable representation of this work with elaborate detail on various measurement techniques. West & Finch (1997) also offer a summary of some of these assumptions.

3. Task, ego, and work-avoidant orientations are theoretically assumed to reflect dimensions of the central trait of competence orientations, and this trait could be seen as a feature of conscientiousness.

4. See Cattell (1973) for a more elaborate summary of these kinds of data.

5. A collection of personality measures for exploring happiness is available at http://www.authentichappiness.org.

6. Juvonen & Graham (2001) offer several chapters from this line of research.

7. Butcher (1996) offers details on the MMPI that are comparable to those McCrae (2002) offers about NEO-PI-R. Jackson (1984) contains details of the PRF and Myers & McCaulley (1985) contains details of the Myers-Briggs Personality Inventory.

8. See Swann (1983) and Fiske (1978) for detailed examples of this dilemma and how personality theorists have addressed it.

9. See Burisch (1984) for an outline of the typical approaches to personality inventory construction.

10. Web sites to learn more about these techniques include that of the National Council on Measurement in Education, http://www.ncme.org, and the Institute for Objective Measurement, http://www.rasch.org.

11. Chapter 3 introduces factor analysis and Figure 3.8 illustrates a unidimensional factor.

12. Nicholls, Licht, & Pearl (1982) outlined this set of challenges using existing measures of sex roles and self-esteem to illustrate their point.

13. Bakeman & Gottman (1997) offer a very clear comparison of these methods.

14. Cohen (1968) compares the original κ with the κ_{wt}.

15. Chapter 4 contains the z-score formula and Figure 3.3 contains a graphic representation of the normal curve.

16. See Ozer (1985) for methods of determining these and related indices.

17. For interested readers, coursework comparing *structural equation modeling* (SEM), item-response theory (IRT), generalizability theory, and Rasch techniques would be helpful.

18. See Cronbach & Meehl (1955) for the initial description of this form of validity. The use of this logic has been expanded to include other questions, but the relationships among dimensions, constructs, and concepts continue to be coordinated in studies of validity (Cronbach, 1988).

19. The original studies using these scales were Nicholls, Patashnick, & Nolen (1985) and Thorkildsen (1988).

20. Cattell (1973) offers an elaborate summary of these ideas.

21. Caprara & Cervone (2000) review this and many other studies of personality.

22. This approach was originally introduced by Campbell & Fiske (1959) for use with personality theory, but has proven to be very useful for many different kinds of social science research. Chapter 4 offers a detailed outline of such matrices.

23. Elaborations can be found in Cattell (1973) and the same logic applies to measuring states.

24. These points were elaborated in a summary by Messick (1979).

25. This model was constructed from information found in McCrae & Costa (1990).

CHAPTER SIX

MEASURING INTELLIGENCE AND ABILITIES

Whereas attitudes reflect a person's beliefs and personality reflects comparisons of self and identity, intelligence and competence involve the classification of abilities and skills. As with all forms of human functioning, measuring intelligence and competence is a complex enterprise. In this chapter and the next, the measurement of reasoning and knowledge will be considered. Concepts of intelligence and competence will be distinguished, but have many common features. *Intelligence* will be used to reflect comparisons between abilities and normative standards. *Competence* will be used to reflect comparisons between skills and task-specific standards. Before going into measurement details, let's clarify this distinction.

Studies of *intelligence* generate normative generalizations about particular skills and abilities across age groups. Investigators theorize about intelligence by classifying patterns of abilities when describing intellectual functioning. They draw inferences about *ability* after describing individual differences in performance. Measures of ability facilitate conclusions about the short-term features of cognitive development whereas measures of intelligence emphasize those features that are more deeply rooted in a person's ontogeny.[1]

WHAT IS INTELLIGENCE?

The concept of intelligence has a long history, which reveals a multifaceted construct that can affect nearly all aspects of human functioning. Just as some personality theorists have assumed that personality is the name given to the whole of human functioning, some cognitive theorists assume that intelligence accounts for all the variance in individual differences.[2] Suffice it to say, measurement experts may not take a strong position in this debate, but most differentiate a variety of techniques for measuring the cognitive dimensions, constructs, and concepts that inform theoretical debates. A brief history of intelligence testing might help you imagine why, aside from the fact that we all prefer to have abilities, this area remains so controversial.

Early in history, the Binet-Simon scale was constructed to identify children who could learn and those who would not learn (Binet & Simon, 1948). The *intelligence quotient* (IQ) was introduced by Wilhelm Stern to represent a child's standing on the Binet-Simon relative to his or her age-mates. Around the same time, Spearman (1904, 1923) introduced the construct of *g* to note the common correlation between measures of cognitive abilities and academic achievements. Spearman's two-factor theory consisted of this general mental engine (*g*) and abilities specific to a particular test (*s*). Comparing relationships between *g* and *s*, Spearman explored individual differences.

Looking more closely at the dimensions of intelligence, Thorndike (1925), Thurstone (1938), and Guilford (1967, 1988) identified primary mental abilities using factor-analytic techniques. Jensen (1984) and Eysenck (1982) also explored relationships between reaction time and scores on complex tasks, finding negative correlations. Jensen's work was linked with Spearman's *g* and intelligence was defined as a correlation between *test performance* and *reaction time*, verifying a biological basis of intelligence. Working as a clinical psychologist, Wechsler (1939) designed measures that distinguished *verbal intelligence* (form alpha), *performance intelligence* (form beta), and *full-scale intelligence* or *g* (the combined scores on forms alpha and beta). He defined intelligence as the ability to act purposefully in relation to one's environment. Meanwhile, Cattell and his colleagues (Cattell, 1963; Horn & Cattell, 1966) identified *fluid* and *crystallized intelligence* and treated each as a set of general capacities that have since been expanded to nine factors. Although it might be interesting to imagine a hierarchy of progress toward a common definition of intelligence, these research programs occurred simultaneously and were occasionally at cross-purposes.

Eventually, Carroll (1989) reanalyzed all the different kinds of data from various intelligence measures to determine if new insights could be obtained. Findings fell into three factors: *broad cognitive ability, general factors* similar to those in the Cattell-Horn model, and many *specific factors* that reflected narrower kinds of abilities. Coordinating these theories, Sternberg (1985) proposed a triarchic theory that has *contextual, experiential,* and *componential* features. The *componential theory* is further subdivided into a *performance* dimension similar to one's information-processing capacity, a *knowledge-acquisition* dimension similar to earlier notions of crystallized intelligence, and a *metacomponent* or managerial function that helps with organization. Newer theories are also looking at how physiological and information-processing abilities come together in *neurophysiological models* (Sternberg & Berg, 1992.) The brief history outlined here obviously offers an oversimplified version of existing theories, but all have informed the intelligence-testing movement.

WHAT IS ABILITY?

Given the premium placed on ability, there are good reasons to verify its definition, and to label how ability is assessed. In education, the measurement of ability has become a high-stakes game from which decisions are made to "kill or keep" programs, teachers, and schools. Ability measures are also used to draw inferences about intelligence and place individuals within educational tracks. In work settings, tests of ability are used to make personnel decisions, assess product or service liabilities, and otherwise hold individuals accountable for their work. Within families and friendship groups, individuals voluntarily compare their abilities as much for entertainment as for anything else.

Generally, *ability* is a normative, abstract explanation derived from patterns in responses to a range of indicants. Three structural components reflect adults' typical understanding of ability (Nicholls, 1990).

- Task performance reflects an individual's skill rather than luck or error variance.
- Performance evaluations include information on task difficulty for a norm group as well as a single respondent.
- Judgments about an individual's capacity are inferred from exploring how much effort was needed to perform the task, when optimal effort is applied.

Information on whether an outcome was determined by skill may seem obvious, but most children and some adults seem to assume that luck or good fortune can influence test performance. Similarly, many children and some adults have trouble differentiating self-referenced and other-referenced notions of task difficulty. Ideally, individuals would identify as difficult tasks that are equally hard for themselves and their peers, but would question their own competence when their peers can easily perform a task they cannot. Despite this awareness, when individuals assume that a task is too hard, they often apply a self-referenced definition of task difficulty and avoid tasks they find personally challenging.

Most children and some adults also have difficulty understanding that their capacity constrains the effect of effort on task performance. They have trouble imagining that to evaluate someone's capacity requires knowledge about the capacity of others. It is easier to imagine tasks in which no amount of effort will improve someone's performance (e.g., leaping to the roof of a three-story building) than to realize that individuals have different capacities and will require different amounts of effort to master the same task. These distinctions are not always easy to see, partly because new knowledge about each dimension is consolidated into a holistic understanding of intelligence and competence. Most individuals spend relatively little energy reflecting on how intelligence is defined, but use their working definitions to make specific context-bound decisions. When evaluating the quality of tools such tacit knowledge about abilities and intelligence is made explicit.

DIFFERENTIATING ABILITY AND SKILL

This definition of ability is widely accepted, but theoretical definitions of epistemology have led some investigators to conflate ability with skill (Glaser, 1963). Two concepts help investigators distinguish the two measurement purposes. *Norm-referenced measures* of ability are expected to facilitate relatively enduring conclusions about individuals' competence in relation to others. *Criterion-referenced measures* of skill require that individuals' performance be compared to task-specific standards. The blueprint, item format, and test layout may not differ for the measurement of ability and skill, but the content of items and interpretation of scores reflect differences in the study of intelligence or competence.

Ability is usually measured using norm-referenced tests in which concepts of skill, task difficulty, and effort are consciously manipulated or standardized. Investigators select a sample of tasks related to particular dimensions. Selected tasks reflect different levels of difficulty and require skill rather than luck. An instrument is administered under conditions designed to optimize effort. Then, individuals' performance is compared to that found in an appropriately selected comparison group to judge their relative standing.

Criterion-referenced scores are not interpreted by comparing a person's performance to the performance of others; therefore, inferences about capacity cannot be supported. The test is calibrated without information on the availability of a particular skill in a target population. Investigators can discover whether individuals adequately demonstrate a particular skill. Skills are identified by analyzing tasks to determine the components needed for mastery. A standard of correctness is established for use as a criterion when evaluating performance.

INFERRING INTELLIGENCE
FROM ESTIMATES OF ABILITY

When investigators explore intelligence, they usually define specific characteristics or structures and determine the origin of those characteristics. Individual differences in responses to particular tasks are combed for patterns in how abilities are clustered in the general population.[3] Tasks related to nonverbal reasoning, reaction time, and abstract problem solving are distinguished from tasks related to verbal and other forms of academic ability. Fluid or performance forms of intelligence are measured when physiological responses are correlated with solutions to novel problems. Crystallized or verbal measures evaluate the retrieval of acquired knowledge. Many adults also accept that social intelligence reflects contextual and experiential factors that emphasize interpersonal relationships. Together these abilities are managed by metacomponents that individuals use to size up a situation and determine how to respond in such settings. Whereas ability is often defined as a series of short-term capacities, intelligence usually involves inferences about the long-term process of integrating clusters of abilities. Ability can be inferred from relationships among skill, task difficulty, and effort, but the structure of intelligence is inferred from relationships among different types of abilities.

When measuring intelligence, investigators typically assume that individuals' placement in a distribution of respondents is unlikely to change unless something in the environment prevents them from developing at a rate that is typical of others in the distribution. Individuals' relative position serves as an anchor for drawing inferences about the role of intelligence in predicting other forms of behavior.

In one debate on the value of intelligence testing, for example, investigators asked whether grades or other indices of crystallized intelligence predict occupational status.[4] They also determined whether life outcomes were predicted by performance on a test designed to assess both fluid and crystallized intelligence (individually administered IQ tests are believed to measure these kinds of intellectual thought). Finding consistency in performance on intelligence tests over time, investigators have noticed that differences attributable to social and economic inequalities are common features of intelligence attributable to acculturation and that heritability plays a recognized role in other dimensions.

Questions about the definition and origin of intelligence continue to emerge from these debates. Most germane to our purposes are the debates about whether intelligence is a latent theoretical construct or a list of names given to clusters of abilities. Latent constructs are those that cannot be directly measured and may be comprised of more than one theoretical dimension. If intelligence is a latent construct, evaluating the fairness of intelligence tests will involve inferences from knowledge of patterns in responses to specific tasks. If intelligence is the name assigned to clusters of abilities, then aptitude tests and other measures of individuals' placement in an intellectual hierarchy are likely to be similar in form and style to the achievement tests used to measure ability. Understanding the devices used to design measures of ability and intelligence can allow investigators to generate useful tests of their assumptions.

■ ■ ■ ■ ■

MAKING CONNECTIONS

Collaborate with others to list as many standardized tests as you can imagine. Then, consider each measure in turn and decide if it addresses intelligence or competence, ability or skill. Are these measures norm-referenced, criterion-referenced, or neither? (Some measures are self-referenced and do not contribute to theories of cognitive functioning.)

ESTABLISHING A THEORETICAL BLUEPRINT

Regardless of whether investigators are interested in measuring skills, ability, or intelligence, a plan is usually developed for defining each dimension. By now it is probably clear that investigators, like architects, design a blueprint in which the dimensions associated with theoretical entities are represented. The nature of the blueprint reflects different theoretical specifications and contains several assumptions. Answers are typically judged right or wrong on most ability and skills tests. Tasks are commonly represented as one parameter, and difficulty levels, steps in a process, or problem types reflect additional parameters.

The Purpose of Blueprints

Generally speaking, the blueprints used to construct tests of abilities and intelligence are likely to differ in the range and specificity of tasks included. Blueprints may be used for attitudes and personality research, but are essential for verifying the different characteristics of ability and intelligence tests. Like attitude and personality measures, intelligence measures rely on the *pan-normalization principle,* but answers are also judged correct or incorrect. This concern with correctness introduces task difficulty into evaluations of item performance. Blueprints that coordinate item content and intended function offer guidance for determining whether a measure is adequately balanced along essential dimensions. Blueprints serve as a guide for adequately representing the content to be measured and linking items to theoretical assumptions.

To minimize distortion associated with repeated use of the same measures, investigators can build an *item bank* or collection of interchangeable items that correspond to the features of a particular blueprint. Respondents' ability to offer correct answers is a salient feature of intelligence, and an item bank can improve test security if enough items are available for each dimension. Multiple tests using the same blueprint can be designed by randomly selecting similarly structured items for each component. Alternate forms can ensure that items passing the evaluation criteria are organized differently across administrations, which can enhance the generalizability of outcomes. Investigators use the guides for both ability and intelligence testing, but rely on different assumptions when doing so.

Measuring Ability. Ability-focused blueprints typically use item difficulty and ability-relevant skills as parameters. Suppose, for example, someone wanted to measure mathematical ability. Differentiating skills associated with computation, geometric problem solving, and algebraic problem solving may be relevant dimensions of mathematical ability. Tasks that vary in the dependence on recall, application, analysis, synthesis, or evaluation can be used to manipulate difficulty levels (Bloom, Engelhart, Furst, Hill, & Krathwohl, 1956).

Whereas teachers might use the content of their curriculum to determine how much weight to put on these different parameters, researchers look at the assumptions in their theories. The sample blueprint in Table 6.1 contains the assumption that all three forms of skill are equally important to understanding mathematical ability; each content area was assessed using 12 items (column totals). Items would be constructed to represent a sample of all possible indicants of these theoretically relevant dimensions. Given that mathematical ability is the theoretical concept to be measured, and computation, geometric problem solving, and algebraic problem solving are dimensions, items of various difficulty levels would also be identified for each dimension. Difficulty weights are represented by the number of items included in each row. Items would vary in difficulty, but to ensure variability tasks that are very easy or inordinately difficult would be left off such tests. Performance on tasks designed to explore different levels within a rubric would serve as indicants themselves or might be combined into total scale scores.

Measuring Intelligence. Blueprints for measuring intelligence typically include many different kinds of abilities. One test may include many different kinds of problem solving, informational, and practical dimensions. Although tasks usually vary in difficulty throughout the test as a whole, individuals would be expected to correctly answer normatively easier items and eventually reach a point where all items are too difficult. Therefore, tasks with similar difficulty levels would be presented together and decision rules would establish how many errors warrant the end of testing.

TABLE 6.1 A Sample Blueprint for a Mathematical Ability Measure

LEVEL OF KNOWLEDGE	MATHEMATICAL CONTENT		
	Computation	*Geometric Reasoning*	*Algebraic Reasoning*
Recall	10 items	2 items	
Application	2 items	4 items	5 items
Analysis		4 items	3 items
Synthesis		1 item	1 item
Evaluation		1 item	3 items

Note: The number of items included in each category reflects the investigators' sense of the importance of each type of knowledge. Levels of knowledge refer to those outlined in Bloom, Engelhart, Furst, Hill, & Krathwohl (1956).

Rather than measure a range of difficulty levels for each dimension of intelligence, task difficulty is used to establish a range of appropriate tasks for use in calculating IQ or aptitude scores. Investigators often use established age-norms to determine a starting point for particular subtests, stopping after respondents offer a pre-specified quantity of errors. A blueprint for typical intelligence tests would include the different forms of intelligence (e.g., fluid, crystallized, social) along one parameter and task structures (e.g., abstract problem solving, verbal skills, social dilemmas) along the other. Tasks within each category would be administered together, but placed in a hierarchical order of difficulty such that respondents would be given easier tasks before more difficult tasks.

MAKING CONNECTIONS

Design a sample blueprint for an instrument that you might construct. What dimensions are important for comparing items? How much emphasis will you place on each dimension? How will you balance items across these dimensions? What would you do to construct an item bank for your measure?

COMMON ITEM FORMATS

Cognitive functioning is measured using a wide variety of item formats. Most item formats can be used to draw inferences about abilities and intelligence. Most commonly, *selection items* offer control over the types of responses that individuals can make, and because standardized scoring can be done quickly, it is possible to sample a broader range of abilities or skills than is likely with other item types. *Supply items* are useful for measuring individuals' ability to recall information or to solve complex problems. Respondents are asked to provide their own ideas rather than select answers from a list. Outcomes are not as highly influenced by guessing as is the case for selection items and investigators can more directly expect respondents to apply, analyze, synthesize, and evaluate material. The most popular forms of selection and supply items will be reviewed along with guidelines for writing such items, and limitations in their use.[5]

Multiple-Choice Items

Multiple-choice formats are probably used more than any other. Structurally, a stem is constructed to introduce the problem and several alternatives represent potential solutions. Along with the correct answer, three or four distracters may be listed and respondents select the correct answer from the list. Investigators interested in an individual's ability to recall or apply information may rely on single-item formants where each item represents an independent set of ideas. However, multiple-choice formats can be used for interpretive exercises as well. Interpretive skills involve the introduction of complex stimuli and a series of questions about such stimuli. Items offer a systematic exploration of respondents' ability to critically respond to the ideas presented. Interdependent collections of items allow investigators to explore respondents' ability to analyze, evaluate, or synthesize different kinds of information about a target stimulus.

Item Writing. Procedures for writing multiple-choice items are quite complex. Table 6.2 offers a synthesis of the guidelines included in 46 authoritative textbooks on writing multiple-choice items.[6] These suggestions reflect trial-and-error lessons regarding the performance of different kinds of stems, the selection of appropriate distracters, and information about how material is typically combined so as to minimize the effects of guessing.

The guidelines were written for educational tests, but they are easily adapted for use in research contexts. For example, when researchers think about the content concerns related to item writing, they typically think about their theoretical goals. They often design measures to reflect study-specific goals rather than borrow measures written for other purposes. When designing measures based on a complex blueprint, researchers still strive to

TABLE 6.2 Item-Writing Suggestions Derived from Assessment Textbooks

GENERAL ITEM WRITING (PROCEDURAL)

1. Use either the best answer or the correct answer format.
2. Avoid complex multiple-choice formats.
3. Format the item vertically, not horizontally.
4. Allow time for editing and other types of item revisions.
5. Use good grammar, punctuation, and spelling consistently.
6. Minimize examinee reading time in phrasing each item.
7. Avoid trick items, those which mislead or deceive examinees into answering incorrectly.

GENERAL ITEM WRITING (CONTENT) CONCERNS

8. Base each item on an educational or instructional objective.
9. Focus on a single problem.
10. Keep the vocabulary consistent with the examinees' level of understanding.
11. Avoid cuing one item with another; keep items independent of one another.
12. Use the author's examples as a basis for developing your items.
13. Avoid overspecific knowledge when developing the item.
14. Avoid textbook, verbatim phrasing when developing the item.
15. Avoid items based on opinion.
16. Use multiple-choice to measure higher-level thinking.
17. Test for important or significant material; avoid trivial material.

STEM CONSTRUCTION

18. State the stem in either question form or completion form.
19. When using the completion format, don't leave a blank for completion in the beginning or middle of the stem.
20. Ensure that the directions in the stem are clear, and that wording lets the examinee know exactly what is being asked.
21. Avoid window dressing (excessive verbiage) in the stem.
22. Word the stem positively; avoid negative phrasing.
23. Include the central idea and most of the phrasing in the stem.

(continued)

TABLE 6.2   Continued

GENERAL OPTION DEVELOPMENT

24. Use as many options as are feasible; more options are desirable.
25. Place options in logical or numerical order.
26. Keep options independent; options should not be overlapping.
27. Keep all options in an item homogeneous in content.
28. Keep the length of options fairly consistent.
29. Avoid, or use sparingly, the phrase "all of the above."
30. Avoid, or use sparingly, the phrase "none of the above."
31. Avoid the use of the phrase "I don't know."
32. Phrase options positively, not negatively.
33. Avoid distracters that can clue test-wise examinees; for example, avoid slang associations, absurd options, formal prompts, or semantic (overly specific or overly general) clues.
34. Avoid giving clues through the use of faulty grammatical construction.
35. Avoid specific quantifiers, such as *never* and *always.*

CORRECT OPTION DEVELOPMENT

36. Position the correct option so that it appears about the same number of times in each possible position for a set of items.
37. Make sure there is one and only one correct option.

DISTRACTER DEVELOPMENT

38. Use plausible distracters; avoid illogical distracters.
39. Incorporate common errors of respondents in distracters.
40. Avoid technically phrased distracters.
41. Use familiar yet incorrect phrases as distracters.
42. Use true statements that do not correctly answer the item.
43. Avoid the use of humor when developing options.

Note: Adapted from "A Taxonomy of Multiple-Choice Item-Writing Rules," by T. M. Haladyna & S. M. Downing, 1989, *Applied Measurement in Education,* 2, pp. 40–41. Copyright 1989 by Lawrence Erlbaum Associates, Inc. Reprinted with permission.

minimize guessing by considering how items relate to one another, the order of distracters, and patterns in how the ideas are represented.

Limitations.   Despite their popularity, multiple-choice items have limitations that constrain their use for measuring the full range of abilities reflective of intelligence. Writing high-quality items is quite time-consuming, so investigators try to be clear about what it is they would like to measure. This format is useful when verbal skills can either be taken for granted or are being investigated. In exploratory kinds of research, investigators may not have enough information about relevant abilities, skills, or forms of intelligence to design strong items.

Investigators learn relatively little about someone's ability to identify the features of a problem, to organize and express ideas, or to synthesize information from more than one source because multiple-choice items also require respondents to produce relatively little knowledge. Test-takers are asked to recognize mistakes and correct answers in a list of options, making different kinds of microlevel judgments. They are not asked to consider all aspects of a problem-solving situation. Macrolevel judgments are made by the investigators who select the nature of the problem and define the parameters for the task.

Matching Items

When investigators want to measure a number of similar factors, matching tasks may be the most parsimonious method. A series of premises are listed in one column and responses are listed in a second column. Respondents match ideas between the two lists. Ideally, the set of premises and responses to be compared are relatively homogeneous.

Item Writing.   To ensure that the premises and responses are sufficiently homogeneous, it is helpful to test the measure on individuals who lack the necessary knowledge. If, for example, a list of actions were to be matched with a list of names, each list should reflect related ideas. Tasks would be well-designed if only those respondents who understand the content could correctly match the two lists.

To facilitate clarity, lists of premises and responses are usually kept short and are often presented in alphabetical order. Directions indicate whether responses may be used once, more than once, or not at all. Making sure the list of responses is shorter or longer than the list of premises, and that responses seem plausible for more than one premise often minimizes the effects of guessing on performance. Keeping the entire matching problem on the same page can ensure that respondents can spend their time efficiently responding to the task.

Limitations.   Matching problems are generally useful for measuring simple factual information. As is the case for all selection-items, individuals are asked to recognize, but not recall information. It can be difficult to find problems with a sufficiently homogeneous set of parameters that are also useful for particular kinds of research agendas.

For matching tasks, forms of systematic error are also difficult to control. Patterns in how alternatives are presented are relatively easy to detect and elimination strategies can make guessing beneficial. Therefore, respondents are as likely to notice irrelevant clues as the intended knowledge.

True-False Formats

True-false formats are commonly used for classifying ideas as correct or incorrect, but have been modified so that respondents may answer "yes" or "no," "agree" or "disagree," "fact" or "opinion," and so forth. Investigators may rely on this format when they can only identify two alternatives for a particular item or when they are faced with items that have more than one correct answer. True-false formats are also useful when there is more than one correct answer for a problem; investigators can record responses to each component separately.

Item Writing.   Items are usually written so that individuals with the requisite knowledge can readily identify correct and incorrect ideas. Those without the requisite knowledge should find the decision difficult. To maximize the test's power for discriminating among people who know the requisite information and those who do not, investigators include one central idea in each statement. They also keep statements grammatically simple and eliminate ambiguity that might interfere with respondents' ability to judge the correctness of the information. As is the case with other item formats, investigators eliminate the availability of clues and double negatives, striving to word items in a positive rather than negative direction. When opinions are evaluated, most investigators are careful to mention the source of these opinions except in cases where respondents are discriminating between facts and opinions. Listing sources can sometimes offer problematic cues about the correct answer.

Cause-and-effect statements involve compound phrases and require special consideration in the item-writing process. It is possible for each side of the statement as well as the causal assertion itself to be true or false. Therefore, investigators who are interested in respondents' ability to identify causal relationships generally start with true propositions for both aspects of the statement. Respondents are asked to evaluate the relationship between two accepted positions, ensuring that they evaluate causality and not the accuracy of each proposition.

Limitations.   Like other selection items, true-false items are difficult for use when measuring individuals' ability to apply, evaluate, synthesize, and analyze complex problems. Although investigators have tried to use this format to measure complex abilities, it becomes difficult to keep items free from ambiguity once the level of thought involves more than the mere recollection of information. To construct items that require more complex forms of thought, investigators would have to anticipate respondents' tacit knowledge.

True-false items also offer little information about individuals' knowledge. Respondents are asked only to make a single judgment. If that judgment is correct, it is easy to infer knowledge. If respondents can recognize that an item is false, investigators are left with little information on whether respondents know correct information; there are no available distracters to offer insight into their reasoning. Guessing is also more likely to influence true-false scores than any other kinds of selection-based measures. Respondents have a 50 percent chance of guessing correctly on each item.

Interpretive Selection Exercises

Most multiple-choice, matching, and true-false items require straightforward responses to items, but investigators may be interested in measuring interpretive abilities. Interpreting text, graphs, maps, photographs, or other complex representations of information can be measured using a series of steps and items to represent each step.

Item Writing.   Most of the rules for writing selection items also apply to the design of interpretive exercises, but identifying the stimulus to be interpreted warrants special consideration. Ideally, stimuli are complex enough to elicit sophisticated thought, but also reflect the investigator's theoretical agenda. Such problems should not require skills other than those the investigator intends to measure. Instructions usually call respondents' attention to the task at hand while eliminating extraneous ideas. Novel stimuli are usually selected because the purpose of this type of measure is to explore individuals' ability to respond to new ideas and problems. Keeping the stimulus material brief, easy to read, and/or graphically clear is essential. Items may reflect different selection formats, but a strong item will elicit only the skills that investigators want to measure.

Limitations.   This approach is constrained by all the factors associated with other selection items. Clues about steps in problem solving may be apparent in item layouts. If investigators construct items to reflect each step, respondents are likely to detect the pattern across similar problem sets. Much of the task is structured to such an extent that respondents may not need to tap all their interpretation abilities; the ability to originate, organize, and express personal ideas remains undetectable.

Unanticipated skills are also likely to influence performance on interpretive selection measures. It can be difficult, for example, to determine if performance on an item reflects individual differences in logical reasoning, verbal comprehension, or visual–spatial thought. Independent measures of each skill may be unattainable because different kinds of thought could be confounded. Nevertheless, investigators who use selection-type exercises to generate process-oriented measures may seek only to verify processes they already understand.

Short-Answer Items

Short-answer items rely on a supply format, but place restrictions on the aspects of a problem to be considered by respondents. Respondents may complete a statement, solve a narrowly defined problem, or answer a question using simple language. Table 6.3 offers some of the common directions that are included in supply items.[7] As you can see, respondents are typically asked to generate phrases, problem solutions, or other abbreviated representations of their knowledge. Scoring rubrics are used to compare answers to correct alternatives, but investigators may also evaluate any extraneous or wrong information included in an answer.

TABLE 6.3   Types of Complex Outcomes and Related Terms for Writing Supply-Style Questions

OUTCOME	SAMPLE ITEMS
Comparing	Compare, classify, describe, distinguish between, explain, outline, summarize
Interpreting	Convert, draw, estimate, illustrate, interpret, restate, summarize, translate
Inferring	Derive, draw, estimate, extend, extrapolate, predict, propose, relate
Applying	Arrange, compute, describe, demonstrate, illustrate, rearrange, relate, summarize
Analyzing	Break down, describe, diagram, differentiate, divide, list, outline, separate
Creating	Compose, design, devise, draw, formulate, make up, present, propose
Synthesizing	Arrange, combine, construct, design, rearrange, regroup, relate, write
Generalizing	Construct, develop, explain, formulate, generate, make, propose, state
Evaluating	Appraise, criticize, defend, describe, evaluate, explain, judge, write

Note: From *Assessment of Student Achievement* (6/e), by N. E. Gronlund, p. 105. Published by Allyn & Bacon. Copyright 1998 by Pearson Education. Reprinted by permission of the publisher.

Item Writing.   When writing short-answer items, investigators make clear requests for single, brief answers. Items usually contain direct questions, but can involve concise forms of completion tasks. If respondents are expected to add missing information (e.g., fill in the blanks), one blank rather than multiple blanks, located at the end of each sentence is preferable; the nature of the question is easily identified. Missing information usually reflects the main idea of the problem rather than tangential information. Extraneous clues, such as those offered by differences in the lengths of blanks or in the use of indefinite articles (e.g., *a* versus *an*), are also minimized. When respondents are expected to include particular details in their answer, the directions usually contain such requests, either in the item itself or before a group of items. Of course, all the rules of grammar and presentation clarity appropriate for other item structures are also relevant for short-answer items. In supply items, investigators also make room for respondents to write their answer rather than select from a list of options.

Limitations.   Short-answer items share many of the limitations associated with measuring complex knowledge using selection-item formats. The content tends to be narrowly focused; item content is sufficiently directive that only one answer will seem obviously correct to knowledgeable respondents. Writing short-answer items is easier than writing multiple-choice items and may also be the best way to measure skills like mathematical problem solving. Nevertheless, short-answer items take more time to score. Investigators tend to weigh the value of obtaining recall and solution-generating measurements against the challenges of establishing an accurate scoring rubric, accommodating spelling and handwriting differences, and allocating the time needed to score each item.

Essay Items

Essay questions are especially useful for exploring individuals' knowledge using a holistic or integrative approach. Respondents supply evidence of their knowledge by establishing parameters for the problem they are investigating, selecting factual information to use in the support of their solution, and structuring their responses to illustrate which ideas are more and less central. The structure of the problem places constraints on the types of essays produced, but investigators who are looking for information on how respondents organize their knowledge are free to set these constraints.

   Restricted-response essays offer boundaries for an acceptable response. Words like *list, define,* or *outline* offer cues about the kinds of information that would be expected in an answer. *Extended-response* questions are intentionally open-ended, requiring respondents to organize, integrate, and develop a line of thought. The creative integration of ideas is constrained by time, page, material, or informational limits, but respondents are expected to analyze, synthesize, and evaluate information to fully reveal their skills or abilities.

Item Writing.   Investigators use essay formats when they are interested in measuring complex thought. The content of the question is structured around theoretical reasons for measuring abilities, skills, and/or intelligence. Selection items minimize cues about preferred answers, but essay items typically include hints that offer sufficient clarity so that respondents understand the point of the exercise. Restricted-response essays generally offer more cues than extended-response essays, but both kinds of questions involve explicit connections between theoretical concerns and the item content.

When items are sufficiently clear, it is usually possible to draft a model answer for use in later comparisons. From this model, a reasonable set of scoring guidelines can be established. In setting guidelines, investigators are careful to label those indicants that are related to their theoretical constructs. They create a point-by-point method of scoring that compares responses to well-defined criteria and maximizes accuracy by using systematic procedures for moving from one essay to the next. Some investigators evaluate one feature for all respondents before moving to another feature. Others establish a highly detailed scoring rubric that can serve as a checklist to ensure accuracy. Ensuring that the same scores are assigned by more than one rater is also an important aspect of verifying that both a model answer and the essays scored are sufficiently accurate.

Investigators consider many different aspects of the testing process when establishing parameters. First, theoretically relevant reasons are identified for giving respondents a choice of questions. Respondents are usually allowed enough time to offer sufficient answers to all the questions posed. Offering time limits can be a helpful cue about how much information is being requested and/or how much time might be devoted to planning and organizing thoughts before writing (or dictating) an answer. Time limits can also induce anxiety so investigators learn to use them judiciously. Finally, investigators try to ensure that their scoring rubric is appropriate for the amount of time allotted for each task.

Limitations.   Essay items are useful for many different purposes. When used to evaluate the content of respondents' knowledge, scoring emphasizes the degree to which factually accurate ideas are organized clearly. When used to evaluate respondents' ability to label and justify their opinions, the quality of evidence brought to bear on the problem may be more important. If the structure of an essay is seen as more important than the content, investigators may permit respondents to choose the content. Each of these purposes is complex, so a relatively small sample of skills and abilities can be sampled in any one essay. Investigators interested in measuring content as well as structural features may also combine essays with other item formats to compare more than one type of information.

The versatility of essay items can also be a limitation when the agendas of investigators and respondents do not coincide. Because respondents are free to express their thoughts, they can offer nonresponsive or poorly articulated answers that may not reveal the breadth of their knowledge.

If investigators do not establish clear parameters for scoring essays, comparisons may be problematic. Respondents who bluff or are highly skilled at writing may receive high content scores without having the requisite knowledge. Those who have poor writing skills or who approach the task in an overly literal style may receive lower content scores than are warranted.

If the structure of an essay is seen as most important, investigators may ignore its content and evaluate how well an individual organizes ideas. Greater emphasis would be placed on respondents' ability to verbalize and convey their thoughts. One caveat involves the fact that verbal production may constrain individuals who are not writing in their native language. Such respondents may have many of the cognitive abilities needed to write a strong essay, but have limited language proficiency.

Choosing a Format

As with all items, investigators usually think carefully about whether they are interested in the factual information an individual brings to a problem or in individuals' ability to organize their thoughts. Selection items may be more appropriate than supply items if verbal production is not central to an investigator's agenda. Supply items may be more appropriate when investigators are interested in how respondents originate, organize, and express ideas.

Assembling a Test

Investigators ask a series of questions when putting together the final draft of a test. They determine whether items offer a representative sample of the abilities that are relevant to their theoretical assumptions. They also make sure that all items are written concisely while still reflecting the intended task. Looking at the soundness of each item, investigators ask whether there is an appropriate difficulty range across items, whether there are defensible answers, and if the items are free of defects. Ensuring that items are independent of one another, investigators verify that clues about the answer to one item are not apparent in other items.

Maximum effort is encouraged when items are arranged in a manner that facilitates efficient responses. Items measuring the same outcome or of the same format are grouped together, and are presented in increasing order of difficulty. Items are arranged on the page to facilitate clarity and investigators try to correct any errors that occur in the development of the measure. Ideally, researchers write clear directions both for the measure as a whole and for any sections that require special instructions. Penalties for guessing may also be referred to in the directions, along with anything else that is likely to distract or confuse a respondent. Most researchers are also careful to administer tests under optimal conditions and to score responses carefully. In experimental studies, these conditions are likely to be manipulated to study cognitive functioning under different circumstances.

MAKING CONNECTIONS

Use the item-writing guidelines to write items matching the blueprint you designed earlier. Will you rely on selection, supply, or a combination of item formats? Why? How will you rank the items when assembling a test? What will your directions look like and where will they be placed?

ITEM-ANALYSIS PROCEDURES

After constructing a test blueprint, determining which item formats are most appropriate and constructing appropriate items, investigators take time to review, edit, and improve test items. This can be very time-consuming because performance evaluations hinge on being able to label correct answers. To ensure that a test is as error-free as possible, items are usually pilot-tested on a group of respondents before being used in research. Looking for patterns in how the items perform in pilot-testing can help researchers anticipate the most obvious problems with item performance, but item analysis is still conducted for all data sets.

When assessing abilities and intelligence, investigators usually begin with dichotomous information on whether responses to an item were correct or incorrect. Points assigned when scoring essays can also be treated in this manner, with each point indicating a correct response. To evaluate the qualities of individual items, investigators often make a few more determinations about how indicants are related to one another than is possible when evaluating attitude or personality measures.[8] Although investigators may use more than one approach to item analysis, techniques have been classified here according to their relative value for responding to ability or intelligence concerns.

Evaluating Items for Ability Tests

When determining if items offer a reasonable indication of individual differences in ability, investigators look at different kinds of evidence depending on whether selection or supply formats were used. Selection items are often evaluated by looking at the distribution of responses, the discriminating power of the items, and the difficulty. For supply items, points may be treated as items or as aspects of the scoring rubric. Looking at Table 6.4, where do you find evidence of each evaluation criterion?

Response Distributions. Looking at the *distribution of responses* to selection items, investigators can evaluate whether each possible choice attracted at least some respondents. Ideally, the correct answer as well as all the distracters will be about equally enticing such that each response was selected by at least some respondents. If an item is mis-scored or poorly written, investigators may find that one of the distracters or positions declared incorrect was selected by the majority of respondents or by respondents who otherwise scored high. If more individuals in the high-scoring group were enticed into accepting a distracter than those in the low-scoring group, the item would be deemed problematic. When distracters are selected by relatively few respondents, there may be unanticipated ambiguities. At best the distracter could be edited, but it may also be replaced.

TABLE 6.4 Output from a Sample Item-Analysis Procedure

ITEM 1	A	B	C	D
Freq	65	123*	16	13
Prop	.30	.57*	.07	.06
Corr	−.17	.29*	−.12	.15

ITEM 2	A	B	C	D
Freq	117	16	18*	66
Prop	.54	.07	.08*	.30
Corr	.10	.05	−.05*	−.11

Note: An asterisk indicates the answer that was scored correct.

Looking at the distribution of responses to supply items, investigators rely on the amount of points awarded and the degree to which mistakes were apparent. To explore evidence of mistakes, investigators typically record common errors as well as correct ideas and determine how often particular types of errors are evident. This type of content analysis can be tedious if investigators construct an overly narrow set of parameters in the scoring rubric. However, balancing the exploration of mistakes as well as the strengths in an essay reflects one of the elegant features of such tools; elaborate forms of social comparison can be generated for normative ability evaluations.

Discriminating Power.   Investigators also look at the *discriminating power* (D) of an item; the degree to which high scorers were inclined to get each item right and low scorers were inclined to get that item wrong. This measure offers a comparison of performance within the group of test-takers. For both selection and supply items, investigators begin by dividing a sample into high and low scorers and identifying a reasonable percentage of the most extreme scores—respondents who scored at the extreme ends of the obtained distribution. Then, a discrimination index is computed by looking at whether respondents who answered each item correctly were also likely to score high on the overall measure and respondents who answered incorrectly also scored low. Mathematically, taking the percentage of high-scoring respondents who obtained the correct answer and subtracting from that the percentage of low-scorers who also found the correct answer, it becomes possible to obtain the percent of disagreement between the two groups. Higher percentages indicate that items have stronger discriminating power.

Guidelines for interpreting the discriminating power (D) of an item have been established using probability studies of item performance. When discriminating power is greater than or equal to .40, the item is usually functioning satisfactorily (Ebel, 1965). If D is between .30 and .39, there is little or no item revision assumed to be necessary. If D falls between .20 and .29, the item is marginal and probably needs revision, and if D is less than or equal to .19, the item would probably be eliminated. Despite these ideals, most tests include items with a range of discriminating power.

Item Difficulty.   A third component of item analysis looks at *item difficulty*. Investigators look at the relative difficulty (*p*-value) of an item to determine what percentage of respondents answered the item correctly. It may be easiest to think of (*p*) as the overall power of a test for determining what individuals know or the proportion of correct answers in a particular sample. By determining the percentage of high scorers who obtained the correct answer and the percentage of low scorers who also obtained the correct answer, researchers can evaluate whether the item was easy, moderately difficult, or hard.

Ideally, more low scorers will answer an item incorrectly and high scorers will answer correctly, but if the item is easy, most respondents are likely to score high and the item taps common knowledge. Moderately difficult items are usually answered correctly by most high scorers and some low scorers. Hard items are usually answered correctly by a relatively small number of respondents. For hard items, in this optimal world, those who do answer correctly also score well on the rest of the test, and such items ideally reflect more specialized knowledge. Starting with information used to calculate discrimination (D), item difficulty (*p*) can be calculated by adding the percentage of respondents in the high and low groups who scored correctly and dividing that number by two to indicate the number of groups.

Difficulty indices for many achievement tests often fall within the range of .60 to .80. These scores may seem relatively high, but item format plays a noticeable role in difficulty scores. Guessing, for example, is more likely to affect scores on selection item formats than on supply formats. Because item performance is assumed to be normally distributed in the population, about half the respondents will typically answer correctly. Ideal estimates for selection items also contain corrections for guessing that are determined, in part, by how many choices are available to respondents.[9]

Generalizations.   Although this process can seem tedious, there are many computer programs available for completing item analysis and making available the necessary information. These steps are dependent on the comparison of each set of item responses with assumptions about the normal distribution. Theoretically, for repeated administrations of the same item to multiple samples, a normal distribution will be apparent in how that item performs.

Evaluating Items for Intelligence Tests

When investigators evaluate items for intelligence tests, they are typically interested in understanding how well items designed to reflect different dimensions of intelligence cluster together. To identify optimal performance levels among respondents, investigators often use items that vary in difficulty, but reflect the same type of intelligence. On a well-designed measure, items allow for the discrimination of individual differences in performance while ensuring that the dimensions of intelligence remain comparable across age groups. This can lead investigators to compare findings from item-analysis procedures used for abilities with those for exploring internal consistency. Typically, intelligence theorists are primarily interested in finding accurate relationships among items reflecting each dimension of intelligence even though they modify difficulty and discrimination priorities when selecting age-appropriate items.[10] The coordination of item difficulty and discrimination indices with variation in item format poses inestimable challenge for investigators committed to designing an effective intelligence test.

Item Difficulty.   Procedures for assessing the difficulty of intelligence test items are the same as those for evaluating ability and skill. On many intelligence tests, investigators typically place a few easy items (those that are likely to be answered correctly by all or most respondents) at the beginning of a test. Moderately difficult items are placed next, followed by items classified as hard for most respondents in a given age group. The resulting collection of *p*-values has meaning only for respondents at the same point in the life cycle. Nevertheless, investigators rely on a well-designed blueprint to ensure that the appropriate number of items with each difficulty level remain in the final measures constructed for different age groups.

To measure fluid intelligence, for example, investigators may select three easy items, five moderately difficult items, and three hard items even though the content of these items taps a different collection of age-appropriate skills and abilities. Respondents would proceed through age-appropriate items until they are unable to offer correct answers. If they answered all items for their age group correctly, they would move to items designed for the next highest age group, proceeding until they make a consistent string of errors. Whereas ability tests are typically designed so that most items are of moderate difficulty, intelligence tests rely on a wide range of difficulty levels to offer definition to intelligence.

Discrimination Indices. To explore the discrimination power of items for intelligence tests, investigators may use more than one method, but a series of recommendations seem to have gained prominence (Crocker & Algina, 1986). First, if investigators are interested in selecting items of moderate difficulty, all discrimination techniques are appropriate. For a crude index, investigators tend to rely on D, the measure frequently considered for ability testing.

Investigators may also be interested in knowing the statistical significance of item discrimination and there are several different correlational methods available for this purpose. Generally speaking, coefficients may be evaluated for significance and incorporated into factor-analytic procedures to explore the internal consistency of a group of items.

More specifically, *point biserial correlations* are used to compare how closely performance on one item correlates with the total test score. A simplified version of the Pearson product moment correlation, the formula (r_{pbis}) is as follows:

POINT BISERIAL CORRELATION COEFFICIENT

$$r_{pbis} = \frac{(M_+ - M_T)}{sd_T}\sqrt{\frac{p}{q}}$$

In this formula, M_+ is the mean score for the respondents who answered an item correctly, M_T is the mean score for the total sample, sd_T is the standard deviation for the total group, p is the item difficulty, and q is $(1 - p)$. This is appropriate for theoretical claims that intelligence is what intelligence tests measure.

When investigators assume that the dimensions of intelligence are latent constructs that are normally distributed, they compute a *biserial correlation coefficient* (Pearson, 1909). This coefficient compares an item's performance to a continuously distributed criterion (usually an estimate of the area in the z-score distribution that is reflected in the item's difficulty index.)

BISERIAL CORRELATION COEFFICIENT

$$r_{bis} = \frac{(M_+ - M_T)}{sd_T}\left(\frac{p}{Y}\right)$$

Once again, M_+ is the mean score for the respondents who answered an item correctly, M_T is the mean score for the total sample, sd_T is the standard deviation for the total group, and p is the item difficulty. Y is the corresponding value for the area represented under the curve of the z-distribution that is associated with p. Looking at numerical representations of the standard normal curve distribution (Appendix A), each column indicates points along the *x*-axis and rows report the ordinates in relation to the *y*-axis. This estimate offers a comparison of actual data with the theoretical distribution to facilitate inferences.

Ordinarily, items are scored dichotomously with 1 indicating a correct response and 0 indicating an incorrect response. Correlating these with a total score or its theoretical estimate usually involves a continuous scale. However, sometimes investigators are interested in comparing an item's performance with a dichotomous criterion (e.g., a respondents' performance on the same item at an earlier point in time). Phi coefficients are useful for establishing this kind of stability in the performance of items that can be scored as correct or incorrect.

PHI COEFFICIENT

$$\Phi = \frac{p_+ - p_x p_y}{\sqrt{p_x q_x p_y q_y}}$$

In this formula, p_+ is the number of people who answered both items correctly, p_x is the percentage of respondents who answered the first item correctly, and p_y is the percentage of respondents who answered the second item correctly, q_x is $(1 - p_x)$, and q_y is $(1 - p_y)$.

Because the phi coefficient is not appropriate for use when scores are created by dichotomizing continuous variables in relation to the normal distribution, investigators avoid using phi coefficients in more complex factor-analytic procedures intended to explore the internal consistency of a group of items. In cases where dichotomously scored items will be subjected to factor analysis, investigators rely on computer programs to compute *tetrachoric correlations*. These coefficients are based on the assumption that items and criterion scores each reflect the dichotomization of normally distributed variables.

In addition to identifying those items of moderate difficulty, designers of intelligence tests are also interested in selecting items at the extreme ends of the distribution. Assuming that each dimension of intelligence is normally distributed in the population, they typically rely on biserial correlation coefficients to select easy or hard items.

To compare the possibility that future samples might differ in intelligence from an obtained sample, investigators also rely on biserial correlations. These offer the most robust estimates of discrimination because they are less dependent than other coefficients on the difficulty level of an item.

If a program of research is relatively far along and investigators can be confident that their current sample is representative of other samples, they may begin to look more closely at the internal consistency in a group of items. Most investigators find that point biserial correlations offer insights into maximizing the covariance between items that can later become beneficial in estimates of reliability and eventually for validity.

Generalizations. Whereas item formats and content tend to be relatively homogeneous in measures of ability, both vary to a considerable degree in most measures of intelligence. Intelligence measures are expected to tap the full range of each dimension, but the limitations of each item format constrains item functioning. Using multiple formats to explore a wide range of abilities poses challenges in item selection that are best addressed using correlational techniques. These techniques have the added benefit of being useful for measures, like those for attitudes or personality, where no correct answer can be determined.

MAKING CONNECTIONS

Administer your test to as many individuals as you can. Which features of item analysis are most appropriate for your particular measure? Evaluate the performance of each item. Using the guidelines for item analysis, how well did each item on your test perform?

RELIABILITY

Indices of reliability for ability and intelligence tests are similar to one another and rely on norm-referenced assumptions. When interpreting a set of norm-referenced scores, investigators consider two classes of indices. To interpret an individual's score, they consider the standard error of measurement. To interpret a group of scores, investigators focus on estimates of stability and accuracy.

Steps for Verifying Reliability

As has been apparent for measuring attitudes and personality, reliability is established using a multistep process. When answers can be eveluted for correctness, three steps are commonly considered.

Interpreting Scores.   You may recall that the *standard error of measurement* is an estimate of the inconsistency in an individual's performance if that individual were to repeatedly take the same test. This estimate is calculated in terms of the units of the scale used in reporting scores. If abilities are measured using raw scores, the standard error of measurement reflects an estimate of variance in raw scores. If scores are converted to IQ units, grade-level equivalents, or z-scores, the estimate reflects variation in those relevant scales. Confidence intervals can be calculated by adding and subtracting the standard error of measurement from an obtained score and this method is used when determining how much an individual's performance might vary.

You may also remember that *reliability coefficients* offer an aggregate estimate of the consistency in measurement of a collection of items across a group of respondents.[11] Some techniques offer an estimate of stability in repeated administrations; others offer a sense of how accurately items on the same administration of a scale correlate with one another. This distinction is much easier to see in measures of ability than those of attitude or personality because responses can be evaluated for correctness.

Estimates of Stability.   Five estimates of stability reflect different features of reliability. All of these approaches estimate variation that arises within the measurement procedure itself. Methods differ in whether they are influenced by day-to-day variation in the person, changes in the specific items on the test, and changes in individuals' speed of work during the test.

Two types of *test-retest reliability* estimate the degree to which scores are distributed in the same way when respondents answer the same questions twice. Sometimes the two tests are administered at the same point in time, offering the most precise estimate of stability without exploring systematic variance attributable to time. An individual's performance may be influenced by practice effects associated with seeing the same items twice and/or fatigue effects associated with the test length. Yet, because there is no formal time interval between testing and only one set of items are selected to represent the dimensions being measured, other known factors that influence stability remain underestimated.

Test-retest correlations may also be calculated when there is a time interval between the two administrations of the same test. When there is a time interval, day-to-day variation in performance is included in the stability estimate. Fatigue and practice effects may be apparent for this estimate, but investigators may want to verify stability in scores before classifying abilities or intelligence. If the time interval is too long, however, new opportunities for learning will influence the outcome and it will become impossible to distinguish the process of calibrating a tool from using it in research.

Two types of *parallel-forms reliability* are also used to estimate stability. In one approach, alternate versions of a test, designed using the same blueprint, are administered at the same point in time. Correlation between these two sets of scores offers an index of stability that is affected by how well items on both tests reflect the dimensions to be explored. Fatigue effects may place constraints on reliability, but practice effects are minimized because the two tests contain different items.

The other type of parallel-forms reliability is calculated after introducing a time interval between administrations of the alternate forms of a test. This approach is affected by all the known types of systematic as well as random error in estimates of stability. Investigators differ on whether they assume that parallel-forms estimates involving a time interval offer more or less robust estimates of stability. As with test-retest reliability estimates, the amount of time between administrations affects the degree to which factors other than the calibration of the tool influence the resulting coefficients. Stability is seen as robust if the correlation is high, but if it is moderate or low, there are many alternative explanations for such variability.

The final method for estimating stability was designed to control the limitations associated with test-retest and parallel-forms reliability. In assessing *split-half reliability,* responses to a single administration of a test are separated into two groups to simulate parallel forms. Most often, even-numbered items are placed in one group and odd-numbered items are placed in a second group. Then, the two sets of items are correlated. In this approach, practice and fatigue effects are minimized because respondents answer fewer items and do so in one setting. If items are selected to ensure that both halves of the test are parallel, another form of systematic error can also be minimized. However, investigators interested in estimates of stability over time are likely to see this approach as more limited in power because these forms of systematic error are controlled rather than incorporated into the coefficient.

Stability estimates offer a sense of whether respondents maintain the same standing with the group on repeated administrations of the same test. Pearson product moment correlations offer a statistical index of how well the two sets of responses are associated for some types of data while nonparametric coefficients may be appropriate for estimates that are dependent on nominal data.

Estimates of Accuracy.   Three measures of *internal consistency reliability* offer estimates of how well responses to items on a single test are correlated with one another. Cronbach's *coefficient alpha* has been previously described (see Chapters 4 and 5) because of its versatility for use with items that cannot be scored dichotomously. This method is also appropriate for estimating the reliability of measures of cognitive functioning. It is especially useful for exploring the internal consistency in a set of multiple-choice items; the performance of each distracter as well as the correct responses is incorporated into the final coefficient.

Two additional techniques are used when answers can be scored dichotomously and investigators are not interested in the performance of distractors. When items offer a homogeneous evaluation of ability or intelligence, *Kuder-Richardson Formula 20* (KR-20) compares the proportion of respondents passing (p_i) the items and the proportion failing the items (q_i). In this formula, n refers to the number of items on the test and sd refers to the standard deviation of raw scores. If you are testing your ability to read formulas, you may have noticed that the standard deviation is squared and could be replaced by the symbol for variance. The reliability of correct and incorrect responses to the full-length test is calculated using the following:

KUDER-RICHARDSON FORMULA 20

$$r_{kr\text{-}20} = \left(\frac{n}{n-1}\right)\left(\frac{sd_t^2 - \sum p_i q_i}{sd_t^2}\right)$$

When investigators can further assume that a homogeneous group of items are also of the same difficulty, the *Kuder-Richardson Formula 21* (KR-21) offers an estimate of accuracy. Rather than compare the proportion of correct and incorrect responses, investigators substitute the mean score (M) on the test for the proportions of correct and incorrect responses.

KUDER-RICHARDSON FORMULA 21

$$r_{kr\text{-}21} = \left(\frac{n}{n-1}\right)\left(\frac{sd_t^2 - M_t\left(1 - \frac{M_t}{n}\right)}{sd_t^2}\right)$$

Investigators acknowledge several limitations to estimates of internal consistency, but consider these limitations in light of their research goals. For measures of intelligence, when it is important to verify that scores are unlikely to fluctuate from day to day, it may be important to estimate stability as well as accuracy. Measures of internal consistency reflect individuals' responses from one particular time period and this performance may not be stable enough for drawing inferences about intelligence (or abilities that are expected to remain stable).

Another limitation concerns the degree to which items are dependent on one another. Items with a common reference, such as those associated with interpretive exercises, may lead to inflated estimates of internal consistency. Respondents who succeed on one item may be more likely to succeed on other items in that set because the items reflect an underlying skill that was not measured directly.

Finally, when items on a test measure more than one dimension of a construct, it may be inappropriate to compute a single measure of internal consistency. On most intelligence tests, for example, items are deliberately selected to represent a wide range of abilities. They also represent a diverse range of difficulty levels. Using factor-analysis methods to create smaller scales may offer a more appropriate method for estimating accuracy. The possibility of constructing a relational circumplex may also be considered when two theoretically comparable dimensions can be identified.

Exogenous Influences on Reliability

Accepting the importance of reliability, both to establish validity and when testing more elaborate research hypotheses, investigators have considered several issues when comparing coefficients. These influences violate the pan-normalization principle and you may recognize some from earlier discussions on measuring attitudes and personality. Try to detect some of the subtle differences in how these issues arise when measuring cognition.

First, the appearance of individual differences in responses within a sample will have a marked effect on a reliability coefficient. As you will notice from looking at the various formulas, estimates of variance play a central role in each method. The formulas for estimating reliability are based on the assumption that responses will be normally distributed. Restrictions in the range of responses will foster low coefficients because the range of scores would be overly narrow. Samples drawn from different populations may also introduce uncontrolled forms of error.

A second influence concerns the degree to which a test was too easy or difficult for the group. If the test is too easy, most respondents will receive the same high score, and if it is too difficult they will receive similarly low scores. The distribution of scores would be skewed in such a way as to restrict the range of possible responses, undermine variance, and minimize the discrimination power of the test. Investigators can calculate different estimates of the standard error of measurement for scores at different points in the distribution, but many respondents may not reveal all their abilities on inappropriately scaled tests.

The test length will also influence its reliability, as will the number of respondents who take the test. Both issues mediate the extent to which extreme responses influence the distribution of scores. If respondents offer different interpretations of each item, parallel items offer more opportunities to reveal a stable set of abilities. If one individual answers differently from the others, that set of responses will have a more marked effect with a small group of scores than with a larger group. Correlations between items form the basis of most reliability coefficients, but, unlike methods of item-analysis, significance testing is not appropriate for evaluating the result and should not be negative.

∎ ∎ ∎ ∎ ∎ ▬▬▬▬▬▬▬▬▬▬▬▬▬▬▬▬▬▬▬

MAKING CONNECTIONS

Find a statistical package like *SPSS* and use it to compute the reliability of your measure. What approach did you use? Why? If possible, compare the results obtained from more than one method for assessing reliability. How different were the resulting coefficients?

VALIDITY

Validity remains an interpretation process commonly explored from different levels, each with unique but sometimes interdependent components. As with other tools, investigators verify content, criterion, and construct validity to explore abilities and intelligence. Verifying these forms of validity for measures of ability seems to be less controversial than doing so for intelligence tests. Over multiple uses of the same measure for the same purpose, investigators may compare different kinds of validity. Change the measurement conditions and the validation process starts anew. When tools are used to generate new knowledge, validity conclusions may not be available until a research program is well underway.

It is also worth remembering that each test score reflects a sample of responses collected at a particular point in time. Inferences about individuals' abilities or intelligence are based only on a sample of relevant indicants. The chain of inferences is shortest for skills tests, a bit more complex for ability tests, and more remote for intelligence tests. Keeping these facts in mind while interpreting scores can minimize the potential for harm caused by making exaggerated claims about an individual's performance.

Content Validity

The content validity of a test can only be evaluated in light of the purpose for using a tool. Investigators evaluate each test blueprint in light of how well it reflects the theoretical constructs to be measured. When considering abilities, the blueprint often reflects a representative range of the dimensions being measured and items are representative of each component in the design. When measuring intelligence, a wide range of abilities tends to be apparent.

Investigators rely on logic to evaluate their blueprints and select relevant items, but they also ask other experts to critique their measure. If experts are given a copy of the test and of the blueprint, they should be able to accurately match items with their place on the blueprint. Experts can also verify whether the content of a blueprint is appropriately comprehensive, dimensions are appropriately balanced, and the resulting measure is of appropriate length, format, and difficulty for the manifest purpose of the tool. Tests are usually laid out so that people taking the test find it reasonable and acceptable for the intended purposes. An exploration of content validity is started before administering a test and continues after the data are collected and item analysis is complete.

Criterion Validity

All of the validity criteria introduced in previous chapters also apply to the evaluation of cognitive functioning. Additional dimensions of criterion validity have been given many different names in books on assessment. In thinking about cognitive measures, it seems worthwhile to mention that *empirical* or *statistical validity* is the term used to represent a combination of three methods when statistical tools are used to verify patterns. Investigators establish *concurrent validity* by determining if scores on a test match a criterion. They establish *discriminant validity* by determining if scores on two unrelated subtests are sufficiently different. In addition, researchers verify *predictive validity* by determining if a test score will forecast a future outcome. Ideally, all three forms of criterion validity would be established, but it is not always practical to measure everything needed to evaluate each type using the same group of respondents.

Concurrent and Discriminant Validity.   The most controversial and challenging part of establishing validity is identifying an adequate criterion for use in comparing test scores. When establishing reliability, investigators often use the total scale score as a criterion, but to establish validity the criterion is usually external to the test itself.

In situations without accepted answers, the same probabilistic techniques used for evaluating attitude or personality measures are used. They may also treat items as dichotomies and rely on nonparametric techniques such as chi square to compare scales. Regardless of the selected approach, strong criterion measures ideally have four qualities. These external criteria should be free from bias, relevant to the purpose for the test, reliable, and readily available.

Not surprisingly, investigators often include as many criteria in their overall research design as possible. Investigators consider concordance for concurrent validity and differences for discriminant validity. Intelligence tests, for example, are designed to measure a wide range of abilities. Therefore, measures of similar abilities (e.g., recognition of synonyms and antonyms) would ideally be correlated while measures of unrelated abilities (e.g., mathematical problem solving and reading comprehension) would differ.

Hopefully, concerns with validity now seem familiar, yet adding a correctness criterion raises another dilemma for verifying validity. After selecting a standard, indicants are evaluated for their proximity to that standard. Indicants should be as close in content to parallel standards, but tests of discriminant validity should consist of a fair comparison. Those within each measure should be different enough to reveal sufficient variance for comparing a new tool and the corresponding external standards. Overlapping content across indicants is problematic, yet theoretically, there would be enough shared variance to warrant comparison. Correlations among new indicants and criterion scores serve as the most straightforward estimate of concurrent and discriminant validity, but regression or Bayesian statistical techniques are often used when multiple subtests are being compared at once.[12]

Predictive and Postdictive Validity.   Because of the degree to which measures of cognitive functioning are used to predict many life opportunities, most of the major standardized tests have undergone rigorous attempts to establish *predictive validity* and sometimes *postdictive validity*. Researchers are wise to follow suit if they plan to use their results to make such life-altering decisions.

When exploring *predictive forms of criterion validity,* investigators often use new tests to predict future achievement. It is also possible to begin with later achievement, drawing inferences about earlier performance to estimate *postdictive forms of criterion validity* (Ghiselli, Campbell, & Zedeck, 1981). Whereas these types of validity sometimes fall within the purview of construct validity, it may be better to imagine two levels when responses can be evaluated for correctness. The first level, considered in this section, involves comparing indicants to a criterion or standard for evaluating correctness. This level essentially verifies the dimensions within a construct. The second level, considered with construct validity, compares scales from one construct with those from other constructs. This second level verifies relations between newly defined and existing constructs.

Investigators modify definitions of achievement depending on whether they are predicting ability or intelligence. These differences, along with variation in measurement error within a tool and across scales, typically lead investigators to see the establishment of predictive validity as a study in its own right. Whenever possible, they use several scales related to the same construct to compare the percentage of variance attributable to each.

To conduct a strong predictive validity study, investigators often obtain a representative sample of respondents and measure their performance on predictor and criterion variables.[13] Just as in other studies, investigators select correlation or regression techniques to compare indicants or related scales. Once all the data are collected, investigators either correlate the predictor and criterion scores or enter them into a multiple regression equation. Although it can be difficult, investigators try to match predictor and criterion scores for each respondent in their sample. For criterion validity studies, researchers can collect predictor and criterion measurements at the same time, using different tools.

Investigators can compare the correlations between scales using the techniques described previously.[14] More often, regression equations estimate predictive validity in cognitive functioning. *Regression lines* are calculated to find the best representation of indicants or scale scores in a scatter diagram. Plotting predictor scores along the x-axis and criterion scores along the y-axis, the regression equation becomes:

REGRESSION FOR PREDICTION

$$\overline{Y}_i = a_y + b_{y \cdot x} X_i$$

In this equation, a_y is the value of Y when X is zero and $b_{y \cdot x}$ is the regression coefficient. Regressing Y, the criterion variable, on X, the predictor variable, we can try to predict future performance from a set of scores collected at an earlier point in time.

Regression also has the advantage of offering a second estimate, unavailable when relying on simple correlations. Postdictive validity can be explored by reversing the direction of the prediction so that earlier performance is predicted from knowledge of later performance. Where a_x is the value of X when Y is zero, investigators can compute:

REGRESSION FOR POSTDICTION

$$\overline{X}_i = a_x + b_{x \cdot y} Y_i$$

It also becomes possible to evaluate the equivalence of means by computing two regression lines. One regression line starts with the first set of test scores and uses them to predict future performance. The other regression line uses test scores collected at a later point in time to predict earlier performance. The point at which the two lines cross is the point at which the means of X and Y distributions are equal ($M_x = M_y$). This mathematical technique for exploring convergence may be most useful for evaluations of abilities because individuals are often told about their relative standing. It becomes possible to estimate how well predictor and criterion variables correspond to similar dimensions.

After predictive validity is established (e.g., r_{xy} forms the requisite patterns), investigators sometimes use the resulting equation to predict the performance of new respondents. Using an individual's raw score on the predictor variable, this is accomplished by taking information about the Y-intercept and beta from the normative sample and inserting the individual's known score, X, into the regression equation. If, for example, a person's score was 25 on an ability test and the regression equation for the normative sample was $Y = .5 + .10X$, the predicted Y score would be 3. Notice that measurement scales for X and Y need not be the same. The beta weight next to the X offers a scale correction for use in predicting Y (or vice versa).

To estimate the *magnitude of error* in this prediction, investigators calculate an individual's *deviation score*, $Y - \overline{Y}_i$. For estimating error in the regression line for X, investigators calculate $X - \overline{X}_i$. Here, deviation scores are the difference between one person's predicted score and the mean predicted scores for the sample. The wider the distribution, the more error is apparent in individuals' predictions.

To determine how much error is apparent in a collection of scores, investigators calculate the *standard error of estimate,* which is also sometimes called the *standard error of prediction.*

STANDARD ERROR FOR PREDICTION **STANDARD ERROR FOR POSTDICTION**

$$se_{y \cdot x} = sd_y^2 \sqrt{1 - r_{xy}^2} \qquad\qquad se_{x \cdot y} = sd_x^2 \sqrt{1 - r_{xy}^2}$$

When the prediction is perfect, r_{xy} will be 1 and all points will fall on the regression line with no error. More realistically, r_{xy} will be greater than 0, but less than 1, and the magnitude of error will need to be interpreted. This standard error of estimate offers an average of the errors in prediction much like the standard error of measurement offers an average of errors in a set of test scores.

Considering the area under the normal curve, it is possible to use the standard error of prediction to estimate the limits within which an individual's predicted score will fall within a given probability. If, for example, we predict that an individual will have a future criterion score of 25, and we know that the standard error of estimate is 2, we can say that the odds are 68.26:100 that the score will be between 23 and 27 (+ or –2). The odds reflect the fact that 68.26 percent of responses are likely to fall within one standard deviation above or below the mean of an individual's scores if they repeatedly took the test. Each individual's score is calculated in light of his or her own estimated mean, which in this case is the criterion score of 25.

Challenges in Establishing Criterion Validity.   To draw inferences about the criterion validity of a new measure, investigators consider several methodological and statistical dilemmas.[15] One major concern is that the reliability of each measure affects the correlation between them. At best, the association $r_{xy} = r_{x\infty y\infty}\sqrt{r_{xx}r_{yy}}$. Knowing the correlation between true predictor and criterion scores ($r_{x\infty y\infty}$), it is possible to see that, as the reliability of the predictor (r_{xx}), and the reliability of the criterion (r_{yy}) change, the validity coefficient r_{xy} is affected. When the reliability of one set of scores is extremely low, the validity will be zero. Investigators sometimes correct for this attenuation, but the reliability coefficients used in such corrections should be appropriately robust for this to be effective.

As was mentioned earlier, most measures of ability or intelligence reflect composites of several variables. Regression is useful for combining these sources of information, but investigators decide whether to weight each dimension equally or differentially. Investigators can also set critical cutoff points that place individuals into master and non-master categories. Whichever decision rules are used, investigators are careful to acknowledge them when reporting their results.

Another challenge will be elaborated more completely in the later discussion of developmental perspectives, but it is important here as well. As is common for criterion-referenced measures, the magnitude of a correlation coefficient is undermined when there is a *restricted range* in a distribution of scores. This can be common in studies for which respondents are selected because they meet a predetermined standard. Predicting college performance only among college students, for example, causes a direct or explicit restriction in the range of possible scores. If individuals who were excluded from college are not sampled, the full range of human functioning cannot be explored and unknown forms of indirect or incidental effects may further compound error attributable to this selection bias.

Such restricted range can also occur when a third intervening variable is used to select participants; relationships between X and Y scores may be incidentally affected by this third variable. Keeping clear which causes of a restricted range are direct and indirect, investigators can sometimes correct for intervening variables as long as they can estimate that variance. Constantly questioning theoretical commitments facilitates this discovery.

Construct Validity

When establishing *construct validity,* investigators are intimately involved in theory construction as well as verifying the measurement features of their new tool.[16] This has been readily apparent in debates about whether intelligence is a latent construct or is "whatever intelligence tests measure." Because levels of inference are features of construct validity, investigators take great pains to make clear their assumptions.

A quick review of central assumptions may be helpful at this point. As is the case for designing an appropriate blueprint, investigators continue to imagine, critique, and refine their definitions of the constructs under investigation. Information on the performance of scales in relation to one another can enhance this process, but findings from a wide range of research programs are also important for exploring construct validity. Construct validity concerns the meaning of the construct (e.g., intelligence, ability), how the construct is related to other constructs (e.g., motivation), and how it is related to specific indicants (e.g., test scores, behavior). Deductive, inductive, and interactionist approaches to defining a construct are also relevant to exploring cognitive functioning.

Defining the Construct.   Even though researchers may evaluate the correctness of answers, they work with hypothetical constructs. Naturally, well-defined constructs clarify how individual measurement operations are interrelated, but these definitions may change as investigators acquire more information. Because constructs are evolving entities, most researchers are tolerant of the variation in reliability that occurs across measures, but strive to select those approaches that demonstrate the viability of their theory.

Investigators can strengthen conclusions about construct validity if they take time to elicit critiques of their assumptions and methods. Eliciting participants' critiques of their theories, methods, and measurement techniques can illuminate practical concerns, whereas expert critics may have additional research evidence to share. Analyzing the process of data collection and interpretation can identify blind spots or faulty assumptions about how respondents think about particular tasks as well as encourage clearer theoretical definitions.

Convergent and Divergent Validity.   In establishing convergent and divergent validity, investigators highlight relationships between the dimensions of a cognitive construct and other variables. As is the case for attitude and personality research, investigators construct *multitrait–multimethod matrices* to explore relationships among methods and measures for verifying and contrasting their measures with existing tools. Hopefully, variables that are similar to the dimensions of a construct will be highly correlated with the indicants of that construct. Variables that are different would show low to moderate correlations. Patterns among scales can be tested using structural equation modeling techniques like path analysis and latent path modeling. (Web sites for learning more about these models are provided in Chapter 4.)

Predictive Validity.   Investigators modify definitions of achievement depending on whether they are interested in the effects of ability (e.g., grades) or intelligence (e.g., occupational success). These differences, along with variation in measurement error across tools, typically lead investigators to see predictive validity as meaningful in its own right. At the construct validity level, investigators are often testing specific hypotheses about how well variables are coordinated in a construct or in a larger concept. Whenever possible, they include several different measures and compare the percentage of variance attributable to each. Because generalizations are normative, investigators also try to collect evidence from more than one point in time.

In longitudinal studies of construct validity, it can be difficult to match predictor and criterion scores for each respondent in their sample. This can be challenging because most longitudinal studies face attrition in participation that investigators cannot control. If the *attrition rate,* the frequency of persons who drop out of a study, is too high, the representativeness of the sample can be compromised. The sample may become too small, or there may be a selection bias in who remains in the study and who drops out. If the duration of a study is short-term, as is often the case when validating ability and skills tests, it may be easier to obtain both predictor and criterion scores than when the duration is long-term.

To conduct a strong predictive validity study, investigators often obtain a representative sample of respondents, measure their performance on predictor variables, and wait for the necessary time to pass before collecting criterion scores on the same group of people.[17] Once all the data are collected, investigators either correlate the predictor and criterion scores or enter them into a multiple regression equation. That is, the same procedures for exploring criterion validity are used for construct validity, but the evidence is typically ag- gregated at this level of analysis.

Most investigators rely on regression equations for exploring construct validity and computers are usually needed to calculate standardized beta weights. Nevertheless, the same process you imagined earlier for individuals can be used to explore relationships within groups of individuals and collections of variable. Error is estimated by looking at ag- gregated *deviation scores*. These scores are the deviation of one set of scores from the mean of the distribution of those scores. To use these scores in establishing predictive validity, the regression equation changes as follows:

DEVIATION SCORES

$$\bar{y}_i = a_y + b_{x \cdot y} x_i$$

In this equation, $\bar{y}_i$ is the deviation of each individual's raw score from the mean of the y dis- tribution. Because the mean of all deviation scores is zero, the intercept a_y is 0 and the re- gression equation in deviation score form becomes $\bar{y}_i = b_{x \cdot y} x_i$. Comparisons among different values for beta become possible when they are interpreted as standard scores. Sim- ilarly, the standard error of estimate can be computed by treating scales as data points. In- vestigators sometimes take this process a step further, replacing x_i with z-scores rather than using raw scores in their analyses.

Not surprisingly, research programs that hinge on the establishment of predictive va- lidity in achievement measures are very costly and are more often done by corporations. Whenever possible, researchers try to use those measures that have been widely accepted to make decisions. Tools normed on a large, representative sample typically offer much more valid assessments than those normed only using one or two research samples. Testing cor- porations also have many more resources for minimizing bias in item functioning and for constructing large item banks.

Ruling Out Intervening Explanations.   Investigators also look for alternative explana- tions that might offer a better account of the phenomena under investigation than is offered by their new construct. For abilities, investigators try to determine if scales measure the in- tended ability and only that ability. If verbal skills are central to math problem solving, for example, investigators consider revising their tools or refining their definition of math. For intelligence, they evaluate alternative explanations for the patterns apparent across mea- sures of ability.

In any research project, intervening variables may account for most of the variance apparent in scores from a new measure. Alternative explanations can reveal forms of sys- tematic error in how a construct is measured that would otherwise be overlooked. Some- times discrepant findings can suggest a need for revision or refinement in a new construct, but wise investigators are also ready to accept that their ideas are misguided.

Using Experimental Evidence.   Cognitive science is a discipline in which researchers actively conduct experimental studies to validate important assumptions about cognitive functioning. This information extends theoretical claims about the structure of cognition to include information about the change mechanisms and intellectual functioning. New measures are included in experimental research either as dependent variables or to cross-validate claims about how cognitive processes affect performance. Verifying predictable patterns in how treatments influence cognition can lead to more detailed definitions of the construct or to rich predictions about its importance. Debates over the definition of *intelligence* need not be resolved, but investigators try to be reasonably confident about their definitions and measurements of abilities.

MAKING CONNECTIONS

Outline a plan for determining the validity of your measure. Which types of validity can you consider with the information you have? What would you do to explore other types of validity? Is it practical to assess all types of validity for this measure? Explain.

MEASURING GENERAL COGNITIVE FUNCTIONING

In this complex chapter, several aspects of theorizing about cognitive functioning have been considered. First, current working definitions of *ability* and *intelligence* were introduced to facilitate comparisons among different measurement approaches. Details on the design and use of test blueprints, and the selection of item formats were outlined. Suggestions for item writing and selection procedures were also summarized. Procedures for item analysis and reliability, not always appropriate for use with attitude and personality measures, were introduced in light of differences in norm-referenced measurement assumptions. Finally, some of the common validity lessons acquired when designing standardized tests reveal the costly challenges of making valid judgments about respondents' abilities and intelligence.

Missing from this analysis are details of how one verifies the existence of relationships among the different dimensions of cognitive processing. Such work would require multiple measures of different aspects of cognitive processes. Theories would focus on how each measure corresponds to the overall process. While this is difficult to describe, investigators typically use tangible responses to specific tasks as an indication of each step in the process.

Also missing from this chapter are details of two additional types of measurement that are used for evaluating cognitive functioning. The next chapter focuses on measuring skills and drawing inferences about competence. The observational and physiological approaches described in Chapter 8 are also combined with approaches described here to draw generalizations about the nature of cognitive functioning. Criterion-referenced tools cannot adequately offer the normative information required for theorizing about intelligence. Many behavioral measures share similarly short-term measurement properties. Nevertheless, researchers have many reasons for exploring the skills and behaviors of participants and drawing inferences about where these come from.

SUGGESTED READINGS

Gronlund, N. E. (1998). *Assessment of student achievement* (6th ed.). Boston: Allyn & Bacon.

Sattler, J. M. (2001). *Assessment of children: Cognitive applications* (4th ed.). San Diego, CA: J. M. Sattler.

Sternberg, R. J., & Berg, C. A. (Eds.). (1992). *Intellectual development*. New York: Cambridge University Press.

Taylor, C. S., & Nolen, S. B. (2005). *Classroom assessment: Supporting teaching and learning in real classrooms*. Upper Saddle River, NJ: Pearson Education.

Thompson, B. (2002). *Score reliability: Contemporary thinking on reliability issues*. Thousand Oaks, CA: Sage.

Thorndike, R. M. (1997). *Measurement and evaluation in psychology and education* (6th ed.). Upper Saddle River, NJ: Merrill.

SUGGESTED WEB SITES

American Testing Company: http://www.americantesting.com

Educational Testing Service: http://www.ets.org

National Council on Measurement in Education: http://www.ncme.org

Psychological Corporation: http://www.psychcorp.com

Riverside Publishing: http://www.riverpub.com

ENDNOTES

1. See Nicholls (1989) for a more elaborate discussion of the differences between ability and intelligence.

2. Gardner (1983) for example, talks about seven different kinds of intelligence, all of which seem to reflect the content domains in which intelligence manifests itself rather than the structure or functioning of intelligence. All of the ideas proposed in his model can be incorporated into the framework provided in this chapter, but different content domains will inevitably lead to the inclusion of different indicants on formal tests.

3. Sternberg (1990) offers details of a series of studies on how individuals define *intelligence.*

4. See Barrett & Depinet (1991) for an outline of the parameters of this conversation as well as a critique of some commonly cited assertions.

5. Although this chapter reflects a synthesis of ideas that are common in many textbooks, Gronlund (1998) offers the most cogent synthesis of the procedures for writing strong items. Chapters 4–6 of that book informed this summary of item styles and limitations.

6. See Haladyna & Downing (1989) for more information on how this list was generated.

7. Although this table is from Gronlund (1998), this kind of approach to item construction emerged from Bloom, Engelhart, Furst, Hill, & Krathwohl (1956).

8. Crocker & Algina (1986) offer a more elaborate description of how these measures are computed.

9. Lord (1952) offered an elaborate study of how reliability is improved by accepting *p*-values that are higher than those estimated by correcting for the possibility of random guessing.

10. Crocker & Algina (1986) offer the most cogent summary of these levels of analysis.

11. See Feldt & Brennan (1993) for more details on how these approaches were derived.

12. *Structural equation modeling* (SEM), *hierarchical linear modeling* (HLM), and *Lisrel* techniques mentioned in Chapters 4 and 5 are appropriate for this kind of comparison.

13. Ghiselli, Campbell, & Zedeck (1981) offer the most straightforward account of the importance of regression to measurement and of its use in studies of predictive and postdictive validity.

14. Chapters 3 to 5 offer progressively more complex representations of this process.

15. Ghiselli, Campbell, & Zedeck (1981) offer a more detailed account of these concerns than is offered here.

16. Cronbach & Meehl (1955) published the first attempt to define this process. Their language is typically used as the standard by which other current conceptions are defined.

17. Ghiselli, Campbell, & Zedeck (1981) offer the most straightforward account of the importance of regression to measurement and of its use in studies of predictive and postdictive validity.

CHAPTER SEVEN

MEASURING COMPETENCE AND SKILL

Whereas *intelligence* was used to name the latent variable that is assumed to reflect *a collection of abilities, competence* will be used to name *a collection of skills.* Semantically, the terms *competence* and *ability* are sometimes used interchangeably (Glaser, 1963). This use reflects one hierarchy in which both ability and intelligence are latent variables that are inferred from the direct measurement of skills. Distinguishing intelligence and competence can also serve to distinguish *norm-referenced* and *criterion-referenced tools.* Before going into detail on how criterion-referenced tools are constructed and evaluated, I'll define task-focused constructs more clearly to illustrate a measurement advantage in distinguishing intelligence and competence.

WHAT IS COMPETENCE?

Differences between person-based and task-based comparisons are noteworthy because they affect the kinds of inferences supported by particular tools. The term *competence,* as it is used here, allows investigators to distinguish *skill as performance on a collection of tasks* from the comparative notion of *ability as a normative capacity* that limits the effect of effort.

In defining *competence* as a collection of skills, it becomes possible to think of human functioning as a broad range of competencies, evaluated in relation to the nature of particular tasks. Investigators who are committed primarily to measuring skill draw inferences about the structure, functioning, and origins of particular tasks. Competence at playing baseball, for example, may be comprised of the skills of pitching, batting, catching, and strategizing. Similarly, mathematical competence may be comprised of a range of particular computation and logic skills that can be isolated or used in combination. Notice that, in these definitions, there are no references to the performance of others. The adequacy of individuals' skill is determined by comparing their performance to a task-specific standard. The emphasis here will be on cognitive functioning, but competence-focused models also extend to the measurement of behavior and physiological processes covered in the next chapter.

ARE INTELLIGENCE AND COMPETENCE DIFFERENT CONSTRUCTS?

Variations in theoretical definitions of *epistemology* have led investigators to the distinction between intelligence and competence. *Norm-referenced measures of ability* are expected to facilitate relatively consistent conclusions about an individual's performance in relation to others such that knowledge acquires meaning in relation to people. *Criterion-referenced measures of skill* require that individuals' performance be compared to a predetermined set of standards, and knowledge is associated with specific tasks. Theoretical inferences about intelligence emerge from the use of norm-referenced tools whereas theoretical inferences about competence emerge from the use of criterion-referenced tools. Practitioners may use both kinds of evaluations when making decisions that affect the lives of individual respondents. They typically use norm-referenced information to make long-term or general predictions about someone's abilities and criterion-referenced information to make short-term or specific predictions about someone's current skill.

Imagining the theoretical normal curve (Figure 3.3), measures of intelligence are designed to place individuals' abilities within a normative distribution of other people's abilities. To explore intelligence, task performance is often a means to evaluating an individual's placement in a group. Investigators draw inferences about the structure and origin of intelligence from looking at distributions of persons in a population. When investigators are primarily committed to such normative models, they may incorporate skill as a bridge construct that addresses what a person can do.

Measures of competence are designed to place individuals' skills within a normative distribution of other skills. The same normal curve may be imagined, but individual differences in performance are a means to the end of evaluating a task's placement in a group of skills. Skills are evaluated in terms of their normative difficulty level whereas abilities are evaluated in terms of their presence or absence within a sample of respondents. While this distinction may seem easy to follow, procedures for designing new tools can be difficult to understand. Procedures for assessing both skill and abilities involve the coordination of person placement, skill placement, and task features, but the balance of these concerns differs.

WHAT IS A SKILL?

Skill is defined as expertise or facility in performing an action. The seemingly straightforward distinction between people-referenced and task-referenced standards becomes progressively less obvious as investigators begin to define the content of particular tools. Test blueprints, item formats, and administration procedures may look quite similar for measuring skills and abilities. Nevertheless, attention is given to very different components of the measurement process when inferences are drawn from these two kinds of tools.

Because criterion-referenced scores are not interpreted by simply comparing a person's performance to the performance of others, investigators using these tools are largely unconcerned with ranking individuals. They are more interested in verifying the stable placement of respondents on a skill continuum. Ideally, persons with particular skills should all be placed at the same point in a distribution of scores and scores would be valid even if all or most respondents were classified at the same level.

Skills to be measured using criterion-referenced tests are identified through a process of task analysis. *Task analysis* isolates components of a skill and the corresponding tasks associated with mastery. Acknowledging that different contexts demand different kinds of task analysis, investigators have distinguished activity analysis, cognitive task analysis, learning analysis, job or procedural analysis, and subject matter/content analysis.[1] These different domains focus on various features of competence and may be used in isolation or in combination. When investigators perform a task analysis, they do the following:

- classify tasks or skills as outcomes or competencies;
- inventory the skills or tasks associated with competence;
- select tasks to reflect each skill;
- decompose tasks into smaller indicants;
- sequence tasks or their components;
- verify the relation of outcomes to competence.

To select tasks for scrutiny, investigators often consider a range of questions. Table 7.1 outlines some decisions that have been made in early selection studies and address five dimensions: (1) the centrality of skills or tasks for achieving a goal, (2) how often skills or tasks are needed, (3) whether skills or tasks will be the same across contexts, (4) whether it

TABLE 7.1   Some Criteria for Selecting Tasks for Analysis

ISSUE	DEFINITION
Universality	Does everyone perform the task or skill?
Difficulty	How difficult is it to learn the task or skill?
Crucialness	What skills are crucial to the task? What tasks are crucial to demonstrating a skill?
Frequency	How often will tasks related to a single skill be performed? How often will skills related to a single task be performed?
Practicality	Is there a practical use for the skill or task?
Attainability	Can a skill be acquired or is it merely a goal? Can a task be mastered or are investigators measuring a process?
Quality	What are the qualitative features of a skill or task?
Deficiency	What does the absence of a skill look like? How does the absence of a skill affect task mastery?
Retention	Will the skill be apparent across contexts? Will the task serve a function across contexts?
Stability	Will subsequent training be necessary for maintaining the skill or performing a task?

is reasonable to expect everyone to learn a task or skill, and (5) the difficulty of the task or skill (Tracey, Flynn, & Legere, 1966).

When determining if a task or particular skill can undergo a task analysis, investigators often:

- verify the referent situation for the task or skill;
- compare tasks or skills to the selection criteria and determine the ranking of dimensions in relation to the construct under investigation;
- consider each skill or task and determine if it is crucial to the desired outcome;
- evaluate the frequency with which each task or skill will be necessary;
- standardize definitions of a skill or task in relation to the components of a theoretical framework and specify the minimum standards or conditions for mastery;
- evaluate the practicality of asking individuals to perform a task or skill and when it will be used;
- evaluate the difficulty of learning or demonstrating the tasks or skills;
- compare tasks or skills in the full model and determine their comparability for inclusion on a measure;
- revise the choice of skills or tasks to offer the strongest account of a theoretical model.[2]

Everyone who has fully mastered the same skill should be able to exhibit all components of that skill and the same can be said for tasks. A standard for passing is often used as a criterion for evaluating an individual's performance, but the measure itself is evaluated in relation to the balance of tasks or skills. Investigators also learn to distinguish evaluations of *process* and *products*. By identifying core quality indicators, investigators evaluate products. By dissecting the steps in task mastery, investigators consider a process.

Using rubrics to evaluate a completed task, investigators often rely on inductive logic to rank the difficulty of particular product-focused dimensions and draw conclusions about the required skill. Product-focused rubrics allow investigators to compare an individual's performance to a predetermined standard that accounts for differences in the structure of a product. Evaluations of different dance routines, for example, may be done using the same rubric even though the content and style of each routine is unique. The resulting criterion-referenced indicants can be interpreted directly in relation to predefined standards. When the details of products differ from one another, a more general set of guidelines can offer a common standard for comparing projects.

Evaluating the steps involved in demonstrating a skill, investigators inevitably ask what the end-point or product should look like. Suppose investigators wanted to measure the process of constructing a noteworthy painting. They might begin by identifying the features that make a painting noteworthy. Working deductively from that point, investigators would then identify important behaviors and characteristics that can be observed. Finding a way to place tasks in a meaningful order allows investigators to rank steps necessary for demonstrating a skill, but not all tasks are completed using linear logic. Many investigators also identify and test common errors associated with demonstrating skills to verify that only the intended inferences explain behavior.

When using task analysis to classify measurable knowledge and skills, taxonomies can facilitate balance in a measure. Taxonomies allow researchers to organize skills or tasks into meaningful categories, useful for selecting appropriate indicants.[3] Taxonomies are selected by specifying a theoretical purpose for classifying tasks or skills. Researchers may explore or revise the assumptions and purposes of existing taxonomies or may invent their own. The practicality of a taxonomy is verified by assessing its comprehensiveness and whether it offers clear guidance concerning how to measure the tasks or skills in question. The selected taxonomy becomes the criterion for evaluating components of every test blueprint generated when exploring a set of competencies.

To illustrate some of the challenges associated with measuring products and processes, product-focused techniques for *computer adaptive testing* will be compared with process-focused methods of measuring *sequential tasks.* Computer adaptive testing involves a conceptual review of *item-response theory* whereas sequential task analysis typically relies on *conventional test development procedures.* These classifications are somewhat arbitrary, but illustrate some of the complex forms of decision making reflected in criterion-referenced tests. Invariably, the final tools for measuring skills are evaluated using interactionist logic, regardless of whether they are intended to evaluate processes or products.

MAKING CONNECTIONS

Identify a form of competence in your field of interest. What skills would be necessary for exhibiting such competence? Do the skills reflect a process or a product? What might task analysis entail? How would you determine performance standards for each skill? Will your measures be unidimensional or multidimensional?

DESIGNING SKILL-FOCUSED TOOLS

Most practitioners prefer using criterion-referenced tools because they work with individuals rather than large groups. To help someone in distress, for example, clinicians often diagnose the availability of particular skills and develop a plan for augmenting missing skills. There are some forms of research that also benefit from this kind of thinking, leading investigators to use criterion-referenced tools. Nevertheless, these tools are quite time-consuming to develop and methods for the design and evaluation of criterion-referenced measures are not often covered in introductory coursework. Despite the difficulty of designing such tools, their use is becoming more widespread in both research and the workplace.

Computer adaptive testing, for example, is becoming common for several reasons.[4] For high-stakes testing, this approach offers better test security because item banks are typically stored on a computer, items are administered one item at a time, and there are no opportunities for respondents to revisit items and identify patterns. In this kind of testing, respondents can work at their own pace and investigators may choose not to record their speed. Respondents stay productive because they work only on items that are likely to be moderately challenging; items are generated to match the skills of respondents such that none are likely to be very easy or difficult.

Researchers also like computer adaptive testing because scoring and test production can be done using a computer and there is little or no ambiguity about a respondent's intended answers. The possibility of metaphorical chads or dimples, erasures, or unreadable answers is eliminated when respondents are asked to make key strokes or mouse clicks to indicate their response. This technology often permits immediate scoring and allows for the pretesting of new items by embedding them in each test. When old and new items are incorporated into a single test, investigators can program the computer to immediately delete faulty items.

A final advantage of computer adaptive testing is the ability to rely on multiple-item formats within a single test. Although computers have limitations, investigators can present items one at a time or in format clusters to help respondents identify the manifest agenda for that item. They can administer items that have dichotomous correct/incorrect answers alongside items that are scaled. Investigators can also include pictures and other kinds of nontextual representations of information that were once too expensive to include on formal tests.

Computer adaptive tests work from the assumption that the constructs to be measured are unidimensional although different tests may be designed to evaluate different constructs. In contrast, *sequential analysis* hinges on the assumption that skills are multidimensional and can be arranged hierarchically. Skills required early in a process may or may not overlap with skills later in the process. Computer adaptive testing may be systematic, but it is not necessarily appropriate when skills are sequential.

Our example of sequential analysis will concern cognitive functioning in a moment-by-moment sequence, but a sequential approach can also involve behavioral assessments, learning processes, or procedural steps. They can also reflect the deconstruction of curricular agendas. Generally speaking, investigators identify tasks to be deconstructed and specific behaviors that make up the task. They then label sequential dependencies by determining the relationship each action has with all other actions. Investigators consider whether relations form subordinate/superordinate hierarchies, coordinated patterns, overlapping elements, or no clear connections. Next, investigators rank behaviors to account for the nature of particular relations and plan a progression for measuring the sequence. They set a formal criterion for determining mastery for each behavior in a sequence and identify any kinds of interventions that might influence test performance. They also try to assess where in a hierarchy of competence individuals are likely to fall at the onset of a study and verify that individuals in a sample show equivalent characteristics. Investigators try to construct items for a sequential test that are mutually exclusive yet exhaustive of the skills required for task completion. On the final tool, skills are ranked in the order in which they are exhibited as a task is completed.

Whereas computer adaptive testing focuses on inferences about a skill, *sequential skills analysis* considers the range of skills that are necessary for task completion. When a sequence is being measured, investigators also evaluate the order in which skills are completed and may be interested in time intervals as well as in the placement of skills in a hierarchy.

Both *computer adaptive testing* and *sequential skills analysis* are classified here as criterion-referenced tools because the evaluation of the tools involves comparison of performance to a set of known standards. This kind of testing necessitates a much clearer understanding of a task than may be available when investigators rely on norm-referenced assumptions. They rely on criterion-referenced measurement when they have a clear definition of the kind of competence they would like to measure.

Fundamentals of Item-Response Theory

To compare individual items to a performance standard, investigators commonly use item-response theory and its derivations. Along with altering the logic associated with the pan-normalization principle, investigators require a new language for representing their procedures.

Mathematical Assumptions.   The mathematics for evaluating criterion-referenced tools can be quite challenging. Currently, *item-response theory* (IRT) is probably the most commonly used method for evaluating item performance, although conceptually similar techniques are also used.[5] A full understanding of this approach involves a change from *least squares statistical assumptions,* commonly underlying most of the methods reviewed so far, to *maximum likelihood estimates* or *Bayesian assumptions.*[6] Computer adaptive testing is greatly enhanced by the change in mathematical assumptions and so will be contrasted with sequential skills tests to exemplify some of the fundamental differences between conventional and IRT approaches to criterion-referenced measurement.

Briefly, *maximum likelihood estimation* is a means by which the parameters of a population distribution are predicted using obtained sample information and estimates of missing information.[7] Investigators make a predetermined assumption about the shape of the population distribution. One kind of assumption that you should already find familiar is the least squares idea that total scores will be normally distributed in a population. Unlike this conventional assumption, IRT involves assumptions about *item characteristic curves* and *proficiency estimates.* Items are evaluated as independent entities because each response is weighted heavily when estimating proficiency and total scores have no mathematical meaning.

Maximum likelihood estimation typically starts with a predefined standard that reflects a great deal of experience with the construct to be measured and little controversy over the definition of the construct. Despite the accepted definition of a construct, investigators rarely have information on all the parameters that give the distribution its predicted form. Using available information along with rather arbitrary, but patterned probability estimates for missing parameters, it becomes possible to test the relative fit or likelihood that particular models explain population parameters. Data from respondents allow investigators to estimate some parameters even if other parameters remain inferred. Not surprisingly, this process is iterative in that investigators can test many different kinds of models before finding one that best fits the available information. IRT is actually one set of models that are used when estimating parameters for item performance. Other theoretical options are also possible even though they will not be reviewed here.[8]

Important Scores.   The previous chapter familiarized you with *raw scores* or the number of items answered correctly and with *formula scores* or those raw scores corrected for guessing. In computer adaptive testing, these scores are uninterpretable because respondents do not answer the same test items and are expected to correctly answer only about half the items they do see.[9] Estimates of a person's *proficiency score* (θ) are not tied to a specific set of items and show a population distribution with a mean of 0 and a standard deviation of 1. To draw inferences about proficiency requires little or no ambiguity in an answer to the question, "proficient at what?" Proficiency estimates of a known skill may be derived from responses to one item or multiple items on a computer adaptive test.

When investigators would like to convert a *proficiency estimate* into the score expected if respondents actually answered every question, they calculate the *item pool score* (IPS). $P_j(\theta)$ reflects an item's true score. Parameters a_j, b_j, and c_j estimate item discrimination, difficulty, and guessing parameters, respectively. Investigators calculate each item's *estimated true score* using the following formula:

ITEM TRUE SCORE ESTIMATE

$$P_j(\theta) = \frac{c_j + (1 - c_j)}{[1 + e^{-a_j(\theta - b_j)}]}$$

Next, an item pool score is calculated by adding each item true score estimate to predict performance on all items in the pool. This is represented by the following formula:

ITEM POOL SCORE

$$\varepsilon(IPS) = \sum P_j(\theta)$$

The minimum item pool score is $c_j(\sum c_j)$ to acknowledge the minimal correction for guessing. The maximum item pool score is the number of items in the pool, an index that is extrapolated from the number of items answered and is sometimes equated with a total score.

Using a subset of items from an item pool score, investigators can also calculate *item subpool scores*. Item subpool scores are commonly used when investigators try to equate two tests. In such a process, investigators may be interested in comparing performance on the exact same indicants of a construct administered using two methods (e.g., computers or paper and pencil), or they may be interested in comparing parallel forms of the same blueprint, as is common when computing reliabilities for norm-referenced tests. The minimum subpool score is the sum of guessing parameters (c_j) for selected items from the total item bank, and the maximum score is the number of items in the subpool.

Important Scales.   The range of scales commonly associated with true score theory are now being introduced into middle and high school science classes and so have been given a cursory review. Nevertheless, a reminder of those scales may serve as a helpful comparison with the parallel IRT scales (Figure 3.3).

Psychometric interpretation of true score theory relies heavily on transformations of respondents' total scores. The percentage correct is computed such that scores range from 0 to 100 percent. These scores can also be converted to standard scores such that all total scores are converted to a scale with the same mean and standard deviation.[10] For *z-scores,* the mean is 0 and the standard deviation is 1. For *T-scores,* the mean is 50 and the standard deviation is 10 (McCall, 1939). The general formula for such calculations is:

STANDARD SCORE FORMULA

$$y = ax + b$$

In this formula, y is the standard scale score, x is a person's raw score, a is σ_y / σ_x and b is $\mu_y - a\mu_x$ such that μ_x and σ_x reflect raw score mean and standard deviation parameters, and μ_y and σ_y are the target mean and standard deviation. Investigators also compute *percentile scores* by comparing an individual's total score to a normative distribution and determining how many respondents typically score lower than the individuals being evaluated. A *percentile rank* involves adding the total frequency of all those scores below an obtained score and half the frequency for the same obtained score. That total is then divided by the number of respondents in a sample. To *normalize a scale,* investigators compare an obtained distribution of scores to the normal curve distribution using a set mean and standard deviation. Investigators may also add a correction for guessing to the total score distribution, but typically do not adjust individual item responses.

With IRT, using a respondent's total score to calculate someone's placement in a skill distribution offers a meaningless estimate. Instead, placement decisions are made using *proficiency estimates* (θ) that are calculated using maximum likelihood or Bayesian modal techniques. To construct a *percentile* or other similar derived linear scale, investigators calculate the percentile for *linear θ-based estimates. Percentile ranks* can also be used to compare proficiency estimates, even though the intervals between estimates are unequal if respondents do not answer the same number or kind of items. Proficiency estimates are ordinarily normalized such that there is a mean of 0 and a standard deviation of 1 for the population of respondents. Guessing estimates of total scores are unnecessary if a guessing parameter is included when estimating the *item characteristic curve.*

In short, investigators using IRT do not think about raw scores and rely instead on *proficiency scores, item pool scores,* or *item subpool scores.* IRT scales ideally result in distributions that have:

- sufficient width to ensure that few scores fall at extreme ends of a distribution;
- sufficient compactness so that only small portions of a skill continuum remain unused;
- average scores that fall near the center of a skill continuum;
- scale units that accurately reflect the tasks being measured;
- a stopping algorithm that is calculated using reported score units rather than proficiency estimates;

Why IRT?   Many researchers who are not involved in large-scale testing use a hybrid of least squares and maximum likelihood techniques because the two systems offer different means for achieving similar ends. For investigators whose work requires criterion-referenced tools, it is worthwhile to rise to the challenge of learning the statistical languages of *maximum likelihood estimation* and *Bayesian statistical theory* because more information on the performance of each test item becomes available. If tests are used to determine someone's qualifications for brain surgery, for example, investigators want the measurement to be as precise as possible.

IRT hinges on four basic assumptions that are often untenable for every variable in a research design, even if they are applicable to some variables. For these models:

- All item parameters are known with certainty.
- The same item parameters apply to all respondents taking a test.
- After controlling for the characteristics of respondents and item parameters, all responses are independent.
- The order of item presentation is irrelevant.

When investigators are working within conventional test settings, IRT and more traditional methods of item analysis typically yield the same results. However, when investigators are using computer adaptive tests, IRT offers many advantages. Briefly, IRT provides more information on item functioning and estimates of proficiency than conventional techniques. Despite these advantages, there are limitations to this approach. Most importantly, all the assumptions that underlie IRT must be rigorously applied. Probably the most difficult assumption concerns the requirement that items assess a *known unidimensional variable* and if a measure is multidimensional, more than one test is designed. In research, constructs may or may not be understood well enough for evaluations based on IRT.

Another limitation concerns the absence of estimates for *item/context effects.* Because IRT assumes that the presentation order has no effect, there are no estimates of learning elicited from exposure to previous items or respondents' emotional states (e.g., anxiety or fatigue) during the test. Investigators try to administer tests using the same environments across participants, but this does not mean that the context is identical. Similarly, limitations of computer displays and respondent experience with computers lead to the likelihood that an item can introduce error through context interaction.

Investigators who use IRT also assume that parameter estimates constitute "true" values, so they do not include systematic error estimates in their analysis. Often relying on computer-simulated parameters, these researchers admit that a model may be incorrect, but do not estimate calibration errors or those associated with ambiguously defined skills. Underestimated calibration errors may be caused by item selection rules, respondents' answers to untested items, and the calibration of untested items. When investigators can assume that such error is random, the concern is alleviated. More commonly, the error is likely to reflect a systematic bias that remains undetected.

Without becoming too involved in the mathematical details of how and why IRT is used, this conceptual overview may help you determine if more measurement coursework would enhance the design of your next research project. Some of the basic vocabulary associated with IRT can illuminate where investigators begin when evaluating skills. Linking conceptual details to computer adaptive testing highlights the benefits of maximum likelihood methods for use in situations where all respondents do not answer the same questions. Contrasting this information with the more conventional techniques of sequential analysis offers a taste of what test developers are excited about while acknowledging that most new investigators will not work with the kind of large-scale testing programs that are generated using IRT and Rasch techniques. Researchers are rarely certain enough about the parameters and definitions of the constructs they are exploring to rely heavily on IRT.

■ ■ ■ ■ ■

MAKING CONNECTIONS

Find an existing test in your field and outline the steps you would take to transform the data set for use with item response theory. What scores would you want to calculate? What scales would be helpful? Would you learn something important from relying on maximum likelihood estimates that could not be discovered using least squares estimation?

ESTABLISHING A SKILL-BASED BLUEPRINT

As is the case for all measurement tools, a blueprint is typically constructed to specify the content of each tool. Blueprints used either for computer adaptive testing or measuring a sequence of skills are likely to contain different kinds of information, but both address the structure of evaluated skills and rules for judging the correctness of a response. The difficulty level of indicants in computer adaptive tests are likely to hold slightly different meaning than that associated with measuring steps in a process, but item difficulty remains an important parameter for writing and evaluating items. Discrimination and guessing parameters may or may not be important and the two approaches rely on different equating procedures for comparing items against a blueprint.

Blueprints for Computer Adaptive Tests

Investigators use computer adaptive tests when they have a single variable that they already understand well enough to construct an item bank.[11] In such banks, items may be clustered into groups with equivalent measurement parameters. Logically speaking, a computer adaptive test is designed so that respondents are asked to answer only those items that offer improvements in decisions of where they fit along a latent competence continuum. The content of each test is adapted to the person taking the test such that respondents do not see items that are predicted to be too easy or too difficult. All respondents will see a different set of items and are expected to get about half of their assigned items right and half wrong. Because total scores for a test have no meaning in this approach, item characteristics are commonly included in a blueprint and each item is treated independently in analyses. Table 7.2 lists the current parameters assumed to be essential for computer adaptive tests.

Because IRT requires all items in a particular bank to be indicants of a unidimensional variable, it is easy to see how investigators have found these procedures useful for measuring discrete skills. Each item is evaluated by comparing features of an *item characteristic curve* obtained when the item is pilot-tested and evaluated in comparison to a predetermined IRT model (see Chapter 4 for definitions and examples of such curves). *Unidimensionality* for a test blueprint cannot be overemphasized because differences across items ideally reflect only those parameters that are necessary for determining skill

TABLE 7.2 Essential Blueprint Parameters for Computer Adaptive Tests

PARAMETER	DEFINITION
Unidimensional construct	Indicants of the skill to be estimated form a scale with one dimension and only one dimension.
Item discrimination (a)	Estimates reveal whether items adequately differentiate high and low levels of skill.
Item difficulty (b)	Estimates indicate the proportion of individuals for each point on a skill continuum who answer correctly.
Guessing (c)	Estimates designate the degree to which responses are affected by guessing or item sensitization.
Task analysis results	The content features that make up a skill are identified and represent multiple levels of difficulty falling along a single continuum.

Note: The letters after some parameters are commonly used in IRT formulas to represent the designated item feature.

placement. If there were more than one skill on a single test, placement decisions would become inaccurate. When investigators want to explore multidimensional constructs, they typically construct *testlets* that involve essentially independent blueprints and scoring procedures for each skill.

To estimate a respondent's proficiency (θ), he or she usually begins a test by answering an item predicted to be at an intermediate level for the members of a relevant population. If answers are correct, items become progressively more difficult until the respondent starts to answer incorrectly or until an accurate estimate of his or her skill is maximized. Incorrect responses lead to progressively easier items. Through this iterative process, investigators are able to maximize accuracy in evaluating skills while minimizing boredom from too many easy items or frustration and confusion from too many difficult items. Knowing this much, it may not seem surprising to learn that *estimates of item difficulty* form an important parameter of a blueprint for this kind of test.

Using conventional criteria, investigators estimate item difficulty by looking at the proportion of respondents in a norm group who answer an item correctly. Using IRT, ideal difficulty distributions are rectangular in shape such that persons with a skill answer correctly and those without a skill do not.[12] *Item-ability regressions* are explored by subdividing a distribution into skill-dependent difficulty intervals. Then, investigators explore the proportion of people answering correctly within each skill interval.[13] This *item-choice algorithm,* coordinating correct responses and item difficulty, allows a computer to generate predictions about which items to assign to respondents so that the full content of a test is covered and each answer offers the maximum amount of placement information.

A second parameter for generating a blueprint involves decisions about the *discriminating power* of an item. You may remember that investigators using conventional criteria often consider the *biserial correlation* between an item and a total test score when determining if high scorers perform better on that item.[14] With IRT, investigators look at the *slope* in the *item characteristic curve* and select items with slopes greater than 1 (see Chapter 4). Slopes less than 1 indicate that items offer little placement information and add a constant to the distribution.

A third, *guessing parameter* is sometimes called a sensitivity parameter and reflects the *asymptote* of an item characteristic curve. Ideally, this parameter is 0, but items can be acceptable if this estimate is less than .2. A guessing parameter is most essential for selection-type item formats, but may also be helpful when there is a potential for one item to teach respondents how to think about subsequent items. Figure 7.1 offers a graphic illustration of a hypothetical item characteristic curve with parameters *a, b,* and *c* marked for that item.

The final set of blueprint parameters concerns the *tasks that make up the skill* being assessed. Each task is usually represented by a category in the blueprint and investigators construct enough items to cover all difficulty levels for each category. Similarly, guessing parameters and discrimination indices are calculated separately for each item.

Blueprints for Sequential Measures of Skill

To explore the order of skill acquisition or the process by which a skill is exhibited, many investigators try to hold the difficulty level of each item constant and place greater emphasis on an item's discrimination power. Starting with a task, they take a microlevel approach to identify the skills involved in task performance and indicants of each skill. The resulting rubric may contain more than one dimension of a skill, but within each dimension, item difficulty is often held constant so that the skill, and not the item structure, is assessed. Table 7.3 contains a sample activity rubric for the process of constructing a noteworthy painting. Notice that one dimension focuses on the subject matter, a second on color usage, and a

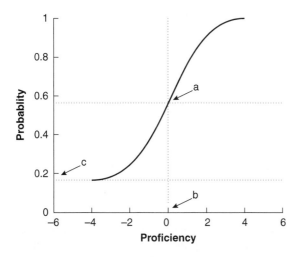

FIGURE 7.1   Graphic Representation of an Item Characteristic Curve

TABLE 7.3   Sample Blueprint for Steps in Producing a Painting

PROCEDURES	QUALITY		
	High *(Original)*	*Medium* *(Typical)*	*Low* *(No polish)*
Step 1: Choice of subject matter			
Tangible objects			
Symbolic			
Expressive			
Step 2: Select a representational style			
Photographic			
Abstract			
Impressionistic			
Surrealistic			
Step 3: Introduce texture and balance			
One-dimensional			
Two-dimensional			
Three-dimensional			
Step 4: Color usage			
Mix of colors			
Subtle tones			
Bold primary tones			
Natural tones			

Note: This is a purely fictional example.

third on the painting's representational style. Within each dimension, items are constructed to be as parallel in difficulty as possible, but across dimensions, difficulty levels vary. Representational style, for example, may be more difficult to put forth than selecting a subject, but within each category the options are parallel.

Measurement of an activity sequence often involves observational formats or secondary analysis of artifacts collected as the demonstration of a skill unfolds. Scoring rubrics invariably match the test blueprint and blueprints contain enough detail so that trained evaluators can adapt them for use as rating scales. Table 7.4 offers a sequence for evaluating metacognitive decision making related to coursework. Notice that questions may be answered dichotomously or expanded in a narrative, but coded into nominal categories.

When sequential methods are used, it is helpful to have more than one person rating each sequence of actions and to compare those ratings (see Chapters 5 and 8 for references to inter-rater reliability). Having students, peers, and instructors rate metacognitive decisions, for example, allows investigators to look for convergence in such evaluations. A team of raters is more likely to notice flaws in instructions and evaluation procedures because inconsistencies would invariably emerge. When ratings are made by evaluators with no personal stake in the outcome, investigators might also be able to detect shortcomings in the abilities of individual raters because poor quality ratings would deviate substantially from others in the collection. The effects of extreme scores can be minimized in subsequent

TABLE 7.4 Metacognitive Steps for Evaluating Study Habits

QUESTION	CODES
Why am I studying this material?	It's assigned, useful, or interesting.
How well do I need to know this material?	Know the gist. Be ready to discuss, to evaluate, or to elaborate.
How fast can I read this?	Slowly, normal pace, fast
How many hours are available for studying?	Less than 1, 1 to 3, more than 4
How many days until class?	Record the number.
How does my ability compare with other students in class?	Superior, equal to, or poorer than others
What is my instructor's intellectual orientation?	Theoretical, applied, Socratic
Can I identify the major terms and topical themes?	Yes/No
Have I studied this topic before?	Yes/No
Have I read anything else by the assigned authors?	Yes/No
Is there a place for me to use the information I am learning?	Yes/No
Have I set short-term goals for studying?	Yes/No
Have I set long-term goals for studying?	Yes/No
Do I feel relaxed and confident about studying?	Yes/No
Am I anxious or tense?	Yes/No
Am I engaging in negative self-talk about studying or about the course?	Yes/No
Can I master this material?	Yes/No

Note: Adapted from "Task Analysis Methods for Instructional Design," by D. H. Jonassen, M. Tessmer, & W. H. Hannum. p. 144. Copyright 1999 by Lawrence Erlbaum Associates, Inc. Reprinted with permission.

analyses by combining scores across reviewers. Estimates of accuracy can be generated from such pooled ratings.

MAKING CONNECTIONS

Imagine designing a criterion-referenced test blueprint. Would you use computer adaptive testing or a sequential skills test? Why? What content dimensions would you include? What item parameters would be important? What could you do to verify your decisions?

PROCEDURES FOR TEST CONSTRUCTION

To build a criterion-referenced test, investigators typically use many of the procedures that have been described in previous chapters, yet alter some of the decision rules. For computer adaptive testing, for example, each item carries a great deal of weight in determining someone's placement along a skill continuum. There is no room in such a tool for poorly functioning items. When evaluating a process, investigators may find themselves repeatedly reviewing the same task as it undergoes completion, essentially treating steps in a process like different skills. If a process is difficult to observe, sequential evaluation of skills sometimes involves inferences such as those made in the metacognitive example of how a task is accomplished. Some of the fine-grained nuances of these design issues will be briefly reviewed here, but the nature of the skills to be measured also plays a role in the procedures used to design actual instruments.

Designing a Computer Adaptive Test

Investigators using computer adaptive tests consider four aspects of the process:

- the design of a blueprint and the construction of items for each blueprint category;
- the design and functioning of the system on which a test will be administered;
- test parameters for beginning, ending, and selecting items during a test;
- the calibration of items and estimates of proficiency.

Comparing Items to a Blueprint. Investigators use common item-writing rules and knowledge of the content being tested to create a large pool of items (Flaugher, 2000). They often rely on paper-and-pencil responses from members of a target population to pretest items and evaluate the item's suitability for particular categories. This cycle is repeated until all categories on a blueprint are represented with enough items to cover the full range of difficulty levels.

Responses from members of a pilot sample undergo two kinds of review. A *test specialist review* relies on conventional or IRT-specific statistics to evaluate each item's performance for the pretest sample. Discrimination, difficulty, and guessing parameters are estimated and compared. A *test sensitivity review,* often conducted before items are pilot-tested, involves the purging of offensive or biased assumptions that may be embedded in the content of an item. Answers from a pilot sample may offer additional evidence for item insensitivity as respondents either skip items or offer ambiguous responses.

To evaluate the quality of a blueprint, investigators select a subset of the original item pool by identifying those items that are strong enough to offer an independent assessment of someone's proficiency. Blueprints may be compared with a taxonomy to ensure that the skill being measured is unidimensional. Then, selected items are compared with a test blueprint to ensure that the final item bank contains the full range of content to be evaluated and that multiple items can represent each level of a skill continuum. Matching indicants and categories inevitably leads to a critique of the blueprint itself as investigators find gaps in their initial plan. Investigators test the balance of an item bank or blueprint by simulating tests for hypothetical persons representing different skill levels. This allows them to verify that every category on a test has enough challenging items for a high scorer and enough easy items for a low scorer to represent the full range of the assessed skill. They can also determine if the task analysis of each skill is appropriately specific. Adding items that are not directly connected to the measured skill can offer a contrast effect during this item-identification process, but are deleted from the final item bank.

Once items are selected, investigators convert the format for computer administration. Then, they may ask participants to take both the computer version and a paper-and-pencil version of the test. Comparing information from both tests, investigators can determine if respondents are placed at the same point on the skill continuum. The IRT model acts as a standard to which the performance of each item is compared. When scores on both kinds of tests match and meet IRT criteria, items are said to have a good fit with the IRT model. When enough items are available to test the full blueprint, a computer adaptive test is ready for use.

System Constraints.   Researchers rarely have all the resources that are taken for granted by testing corporations. However, they still face some of the same decisions about the computer systems and environments in which their test will be administered. Computer adaptive testing requires a system that will *present items, record responses,* and *collect other required data* such as reaction times or the number of keystrokes associated with a response.[15] To evaluate system components, investigators ask the following questions:

- How does the computer system operate?
- What hardware constraints are important?
- What software components would be beneficial?
- What human factors are likely to affect scores?

When relying on computers as research tools, investigators ask themselves whether their equipment should be connected to a server. They also explore hardware constraints that will influence the timing of item presentation, devices for responding, and the display characteristics. Ideally, the presentation of items should be quick, responding devices easy to use, and the display clear. For some systems, it may be easier to achieve these goals if computers are connected to a server. If portability is important, investigators will benefit from freestanding computers.

For long-term use, investigators also concern themselves with whether hardware will have sufficient power and how power shortages will be accommodated in the storing of responses. They also decide whether printers and removable storage devices will be necessary. To establish station equivalence, investigators are careful to check the calibration of all components on the computer and to regularly check that calibration while the system is in use.

Software continues to be easier to find, use, and modify for research purposes. This means that investigators can use a much wider range of item formats and response methods with relatively little effort. One test may contain multiple item formats and investigators notice little difference in performance as long as each format is presented in a clear and concise way. Selection and supply items can also take many different forms as long as investigators can find a way to record responses. When making software decisions, investigators are wise to imagine the perspectives of respondents and to develop simple routines for *recording responses, monitoring progress,* and *restarting a system* should a session be interrupted or multiple users require the same equipment. It is also helpful to have the computer *acknowledge responses* by changing the display when individuals respond.

Human factors are less easily anticipated, but most investigators try to maximize performance by imagining respondents' perspectives. Considering the conditions under which a test is administered, investigators may ask if the *setting is comfortable,* if the *lighting is adequate,* and if respondents *have as much space* as they might need to move around. *Minimizing distractions* in a test environment is usually important, but researchers may sometimes want to alter the environment as part of an experimental manipulation.

On a more emotional level, investigators may want to imagine the degree of comfort participants bring to the use of computers. By *offering practice problems,* they can teach respondents about the process of answering and the kinds of questions they will be asked. Investigators may identify *individual differences in respondents' abilities* such as color-blindness or problems with eye–hand coordination that are tangential to the test situation. At the very least, investigators usually offer advice to respondents on *how they might find help,* either on the computer screen itself or by attracting the attention of a research assistant.

Determining a Test's Structure.   Three decisions are essential to administering a computer adaptive test. Investigators decide (1) what item is used to start a test, (2) how subsequent items will be selected, and (3) when to stop presenting items. You may remember that investigators are looking for a proficiency estimate (θ) for each respondent by selecting those items that will maximize the prediction of performance, minimize the number of items presented, and represent all content aspects of the test. Norm-referenced tests strive to maximize variation in individuals' performance by asking all respondents to answer easy, difficult, and moderately difficult items. Criterion-referenced tests of this kind strive to minimize the variance in each person's answers and ask them to respond only to those items necessary for accurately defining their placement.

The *first item given* to a respondent is usually determined by estimating the probability of proficiency using information about the population from which the respondent is a member. Sometimes age is the population parameter, but gender or knowledge from previous tests may also be used to determine a starting point. Decisions about how to start are drawn from statistical probabilities as well as knowledge of respondents' characteristics.

The start items may be selected from different points on a blueprint even if they reflect the same difficulty level. Investigators often have a range of items to use first so that multiple respondents with the same characteristics do not always start with the same item.

Determining *which item to present next* is dependent on whether respondents answer an initial item correctly or incorrectly. Subsequent items are selected to offer the maximum amount of proficiency information while offering a balanced representation of the content of the test. After each response, proficiency is estimated using the distribution of prior responses as well as information about the blueprint to determine the next item.

To determine *when to stop,* investigators often use one of two methods. They may use a *fixed number of items* as the stop criterion or a *fixed level of accuracy* for a proficiency estimate. If a fixed number of items is the stop parameter, respondents are given items that will improve the accuracy of their placement but answer the same number of items as everyone else in the sample. When an accuracy parameter is used, the iterative process of generating items for respondents continues until the accuracy standard is met.

Calibrating Items. The process of calibrating items involves three goals:

- characterize variation among items in relation to a standard;
- determine practical item-selection rules;
- calibrate items in relation to a common scale.

Investigators expect all items on a test to measure the same thing and use a family of procedures to evaluate what happens when a respondent meets an item.[16] Our assumption is that items represent skills on a latent competence variable. Three different models illustrate how investigators try to fit an IRT model to obtained data and use that information to designate performance characteristics for each item. Once an item is calibrated in relation to a given collection of item parameters, future respondents' performance can be evaluated using initial placement information for that item. Maximum likelihood parameters associated with each item allow investigators to predict respondents' performance on future items using information about their performance on even one start item.

The selected models evaluate item functioning. The simplest IRT model offers a theoretical *proficiency estimate* (θ) by using the *item difficulty* parameter *(b).* This *one-parameter logistic model* (1-PL) is sometimes called the Rasch model and is represented with the formula:

ONE-PARAMETER LOGISTIC MODEL

$$P(\theta) = \frac{1}{1 + e^{-(\theta + b)}}$$

One limitation of this model is the assumption that the discriminating functions are parallel for all items. A two-parameter model was introduced to acknowledge the fact that items of various difficulty levels are also likely to differ in their *discrimination power (a).* Put another way, the *slope* of an *item characteristic curve* is likely to differ across items. This *two-parameter logistic model* (2-PL) includes estimates for item difficulty and discrimination and is represented in the following formula:

TWO-PARAMETER LOGISTIC MODEL

$$P(\theta) = \frac{1}{1 + e^{-a(\theta+b)}}$$

Allowing for the possibility that respondents may inflate their score through *guessing (c)* on selection-type items, a *three-parameter logistic model* was also designed. The third guessing parameter is graphically represented as the *asymptote* or the point at which an item characteristic curve hits the *y*-axis. Not surprisingly, investigators would like to see a 0 or near 0 number for estimates of this parameter. In the formula below, *c* is the binomial floor on the probability of answering an item correctly and the other parameters are the same as those for 1-PL and 2-PL models.

THREE-PARAMETER LOGISTIC MODEL

$$P(\theta) = c + \frac{1 - c}{1 + e^{-a(\theta+b)}}$$

Investigators may select any one of these models to explain the distribution of item responses, but those who consider more parameters may gain a better sense of how items can maximize the likelihood of accurately predicting proficiency. In selecting a model, most researchers also strive for parsimony and practicality. At this point, an item seems most useful if the item characteristic curve has a slope that is greater than 1, indicating that the item contributes to explaining an individuals' proficiency (slopes are near 0 or flat when the item contributes nothing to a test). The asymptote is ideally less than .2, and difficulty conforms to the position on a skill continuum. Parameters *a, b,* and *c* are usually calculated separately for each item and those calculations are used for estimating the proficiency of subsequent respondents. Figure 7.2 contains graphic representations of item characteristic curves for 1-PL, 2-PL, and 3-PL logistic models.

Determining Proficiency.   Item characteristic curves allow investigators to estimate a respondent's *proficiency* (θ).[17] Investigators can do this by relying on obtained data to predict future performance, using what is sometimes called the *brute force* method. Or, more commonly, investigators use an *analytic solution* in which they rely on an algorithm to approximate accuracy of the resulting estimate of θ. The algorithm operates like a predetermined standard or criterion for making comparisons.

Two algorithms are commonly used. The *maximum likelihood method* estimates proficiency by finding the *mode of the likelihood distribution. Bayesian modal estimates* add a *posterior distribution* of prior population information when calculating the mode. Regardless of the approach, *proficiency* is usually scaled with a mean of 0 and a standard deviation of 1 for a reference population of respondents. Using *maximum likelihood estimates,* investigators typically estimate the proficiency of a respondent using the following formula:

METHOD OF MAXIMUM LIKELIHOOD

$$P(x_i \mid \theta_i, \beta) = \prod_j P_j(\theta_i)^{x_{ij}} Q_j(\theta_i)^{1-x_{ij}}$$

In this formula x_i is the vector of item responses for person i where correct answers are scored as 1, and incorrect answers are scored as 0. In x_{ij}, j refers to the items administered. β_j is the parameter vector (a_j, b_j, c_j) for the item j with a matrix of all items labeled as β, and $Q(\theta) = 1 - P(\theta)$. Put another way, $P_j(\theta_i)^{x_{ij}}$ is the item characteristic curve for

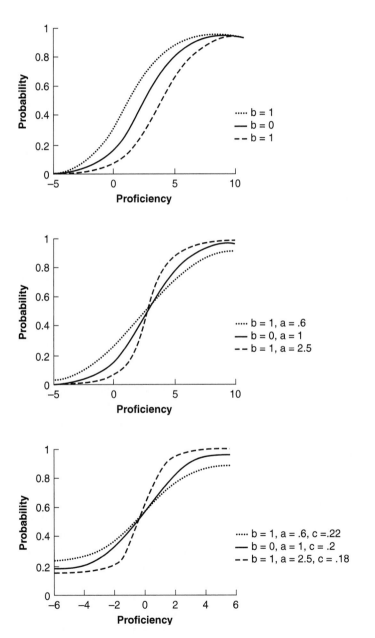

FIGURE 7.2 Comparison of 1-PL, 2-PL, and 3-PL Item Characteristic Curves

correct responses and $Q_j(\theta_i)^{1-x_{ij}}$ is the item characteristic curve for incorrect responses when x is 0 or the midpoint of the standardized distribution.

Adding a posterior distribution to the estimate, the formula for *Bayesian modal estimates* is:

BAYES MODAL ESTIMATES

$$p(\theta \,|\, x_i) \propto L(\theta \,|\, x_i)p(\theta)$$

In this approach, $p(\theta)$ reflects the estimate of θ prior to the observation x_i. This prior distribution is included in a multiplicative index of item parameters. When investigators minimize the width of a posterior distribution, they can make more accurate predictions. Lengthening a test with more items of similar difficulty can improve the accuracy of the prediction, but adding items that are too easy or too difficult will be like adding a constant to the estimate.

Equating Tests. Especially when respondents are not answering the same set of items, investigators spend time verifying the equivalence of tests and the interchangeability of items. When doing so, they consider several specifications. Researchers ask:

- When balancing content, do two tests measure the same construct?
- Can equity be achieved such that all individuals of a given proficiency level show an equal conditional distribution of scores?
- Do tests have the same parameters such that scores across populations are invariant when transformed to a common scale?
- Is the transformation of scores symmetrical such that equating X to Y is the same as equating Y to X?[18]

When equating a test, investigators start with old and new forms of the test and administer each to independent samples of respondents. Next, they compare data from these samples in one of three ways. Researchers may compare independent samples of persons taking old and new versions of the tests to one another, or compare the samples to an intended population. More commonly, however, investigators compare old and new forms of a test to a third *equating test.*

Four kinds of equating decisions are commonly made. Equating tests can either be administered as an *intact section* of one of the tests, or by using a *mixed format* to pepper items throughout an old or new test. The equating test can be taken by all or a subsample of respondents. In addition, answers to an equating test may or may not be included in a respondent's total score. Finally, some equating tests are comprised of anchor items that have a different format from both the old and new test, and those anchor items serve as a basis for comparison.

Investigators usually compare data using one of three kinds of mathematical models.[19] *Equipercentile equating* involves distribution-matching procedures. After converting proficiency estimates to standard scores, investigators may simply compare the shapes of each distribution. If they use a *chained equipercentile approach,* they do not make direct comparisons between two samples, but compare each sample to an anchor test score. *Frequency estimation* is also used, treating the respondents of old and new tests like a single sample and comparing the distributions to a population estimate.

Linear equating uses only a portion of the items from old and new tests to explore relationships between standard deviation units. In this approach, investigators verify that parallel items fall in the same deviations of a skill continuum. Measurement theorists have generated different models for completing these equating transformations and for drawing comparisons with a normal curve distribution. Variations in approaches reflect different underlying distribution characteristics.

For *item-response theory equating,* investigators assume that there is an available mathematical function to describe the probability that a respondent will answer correctly and for estimating proficiency scores.[20] By adding the item response functions for all items answered, the tests are equated. Put another way, investigators compare item pool scores for old and new tests to determine if they elicit the same proficiency score (θ).

Generalizations.   This is an obvious oversimplification of the mathematics involved in computer adaptive testing. Investigators also have complex methods of estimating item parameters using *marginal maximum likelihood* techniques. However, this introduction to IRT should offer enough information to help you see that investigators can test the calibration of single-item measures and treat each item as independent of other items when administering a test.

MAKING CONNECTIONS

Design a short computer adaptive test. How many items will you need? What parameters are important for each item? What will you do to pretest your measure? How will you ensure that items are balanced in relation to the blueprint?

Designing a Sequential Skills Test

To design a criterion-referenced tool for evaluating a sequence of skills, investigators often find a way to recreate the process of completing a task and construct separate indicants for each component of the process. Imagine, for example, following a family cook around the kitchen while he or she is making a favorite family recipe. Rather than letting this chef toss ingredients into a mixing bowl, you may want to collect the pinch of this or the dash of that measured out so effortlessly. For each step, you might want to evaluate the nature of all the ingredients that are in the recipe, the cooking instruments that are being used, the method by which instruments and ingredients come together, and the steps for cooking or baking the treat. A template of what to look for can guide the efficient documentation of what might otherwise be a lost treat.

Once this kind of task analysis is conducted, investigators often look at each documented indicant to determine if all indicants are necessary of if some indicants can be inferred from another. For one family recipe, measuring salt, baking powder, and flour for a dry ingredients bowl could constitute three documented steps. When dry ingredients are mixed with the wet ingredients, it may be unnecessary to remeasure salt, baking powder, and so forth. Instead, an observer might cluster smaller steps within larger steps to create a sequence of actions that are of relatively similar difficulty levels.

For the final tool, investigators typically work from a clear theoretical framework that outlines how test items are related to one another. All three parameters associated with computer adaptive testing are also associated with sequential skills analysis, but they take a slightly different form. Sequential analyses also scale and equate items in a succession of tasks.

Item Difficulty.   In measuring skill, investigators are not striving to maximize variance in item responses. They typically calculate the difficulty level of an item (*p*-value) by evaluating the proportion of respondents who answered correctly. Most items are expected to reflect easy or moderate difficulty levels. Investigators might also expect the same difficulty levels across items measuring a single skill, but different levels across a sequence of different skills. Hitting a ball, for example, may be more difficult than throwing one.

Looking at difficulty patterns for a group of related items, investigators can determine if their theoretical representations are appropriately challenging. If all items reflect an easy level of difficulty, for example, investigators might wonder about their reasons for measuring a particular skill. Yet, if the skills are necessary prerequisites for a more elaborate sequence of skills, as is common on Guttman scales, prerequisite items would have easy difficulty levels.

Item Discrimination.   When measuring skills, it is not reasonable to compare high and low scorers in a sample because such comparisons offer no information about what an individual can do. Instead, investigators evaluate how well particular items assess individual differences, estimating whether factors extraneous to the desired skill have contributed to test performance. They try to minimize extraneous influences by comparing actions from more than one group of examinees (see, for example, Millman & Popham, 1974). If a template can be consistently applied and differences in skill can be detected for each item, the value of that item increases. If the template can be appropriately applied to a completely irrelevant skill, investigators reevaluate the content of the template and look for items with greater discriminating power.

Instructional or Treatment Sensitivity.   A second method of estimating an item's discriminating power involves determining if respondents perform better after receiving instruction. In experiments, researchers may compare the performance of respondents who received instruction with those who do not (Cox & Vargas, 1966).[21] Treatment sensitivity studies are parallel to adding a guessing parameter in computer adaptive testing. Both techniques attempt to estimate systematic error variance. Comparing an individual's pretest and posttest scores can result in a *difference index* (*D*) ranging from −1.00 to 1.00, where high values are desirable.

To compare groups, investigators use an indicator of mastery to explore the role of forces other than a skill in test performance. This *sensitivity index* (*B*) allows investigators to draw comparisons among the performance of groups that do and do not receive instruction (Brennan, 1972).

SENSITIVITY INDEX

$$B = \left(\frac{U}{n_1}\right) - \left(\frac{L}{n_2}\right)$$

In this formula, n_1 is the total number of respondents who scored above a predetermined mastery cutoff, and n_2 is the total number below. U is the number above the criterion who correctly answered the item being evaluated and L is the number below the criterion who answered correctly. Assuming that instruction has an effect on performance, comparing the B-value for groups that do and do not receive instruction should ensure that there are respondents who score low. This sensitivity index offers information on whether the tool measures only common knowledge or whether specialized forms of knowledge are also assessed.

In addition to these two methods for assessing the effects of instruction, investigators also use more complex statistical methods that reflect the coordination of group characteristics. Gender, for example, may serve as a theoretically relevant predictor of performance and could be included in regression equations designed to test possible differences.

Indices of Agreement. Sometimes when investigators are building an item bank, they are interested in whether items are interchangeable. The most straightforward way of testing whether two items measure the same content is to use *chi square techniques* (χ^2) to compare responses; respondents who answer one item correctly should answer all interchangeable items correctly. (See Figure 7.3 for a sample of how responses are typically laid out and for the χ^2 formula.) In the formula, a, b, c, and d are the cell frequencies and n is the number of persons in the sample. The resulting coefficient is compared to a critical value of χ^2 with

**FIGURE 7.3 Sample Distribution Layout
and χ^2 Formula**

	ITEM 1	
ITEM 2	+	−
+	a	b
−	c	d

$$X^2 = \frac{n(ad - bc)^2}{(a + b)(c + d)(b + d)(a + c)}$$

one degree of freedom and the desired alpha level. (Appendix A contains χ^2 criterion scores.) A significant outcome in a χ^2 test would indicate that the two items can be equated.

Once investigators have verified the similarity among test items, they may test the magnitude of that similarity. Computing the *proportion of agreement* is one direct way to accomplish this (Harris & Pearlman, 1977). Using information from the cross-tabulation included in Figure 7.3, investigators identify the proportion of respondents who consistently answered the two items, either by correctly or incorrectly answering both problems, $P = (a + d)/n$. Investigators also use *weighted kappa coefficients* (see Chapter 5) when they are looking for hierarchical patterns of agreement, *Yule's Q* for distributions that can range from –1 to 1 with 0 indicating no effect, or *phi coefficients* for a 2 × 2 matrix of scores.[22]

YULE'S Q

$$Q = \frac{ad - bc}{\sqrt{(ad + bc)(ad + bc)}}$$

PHI COEFFICIENT

$$\phi = \frac{ad - bc}{\sqrt{(ac + bd + ad + bc)(ab + cd + ad + bc)}}$$

In these formulas, as in Figure 7.3, the letters refer to different cells in the cross-tabulation or confusion matrix representing the distribution of responses.

As with IRT, investigators can also determine if items are interchangeable by comparing the difficulty of the two items. Investigators modify their use of χ^2 to determine if differences in difficulty are small enough to be attributable to sampling errors. Using the points of mismatch between the two sets of responses, investigators compute the following:

CHI SQUARE TO EVALUATE MISMATCHES

$$X^2 = \frac{(|b - c| - 1)^2}{b + c}$$

Again, the computed statistic is contrasted to the value of χ^2 with one degree of freedom and a planned alpha level. In this case, investigators prefer to find nonsignificant results; significant values indicate that there are marked differences in the difficulty of the two items.

Generalizations. Investigators typically tailor their procedures for item analysis to the particular questions raised by the performance of particular items. There is marked disagreement on whether these procedures should be used to eliminate problematic items or whether these steps offer insight into the evaluation of instruction.[23] To make such decisions, researchers often coordinate the larger purpose of their investigation with item performance information. Researchers may or may not decide to eliminate or aggregate items, but when making such decisions they are careful to establish a fair test of their predictions.

It remains unethical to eliminate information until predicted findings are obtained (this ethical stance is discussed in Chapter 2).

MAKING CONNECTIONS

Design a sequential skills test. How did you identify the skills to be evaluated? Does your test involve a sequence of tasks related to a single skill or multiple skills related to a competency? How were items constructed? What item parameters are important?

RELIABILITY

For skills tests, indices of reliability require a set of standards or criteria to which individual scores might be compared. Newer work on computer adaptive testing introduces probabilistic standards for use in making comparisons whereas sequential skills tests tend to rely on conventional criterion-referenced approaches. Comparing these two approaches may reinforce your understanding of the differences between accuracy and stability when estimating precision.

Precision and Computer Adaptive Testing

You may remember that, with traditional test theory, two indices are central to evaluating the accuracy with which a tool functions. Reliability involves an aggregate estimate of how indicants perform in relation to a total test score. Ordinarily, the standard error of measurement uses the reliability coefficient to estimate scaled errors in a collection of scores and allows investigators to compute a confidence interval for use when interpreting an individual's total score. Both reliability coefficients and standard error estimates treat error in a total score as distributed equally across items. Although precision remains important, these techniques are inappropriate for use with item-response theory. The precision of measurement in IRT typically varies as a function of proficiency scores (θ) and it is problematic to assume that error is distributed equally across items.[24]

Key Concepts.   Rather than talk about one or two estimates of precision, researchers using IRT consider *error in the proficiency estimates, error in expected-score estimates,* and *error associated with alternate forms and test-retest estimates* of stability. Investigators can also approximate an estimate of internal consistency in a group of items, but lose accuracy when doing so.

Investigators using IRT typically report a table or a graph that represents precision at different levels of proficiency. They can report standard errors or error variances for each proficiency level. More commonly, they rely on an *information function* that reveals the expected value of the inverse of the error variance. The formula for representing the *information function* for each item is as follows:

INFORMATION FUNCTION

$$I(\theta) = \sum_j \frac{(P_j')^2}{P_j(\theta)Q_j(\theta)}$$

The information function is typically additive across the items actually answered by respondents. Investigators can treat each indicant separately and report the *item information curve* for that indicant or add curves for all the items to compute a *score information curve*. When aggregating curves, researchers transform the item function formula into the following:

INFORMATION INDEX

$$I(\theta) = E\left[\frac{1}{\sigma_{e*}^2}\right]$$

In this formula σ_{e*}^2 is the error variance of the IRT estimate θ. This approach to estimating error allows investigators to account for differences in measurement error across proficiency levels. When using actual data rather than simulations, investigators replace the concept of an observed score x_j with the *maximum likelihood estimate* θr the Bayes modal estimate $\theta*$ using the proficiency in a population of respondents as a prior distribution.

Estimating Error for Proficiency.   To estimate error in proficiency matrices, investigators typically run simulations in which they use the full item pool, the item selection algorithm, and any item-exposure control systems that will be incorporated into a test. The full theoretical reliability in which simulated scores are compared to true scores can be explored because the proficiencies (θ) are known rather than estimated. *Actual errors of estimate, error variance,* and corresponding values of *the information function* can be computed for many different proficiency levels. By averaging the squared differences between observed estimates and known values of θ for each hypothetical respondent, investigators can estimate actual error variance. Inverting those variances and using them to create an information curve for the system offers a sense of how error is distributed across proficiency levels.

Figure 7.4 offers two kinds of information curves. The first one involves a test with a stopping rule that reflects *fixed error variance.* Respondents stop answering items when σ_{e*}^2 reaches a predetermined point (e.g., .2, or .3 when guessing parameters are included). The second graph reflects a test where investigators used a *fixed test length* stopping rule such that all respondents answered the same number of items. Ideally, a relatively flat information function distribution is helpful for tests used to estimate competence for a wide variety of persons and is most easily accomplished when investigators use a *fixed error variance* stopping rule.

Estimating Error for Expected Scores.   When investigators want to compare results from a computer adaptive test to those from a preexisting measure, they often find it more conve-

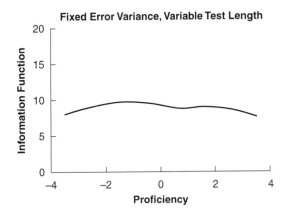

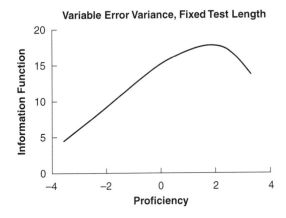

FIGURE 7.4   Sample Information Curves for Two Stopping Rules

nient to transform the proficiency estimates into *expected scores* that include only items on the test of interest. A respondent's expected score is calculated using the following:

EXPECTED SCORES ON A COMPUTER ADAPTIVE TEST

$$E[score] = \sum_{j} P_j(\theta)$$

Note the similarity between this and the item pool score presented earlier. These expected scores are identical to the *subpool scores.* Investigators would read *E[scores]* much like a total score such that an *E[score]* of 50 would indicate 50 correct answers even though respondents may not have answered 50 questions. To compare proficiency and expected scores, investigators can construct a *test characteristic curve* that has the same properties as an item characteristic curve but relies on test scores in a proficiency matrix (θ) and *E[scores]* derived from the specific items to be compared.

Because error distributions for *E[scores]* and proficiency scores (θ) are not equal, it becomes difficult to compare the two when estimating the precision of *E[scores]*. Aware of the inaccuracy of doing so, most investigators solve this problem by relying on conventional *standard error of measurement* estimates for the distribution of *E[scores]* and treat the scores as if the distributions should ideally be normal. Once *E[scores]* for the computer adaptive test are computed, most investigators assume they form a metric comparable to that for a more conventional test. The two sets of scaled test scores can then be compared using conventional correlational or regression techniques.

Marginal Reliability.   There are also occasions when investigators find themselves wanting an IRT estimate that is comparable to conventional estimates of the internal consistency of a test. Investigators can calculate *marginal reliability* in which they average the measurement error across indicants to create a comparable internal consistency estimate. The *marginal measurement error variance*, $\overline{\sigma}^2_{e*}$ for a population with a proficiency distribution $g(\theta)$ can be estimated with the following:

MARGINAL MEASUREMENT ERROR VARIANCE

$$\overline{\sigma}^2_{e*} = \int \sigma^2_{e*} g(\theta) \, d\theta$$

Using this information, the *marginal reliability* is calculated as:

MARGINAL RELIABILITY

$$\overline{p} = \frac{\sigma^2_\theta - \overline{\sigma}^2_{e*}}{\sigma^2_\theta}$$

In this formula, $\overline{\sigma}^2_{e*}$ is the average of the error variance values σ^2_{e*}. The error variance is allowed to differ across proficiency levels, and the row of σ^2_{e*} for all the different proficiencies (θ) would reflect the row's marginal average. Rather than assume all items share equal error variances, investigators use this integration (averaging) over possible estimates of θ to offer a more precise estimate of error variance. Nevertheless, they remember that these estimates lead to a loss of information about how well items perform across persons.

Stability Estimates.   As with other kinds of measures, investigators also look for strong stability in how individuals are classified over time or on alternate forms of the same test. To explore whether *alternative forms* of the same test will yield the same proficiency scores, investigators try to create two item banks rather than ask respondents to complete the same test twice. This limits the possibility that some of the same items will appear on repeated testing with a single item bank. Conventional correlational techniques can evaluate the degree to which respondents achieve the same scores on both measures. For low correlations, investigators can verify that the two measures are equated and then systematically evaluate other sources of error.

Stability over time serves as an index of reliability when investigators have no reason to assume that respondents' placement in a distribution of scores would change between testing sessions. For computer adaptive testing, there are at least two reasons why these correlations are less than 1. Tests always include an irreproducible form of measurement error and there might be reasonable levels of change between the two testing sessions even though the change may not be the same for all respondents in a sample. Researchers who use computer adaptive testing are primarily interested in high levels of test-retest reliability and internal consistency. They continue revising a test until such consistency is accomplished.

The time lag between testing usually mirrors that assumed to match the theoretical use of a test. A brain surgeon should probably retain skills for multiple months or years and test-retest reliability would account for long-term goals. A child's reading skill often changes quite quickly during the primary grades so test-retest estimation would involve a short time interval.

Conventional Criterion-Referenced Approaches to Reliability

Most norm-referenced techniques for interpreting scores and estimating reliability are inappropriate for use with criterion-referenced tests because the goal is to obtain a restricted range of responses (Popham & Husek, 1969). Variance is restricted because most respondents, 80 to 90 percent in many cases, are expected to pass the test. Most of the formulas discussed so far are inappropriate because they hinge on theoretical claims about normally distributed variance in total test scores. Deviations from the assumptions of norm-referenced testing also undermine the value of using the standard error of measurement to interpret sequential scores.

Interpreting Scores.   Criterion-referenced tests are interpreted by looking at three factors. First, criterion-referenced interpretation reflects the percentage of respondents whose scores meet or exceed a predetermined standard. A mastery interpretation evaluates how far individual scores fall beyond a standard. In addition, domain-referenced interpretation reflects the adequacy with which a skill domain is represented in a particular score. These interpretations are parallel to the standard error of measurement and most investigators incorporate all three considerations when evaluating individual and group differences.

Estimating Accuracy.   *Threshold loss indices* have been derived to estimate the internal consistency of items on a single administration of a test.[25] These techniques treat all inconsistent classifications as equally serious and are derived from proportions of agreement or kappa formulas. Each approach is rather tedious, but can be useful to investigators who want to incorporate evidence of false-positive and false-negative decisions into their reports. Threshold loss estimates tend to focus more on errors of classification without estimating other forms of measurement error.

Taking into account the measurement-error variance and classification errors in a group of scores, investigators can also estimate reliability using *squared-error loss* techniques (Feldt & Brennan, 1993). In estimates of reliability, investigators replace the norm-referenced concept of variance as the expected squared deviation *from the mean* with the expected squared deviation *from the cutoff score*. Livingston's coefficient k^2 offers one such estimate for criterion-referenced tests. This coefficient can be computed using the number or proportion of items answered correctly. The formula for proportions is:

LIVINGSTON'S COEFFICIENT k^2

$$k^2 = 1 - \left(\frac{1}{n_i - 1}\right)\left[\frac{\dfrac{\sum M_i(1 - M_i)}{n_i} - sd^2(M_p)}{(M - \lambda)^2 + sd^2(M_p)}\right]$$

In this formula, λ is the cutoff score or the proportion of correctly answered items that verify mastery, n_i is the number of items, n_p is the number of persons, M_i is the items mean over persons, M_p is a person's mean score over n_i items, M is the sample mean over persons and items, and $sd^2(M_p)$ is equal to $\dfrac{\sum (M_p - M)^2}{n_p}$. If $\lambda = M$, this formula is identical to the KR-20 formula (see Chapter 6).

Also available are *Brennan & Kane indices of dependability*.[26] These coefficients involve different kinds of estimates of error variance that offer corrections for change in squared-error loss techniques.

Estimating Stability.   To determine if a test correctly classifies respondents as master or nonmaster, investigators modify test-retest and parallel forms reliability techniques. In one type of estimate, investigators evaluate whether respondents receive the same classification when repeating the same test or an alternate form. They can simply look at the percentage of agreement or use statistical methods to determine whether respondents are more consistent than would be apparent by chance alone. *Phi coefficients, χ^2 tests,* and *other nonparametric statistics* are appropriate indices for this evaluation. Researchers can also use Cohen's *weighted kappa* to estimate the proportion of persons who were consistently classified while taking into account the degree of variance in misclassifications.[27]

Although investigators can explore stability, there are many reasons why stability estimates are not valued. The most obvious issue concerns how well respondents' *true* skill is estimated. Ideally, items are adequately difficult and align with the intended skill, but stability estimates cannot verify such features.

In addition, stability estimates do not incorporate evaluations of how well a group of respondents is representative of a larger population. It would be more helpful to compare an obtained distribution of responses to that from a population of respondents. If a sample is too homogeneous, investigators cannot learn whether the test allows for the discrimination of masters and nonmasters.

As was apparent for computer adaptive testing, to compare total scores to particular standards fails to incorporate clear information on the rigor of the classification standards. If one investigator decided that respondents who answer 80 percent of the items correctly meet a standard, but another decided that respondents must answer 90 percent of the items correctly, comparison of reliability coefficients would be problematic. Similarly, comparison would be problematic if one measure contained a relatively few number of items and another contained many items. These limitations encourage investigators to use multiple indices of reliability when verifying that a measure maintains stable properties on repeated administrations.

Factors Influencing Reliability. Many of the factors that influence reliability for norm-referenced tests also influence the reliability of criterion-referenced tests. The number and representativeness of items on a test influence most estimates of reliability. Similarly, the sample's representativeness and, to some degree, the sample size also influence accuracy. Practice and fatigue effects play a role in stability estimates.

Unique to criterion-referenced tests, indices of agreement are affected by the rigor or leniency of mastery criteria. Performance on a sequential skills test is not interpreted in relation to predefined probability assumptions (although distributions tend to be negatively skewed), rendering conventional approaches to estimating reliability less useful for obtaining information on a test's discriminating power. To accommodate this difference, skills are often classified in relation to total scores rather than proficiency estimates of each indicant. Investigators who are limited to conventional techniques may estimate how often particular skills are replicable over time, but more advanced forms of IRT and Rasch analyses are also being developed to help with this dilemma.

MAKING CONNECTIONS

Using the computer adaptive or sequential skills test you designed earlier, outline a plan for estimating precision. Will you compute an aggregate reliability coefficient? Why or why not? How will you determine if items form a unidimensional construct or are internally consistent? What will you do to estimate stability?

VALIDITY

All the validity issues discussed in previous chapters are relevant to the evaluation of criterion-referenced tests as readily as to other types of measures. Because strong indicants do not necessarily result in a normal distribution of scores, investigators use regression and structural equation modeling techniques with transformed indicants to account for restricted ranges or dichotomous scoring. With computer adaptive testing, investigators explore relationships among items more readily than among item pool scores, but item pool scores can be used in more complex regression or structural analyses. Exploring a sequential analysis of skills typically involves the use of χ^2 techniques, logistic regression, or other nonparametric devices for exploring categorical data. Issues related to these styles will be contrasted to show that established criteria or standards are central to the validation process.

Content Validity

As with content validity for other measures, investigators compare the performance of indicants with parameters on a blueprint to determine if there is an adequate balance of the construct. Investigators using criterion-referenced tools often spend more time in the task-analysis phase of design than is the case for other kinds of measures because every item has a marked influence on the outcome. The weight of each item raises extra validity questions for both computer adaptive testing and sequential skills tests.

Computer Adaptive Testing.   The basic question of whether an item bank adequately represents the skills to be assessed remains central to computer adaptive testing.[28] Because respondents do not typically see all the items, investigators look for ways to evaluate relations between item content and item-selection procedures. Decisions about whether to maximize precision, acknowledge posterior distributions, or follow a predetermined item-generation tree result in different kinds of content by item-selection interactions. Nevertheless, if balance is not adequately considered when generating items, there could be distortion in how a skill is represented across proficiency levels.

Investigators also try to ensure that respondents do not see the same item twice or that items with high discrimination indices are not overused. Instead, computers are typically set to generate items with the same overall frequencies across participants. This could mean that some participants would not respond to those items that maximize the accuracy of their proficiency estimates. Rather than determining where a person's proficiency falls along a continuum, investigators could introduce an uncontrolled form of error. Therefore, most investigators try to eliminate distortion in how well items represent the skill being measured.

Another concern involves the degree to which computers influence respondents' performance on particular items (Green, Bock, Humphreys, Linn, & Reckase, 1984, studied such effects). This is sometimes referred to as a *mode effect* where *mode* refers to the method of presentation rather than the most frequent score. Mode effects are typically detected when *differential item functions* become apparent across individuals or groups. Such differences could appear for at least one of two reasons. Most problematically, variance could be attributable to a multidimensional rather than a unidimensional scale because it reflects a mismatch between item content and the definition of the construct being measured. Error could also result from differences in respondents' computer literacy or comfort when acquiring information from a computer. Unfortunately, these differences are not likely to be random or sufficiently systematic that investigators could offer accurate estimates of such effects.

Rather than simply label these types of error, as might be the case for norm-referenced measures, computer adaptive tests are typically revised until every item functions at an optimal level. Investigators commonly pretest items by generating parameter estimates in one of two ways. When *initial calibration* occurs, responses to a completely new test are generated without comparison to other items on a test. This often occurs when investigators are replacing a paper-and-pencil measure with computer-generated items because there are no existing scales to use when calibrating items. Investigators also use *on-line calibration,* in which respondents are given new items alongside previously evaluated items. Responses to the two sets of items are then compared to determine if they have the same characteristics and if the content can be equated. Without going into too much detail, investigators have identified three methods for estimating unknown item parameters. They may consider *joint maximum likelihood* to determine the probability of a response matrix in a sample of respondents, *conditional maximum likelihood* when they are limited to a 1-PL model, or *marginal maximum likelihood* when they want to account for individual differences in the number of items each respondent answered (see Wainer & Mislevy, 2000, for details on these approaches).

Sequential Skills Tests.   When measuring skills in order to draw inferences about task performance, investigators rely on the task-selection criteria and analysis procedures to label particular skills associated with a desired outcome. They design or borrow a taxonomy of task features for use when evaluating the balance of a blueprint. There are no clear mathematical ways for comparing the components of a task, taxonomies, and sequential blueprints, but content validity can involve logical attempts to document these associations.

Perhaps the most difficult aspect of designing a sequential tool is verifying that skills are weighted appropriately and that there is sufficient balance in the range of indicants used. Theoretical frameworks are central to this process, but investigators can look at patterns in how skills align with one another to verify that the patterns follow intended hierarchical, coordinated, overlapping, or independent relations. In short, content validity for a sequential skills test involves the verification that a task is comprised of the skills included on a particular blueprint and only those skills.

Criterion Validity

Many of the common methods for exploring the structure of a measure and verifying that a desired construct and only that construct is measured are appropriate for use with criterion-referenced tools. Again, the major difference hinges on the fact that variance is restricted in these tools, constraining the range of methods available for exploring error. Because computer adaptive tests are designed to reflect a known construct, investigators are most concerned with predictive validity. The unidimensionality of the construct renders concern with concurrent and discriminant validity unnecessary although it is important to verify that the intended skill and only that skill is measured. Evaluating sequential skills tests primarily involves issues of concurrent and discriminant validity, although once a task is fully understood it may become possible to consider predictive validity when verifying an intended sequence.

Computer Adaptive Testing.   Trying to remove social comparison from the evaluation of a tool's performance, investigators explore precision by *estimating the standard error of ability.* At the validity level, investigators typically use information on placement decisions to evaluate the predictive validity of a computer adaptive test and at least one independent outcome variable. In doing so, four potential limitations of a test become apparent; investigators consider criterion problems, restricted range issues, bouncing beta issues, and differential validity across groups.

Investigators using computer adaptive tests start with the assumption that they have a known unidimensional skill and that the test will assess only individual differences in that skill. Unfortunately, this can lead to the dismissal of possible criterion problems. More reasonably, investigators verify the absence of such problems by computing linear regression equations to determine if test performance predicts a desired theoretical or practical outcome. Investigators ask whether the desired outcome can be adequately quantified and may also examine whether outcome variables are measured independently and systematically. They strive to eliminate bias from evaluators who are familiar with the manifest agenda and consciously or unconsciously distort outcome data.

Ideally, prediction studies conducted to evaluate a criterion acknowledge assumptions about the stability of a skill. This may require longitudinal research that verifies stability in respondents' scores, yet researchers can find that sample attrition distorts their findings. Suppose, for example, a group of individuals expect to fail a test and drop out before completing all the assessments. The remaining sample is likely to show a restricted range of responses and investigators may not fully discover how the tool functions.

On a related theme, when investigators use exogenous criteria such as previous test scores to select participants, they could restrict the range of variance to such a degree that parametric statistical analyses cannot be performed. When such restrictions are apparent, the slope of an item characteristic curve may not change, but the standard error of the slope increases substantially. This increase may mean that scores will not deviate far enough from 0 to offer information on an item's functioning in relation to a skill continuum.

Bouncing beta is the nickname given to the fact that sample characteristics sometimes influence the beta coefficients emerging in regression analyses.[29] Investigators may notice sample characteristics that result in notable differences in test performance, but this may also remain undetected. In education, for example, schools differ in their grading practices to such a degree that beta coefficients are likely to vary from school to school and year to year. Some investigators combine samples to create an aggregate set of predictions, improving variance in their tools, but obfuscating potentially known causes for the variance. More recently, investigators use Bayes estimates to offer better cross-validation than has been evident with ordinary least squares regression. Comparisons of the resulting regression lines seem to reveal more realistic fit indices.[30]

Most investigators come to accept *differential validity* in how tests function. Some respondents may differ in their experience and comfort with computers and so will show a systematic variance in things like response time and error rates. Other respondents may have enduring characteristics that make them genuinely different from one another. Because computer adaptive tests are usually intended to measure universal skills, these differences are assumed to reflect faulty measurement rather than interesting knowledge. Investigators work to modify the ease of computer tasks or the content and style of items sufficiently to eliminate extraneous factors that could influence performance.

Sequential Skills Tests.   When exploring criterion validity for a sequential skills test, investigators can use procedures for validating a Guttman scale (see Chapter 4). Ideally, the succession is organized so that respondents who demonstrate later skills also show mastery on all previous skills. When investigators create a multidimensional test, separate sequences may be apparent for different clusters of skills.

Consider the metacognitive skills outlined in Table 7.4. Those skills may cluster into general thoughts about studying and competence, more specific skills associated with labeling course expectations, and even more detailed goal-setting skills. That sequence could also be extended to emphasize strategies for specific homework tasks. Within each cluster, indicants may be sequentially arranged, coordinated, contain overlapping ideas, or be unrelated to one another. Investigators often use common correlational or χ^2 methods for exploring these possibilities. Concurrent validity is likely to be apparent for indicants related to successful task mastery and discriminant validity is associated with independent skills.

This decision-making process can also be extended to the test as a whole, comparing skills with taxonomies and evaluating the balance of indicants. Taxonomies are intended to help investigators determine if they have evaluated a skill from all relevant angles, even if those angles show no clear relations with one another. This was apparent for the rubric designed for evaluating a noteworthy painting.

Construct Validity

As you now probably understand, investigators explore construct validity by looking at the meaningfulness, appropriateness, and usefulness of inferences from a test. Using ordinary least squares regression and structural equation modeling, investigators explore relations between indicants and skills to draw inferences about competencies. These techniques work from the assumption that measurement error in test scores is the same for all scores. Because IRT is used to calibrate items with known error parameters, it may be more reasonable to assume that error is equally distributed for tests that are dependent on this approach than for other forms of tests. This leads some investigators to argue that tests designed using IRT are more accurate than tests evaluated using conventional evaluation techniques.

Computer Adaptive Techniques. Three concerns are commonly explored at two different levels when investigators evaluate construct validity for a computer adaptive test. At the item level, investigators verify that indicants reflect a unidimensional construct, indicants at particular difficulty levels are equivalent, and performance across items is not affected by the mode of presentation.

At the test level, investigators compare a unidimensional construct to other related constructs to explore mode effects. Multitrait–multimethod matrices can determine whether constraints of computers are affecting performance and verify that only the intended construct is being evaluated. With computers, respondents are forced to answer one item before seeing another, and they cannot backtrack or revisit earlier responses. Computer screens also offer limited amounts of space in which to lay out items. Time pressures can also be more prevalent for methods in which respondents answer all relevant items or only those that will help verify their placement on a skill continuum. If participants who respond to several different measures receive the same placements regardless of the mode of presentation, investigators may rule out computer literacy effects.

Testing *congeneric measurement* or the equivalence of measures, investigators may also compare the equivalence of variance–covariance matrices or determine if patterns in obtained data conform to theoretical predictions. Confirmatory factor analysis can be used to explore patterns in factor loadings and identify any unique error variances between two versions of the test. This allows investigators to compare a restricted model that treats both tests as equal with an unrestricted model that does not impose the equality constraints. Comparing the goodness-of-fit indices (G^2) for these two models allows investigators to determine the best fit for the data.

To verify the definition of a construct, investigators are likely to evaluate whether the dimensions of a construct and only those dimensions are measured using different methods. They determine if data conform to predicted theoretical patterns using experimental designs and least squares methods of analysis, or descriptive designs and structural equation modeling or interscale correlations. Allowing for the fact that analyses contain item pool estimates rather than total scores, investigators can include such estimates in regression analyses.

Sequential Skills Tests.   For sequential skills tests, exploring construct validity is rarely a straightforward process. The nature of tasks being analyzed, theoretical assumptions about skills, and the ease with which skills can be detected using indicants all play a role in how direct measurements and inferences are combined. Nevertheless, all investigators look for patterns in how the dimensions of task analysis are related. Returning to the metacognitive measure, for example, investigators might ask how indicants align with a theoretical framework for exploring metacognition. They would evaluate whether the dimensions for grouping indicants are exhaustive and mutually exclusive.

Investigators also use criterion-referenced techniques to explore relationships between their new construct and other constructs in a theoretical framework. Because they work from a predetermined standard, challenges to the standard itself can be a feature of construct validity. To explore this, the validation process looks very much like the research process in that hypotheses are tested and relationships among constructs are explored.

In the metacognitive example, investigators could use different kinds of research designs to test relations among constructs. Investigators would look for evidence outside the parameters of their tool to verify that metacognition typically takes the form of thoughts about competence and studying, labeling course expectations and specific kinds of goal setting. They might construct experimental manipulations to see what reactions are elicited or look for convergence and divergence in other ratings.

Threats to Validity

You may recall that threats to validity can occur at the measurement and research design levels of a study (Chapter 1). Because criterion-referenced tests start with a predefined standard, and the assumption that their tools are universally valid for assessing a skill or set of skills, both kinds of threats have the potential to undermine the functioning of such measures. For computer adaptive testing, the most serious threat emerges when departures from unidimensionality occur within an item bank. For sequential skills tests, multidimensionality is essential for differentiating skills, but sequential departures pose serious threats.

Computer Adaptive Testing.   Investigators accept that threats to validity can occur at one of three levels in the tool itself. Item performance can be inadequate in that unsuitable proficiency predictions are generated. The mode of presentation can be confounded with measured skills so that inferences fail to correspond to the designer's intent. In addition, the item-selection algorithm may not generate a sufficiently balanced or fair test. These possibilities are raised to evaluate within-group multidimensionality or between-group multidimensionality outcomes.

To explore *within-group multidimensionality,* investigators often use modifications of factor analysis. *Full information factor analysis* is a marginal maximum likelihood procedure for evaluating dimensions of an underlying skill continuum. This approach evaluates how many factors are present within a test while considering the details of item parameters such as difficulty, discrimination, and correction for guessing. Factor loadings reflect regression coefficients of the item-response process on latent variables and are computed using item-response data rather than correlations. Changes in the goodness-of-fit are explored as additional factors are added to the model. The process is iterative in that investigators start with one factor and repeat the process until there is no improvement in the goodness-of-fit (G^2). Once satisfactory loadings are obtained, investigators match acceptable items to the blueprint or create several unidimensional testlets.

Between-group multidimensionality may be evident if items show differential functioning across groups. This raises the problem of whether items mean different things to people with different characteristics. Investigators use multiple measures of the same constructs and determine if performance is stable when some, but not other, tools are used. If stability is evident for most tools, an unstable tool may need revision. If all tools are unstable, item content, blueprints, and theoretical assumptions may be called into question.

Sequential Skills Test. Validity of sequential skills analysis is commonly threatened when investigators fail to label enough dimensions to fully represent each skill in an intended hierarchy. Once investigators select a task and criteria for analysis, they can still adhere inconsistently to the analytical logic. Not all taxonomies include internally consistent parameters and investigators who simply choose a popular taxonomy may find that the structure does not fit their theoretical problem.

A lack of fit between parameters of a taxonomy and the task to be analyzed may be evident within and between groups, just as was possible for computer adaptive testing. Within a group, individuals may have different skills or may apply the same skills in an order that differs from the one documented. Between groups, the same kinds of variance could occur, but the errors would reflect characteristics of samples rather than of individuals. Such mismatches introduce pressure to either revise theoretical assumptions, indicants of particular skills, or the skills associated with particular tasks.

Generalizations

As is the case for other tools, validating criterion-referenced evidence is quite complex. In some ways, investigators who use criterion-referenced measures may be better able to see the error in their tool because they start with the assumption that their criterion has known parameters. When evidence of invalidity is sufficient, the particular criterion may change and the tool will be completely revised. More commonly, investigators question their choice of indicants and decisions about relations between indicants and skills.

■ ■ ■ ■ ■

MAKING CONNECTIONS

Use one of the measures you have designed to outline a plan for exploring validity. How would you verify that the content of your measure actually reflects the intended tasks and skills? What comparisons would you make? What would you do to establish criterion validity? Would you focus on predictive validity or compare concurrent and discriminant validity? How would you explore construct validity? What threats would you worry most about when evaluating your tool?

MEASURING SPECIFIC COGNITIVE FUNCTIONING

Whereas most of the tools discussed in previous chapters are used with the assumption that constructs are evolving, dynamic entities, criterion-referenced tools start with a known, accepted construct. Investigators may start with the assumption that they know what a skill or task looks like and attempt to deconstruct that entity in the measurement process. Starting with a known skill, investigators can draw inferences about the tasks that make up a skill and about how the skill is coordinated with competence. Not surprisingly, the decision to start with a skill or a task holds many implications for the design of test blueprints, indicants, and modes of presentation. Procedures for calibrating items, exploring error, and validating measurements are also affected by this decision. Certainty about a definition offers the advantage of illuminating common measurement techniques.

SUGGESTED READINGS

Cizek, G. J. (2001). *Setting performance standards: Concepts, methods, and perspectives.* Mahwah, NJ: Erlbaum.

Embretson, S. E., & Reise, S. P. (2000). *Item-response theory for psychologists.* Mahwah, NJ: Erlbaum.

Hollnagel, E., & Dobson, D. L. (2003). *Handbook of cognitive task design: Human factors and ergonomics.* Mahwah, NJ: Erlbaum.

Mills, C. N., Potenza, M. T., Fremer, J. J., & Ward, W. C. (Eds.). (2002). *Computer-based testing: Building the foundation for future assessments.* Mahwah, NJ: Erlbaum.

Sands, W. A., Waters, B. K., & McBride, J. R. (Eds.). (1997). *Computerized adaptive testing: From inquiry to operation.* Washington, DC: American Psychological Association.

Schraagen, J. M., Chipman, S. F., Shalin, V. J. (2000). *Cognitive task analysis.* Mahwah, NJ: Erlbaum.

Shepherd, A. (2000). *Hierarchical task analysis.* New York: Taylor & Francis.

Sijtsma, K., & Molenaar, I. W. (2002). *Introduction to nonparametric item-response theory.* Thousand Oaks, CA: Sage.

Wainer, H. (with Dorans, N. J., Eignor, D., Flaugher, R., Green, B. F., Mislevy, R. J., Steinberg, L., & Thissen, D.) (2000). *Computerized adaptive testing: A primer.* (2nd ed.). Mahwah, NJ: Erlbaum.

SUGGESTED WEB SITES

Assessment Systems Corporation for MicroCAT: http://www.assess.com/Software/microcat.htm

Assessment Systems Corporation for PARSCALE: http://www.assess.com/Software/parscale.htm

Eric Clearinghouse for Assessment and Evaluation for Item Response Theory: http://ericae.net/irt/

ENDNOTES

1. Jonassen, Tessmer, & Hannum (1999) offer a more detailed presentation of different kinds of task analysis and examples of such approaches to instructional design.

2. These decisions were adapted from Jonassen, Tessmer, & Hannum (1999).

3. Jonassen, Tessmer, & Hannum (1999) offer several different examples of taxonomies, but researchers ordinarily generate this from their theoretical reasons for measuring skill or task performance.

4. Wainer (2000) contains many of the basic details of computer adaptive testing.

5. Wainer (2000) offers a very readable outline of how item-response theory is used in the evaluation of computer adaptive tests. This book also distinguishes IRT from Rasch techniques in a way that reveals why it seems to be the method of choice for use with criterion-referenced measures. This debate between groups of scholars, however, continues to introduce new information about how indicants can be evaluated.

6. Although maximum likelihood and Bayesian statistical approaches will not be fully distinguished here, they differ in how error is treated. *Maximum likelihood techniques* focus primarily on the parameters being estimated and do not fully account for uncertainty in the model parameters. Each parameter is treated as if it contains no error. *Bayesian approaches* work from the assumption that parameters are random variables, complete with the same kind of error embedded in all variables. To keep the representations of key parameters clear, I have adopted the simplest approach and encourage interested readers to find Patz & Junker (1999a, 1999b) for more details on Bayesian approaches to IRT. Similarly, nonparametric approaches to IRT are also available (Sijtsma & Molenaar, 2002).

7. This summary was constructed with the help of Pedhazur (1982).

8. Thissen & Mislevy (2000) offer a review of various algorithms; books related to Rasch or generalizability theory are likely to offer additional examples.

9. Dorans (2000) offers a more direct comparison of different scores, scales, and equating procedures.

10. The early versions of this kind of conversion are reviewed in Hull (1922).

11. Wainer (2000) and Lord & Novick (1968) offer more explicit details on these and other related issues for IRT.

12. See Chapter 4 for sample item characteristic curves and the curve for Guttman scales to exemplify some features of the IRT difficulty estimates. The two differ in that each item on a computer adaptive test is treated independently of all other items.

13. Kingston & Dorans (1985) outline this process in greater detail.

14. Flaugher (2000) draws these comparisons, but the conventional procedures are described in Chapter 6.

15. Green (2000) offers more details on the kinds of system-related dilemmas faced by investigators using computer adaptive testing.

16. Wainer & Mislevy (2000) offer a very clear representation of this process using mathematical examples.

17. Wainer & Mislevy (2000) offer a much more elaborate description of this process.

18. Many new scholars incorrectly assume this is the same as using regression on a set of scores.

19. Dorans (2000) offers much more detail on these comparisons.

20. Lord (1980) offers the technical details on how these were derived.

21. Crocker & Algina (1986) offered a strong review of these and other methods for evaluating item performance on criterion-referenced tests.

22. Bakeman & Gottman (1997) offer this comparison of Yule's Q and Phi coefficients.

23. See Crocker & Algina (1986) for an outline of these ideas.

24. Information on reliability was obtained from Thissen (2000).

25. See Subkoviak (1984) for a review of these techniques. They are more technical than is appropriate for this book.

26. See Feldt & Brennan (1993) for more information on these formulas and their difference from k^2.

27. This statistic is available in Cohen (1968), but does not seem to be acknowledged by investigators who have used *kappa* as the "straw-man" for a critique of stability in estimating reliability. The formula is included in Chapter 5.

28. Most of the procedural information on validity used in this chapter was drawn from Steinberg, Thissen, & Wainer (2000).

29. Rubin (1980) introduced this dilemma and offered some preliminary suggestions for minimizing the effects.

30. More technical detail and visual examples of these differences are available in Steinberg, Thissen, & Wainer (2000).

CHAPTER EIGHT

MEASURING BEHAVIOR AND PHYSIOLOGICAL REACTIONS

Most of the measurement techniques reviewed thus far have relied heavily on verbal tasks, but measures of behavior and physiological characteristics are also commonly used. Investigators who are primarily interested in stable patterns of behavior or physiological functioning are likely to record indicants of interpersonal and intrapersonal functioning. In addition to providing useful information in its own right, observational evidence is sometimes used to verify changes in attitude or balance assessment profiles of persons (see Chapters 3 through 7). Skills and abilities can be characterized in behavioral as well as cognitive terms. Inferences about multiple forms of human functioning are also drawn from physiological measures.

This chapter samples psychometric techniques for measuring behavior and physiological responses. Later, observational methods will be revisited to illustrate their use in measuring human development and in ethnographic accounts of lives in progress. Here, the emphasis will be on stable patterns, but later chapters will emphasize growth and nondevelopmental forms of change. Some physiological tools will be described here, but more complex tools will not be reviewed because they require a greater degree of physiological knowledge than is common in the social sciences. Investigators typically collaborate with physicians when their theoretical assumptions require elaborate physiological measures.

MEASURING BEHAVIOR

To measure behavior, investigators often look for ways to freeze *actions, events,* and *processes* for later analysis. Exploring events that unfold in time, naturally occurring behavior in everyday settings can be coded on the spot or recorded using video equipment. Through systematic observation, investigators endeavor to identify common patterns and idiosyncrasies. Although most observational research is informed by the psychology of perception, methods differ, depending on the parameters of a research tradition. Specifically, techniques differ depending on whether investigators are theorizing about human functioning, the effects of environments on people, and/or how to improve daily or professional practice.[1]

Methods used to achieve these different goals reflect different degrees of *systematization,* repeated use of predetermined coding methods, and *function,* combinations of actions, events, and processes (Table 8.1). Psychometricians typically emphasize systematization and formality whereas developmental and ethnographic researchers either blend methods or rely on open-ended scoring techniques that reflect either narrower or broader conceptions of context.

Regardless of these differences, all observation techniques require a predetermined target. Most investigators assume that stimuli and the environments in which behavior is elicited restrict stable identification and classification patterns. They typically accept that their findings are influenced by observers' interests, theoretical perspectives, and research questions.

The observer in this kind of research is the primary instrument, but tools are used to help observers focus and guide their attention as well as record their perceptions. Therefore, when evaluating observational research, most investigators remember that observers are people with biases, abilities, and beliefs that can be influenced by training, but only to a certain degree.

Imagine the structure of a birthday party. The party's duration might be the event, beginning with the arrival of guests and ending with their departure. The different sequences of events associated with particular activities would reflect the processes within the event and would be made up of actions. The process of wishing someone a happy birthday might include actions such as singing, cutting cake, scooping ice cream, and eating the sweets. The entire sequence might be evaluated along predefined dimensions, and each action could be coded or counted.

Technology is often used to adjust for observer biases by offering opportunities to sufficiently freeze events so that investigators can thoughtfully reflect on them. Multiple raters can evaluate the same event and come to agreement about what is observed. Filming birthday parties, for example, allows researchers to later evaluate who did what, how often, and in what order. Investigators may also design instruments that direct attention to specific features of a frozen situation. Investigators interested in evaluating emotional displays at particular points during a party may use a checklist or rating scale to record their judgments.

As is the case for any measurement tool, different recording techniques contain a structure and biases that hopefully align with theoretical assumptions. Unfortunately, the structure of the tool can distort the recording of events, processes, and actions. Like other

TABLE 8.1   Sample Functions Served by Observational Tools

PROCEDURES	FUNCTION
Tacit procedures	Used for describing how individuals make sense of their experience.
Situation-specific procedures	Used for facilitating or limiting involvement in everyday activities.
Question-specific procedures	Used for evaluating or altering events.
Sequential verification	Used for theorizing about behavior.

tools, the structure of the behavioral measures introduces systematic error that is often diffi-cult to control. When investigators are aware of this kind of distortion, they are likely to offer appropriate hedges when reporting their findings, acknowledging that distortion cannot be eliminated. Replicating findings still offers the best means for validating conclusions.

MAKING CONNECTIONS

Consider a research question in your area of interest that involves behavior. How systematically would you want to measure behavior? What assumptions will you make about the function of the recorded behavior? How could you verify those assumptions? What biases, skills, and as-sumptions would you want to constrain when conducting observations?

Matching Theoretical Concerns with Indicants

Psychometric measurement assumptions are the most formal and systematic of those rep-resented in this book. Nevertheless, even within this system of thought, indicants take many forms and differ depending on the theoretical assumptions being tested. This variability car-ries over into the measurement of behavior. Indicants in observational research can refer to specific events, processes, actions, or abstract phenomena, but are constrained by the con-text in which they are identified. Observing and recording behavior requires a careful matching of questions, contexts, and definitions of reality. Because indicants take many forms in observational research, parameters for those forms are usually considered when matching indicants with theoretical concerns. These forms reflect the following assump-tions about how context, reality, and behavior relate to measurement.

Levels of Context.   Decisions on the parameters for *defining the environment* are central to observational investigations. Contexts are difficult to define, but investigators use terms like environment, situation, and practices to reflect various levels of consideration. One common model contains four levels of context: local contexts, historical contexts of a spe-cific event, historical contexts of a setting, and the context of the research approach (Ever-ston & Green, 1986).

Local contexts contain several levels of organization that simultaneously influence immediate behavior. In understanding students' motivation to do homework, for example, their beliefs about school, particular classes, and the task at hand converge to influence their willingness to apply effort (White-McNulty, 2002).

The *historical context of a specific event* focuses on how processes differ in content, unfold over time, and vary across situations. Investigators usually look for possible rela-tionships among contexts and ask how events can be selected so that a representative sam-ple of behavior is available for analysis. As is the case in most forms of measurement, investigators try to anticipate systematic variance when linking their observations to theo-retical claims. To explore homework behavior, for example, investigators might look at the nature of the classes in which homework is assigned, patterns of homework within and be-tween classes or across schools, and the nature of the assignments.

The *historical context of the setting* offers information on the expectations, traditions, networks, and lines of communication established well before particular behaviors are observed. At this level, investigators determine if the features of the designated context are unique or if they are embedded within a more stable setting. Returning to the homework study, investigators could explore the traditions associated with homework, parent and teacher expectations, and particular homework rituals that are common to the setting.

Finally, the *context of the research approach* reflects the expectations and norms of the discourse community with whom investigators plan to share their results. Four dimensions are related to the research context: Investigators coordinate the theory guiding decision making, recognizable values about the topic and situation, the tools for recording events, and specific research questions. The homework study might focus on intrapersonal or interpersonal processes, different features of homework behavior, recording tools, and definitions of evidence. Decisions about each parameter usually differ, depending on how findings will be used. (See Chapter 1 for some of the discourse communities that engage in research on human functioning.)

Other models for defining context can be defined, but these levels are commonly considered across many disciplines. Investigators form a lens through which they study how individuals and groups function in everyday settings as well as factors that constrain and support such behavior. Those who are interested in comparing findings across studies also remain explicit about establishing the functional equivalence of different settings.

Representing Reality.   Working *definitions of reality* are also established before conducting observations. Like context, definitions of reality are controversial. Philosophical and theoretical definitions of research are central to defining observable reality. (See Chapter 1 for some of these philosophical concerns.) Some fields accept concrete definitions of reality that are tangible and observable by anyone taking time to notice. Other fields consider progressively more abstract assumptions. Concrete definitions emphasize direct relations among indicants whereas more abstract definitions focus on how indicants are related to latent or unobservable constructs.

Regardless of these theoretical assumptions, most investigators realize that each tool represents only one set of possible observations among many alternatives. Measurement parameters are sometimes manipulated deliberately to test theoretical questions, and one investigator might wrestle with multiple definitions of reality.

Definitions of reality are important primarily because they influence the *degree of selectivity* in the measurement process. The particular questions to be explored and the setting to be observed are part of all measurement tools, but distinguishing these parameters is especially challenging for observational research. The "slices of reality" or nature of observed activities are usually anticipated in psychometric forms of observation, but surprising patterns may also emerge during the assessment. Selectivity decisions influence investigators' choice of observational procedures, placement of observers in a setting, and data reduction decisions. Reports are derived from predetermined assumptions about what is worthwhile to know and to measure.

Characteristics of Indicants.   To match theoretical concerns, investigators also think about the parameters of each type of indicant or observation. Whereas items on attitude, personality, and intelligence scales are relatively straightforward, the same cannot be said for measures of behavior. Some common comparisons that inform decision making are listed below. Notice how components of the list contain different levels of logic or multiple definitions of context. Indicants can reflect:

- naturally occurring events or units, perceived as breaks in streams of behavior that conform to dynamic, temporal structures;
- patterns that are identified inductively or deductively from a record of events or behavior, and derived statistically or by comparing indicants to theoretical parameters;
- descriptive or evaluative judgments of behavior;
- phenomenological or morphological features derived from inferences, similar in form or structure;
- discrete representations that are counted or continuous recordings that involve ratings;
- a single rating of complex stimuli or multiple ratings of simple stimuli;
- a single behavior or event that is further reduced so each unit of meaning is counted;
- behaviors with a common cause, even if the details of each action differ;
- behaviors that serve the same function, even if the details differ across situations;
- a set of situations that are comprised of rule-bound, recurring elements;
- global, molar properties of behavior or specific, molecular properties;
- time sequences or events with similar form and content (Fassnacht, 1982).

Because this list is so complex, no one indicant can reflect decisions on all these levels; investigators typically make theoretically grounded choices when designing a new set of observational methods and tools. Each unit of observation is measured by recording entities that are not overtly manipulated.

To accommodate the complexities of behavior, more than one kind of indicant may be used in an investigation. Returning to the birthday party, investigators might observe the various emotional displays from one level and the sequence of events over time from a second level. Indicants from these two coding schemes would not be parallel, but indicants within a level (e.g., emotional displays or sequences of events) would reflect the corresponding level of specificity.

Behavioral units that reflect diverse agendas sometimes contain overlapping features. Investigators may study this by designing different classes of codes for their observations, tallying observations in each class, and comparing the resulting distributions. Furthermore, coding classes may represent different levels of context as well as more general and specific levels within a particular behavioral sequence or event. Generally speaking, the form and content of indicants may vary even within a single study to serve different functions.

Procedures previously described for measuring attitudes and personality can sometimes be used with behavioral data.[2] Like items on a test, indicants with similar features can be combined into scales, and correlated with other scales. They can be counted, transformed, and otherwise aggregated to form larger classes of units. In addition, new descriptive units can be created out of patterns found in existing units to better capture the theoretical constructs under investigation. Unfortunately, however, factor-analytic techniques are inappropriate for the categorical data that emerges from observational tools, and investigators often rely on theoretical relations and inter-rater agreement to determine which indicants belong on the same scale. Before conducting observations, investigators try to anticipate how their data will be analyzed because that process constrains the characteristics of acceptable indicants.

Sampling Methods. To determine which indicants to sample, investigators often distinguish event-sampling and time-sampling methods. *Event-sampling* uses the boundaries of an event to determine when to start and stop their observations. *Time-sampling* typically involves units of time such as seconds, minutes, hours, or days to mark sequences of observation. Start and stop times are determined by other parameters of the design or are randomly selected from a range of possibilities.

There are at least three important decisions for *event-sampling*; observers typically wait until an event occurs before coding its properties, use the time an event begins and ends to determine boundaries for coding, and evaluate time durations of behavior as the patterns change. A birthday party can be identified as the event to be sampled and investigators might try to record all aspects of that event. They could use the time the first guest arrives to mark the beginning of the event and the time the last guest leaves to mark the end of the event. Within the event, investigators might evaluate more narrowly focused events delineated by particular activities. Activities such as games, eating cake and ice cream, or gift-giving also have beginning and end points that can be used while recording behavior.

Time-sampling usually involves intervals for delineating judgments, but can serve sequential or nonsequential functions. An investigator might randomly select an optimal time to begin observing across participants. Deciding to capture the behavior of five-year-olds, for example, investigators may contact parents or school officials to determine who to observe and arrange a meeting time, using established parameters for these decisions. Some children might be observed in the morning, others in the afternoon or at bedtime. Parameters for how often behavior is recorded and the duration of each observation period would correspond to theoretical reasons for measuring behavior, but are usually kept constant across participants. With such a schedule, investigators may or may not observe a birthday party because the observation period would reflect the time of day rather than an event.

Investigators also combine time- and event-sampling techniques. Cross-classifying behavior into more than one class of codes may involve time and event factors or focus primarily on the qualities of behavior in each segment of a sequence of events. Investigators who sample time intervals during the birthday party would use both event- and time-sampling methods.

Before collecting research data, investigators generally pilot-test their tools. This allows them to explore the practicalities of using time- or event-sampling. The most reasonable units for recording indicants of behavior are identifiable and the effectiveness of the corresponding recording method can be evaluated.

Classification Systems. Two kinds of classification systems are commonly used to record observations. *Categorical systems* involve known indicant parameters and *descriptive systems* involve generative parameters. A categorical system may be used for our birthday party example because these events often follow a similar script. Investigators may predict that the emotions of five-year-olds will peak as gifts begin to be exchanged, but record emotional displays using a predetermined list of common emotions. To explore differences across birthday parties, investigators may be more enlightened by a descriptive system in which they list everything they notice. Recording as much information about the event as possible could reveal commonalities and differences.

Essential Considerations.   To construct an observational measure, investigators try to carefully define three dimensions that, in other types of research, are often thought of as design concerns. They explicitly define parameters for the context to be observed, a working definition of reality, and the units to record.

Without establishing clear parameters, it becomes very difficult to conduct reliable and valid observations, especially if the initial parameters are to be systematically modified over the course of a research program. If parameters for data collection remain murky, the analysis of findings becomes difficult, if not impossible to interpret.

Investigators also determine whether to use categorical or descriptive systems to record their observations. This decision is often contingent on how much information is already available. If investigators cannot predict the actions, events, or processes that might transpire, they usually rely on a descriptive system. Categorical systems can be more parsimonious when investigators know what to observe.

MAKING CONNECTIONS

Imagine conducting observations. How many dimensions are central to your question? What parameters are essential for defining appropriate indicants? What contextual considerations will likely influence relevant dimensions? Are all contextual levels important? How would you define reality? What levels of inference would be necessary for coordinating indicants and theoretical constructs? Should your question be revised to clarify these parameters? What structural features will you consider when defining codes?

Designing Tools: Categorical Classification Systems

Investigators who use *categorical classification systems* are usually interested in the normative features of multiple contexts and find the qualities of changes that occur within an individual less interesting. This is common when investigators endeavor to identify explanatory principles. Investigators define the structure of a situation or set of behaviors that make them functionally equivalent and look only at replicable findings.

Beginning with a finite set of predetermined categories, investigators evaluate only the items included on the recording tool. Categories on the tool are often mutually exclusive, but reflect behaviors that are derived from investigators' philosophical, theoretical, and empirical assumptions. Investigators may also begin with experience-based beliefs about a process, event, or group under investigation, but their tool is self-contained in that no new categories are added while the system is in use.

Categorical tools are valuable when coding is done at the time the behavior occurs because observers can tally or rate the behavior on site. When codes can be easily memorized for use alone or in combination, observers can accurately record behavior as it is observed. In these circumstances, behavior is recorded using symbols, tallies, or checklists.

Technology (e.g., audio- or videotaping) is also used to record behavior during predetermined time frames. Procedures are more likely to be replicable if investigators limit the amount of memory needed to use recording tools, record as much detail as possible, and minimize interruptions during the observation period.

When establishing replicable procedures, investigators set boundaries for observations. You may recall that, in event-sampling, boundaries are determined by the parameters of events so that the onset and closure of an event mark the beginning and end of the observation period. The selection of events (e.g., birthday parties, evidence of conflict, or concentrated effort on a task) is usually tied to the theoretical reasons for observing behavior.

In time-sampling, units of time form beginning and ending points as well as discrete intervals within the observation period. During each time interval, observers can record the existence of particular behaviors or the amount of time target participants are engaged in such behavior. For many time-constrained purposes, frequent and brief observation periods seem more useful than lengthy periods. Nevertheless, decisions about the length of an observation period usually correspond to the complexity of the behavior being observed.

Occasionally, event-sampling is used in combination with time-sampling to establish boundaries. In later stages of a research program, investigators may combine methods to test strong hypotheses about relations between behaviors.

Regardless of the parameters of categorical classification systems, this approach is defined as *systematic* because investigators capture the dynamic qualities of repeated, short samples of behavior. In a deliberate attempt to record particular behaviors, category systems, checklists, and rating scales make regularities, laws, and normative information more readily available.

Category Systems. Investigators who use category systems rely on a finite set of categories and classify behavior as indicative of one of the categories listed (Table 8.2). In this respect they often make one complex judgment rather than many simple judgments. The categories are usually derived deductively from coordinating theoretical and practical concerns. As is the case for item writing, inductive approaches may also be appropriate if data from related studies are available.

Suppose an investigator wanted to determine individuals' involvement in teamwork by observing differences in employees' work habits. The researcher is likely to define categories of habits from reviewing existing research and noticing the typical patterns that occur in the target environment (Table 8.2). Details of the tasks would not be necessary for determining if a person is avoiding work, working alone, or working with others. Investigators could sample behavior by identifying work-related events or randomly selecting different periods of time to evaluate work habits. Judgments might involve the coordination of particular actions evident during the designated period or global decisions about the typical habits of each target.

Category systems commonly reflect descriptions of behavior rather than inferences about behavior. Investigators observing the work habits would not be able to determine why they noticed differences in work style or the structure of "not working," "working alone," or "collaborating with others." Furthermore, they would not be able to determine the larger

TABLE 8.2   Sample Category System for Observing Work Style

WORK STYLE	TIME 1	TIME 2	TIME 3
Not working	Observed		
Solitary work		Observed	
Collaborative work			Observed

purpose for the habits they detected. An individual could be engaged in solitary work because the task requires this style or because they do not like their coworkers. Additional details on the actual behavior being evaluated would be required to justify more general inferences and conclusions about such behavior.

Items in a category system tend to be discrete and easy to discriminate because they represent clear units. Nominal measurement scales are common as investigators simply identify the best category for representing the behavior unfolding in front of them. The behavior may be live or recorded, but unusual events remain unscored.

Category systems are frequently used for time-series analysis in which designated intervals can mark the beginning and end of the observation period. Within a given period, time can mark the assignment of codes. Information on events within an interval can be lost, but if intervals are appropriately set, the tool would offer necessary information. If, for example, someone started with a 12-minute observation period, that time could be subdivided into three-minute segments after which observers would assign a code to the behavior they observed. For each 12-minute interval, observers would make four judgments. In the analysis phase, investigators would compare the frequency of recorded behavior across individuals.

Checklists.   Checklists work much like category systems in that investigators construct items for observers to use when recording behavior. Observers usually tally the listed behavior they observe no matter how often that behavior occurs. Table 8.3 offers a sample checklist for evaluating the behavior of graduate students in two contexts. Multiple checks can be used to indicate multiple occurrences of the same behavior. Only behavior on the checklist would be recorded with a nominal scale. Then, responses would be tallied to form an ordinal scale and draw normative conclusions about the frequency of behavior.

Checklists are useful for recording discrete forms of behavior. When used in combination with time intervals, checklists can offer information on the sequence as well as content of events. Sets of similarly structured indicants could be grouped together on the page and differentiated from indicants with different features. This is apparent in Table 8.3 where participation, encouragement, and distractions are treated as three dimensions of group behavior among graduate students. Strong checklists lend themselves to time-based, event-based, or combined forms of coding, especially when observers are not required to make complex inferences about behavior. They may not be ideal when investigators endeavor to record novel behavior or evaluate complex patterns.

TABLE 8.3   Sample Observational Checklist for Recording Behavior among Research Assistants

HOW OFTEN DO MEMBERS . . .

PARTICIPATION

Group behaviors	Laboratory Meetings	Social Meetings
Offer their opinions.		
Give short lectures.		
Offer constructive ideas.		
Acknowledge others' comments.		
Respond to another's comments.		
Ask questions.		

ENCOURAGEMENT

Group behaviors	Laboratory Meetings	Social Meetings
Say or do something cheerful.		
Compliment others.		

DISTRACTION

Group behaviors	Laboratory Meetings	Social Meetings
Do unrelated tasks.		
Make irrelevant comments.		
Change the topic of conversation.		
Refuse direct requests.		
Insult someone in the group.		
Compliment themselves.		

Rating Scales.   Rating scales are similar in many ways to category systems and check-lists, with one major difference. Instead of determining if or how often a behavior occurs, observers make weighted judgments about the events unfolding in time. These features do not lend themselves to use in time-sampling but are commonly used for event-sampling situations. With rating scales, investigators may make magnitude judgments (e.g., low to high), evaluative judgments (e.g., good to bad), or frequency judgments (e.g., rare to often). Table 8.4 contains a rating scale for evaluating individuals' level of involvement in research

TABLE 8.4   Sample Observational Rating Scale for Evaluating Involvement Behaviors

SIGNS OF INVOLVEMENT	NEVER	RARELY	SOMETIMES	FREQUENTLY	ALWAYS
Chooses an activity voluntarily					
Invents an activity					
Completes an assigned activity					
Shows work to others					
Asks for help only if needed					
Shows gestures of enjoyment (e.g., smiles)					
Continues working when asked to stop					

activities. As you can see, item formats used on attitude and personality measures can be applied to ratings of behavior.

As is the case for attitude and personality measures, investigators disagree on whether ratings reflect ordinal or interval scales. Most rating scales reflect continuous rather than discrete forms of data. With training, observers ideally strive for equivalence in the distance between points, but this may not be easily accomplished or sustained over the course of a study.

To ensure consistency, most observers are taught how to match samples of behavior with ratings. This training, if done well, can lead multiple raters to assign the same value to a particular behavior, and encourage investigators to label their measurement scale as interval rather than ordinal. Uncontrolled systematic error remains likely across observers.

Unlike checklists and category systems, rating scales are amenable to situations in which observers are inclined to make strong inferences or to draw conclusions about global constructs. Although investigators sometimes rate entire blocks of time or events, they may not rely completely on rating scales for their study. The most common use of this technique occurs at the end of an observation period as a means of summarizing more direct assessments of behavior.

Limitations of Categorical Systems.   With the exception of rating scales, most categorical systems are predicated on the assumption that strong instruments allow for a literal reading of events with a minimal degree of inference. This high degree of systematization offers a detailed record of actual behavior that can be useful for situations demanding on-the-spot coding.

Pragmatically, it is sometimes necessary for observers to watch behavior, leave the situation, and then record their ratings. The delay between action and recording inevitably creates a dependence on investigators' ability to remember what they saw. Whenever possible, this should be avoided, but, if it is necessary, the time interval between observations and assessment is usually short. Observers are inclined to lose or distort their understanding of events if there is much delay between the acts of observing and rating events. Most investigators find themselves better off using video equipment to record behavior for later coding than accepting such delays.

Rating behavior without recording the details of the evaluated events can be problematic. Without at least describing the parameters of an observational period, variation in ratings cannot be directly linked with variation in action or events. If the extent to which events unfold in an anticipated manner remains unverified, misperceptions in the meaning of codes can emerge.

Off site, in the analysis phase, investigators usually combine observations in different ways to draw relationships with particular constructs and to answer their research questions. Unfortunately, when observations are placed in categories, behavior can appear to be more isolated than was actually the case. Discrete scoring of behavior can make it difficult to identify meaningful representations of the order of events and to draw inferences about the structure, function, and processes associated with the observations. Investigators sometimes combine such measures with markers of time to record an order of events, but information can get lost if it is not represented as part of the coding system.

Categorical methods are costly when one considers the amount of time and training needed to ensure that observers can reliably identify and/or evaluate the same events. It is also difficult for observers to remain unobtrusive and eliminate individual differences in their biases about observed events. The amount of time and energy necessary for effective measurement is decreased when meaningful or productive classifications can be anticipated, but that is also a time-consuming process. For these reasons, investigators often use classification approaches in combination with descriptive systems or add a classification study to the end of a more elaborate research program.

MAKING CONNECTIONS

Imagine either an event or a time sequence and design a plan for recording behavior. Will you use a category system, checklist, or rating scale? What parameters would you place on each category? Would observers be making complex or simple judgments? Try asking someone else to make observations using your newly designed tool. Did the observer have trouble classifying behavior? What modifications would you make to the categories or recording system you devised?

Designing Tools: Descriptive Systems

Descriptive classification systems are typically used to explain a developing process and/or to identify general principles from specific behavior. This type of evaluation facilitates in-depth analysis of evolving streams of behavior. Descriptive systems are most useful when investigators are still exploring abstract phenomena to render more concrete representations of theoretical constructs. Investigators can systematically alter their definitions of context, reality, and indicants, revising their coding plan until they find the most parsimonious representation of the framework under investigation. Proximal goals include comparing persons and contexts to identify sequences of behavior. A common distal goal is to design a useful categorical system for more elaborate experiments.

Imagine trying to understand how Guatemalan children celebrate birthdays. Investigators unfamiliar with the norms of Guatemalan culture might impose an inaccurate structure on such events by using a category system, checklist, or rating scale designed for the United States. Thoughtful investigators might ask about the cultural significance of birthdays in Guatemala, establish a working definition about the reality of birthday celebrations, and start identifying indicants to record events associated with birthdays. Initial recordings might involve educated guesses about whether sequences of time or events might best represent birthdays. A new five-year-old girl could be declared princess of the day, but participate in no specific birthday activities. Such a child could also participate in a sequence of events that are repeated across birthdays. To explore these possibilities, investigators might compare the behaviors of several five-year-olds on their respective birthdays and look for many different Guatemalan cities in which to replicate this observation process.

Several questions can be addressed with a descriptive approach. Investigators can ask how two contexts are functionally equivalent. They may also identify those behaviors that are stable across situations, distinguishing recurring behavior from situation-specific actions. Out of these investigations, researchers represent theoretical ideas and may find those that can be recorded with categorical classification systems.

In the case of birthdays in Guatemala, an investigator might use evidence of each child's date of birth to verify the functional equivalence of the time period or events to be sampled. They may record all the events on each child's birthday and look for patterns across descriptions. Those events common across families and cities could become indicants on a more systematic categorical evaluation of birthday rituals among Guatemalan children.

Most descriptive systems involve a heavy reliance on technology that records frozen behavior. This allows investigators to review events and elicit advice from individuals who may not have been present for the actual behaviors. Such retrospective analysis can maximize consistency in scoring. Naturally occurring boundaries can be established for observations of particular events, contexts, and situation-specific behavior. Investigators can alter their definitions of context and reality without conducting new observations. They may rescore recorded events several times as they develop a richer understanding of the evidence.

Labeling all the known starting points is a common method for finding order in a set of observations.[3] Sampling relevant behaviors and starting points allows investigators to generate reliable patterns. When categories from other lines of work are available, they may be incorporated into this planning phase and edited in light of new behavior samples. The resulting categories need not be mutually exclusive, but reliability in coding is easier to establish when categories are kept distinct. Investigators may also use more than one category when evaluating behavior, and combine them in later phases of the analysis. More accurate scoring may also occur if positive evaluations of an event are kept separate from negative evaluations, even if the two coding categories are later combined.

Evaluations of behavior often begin with descriptions of a coding scheme generated by writing a narrative summary of different observational sessions. Investigators who know very little about Guatemala, for example, may simply start with stories of what they observe on birthdays. If investigators also keep a log of any new behavior they notice, the two kinds of information can be combined when designing a coding system. Noticing the contexts for new behavior and where such behavior occurs in a sequence of events, new categories can emerge in the resulting patterns.

In the development and revision process, categories may be combined to reflect co-occurring relationships. For sequential analysis, the order of categories is evaluated to verify similarities in how events unfold in time. Investigators can explore the structure, process, and function of behavior to draw inferences about events, causes, and actions. Such conclusions are easier when the classification system consists of mutually exclusive categories, but behavior is sometimes classified into co-occurring categories. Classifying behavior into more than one category reveals co-occurrence. Coding systems can also remain generative in that investigators can continually add codes as long as they are sure to score all samples using the same final rubric. These decisions are guided by investigators' perceptions, training, and theoretical framework, and are constrained by the goal of finding replicable and valid outcomes.

Descriptive classification systems are used for many purposes, two of which will be described here. In *linguistic systems,* investigators are more interested in the language used during an event than in the context that precipitated the event. In *sequential analysis,* investigators are usually concerned with consecutive patterns in how behavior unfolds over time.

Linguistic Observations. Linguistic analysis typically involves coding schemes that represent the features of language evident in the flow of talk.[4] Relying on transcriptions of audio- and videotapes, investigators may eliminate contextual details from the coding process. Transcriptions may still take different forms. Linguists interested in how particular words are combined may be most interested in transcriptions that focus on chunks of discourse. In such transcripts, episodes and utterances differ depending on the kinds of details being explored (e.g., sentences, phrases, phonemes). Investigators interested in conversational communication may be most interested in turn-taking issues, how individuals hold one another accountable for speech, and the patterns evident in naturally occurring talk units. Studies of the relations between speech and gesture may focus on pauses, gestures, hesitations, and patterns in prepositional structures. Of course, these are only some of the many combinations of linguistic concerns that will influence how investigators transcribe the information contained in conversational observations.

Coding transcriptions, investigators typically rely on molecular level codes that can be combined into molar level units. Molar units are commonly generated inductively by looking at patterns in molecular coding. These decisions are made by considering features of a theoretical framework and drawing inferences about relations among indicants and theoretical constructs. Investigators may analyze the same data from more than one complementary perspective, but rely on rule-governed logic to make their decisions.[5] Not surprisingly, most of the effort goes into identifying well-defined categories, using those categories consistently when scoring protocols, and ensuring that others can see the same behavior as an observer.[6]

Sequential Observations. In sequential observation, investigators explore how behavior unfolds in time on an event-by-event basis.[7] They identify a single type of event or discrete time period and the sequence of apparent behavior. Investigators may label action in successive seconds or record the order of actions, events, or processes. Coding schemes are written by looking at successive points in time and labeling the order of events. Once codes are defined, observers are trained to use them until everyone can produce essentially the same protocol. In early stages of research, investigators describe the sequence of events, but eventually generate hypotheses to determine the structure, function, and processes of unfolding behavior.

Investigators define sequential coding schemes by starting with a clear question and remaining committed to that question. They resist temptations to progressively broaden a coding scheme and use theoretical rather than mechanical concerns to guide decision making. Codes in this type of behavioral analysis typically emerge from social processes, generated using knowledge of cultural traditions and/or negotiations among people. Inferences are common rather than rare, yet most investigators are careful to concretely represent each coding category.

On another level, sequential analysis requires observers to coordinate knowledge of social processes with the behavior that unfolds in front of them. Observers are expected to interpret rather than simply detect behavior, acting as a kind of cultural informant as well as the instrument. This process cannot be successful if raters rely too much on concrete, physical changes and fail to consider the meaning of speech and gestures to the parties involved; humans have interpretive abilities that machines do not. Ordinarily, a few illustrative examples for each interpreted entity are sufficient to help observers accurately record indicants.

Imagine, for example, a comparative study of emotional displays between 5-year-olds from Guatemala and the United States. A few examples of common sequences might be more than adequate for helping observers recognize the excitement and delight of having a birthday. Labeling emotions without labeling concrete gestures is usually sufficient for well-trained observers. Put another way, if a coding scheme is sufficiently clear, categories would be simple and indicants would have parallel features. If related codes are reasonably distinct and contain the same level of complexity, trained observers can use them with a high degree of accuracy even if all relevant behaviors are not literally represented.

When investigators see subtle differences in behavior, it is better to rely on molecular levels of coding than molar levels. It is easy to find meaningful ways to combine codes, but quite difficult to split them. There may also be situations in which unanticipated patterns emerge in molecular level coding that would not be apparent at a molar level. While designing a coding system, investigators commonly find different levels and functions for classes of codes. If the codes are mutually exclusive and the scheme is sufficiently exhaustive, it becomes reasonable to think about combining codes at a later point in time or comparing associations among codes.

Limitations of Descriptive Classification Systems.   Descriptive classification systems are complex and challenging to use. The flexibility of such systems can both be a virtue and a problem for investigators interested in exploring behavior. Investigators can become highly dependent on the quality and availability of recording technology because reusable records are inordinately helpful while coding. Investigators who are working with a newly emerging theoretical framework can find it arduous to evaluate the quality of theoretical ideas and design measures that yield reliable indicants of behavior. As a program of research evolves over time, the frustrations of trial and error can eventually yield highly valid results if investigators make systematic decisions. The flexibility of descriptive classification systems can yield rich sources of information for investigators to ponder as they imagine the structure of a theory, the function of theoretical models, and the processes by which behavior evolves over time.

MAKING CONNECTIONS

Design a descriptive classification measure. Would a linguistic or sequential approach to recording behavior be appropriate? What features are essential for your system? Ask someone else to make observations using your plan. Did the observer have trouble classifying behavior? What modifications would you make to your coding or recording systems?

Evaluating the Qualities of Indicants: Sources of Error

Rather than explore issues like item difficulty, item discrimination, or internal consistency, investigators using observational measures evaluate the qualities of their coding scheme. Most investigators look for sources of error in the design and implementation of observational techniques. They typically recognize that error does not occur in the "slices of reality" observed, but in the representational system or observational process. Consistent with other measures, error can be found in a theoretical framework, data-collection procedures, and the structure and content of indicants. Error can also be found in the accuracy with which observers fulfill their responsibilities.

One major source of error can emerge in the treatment of the people being observed. Observers introduce a source of error simply by their presence in a situation. In the opening of his book, Malinowski (1992) included a vivid reminder of how the mere presence of an observer can change the events that transpire: A photo called "a ceremonial act of the Kula" shows the last person in line looking at the camera rather than at the ritual in which he was participating, vividly illustrating that observers can alter events. Similarly, participants are likely to change their behavior if they know they are being observed. In addition to simply watching an observer, they may exaggerate or show off their abilities, or experience unusual levels of anxiety. Participants also have agendas that may not be readily apparent to an observer, but influence behavior. Respecting participants' interests and comfort levels is essential for generating fair observations of behavior, but respect is also essential for generating an accurate representation of events.

Errors also arise when parameters of a theoretical framework are poorly defined. Observers may experience difficulty offering a consistent accounting of events when they are unsure of what is being observed, when to notice behavior, or why they are making observations. Observers are more likely to commit logical errors that distort judgments because their own theoretical, experiential, and personal values may distort their perceptions. They can also be influenced by primacy or recency effects in that behavior observed early in a session or in previous sessions can lead to biased perceptions. It is also possible to experience a drift in coding standards over time and across situations. When using rating scales, observers can reveal a tendency toward leniency or gravitate toward the middle of a scale when evaluating behavior. These are only some of the ways in which the interests of the observer can create an unchecked form of bias in the observation process.

Several kinds of error can also emerge from the sampling process. Observers may select an unrepresentative sample of events to observe or choose inappropriate points in time to begin the sessions. They may also draw faulty generalizations about unique behavior, leaving the impression that such behavior is typical. By failing to establish the functional equivalence of events or contexts for observation, investigators can also find a distorted representation of processes and behavior. In addition, they can select an unrepresentative sample of persons to observe, resulting in a biased sample of behavior.

A fourth class of errors can involve procedures for conducting observations. If the techniques for recording observations are inaccurate, unsystematic, or poorly designed, error may be a common occurrence. For example, observers may be asked to make classifications that are too broad to offer insight into individual differences (e.g., determining if children on a playground are playing). The amount of time scheduled for observations may also be too long or too short for the essential behavior to occur and/or fully unfold. Furthermore, behavior can occur at such a fast pace that observers are unable to record all actions, processes, or events. And, when details of behavior overlap to a marked degree, observers may have difficulty distinguishing among codes or categories.

Minimizing Error.   Ordinarily investigators try to minimize most sources of error by becoming familiar with the setting in which observations are to be conducted before designing procedures and coding systems. Sometimes the procedures and sampling techniques are set well before data collection begins, but in many cases the specific procedures evolve over the course of a study or research program. Investigators remember that their primary agenda is to obtain representative samples of the events, processes, and actions necessary for drawing accurate conclusions about more abstract phenomena. They regularly evaluate sources of error in their practices, strive to minimize those sources, and modify procedures to match theoretical agendas. Categorical classification systems may be appropriate for testing hypotheses about behavior, but descriptive classification systems are often necessary prerequisites for such agendas.

MAKING CONNECTIONS

Look at the plans you made in the previous two exercises and compare those plans to the types of error described here. What kinds of error did you minimize? What kinds of error still need to be considered? How would you modify your plans to minimize error?

Reliability for Observational Techniques

Generally speaking, reliability is a means of convincing others that what was observed is not idiosyncratic to the observers. In some cases, investigators try to keep observers naïve about the hypotheses being tested and explore agreement between independent records. In other cases, they compare observers' records to a predetermined standard. The degree to which investigators rely on event-triggered, time-triggered, or cross-classification systems will have some influence on how they use different formulas for calculating reliability. Nevertheless, general concerns for maximizing accuracy and stability remain the same.

When investigators explore issues of accuracy and stability, at least three kinds of reliability techniques are considered. Investigators consider intraobserver reliability, interobserver reliability, and normative reliability. *Intraobserver reliability* evaluates whether observers drift in their judgments, a phenomenon that should be minimized in the measurement process. *Interobserver reliability* is the degree to which multiple raters essentially construct identical protocols. *Normative reliability* involves the degree to which persons are accurately classified by the measurement tool, regardless of which observer rates their behavior. Taking each of these considerations in turn, it should be easy to see that they are highly interdependent.

Intraobserver Reliability. Because observers tend to alter their standards over time, decay in reliability is almost inevitable.[8] Observer drift is usually apparent when scores between two observers are compared and the points of disagreement are scrutinized. It is also possible to compare observers' responses to a standard protocol if one is available. Investigators can respond to observer drift if they designate a person to monitor reliability, rotate the responsibilities for coding and monitoring trained observers, and define strategies to minimize fatigue. When behavior is recorded using technology, for example, it is possible to subdivide the coding responsibilities so that each trained observer is responsible for coding only some categories.

Interobserver Agreement. Investigators typically compare independent ratings to explore interobserver agreement. They verify that two observers record indicants of behavior in the same way. Training observers allows investigators to calibrate the measurement process, improving the quality of the coding system as well as the skill of observers. Several methods are used to calculate agreement for categorical data, but *kappa coefficients* (κ) seem to be the most effective means for considering chance as well as other forms of agreement (see Chapter 5). Pearson correlations (r) are commonly used for comparing ratings that involve continuous data (see Chapter 3).

Investigators sometimes rely on simple calculations of the *percentage of agreement* between two observers. Constructing a "confusion matrix," it is possible to document the points of agreement and disagreement between coders. Table 8.5 offers an example from a study on children's verbal representations of fair contest practices, generated using cross-tabulations in *SPSS*. This comparison reflects the agreement between two raters who offered holistic evaluations of children's ($n = 136$, ages 6 to 14) verbal protocols (see Thorkildsen & White-McNulty, 2002, for the findings). The kappa coefficient for these data was $\kappa = .98$, whereas the percentage of agreement was .99 with disagreement on two protocols.

Notice that the *percentage of agreement* is slightly higher than the *kappa coefficient* for this comparison. This occurs because the percentage of agreement includes the degree to which chance alone is likely to influence concordance and overestimates reliability. Unfortunately, there are times when the percentage of agreement is the only available estimate of reliability. Investigators may cross-classify events, for example, by using more than one category for a particular behavior. Because scoring is not discrete, they are limited to using percentage of agreement for each category. It would be difficult to consider variation in how observers coordinated multiple criteria when assigning codes. If limited to this index, some investigators also report the frequency of disagreement.

You may remember that *Cohen's kappa* (κ) allows for a correction in chance agreement as well as disagreement within a measure (see Chapter 5). Although it may be important to examine confusion matrices to determine where the points of disagreement fall, the coefficient itself can also be weighted to consider the degree of disagreement. Kappa formulas can be adjusted to include more than two observers, estimate how far off the diagonal disagreements fall in ordinal or interval classifications, and/or consider how well an obtained distribution matches theoretical predictions.

In Table 8.5, the two protocols that received different ratings by each evaluator were different by one level rather than more than one. These data represent findings from developmental research in which each level represents a progressively more complex form of reasoning. Information on points of disagreement was included when calculating the kappa coefficient, although ratings on this ordinal scale were very close. Suppose, however, one rater found a protocol to reflect the least complex set of ideas and the other scored it as the most complex combination of ideas. The degree of difference along the ordinal scale would influence the error term when calculating kappa.

Sometimes investigators convert tallies into the proportion of total observations. When that is appropriate, investigators can use *Pearson correlation coefficients* to compare agreement between observers (see Chapter 3). As is the case for kappa coefficients, the resulting coefficient offers an aggregate index of how chance and error influence agreement. When such agreement is high, investigators need not go back and explore points of disagreement, but when it is low, they will need the assistance of a scattergram to determine sources of error.

Table 8.6 includes data from a verbal protocol in which proportions were used to accommodate the fact that older children and adolescents talked more than younger children even though they raised similar issues. For each category, proportions were calculated by

TABLE 8.5   A Sample Confusion Matrix Comparing the Evaluations of Two Raters

	RATER 1				
RATER 2	*Level 1*	*Level 2*	*Level 3*	*Level 4*	TOTAL
Level 1	44				44
Level 2	1	19			20
Level 3		1	23		24
Level 4				48	48
Total	45	20	23	48	136

Note: Points off the diagonal represent points of disagreement.

TABLE 8.6 **Mean Proportions of Speech Acts When Evaluating Fair Contest Procedures and Inter-rater Reliability Coefficients**

VERBAL REFERENCES	MEANS				STANDARD DEVIATIONS				INTER-RATER RELIABILITIES	
	Skill		Luck		Skill		Luck		Skill	Luck
	R1	R2	R1	R2	R1	R2	R1	R2	r	r
Credit allocation	.05	.05	.09	.07	.03	.03	.05	.05	.74	.83
Odds of winning	.11	.10	.25	.30	.04	.04	.07	.08	.83	.82
Incentives for working	.02	.02	.04	.04	.03	.03	.04	.04	.94	.96
Total	.18	.17	.38	.41	.10	.10	.16	.17		

Note: This represents two independent samples of 20 percent of the protocols, one for skill contests and one for luck contests. R1 refers to rater 1 and R2 refers to rater 2. Only three of seven categories are reported here so totals will not equal 100 percent.

dividing a participant's tally score by the total number of speech acts they uttered. Those proportions were calculated separately for each rater and later correlated. Reliabilities were calculated using Pearson coefficients (r) to accommodate the interval nature of these data.

To fully explore types of agreement, investigators sometimes distinguish the *identification of codable units* from the *classification of behavior* using a coding scheme. The former is a more methodical process. In event-sampling, for example, it is helpful to verify that observers all detect the same events before evaluating coding accuracy. This can be difficult in that observers have the potential to disagree on the start of events, the end of events, or both boundaries. Investigators sometimes use time to establish the start and end points, and label homogeneous stretches of time or episodes. Recording the duration of each pattern and marking the point at which behavior changes also involves the use of clocks to determine units while coding events. Setting time intervals with starting and ending points is also helpful for setting boundaries. Determining agreement in the boundaries used to cross-classify events is difficult because differentiating two sets of event-based criteria can be nearly impossible. If two events occur simultaneously, investigators resolve the challenge of cross-classification by simply recording the extent to which observers see the same set of events. When observers are left to define the event, they may not choose the same start and end points. After all these decisions are made, observers can begin to classify behavior.

After coming to agreement on the units for analysis, it becomes appropriate to explore agreement in the frequency of codes within each unit. Investigators do this by asking two respondents to code all or some appropriate percentage of the behaviors to be evaluated. They compare the two sets of codes to illuminate points of agreement and disagreement.

Normative Reliability. Investigators sometimes explore normative assumptions about reliability in one of two ways. Using a standard template to which observer ratings can be compared, investigators can explore relationships between a sample and a set of standardized norms. Kappa coefficients can permit a comparison of the two distributions. If there is homogeneity in the proportion of scores in each margin such that column and row totals are distributed equally, or uniformity in the two margin distributions such that the column totals are distributed in similar patterns to the row totals, it becomes possible to use *S-coefficients* or *Scott's π*.[9]

S-coefficients were designed to explore the degree of agreement between two different methods of obtaining parallel information (Bennett, Alpert, & Goldstein, 1954). Raters are assumed to be independent and the margin totals (columns and rows) are assumed to be equal and uniform. These can be calculated with the formula:

S-COEFFICIENTS

$$S = \frac{k}{k-1}\left(P_O - \frac{1}{k}\right)$$

Here, k reflects the number of categories in a $k \times k$ agreement or "confusion" matrix. P_O reflects the observed proportion of agreements or $\sum_{i=1}^{k} p_{ii}$. In this formula, the correction for chance is defined as $1/k$. This S-coefficient would not be useful for exploring the data in Table 8.5 because the number of participants classified at each level differs.

Scott's π (Scott, 1955) was designed to expand assumptions that column and row totals must be uniform (the same across the different levels in Table 8.5). Proportions for each category are assumed to be the same for the two raters, but each category need not have the same proportion as every other category. It is assumed that raters will classify participants using the same proportions. To calculate *Scott's π* investigators compute the following:

SCOTT'S π

$$\pi = \frac{P_O - \sum_{i=1}^{k}\left(\frac{p_{i+} + p_{+i}}{2}\right)^2}{1 - \sum_{i=1}^{k}\left(\frac{p_{i+} + p_{+i}}{2}\right)^2}$$

Here, p_{i+} is the observed marginal proportions for rater 1 and p_{+i} is the observed marginal proportions for rater 2. *Scott's π* could be useful for the data in Table 8.5 because it is assumed that the two raters will classify the same proportion of participants for each level.

In these analyses, investigators look for whether distributions of behavior conform to a standard pattern rather than compare obtained data to probabilistic assumptions about individual differences. Some investigators assume such comparisons offer a more adequate estimate of normative reliability because those standards are expected to hold across samples.

A second type of normative reliability emerges from *generalizability theory*.[10] Some investigators may not be interested in whether each observation made by two observers match. They would prefer to look at comparisons across codes and participants to make generalizations across observers. In essence, they ask whether the aggregate collection of codes and participants form a predicted normative pattern. Using *intraclass correlation coefficients* and a computer, these investigators conduct analyses using a modified version of Cronbach's α coefficient (see Chapter 4). This analysis reveals whether a collection of codes adequately discriminates people in a manner anticipated by the investigator.

Limitations in Reliability. To explore reliability in observational measures, most investigators start with criterion-referenced assumptions and explore how well behavior matches a standard. Many of the limitations of criterion-referenced measures are also relevant here because indicants typically represent nominal scales of measurement (see Chapter 7). Using tallies and converting them into proportions offers one means for transforming a nominal scale into an ordinal scale and then into an interval scale, but it still remains problematic to explore relationships between coding categories. Accuracy cannot be verified by treating codes like items on a scale because each indicant represents only a nominal judgment about the presence or absence of an action, event, or process. The logic of verifying internal consistency or exploring a relational circumplex does not carry over to this collection of tools.

Some investigators believe that verifying interobserver agreement does not qualify as a measure of reliability.[11] Two observers at a birthday party could both use each code with the same frequency but focus on different actions while making their decisions. Because codes are not directly linked with behavior, it is not possible to estimate the resulting systematic error that could occur. These investigators note the existence of systematic error and modify their conclusions to reflect this awareness.

Rather than reject the possibility of reliability, it seems helpful to distinguish between accuracy and stability. Verifying accuracy in the calibration of a measurement tool is possible with information on interobserver and intraobserver agreement. Information on stability is less adequate, but can be estimated by comparing a coded protocol to a theoretically determined standard and determining how well the two sets of indicants agree. Stability can also be evaluated by comparing the distribution of scores across two samples of behaviors or participants.

Comparing distributions of responses to a standard protocol offers one means for comparing indicants to standards, but the many forms of reliability involving norm-referenced assumptions remain inappropriate for this type of scoring system. The idea that behavior within an event or across a relevant time sequence would be normally distributed in a sample will be untenable if a coding scheme is representative of the behavior to be observed and participants are selected because they are likely to exhibit such behavior. Everyone would be expected to engage in at least a reasonable proportion of the behaviors being recorded.

■ ■ ■ ■ ■ ▬▬▬▬▬▬▬▬▬▬▬▬▬▬▬▬▬▬▬▬▬▬▬▬▬▬▬▬▬▬▬▬▬

MAKING CONNECTIONS

Consider the reliability of your measures. What steps would you take to maximize intraobserver reliability? What steps would you take to ensure interobserver agreement? How would you evaluate accuracy and stability considerations? Can you make normative predictions about the patterns that should appear in your results? How could you use that information to explore normative reliability?

Validity of Observational Techniques

Behavior can be measured for many reasons, but applied research commonly includes tacit or *situation-specific procedures* more often than *question-specific procedures* or *sequential verification.* Without considering all levels, however, investigators may not fully consider validity. Exploring validity for observational measures involves theorizing about general patterns and includes all levels of consideration.

Content Validity.   In observational research, the coding schemes and recording methods serve as a blueprint for organizing evidence. On the blueprint, coding categories form one set of parameters and the structure for determining which events to sample and for how long become the second. Procedural parameters outline whether observers record time, tally behavior, or make ratings and so forth.

Content validity is established by comparing the weighting and proportions of recording formats for different dimensions of a classification system. This includes balancing codes in relation to theoretical dimensions as investigators generate predictions of which codes will be used more and less often.

To study conceptions of fair contests, for example, we predicted that children would discuss the parameters of contest rules more often for luck-based contests than skill-based contests and that the balance of their speech acts would reflect intrapersonal concerns with mood, talents, and interests (Table 8.6). Looking at mean totals, this prediction was sufficiently upheld to validate the content of children's speech.

As is the case for other kinds of psychometric measures, content validity hinges on how well indicants represent theoretical constructs. Many of these decisions depend on the levels of specificity to be observed, recorded, and combined using data reduction techniques.

Criterion Validity.   To determine if the dimensions within a measure offer a solid representation of theoretical constructs, investigators compare anticipated patterns among codes to obtained data. Using cross-tabulation and χ^2 methods, they can look for concurrent validity by comparing codes that reflect common dimensions of behavior and determining how often two codes are used in tandem. Nonsignificant relationships between distributions of two coding categories can offer evidence of their relative independence, supporting discriminant validity.

When children's conceptions of fair ways to organize contests were compared to their ability to differentiate skill and luck tasks, for example, the resulting $\chi^2_{(1,n=136)} = 98.37$, $p < .000$. The linear pattern between two sets of scores showed a strong degree of concurrent validity (Table 8.7).

With data collected using nominal or ordinal scales, there are fewer statistical techniques for comparing dimensions than is the case for interval data. Investigators maximize opportunities for comparison by converting nominal indicants into frequencies or proportions. They may also ask raters to evaluate behavior using more than one indicant of the same dimension and add or average those ratings to approximate an interval distribution. Once these conversions are completed, most of the available methods used for other measures are applied to observational data. After frequencies are converted to proportions, for example, investigators may conduct a factor analysis to verify concurrent and discriminant

TABLE 8.7   Comparison of Two Scales of Speech Acts to Explore Concurrent Validity

FAIR CONTEST PROCEDURES	DIFFERENTIATING SKILL AND LUCK				TOTAL
	Level 1	*Level 2*	*Level 3*	*Level 4*	
Level 1	27	14	3	1	45
Level 2	4	12	3	1	20
Level 3		5	8	10	23
Level 4			5	43	48
Total	31	31	19	55	136

validity. When there are relatively few categories to consider, they may also compute simple correlations among the obtained data. Remembering the limitations of nominal, ordinal, and interval scales is necessary for making wise decisions about the value of factor analysis and other methods of data reduction.

Because most observational measures involve nominal forms of measurement, predictive validity is usually obtained by comparing an existing distribution of observations to a set of predetermined standards. Investigators use nonparametric statistical techniques for comparing a theoretical distribution to an obtained distribution. Computer programs often compute statistics that rely on the assumption of equivalence in cell frequencies, but it is possible to replace that probability distribution with a theoretically derived set of assumptions. Investigators sometimes use forms of *logistic regression* or *transform their data* to approximate the kind of interval scale required for other forms of regression.

Construct Validity.   Investigators typically explore construct validity by including observational measures in more complex research designs. You may remember that attitude measures are often used to predict behavior and observations are included in studies of traits and states. Evaluations of specific actions often include the reasoning associated with those actions and multiple kinds of evidence are coordinated to draw conclusions.

By now it should be clear that validation occurs in many ways. Investigators can combine self-report, observational, and standardized test data in factor analysis to determine the degree to which convergent and divergent validity are apparent in the dimensions that make up each latent construct. They can also explore predictive relationships among different methods of measuring the same construct by including them in regression equations, hierarchically linear models (HLM), or structural equation models (SEM). Ideally, parallel measures of each dimension are positively associated and measures of alternative dimensions are negatively associated or uncorrelated according to the dictates of a working definition.

Theoretical Validity.   As you probably remember, theoretical validity is an essential feature of all measurement plans and typically involves the integration of different kinds of tools. In this last psychometric chapter, generalizations that may initially have seemed overly abstract can now be grounded in greater detail. Although early definitions of construct validity involved the assumption that constructs are technically theories rather than variables, current methods offer a confusing representation of theoretical complexity. For this reason, *theoretical validity* is differentiated from *construct validity* and *theoretical concepts* are distinguished from *theoretical constructs.*

Theories, in this view, can be simple or complex. Thinking about the most general level of validity, knowledge of the structure of constructs is combined into explanatory concepts. Just as the function of latent variables in a larger theoretical model is nested in other parameters, processes associated with the origin, sequence, endpoints, and consequences of a theoretical model are also invariably nested. Theorists are interested in explaining how these nested features are coordinated. Changing one feature of this kind of dynamic system invariably affects other features.

Experimental research in which specific features of a larger system are isolated and/or manipulated facilitates conclusions about particular patterns and offers evidence for relations between theoretical constructs and concepts. Observational research lends itself to clear representations of theoretical validity because actions are concrete, repeated, and laden with meaning. People learn to identify patterns of action at a very young age, making similar kinds of interpretations of related events. Like others, most investigators want to know more than which actions took place during a particular time or event sequence. They want to know why such actions occur, the events leading up to such actions, and the consequences of such actions. These questions can invariably be answered only in light of valid measurement and by comparing behavior with other variables in the formation of concepts.

Theoretical validity emerges over the course of a research program rather than from a single study. All aspects of measurement and research design come into play when researchers are verifying relationships between cognitive, affective, and conative processes as well as between intrapersonal, interpersonal, and extrapersonal experiences.

MAKING CONNECTIONS

Look at the qualities of the measures you designed and evaluate their strength and limitations. What procedures would you use to explore the validity of each measure? Could you cross-validate information from two measures? What levels of validity could you explore?

MEASURING PHYSIOLOGICAL REACTIONS

Early in the history of the social sciences, investigators tried to measure many variables by drawing associations with physical reactions. Now that there are other available techniques, it is sometimes easy to forget that physiological measures can still be useful for some purposes. In many cases, investigators use tools that work like a physiological yardstick to draw comparisons with psychological characteristics. Some of these tools yield data that conform to the properties of a ratio scale, with an absolute 0 as well as equal intervals. Other tools yield interval data that offer information about patterns in individuals' physiological arousal. Investigators whose research program would be augmented by these tools usually collaborate with others who have some form of medical or physiological training. The remainder of this chapter, therefore, serves only as a reminder of some of the common techniques that have been used by social scientists to measure human functioning.

Measures will be classified into three categories: *psychophysical scaling, measures of isolated physical properties,* and *measures of the central nervous system.* Specific tools represent a narrow range of those available, but have been used in social science research. They have been used to explore attitudes and attitude change, personality types, and cognitive functioning.

Psychophysical Scaling

Historically, investigators who were highly committed to validating psychological variables by linking them with physical processes began by measuring the physical attributes of individuals with different characteristics and comparing those attributes. Investigators are cautious about using *psychophysical scaling* in which physical and psychological dimensions are combined to draw inferences. Measuring attributes like brain size, body type, and physical size offered little insight into individuals' psychological functioning, but some of those methods influenced today's measurement procedures. Magnitude estimation tasks, for example, were a later development, but became one device for connecting physical and psychological characteristics while minimizing previously exaggerated inferences.

Magnitude Estimation Tasks. Investigators using *magnitude estimation tasks* present physical stimuli such as tones, smells, or lights and ask respondents to make psychological judgments about the resulting sensations. Common eye and hearing examinations reflect this form of measurement. Manipulating the magnitude of stimuli invariably produces different sensations and respondents are asked to draw psychological inferences about those sensations. Once the sensation scales are constructed, they are used as a kind of ruler to compare responses across participants.

In one kind of magnitude estimation task, respondents were asked to compare a stimulus to the brightness of lights. Investigators have also asked respondents to evaluate the same stimuli using light intensity and tone loudness to cross-validate such ratings (Dawson, 1982). Some investigators (see Stevens, 1956; Stevens & Galanter, 1957) have asserted that such measures represent ratio measurement scales, but others have supported the idea that, at best, this method yields interval data (Dawson, 1982).

Limitations of Psychophysical Scales. In these measures, respondents rather than investigators draw inferences between their internal states and external stimuli. Because respondents' physiological reactions are not directly measured, these methods are limited by respondents' ability to interpret their internal reactions. Calibration of such tools involves the same dilemmas associated with the observational measures, where respondents serve as untrained observers.

Measures of Isolated Physical Properties

Investigators have also designed tools to directly measure particular physical reactions. These tools typically rely on elaborate laboratory equipment to monitor individuals' physical reactions to stimuli. Respondents are shown an external stimulus and a machine measures physiological changes in one part of the body.

Pupillary Response.   Some investigators have measured the degree to which pupils dilate or constrict in response to a stimulus. Generally, when a visual stimulus is interesting, pupils tend to dilate, but in some conditions they constrict. This method has been somewhat controversial because in studies of whether pupils tend to constrict in the face of aversive stimuli, findings have been inconsistent. Nevertheless, exploration of *pupillary responses,* when used in conjunction with other measures, can facilitate inferences about respondents' emotional arousal.

Eye or Head Tracking.   Investigators also measure the extent to which stimuli elicit *eye or head movement* when evaluating attention processes. In studies of infant vision, for example, peripheral vision was explored by placing infants in a dark room, flashing lights just outside the range normally attributed to direct vision, and watching to see if babies turned their heads to see the light more clearly. Similar work has been done by tracking students' eye movements to understand more about their study strategies. The equipment needed to track these physical reactions can be a little daunting to respondents, and typically involves laboratory work. Nevertheless, investigators learn how to compare respondents' self-reported actions and their actual behavior to understand the relationships between perception and other psychological variables.

Electrodermal Activity.   A measure of skin resistance, the *galvanic skin response* involves a measure of skin's ability to conduct electricity when the sweat glands become active. Sweat glands are under the control of the sympathetic nervous system and using a galvanometer, voltmeter, or other newer technologies, investigators record sweat secretions by placing electrodes on the hands or on another relevant place on the body. Although investigators have tried to differentiate positive and negative attitudes using this measure, it lacks the precision necessary for making such discriminations. At best, investigators can draw inferences about the presence or absence of arousal. The arousal may be attributable to surprise, novelty, or other forms of change, but the factors that initiate such arousal can only be inferred.

Facial Electromyographic Activity.   Another method that has been used to explore emotional states involves the measurement of contractions in facial muscles. Using *electromyographic techniques* (EMG), investigators have differentiated zygomatic muscles (associated with smiling) and corrugator muscles (associated with frowning). Measuring the subtle changes in different forms of muscle movements in response to stimuli offers an indication of whether respondents experience pleasure or discomfort.

Limitations of Isolated Measures.   Reactions attributable to isolated body parts have offered more information about relationships between psychological variables and physical arousal than self-report measures alone. Nevertheless, it is difficult to gain an integrated sense of whether isolated physical reactions are strong enough to influence behavior. There is also a high degree of inference between measures of physiological reactions and psychological attributions that is difficult to verify with other measures. As some cognitive scientists have put it, knowledge of biology is essential for understanding consciousness and mind, but knowledge of one feature does not offer sufficient information for understanding the other.[12] By analogy, measuring only an isolated feature of an individual's physiology is likely to offer an incomplete picture of either side of this intellectual equation.

Measures of the Central Nervous System

Newer technologies offer relatively nonintrusive measures of the central nervous system and corresponding brain functions.[13] The information gleaned from these tools has investigators from many fields excited about the potential information to be acquired by drawing associations between physiological states or reactions and psychological variables. The field of cognitive science, for example, has become replete with the assumption that to understand concepts of mind and consciousness, it is essential to move well beyond questions of the presence or absence of arousal and explore evolutionary processes, genetic codes, biochemical reactions, and neural pathways as well as tangible expressions of reasoning, emotion, and behavior.[14] In addition, nonintrusive measures of functioning in the central nervous system are becoming more widely used to draw conclusions about personality, attitudes, and behavior. To give you some indication of just how complex the array of choices has become, some of the current measures used to draw inferences about the central nervous system will be outlined.

Electroenchephalograph (EEG).   Investigators often look at baseline mental functioning using an *electroenchephalograph* (EEG). This measure is represented by waveforms consisting of several frequencies. Investigators compare differences in waves, most often alpha waves, to determine the degree of cortical arousal. Averaging the responses of repeated short samples, taken under different conditions (e.g., while asleep, awake, stimulated) can offer a sense of how the brain functions under these conditions. Studies of abnormal brain functioning (e.g., after a traumatic brain injury or in light of birth defects) have facilitated hypothesis testing about which patterns are essential for different kinds of mental activity. *Functional magnetic resonance imaging* (fMRI) and other newer technologies are becoming more widely used to explore similar changes in biochemical functioning.

Cortical evoked responses (CER).   Extending the logic of comparing brainwaves, some investigators also explore changes in brain activity that occur in response to brief presentations of a stimulus. Participants' brain activity after a stimulus is introduced is compared to the results of an EEG to explore the patterns of peaks. Early peaks are assumed to be elicited by the stimulus itself whereas later peaks are assumed to reflect attentional or other more elaborate cognitive processes. Systematic variations in the intensity of a stimulus, the overall arousal level, and the rate of stimulus presentation are often averaged over many trials to draw conclusions about the processing of information.

Brainstem auditory evoked response (BAER).   Similar to the cortical evoked response, seven positive waves associated with the brainstem are measured to determine the influence of auditory stimulus on brain functioning. Over a large number of trials, waves are measured within the first ten ms of a stimulus presentation. The results are averaged and the initial latency (time from stimulus to peak) or interpeak latencies (time between peaks) are evaluated. The *brainstem auditory evoked response* (BAER) offers a sense of typical auditory functioning, which is likely to influence how well individuals can respond to auditory information.

Audiomotor reflex (AMR).   Investigators also measure an individual's *audiomotor reflex* by introducing auditory, visual, cutaneous, or electrical stimulation. This introduction produces a phasic startle reaction that offers information on connections between the brainstem and other processes such as movement in facial nerves. Learning about startle reactions offers further evidence of the sensitivity of the central nervous system to stimuli in the environment.

Cardiovascular Measures.   Psychological variables such as stress or personality type have often been inferred from indicators of variation in the cardiovascular system. Individual differences in *blood pressure, heart rate, respiration volume,* and *weight loss* have been used to draw inferences about respondents' internal states, dispositional reactions to their environment or to change, and the overall strength of their central nervous system.

Blood Chemical Measures.   Looking at information gleaned from *blood tests,* some investigators also explore the levels of particular chemicals in the blood to draw conclusions about psychological variables such as stress, emotion, or personality type. One chemical, monoamine oxidase (MAO) has been associated with hostility. Other circulating catecholamines have been associated with high indices of Type A behavior. These biochemical differences have led investigators to conclude that individuals vary in the responsive/reactive functioning of their sympathetic nervous system.

Limitations of Measuring the Central Nervous System.   Although investigators can measure many more physiological reactions today than they have in the past, it becomes difficult to verify how well these tools correspond with other forms of human functioning. It is easy to see that behavior is highly influenced by physiological reactions. People with diabetes, for example, typically alter their life to accommodate the dramatic changes in blood sugar they confront at unexpected intervals. Anticipating the change can prove beneficial if steps can be taken to accommodate the impending reactions. Nevertheless, more information is available concerning when and how physiological processes break down than when all functions fall within the normal range.

Many investigators have difficulty finding adequate resources for designing studies with an adequate control group and disease-focused models often drive research agendas. Even if they were asked, people with few physical problems may be reluctant to participate in such laboratory investigations out of fear or because of the impending expense. Despite the ratio scale of many medical tools, normative data is often sorely lacking.

■ ■ ■ ■ ■ ■

MAKING CONNECTIONS

Find a study in your general field that includes a physiological measure. What tools were used to measure physiological reactions? What other variables were included in the study? How did investigators support their inferences about the relationships among variables?

MEASURING ACTIONS AND REACTIONS

The process of measuring behavior and physical reactions with sufficient clarity is an arduous task. In both cases, it can be difficult to identify normative standards for use in making comparisons. When such standards are accepted, there are still many decisions to be made about the definitions of indicants, the appropriate levels of inference for associating indicants with theoretical constructs, and how constructs can be combined to form defensible concepts. Nevertheless, these challenges, when appropriately met, can offer rich insight into how individuals coordinate intrapersonal, interpersonal, and extrapersonal information.

SUGGESTED READINGS

Bakeman, R., & Gottman, J. M. (1997). *Observing interaction: An introduction to sequential analysis* (2nd ed.). New York: Cambridge University Press.

Everston, C. M., & Green, J. L. (1986). Observation as inquiry and method. In M. C. Wittrock (Ed.), *Handbook of research on teaching* (3rd ed., pp. 162–213). New York: Macmillan.

Fassnacht, G. (1982). *Theory and practice of observing behavior.* London: Academic Press.

Green, R. G. (1997). Psychophysical approaches to personality. In R. Hogan, J. Johnson, & S. Briggs (Eds.), *Handbook of personality psychology* (pp. 387–414). New York: Academic Press.

Pellegrini, A. D. (1996). *Observing children in their natural worlds: A methodological primer.* Mahwah, NJ: Erlbaum.

Sackett, G. (1978). *Observing behavior.* Baltimore, MD: University Park Press.

Sattler, J. M. (2001). *Assessment of children: Behavioral and clinical applications* (4th ed.). San Diego, CA: J. M. Sattler.

ENDNOTES

1. Rosenblum (1978) offers an elaborate summary of this set of concerns. Everston & Green (1986) also offer a cogent summary of how observational research is used in educational contexts. Their classification model is relevant to several chapters in this book. Readers interested in specific tools used in educational research will also find their review of research quite valuable.

2. Chapters 3 to 7 outline many of these procedures, although all measures cannot be meaningfully translated into observational tools.

3. These suggestions were extracted from Bakeman & Gottman (1997), who offer a great deal of concrete advice on how to proceed through the coding, recording, and analysis phases of observational research.

4. Everston & Green (1986) offer a more elaborate examination of linguistic analysis of observations.

11. Glaser & Strauss (1967) offer one set of guidelines that is still used today.

12. *Atlas.ti,* http://www.atlasti.com, and *QSR NVIVO* (formerly *NUD-IST*), http://www.scolari.co.uk, are two

very useful software packages for helping investigators keep track of this kind of coding. More details on how this is accomplished are provided in later chapters. The designers of these software packages did not intend for them to be used by psychometricians, but the tools are very helpful for keeping track of linguistic coding.

7. See Bakeman & Gottman (1997) for more elaborate guidelines on this type of observation.

8. Taplin & Reid (1973) conducted a study in which the monitoring of observers influenced the propensity for observer drift. Regardless of the monitoring program they used, reliability inevitably declined. Despite this decline, random rather than systematic checking of observer vigilance was most effective in minimizing such drift. Bakeman & Gottman (1997) have since tested the suggestions included here.

9. Zwick (1988) offers a strong case for using these options rather than assuming that kappa coefficients are appropriate for all forms of inter-rater agreement.

10. This work was initiated by Cronbach, Gleser, Nanda, & Rajaratnam (1972). Other elaborations on the use of this approach can be found in Fleiss (1986), Hartmann (1982), and Suen (1988, 1990).

11. See Bakeman & Gottman (1997) for this type of claim. They are also interested in sequential analysis and are not as interested in global comparisons of an observer's protocol to a theoretical standard.

12. See Edelman (1992) and Damasio (1999) for more detailed descriptions of these assumptions.

13. Green (1997) outlines many uses for such physiological tools while exploring how personality characteristics are measured using physical symptoms.

14. Edelman (1992) and Damasio (1999) offer different versions of the same claim. Luciana & Nelson (2002) and Nelson et al. (2000) have completed studies using the fMRI to explore how adolescents' brain development is associated with behavior.

CHAPTER NINE

ASSUMPTIONS OF DEVELOPMENTAL MEASUREMENT

Given that the various social sciences are predicated on different ontological and methodological assumptions, measurement plans are constructed to reflect decisions in particular discourse communities. This chapter is the first of four that emphasize the measurement of change commonly used in discourse about human development. This broad overview of common assumptions will be followed by more detailed chapters about various epistemic and methodological questions concerning growth and development.

Developmental research involves the coordination of conceptual patterns and causes while offering scientific explanations for variation in human functioning. Most developmental researchers emphasize distinctions between explanation and description that differ from those associated with psychometrically-driven experimental research. Accepting the dynamic nature of development and that people are situated in historical time and local contexts, developmentalists do not search for universal laws that will hold for people of all ages.[1] Developmental research is descriptive and, ideally, such work offers insight into general explanatory models. Long-term research agendas inevitably coordinate backward-looking theoretical claims that are grounded in historical assumptions with forward-looking plans to discover new empirical, methodological, and theoretical explanations for human functioning. Research programs as well as people develop, and change is fundamental to such growth.

Developmental researchers use a variety of techniques to accomplish their goals. Investigators use *psychometric measurement tools* when they want to determine how individuals perform in relation to a set of norms or standards. Measurements that reflect stable classifications of individuals or aspects of functioning are seen as valid evidence for stability in human functioning. To describe as well as explain behavior, developmental researchers may use psychometric tools in experimental designs and explore relationships between variables that are deliberately manipulated. Details on the shared features of human functioning can serve as anchors to which more dynamic features are compared. Findings from psychometric tools can facilitate descriptions of typical attitudes, personalities, abilities, emotions, and/or behavior. Combining such measures with evidence of change can facilitate rich explanations of the structure, function, and process of development.

STUDYING A DYNAMIC SYSTEM

Investigators use *developmental measurement* when they want to measure change, aware that change can take many forms. When identifying incidents, they may rely on many of the same rules found within the psychometric tradition. Nevertheless, developmentalists are aware that the nature of dimensions and relations among indicants might change over time. Furthermore, indicants that are essential to describing functioning at one age may entirely disappear or take another form at another age. As individuals acquire more abilities, they often move through a cycle of complex functioning followed by simplicity and back to complexity in ever-widening circles. Common jokes about needing the same care from others at the beginning and end of life illustrate our awareness of such cycles. To measure such cycles, the qualities of indicants as well as the calibration of tools change.

Although most social scientists prefer to emphasize growth, decay also reflects important change in human functioning. The iterative nature of exploring change can lead new investigators to mistakenly assume that research always involves a linear progression toward improvement. If development is a form of improvement in human functioning, decay is the antithesis of that improvement.

How Is Change Explored?

When investigators explore change, they are confronted with one of three kinds of measurement decisions. They decide whether or not to:

- manipulate the design of research to include temporal or age-related variables;
- change tools or indicants over time to reflect evolving concepts;
- change the calibration of tools to reflect emerging or retreating dimensions.

Manipulating a Design.   Differences between two sets of scores do not necessarily reflect growth. Therefore, investigators design studies to explicitly measure change, and often use the same measurement tools across participants. The same variables could be measured either by sampling participants of different ages at the same point in time or by repeating measurement at different time intervals. *Cross-sectional designs* typically include multiple samples of individuals from different age groups. *Longitudinal designs* tend to involve repeated measures with the same participants. To draw inferences about development, investigators also include some means of verifying that change is not random. Growth and decay are distinguished by testing predictions about the direction of change.

Changing Tools.   When investigators change tools over time, they try to ensure that the same constructs are measured using age-appropriate indicants or methods of extracting information. Ideally, indicants offer a reasonable match for participants' age and abilities as well as the context under consideration, even if a construct may be pan-contextual. Imagine, for example, trying to understand children's play, both before and after they develop the ability to use fantasy.[2] Before fantasy becomes common, children may have little interest in things like boxes or other kinds of household objects. Once they are able to pretend that a box is a house and a towel is a blanket, the nature of play is likely to change. New measurement tools that would serve no purpose when children are unable to pretend may be necessary for capturing the content of the stories and games they generate.

Recalibrating Tools.   There are also times when investigators need not add or replace tools, but will be compelled to recalibrate an existing tool for appropriate comparisons. The most obvious example of this involves the use of vocabulary on surveys. What seems like a simple statement to one person may contain more than one idea to another. Some ideas may be so coordinated in a designer's mind that he or she cannot imagine a time when the information was not understood.

Young children, for example, are not as insulted as older children and adolescents by feedback indicating a need for more effort.[3] Young children simply accept their lack of skill and see effort as the only means of changing the situation. After about age 13, most individuals are likely to see two reasons for requiring greater effort. Such feedback can imply a lack of capacity for acquiring new information or a sense of laziness.[4] Many older participants assume that pressure to work harder emerges when they have low ability. They also know that their ability is likely to constrain the effects of effort on performance and differ in their willingness to remain task-focused. When focused exclusively on their capacity, older learners are likely to believe that no amount of effort can improve ability. Individuals who operate this way tend to differentiate effort, skill, and capacity in ways that younger children do not. This new knowledge leads to more complex inferences that can include a sense of insult when being told to work harder. This insult, of course, is most injurious when adolescents or adults assume they have already been working hard.

To measure these reactions, investigators have isolated representations of capacity, skill, and effort when measuring motivation. Theorists often remain aware that young children are likely to have difficulty distinguishing these motivational dimensions because they treat all three issues interchangeably or focus on unrelated aspects of the question.[5] The same constructs could be used for all participants in a feedback study, but it would be more informative to recalibrate the tool across different age groups. Isolating the dimensions of capacity, skill, and effort might seem repetitious to young children, but would be easily distinguished by older participants.

Theoretical Parameters

Decisions about what to isolate raise different design and measurement concerns. Researchers may theorize about different features of a larger developmental system, but they hold different assumptions about how individuals and environments are fused in ontogeny. These assumptions foster a wide range of topical variability in studies of human development. Despite holistic assumptions about development, investigators tend to isolate features of the system for scrutiny. Looking at the *Handbook of Child Psychology,* for example, four volumes of review chapters cover topics like cognition, perception, and language as well as social, emotional, and personality development.[6] Chapters also reflect general theoretical assumptions about common beliefs in the field and practical work on intervention research.[7]

For each topic, only some substrates of a developmental system may be relevant to understanding a particular form of human functioning. To illustrate this point, two general approaches to theorizing will be contrasted here (Figure 9.1).

An Ecological Developmental System

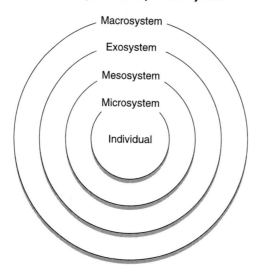

An Individualistic Developmental System

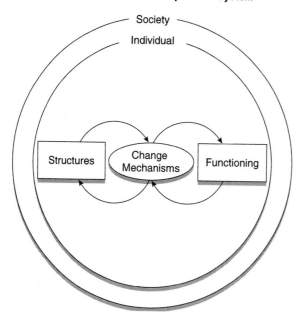

FIGURE 9.1   **Common Models for Studying Human Development**

Ecological Theories.   An ecological approach assumes that individuals cannot be isolated from the context in which they function.[8] The *microsystem* represents all patterns of an individual's functioning, including activities, roles, and interpersonal relations that occur when developing persons are in a given setting. The *mesosystem* indicates the forces that directly affect socialization and development. An *exosystem* consists of contexts that do not include the developing person, but exert pressure on his or her development. Finally, the *macrosystem* is the culture that includes microsystems, mesosystems, and exosystems.

Individualism.   Focusing more intently on the individual and the microsystem in which the individual functions, investigators may emphasize *development within a person* while assuming that development occurs in context. Intrapersonal structures show a bidirectional relation with functioning that invariably undergoes change. Investigators may look for common patterns across contexts rather than assume that contexts cause change.

Comparing Psychometric and Developmental Measurement

Both ecological and individualistic assumptions about development require tools that are sufficiently sensitive to detecting change. To understand the dilemmas posed by this task, let's recall the virtues and limitations of psychometric tools. Remember that assessment tools allow investigators to compare individual scores to a predetermined set of norms. Psychometric tools are also used in research to compare aggregate estimates of performance to probabilistic predictions. For these purposes, tools must *maintain their calibration* over time and contain an adequate degree of *internal consistency* in how indicants are related to one another. To validate constructs and concepts, psychometricians look for *stability* in the distribution of scores.

Developmental measurement has some similarities with psychometric approaches, but also differs in many respects. Developmental tools are designed to record *changes* in individuals, families, communities, and society such that issues of *calibration, internal consistency,* and *stability* take on different meaning (Bronfenbrenner, 1979). These researchers typically assume that *an individual's ontogeny* is one outcome of a *dynamic developmental system* that is constantly in motion and involves the fusion of person and context.

To help you see the challenges of measuring change more clearly, the developmental chapters will emphasize individual development, leaving the measurement of *mesosystems* and *exosystems* for the interpretive section that introduces ethnographic tools. Considering all levels of an ecological system is generally too large an undertaking for new investigators, but designing studies that isolate one narrow part of a system can lead to successful thesis work.

Components of Individual Development

Exploring development typically involves evaluating bidirectional relationships between a person's internal structures and the functioning of those structures in multiple levels of organization.[9] To study these relationships, investigators typically isolate levels of the larger developmental system that serve some socially useful purpose. Studies of motivation, for example, involve the exploration of personal needs, intentions, goals, strategies, attributions, and behavior as well as the conditions under which these ontological processes are elicited. Some aspects of motivation change as a function of the situation parameters, but other aspects reflect more enduring kinds of growth. Investigators interested in growth may use specialized designs and/or specialized tools to verify the direction and stability of change necessary for explaining the development of motivation. More generally, the study of individual development commonly involves the differentiation of three components that can be isolated or considered in combination (Figure 9.1b).

Structure.   *Structure* is a substrate of a person such as limbs, nervous tissue, muscle, or mental maps that are measured using most of the tools reviewed in previous chapters. Structures also reflect an individual's role or social position in a particular context. Furthermore, structures can account for individuals' understanding of their environments.

When investigators study structures, they typically isolate components of a developmental system and explore both related and unrelated dimensions (see Chapter 10). Relations can be hierarchical such that less complex dimensions are gradually incorporated into more complex dimensions in additive, multiplicative, or qualitatively different ways. Dimensions may also be completely coordinated or completely independent of one another while remaining part of a more general structure. Furthermore, dimensions may show some degree of overlap, but also serve independent purposes within a structure. This logic is consistent with psychometric definitions of constructs. Put another way, developmentalists assume that definitions of constructs are not stable and look at structure to determine which dimensions belong to a construct for a given point in development. When measuring internal structures, for example, investigators may use one or multiple tools and look for relations among the dimensions to identify the structure of a construct.

Functioning.   Investigators often identify structures by trying to explain the actions and reactions detected in the study of human functioning. Put more formally, *functioning* involves actions related to structures and is influenced by identifiable *levels of organization* for such structures as well as between them.[10] Many investigators choose to isolate particular ontological structures because they notice a practical dilemma associated with functioning. A flurry of research on aggression, for example, was stimulated by the awareness that children were frequently hurting one another, eliciting a desire to understand the structure of aggression well enough to change such social functioning.

There is a reciprocal relation between structure and functioning; functioning in the world is assumed to cause structural change and changes in structure cause changes in functioning. For example, adolescents who actively engage in sensation-seeking are more likely to participate in high-risk behavior than those who do not, and the nature of that experience affects the structures they form for dealing with the resulting stimulation. Their behavior affects the mental maps they construct for organizing their social sensory experience, which in turn affects the degree to which they will engage in high-risk behavior in the future. Over time, these cycles influence adolescents' opportunities for risk-taking and incorporating that experience into their identities.

Whereas structure is usually seen as the substrate of a person's ontogeny or the levels of organization in which ontogeny is embedded, functioning in a system can take many

FIGURE 9.2 Possible Dimensions for Exploring Functioning in Development

		PERSON	
		Endogenous	*Exogenous*
STRUCTURE	*Endogenous*		
	Exogenous		

forms.[11] Figure 9.2 offers one means by which investigators have diagramed functioning. In that model, functioning can be endogenous or exogenous to both particular persons and social or ontological structures. If functioning is endogenous both to a person and a structure, most investigators are focusing on individuals rather than the entire developmental system. If functioning is exogenous to people and structures, investigators are studying the broader context in which functioning occurs. Theorists also have subtle ways of coordinating structures and functioning that reflect topical expertise.

When looking at functioning that is endogenous to both a person and a structure, fusion in more than one organizational level is possible. Within a family, for example, a boy's feelings of closeness with his sister can influence his willingness to disclose sensitive thoughts to his sibling. The boy's feelings are internal to himself and he is embedded in his family structure.

Suppose functioning is exogenous to a person as well as a structure. A child who is undergoing a family tragedy, for example, may have difficulty solving a math problem in school. Both the tragedy and the child's emotional reactions to it are external to the child's problem-solving performance, even though the child's functioning may be influenced by both exogenous sources.

Functioning can also involve more complex relations. If functioning is endogenous to the person while still being exogenous to an ontological structure, the emphasis is on how people function. During a cognitive task, for example, neurochemical or hormonal secretions can constrain the retrieval of information, but remain outside the structures or conceptions someone uses to organize his or her knowledge. If functioning is external to the person but internal to a structure, more emphasis is placed on the context in which functioning occurs than on the ontological structures of a person. Again assuming the family is an organizational level with a developmental structure, a boy's position in his family's birth-order hierarchy will influence how family members treat him.

Careful study of human functioning is much easier to execute than careful study of developmental structures. Measures of human functioning can often be grounded using readily apparent observables such as actions, biochemical events, or self-reported judgments. Measures of structures often involve at least one level of inference derived from testing predictions about the dimensions that drive functioning. It is difficult, for example, to see the thoughts an individual brings forth to understand a particular situation. When predicting that particular thoughts will lead to action, investigators can manipulate contexts to test their predictions and draw inferences.

Change Mechanisms.   When combining descriptive and explanatory information, investigators draw inferences about change mechanisms within a system. *Change mechanisms* are the causal links embedded in developmental concepts to explain relations between structural and functional constructs. Such mechanisms are usually inferences about associations between structures and functioning. When investigators can isolate and measure structures and functioning with the same degree of precision, these measurements can serve as anchors for drawing conclusions about change mechanisms.

Labels for change mechanisms or developmental processes are usually derived from evidence, but the actual mechanisms are typically unseen by investigators. Mechanisms of change may reflect discrete, successive, multilevel, and/or integrated categories in one or more levels of a social system. To complicate matters further, such developmental systems involve co-occurring biological, psychological, relational, sociocultural, and geographical ecologies. Within a program of research, investigators isolate those features that can yield practical as well as theoretical insight and document the change that occurs within each level of organization.

Differences in Tools and Their Use

As is the case for psychometrically derived research, the parameters of developmental systems are generally defined by theoretical frameworks used to distinguish various constructs and how the dimensions of those constructs are related to one another. Yet, developmental research relies on the assumption that change is more salient than stability and that norms will be dynamic rather than static. Developmentalists explore the relationships between structure and functioning to determine changes in each dimension as well as how the two components facilitate more general forms of ontological change.

To solve the measurement dilemmas generated by these distinctions, it is helpful to consciously distinguish the calibration, internal consistency, and standardization of a tool. *Calibration* reflects a tool's ability to accurately reveal the structure of human functioning for each respondent. *Internal consistency* reflects the degree to which indicants of the same dimension are highly correlated. *Standardization* reflects the ability of a tool to measure human functioning in predictable ways. These measurement concerns remain central to the reliability of a tool, but investigators often place different emphases on issues of accuracy and stability depending on their theoretical interests.

■ ■ ■ ■ ■ ■

MAKING CONNECTIONS

Identify a theory in your area of research that is supported using the measurement of change. What are the essential features of that theory? What dimensions undergo change? What assumptions are made about those dimensions? What inferences are made about participants? Do the inferences focus on individual or group differences?

DIMENSIONS OF CHANGE

Most developmentalists study how structures function and how functioning is structured with a particular emphasis on change. Isolating the dimensions of change and briefly explaining why they are important can help prevent confusion as measurement techniques are introduced. Although investigators rarely explore the whole of a developmental system, they may explore a small part or help other investigators see gaps in their theories.

Levels of Organization

To be sufficiently sensitive to change, researchers would be wise to label the levels of organization apparent in their theories. Some investigators assume that constructs have theoretical meaning only if they can be applied to all settings, points in time, and spheres of a person's life. They theorize about *pan-contextual components* of development. Others recognize that universal constructs lack practical explanatory power and may be so general as to be uninformative. These investigators may offer highly contextualized descriptions of development and elaborate detail about changes in a specific sample. Not surprisingly, there are also investigators who adopt an intermediate position, labeling the levels of organization that are embedded in their theories and identifying commonalities and differences.

Given these different approaches, what do investigators mean when they talk about organizational levels in their theories? Levels of behavioral contexts can be subdivided into the local context, historical context of the setting, and historical context of the event being observed (see Chapter 8). More generally, levels of organization direct attention to the ways in which people are fused with the environments in which they live.

Investigators who focus on *biological levels* look for structures that explore species variation in physiological characteristics as they are expressed in generations of living organisms. *Psychological levels* of organization are concerned with the study of the human mind, its functioning, and how mental factors govern particular situations or activities. *Relational levels* involve the study of interactions among persons, and *sociocultural levels* involve the combination of social spheres like family, school, and community with cultural factors such as those apparent when considering different regions of the world or ethnic variation within the same locale. *Geographic levels* reflect climates and other geographical constraints that influence development. Together, these conditions are assumed to be fused with *history* in such a way as to be indistinguishable within *a person's ontogeny.* Investigators isolating different areas of development define those levels of organization that are assumed to have the most direct effect on the topics under investigation.

Plasticity versus Stability

The primary concern of most developmentalists involves relations between plasticity and stability. *Plasticity* is assumed to reflect the malleability in structures and functioning with high levels indicating frequent and/or intense change. *Stability* reflects the possibility of little movement, homeostasis, or equilibrium in structures or functioning over time, settings, or populations. Investigators want to know how the levels of organization relevant to the system under investigation affects development and whether structures and functioning show motion with respect to different contextual demands. Investigators interested in development tend to adopt different assumptions and measurement techniques for exploring relationships between structures and functioning, but share a common interest in understanding the nature of change.

Developmental Commonalities.   As was apparent earlier, some investigators explore *developmental commonalities* by working within the psychometric tradition. They tend to emphasize stability in the degree to which individuals' relative rank within a set of scores remains stable over time. A distribution may shift upward or downward, but stability in the placement of individuals is seen as evidence that the measure is valid.

Psychometrically oriented investigators are usually interested in labeling *developmental changes among individuals.* They focus on universal, age-linked trends that are common across most individuals in a population.[12] Exploring how intraindividual differences are common within each age group, they may assume that interindividual differences in that age group reflect error variance and/or moderate forms of variation (e.g., spurts or delays). Such investigators can use psychometric tools but include age or some other indicator of change as a variable in their design. Thinking like psychometricians, they are interested in interindividual differences in personal characteristics, the characteristics of different populations (e.g., genders, age groups, cultural groups) and/or case studies of particular individuals or groups. Using psychometric tools in combination with statistical methods for comparing groups, the stable or dynamic aspects of functioning can be detected.

Developmental Systems.   Investigators who focus on *developmental systems* often start with the assumption that plasticity is central to human functioning. They explore whether structures and functioning evolve over time to determine how stimulation and experience alter a developmental course. They look at the degree to which trends of development can be bent, rebent, or otherwise subject to manipulation.

Researchers interested in systems simultaneously explore inter- and intraindividual variation in development. They accept that plasticity is apparent within as well as between persons and strive to identify *variation in developmental changes* rather than differences among individuals. By evaluating the rates of change in measures administered at more than one point in time, investigators try to explain the resulting change. As is apparent in Figures 9.3 and 9.4, if there is a high degree of stability in the interindividual performance, all participants can be assumed to change in the same way. A general developmental theory would be supported because plasticity assumptions would be predictable. The greater the degree of instability in scores obtained within and across persons, the greater the degree of plasticity in development and the greater the need for theories and tools that account for such variation.

General Commitments.   Using psychometric assumptions, investigators may label the existence of change, but pay little attention to the direction of such change. In developmental research, the direction of change (e.g., whether differences flow in the positive or negative direction) is as important as the presence or absence of change because investigators

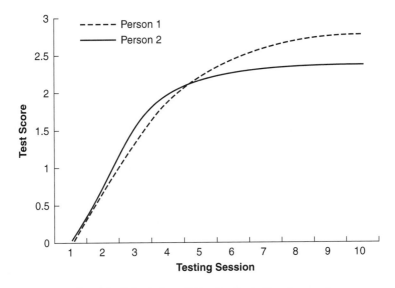

FIGURE 9.3   Graphical Depiction of Continuity in Development

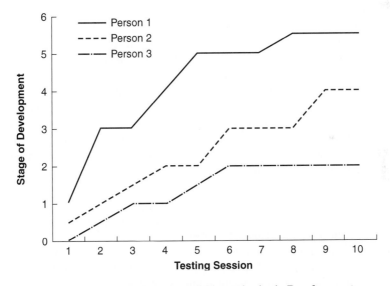

FIGURE 9.4   Graphical Depiction of Discontinuity in Development

are interested in knowing where plasticity begins and ends. Investigators may compare individuals' change scores with one another or compare mean change scores between groups, but the purpose of such inquiries is to identify the qualities of change and to evaluate the adequacy of developmental claims.

Continuity versus Discontinuity

In determining how to compare differences between change scores, investigators consider the nature of expected patterns in their data. These predictions are important because they allow investigators to theorize about growth or development. Four possibilities are commonly considered.

Continuity.   If change is assumed to reflect general improvements in functioning over time, investigators draw inferences about *continuity*. Most commonly, researchers assume that development forms additive or multiplicative patterns similar to those in Figure 9.3. Associationist theories of learning often begin with the assumption that knowledge acquisition follows this kind of pattern. Early developing skills are assumed to be necessary building blocks for later developing skills. Eventually, the change process ceases as an individual achieves equilibrium, fully balancing all relevant skills and reaching a state of adaptive functioning. When particular structures or functioning cease to be adaptive, the change process can begin again or individuals can resist adjusting to the systematic tensions by repeating what becomes maladaptive cycles. The slope or rate of change may differ across individuals, but the nature of the change typically remains incremental.

Discontinuity.   *Discontinuity* is apparent when development occurs in a steplike fashion (Figure 9.4). In studies of moral reasoning, for example, these kinds of patterns are highly salient.[13] More adaptive functioning emerges in rather abrupt changes followed by periods of relative homogeneity in performance. Theoretically, there is relatively little evidence of a transition between one step (sometimes called a stage) and the next, but in practice investigators can detect signs of new thinking before a new stage fully emerges. Functioning within a step is fully adaptive in that all relevant skills seem to appear at once rather than in an incremental fashion. Investigators use the term *discontinuity* to refer to this sudden detectable change because the changes often reflect qualitative as well as quantitative differences. As with continuity patterns, the characteristics that show discontinuity may or may not be responsive to external pressures to change. Individuals may cease to change when a system is changing around them and find themselves responding in maladaptive as well as adaptive ways.

Invariance.   A third possibility is that competencies develop early in life or are present at birth and remain invariant across the lifespan (Figure 9.5). In such cases, investigators would find a high degree of stability in functioning and such stability would remain resistant to reasonable attempts to alter development. Once an individual learns to walk, for example, that knowledge is usually retained unless some sort of physical impairment occurs and the decay process begins. Studies of *developmental invariance* offer essential information about stability that investigators can use to anchor their theories of change.

Decline.   Studies of development can also reveal changes that reflect a *developmental decline* in abilities as easily as improvement. When individuals find it more adaptive to regress to earlier points in development, they may do so in ways that reveal continuity or discontinuity. Reasons for regression can be multifaceted and include illness, adaptive responses to

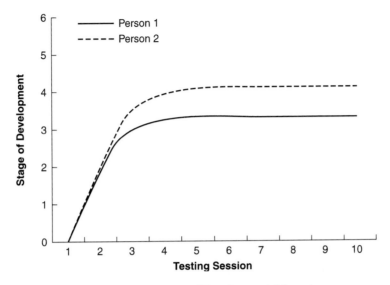

FIGURE 9.5   Graphical Depiction of Developmental Invariance

environmental pressures for a lower level of functioning, or maladaptive responses to excessive amounts of stress. Regardless of these reasons, investigators who begin with an interest in plasticity are more likely to explore these changes than those who begin with an interest in stability.

Quantitative versus Qualitative Differences

Decisions about change also reflect the exploration of quantitative and qualitative differences within and between people. Although the two sets of measurement concerns are often addressed in tandem, investigators also isolate one or the other when they need information to address a specific feature of development.

Quantitative Variation.   *Quantitative differences* are those of frequency, magnitude, or intensity. Additive indicators of development are apparent when investigators measure the frequency of key dimensions. Variation in the rate of development—changes in actual scores or differences between scores—offers an indication of how fast development occurs.

Patterns in the numerical function of scores (e.g., additive, multiplicative, exponential) offer insight into what the rate of change over time looks like within and between persons. Patterns may reflect discontinuity, but incremental increases in test scores are often used to verify continuity in development. Measures of the magnitude of change ideally reflect an interval or ratio scale and contain a sufficient range for detecting variation in performance.

Qualitative Variation.   *Qualitative differences* involve surface appearances that indicate variation in the mechanisms underlying development. Such differences are challenging to define, partly because investigators' experience with number systems and the use of numbers to represent abstract ideas can mislead them into focusing on quantitative changes. Researchers may miss the fact that constructs change in structure and cannot always be measured using the same indicants.

At the qualitative level, differences in the degree to which behavior is stable are used to distinguish *adaptive* and *transition* phases of development. Ordinarily, when individuals are in an *adaptive phase*, their functioning is homogeneous in that they bring all skills to bear on relevant decision making and their behavior is relatively consistent. Drawing inferences about structure, investigators look for such homogeneity to verify qualitative changes. A *transition phase* is evident when individuals' capacities show unevenness. Erratic or inconsistent functioning is likely when individuals are pushed to the limit. Eventually, skills necessary for the next transition are acquired and homogeneity in adaptive functioning increases while old forms of functioning disappear.

Domain Specificity.   Developmental theories can explain *domain-general* functioning such that at any point in time, functioning is influenced by a single set of factors. They can also explain *domain-specific* functioning that is influenced by different mind/brain structures or levels of organization. Researchers interested in identifying universal human characteristics seem to be more concerned with domain-general evidence whereas those interested in describing the plasticity of development seem more committed to domain-specific evidence. Some investigators have adopted an intermediate set of assumptions. They identify the degree to which development is modular such that certain areas of the organism are dedicated to performing certain functions in relatively invariant ways.

General Stability Concerns.   Investigators may also use evidence of stability in behavior to distinguish *traitlike* and *statelike* characteristics. Traits are more enduring characteristics whereas states are responses to more immediate contextual constraints. Researchers interested in development compare the enduring features of structures as well as the enduring features of functioning when theorizing about development as traitlike. They may compare the dynamic responses of both structures and functioning to theorize about statelike features. Not surprisingly, some problems also reflect a combination of trait- and statelike characteristics.

Stability in Qualitative Concepts.   When defending qualitative assumptions, investigators have sometimes used the word *stage* to represent the differences. This term tends to be used in one of three ways: as a metaphor, as a description of behaviors that undergo age change, and as an explanation of age-related changes in behavior.[14] Terms like *level, phase,* or *period of development* have also been used to differentiate the definitions of *stage* as an explanatory structure from the definitions of *stage* as a metaphor or description of behavior. Ordinarily, *stage* has been reserved for explaining age-related changes in thoughts, feelings, and behavior.

Explanations for qualitative change incorporate a complex definition of *stage*. Cognitive developmental theories, for example, have adhered to five empirical criteria. Stages, in this view, should form an *invariant sequence* in that the order in which individuals pass through each stage remains the same and individuals do not "regress" to earlier stages after passing to a more advanced stage. Stages are qualitatively different from one another in that they are characterized by a unique complement of *cognitive structures* that are sufficiently different from previously operative structures. Each stage represents a *hierarchical integration* of skills that were part of the preceding stage but are transformed in the next stage. The *consolidation* of new and old skills means that each stage is simultaneously an achievement phase for stagelike abilities and a preparation phase for new, more advanced abilities. In the consolidation process, *horizontal décalage* involves the means by which individuals gradually coordinate all aspects of their experience with the cognitive structures of the current stage. *Equilibration* is the process by which one stage is transformed into another; a stage dissolves into disequilibrium when internal and external pressures render it no longer adaptive.

To empirically verify the assumptions of invariant sequence, integration, and consolidation, investigators often conduct cross-cultural studies. Such work facilitates the identification of culturally universal sequences in the acquisition of representative behaviors. Cognitive structures and equilibration remain abstract concepts that cannot be measured, yet investigators try to empirically describe the content of particular cognitive structures. Similarly, looking at the degree to which reasoning, affect, and behavior are aligned in a particular situation can facilitate inferences of whether an individual is currently in a state of equilibrium or disequilibrium, but the process cannot be directly observed.

Debates about the nature of stages have occurred at a time when investigators were writing as if individuals can be studied independently of the context in which they live. That assumption has been significantly challenged, but the measurement concerns still hold up to scrutiny. Investigators need not remain committed to a person-centered definition of *stage* to explore qualitative forms of change. Scholars have added qualitative information about the nature of research contexts to strengthen their claims. They have explored variation across samples of the human population, or subdivided the whole of humanity into more microlevel populations that were then studied in depth. Such forms of *developmental contextualism* require qualitative methods that are appropriate for each organizational level.

Change in a Dynamic System

Investigators who coordinate all aspects of change generally accept that development is ongoing throughout life. Individuals gain knowledge in regenerating loops that move from complexity to simplicity to complexity as they consolidate information about their experience.[15] Some investigators focus on smaller dimensions of the larger system, but assume that pressures from other levels of organization encourage development. Developmental loops can be nested or layered as individuals discover more about themselves, their relationships with others, and how their concerns fit within a larger society. Such loops, in this view, form a dynamic system in that individuals' histories, along with spatial and temporal dimensions of various organizational levels, are assumed to influence development. Researchers label patterns in how individuals change over time and describe how order emerges from interacting components of a complex developmental system.

■ ■ ■ ■ ■ ■

MAKING CONNECTIONS

Look again at the theory you identified. How many dimensions of change are apparent? What levels of organization were measured? Were investigators primarily interested in understanding stability or plasticity? Was the resulting change a continuous or discontinuous process? Were the differences qualitative or quantitative? Did investigators draw inferences about an entire developmental system or one part of such a system?

TYPES OF CHANGE

Developmentalists take it for granted that individuals, families, communities, and societies are sufficiently fused in history that change is inevitable.[16] Inferences about the multiple dimensions of human development are facilitated by isolating types of change and the resulting patterns attributable to each level of organization. Three types of change associated with representations, time, and human diversity will be introduced here, and theoretical examples will be used to clarify common measurement dilemmas.

Representational Change

Studies of *representational change* usually focus on the qualities of particular structures and changes in individuals' intentional control over such structures. Controversial decisions about essential levels of organization (e.g., person, family, community) are central to theorizing about a particular concept and exploring the integration of structures and functioning. Measuring at least one dynamic relation between persons and context facilitates conclusions about plasticity, yet constraints on development also involve unmeasured biological, psychological, relational, sociocultural, and geographical factors. Ordinarily, it is assumed that representational units are tightly fused in ontogeny. By isolating relations among measured variables, investigators use sampling and design procedures to control for unmeasured factors. Some investigators identify the components of commonly occurring structures and theorize about the functioning driven by such structures. Others measure the dimensions of functioning and draw inferences about the structures that drive such actions.

Labeling the practical knowledge gained from understanding a particular representational system helps researchers decide which structural features to study. When thinking about how family life influences school performance, for example, investigators may want to isolate details of how the family structure is embedded within a community as well as how an individual is placed within the family structure. Researchers might explore the relative plasticity of structures apparent at each organizational level and the degree of stability in their functioning, but they would not ask if school achievement is caused by nature or nurture. (The obvious answer is that mesosystemic and microsystemic concerns are both important and their influence on development is so tightly associated that one cannot exist without the other.) Instead, researchers might identify those components of the family, school, and community mesosystem that appear to be related to the functional outcome of school performance.

Another rejected idea is that there might be a critical period for intellectual development in which biological constraints dominate ontogeny. Notions of critical periods do not account for relations in levels of organization or for the complete integration of person and context. Investigators may report ages for which functioning is common, but that is not usually understood to mean that individuals must be of the designated age before functioning is possible, or that all individuals at a given age will achieve the same level of functioning. Measurement, in other words, involves multiple dimensions with representational constraints that collectively yield an explanatory model. The resulting developmental concepts typically reflect bidirectional relations between structures and functioning.

Change, in this type of analysis, involves an exploration of whether elements in particular models remain apparent under different circumstances. Investigators often identify relational units and mark the presence or absence of these units in a larger system. Instead of assuming that all change is for the better, leading to greater maturity, investigators who emphasize representational change look for the conditions under which particular behaviors are or are not adaptive. They also evaluate mechanisms for change, assuming that everyday functioning has integrity of its own, but that something drives the development of new representations.

Temporal Change

Investigators also measure *change over time* in both structure and functioning. They may search for explanatory mechanisms that reveal the process of change or determine the evolution of particular outcomes (e.g., specific events, depictions, or structural dimensions). Studies of temporal change are also embedded in history and all assessments of change are integrated with concurrent historical events. No level of organization functions as a consequence of its own isolated activity and change occurs simultaneously in all levels. When interested in the effects of time, investigators focus on intrasystemic continuity or discontinuity in the rate, scope, and substantive components of the dimensions being measured. Discontinuity in one level may be coupled with continuity in another level. Temporal change may reflect qualitative, quantitative, or an interaction of the two types of measurement.

Age is often used as a ruler for comparing the rate of temporal change within and between persons. Dates or periods during the year can link events to behavior. Clocks are used to measure more proximal kinds of change. Regardless of the tools used to measure time, investigators test whether rates of change are constant or variable across persons as well as different levels of organization.

Diversity and Individual Variation

Whereas investigators interested in domain-general theories may dismiss findings that are highly dynamic, others are highly committed to the study of diversity among people, relations, settings, and time of measurement. It is accepted that change apparent at one point in time may not occur at another. Similarly, change in one set of variables may not be apparent in another set of related variables, and change in one group of people may not occur in another.

Studies of individual differences, measured at one point in time within and across organizational levels, offer evidence for plasticity and the potential for change within a developmental system. Theoretically, this work offers evidence for how individual characteristics affect the fusion of agents within a total system. One person's actions or physiological characteristics could produce differential actions and reactions within the system. Most humans consider the characteristics of individuals when determining how to treat them, and the resulting treatment influences the degree of congruence between a person and context.

Most psychometric tools are helpful for measuring diversity and individual differences if investigators know what to measure. Participants' performance can be compared to a set of norms or, more importantly, investigators can learn how individuals differ from one another. To determine if variance in a data set is attributable to predictable individual differences, investigators look for patterns across more than one sample selected to reflect anticipated differences. Researchers learn whether variation is best attributable to diversity in people, relationships, settings, or time of measurement. They can also decide when there is an appropriate fit between the characteristics of a person and the context in which that person functions.

Theorizing about Change

Within a single study, most investigators would have a hard time measuring all aspects of change. Discriminating temporal and representational sources of variance would be difficult. Individual differences attributable to the onset of a developmental cycle, for example, could obfuscate which aspects of change are being observed.

The risky nature of testing developmental theories has sometimes led new investigators to avoid measuring change. This can be problematic if theorists forget that experimental findings are sometimes better attributed to unmeasured maturation rather than predicted causes. By failing to consider the effects of maturation, many investigators have spent inordinate numbers of years drawing inferences about the value of treatments that were ultimately shown to be ineffective. Similarly, descriptive research that does not acknowledge developmental possibilities may foster overgeneralizations about the value of short-term events. Rather than avoid the complexities of measuring change, it might be more useful to introduce at least one type, remaining aware of such limitations when drawing conclusions.

Once investigators understand developmental complexity, they can generate exciting evidence for theorizing about change. Some researchers conduct multiple studies on the same set of ideas, altering only assumptions about change while comparing the results. Other investigators focus on one type of change and, once they are confident of their findings, they study another. A third group does not distinguish different types of change and simply theorizes about the relationship between structure and functioning without linking their findings to representational, temporal, or diversity issues; they usually begin with a specific practical problem to solve and look at how change is represented in that problem.

- - - - - ▬▬▬▬▬▬▬▬▬▬▬▬▬▬▬▬▬▬▬▬▬▬▬▬▬

MAKING CONNECTIONS

What types of change are important in the theory you selected? Did investigators theorize about representational change? Were they interested in temporal change? Could change be attributed to development? Should differences be treated as an index of diversity among individuals or groups?

▬▬▬▬▬▬▬▬▬▬▬▬▬▬▬▬▬▬▬▬▬▬▬▬▬▬▬▬▬▬▬▬▬

MEASURING CHANGE

To measure change, investigators typically separate the representational, temporal, and diversity aspects of their theories. They take stock of the known content of each variable's dimensions and design studies to account for gaps. Because classes of theoretical agendas have led investigators to make different kinds of measurement decisions, four especially common classes will be used here to stimulate measurement possibilities. Different measurement concerns become apparent when investigators consider associationist, constructivist, cultural, and developmental systems theories.

Those who explore *associationist theories* presume that the pairing of experiences causes changes in human functioning; studies of reward-and-punishment contingencies are based on such paradigms. Investigators who study *constructivist theories* assume individuals actively invent personal realities out of their internal and external activities; cognitive developmental theorists accept these assumptions and explore how individuals form semantic representations or schema. *Cultural theorists* incorporate multiple levels of organization with details of individual growth to draw conclusions about the fusion of person and culture. *Developmental systems theorists* look for ways to illustrate how levels of organization are fused in ontogeny; they may rely on measurement techniques used by associationists, constructivists, and sociocultural theorists to identify relations in all three kinds of evidence. Let's compare measurement questions that emerge when these theoretical classes are compared with types of change.

Measuring Representational Change

Representational change can be attributed to differences in the structures or conceptions that individuals use to organize their experience. Such changes are evident in individuals' conceptions of how the world works, their role in events, and their intentional control and behavior. Representational changes are also apparent in how individuals act within and between levels of organization and the theoretical classes incorporate various definitions of how structure, functioning, and change mechanisms are coordinated in representations.

Associationist Theories.   Associationists are primarily concerned with structures that reveal how changes in magnitude offer cues about human functioning. Early associationists were interested in relations between stimuli and behavior; they were more preoccupied with observational and physiological data or measures of ability than with measures of attitudes or personality. Others extended this logic to explore attitude change and the development of personality. Many associationists are more interested in changes in functioning than structure, and are busy trying to predict and control functional variation. In prevention research, for example, investigators typically label problem behavior and strive to change that behavior. They do not always explore the underlying causes of behavior or the structures that perpetuate such behavior; changes in functioning are sufficient for verifying associations between stimuli and responses.

Constructivist Theories.   Constructivists look for evidence of how individuals make sense of their experience and see tangible forms of human functioning as only one sign of development. Behavior in such models is usually something to be explained rather than manipulated, and the explanations often involve latent constructs. Measures of attitudes, personality, and abilities are as important as measures of behavior or physiological change in this approach. Changes in functioning are assumed to offer evidence for changes in structure and investigators try to explain such structural variation.

Cultural Theories.   Cultural theorists have added a third dimension to the relations between structure and functioning, assuming that the context in which individuals are embedded plays a more central role in their behavior than the characteristics of the person. Generally speaking, culture reflects the characteristics of groups that are separated by time or geographical location. In group psychology, for example, it is taken for granted that the behavior of individuals is dominated by group norms rather than personal norms. Investigators look for evidence of how individuals adapt to group expectations and cultural assumptions. Information on attitudes, abilities, and behavior is more salient in these measurement plans than information on personality and physiological characteristics. Cultural theorists, more than others, focus on the levels of organization in their measurement plan. The structure and functioning of groups becomes more salient than the structure and functioning of individuals.

Dynamic System Theories.   To theorize about development as a dynamic system, researchers may include concepts from associationist, constructivist, and sociocultural theories. Because they assume that person and context are fused in ontogeny, it becomes problematic to study persons or contexts in isolation. Instead, investigators typically define a problem that requires a solution. They then isolate aspects of the more general developmental system that are related to such a problem and explore those features in greater detail.

Consider the dilemma of why many students are disengaged from thoughtful learning in school. Investigators might be obligated to explore aspects of students' functioning at home, in school, and in peer groups to determine which features of each organizational level interfere with learning. They may also evaluate the structure of individuals' attitudes, personality, abilities, physiological responses, and behavior to determine why disengagement is more adaptive than engagement in school tasks. A comprehensive measurement plan would include the exploration of structure and functioning within and across individuals who are embedded in different educational contexts. Investigators are unlikely to do a comprehensive job in a single study, but may develop a larger research agenda to compare and contrast information across all aspects of the particular dilemma being explored.

Representational Structures.   Regardless of their theoretical approach, investigators interested in representational indices of development use conceptual units as the primary indicants of structures. They explore relations among conceptual units and functioning to theorize about structural change. Investigators exploring systems that are broad in scope may identify indicants embedded within each organizational level. They may explore how individuals coordinate reasoning, emotion, and behavior in one type of situation, or study one of these dimensions across different contexts. When deciding which representational units to measure, investigators typically rely on a concept-driven theory that has at least some concrete dimensions. Often researchers make these decisions by imagining the practical value of the knowledge generated from their inquiries.

Measuring Representations.   Many concepts can and should be measured using different kinds of tools and/or indicants of the relevant representational units. When looking at representations of behavior, for example, investigators can measure frequency and/or intensity. They usually decide whether behavior can be sampled directly or latent variables are necessary for drawing inferences from indicants. Mental maps, for example, are latent constructs that cannot be observed, but inferences about the existence of particular kinds of knowledge can be drawn from looking at someone's test performance. Investigators also decide whether to make the purpose of measurement clear to participants or to keep it covert.

This set of concerns probably seems similar to those introduced along with psychometric assumptions, and they are similar. In developmental research, however, investigators are carefully monitoring representational changes within individuals to draw inferences about whether particular measurement tools capture structural change while facilitating conclusions about human functioning. It is important in developmental research to recognize that dilemmas apparent at one age may not be apparent at other ages.

Think, for example, about how the content of what individuals find humorous changes over the lifespan.[17] Young children place a great degree of primacy on linguistic puns and/or bodily functions in their humor whereas adults gradually add more subtle forms of humor to their repertoire and may no longer find children's humor funny. It would be problematic to measure emotional pleasure across age groups using the same kinds of jokes; if individuals find children's jokes crude or annoying as they get older, they would not be experiencing the same kind of pleasure that could be generated with children who are still thinking about how their bodies work. Accurate measurement could require sensitivity to these changes in structure and function.

The challenge of accurately representing human functioning is compounded by the necessity of measuring how individuals coordinate reasoning, emotion, and behavior. Often, levels of organization are fused in ontogeny and investigators label relevant levels when defining indicants; they look for patterns across as well as within levels. Many investigators realize that participants cannot always talk about their experiences, either because they are unaware or do not have the communication skills necessary for highlighting relevant behaviors, thought processes, or emotional reactions (see Messick, 1983, for discussion of such

measurement limitations). To account for this fact, researchers rely on complex methods and
measure relations between structure and functioning from many different angles. Details of
how evidence is gleaned from multiple sources will be outlined in the next chapter.

Measuring Temporal Change

Temporal change reflects the fact that persons and context are embedded in history to such
an extent that no level of organization functions as a consequence of its own activity. Temporal studies help investigators describe the evolution of representations over time. Definitions of time reflect researchers' theoretical agendas, emphasizing macrolevel qualities for
some purposes and microlevel qualities for others. Investigators who equate change with
quantitative measures of magnitude find themselves relying on temporal measurement
plans because they can study an individual's responses to the same measure administered at
more than one point in time. Temporal scores can also be compared to draw conclusions
about fluctuations in group performance over time.

There are also times when investigators want to compare the rate of change or the
slopes of a distribution of scores to verify plasticity in development. Looking only at the
rate of change does not facilitate comparisons of who demonstrates more or less of an attribute; at the initial time of measurement, individuals may score at different points in the
distribution, but change at the same rate over time (see Figure 9.6). Knowing the distance
between scores facilitates conclusions about how fast or slow development occurs; the
slope of the resulting distribution may be the same across individuals despite differences in
the value of each score in the distribution.

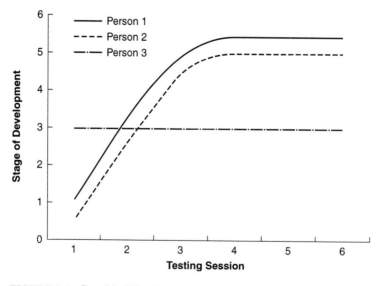

FIGURE 9.6   Graphical Depiction of Rate Over Time

To verify spurts or delays in how individuals organize their experience, investigators sometimes rely on hierarchical modeling techniques. These techniques account for individual differences in scores at the onset of a study as well as the rate of change over the duration of the investigation. The flatness of a distribution is used to indicate stability or lack of change. Distributions with a sharp slope offer evidence for a relatively fast rate of change. The degree to which peaks and valleys are apparent in a graph can reveal further evidence of plasticity. Figures 9.3 through 9.6 exemplify different temporal distributions.

Associationist Approaches.   Investigators using associationist theories value evidence of continuity in the change process. They typically start with baseline assumptions regarding the stability of some characteristics and the malleability of others. Those who assume that attitude change is incremental, for example, may start by measuring general beliefs and then work to alter those initial beliefs by exposing individuals to stimuli that challenge or confirm such predictions.

Constructivist Approaches.   Constructivists use temporal change to confirm explanatory theories of how structures evolve within persons. To verify many of the assumptions in confirming stages, for example, it is necessary to establish that qualitative differences form an invariant sequence. Distributions that reveal discontinuity in development are common in many constructivist theories. Evidence of continuity may also be valuable when investigators look for stability in functioning to theorize about stability in structures. In addition, short-term instability is sometimes seen as evidence that an individual is in transition, especially when such inconsistencies in performance align with predicted qualitative differences in structures. Generally, trends are assumed to reflect a greater integration of ideas.

Cultural Approaches.   Cultural theorists often explore group differences in both the rates of change and in the magnitude of particular score distributions. Because they want to know if different groups of people show similar kinds of change, they evaluate whether a tool designed for one kind of cultural group is appropriate for use with another. Cultural theorists may rely on the same measurement plan designed by associationists or constructivists, but focus primarily on changes across contexts or levels of organization.

Systems Approaches.   Many investigators who explore developmental systems assume that development moves from simplicity to complexity to simplicity to complexity throughout the lifespan. This set of assumptions requires a measurement plan that is sensitive enough to detect complexity and malleable enough to also detect simplicity in performance. Most investigators accomplish this by relying on more than one tool for measuring each construct and select those that are sensitive to structural as well as functional change over time.

Temporal Variables.   Temporal evidence is used to draw conclusions about stability and plasticity in functioning, but can also support inferences about the structures that determine internal and external activities. If participants' functioning remains literally the same over time and across situations, investigators assume that functioning is absolutely stable. (See scores for Person 3 in Figure 9.6.) If a person's relative position in a distribution of participants remains the same even though everyone's scores change, investigators assume that functioning is normatively stable. Looking at individual differences across participants over time offers a sense of whether changes in functioning are best understood as linked to age, history, or the interaction of age and history. Rather than assume history is a threat to validity, as was mentioned in Chapter 1, developmentalists strive to understand its role in the change process.

Temporal evidence is also used to confirm assumptions about stability and plasticity in structure. Coherent structures are assumed when predictable patterns are apparent in how individuals interpret environmental information, decide on a course of action, and use information for inner and outer activity. Stability in structures is evident when individuals' history and maturation experiences result in lawful, consistent predictions of their overall functioning. Plasticity is evident when inconsistencies are apparent over time, but ideally these inconsistencies should also show evidence of lawful continuity or discontinuity. Random fluctuations are usually seen as evidence for a faulty theory. Chapter 11 contains more information on how investigators collect and interpret temporal information.

Measuring Diversity

Diversity in the human population is as essential to survival as homogeneity, but it can be difficult to determine when differences should be attributable to age or phases of development and when they should be defined as independent of such trajectories. Not all differences reflect development. Individual differences in scores may simply reflect human variability in attitudes, personality, ability, physiological characteristics, or behavior. Variability may also reflect differences in the quality of relationships, settings, or circumstances, and the time at which investigators obtained their measurement. When measuring *diversity and individual variation,* most investigators assume that variation in one set of dimensions, at one point in time, may not occur at another. Yet individual differences within and across levels support inferences about the plasticity of human development and the potential for change become salient.

Associationist Theories.   Many associationist theories contain evidence of individual differences. In studies of extrinsic rewards, for example, what is rewarding to some participants may not be to others. If the desirability of the reward is associated with changes in behavior, individual preferences can limit developmental inferences. Understanding what accounts for individual differences can minimize how much time is spent drawing and disconfirming developmental claims.

Associationists may control for individual differences by measuring a baseline of human functioning and incorporating the resulting variability into later statistical analyses. Lawful patterns of change can be evident in repeated measures of the same constructs. Chains of variation in functioning may differ from person to person, but the structural mechanisms that produce such change might remain stable.

Constructivist Theories.   Constructivists generally acknowledge the existence of individual differences in the rate of development, but often look for a standard developmental course. By minimizing the effects of individual differences, they search for homogeneity within each stage or phase of human functioning.

Some theorists go so far as to differentiate ontological structures from the knowledge or content that emerges in functioning. In studies of moral development, for example, researchers have assumed that the structure of someone's reasoning at a given stage is independent of the content of their moral decisions. Structure and functioning are also less dependent on one another at earlier stages in the development process, but become fused as the individual matures. Some of these theorists assume that young people may engage in behavior that does not align with their moral values, but, as they develop, individuals accept the responsibility for their actions and endeavor to behave in ways that are consistent with their values. Maturity, in this view, is defined as the fusion of structure and functioning in ontogeny, but evidence for that fusion may reflect individual differences in knowledge or content.

Cultural Theories.   Whereas associationists and constructivists are often interested in individual differences, cultural theorists are primarily interested in cultural variability and culture is defined, in large part, by the differences attributable to group norms and expectations that play a central role in development. Some cultural theorists go so far as to assert deterministic theories in which societal norms and values are believed to cause individual differences in behavior. Women, for example, have been described as behaving in culturally generated ways because their gender causes them to be treated differently from men. Differences attributable to ethnic variation have also been attributed to environmental causes that are in the settings in which individuals function. To measure these effects, group norms become the primary representational unit and investigators look for information on how groups are organized and how they differ.

Systems Theories.   Developmental systems theorists incorporate individual differences directly into their theories. They assume that all of life's experiences are fused in ontogeny and that there is a wealth of variation in personal experiences as well as in the physiological responses to such experiences. To explore particular facets of a system, therefore, it becomes important to identify diversity within a particular age group or period of development as well as change over time and across periods in the life cycle. These investigators may use design constraints to compare individual and developmental differences. They may also use psychometric tools to explore group norms and developmental tools to explore changes in structure and functioning.

Measuring Diversity.   To draw appropriate inferences about the role of human diversity and individual variation, many investigators conduct cross-sectional studies in which participants from different age groups complete the same measures. When findings from cross-sectional studies reveal individual variation without revealing age-related differences, investigators can attribute these findings to group differences. When findings from cross-sectional studies reveal age-related differences, investigators tend to conduct longitudinal studies to help them evaluate such variation more closely. Psychometric tools can be used to explore individual differences, but investigators interested in development tend to value descriptive research more highly than their colleagues working in fields where the primary agenda is to predict and control human behavior. Chapter 12 outlines some of the methods used by investigators interested in development when studying diversity in human functioning.

MAKING CONNECTIONS

What did the theorists you read do to measure change? Did they measure changes in structure, functioning, or both? Did they measure change in representational units? Was there evidence of temporal change? Was there evidence of individual or group differences that do not seem attributable to development?

A PROGRAMMATIC EXAMPLE

It may be helpful to see how investigators use a practical question to guide their studies of change. Our intentional theory of motivation began with the awareness that children do not have the full capacities needed to formulate adultlike goals, even though their behavior seems guided by clear agendas. Over the years, our research team has explored many types of change. Studies of young people's conceptions of ability, effort, task difficulty, skill, and luck were undertaken to determine age-related differences in their representations of task and ego orientations.[18] Even very young children seem to sustain high levels of task orientation, but ego orientation reflects developing awareness of the self in relation to others. Although we did not conduct temporal studies, conceptions of key achievement attributions could be evaluated over time to monitor how young people represent their orientations. Measures of young people's competence orientations were modified to match the skills and abilities of each age group while preserving the definition of the constructs under investigation. Using these and other measures, we explored diversity by conducting cross-cultural and cross-contextual studies with adolescents, and gender differences with fifth graders.[19]

In this program of research, we distinguished representational change and diversity. Structured interviews were used to explore age-related differences in young people's representations of competence-related attributions (Nicholls, 1989). Surveys completed by American and Chinese adolescents were compared to explore cross-cultural differences (Lau, Nicholls, Thorkildsen, & Patashnick, 2000). Experimental designs were used to compare the reasoning of students facing different kinds of pressures (Jagacinski & Nicholls, 1990; Nolen, 1988). Similarly, surveys adapted for use with fifth graders were used to explore persistent gender differences (Thorkildsen & Nicholls, 1998). Conclusions about the semantic representations of children and adolescents support inferences about the structures associated with task and ego orientations and whether there might be cultural or gender-based diversity in the nature of these orientations.

Knowing that young children did not show sufficient representations of ability, effort, and skill to fully understand ego orientation, we also began to explore conceptual change in how young people coordinate motivational attributions and fairness concerns.[20] Those studies were conducted using structured activities to test hypotheses during the course of each interview. In addition, observational studies were conducted with second graders to offer a holistic exploration of how individuals coordinated issues of ability, effort, and skill (Thorkildsen & Nicholls, 2002). At this point, there is sufficient conceptual knowledge to warrant the undertaking of a longitudinal study exploring the coordination of representational and temporal change.

It might be helpful to know that this body of work has accumulated over the course of 30 years. The historical context in which it has been undertaken has not been particularly supportive of systematic data collection. Nevertheless, it is possible to see that task, ego, and work-avoidant orientations have meaning to most children and adults, but investigators would be wise to recalibrate tools for use prior to age ten, between ages 11 and 16, and after age 16. We have had relatively little problem establishing the internal consistency of indicants within a measure, but have not spent enough time conducting longitudinal research or evaluating how mesosystemic pressures affect developing conceptions of competence. Setting proximal and distal goals has been essential to verifying those viable developmental claims apparent in this work.

MEASURING DEVELOPMENT

As you will have noticed, investigators who study development consider a wide array of complex issues when designing and selecting measurement tools. Investigators may use psychological tools, but adjust their research design to remain sensitive to possible structural changes in how individuals organize their experience. Investigators may also design tools that are sensitive to structural changes and remain sensitive to the possibility that assumptions about functioning are also likely to change in meaning.

Investigators who work on research teams may focus on a small piece of a larger macrosystem while learning from others about the features they do not study. In this sense, new investigators can learn about other parts of a system without being obligated to evaluate all aspects of the system in their own research. Understanding how investigators measure all parts of an ecological system can foster wise decision making when coordinating evidence, even in areas that are not central to a particular study. Linking the study of developmental systems to practical concerns offers a straightforward means of establishing parameters for exploring human functioning over time.

SUGGESTED READINGS

Asendorpf, J. B., & Valsiner, J. (1992). *Stability and change in development: A study of methodological reasoning.* Newbury Park, CA: Sage.

Bjorklund, D. F. (2005). *Children's thinking: Cognitive development and individual differences* (4th ed.). Belmont, CA: Wadsworth/Thomas Learning.

Bornstein, M., Lamb, M. E., & Pierson, H. (1999). *Developmental psychology: An introduction* (4th ed.). Hillsdale, NJ: Erlbaum.

Damon W. (Series Ed.) & Lerner, R. M. (Vol. Ed.). (1998). *Handbook of child psychology: Vol 1. Theoretical models.* (5th ed.). New York: Wiley.

Damon W. (Series Ed.), Kuhn, D., & Siegler, R. S. (Vol. Eds.). (1998). *Handbook of child psychology: Vol 2. Cognition, perception, and language.* (5th ed.). New York: Wiley.

Damon, W. (Series Ed.), Eisenberg, N. (Vol. Ed.). (1998). *Handbook of child psychology: Vol. 3. Social, emotional, and personality development.* (5th ed.). New York: Wiley.

Damon W. (Series Ed.), Sigel, I. E., & Renninger, K. A. (Vol. Ed.). (1998). *Handbook of child psychology: Vol. 4. Practice.* (5th ed.). New York: Wiley.

Wohlwill, J. F. (1973). *The study of behavioral development.* New York: Academic Press.

SUGGESTED WEB SITES

American Psychological Association: http://www.apa.org/science/faq-findtests.html

American Psychological Society: http://www.psychologicalsociety.org

Jean Piaget Society: http://www.piaget.org

Society for Research in Child Development: http://www.srcd.org/about.html#standards

ENDNOTES

1. Overton (1998) offers an historical description of the field and how developmental researchers have come to this coordination of philosophy, concepts, and methodology.

2. Work by Bronson (1983), Brownell & Brown (1992), and Watson & Fischer (1980) focuses on this topic.

3. Nicholls (1989) outlines in elaborate detail many of the developmental explanations that support this practical assertion, but there is also a wide range of experimental studies on the nature of feedback to support this initial conclusion.

4. As with all developmental claims, it is not wise to become too concerned with the age of onset. Conceptual changes in individuals' understanding seem to follow the same general pattern even if some children learn things sooner or later than others. When communicating developmental findings, I tend to exaggerate the age of onset to find the point at which practitioners can assume that all the people they work with have the noted understanding. Some investigators try to label the earliest point at which they detect such differences, but that is likely to differ across contexts and cultures.

5. This was apparent in structured interviews where first graders and many second graders were unable to see the difference between practices that rewarded or encouraged effort and ability (Thorkildsen, Nolen, & Fournier, 1994).

6. Volumes 2 and 3 are encyclopedias of current topical research in these areas (Damon & Eisenberg, 1998; Damon, Kuhn, & Siegler, 1998).

7. Damon & Lerner (1998) edited a volume on theoretical models and Damon, Sigel, & Renninger (1998) edited the volume on practice.

8. Bronfenbrenner (1979) put forth this general model that continues to be widely used.

9. Bjorklund (2000) offers a clear summary of these levels as they relate to cognitive development.

10. Levels of organization were introduced in Chapter 1, but are defined later in this chapter and presented in more detail in Chapter 10.

11. See Bjorklund (2000), Hartmann (1992), or Lerner (1996) for different elaborations on this same set of assumptions.

12. See Asendorpf & Valsiner (1992) for another version of these assumptions.

13. Kohlberg (1969) produced a groundbreaking study that reflects a comprehensive treatment of stages.

14. See Brainerd (1978) for a thorough treatment of this issue and the subsequent critiques of his perspectives included in the same issue of a journal called *The Behavioral and Brain Sciences.*

15. Thelen & Smith (1998) offer a much more elaborate representation of this approach to studying development.

16. Lerner (1996) makes this point most directly.

17. McGhee (1974) and Zigler, Levine, & Gould (1967) offer examples of how humor develops in children.

18. Nicholls (1989) offers a comprehensive review of these studies.

19. See, for example, Duda & Nicholls (1992), Lau, Nicholls, Thorkildsen, & Patashnick (2000), Nolen (2003), and Thorkildsen & Nicholls (1998).

20. Thorkildsen (1989a, 1989b, 1993, 2000), (Thorkildsen & Schmahl, 1997), (Thorkildsen & White-McNulty, 2002) draw parallels between students' conceptions of motivational attributions and fair instructional practices.

CHAPTER TEN

REPRESENTING STRUCTURE AND FUNCTIONING

To take a closer look at measuring representational change, this chapter will emphasize dilemmas associated with identifying structures. Theoretically, a *structural core* is embedded in a person's ontogeny and investigators look for the *organizing principles* of that core. This core is assumed to shape individuals' knowledge and gives it the coherence and predictability necessary for regulating emotion and behavior. Structures may change, but labeling the essential organizing principles offers a means of comparing structures over time, among age groups, and across different levels of organization.

Because structures cannot be directly observed, some investigators measure indicants of dimensions that are assumed to make up a structure and draw inferences by describing relations among particular indicants. Variability in the measured dimensions is assumed to reflect *representational change*. More complex representations are captured by formulating theories of how structures and functioning are integrated.

Developmentalists differ in whether they rely on descriptive or experimental research designs for studies of representational change. Descriptive designs may involve the measurement of many related dimensions and the study of relations among them. Manipulating indicants in an experiment and noting the resulting patterns allows for inferences about change in the structures represented by those indicants. Functioning is often measured systematically while experimental manipulations facilitate tests of the latent structures assumed to control how individuals behave in the world. This type of experimentation shows the same logic as is common in studies with psychometric tools, but the manipulation of ideas occurs at a microlevel. Investigators test possible relations between dimensions, constructs, or concepts *while* collecting data and look for ways to cross-validate their assumptions. Such microlevel experimentation is more helpful for developmental research if all dimensions, including those that may otherwise be inferred, are represented with indicants.

Reports of how developmental researchers combine tools to explore representations can sometimes mislead new scholars into equating the study of structure and functioning with multitrait-multimethod approaches to exploring validity. Investigators typically use a combination of tools to fully explore developmental systems, but many psychometric assumptions about stability and internal consistency can be untenable. Let's look more closely at the differences in these assumptions.

COMMON STRUCTURAL FEATURES

Probably the central difference between studies of representational change and studies rely-ing on more traditional research designs concerns questions of when and how variables are manipulated. In many types of representational research, experimentation occurs while in-vestigators are making observations or interacting with participants. Investigators often ma-nipulate indicants rather than variables and are expected to generate and test hypotheses while collecting data. In an interview, for example, questions may be reworded or combined in different ways to test predictions about young people's responses. Investigators generally start with a plan for exploring particular structures, but it is assumed that they will uncover surprising findings. By exploring individuals' responses to each indicant and testing partici-pants' understanding of them, it becomes possible to detect areas of stability and change within and across participants. Common psychometric approaches to measurement are often modified for use in developmental research because they reflect clearly defined constructs that may change. Later in the theory-building process, investigators may also use psycho-metric tools to verify rather than identify relations between structures and functioning.

COMMON STRUCTURAL FORMS

Structures or representations of development can take many forms. Because of this multi-faceted nature, they are often represented as collections of concepts.

Hierarchical Structures

Even people unfamiliar with the complexity of development are likely to recognize *hierar-chical structures* (Table 10.1). Students' conceptions of learning practices, for example, start with a simplicity that seems to evolve into more complex representations of the same problem (Thorkildsen, 1989a, 1993). At each level, these evolving conceptions reflect the construction and recombination of dynamic dimensions. Even though they may choose the same actions, older individuals raise more complex issues and coordinate more sophisti-cated concepts than younger individuals. This coordination is evident in students' justifica-tions for how learning situations ought to be organized. The overall structure of their justifications for selecting instructional practices shows a subtle increase in sophistication across age groups. Other hierarchies may reflect more obvious transformations when change occurs in qualitatively different behavior as well as thought. The discontinuity in performance across groups or over time would reveal a seemingly magical appearance of new skills.

Completely Coordinated Structures

Structures can also reflect concepts that are *completely coordinated* such that one concept cannot be evident without the other. Many theories of the relation between emotion and ac-tion reflect such structural assumptions. Broad smiles, for example, are assumed to reflect some sort of pleasure and rarely occur in the absence of such emotion. The physical behav-

TABLE 10.1   Conceptions of Fair Learning Practices

LEVEL	CONCEPTION
1. Equality of rewards	The point of completing schoolwork is to gain rewards and equal allocation of rewards is seen as more important than ensuring that slower workers finish assignments. Children do not associate finishing schoolwork or the associated rewards with understanding or learning.
2. Equality in the quantity of schoolwork completed	Equality in the amount of schoolwork completed is emphasized. Practices that produce this are judged as fair. As with Level 1, children do not associate finishing schoolwork or associated rewards with learning.
3. Equality of learning	Learning is the most important good to be distributed in school and everyone should learn the same material equally well: Simple equality of learning is fair.
4. Equity of learning is partially differentiated from equality of learning	Children vacillate between endorsing practices that promote simple equality of learning (as in Level 3) and equity of learning (as in Level 5), wherein the more able students learn more.
5. Equity of learning	Equity or meritocratic systems, wherein those capable of doing so learn more than the others, are seen as fair.

Note: From "Justice in the Classroom: The Student's View," by T. A. Thorkildsen, 1989, *Child Development, 60,* p. 331. Copyright 1989 by the Society for Research in Child Development. Reprinted with permission.

ior and emotional state are assumed to be completely coincident, reflecting reasoning, feeling, and action.

Completely Independent Structures

Constructs within a structure can also be *completely independent,* but work together to influence human functioning. For example, academically talented individuals can lack motivation and students with low abilities may sustain high levels of motivation despite common-sense beliefs to the contrary. Achievement motivation and academic abilities form bidirectional relations that influence functioning even though the concepts embedded in the relevant structures seem theoretically independent.

Overlapping Structures

As is apparent in theoretical representations previously introduced, structures can also be comprised of *overlapping constructs* that, when coordinated, influence human functioning. Individuals' athletic flexibility, for example, is often influenced by the overlapping characteristics of height and weight. Tall people tend to weigh more than short people, fat people more than thin people, and so forth. The two constructs do not completely overlap even though the coordination of height and weight plays a role in an individual's sense of balance, willingness to engage in particular kinds of movement, and the muscles they use to get around.

Anticipating Structural Features

Prior to collecting data, investigators who study representational change are rarely able to fully imagine the nature of the structures they are investigating. Typically, they make educated guesses about the dimensions of a structure and collect some sort of evidence on relations among predicted dimensions and those they discover while collecting data. The importance of having a strong theoretical grounding cannot be emphasized enough because such knowledge increases the likelihood that investigators will recognize meaningful patterns. During this discovery phase, researchers may observe or interact with individuals they know well or rely on some sort of trial and error during the research process. Once in a while, other investigators have also measured variables that offer clues about particular structures.

Comparing work by two developmental psychologists, for example, it is possible to see that young children confused the concepts of effort and ability in interviews that were designed to explore conceptions of positive justice.[1] Both studies were conducted at similar points in time, but in two different hemispheres of the world. Only careful consideration of the methods used in each study reveals such interesting and potentially useful parallels in conceptions. Those parallels seem to reflect organizing principles that influence functioning in school. Similar parallels were also evident when children's conceptions of fair contests were compared to their understanding of luck and skill (Thorkildsen & White-McNulty, 2002).

Some investigators avoid studying representational change because the challenge of finding significant results is too daunting. Other researchers have developed procedures that streamline the identification and verification of potential structures. Out of this process has come a series of questions that, when considered, can minimize the tendency to find misrepresentations rather than representations of structures and functioning.

■ ■ ■ ■ ■ ▬▬▬▬▬▬▬▬▬▬▬▬▬▬▬▬▬▬▬▬▬▬▬▬▬▬▬▬▬▬▬▬▬

MAKING CONNECTIONS

Try to identify the dimensions that comprise a structure in your area of interest. What kinds of relations would you expect to find between those dimensions? What indicants would you use to represent each dimension? Would you expect some indicants to change? How?

DILEMMAS IN DEFINING STRUCTURES

The complexity of a research problem dictates whether researchers are faced with more or less multifaceted structures.[2] Nevertheless, answers to a few fundamental questions can help investigators draw accurate inferences even though some questions will never be fully answered. Careful attention to lessons previously learned can improve the likelihood that new research efforts will bear theoretical fruit.

Common Questions

The process of labeling structures can seem daunting, but investigators have been able to find meaningful results by considering seven guiding questions. These questions do not form a progression of steps, are often revisited each time new data became available, and may not lead to definitive answers.

Where Do Investigators Begin when Defining a Structure?   Many investigators believe that structures are theoretical entities that cannot be measured, although there are likely to be symptoms apparent in human functioning. To determine if measurable entities correspond to a particular structure, investigators may find characteristics that correspond to a point in time, an event, or an age group. With this starting point, the problem under investigation ordinarily undergoes logical analysis in which epistemological assumptions are spelled out and a survey of existing work is conducted to design a measurement plan.

To explore children's conceptions of the fairness of institutional practices, for example, I began inquiries using the entry into school as a starting point. School is the first institution outside the family in which most children actively participate, and students usually function in school without the direct supervision of their parents. By analyzing common situations representative of those in school, it became possible to formulate a plan to begin exploring children's conceptions. My guiding practical question focused on whether young people had sufficient understanding of equal educational opportunity to understand common social inequalities. I discovered that most children are not sufficiently aware of differences between schools to recognize inequality in resources but they do understand fairness for learning, test, and contest situations within their schools.[3] Exploring conceptions for each of these types of situations, emerging structural patterns aligned with patterns in young people's conceptions of key motivational attributions. Knowledge of attributions constrained children's interpretation of their experience. By starting with empirically verifiable assumptions, the components of a more general value system have been articulated and these personal standards seem to compel students' sense of agency in school.

Should the Surface Characteristics of Functioning Be Distinguished from Structural Similarities and Differences?   Historically, there has been an inordinate amount of pressure on researchers to define constructs using readily identifiable indicants. The phrase "intelligence is what intelligence tests measure" reflects this assumption that inferences are not appropriate for theorizing about human functioning. Many developmental researchers challenge this assumption and recognize that structures are largely inferential entities. They assume that measuring functioning alone offers little insight into why people do what they do. As a result, investigators explore representational change by making predictions about the relation between structure and functioning. When constructs within a structure can be distinguished from one another or structures can be distinguished from functioning, investigators have found evidence of *differentiation* necessary for development.

Asking about the process of differentiation, researchers have discovered that there may be many different structural causes of seemingly similar indicants of functioning. On the surface, for example, a smile might be an indication of pleasure, but this pleasure may reflect mirth, the recognition of a contradiction, or joy. The nature of the smile may or may not change as a result of these different reasons, but the same surface behavior may reflect the expression of different structures. Without exploring similarities and differences in the conditions that elicit a smile or self-reported reasons for smiling, investigators may not understand that the same surface characteristics can be elicited for different reasons.

Investigators consider the fusion of structure and functioning differently depending on the theoretical framework used to organize their inquiry. Many associationists, for example, assume that structure is completely fused with functioning and that investigators need not distinguish the two.[4] Most constructivists, on the other hand, go to great lengths to differentiate the surface characteristics of reasoning, emotion, and behavior from the structural characteristics that underlie such functioning.[5] Surface characteristics, in this view, are merely symptoms of an underlying structure; stability in individuals' functioning may facilitate the identification of patterns necessary for defining structures. Cultural theorists are often so interested in the functioning of groups that they spend little time drawing relationships between structures and functioning within persons (see, for example, Shweder, 1991). Developmental systems theorists often coordinate more than one kind of structure with functioning while describing the integration of different structures in a larger system (Thelen & Smith, 1998). Adding the details of human functioning in different contexts to this complexity, it becomes easy to see why most researchers spend their career working within one system of thought.

What Does It Mean to Explore Integration in Development?   An essential feature of representational change concerns the presence of a coherent whole in combinations of dimensions, constructs, and concepts. A coherent structure contains the stable integration of concepts that can be called forth, at least for a time, to help individuals make sense of their experience. This stability may be apparent for most of an individual's life, as is the case for structures that show developmental *invariance*. The whole may also be stable only as long as a particular structure remains intact, as is common for structures that show *discontinuity* in development. In addition, a structural whole that shows developmental *continuity* may remain intact but become more versatile as individuals develop. Studies of continuity indicate that individuals are likely to add new skills or new information to existing structures that ultimately control their utility for guiding daily functioning.

More formally, *integration* involves the degree to which organizing principles are fused in a structural core and/or are coordinated within a structure. Functioning, in such work, offers clues about the nature of structures. It is a means to the end of understanding the organizing principles that facilitate the integration of biological, psychological, relational, sociocultural, and geographical influences on behavior.

As is the case for questions of differentiation, integration in developmental research holds different meaning across theoretical classes.[6] Investigators differ in whether they are interested in how the dimensions of constructs and the constructs themselves are organized into structures that affect human functioning. Those who acknowledge the dynamic qualities of both structure and functioning assume that the two are fully integrated when, despite external pressures, stability and consistency are apparent in daily functioning. Investigators who primarily study functioning often assume that structures and functioning are always fully integrated, and explore the relationship between external pressures and functioning to theorize about behavioral change. Functional integration often reflects the coordination of internal and external demands whereas structural integration involves the isolation of internal and external demands while coordinating dimensions within each.

To What Extent Are Stability and Consistency Evident when Defining a Structure?
To fully understand components of a larger developmental system, investigators try to explain both differentiation and integration. They do so by making predictions about how structures and functioning might change, which aspects of a system are likely to remain stable, and the necessity of external stimulation for compelling change.

These steps constitute one of the most difficult aspects of developmental research because verifying structures in a changing system requires careful measurement and clearly defined organizing principles. If structure and functioning are so tightly fused in ontogeny that the two dimensions cannot be differentiated, investigators need only explore how individuals function in society. Trial and error has taught many investigators to assume that functioning offers, at best, an imperfect representation of core structures that control thoughts, feelings, and actions. Yet, these studies are important. Human functioning differs from one context to the next, and exploring why and how those differences emerge fosters knowledge about what may and may not be predictable.

Many developmental theorists have concluded that structures are apparent when there is stability in human functioning across more than one context. This notion of stability involves the resistance of functioning to external influence. It does not simply reflect consistency in someone's placement within a distribution of scores over time. Resistance to change serves as evidence that someone's structural core is sufficiently stable that it shows signs of equilibrium.

At another extreme, there are developmental researchers who find stability to be logically impossible because development is theorized to be a dynamic process that involves the fusion of many levels of organization. Such investigators look for evidence of the pervasiveness of a structure in functioning, but expect functioning to be responsive to external pressure.

Regardless of their views on the role of stability, most developmentalists agree that structures are in a state of equilibrium when there is consistency in how an individual uses them. Such consistency can be apparent in more than one mode of behavior and/or in the same type of behavior over different contexts. Understanding how to read, for example, should carry over from books to signs, and from one book to the next. The structural core associated with reading is fully embedded when this kind of cross-situational consistency is possible.

Investigators also disagree on the pervasiveness of functioning necessary for verifying the existence of a structure. If there is absolutely no evidence of consistency in use, investigators may conclude that they are not observing an organizing principle. If consistency is apparent in all forms of human functioning, investigators may assume they have identified a central structure. Disagreement emerges when there is some evidence for consistency, but it is not pervasive. Some investigators assume that inconsistency is evidence for a partial structure and strive to determine the larger system in which that partial structure is embedded.[7] Others take inconsistency as an indication that developmental hypotheses should be rejected (see, for example, Brainerd, 1974). Not surprisingly, there is no room for a poorly designed measurement tool in this kind of analysis.

To What Extent Is a Structure Expected to Spontaneously Appear and Reappear across Contexts and Persons?   In addition to debates over the role of stability, there are also debates on whether representational change should occur spontaneously. Most researchers exploring representational change look for evidence that a structure (1) is self-constructed, (2) is deeply held, and (3) requires no external stimulation to be apparent in human functioning. *Spontaneity* is assumed to reflect individuals' ability to use structures when responding to novel problems. Structures are verified by automatic processes because spontaneous appearance suggests at least a modicum of control over functioning. Criteria like this help investigators determine if respondents are imitating actions they observe or if those actions are embedded within their ontogeny. Changes in the indicants of a structure are usually taken as a sign that structures are undergoing development.

Although investigators use evidence of stability in functioning to anchor the measurement of change, rules for balancing issues of stability, consistency, and spontaneity remain hotly contested. Investigators have offered many solutions to the methodological question of how and if all three criteria can be explored. Features of their theoretical framework are typically linked to the details of everyday events, using functioning in actual settings as a guide for labeling systems worthy of exploration.

If Structures Are Dynamic, How Can Investigators Be sure that Differences Are Appropriately Attributed to the Relevant Structure?   Because investigators cannot identify the precursory behavior that influences functioning, determining the cause of structural differences is nearly impossible. Put another way, it is not realistic to completely control all combinations of intervening variables in designs that involve human functioning. Investigators can usually describe the nature of differences, but not the actual causes of change.

The difficulty of directly measuring causal assumptions has led some theorists to focus exclusively on studies of human functioning and avoid exploring structural differences, yet most developmentalists explore structures. They conduct a logical analysis of each concept, design tools to measure relevant dimensions, and monitor the patterns in individuals' responses. To adequately measure all forms of functioning, most investigators design problems and activities that participants find compelling and interesting. Investigators may also ask respondents to report on their thought processes or otherwise reflect on how they organize their experience. When participants are fully engaged in relevant activities, investigators can rigorously test the limits of participants' knowledge.

Many investigators are as interested in the meaning participants make of their thoughts and behaviors as in the functioning of such behaviors. It is the meaning-making enterprise that typically offers clues about how individuals organize their experience. Therefore, tools are designed to measure particular aspects of a problem under investigation, and investigators look for integration in individual and group performance on multiple measures of related constructs. When there is convergence in participants' performance on multiple tools, this evidence suggests that performance may be linked to a structural core. Differences could be caused by faulty measurement, alternative structures, or confounding variables. After ruling out each possibility, investigators may revise their theories.

How Do Structural Characteristics Retain Unity across the Lifespan if the Nature of a Structure Is Dynamic? Developmentalists differ in whether they expect a particular structure to remain present across the lifespan, but most look for the same organizing principles for a given problem. More primitive forms of functioning may require different measurement tools than more advanced forms of functioning, but structures enable individuals to adapt to the environment in which they live. Some structures may be more and less necessary at different points in the life cycle. Similarly, some forms of human functioning may be more and less necessary at different points in time.

Effective measurement across the lifespan involves knowledge of the organizing principles that guide the appearance and disappearance of structures and forms of human functioning. Such principles are usually identified by describing the concepts embedded in each structure and using those definitions to explore functioning at different ages. New dimensions may be added and obsolete dimensions deleted from a plan to accommodate changes in meaning.

Some investigators begin with the structures apparent in adults and work backward to determine how those structures are apparent in the functioning of children. Others start at the beginning of the life cycle and note the emerging structures that become apparent as infants become toddlers, toddlers become children, and so forth. For structures that develop in the middle of the life cycle, other characteristics are used to verify their existence and relevance. Adolescence, for example, is often defined as the period in life that emerges at the onset of puberty. Individual differences in this onset are often controlled when investigators theorize about ontological structures in this phase of life.

Choosing among Dilemmas

Before designing new studies, it is helpful to explore existing research in a field. Comparing existing research methods also illuminates how well or poorly a particular line of inquiry has been followed through. New investigators may not need to determine a beginning point for a structure if experienced researchers have solved that problem. They may still make a valuable contribution by exploring unarticulated relations between parts of a structure or between a structure and different kinds of functioning. Similarly, measurement tools may be available for some forms of human functioning, but not others. Looking at what others have accomplished can save time, but might also reveal the blind alleys that have been started and abandoned. Investigators learn from mistakes as well as successes.

The remainder of this chapter illustrates how investigators go about exploring less well-established forms of representational change. They typically begin by conducting cross-sectional studies to identify representational differences, leaving the analysis of change for longitudinal research.

■　■　■　■　■

MAKING CONNECTIONS

Imagine a concept in your field that seems central to individuals' interpretation of their experience. Rather than imagine why such concepts may or may not exist, try to imagine how that concept is fused in a person's ontogeny. Which dilemmas associated with defining a relevant structure would offer a starting place for understanding development? How much knowledge do you already have about the concept you selected? What would you like to know more about?

QUESTIONING THE OVERDEPENDENCE ON JUDGMENTS

Comparing assumptions of psychometric measurement and developmental questions has helped many new scholars understand both traditions more clearly. Most psychometric tools rely on *judgments* about reasoning, emotion, and behavior, made either by participants or by investigators. Tools may be designed using external, inductive, deductive, or interactionist forms of logic, but indicants on each tool reflect an appraisal of someone's functioning. Most psychometricians do not explore the logic underlying decisions embedded in each tool. Developmental researchers, in contrast, try to explore the organizing principles of the structural core that guides human functioning as well as indicants of that functioning.

Reliance on judgments alone has produced sufficient levels of frustration that developmentalists commonly use psychometric tools in combination with other techniques.[8] Let's explore some common limitations of direct observations, interviews, and tests. With such shortcomings in mind, you may acquire a richer understanding of what can and cannot be learned from experimental designs and static tools.

Limitations of Direct Observation

Psychometricians developed systematic approaches to observational research because naturalistic observations alone tended to obfuscate important aspects of human functioning (see Chapter 8). In strict observational studies, interaction is necessarily one-sided, with participants determining a course of action and investigators making judgments about those actions.[9] Measured behavior is assumed to occur spontaneously and investigators record the type and/or frequency of actions. Formal recording tools limit investigators' ability to look at qualitative differences in such actions or the underlying reasons that compel behavior.

Investigators Determine the Measurement Agenda.   Psychometric tools are not flexible enough to detect unanticipated trends of thought, feeling, and action because investigators' concerns dictate the kind of observations generated. Participants' actions may not be accurately recorded if they fail to conform to the patterns anticipated by researchers. Investigators recording behavioral sequences, for example, find that participants do not always follow the sequence or reveal their motives. Participants can also juxtapose rather than synthesize internal and external pressures if they become preoccupied with researchers' expectations or do not consciously choose a course of action.

Situations are not Identical.   Another challenge involves sufficiently standardizing situations so that observed behavior can emerge in comparable settings. Findings obtained with one participant may not be similar to those of another because situations rather than personal characteristics vary. It is virtually impossible to ensure that conditions remain the same for all participants and investigators cannot adequately observe numerous participants at one time. Such challenges are especially salient for larger samples.

Using Actions to Draw Inferences about Reflection.   Observational research is commonly conducted with children because of their limited verbal skill. Unfortunately, the very limitations in children's ability to communicate their thoughts also restrict their ability to show investigators what they know. Not all ideas are sufficiently grounded in concrete reality to warrant observation, and, when they are, children may not have the resources to find them. In addition, not all children are willing or able to share their thoughts and reactions with adults; most adults rely on a mixture of behavioral and verbal information to interpret children's behavior.

Consider the case of my niece, who at the age of 16 months was learning to talk. Amelia could pronounce single words but had not yet learned to combine words. Her mother, hopeful that Amelia would be able to say "Aunt Terri" before I left for a few months, began to coach her daughter. Amelia was confused by the phrase and, going against the norms of her age group, refused to merge the two words into a single word with multiple syllables. Instead, she took me to her room, pulled out a favorite animal book, and opened it to a page of insects. Pointing to the ant and then to me, Amelia tried to explain her confusion to this baffled aunt. After several repeated tries and the kind of guessing game that is common between adults and children at this age, Amelia convinced me that she understood two word phrases, but could not understand how I could be an ant. A few weeks later, before I left, Amelia proudly pronounced "Aunt Terri" with fits of giggles. Without relying on interaction, it would have been impossible to detect the source of Amelia's resistance, yet even that offered only an incomplete sense of the structures she used to organize her thoughts. We will never know how long it was before Amelia constructed the idea that there might be two kinds of aunts/ants. Certainly, Amelia's later discovery that she was my niece produced fits of giggles reminiscent of the time when I was "Ant Terri." Adults commonly experience such dilemmas when working with children, but such confusion could just as easily occur between adults.

Discerning Playful versus Serious Action.   Another dilemma in drawing inferences about children's behavior involves the difficulty of distinguishing play from more serious commitments. Amelia had been intentional in her attempt to show me what she knew, but she may simply have been playing with a pun she had discovered. Her resistance to calling me "Ant Terri" and anger at my initial lack of comprehension suggested she was serious about her question, but now that she is much older playful reactions are as common as serious questioning in ways that obfuscate the difference.

Generally speaking, children are slow to construct personal explanations (Piaget, 1951). Initially, children assume adults know what they are thinking, but they gradually start to feel ashamed or fearful of being wrong. This change can lead children to hide their intellectual curiosities by behaving in deceptive ways. Once children begin to recognize that they hold personal perspectives on the world and find others' opinions interesting rather than judgmental, they may be more willing to show adults what they think. This discovery need not prevent investigators from learning how children interpret the world, but is often considered when designing tools that distinguish play and serious behavior.

Developmental Solutions.   Investigators may address some limitations by relying on design or less formal measurement techniques to cross-check their assumptions. Some address limitations by keeping diaries of naturally occurring events, recording only those that are new and interesting. They may also use time-sampling and event-sampling techniques to identify those behaviors that require explanation. Observational research may be essential for generating hypotheses even though it is time-consuming and difficult to interpret. Interpreting my "conversations" with Amelia was made easier by the kind of protracted interactions possible in family contexts, but most observational research does not involve such opportunities. Investigators are likely to draw inferences that match their data, but the data may not accurately convey participants' experience.

Limitations of Interviews

Psychometric interview techniques also offer limited information about structures and operating principles if they reflect *verbal surveys*. In verbal surveys, questions are posed in exactly the same way across participants and restrictions are placed on the kinds of answers participants are permitted to offer. These methods may be standardized, but linguistic limitations linked to participants' language proficiency become obvious, and other limitations are more subtle.

Meaning Is not Standardized.   Assuming that investigators and respondents share a common language, participants' cognitive or affective functioning is sometimes assessed through conversations. Standardizing how questions are posed and answers recorded does not allow investigators to probe into participants' personal explanations for their responses. Standardized presentation of items obfuscates the fact that respondents do not always understand questions in the same way. Knowing someone's answers to a set of questions does not offer a clear sense of where those answers came from or what they mean to the person providing them.

New Knowledge Can Be Introduced.   Investigators may also ask questions that respondents have never imagined. In answering, respondents may draw conclusions about organizing principles that are not central to their structural core. Individuals differ in how readily they construct personal explanations for how the world works and their position in such a world. If investigators focus on literal interpretations of standard questions, they limit their ability to identify respondents' inexpressible thoughts or tendencies of mind. Investigators who patiently encourage respondents to reveal their thoughts, no matter how primitive, are more likely to identify subtle, intuitive conceptions that can sometimes be felt when interacting with a child. Such thoughts are unlikely to be detected on standard survey or test questions.

Developmental Solutions. As will be clearer later in the chapter, investigators typically use a variety of means for communicating their questions. They also ask respondents to justify their answers and minimize the number of restrictions placed on such responses. Allowing participants to also raise issues, and looking for patterns in responses across participants facilitates surprises as well as the verification of predictions.

Limitations of Surveys and Tests

Like interviews that rely on invariant questions, the language in standardized tests and surveys place restrictions on participants' thinking. The limitations of verbal surveys also apply to paper-and-pecil or computer adaptive surveys and tests, but the style in which tests and surveys are written poses another challenge.

Linguistic Cues. Tests and surveys offer a false impression of respondents' natural mental inclinations because the wording of questions often provides clues about the intended answers. In Piaget's (1951) work, for example, the question, "What makes the sun move?" was posed to children. Embedded in this question is the idea that a force external to the sun rather than the rotation of the earth causes the sun to change position in the sky. If respondents are accustomed to thinking about the earth's rotation, or to imagining the sun as an internally driven, freestanding entity, it may be difficult to interpret this question. When data consist of answers alone, without justifications for those answers, investigators cannot explore these possibilities.

Developmental Solutions. Investigators sometimes rely on indices of item difficulty to help them select appropriate items for surveys or tests. They may also reconstruct scales across age groups by looking at item correlations and relying on item-response theory or Rasch techniques to evaluate the interchangeability of items. These solutions permit investigators to cluster items around dimensions they know to exist, but do not fully solve the problem of exploring representational change. Therefore, surveys and tests are more often used to verify rather than identify assumptions about structures and functioning.

Confounding Inferences in Experimental Designs

Although developmentalists use a form of experimentation in their work, traditional experimental designs that rely on psychometric tools also pose limitations for investigators' ability to understand how respondents organize their experience. Experiments are useful for identifying general processes in human performance, but are not usually sensitive enough to detect subtle types of change within persons. Typically, investigators assign participants to treatment and control groups with the assumption that human characteristics will be randomly distributed in the sample and the two groups will be roughly equivalent. Introducing a treatment and establishing criteria for judging the presence or absence of a concept before and after that treatment, investigators draw conclusions about whether the treatment causes differences. In such models, performance on a task is seen as a direct indicator of the presence or absence of a concept or structure.[10] Comparison of task performance to a set of age-related norms becomes the device by which representational change is inferred. In this type of research, concepts are defined as simple, undifferentiated units of psychic matter and structures are comprised of concepts that are assumed to cause functioning.

Inferences Fall Far from Indicants.   For investigators interested in relationships between structure and functioning, such experimental approaches are limiting because investigators rely on educated guesses about what would be stimulating or meaningful to their respondents. Such techniques do not enable investigators to identify how individuals represent their own experience because only the presence or absence of predefined concepts is assessed; unanticipated conceptions are not likely to be noticed.

Developmental Solutions.   Near the end of a research program, after investigators have identified the salient dimensions of particular structures and designed tools to measure each dimension, experimental research may be helpful. With a clear sense of the dimensions to be measured, experiments make it possible to verify relations of theoretical and practical interest. However, such work is rarely helpful for the exploratory phase of identifying representational differences because investigators are not fully aware of what is to be measured and there is little or no opportunity to directly test predictions during the data-collection process.

Potential Theoretical Blind Spots

As investigators identify the organizing principles and the structural core of their theoretical framework, they begin to adopt a more definitive theoretical position concerning the developmental processes they are exploring. Associationists and cultural theorists are most likely to rely on descriptive and experimental research designs using psychometric tools. Associationists are looking for linear chains in functioning whereas cultural theorists look for evidence linking functioning to identifiable cultural causes. Both groups of researchers are interested in labeling general processes of human functioning and so find psychometric approaches to be as helpful as developmental approaches. Constructivists, on the other hand, are interested in explaining individual differences in functioning and are more likely to build experimentation directly into observational or interview tools.

Search for Blind Spots.   Theoretical leanings can foster blind spots in the measurement plans that investigators might design. If left unchallenged, investigators can become overly dependent on one type of tool or fail to look for more enduring patterns in their data. It would be easy, for example, to continue my work on children's conceptions of fairness by designing interesting structured interviews on topics related to schooling. Such work would be fun, but without making theoretical connections between studies this work would not add up to something that is theoretically meaningful.

Developmental Solutions. Investigators striving to understand developmental systems are likely to use a combination of all available methods, depending on which organizational levels are theoretically relevant. Reliance on multiple methods permits investigators to look for disconfirming as well as confirming evidence for their theoretical claims. Building one design using tools that will offer a rigorous test of predictions can help investigators generate causal theories for understanding representational change while accepting that their theories could later be proven wrong.

MAKING CONNECTIONS

What theoretical paradigms are commonly used to explore the concept you selected? Do you know of relevant research based on psychometric methods? Looking at such a study, are there noticeable shortcomings in the design or measurement procedures? Would the researcher's question have to change for the study to fall within a developmental framework?

MEASURING JUDGMENTS AND EXPLANATIONS

At the onset of a research program, investigators often conduct a logical analysis of how knowledge might be organized. They synthesize information from an extensive array of data collected in different contexts, including naturalistic observations, reasoning about actual and hypothetical events, and self-reported beliefs about the self and society. While gathering information, investigators challenge the knowledge of their respondents, verifying the strength of individuals' commitments to particular positions while maximizing spontaneity. Developmentalists take time to include the subjective meaning of experience for the participant and identify forms of human functioning that occur throughout life. Eliciting both primitive and advanced forms of functioning, investigators are able to identify age-related standards or structural norms for use in later analysis. By keeping activities interesting, realistic, and easily understood, investigators endeavor to test the limits of individuals' knowledge, identify organizing principles for constructing knowledge, and verify the relationships between structures and functioning in development.

No single method is adequate for accomplishing all these goals, but in addition to the judgment-based methods associated with psychometric tools, developmental researchers have relied on methods that integrate judgments and explanations. These methods were primarily derived for use with children because children have a difficult time explaining their thoughts to adults. However, if the tasks are sufficiently engaging for older participants, the methods can still yield interesting and useful results.

Most techniques for exploring representational change involve the integration of experimental techniques with other, more interactive, approaches to measuring human functioning.[11] Respondents are typically given a task and asked to invent a response to that task. The task is then modified, and new stimuli or a variation of the original stimulus is presented. The order in which tasks are presented and the nature of those tasks differ, depending on individuals' responses, until the investigator has explored all relevant angles of the problem. Investigators typically rely on all their insight and abilities to understand what respondents say or do and to test the limits of respondents' reasoning. When investigators explore all detectable possibilities during an interview, they have little time to synthesize patterns in the evidence gathered. Piaget and his colleagues, for example, worked with the following five different methods over the course of their investigations. Methods were sometimes used in isolation or in combination, and the purpose of these activities was to identify commonalities in young people's reasoning that might not otherwise be understood by adults.

Verbal Behavior about Events Remote in Time

Investigators have asked respondents to talk about past or future events to determine the expansiveness of children's abstractions. Discussing events such as where the world came from, why the dinosaurs died out, or what would happen if schools were eliminated can illuminate individuals' understanding of reality and causality. With adults, this type of interview can also help investigators discern which features of the world are more and less salient in personal experience.

Remote events may be concrete and readily observed, or they may reflect abstract ideas. Both children and adults are likely to understand concrete representations, but, depending on the degree of abstraction, it may be difficult for children to imagine ideas that cannot be grounded in something tangible. When asked to imagine a world with no schools, for example, only a small percentage of children were able to articulate another means of learning about the world (see Nicholls, McKenzie, & Shufro, 1994). Concepts like freedom are highly abstract, and when children think about this important value, they are most likely to offer examples grounded in actions rather than general principles. Adults may use a mixture of languages to communicate to different audiences, but most are able to speak in principled terms.

Verbal Behavior about Immediate Events

Asking respondents to talk about the events in front of them, explaining why something occurred as it did or elaborating on beliefs about particular events, can offer information on current levels of functioning. When children are told a story and asked to imagine what occurs next, inferences can be drawn about their intentions or goals. In studies of aggression, it has been possible to identify variation in how different children interpret the same events using such techniques (Graham & Hudley, 1994). Other investigators have stopped children while they were involved in an activity to ask them about their reasons for doing what they are doing.

Problems focusing on current events, even if they involve imaginative thinking, are somewhat easier for children than problems requiring the visualization of remote events because they can be grounded in tangible, direct experience. Without careful planning, both immediate and remote events can be presented in such an obtuse manner that respondents may find themselves confused. Therefore, investigators select stimuli that are sufficiently clear that respondents and interviewers are imagining the same set of concerns during their conversation. Reasoning about immediate events is likely to be interpreted in the same way by children and adults because it requires the direct evaluation of experience. Adults, more than children, may make spontaneous connections between immediate events and more abstract aspects of their experience.

Mixing Verbal and Nonverbal Behavior

Investigators also ask respondents to do something and explain why they did what they did. Sometimes this involves solving a particular problem. Other times it involves manipulating objects at the investigator's request. When considering fair ways to organize test situations, for example, children were asked to manipulate magnets on a bar graph to show the scores of hypothetical students with high and low levels of competence (Thorkildsen, 1991). In doing so, children conveyed their understanding of different performance conditions as well as different types of learners. Children also justified their decisions and, in doing so, revealed the logic they used to make decisions.

Combining verbal and nonverbal behavior is especially helpful for determining if respondents understand the investigators' instructions because respondents can show what they know as well as describe their experiences. This approach is also useful when the subject of inquiry involves a mixture of concrete and abstract ideas. As with other tasks, children and adults are both likely to complete the manipulation step, but may give more and less abstract justifications for their decisions.

Nonverbal Behavior

To explore the coordination of structures and functioning in everyday events, it may sometimes be necessary to observe nonverbal compliance with investigators' requests. In these studies, investigators ask respondents to show them how particular tasks are done or to do particular things. Tests used with preschoolers, for example, often require children to exhibit gross and fine motor skills or to write and draw.

Adding an experimental component to the observation process, investigators typically introduce instructions to regulate behavior. Asking respondents to perform particular activities and/or monitoring gestures during the course of an investigation can offer clues into reasoning that would not otherwise be tested. This is especially helpful with children who cannot talk because their ability to follow instructions can be measured, revealing how well they understand the events going on around them.

Clinical Concentric Studies

Using a *bracketing process,* investigators sometimes determine thresholds that reveal the acuity with which individuals perceive the world around them. In such techniques, investigators present a series of stimuli of different values, requiring participants to judge each stimulus in comparison to a predetermined standard.

Suppose investigators wanted to understand how well children could read. They might include a range of reading tasks that could reveal different skills. Letter–sound recognition might be different from the ability to decode nonsense words or add missing words to a closed passage. Respondents would be evaluated in relation to a particular set of answers that are tagged to normative assumptions about how reading develops.

As is the case with structured interviews, investigators typically alter the presentation of stimuli according to the information offered by the respondent. They find ways to manipulate stimuli to offer insight into the depth as well as the breadth of a respondent's functioning. The concentric nature of this process is apparent when activities are grouped so that the same skills are required for addressing different problems. Investigators explore one set of behaviors, abilities, or emotional reactions from different directions. In doing so, they can minimize at least one form of systematic *measurement error* and *nonresponse error* because respondents are able to clarify their understanding and investigators are able to explore their hunches about what an individual does and does not understand.

Designing Activities

To study development, participants hopefully feel free, intellectually and socially, to move on their own. By anticipating the questions participants might naturally ask, investigators can stimulate such freedom. Allowing respondents to speak first during an interview can help investigators learn the vocabulary they find most salient. When beliefs are strongly held, respondents are usually resistant to countersuggestion and investigators can use a range of approaches for testing such convictions. If respondents are highly suggestible, investigators usually take this to mean that individuals are relatively uncertain about their beliefs, about the nature of the questions asked, or about the instructions delivered. Modifying the way tasks are introduced can rule out clarity issues, supporting conclusions about participants' convictions or abilities.

Clues about Intended Answers.   Investigators benefit from scrutinizing activities and materials to determine if suggestions may offer clues about acceptable answers. Without training, investigators, especially beginners, are inclined to embed verbal suggestions and/or suggestion by perseveration into their activity (Piaget, 1951). *Verbal suggestions,* like those found in poor-quality items on psychometric measures, include compound statements or cues about what the investigator expects to find. *Suggestion by perseveration* is evident when questions are introduced in an order that leads the respondent to a particular set of conclusions. Linear chains of questions or sequential patterns can encourage the establishment of mental blocks or less creative answers than might otherwise be apparent. They can also encourage respondents to passively acquiesce to the manifest agenda of an investigator rather than to reveal thoughts and behaviors that might naturally occur in other settings. To avoid this, investigators often test the consistency of responses by altering the order in which questions appear or by confirming answers later in the interview. If respondents are concentrating on communicating their knowledge, they are unlikely to notice when investigators repeat questions to verify their understanding.

Putting Respondents at Ease.   Investigators who delve into someone's reasoning usually spend time helping respondents feel comfortable with the agenda before engaging in more formal activities. Presenting tasks that are easily performed by individuals within the same age group or those easily performed by younger participants serves as one comfortable place to begin conversations. Everyone can see a clear solution and reinforce the purpose of the conversation. If investigators are willing to admit to their own fallibility, respondents are also less likely to feel intimidated by the subsequent suggestion and countersuggestion process. Seeking corroboration during the interview to verify the appropriateness of opening questions can ensure that common ground is established and maintained for the conversation. Hopefully, participants will feel free to display their own natural orientations without fear of ridicule or repercussions.

It is important to let participants talk freely and resist the temptation to interrupt or sidetrack the resulting thought processes, especially when working with children. Children, more than adults, are ready to believe that investigators are not necessarily interested in understanding their perspectives. Investigators who can convince participants about their sincere interests are likely to find rich information emerging from their activities.

Verifying Comprehension during an Interaction.   During the course of structured interviews or activities, most investigators ask alternative variations of major questions. They also offer countersuggestions and probe into individuals' responses to test the limits of their abilities. Suggestions and countersuggestions may also take place while evaluating nonverbal behavior. Listening carefully to the questions respondents pose either in natural settings or around those asked by the interviewer can also illuminate how individuals see the world. When respondents are sufficiently comfortable, they are also likely to challenge and clarify the investigator's agenda. Investigators who feel threatened or intimidated by such pressure are unlikely to be ready to undertake this kind of work.

Testing Predictions while Collecting Data.   Most structured activities used to understand development are experimental in that investigators set a problem, make hypotheses, and adapt conditions to test hypotheses. Investigators also control for intervening hypotheses by testing relevant possibilities in a conversation. When participants try to lead investigators in new directions, investigators invariably follow the lead while paying attention to the whole of the problem under investigation.

Seasoned investigators know how to listen to a respondent's agenda and then comfortably lead them back to their own plan for the day. At every moment, they construct working hypotheses and strive to establish their plausibility. As researchers gain skill, they can recognize greater subtleties in the speech and gestures of their respondents. They learn to avoid overinterpreting what respondents say or minimizing opportunities to display competence. It is important, in this kind of work, to remain skeptical of the things respondents say without becoming cynical. Investigators do so by focusing primarily on the trends of thought that remain consistent in respondents' answers. Remembering that respondents differ in confidence and ability to articulate their thoughts, investigators can adapt activities to account for individual differences.

MAKING CONNECTIONS

Design a set of activities for measuring individuals' representations of a concept in your field. What stimuli would you use? How would you explore individuals' understanding of the concept? How many examples of each structural dimension would you incorporate into your activity plan? Would your activities fall within one or more than one of Piaget's methods?

INVESTIGATORS' SKILLS

In reading reports of developmental research, you are likely to find allusions to the importance of special training in the successful completion of structured interviews and activities. It is wise to take seriously this caution because the successful calibration of many developmental tools requires a high degree of skill and sensitivity to the age groups under investigation. Investigators are also expected to monitor their own anxiety and explore how they react when personal assumptions and defenses are challenged. They generally remember that participants are evaluating an investigator's behavior and motives as readily as investigators are evaluating those of the participant.

Children are especially sensitive to the emotional states of adults with whom they are in close contact. Infants and toddlers learn to communicate by anticipating adults' behavior, but most individuals take time to size up the strangers in their midst. Training is often organized around three categories of concerns. Such activities usually focus on job skills, personal attributes, and work-related knowledge.[12]

Job Skills

Essential *job skills* include a person's ability to establish relationships of trust, compassion, and concern while setting appropriate boundaries for the interaction. Three principles are worth keeping in mind.

Generate Spontaneous Hypotheses.   It is assumed that investigators have sufficient theoretical and practical knowledge to be able to generate appropriate hypotheses during particular activities and gather evidence from watching, listening, and testing possibilities. Investigators also learn how to communicate with participants at a level that is easily understood. They find ways to accept feedback from respondents and minimize pressures that will elicit feelings of anxiety and discomfort.

Communicate Clearly.   One of the most difficult challenges involves learning to communicate without sending contradictory messages. Ideally, respondents accept that the valuable ideas discussed are their own. This is only possible if there is a shared agenda and communication between investigators and respondents is open and honest. Put more casually, participants and investigators ideally agree to play the same game.

Manage Time and Stress.   Collecting data is stressful, so most investigators cultivate a well-developed sense of timing, an ability to be flexible in the face of surprises, and a willingness to remain practical before interacting directly with participants. They also learn to persist in the face of uncertainty, ambiguity, frustration, and loneliness. It is unlikely that everyone will be overjoyed with the plans an investigator has for each participant. Anticipating this possibility, most investigators try to be sufficiently skilled to constructively address surprising or conflict-laden interactions without making participants feel uncomfortable.

Personal Attributes

Personal attributes that are important to successful work in development include many that are relatively rare. Investigators who are well-qualified for such work show intelligence, wisdom, and compassion while collecting data.

Cognitive Complexity.   Most investigators show a high degree of cognitive complexity and intelligence when observing, anticipating, and evaluating their experiences. This inevitably involves the ability to bring multiple skills to bear on problems as they arise in the research enterprise.

Self-Understanding.   Along with cognitive complexity, successful investigators also take for granted stable levels of self-awareness, self-acceptance, and control over their psychological defenses. They remain ready to learn from participants as often as they make judgments about actions, reasoning, and feelings. In doing so, investigators moderate their own needs for affiliation, competence, and power and are likely to imagine being informed by those with whom they interact.

Interpersonal Competence.   The most beneficial forms of interpersonal competence include openness and honesty. To call forth the best performance from participants, skilled investigators are likely to elicit high levels of achievement, find comfort in intuitive methods of extracting information, and show high levels of imagination as they generate possibilities. Such attributes place limits on the likelihood that investigators might lash out at participants who surprise them. Successful investigators do not overreact to the things participants say or do, and would not compromise data collection by introducing inappropriate issues.

Work-Related Knowledge

Work-related knowledge involves many of the themes raised in Chapter 2, but warrant particular emphasis in contexts that are dependent on high-quality interactions with vulnerable populations. This aspect of training reinforces professional and discipline-related skills and abilities.

Know the Context.   Most investigators develop elaborate organizational and interpersonal knowledge of the contexts in which they work. They explore the roles individuals are expected to fulfill and their own and others' responsibilities.

Understand the Change Process.   Knowing the fundamental principles associated with change and the effects of change on the people involved is essential to remaining sensitive enough to detect individual responses. Investigators try to remember that participants face risks while participating in research and may differ in their ability to remain flexible in the face of challenges to their thoughts, actions, or emotions. Treating participants with respect and designing projects with the principles of justice and beneficence in mind can maximize the likelihood that quality information will be obtained.

Anticipate Individual Differences in Participants' Interests and Agendas.   Knowledge of the range of personality dynamics that are likely to be apparent in a given context is also important to remaining sensitive to the needs of participants and those in the workplace. Staying informed about the ethical norms and standards for professional practice helps investigators consider the greater good of their research and the welfare of participants.

Verifying Qualifications

Exploring the strength of job skills, personal attributes, and work-related knowledge is essential for conducting strong developmental research because measurement requires a skilled investigator. Most developmentalists typically undergo a wide range of training activities to help them learn about themselves and listen carefully to research participants. Strong measurement is possible only if investigators can balance their own issues of power, competence, and affiliation well enough to consider participants' perspectives and elicit rich responses from them.

Training is especially critical in that most developmental research involves interactions with vulnerable populations. Children and adolescents are vulnerable because they are not in a position to make fully autonomous decisions about the risks associated with research procedures, especially for techniques that depend heavily on probing into participants' imaginations. Most investigators remain highly self-conscious of the power they have in such interactions.

MAKING CONNECTIONS

What qualifications enable you to study development effectively? What skills would you need to learn? What personality attributes allow you to be well-suited for this kind of work? What attributes would you want to change? What theoretical/practical knowledge prepares you for collecting developmental data? What knowledge would you have to acquire? Where could you learn skills you do not yet have? How will you address the power differential that is likely to be apparent in your interactions? What will you do to elicit respondents' trust and convey your research purposes?

CALIBRATING TOOLS

To calibrate interview and observational methods that are embedded with experimentation, investigators try to anticipate the responses of participants, plan probing questions to explore the roots of participants' answers, and design countersuggestions for use in testing the strength of individuals' beliefs. Across participants, investigators may find one of five different kinds of reactions to stimuli and should learn how to differentiate among them.[13]

Liberated and Spontaneous Convictions

When at their best, participants typically offer liberated or spontaneous convictions. *Liberated convictions* are apparent when investigators ask a question that respondents have never asked themselves, but draw an answer from their own minds. Although the wording of such questions may influence individuals' responses, participants use original thought to reveal their reasoning. *Spontaneous convictions* are apparent when a respondent has asked and answered an investigator's question prior to the activity and is revealing fully formulated answers. Most children and some adults cannot tell a researcher if they have previously considered a question, but investigators can make educated guesses as to the degree of spontaneity in someone's answers.

Both liberated and spontaneous reactions are highly resistant to suggestion because the roots of beliefs or behaviors emerge from deep within the structural core of how individuals organize their experience. Some responses may be apparent across a substantial group of participants of the same age. As new responses are constructed, such beliefs or behaviors are likely to show a gradual decrease; respondents are unlikely to suddenly abandon early developing convictions. During a developmental transition, traces of old and new ways of organizing experience are likely to be in respondents' initial answers before investigators probe those answers, and in respondents' naturally occurring questions. To determine if reactions are spontaneous rather than liberated, investigators typically conduct direct observations. No questioning styles or experimentation techniques facilitate distinctions between liberated and spontaneous convictions.

Constrained Convictions

The remaining three types of responses are unhelpful in the research enterprise although investigators learn from their presence. Participants can offer random responses, show signs of romancing, or offer a suggested conviction. *Random answers* typically reveal a lack of interest as participants persevere in avoiding a question. *Romancing* is apparent when participants respond by engaging in magical thinking or otherwise inventing stories that are seen as plausible simply in the telling. *Suggested convictions* are those in which participants endeavor to please the interviewer by offering those responses the investigator is assumed to want. Such convictions are most common when investigators use a series of questions to lead respondents to a set of answers or when investigators perseverate on a topic.

Depending on the age of the participant, some of these devices can be deliberate attempts to poke fun at an investigator and the research tasks. However, in early and middle childhood, constrained responses are common indicators that children fail to understand investigators' questions and have invented replacement questions. As with guessing, traces of earlier convictions and/or anticipations of future convictions may appear in participants' answers. Successful calibration of developmental interview or observation techniques hinges on an investigator's awareness of these possibilities and most design methods for differentiating one style of responding from another.

Thinking Out Loud.　Temperamentally speaking, some participants are highly susceptible to change, thinking aloud rather than to themselves. Investigators generally take time to discriminate this tendency to talk through a thinking process from random or suggested answers because the end results in a conviction. It is also this willingness to share thought processes that can help investigators identify change mechanisms.

Distinguishing Random and Suggested Convictions.   Investigators can distinguish *random answers* from *suggested convictions* in one of several ways. Like random answers, suggested convictions are fleeting in that countersuggestions easily lead to revised positions. However, suggested convictions are likely to have a kind of coherence that is not apparent when answers are random. One way investigators test for such possibilities is to identify coherence by asking essentially the same questions using different examples or at different points during an interview. When respondents are following behavioral instructions, similar attempts to establish internal consistency can be incorporated. Many investigators also probe individuals' responses to determine if there are strong commitments. When answers are highly inconsistent it is likely that respondents are answering randomly. If there is coherence, but that coherence does not seem well-supported with justifications or patterns of behavior, the conviction is likely to be suggested.

Recognizing Romancing.   In contrast to random answers and suggested convictions, *romancing* tends to result in rich, coherent responses, albeit those grounded in fantasy. In interviews, participants will resist countersuggestions that do not fit with the story they are inventing. Investigators cannot learn much from analyzing the roots of an answer because the ramifications of the story will be deeply rooted in fantasy. Instead, romancing is detectable primarily by comparing the responses of one person against those of a group of people the same age. Generally speaking, romancing is apparent when few respondents offer the same answers, but this rule has a caveat. If questions are incomprehensible at a given age, there may be consistency in children's tendency to create fantasies, and if children are immersed in the same environments, their stories may show marked similarities. Incongruity alone is not sufficient for determining the extent of romancing.

Investigators can contrast romancing with other forms of conviction by looking for evidence of stagelike qualities in responses. If, at a particular age, features of the predicted answers disappear entirely and are replaced by an entirely different set of answers, investigators could see this as evidence for romancing at that age or as evidence for two different stages of reasoning. In discontinuous forms of development, investigators could more easily rule out the possibility of romancing if a third, intermediate stage were apparent in which elements of both stages were apparent in participants' reasoning. If a continuous developmental progression were in evidence, intermediate positions would not be apparent. Romancing would be detectable if inconsistent ideas, that would not seem plausible on later reflection, were apparent in individuals' answers. Rather than engage in romancing, some individuals will cling to more primitive forms of thought and behavior, even if their conceptions are changing, until the new representational models are fully intact.

The Importance of Justifications

These examples of how individuals might respond should convey the idea that calibrating tools in developmental research involves a grounded form of sensitivity to the perspectives of the individuals whose functioning is being explored. Most investigators are as interested in how conceptions are organized within the person as they are in declaring the presence or absence of a particular concept.

Calibrating tools for use with children is more difficult than for adults because children's methods of communicating are still developing. Children rely on gestures and actions as often as words to share their knowledge. To understand intentions, most investigators collect as much information as possible from each respondent using multiple tools. This allows them to look for internal consistency in judgments across tasks. Many investigators also look for stability in judgments when participants are offered challenges and countersuggestions.

Developmental experimentation is most effective when respondents justify or otherwise explain their behavior. Comparing judgments and explanations, developmentalists find patterns in performance within a particular task. It is tautological, in developmental research, to assume that an individual's limited verbal or behavioral skills *cause* differences in performance because skills and performance on research activities are expected to be highly associated. At best, developmental work offers a qualitatively ordered hierarchy of stages, levels, or phases of development in which tools are calibrated using feedback from respondents and patterns of responses across participants with similar characteristics. Investigators can verify which representational features are simple or complex, but they cannot demonstrate the causes of structures or functioning. Inferences about change mechanisms require longitudinal research designs and temporal measurement techniques, although investigators may speculate using cross-sectional evidence.

MAKING CONNECTIONS

Imagine administering the activity you designed to one or two individuals in an age group. Write a brief set of predictions about how individuals are likely to respond. What probing questions would you ask when exploring the roots of individuals' responses? What countersuggestions would you make? How would you minimize perseveration? What reactions would you expect and how will you respond in the face of such reactions? With these predictions in mind, administer the tasks to one or two individuals and compare your predictions to the actual experiences.

STANDARDIZATION

If tools are calibrated using feedback from respondents, issues of standardization pose problems that are not apparent with psychometric tools. To be able to compare responses, investigators typically find ways to ensure that respondents understand and interpret the stimulus materials in the same way. This process invariably requires adjustments to the order of presenting problems, wording, and the details of particular activities rather than assurances that everyone has been given exactly the same stimuli in the same order. To be sensitive to age-related change, investigators may also find themselves posing different questions to different groups of participants while ensuring that the meaning of each question remains stable. Parallel procedures are used when giving instructions to elicit measurable behavior. Similarly, differences in the temperament of individuals can lead to different styles of interaction, essential for ensuring that tasks are fully understood.

Variation in Theoretical Commitments

Standardization takes on different definitions, depending on the theoretical framework that drives the research. *Associationists* are usually interested in developmental ordering, and see structure and functioning as so tightly fused that surface characteristics reveal structural characteristics. They are likely to value standardization in how activities are presented and in the wording used to give instructions. *Constructivists* look for a common order of responses but expect surface characteristics to vary. Standardization involves verifying the meaning of activities to participants while exploring features of the same concepts across persons. Variation in the presentation order can also offer insight into how well meaning is standardized. *Cultural theorists* assume that performance will be similar within groups, but that even structural features may differ across groups. New tools may be essential for understanding intergroup variation, but the same tools are typically used within a particular culture so that data can be aggregated to obfuscate individual differences. *Developmental systems theories* incorporate features of associationist, constructivist, and cultural theories and may alter their definitions of standardization accordingly.

Differentiating Trivial and Essential Forms of Standardization

In many of these frameworks, standardization is possible if investigators focus on individuals' understanding of the particular concepts under investigation rather than the exact methods of presenting questions or instructions. Most developmentalists distinguish essential features of standardization from more trivial features, looking at what participants understand rather than ensuring everyone hears the same vocabulary under identical conditions. The idea is to standardize activities only to the extent necessary for eliciting respondents' knowledge of the same concepts without alienating them or obscuring their abilities. Investigators accomplish this by designing a wide array of materials and methods for identifying functioning. They alter methods that are overly dependent on verbal production, are overly abstract or distant from the experience of respondents, or do not permit respondents to reveal the whole of their knowledge. Developmentalists may also combine techniques to fully test the limits of children's reasoning.

Maximizing Interaction

Using interactive tasks, it is especially difficult for investigators to learn not to talk too much, suggest responses, or sidetrack respondents' ideas. Most developmentalists are cautious when modifying the presentation of materials to ensure they offer an adequate test of predictions. With training, they learn how to avoid overly leading questions or suggesting answers. Liberated or spontaneous convictions reveal participants' functioning and, over the duration of an activity, similar indicants can reflect trends of thought or action. When participants' responses reflect fantasy, coherence may be apparent in their answers, but those answers do not correspond to normative trends of thought. Random and suggested convictions are typically so fleeting that trends of thought would not be apparent.

Skilled investigators are careful to balance the significance of each indicant, trying not to overestimate or underestimate participants' abilities. Measuring functioning across similar groups of participants, investigators can separate the common, recurring findings from idiosyncratic, occasional responses. This is most likely if respondents are encouraged to do most of the talking.

Bracket Indicants for an Age Group

Invariably, investigators learn to *bracket* tools after finding the midpoint of an age range for which they are useful. They try to remember that participants are giving answers or revealing behavior that is in response to the research plan; functioning is not completely spontaneous. Instead, investigators plan clusters of activities to test predetermined possibilities while remaining flexible about anticipated events. Predicted age differences are often bracketed, but the nature of the activities may also facilitate this clustering.

When collecting data, investigators are so preoccupied with understanding respondents' perspectives that bracketing is nearly impossible. It is difficult to notice age-related patterns while generating hypotheses to be tested and formulating gentle ways of communicating with participants to test specific hypotheses. Most developmentalists determine if the logic of each respondent is fully available during the activity and later look for emerging patterns across participants. Including questions that are optimally challenging for particular age groups as well as a few that are relatively easy and difficult, most investigators pay careful attention to how participants respond to these questions in much the same way as psychometricians may look at item difficulty. Clusters of responses can then be bracketed into clusters with scalelike properties.

The Value of Comparison

Standardization, along with calibration, facilitates investigators' ability to verify that concepts are not borrowed through imitation, but are products of a respondent's structural core. As children learn to think like adults, some standardization techniques are invariably simplified because most adults are better able than children to communicate their reactions. Investigators may use activities that are appropriately bracketed for each age group and different activities across age groups to draw generalizations about representational change. Progressively greater levels of standardization invariably place restrictions on the calibration of tools by limiting the flexibility of the tasks. Empathic or intuitive approaches are less common and investigators are less responsive to individual differences in functioning.[14] Balancing theoretical and measurement assumptions using different methods can maximize reliability in studies of representational change.

MAKING CONNECTIONS

Are you ready to standardize procedures for administering your activity? Why or why not? What type of individual variation was apparent in how respondents interpreted your activities? How will you make fair comparisons when identifying trends of thought?

GENERALIZABILITY

To make generalizations about representational differences, most developmentalists verify the order in which different conceptions develop. This requires measurement of the same conceptions at different ages and verification that all relevant dimensions and only those dimensions are sampled for each concept. Four major considerations have been identified in available research programs.

Generalizability as the Verification of Order

When order is important, the most common approach to exploring generalizability involves comparing measures of different kinds of functioning against one another.[15] *Generalizability as a verification of order* involves uniformity in answers for each relevant age group and differences across age to verify the origin of a logical sequence.

Comparing the Manifest Order Using Emprical Patterns.   Investigators can compare responses of participants by creating transcripts or coding techniques that essentially remove identifying characteristics. Mixing indicants from a variety of age groups while coding data, raters are unlikely to be influenced by preconceived knowledge of how age groups differ. If problems are presented in appropriately counterbalanced orders, this may also be untangled, placing responses from each participant in a standard order. These "blinded" transcripts invariably take away the original logical order of the activity. Raters are less likely to impose artificial coherence on answers that may not be connected in the minds of respondents. Looking for trends of thought across protocols, investigators consider patterns evident in the data to reflect representations of participants' structural core.

Limitations of Direct Comparisons.   Some theorists note a major limitation of directly comparing two conceptions against one another to verify order.[16] Although investigators can look for synchrony between concepts, they have difficulty determining if one type of conception is necessary for another. On one level, it is difficult to verify that the measurement scales used to verify two different conceptions are compatible; most scales may be transformed to approximate an interval scale, but ratio scales are rare. Without verifying the compatibility of scaling, investigators can only explore synchrony to verify that conceptions are related to the same structure. They do so by ruling out alternative predictions, not by verifying that the order obtained for one measure is somehow causally related to the order obtained for another.

Age as a Ruler.   One means of making direct comparisons involves using age as an index of order. This is most commonly used to evaluate participants' functioning. If there is no correlation between age and a new classification system, investigators reject developmental claims and explore individual differences. When patterns follow age trends, investigators start theorizing about development.

Differences in theoretical frameworks foster various commitments to using age as a proxy for representational change. Investigators holding associationist theories are more likely to use age as a ruler for verifying the order of conceptual development. They avoid the problem of establishing synchrony among concepts, and do not distinguish structure and functioning. Other theorists may start exploring developmental claims when age differences are apparent, but this is treated as only one of several clues about such sequences. Developmentalists recognize that some forms of development are not closely tied to age.

Generalizability as Synchrony of Concepts

Investigators solve problems with direct comparisons by establishing criteria for verifying measurement equivalence across age groups. Coding schemes can be established so the definitions of each variable remain the same, but indicants reflect age-appropriate language or behavior. In this way, investigators emphasize synchrony in structure and functioning without worrying about the ages at which particular kinds of functioning appears.

Are Related Concepts in Temporal Synchrony?   Investigators can verify synchrony in one of two ways: They can determine if two conceptions are *apparent at the same time* or if two conceptions *develop at the same rate.* In representational studies, it is usually premature to draw inferences about the rate of development, but before exploring temporal relations it is helpful to verify the sequence of representational differences using cross-sectional designs. In such designs, the relations between two variables are typically plotted using age and scores on the measured dimension as parameters. Investigators can determine if a common underlying structure is apparent and if age is partly related to functioning.

Bootstrapping.   Using *bootstrapping methods,* investigators often combine results from several tools to compare the sequence obtained using a new measure with at least two others. This makes it possible to propose and test models of the relations among measures and is accomplished by making predictions regarding developmental priorities. Most commonly, investigators use structural equation modeling or regression techniques in which indicants rather than scales are compared.

Three findings are common in developmental research (Figure 10.1). *Complete priority* is evident when one conception must be fully developed before another can begin. Investigators would not expect high correlations between the old and new conception, but, for a later occurring conception to be apparent, an earlier one is also present. *Partial priority* is evident when the development of one conception is underway before another can begin to emerge. Here there might be some correlation between indicants of earlier appearing concepts, but other indicants would not be associated. *A lack of priority* or *the presence of synchrony* occurs when the development of two conceptions starts and ends at the same time. Correlations between indicants of both concepts would be high.

When investigators have ordinal data, they can rule out the complete priority hypothesis, but cannot differentiate partial priority from synchrony. When investigators measure concepts using an interval scale, they can verify the presence or absence of priority, partial priority, and complete synchrony, but cannot verify the causal relationship between conceptions.

Generalizations about Stages

Most stage models tend to underrepresent differences within a stage and similarities in responses across stages. In this respect, they may not offer enough information for fully understanding representational change. Ordinarily, patterns in responses do not suddenly

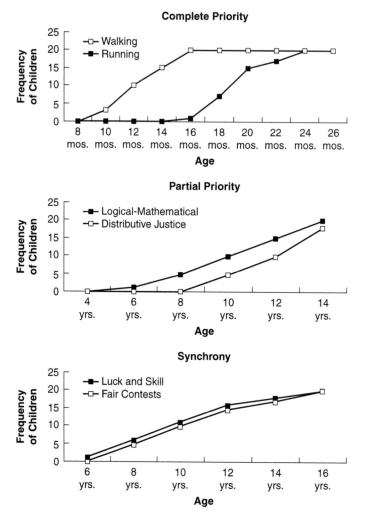

FIGURE 10.1   Sample Bootstrapping Outcomes When Two Related Concepts Are Compared across Age Groups.

appear or disappear, and even when development is discontinuous, inconsistent answers contain symptoms of reasoning common in early and later periods in development. For these and other theoretical reasons, investigators usually conduct longitudinal studies using age as a ruler to verify claims about development.

Some investigators also explore the details of individual differences in functioning to challenge theorists who look only at change across structures. Guidelines for calibrating and standardizing representational measures continue to be used for such generalizations as well as for stage-driven theories. When comparisons with age are finally explored, developmental claims are accepted as if age is associated with changes across measures.

Put simply, when convictions are strong, participants are usually resistant to suggestion. When convictions are in transition, participants will offer inconsistent responses. Age trends in these patterns are usually apparent if developmental claims are supported, but investigators may only find evidence for individual differences.

Generalizations Involving Children

Working with children poses a special set of dilemmas that constrains the validity of generalizations. The egocentrism of children predisposes them to minimize attempts to defend their original thoughts or to articulate elaborate justifications for such thoughts. Investigators find children's thoughts and actions to be at least partially original because children selectively imitate rather than mimic ideas in their environment with a reasonable degree of spontaneity. However, it is difficult to determine when children are imitating the perspectives in their environment and when they have begun to construct a more solid structural core. Generalizations are improved as a theoretical framework becomes better established because investigators can design multivariate measurement models to evaluate individual and contextual levels of functioning and how they are integrated.[17] Put another way, investigators are better able to discern how relationships among multiple levels of organization are fused in the full ecology of people at a given age or across ages. Looking at how development is embedded within a culture, investigators can also explore how people pool and accumulate their discoveries and conventions.

Generalizations about Generalizations

Regardless of their theoretical assumptions, when generalizing from the patterns apparent in participants' actions and reactions, investigators are careful to consider the world in which respondents are adapted. They consider the individuals' own world of thought as well as the society that influences such thought. Individuals learn both by inventing their own perspectives and by accepting the positions held by others. Designing tasks that cannot be solved simply through imitation can facilitate attempts to distinguish the structural core that directs functioning from more fleeting external pressures that invariably lead to imitation. Association studies can determine how imitation and structural variability are fused in functioning.

MAKING CONNECTIONS

Identify trends of thought in the responses you obtained for your activity. Was it relatively easy to find consistency in individuals' responses? Were there inconsistencies? Would it be possible to draw generalizations from these trends? Is there a developmental framework (e.g., associationist, constructivist, cultural, or developmental systems theories) that most closely aligns with your data?

REPRESENTING DEVELOPMENT

Defining representations requires investigators to choose among many dilemmas associated with exploring these relationships; it would be nearly impossible in a single study to explore all of the dilemmas associated with measuring representational differences. Investigators also need training in relevant job skills and theoretical knowledge as well as attributes that are conducive to putting respondents at ease in a measurement session.

Collecting evidence from multiple sources and looking for patterns in that evidence allows investigators to identify those structural dimensions and levels of organization that offer the most important theoretical and practical information. With the generation of expectations, it becomes possible to design activities that test the limits of individuals' abilities and explore the levels of organization in which those abilities are most salient. Investigators calibrate tools by considering respondents' perspectives on the concepts to be measured rather than rely on predetermined, context-free standards. As a theoretical framework emerges, calibration becomes less ambiguous and standardizing the presentation of activities is easier. Most investigators still take time to ensure that new respondents understand the activities as intended, but can more readily anticipate the kinds of responses that are likely. The more emphasis investigators place on standardization in presenting and interpreting activities, the less rigorous the calibration of each tool becomes.

Investigators usually try to elicit either liberated or spontaneous convictions and look for trends of thought, feelings, or actions in the indicants apparent in each participant's responses. These trends offer information on whether structures reflect simple or complex representations of particular concepts. Differences across age and comparisons between different abilities are made to establish whether findings can be generalized across samples, contexts, and problem types. Verifying structures often gives rise to evidence of representational change, but, before investigators can be convinced of such change, it is important to conduct longitudinal research.

SUGGESTED READINGS

Agresti, A. (2002). *Categorical data analysis* (2nd ed.). New York: Wiley.

Baltes, P. B., Reese, H. W., & Nesselroade, J. R. (1977). *Life-span developmental psychology: Introduction to research methods.* Monterey, CA: Brooks/Cole.

Bronfenbrenner, U. (1979). *The ecology of human development: Experiments by nature and design.* Cambridge, MA: Harvard University Press.

Case, R., & Okamoto, Y. (2000). *The role of central conceptual structures in the development of children's thought.* London: Blackwell.

Denison, D. G. T., Holmes, C., Mallick, B. K., & Smith, A. F. M. (2002). *Bayesian methods for nonlinear classification and regression.* New York: Wiley.

Ericsson, K. A., & Simon, H. A. (1996). *Protocol analysis: Verbal reports as data.* Cambridge, MA: MIT Press.

Hosmer, D. W., Jr., & Lemeshow, S. (2000). *Applied logistic regression* (2nd ed.). New York: Wiley.

Marcoulides, G. A., & Moustaki, I. (Eds.). (2002). *Latent variable and latent structure models.* Mahwah, NJ: Erlbaum.

Piaget, J. (1951). *The child's conception of the world.* Savage, MD: Littlefield Adams.

Seber, G. A. F., & Wild, C. J. (2003). *Nonlinear regression.* New York: Wiley.

Thelen, E., & Smith, L. B. (1998). Dynamic systems theories. In W. Damon & R. M. Lerner (Eds.), *Handbook of child psychology: Vol. 1. Theoretical models of human development* (5th ed., pp. 563-634). New York: Wiley.

Vasta, R. (Ed.). (1982). *Strategies and techniques for child study.* New York: Academic Press.

SUGGESTED WEB SITES

Sage Publications Software for *NVIVO:* http://scolari.co.uk
Scientific software for *Atlas-ti:* http://www.atlasti.com.

ENDNOTES

1. Compare details reported in Damon (1977) and Nicholls (1978) for an example.

2. See Damon (1977) and Thelen & Smith (1998) for other versions of this argument.

3. Thorkildsen (1989b) offers a direct test of this possibility.

4. Larsen (1977) reviews research based on these assumptions.

5. Damon (1977), Flavell (1963), and Piaget (1951) outline these assumptions.

6. Lerner (1996) and Larsen (1977) outline some of these tensions.

7. Piaget (1951) offers the most widely cited examples.

8. Larson (1977) offers a summary of these points. Damon (1977) and Piaget (1951) offer elaborate examples of such methods in use.

9. These assertions were initially found in the work of Piaget (1951), but are reported in several other books on developmental research methods.

10. Larson (1977) offers a review of studies conducted with these assumptions.

11. Piaget (1951) outlines some of the rules used, but others have combed his work to identify common techniques he used to address different problems (e.g., Damon, 1977; Flavell, 1963).

12. These are modified from Lowman (1985) and are intended to supplement those themes raised in Chapter 2.

13. Piaget (1951) offers a detailed summary of these reactions and many examples of such thought.

14. Lowman (1985) introduces these assumptions about clinical methods that were revised in Piaget's (1951) work to include experimental components.

15. Flavell (1963) offers a description of how Piaget's work on perception was standardized using bracketing techniques that involve comparing intellectual and perceptual functioning to determine how one type of functioning influences another. Theoretically, these two kinds of functioning are fused in ontogeny such that descriptions and explanations of one invariably involve the other. Piaget (1951) outlines rules for interpreting such findings.

16. Dixon (1998) offers a clear summary of many of the pitfalls with this approach to establishing generalizability.

17. Lerner (1996) and Thelen & Smith (1998) offer some current examples of this approach to development.

CHAPTER ELEVEN

MEASURING TEMPORAL CHANGE

Change is such a fact of life that even when asleep a person's central nervous system is never in a state of rest. Investigators interested in development accept that change rather than stability is the norm, but that not all forms of change are theoretically interesting. Interesting forms of change are those that follow relatively stable patterns and facilitate an understanding of how humans function in the larger ecology. This type of change may be measured using indices of time, number of trials, and/or the magnitude of stimuli needed to produce a reaction. Less interesting forms of change include those that are completely random or follow regenerating cycles that show evidence of oscillation but not of progress. Physiological adaptation, habituation, or sensitization are examples of changes attributable to the passage of time, but are not particularly interesting to developmental researchers. In fact, these forms of change are sometimes used as a substitute for time in studies that involve the manipulation of variables because the oscillation is predictable but not evolving. Emphasizing the central features of developmental change, this chapter will focus on measuring those forms of change that are concerned with integrating structure and functioning.

STEPS IN THEORY BUILDING

As you may recall, there are three phases commonly associated with constructing developmental theories. Investigators focusing on temporal change try to coordinate all three phases when designing and comparing tools. They do so by synthesizing findings from at least six different theory-building steps.[1]

Representational Change

Three steps are associated with measuring representational change and are not typically addressed in a linear order. To identify representations of individuals' structural core, investigators discover and synthesize theoretical dimensions evident in a developmental system (Figure 11.1).

Measuring Structures First. To *identify and measure structures,* developmental researchers sometimes look for uniform, consistent patterns that can be attributed to the features of participants' ontogeny. Investigators may start by representing and measuring the logical dimensions of theoretical structures and explore changes in those structures across

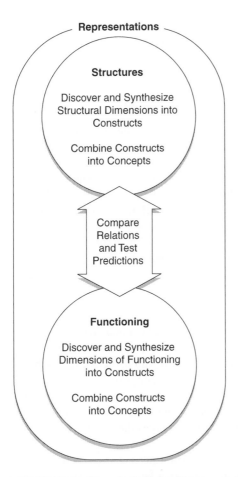

FIGURE 11.1   Steps in Defining Representations

age groups and time. Later in the theory-building process, investigators may make predictions about how structures influence functioning and test those predictions.

Measuring Functioning First.   Investigators may also start by *identifying and measuring functioning* and use existing knowledge to generate theories about individuals' structural core. In this approach, investigators look for patterns in the dimensions of functioning and measure those dimensions. They draw inferences about the structural core that guides functioning by describing dimensions or introducing pressures to induce change, and exploring the resulting effects.

Measuring Representational Differences.   Explorations of structure and functioning across age groups allow investigators to draw conclusions about *representational differences* attributable to development. To fully explore differences, investigators measure all relevant aspects of structures and functioning and look for similarities and differences in how indicants are associated. Claims about the relations between structures and functioning are used to make inferences about the constructs and concepts of a developmental system.

Individual Differences

Investigators also explore *individual differences within age groups* to determine patterns in the starting point of a trend, the asymptote or convergence of manifest and latent variables, and the nature of curvature parameters (e.g., continuous or discontinuous). To fully understand a system, it is helpful to think of individual differences as embedded within each cluster of representational differences and representations of development as evolving over time. Given that representations of different concepts also vary in form, it becomes difficult to fully illustrate the coordination of individual differences and representational change within a system. Stable characteristics like gender or ethnicity are often combined with more dynamic features of personality and social position in studies of associations between enduring person characteristics and representational differences.

Temporal Change

Once investigators have found sufficient evidence of common representations in cross-sectional studies, they can add theoretical detail using *evidence of temporal change* (Figure 11.2). When individual differences are associated with particular representations, separate longitudinal studies for each dimension of a personality characteristic can be conducted. If gender differences are salient, for example, investigators might identify separate relations between structures and functioning for males and females. They would conduct independent studies for each gender and compare and contrast the results.

Limiting Causal Inferences.   Inferences about causal relations between personal characteristics and representations are rarely supported because characteristics cannot be randomly assigned to participants.[2] It is not possible to confirm that gender *causes* differences in motivation, even if the structure of motivation may differ for males and females. At best, investigators can describe the relations between stable personal characteristics and other variables. Investigators can use quasi-experimental designs to explore similarities and differences in the change process and determine if variance in a set of changing dimensions predict individual differences. Studies of differences in how individuals coordinate task and ego orientations over time, for example, may foster consistent predictions of gender.

Identifying Change Mechanisms.   To fully support developmental conclusions, it is not enough to find differences among age groups. The sixth step in theory-building involves inferences about the *mechanisms that cause change* drawn from longitudinal research evidence. Temporal research enables investigators to compare individual and group differences, and investigators may use a mixture of experimental and descriptive methods.

Correlational studies of age changes in particular types of functioning are sometimes used to explore interrelationships among the structural dimensions of a dynamic system. Experimental studies in which investigators introduce external pressures to initiate or maintain change can also permit inferences about the relation between structures and functioning.

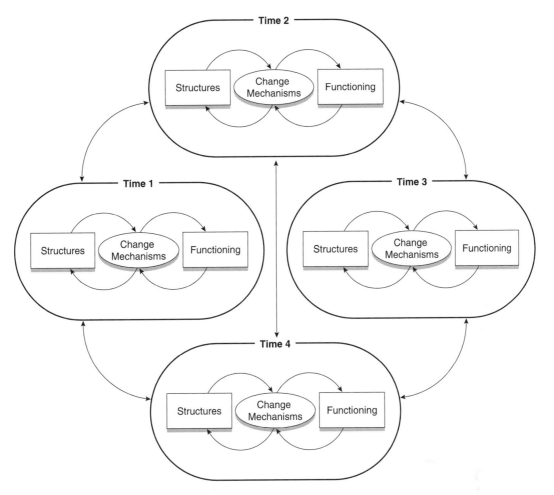

FIGURE 11.2   Temporal Change

Multiple Designs, Multiple Tools

When looking at how change is initiated, maintained, and halted, several designs are coordinated. Individuals' standing in a distribution can differ as a function of their evolving structural core, more enduring personal characteristics, or a given point in time. Therefore, aggregate levels of change, tied directly to age, can obfuscate important differences. To address this challenge, investigators commonly use a variety of designs and measures to isolate patterns within a system. They often rely on multiple studies to identify recurring patterns. In doing so, investigators are able to detect subtle forms of change and can find support for assumptions about the nature of structural cores and how they affect functioning.

The Iterative Nature of Developmental Research.   Developmental research is *iterative* in that findings from one line of investigation can easily lead investigators back to more descriptive phases and to revisions in some or all of their conclusions. Information derived from any one of the six research steps may lead investigators to revise theoretical definitions of structures, functioning, and mechanisms of change apparent in a developmental system. Theoretical alterations made for one step invariably involve alterations at many of the others.

Verifying the Practicality of Longitudinal Research.   To estimate the value of longitudinal research, investigators often ask if findings would help them understand important changes in a given developmental outcome.[3] Investigators commonly target outcomes that reflect valuable life skills. Studies of how individuals learn to regulate their own behavior, for example, have emerged from looking at levels of aggression, prosocial interactions, and conflict resolution. Findings serve a practical as well as theoretical purpose in that aggressive individuals are typically expected to modify their behavior whereas prosocial conduct may remain unchallenged.

Shortcomings of Premature Research.   Unfortunately, concern with parsimony has led many investigators to look at only part of the developmental system, attributing causal agency to adults rather than to children, to families rather than cultural factors, or environmental rather than biological factors. Although adults would not claim to "learn" children, for example, many feel little shame when proudly claiming to "motivate" them. Similarly, bosses talk about motivating their subordinates and political leaders their followers. This reflects some awareness that motivation is influenced by the contexts in which individuals reside, but eliminates personal agency and responsibility from the story.

Investigators with a strong commitment to understanding development try to move beyond such dichotomies by remaining aware of distal as well as proximal effects on functioning and of less popular as well as more popular topics of inquiry. They recognize the importance of controlling variables in a research design and realize that such commitments invariably place limits on how much can be accomplished by each study.

Types of Temporal Change

The rest of this chapter will raise issues of how dimensions of a structure and the resulting functioning *change in integration* and *change over time.* The former is sometimes characterized as qualitative and the latter as quantitative, but investigators often use numbers to represent ideas for both kinds of measurement. Investigators sometimes replace measures of time with the number of trials or magnitude of stimuli necessary for producing a reaction, but the same general algorithms apply to temporal problems.

MAKING CONNECTIONS

Identify claims in your field about change over time. What techniques have investigators used to verify these claims? Did investigators distinguish changes in both structures and functioning? Are the two issues coordinated in existing theories? How do investigators account for individual differences?

CHALLENGES OF MEASURING TEMPORAL CHANGE

Studies of change are highly complex, no matter what organizational level of a developmental system is being considered. Six of the most challenging measurement considerations will be introduced here, but each study poses its own set of hurdles. Investigators learn to:

- accept that not all variables in experimental designs can be manipulated or randomly assigned to participants;
- find ways to account for individual differences in the onset of a developmental sequence;
- realize that difference scores can be unreliable;
- understand that stimuli may not hold comparable meaning across ages or over time;
- find measurement scales that are sufficiently sensitive to change;
- accept that longitudinal data is expensive and difficult to collect.

Each of these concerns will be introduced here, but you may want to read more on how investigators have worked around as well as with such challenges before designing a longitudinal study. Knowledge of available research can save inordinate amounts of energy and cost.

Design and Variable Constraints

When inventing new tools, investigators often consider the design in which growth is being explored. At the beginning of psychometrically-driven experimental research, two groups are assumed to have identical means on randomly assigned variables,[4] then a treatment or intervention is introduced. Independent variables are measured to draw inferences about individual differences. Dependent variables are measured to verify the outcomes of a treatment in repeated trials. Predictions are tested by comparing differences among treatments or by exploring patterns in thoughts and actions over time.

Randomization Constraints.   Because developmental research contains limits on an investigator's ability to draw causal inferences about changes attributable to human characteristics, determining causality is nearly impossible. Many human characteristics such as age, gender, ethnicity, height, and so forth cannot be randomly assigned within a particular study or manipulated to produce change. Therefore, differences attributable to age do not support inferences that change will occur *because* individuals age in time. Age does not have the random properties necessary for inclusion as a manipulated variable, but inferences about descriptive patterns are still reasonable.

Developmental Solutions.   Most investigators solve the constraints of measuring change by rearranging well-measured variables in their research design. They may use age or some similar temporal index as a dependent measure to facilitate inferences about the cause of change. The existence of change is taken for granted and investigators identify the structures or functioning in which change occurs. Age remains the most frequently used index of change because it offers a ratio scale and a highly flexible estimate of growth.

Sometimes age is so tightly fused with other outcome variables that it is difficult to discriminate the two. This problem has not been completely solved, but investigators continue to compare findings from analysis of covariance and path analyses with those obtained from regression models or simple tests of difference scores (Gottman, 1995). Such comparisons can facilitate independent representations of concepts ordinarily fused with age. As tools become more accurate, investigators minimize the need for statistical corrections or estimates of the percentage of variance accounted for by each theoretical dimension. In turn, maximizing accuracy in the measurement process has facilitated comparison among methods of analysis. Despite these generalizations, each study poses different challenges that hinge on how many levels of organization are evident in each construct or concept.

MAKING CONNECTIONS

Are there studies in your field that rely on age as a dependent variable? Do investigators use other temporal measures instead of age? What variables are measured in such studies? What measurement scales are used for these variables?

Control for Initial Differences

Investigators who are comfortable using age scales as one outcome in their design still face the challenge of finding an *appropriate place to begin* exploring development. The duration of change may be the same across participants once individuals start to develop, but not everyone is likely to start developing at the same time. Investigators who rely on age as a means of determining when to start and end their observations may be aggregating individual differences in functioning so as to obfuscate differences in the onset of development.

It is not always possible to control for initial differences and investigators learn to explore indicants from many angles to verify common parameters. Ideally, if age changes are apparent despite uncontrollable error it becomes easier to attribute differences to changes in ontological structures. Common forms of uncontrollable error include that attributable to initial differences, situational factors, stimulus conditions, sampling error, and measurement error. Keeping in mind the effects of this noise on the validity of conclusions about temporal change, by controlling as many confounds as possible investigators can gradually improve the precision of their measurement.

MAKING CONNECTIONS

Find a study with a longitudinal design. What did investigators do to verify a common starting point before comparing change across participants? Did they offer an elaborate explanation or avoid the issue?

Difference Scores

To explore changes within a person, investigators can be enticed into using *difference scores,* obtained by subtracting a later score from an initial score to record the magnitude of change.[5] This is a controversial decision that hinges on the calibration of the tool being used.

Problems with Difference Scores.   When difference scores are computed, investigators can compound error evident in the measurement of both the initial and subsequent scores by introducing a third type of error that emerges from the correlation between scores (Cronbach & Furby, 1970). If two sets of scores are completely random, each contributes 50 percent of the variance to the difference score. The square of the correlation between the two sets of scores indicates the contribution of each (Fiske, 1971). If scores were completely random (which they generally are not), the resulting difference scores are likely to be correlated –.71 with initial scores and +.71 with final scores. Such algorithms suggest there is plenty of room for uncontrolled error if one relies only on simple differences.

Faulty Assumptions.   Researchers who have studied distributions of difference scores typically assumed that the internal consistency of each measure remains the same across administrations and variances for individual scores will be equal over time. These investigators also assume that true score variance should be the same over time so that the correlation between initial scores and change scores will always be negative. Finding that development often progresses from simplicity to complexity to simplicity, these assumptions have been challenged, and investigators have found that:

- no two sets of scores are completely random; correlations between initial and later scores could be negative, 0, or positive;[6]
- initial scores across individuals do not always fall at the same place in the distribution;
- the more highly correlated the initial and subsequent scores, the less reliable the difference scores become; there is potential for a serious *restriction in the range of variance* that constrains the measurement of differences.

Put another way, if the average reliability of two scores equals the correlation between them, variation in difference scores will reflect only error variance.

Scaling Dilemmas.   In situations where the measures themselves are each error-laden, respondents with low scores for the first measurement will invariably show higher scores on subsequent trials (Figure 11.3). Similarly, respondents with high initial scores will invariably show lower subsequent scores. These *regression toward the mean* effects can have a marked influence on the conclusions of a study when investigators rely on the standard deviation as a metric for change.[7] The resulting difference scores reflect a mathematical tautology, and these facts can easily lead to faulty conclusions about a theoretical framework. Findings may have no relationship to the substance of the constructs being measured because they are not grounded in the obtained data. Investigators can solve this problem by using a metric other than the standard deviation to represent change (e.g., the rate or duration of change) or by conducting numerical transformations to alter the measurement scale sufficiently to improve the range of possible scores.

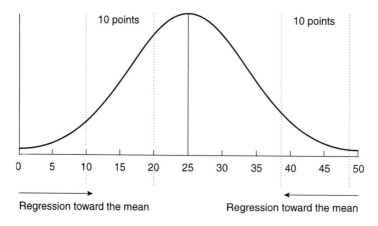

FIGURE 11.3   Some Shortcomings of Difference Scores

Another shortcoming of simple difference scores is the *obfuscation of information about a respondent's relative placement* in a distribution of scores. Look again at Figure 11.3. On that 50-point measure, the difference between 10 and 20 would be treated the same as the difference between 39 and 49. Rarely can measures of human functioning be so well calibrated that the ten-point difference at each end of the distribution would have the same relative meaning. In addition, it is often more difficult for respondents initially near the top end of the score distribution to gain ten points than if they were initially placed near the bottom. Simply comparing difference scores obfuscates these probabilities.

New Alternatives.   How can measures of change be explored if difference scores are so problematic? The most common methods currently in use involve the analysis of growth curves. In such analysis, investigators measure the variables undergoing change at least three times and look at the details of the resulting trends. They can detect where in a distribution of scores growth is evident. If there are sufficient measurement attempts, investigators may be able to identify (1) individual differences in the starting points, (2) the rate of change, and (3) the shape of the resulting distribution. Conclusions can be more accurate if investigators identify exogenous variables that account for individual differences in each of these three parameters. Stable starting points, rates of change, and shapes of score distributions may also be identified across persons within the same age group.

MAKING CONNECTIONS

In the longitudinal study you selected, did investigators use growth curve analysis? Did they measure each variable at three or more points in time? Were difference scores calculated?

Comparability of Stimuli

Findings from studies of representational differences are essential for the development of tools for longitudinal research. The same stimuli given to individuals in two different age groups can take on different meaning. Such variables can be a potential problem or a source of valuable information. Using information gleaned from studies of representational differences, investigators try to anticipate how participants will respond to stimuli, modifying particular tools or recalibrating them as needed. Some studies describe these differences in interpretation, but other studies may control for such differences by standardizing the meaning of stimuli.

When designing tools for temporal research, most developmentalists accept standard definitions of structures verified in previous studies and ensure that stimuli elicit theoretically relevant dimensions. If investigators have found central dimensions, changes in the surface features of measurement tools should not have a profound effect on the outcome of the study. Logical as this might sound, it is important to check for stability across measurement techniques rather than assume tools are infallible.

Investigators check for comparability of measurement techniques in many different ways, three of which are introduced here. Investigators may (1) rely on direct observation of functioning, (2) conduct pilot studies and elicit respondents' critiques, and (3) use training trials to teach respondents about how to define the task.

Direct Observation. *Direct observation* is most often used when investigators can find patterns of thought, feelings, and actions that are immediately obvious in particular settings. As was apparent earlier, observations of daily functioning are assumed to provide clues about the underlying structural core that directs individuals' functioning. Ideally, predictions concerning differences attributable to measurement techniques are not supported. For example, inferences about a structure gain support when the same conclusions emerge from observational work, interviews, or other forms of testing. Similarly, exploring participants' reactions to different stimuli allows investigators to draw conclusions about the comparability of particular techniques.

Pilot Tests. *Pilot studies* in which participants openly critique activities after completing them can facilitate the revision of stimuli to ensure that meaning is standardized. In those cases where respondents are asked to talk about their reactions, many investigators plan questions to explore participants' comprehension. These questions, repetitious as they seem, often require respondents to explain the purpose of research activities and the features of the stimuli being presented. Answers to these questions allow investigators to verify commonalities or to probe interpretations they had not anticipated.

Training Trials. Investigators may also use *training trials* to offer direct advice about task demands. This offers participants the opportunity to ask questions and practice with stimuli-and-response options before their responses are formally measured. In this way, investigators can explore individual differences in how a task is understood, but end the training with a set of clear agreements about how to calibrate their tools.

Multiple Approaches.   In combination, these techniques can minimize obvious differences in how stimuli are interpreted. Depending on the nature of a task, investigators may use one, two, or all three approaches to ensuring their stimuli have comparable meaning across participants. To discover if stimuli change in meaning over time, investigators often rely on all three methods and record any necessary modifications.

MAKING CONNECTIONS

In the paper you are reading, what did investigators do to evaluate whether stimuli were comparable across time? Were they interested in whether stimuli changed in meaning with age? Were stimuli altered to facilitate comparison among variables?

Appropriate Measurement Scales

Another constraint in using simple experimental designs for evaluating change involves the units of measurement representing each variable. Investigators conducting experimental research often look at differences between groups, using measures of central tendency rather than individual scores as an index of performance. Such aggregate scores minimize some measurement error, although extreme scores can still distort those indices in small samples. Unfortunately, emphasis on aggregate scores creates problems for developmentalists for reasons other than those commonly attributed to experimental research.

Limitations of Aggregate Scores.   Information on development is obfuscated in *experimental designs* because it is too quickly assumed that variables introduced to produce change in fact cause the obtained differences between groups. When designs rely on the difference between baseline and post-intervention variables, there is no information on the stability of a trajectory. Differences between two sets of scores could reflect environmental factors as easily as ontological ones and there is no way to fully verify this difference.

Sequential and *time-series designs* contain more features of longitudinal research than traditional experimental designs. After making baseline measurements, outcomes are repeatedly measured to explore the reliability of patterns. Unfortunately, the nature of these designs can also mask important developmental findings as easily as reveal them. This is especially likely when tools show low reliability and aggregate scores represent each variable. If there are no anchors for supporting developmental inferences and no acknowledgment of individual differences, change may be detected without revealing a clear explanation.

Imagine measurement in drug trials. As individuals take a particular drug over time, their scores on behavioral or other psychological measures might change. This change could occur until an illness is healed, after which a drug would have no noticeable effect, or until an individual's system accommodates to the drug and no longer fluctuates as a function of the dose. In one case, removing the drug will not necessarily show an effect; in the other, behavior would change. Neither of these studies would support inferences about ontological development despite the appearance of stability or change. The design alone could not facilitate conclusions about relations between a person's structural core and daily functioning.

Limitations Attributable to Measurement Scales.   The nominal, ordinal, interval, and ratio scales introduced earlier add to the complexity of accurately measuring essential developmental variables. Consider the following possibilities.

- When findings are represented in nominal terms, investigators sometimes note ordered sequences, but the numbers representing those sequences do not form a sufficiently continuous scale for inclusion as a dependent variable. The process of learning to walk, for example, has been documented and ordered, but each step in that process is disconnected from every other step.
- Investigators find continuous variables that do not follow a coherent order. The flow of blood through the body, for example, can be interpreted like computer-generated loops with continuous oscillation that may have no perceivable direction.
- Other scales show a hierarchical progression, but can only be represented using an ordinal scale that reflects greater levels of integration. Representations of stages may not yield scales with equal intervals.

Each of these constraints limits conclusions about whether functioning increases monotonically with age, shows increasing and decreasing patterns, or changes in an irregular fashion. Without relying on some measures with at least an interval scale, investigators cannot attribute changes to differences in development.

Developmental Solutions.   Investigators typically address these dilemmas by exploring associations among variables. Because age can be calculated using a ratio scale, investigators often explore how other dimensions align with age to draw inferences about change. Ideally, age is only one of several indices of change. When age is not practical for exploring change in particular organizational levels, researchers look for proxies that serve the same temporal purpose.

MAKING CONNECTIONS

Outline the design of a longitudinal study in your area. What scales would you use to measure each variable? Would measures of change involve age, time, number of trials, magnitude of stimuli, or some other index of time?

Finding Enough Longitudinal Data

Longitudinal data, although essential for drawing inferences about change, is difficult and expensive to collect. To maximize value, investigators often conduct several cross-sectional studies of essential dimensions before attempting long-term measurements.

Premature Attempts to Explore Temporal Change.   If investigators are unaware of all the dimensions of a construct, they may lack the necessary indicants for interpreting their findings. Developing a convincing theoretical framework before collecting data is one means used to improve the chances of finding successful outcomes. This is often accomplished by conducting descriptive studies using cross-sectional designs or experimental studies to explore individual differences.

A second consequential device involves the selection of what to measure at each point in time. If investigators assume that dimensions reflect simple concepts, but participants hold complex representations, findings with a simple tool will not accurately represent participants' functioning.

Developmental Solutions.   To facilitate accuracy, investigators typically imagine where, on an ideal distribution curve, the sampled activities and events are located. Designing measures to tap each dimension and pilot-testing those measures can save time and cost. By balancing the tension between measuring each variable with adequate complexity and not overloading participants with activities, key concepts can be measured with sufficient depth to facilitate normative conclusions.

MAKING CONNECTIONS

Is the field in which you are working ready for longitudinal research? What challenges have investigators responded to? What challenges were overlooked? What would you do differently if you were to plan a longitudinal study?

DIFFERENT FORMS OF TEMPORAL CHANGE

As you can see, age and other temporal indicators are hardly neutral variables. Age may be but one of many dimensions along which organizing principles vary, but it remains the strongest scale for supporting conclusions about development. Being able to associate age and human functioning can support inferences about intrapersonal variation. Changes in levels of organization outside the individual may or may not be associated with changes occurring inside a person, so both levels are often measured and compared. Some determining events may be traced to age, but cannot always be distinguished from it and investigators look for methods of isolating dimensions of such confounded variables (Wohlwill, 1973).

Age or Proxies for Time?

Despite the value of considering age as an intrapersonal variable, critics complain about such approaches. They highlight the fact that age lacks explanatory power because causality cannot be inferred from studies in which age is treated as an independent variable. Variables like personal history may offer a better explanation than age for some of the structural dimensions emerging within a person, even though history is lawfully related to age. Techniques like the number of trials or magnitude of stimuli necessary for producing a reaction can evaluate change that may not be tied to growth. Furthermore, studies of a system's microlevels may require more fine-grained measures of time than those of macrolevels.

Developmental or Nondevelopmental Change?

Investigators have challenged the use of age as a proxy for development by asking if events attributed to development would occur merely with the passage of time.[8] They identify transformations that occur in repetitive cycles having little to do with changes in individuals' structural core.

Consider the evolution of a friendship. Individuals may find themselves in proximity; engage in a contact event; begin subsequent interactions with polite, small talk or parallel play; participate in a selection of activities reflecting common interests; and eventually move on to more heart-felt conversations. Such progressions are likely to occur among all age groups old enough to begin establishing independent friendships. These recurring cycles may be measured when exploring macrolevels of a developmental system; friendship can offer many developmental benefits and individuals' choice of friends can reveal much about their interests and personalities. Nevertheless, investigators are wise to remain cautious about assuming that friendship cycles are highly stable or that changes in someone's choice of friends reflect changes in his or her definition of friendship.

Why Use Age?

Despite such critiques, investigators continue to use statistical tools to explore the percentage of variance accounted for by age in designs where age is an independent variable. They also use age or the amount of time passed to calculate individual differences in the rate of change or the duration of change. Age remains the most reliable indicant for change in human functioning because it offers a ratio scale for finding factorial communalities in evolving patterns of related thought and/or action. Carefully calibrating tools to minimize constraints, standardizing the parameters used to measure change, and considering the generalizations that can be supported facilitates the systematic exploration of complex, dynamic systems. Isolating whether changes occurring outside a person are associated with those occurring inside can strengthen attempts to theorize about how individuals coordinate internal and external activities when choosing a course of action.

■ ■ ■ ■ ■

MAKING CONNECTIONS

What techniques would be appropriate for measuring change in your area of research? Is there an appropriate ratio scale? Would measures of change be considered a sign of development? How can you tell the difference between cyclical change and signs of growth in human functioning?

CALIBRATING TEMPORAL VARIABLES

Researchers have taken many different approaches to calibrating tools for measuring change, only some of which are used today. They try to differentiate issues of change, stability, order, and chaos. In development, these central ideas are often defined as follows:

- *Change* is typically seen as the dynamic feature of structures and functioning.

- *Stability* serves as the anchor in a structure or in functioning from which comparisons are made.
- *Order* reflects the degree to which change is sequential.
- *Chaos* highlights the random features of change.

These parameters reflect different measurement purposes and require different calibration techniques. Investigators try to keep their research programs flexible to accommodate all four parameters, while realizing that each tool can encompass only some concerns.

Limitations of Change as Integration

One disregarded calibration method involves leaving age or time out of the measurement process by looking at qualitative changes among related variables. This reflects early attempts to measure *change as integration.* Adding to the confusion, some investigators have referred to structural standards as age equivalents. Nevertheless, the initial agenda involved focusing on the structure of key variables. Researchers commonly used descriptions of selected structures and corresponding functions to measure change without introducing indicants of time. Piaget's stages, for example, are not intended to be age-linked benchmarks, and when investigators tried to calibrate performance on Piagetian tasks with age, correlations were at best moderate and, more typically, low. Such correlations have been inaccurately used to argue that Piaget's stages are invalid although stages were not designed to be a proxy for age.

Cautions about Structural Rulers.   Constructing a structural ruler that does not involve age can offer informative descriptive information, but it is difficult to completely eliminate temporal dimensions of such work. Using structural integration as an index of change does not occur often, primarily because investigators acknowledge that structures themselves are dynamic and may not serve as a sufficiently stable anchor for drawing comparisons. In previous studies, many investigators found spurious linear relationships that were difficult to replicate. They had limited information about whether external pressures or individuals' structural core drove development. It has also been difficult to determine if investigators were measuring two parallel constructs or if both sets of measures reflected the same latent construct. These problems are most salient when constructs are difficult to define; investigators cannot be sure of the standards to which their instruments are calibrated.

Rejected Integration Assumptions.   In intelligence testing, for example, references to a person's mental age were once common. *Mental age* (MA) was calculated by comparing a respondent's performance on test items to norms established for each chronological age group. If someone correctly answered all the items designated for their age group, their mental age would match their chronological age; differences in performance would be used to identify an appropriate mental age for each respondent. While these figures could be calculated and compared, the resulting labels offered little information about a person's skills or abilities; the apparent stability in MA scores obscured differences in the structures and functioning that underlie such scores. Investigators only knew if respondents were or were not able to answer questions like others in their age group.

If respondents showed behavior that was uncharacteristic of age-group norms, they were often deemed low in competence, even if their responses required greater sophistication than was anticipated by those designing the test. As investigators learned more about how development proceeds through cycles of simplicity and complexity, it became increasingly apparent that age-appropriate norms would and should invariably remain a moving target. Ideally, norms change in historical time whenever individuals are responsive to changes in their immediate environment. This awareness eventually led to the invention of new approaches for calibrating tools although it remains difficult to find one tool that simultaneously addresses simplicity and complexity in cognitive functioning.

Developmental Solutions.   Whereas this chapter focuses primarily on calibrating tools for use in temporal studies, the next chapter will highlight calibration techniques for exploring individual differences. To study development, many investigators consider both kinds of calibration in cohort comparative studies. They may repeat their studies with different cohorts of participants situated at more than one point in historical time. Each tool is calibrated to explore individual differences and temporal change within and across cohorts. While labor-intensive, such studies are highly informative because the strengths of time-series designs can be coordinated with evidence of changes in structural integration.

Change

Calibrating change can take several different forms. Investigators can explore the (1) magnitude of change, (2) rate of change, and (3) duration of change. The *magnitude of change* is usually computed using difference scores and reflects values on an interval or ratio scale showing how much a score has increased over time. Graphically, magnitude might reflect the peaks of performance within or across participants. The *rate of change* reflects how fast or slow development occurs within a specified period of time or cycle. The length of a developmental cycle from onset to completion reflects the *duration of change.* Investigators select those definitions of change that best meet their theoretical assumptions and calibrate tools accordingly.

Change as Residual Scores.   Change has sometimes been estimated by calculating *residual scores* or how individual scores deviate from a regression line. Residual scores were conceived from the assumption that all people start out with equal characteristics and initial measurements reflect identical estimates of how much they changed on the attributes being measured. Unfortunately, this offers a biased estimate of theoretical residual change because the method assumes an infinite sample size; the resulting score contains measurement error and uncertainty caused by the fact that data are estimated using a finite sample size. Furthermore, the assumption that everyone begins in the same place is problematic.

More specifically, definitions of equality at the onset of a temporal sequence could reflect different parameters. Measurement may reflect a respondent's theoretical initial status, observed initial status, background characteristics, cultural attributes, or combinations of these dimensions.

Growth Curve Parameters.   Rather than simply calibrate tools by focusing on the amount of change over a specified time interval (e.g., by subtracting the latter score from an earlier one) or on residuals, investigators have begun to consider three parameters:

- respondents' initial scores $\xi(0)$, or where they were on a scale at time zero;

- differences in the asymptote λ, or how the manifest end-point aligns with latent estimates of growth;
- differences in the curvature parameter r, or estimates of how far individual growth deviates from a latent trend.

The duration and rate of change can be incorporated into these parameters by ensuring that everyone is measured over the same time interval or by transforming scores to incorporate time into the values used. These parameters facilitate the computation of exponential growth curves. Scores may show identical quantities when the magnitude of change is calculated using difference scores, but also reflect marked variability in each of these growth curve parameters.

Why multiple data points?   Investigators measure each variable at more than two points in time to obtain sufficient information for representing the growth of individuals. Details of growth curve analysis can help investigators draw more accurate conclusions about development than would be possible by looking at difference or residual scores.

To measure the *rate of change,* investigators may control for the *duration of change* or vice versa. By correlating a change parameter with respondents' *initial status* and determining if the relationship is *negative* (conforming to the law of initial values), *0* (confirming the overlap hypothesis), or *positive* (revealing a fanspread in which variance increases over time), estimates of change remain sensitive to the time at which the initial level was measured.

By calibrating measures of change while considering all three parameters of a growth curve, incorrect assumptions about the onset and rate of growth can be avoided. Potential individual differences in "true change" can be embraced by using common initial points in a growth curve, and allowing for fluctuation in the asymptote and curvature parameters. Calibration is strongest when there is a sufficiently low initial status with change and asymptote parameters accounting for the whole of individuals' growth.

Stability

Calibrated as the absence of change in those constructs that should not develop, definitions of *stability* also vary. Stability can occur for a relatively short or long duration. Some dimensions may remain unchanged while others stay flexible. Stability may also indicate that structures and/or functioning become normatively permanent.

Short Duration.   Investigators learn about structures from exploring stability in functioning at different ages, and when stability is obtained for a relatively *short duration,* individuals often reach a state of equilibrium after a period of growth. You may recall that discontinuous patterns of development show periodic plateaus in which individuals achieve a temporary state of equilibrium before internal or external pressures compel them toward new forms of growth. Continuous growth may not show stability, but performance would show additive improvement.

Unchanging Dimensions.   Stability is also evident for human characteristics that remain sufficiently *unchanged.* Many physiological characteristics like gender or ethnicity do not change, but offer essential information about a developmental system. Using designs in which change is recorded by measuring the number of trials or magnitude of stimuli, nondevelopmental constructs or dimensions serve as helpful comparisons for more dynamic variables.

Normative Stability.   Designs involving some variability in time, but relatively low or insignificant amounts of variance are also evident. *Normatively stable* variables that change slowly or follow predictable patterns can serve as comparative benchmarks in more complex designs. Estimates of IQ, for example, have often been used to predict academic potential and serve as anchors to which changes in ability are compared.

Why is stability important?   By calibrating some tools to measure stability and others to measure change, investigators are better able to theorize about how the two signs of development operate in their design. As is apparent when exploring seemingly chaotic patterns, there are also times when calibrating one tool can involve both stability and change.

Order

Calibration of the order in which change occurs was introduced in the previous chapter, but, when time is added as a theoretical dimension, a new dilemma becomes evident (see Gardner, 1995). You may recall that order can reflect *complete priority,* such that one form of change must occur before another begins, *partial priority,* such that there is some overlap between the onset of one form of change and another, or *synchrony,* such that two forms of change occur at the same time (see Chapter 10).

Three parameters are important when calibrating order. Investigators consider the standard error estimates, power when variables are compared, and expected values of aggregate indices.

Calibration Challenges.   Calibrating tools is easiest when indicants used to classify individuals' thoughts, feelings, or actions record only the present latent state and are independent of prior states or coding decisions. When *complete independence* is possible, investigators can assume that accuracy in scoring is the same across participants. Nevertheless, most developmental work reveals orders that are *time-dependent.* Time affects manifest and latent states such that initial classifications often influence subsequent classifications. At the concrete level, when observers are recording a sequence of events, they can develop expectations that create sequential dependencies over and above those that are predicted by the latent construct dependencies. Similarly, the nature of the theoretical dimensions being sampled may not be entirely independent.

The dependent nature of manifest and latent states has the potential to generate misclassifications that are significantly more serious in developmental research than those introduced when working with psychometric tools. In psychometric forms of measurement, investigators can assume that errors in judgment are likely to be randomly distributed within a measurement plan. Such *random error* will inflate the *standard error estimates* and instigate a *loss of power* in subsequent significance testing, but it does not usually distort the parameters that are interpreted when generating conclusions. Investigators using such tools minimize the effects of bias by collecting numerous indicants across many different participants to increase power and reduce standard errors.

In sequential or time-series analysis, scoring misclassifications will distort three, rather than two parameters because not all error is random. That is, the *standard error estimates* and *power* are distorted, but so are the *expected values of aggregate measures* (e.g., means, standard deviations) of particular dimensions. Collecting more indicants across different participants cannot remedy bias in the expected values of conditional probabilities used to interpret findings. This distortion is serious enough that investigators can even discover that their manifest data show patterns that are the opposite of those predicted from latent assumptions. The size of the bias tends to be proportional rather than symmetrical to any skew in initial rates.

Developmental Solutions.   To address the challenges of calibrating order, investigators typically rely less on aggregate representations of findings and more on stable patterns found within and across individuals. Starting with each individual's responses and sorting participants into groups showing similar characteristics, it becomes possible to emphasize individual differences in dimensions that would not otherwise be detectable.

When exploring age-related patterns in individuals' fairness reasoning, for example, interviews were transcribed and answers were organized using a standard template. This made it possible to look across protocols and compare answers to particular questions. Looking for similarities and differences in individuals' answers, protocols could be classified into groups with different characteristics. Individuals within the same group tended to reveal similar manifest states that permit common inferences about latent variables. Persons would be placed in different groups to reflect variance in their characteristics. The inferences used to represent these manifest differences reflect group differences corresponding to different dimensions on one or more latent variables.

Chaos

For some forms of development, investigators have found chaos theories to be more useful than those exploring linear, curvilinear, and simplex patterns. Whereas other models compare indicants to randomly generated parameters, investigators who use dynamic modeling techniques recognize that deterministic forces lead to change. They assume that "chaotic regimes are not predictable, yet they are constrained" (Gottman, 1995, p. xii).

Patterns in Chaos?   The forces that lead to change may not be predictable, but, when they are present, the course of change typically follows systematic patterns. As several dimensions change simultaneously, the appearance of chaos can lead investigators to incorrectly assume that change is unsystematic and that efforts to explore development are futile. To avoid this trap, investigators often distinguish *change mechanisms* or forces that compel change from *indicators that change has occurred*. They attempt to measure both the force that compels change and the products of such force.

It can be difficult to measure dynamic forces, but predictions about the content of such entities are emerging. In studies of moral engagement, for example, investigators have noticed that individuals' values and beliefs influence how they perceive and interpret their experiences and are part of a force that compels agency and action.

Developmental Solutions.   With newer statistical techniques, investigators are able to test different models to determine the effects of simultaneous change in more than one parameter. This facilitates tests of dimensions that may or may not be embedded in change mechanisms. Investigators typically include one or two anchor variables that do not change and several related variables that do. Each dimension is often measured using more than one set of indicants to support theoretical outcomes and overrule the dominance of measurement error. The design of each tool is kept as simple as possible so that estimates of individual as well as group differences can be tested without relying exclusively on aggregate scores.[9]

Procedures for Calibrating Tools

Most of the calibration techniques for estimating change are implemented after data are collected. This is one major deviation from calibration techniques associated with measures of representational differences. In longitudinal research, investigators are often able to streamline the measurement of key variables using findings from representational studies. Then, they try to find a common initial base to use as the starting point for their investigations. Keeping the collection of indicants as simple as possible can minimize some forms of measurement error and facilitate more accurate conclusions about the magnitude, rate, or duration of change.

■ ■ ■ ■ ■

MAKING CONNECTIONS

Find a study that involves temporal change. What did investigators do to calibrate their tools? Which dimensions changed? Which dimensions remained stable? Were three order parameters considered, or only two? How did investigators coordinate issues of stability, order, or chaos when making decisions? How do you know?

STANDARDIZING TEMPORAL VARIABLES

As with calibrating tools, the process of standardizing measures also differs, depending on the kind of information investigators are trying to acquire (Gardner, 1995). Three standardized techniques reflect different purposes for exploring change: sequential analysis, time-series analysis, and dynamic modeling. The first two approaches hinge on assumptions about linear and curvilinear relations. The third approach reflects the belief that change is patterned, but nonlinear.

Assumptions about Time

When designing a measurement plan, investigators evaluate their operating assumptions about time. Common assumptions can be grouped into stochastic and nonlinear categories.

Stochastic Assumptions. *Sequential analysis* is commonly used to explore changes in structures over time and requires information about the history of events included in the analysis. These investigations involve a rich exploration of order, and reveal those entities appearing first, second, third, and so forth. Investigators commonly use sequential analysis to explore behavior and make predictions about future functioning.

Time-series analysis also involves the exploration of linear and curvilinear patterns. Investigators typically compare obtained data to predicted variance, and often rely on measures that can be calibrated against known standards or norms such that time is the only variable that changes.

In both sequential and time-series analyses, investigators use *stochastic processes* of finding random distributions of probabilities for estimating latent states. They measure manifest states and compare those obtained scores to latent or true scores. Next, the resulting probability model is used to calculate *expected values of conditional probabilities* and those probabilities are used as the standards for comparison. As mentioned previously, when measurement is inaccurate and tools are not properly calibrated, the resulting statistics can lead to contradictory interpretations; standardization and calibration processes are highly interdependent.

Nonlinear Assumptions.   In *dynamic modeling,* investigators give up the assumption that development is linear and write multidimensional equations to clarify a theory. They may accept that gradual change in one parameter can produce major changes in another. Computer-generated equations can be constructed to use as a standard for comparing obtained data and labeling the best fit. Investigators may also go beyond their data to calculate predictions of how a theoretical system would function under different parameters and initial conditions. When programming is adequate, the effect of simultaneous changes in multiple parameters can be estimated before investigators spend inordinate amounts of time collecting data. Nevertheless, stronger predictions of how structures and functioning are coordinated within individuals are possible when investigators acquire more relevant information about each dimension.

Change in Integration

Measures of qualitative change in these types of data typically involve sequences of thought, feeling, and action that may not form continuous patterns. Individuals' structural core may show marked differences without revealing changes in functioning, functioning may differ without requiring changes in structure, or the two dimensions may both have evolved. For these reasons, investigators explore *changes in integration* to draw inferences about the developmental system.

Challenges in Standardizing Measures of Integration.   Most investigators know that measuring changes in integration involve no foolproof methods for verifying the standardization of their measures. The major difficulty involves finding a criterion to which observations can be compared. Investigators have identified the following challenges:

- Comparing new criteria with the criteria embedded in available tools can offer partial evidence that new tools yield the same indicants when used in identical situations, but this analysis requires a great deal of prior knowledge.
- Comparing repeated measures of a single tool used under identical conditions can yield sufficiently stable findings to support claims of reliability, but if change occurs quickly or respondents experience fatigue, comparisons may contain systematic error.

- Looking at the percentage of agreement between two sets of qualitative ratings offers evidence of stability in scoring, but does not indicate whether both coders make the same kinds of misclassifications or migrate from an initial standard.

Inter-Rater Reliability. Investigators usually reconcile these limitations by accepting them and using more than one technique for standardizing variables when it is possible to do so. Using classification frequencies, investigators commonly verify their classification decisions by comparing the evaluations of multiple raters and using kappa coefficients (κ) to estimate the degree of error.[10] They can estimate how far scores deviate from a standard and how much agreement occurs among raters. Confirming their conclusions by exploring a confusion matrix, it becomes possible to determine how far two sets of ratings deviate from one another.[11]

Because kappa coefficients (κ) rely heavily on probability estimates, they are problematic when a low incidence of each dimension is expected; even a few misclassifications are likely to distort the outcome. This has led to the generation of transformation techniques. For example, investigators sometimes convert the coding of each indicant into a proportion of the total number of indicants coded. They correlate those proportions evident across different raters to verify the extent of agreement. Used in combination, inter-rater reliability techniques offer different information that can be useful in verifying replicability in the measurement of qualitative change.

Change in Rate, Magnitude, or Duration of Time

Whereas integrative change focuses on the characteristics of measured variables, investigators explore change in the rate, magnitude, or duration of time using tools that reflect interval or ratio scales. Group or individual differences in the *rate of change* involve evaluations of the slope of growth curves and/or asymptotes. The *magnitude of change* is considered in relation to the peaks of a distribution, and the *duration of change* reflects a comparison of the onset of a growth cycle and the completion of that cycle. Such quantitative measures address how fast or how long a growth process may last.

Deviations from Psychometric Approaches. In psychometric research, investigators often standardize measures by calculating test-retest reliability to determine if distributions remain constant over time. High correlations are seen as an indication that tools are appropriately standardized. In developmental work, this technique is problematic for several reasons. Most consistently, investigators have learned that measures of change may not be correlated over time, and detected differences may be quantitative or qualitative. Correlation matrices, for example, offer relatively little information on the relationships among repeated measures. Sometimes investigators accept that a little information may be better than no information.

Developmental Solutions. To standardize the *rate* or *magnitude of change,* investigators who can identify a criterion to which they can compare their obtained data have the easiest time. More realistically, developmental researchers compare obtained data to probability distributions that match their theoretical assumptions. Different kinds of distributions can be generated using theoretical assumptions as a guide. Parallel to correlations of change scores with initial indicants, investigators look for evidence that quantitative dimensions behave in the same way across persons. Standardizing the *duration of change* is easier than rates or magnitudes because investigators can use measures of time that have a ratio scale, permitting direct comparison among scores.

Coordinating Qualitative and Quantitative Measures

Investigators who explore developmental systems generally coordinate both qualitative and quantitative information about change. Estimates of integration are invariably qualitative while estimates of time are quantitative in form. Investigators may rely on previous investigations of how structures change and add to their design measures of how functioning differs across contexts. They may also start with existing knowledge about functioning and systematically explore structural change in individuals. To do either successfully, it is helpful to use more than one tool, each calibrated for a different purpose. Comparing information from multiple measures in the standardization phase of research facilitates confidence in the reliability of each tool. Investigators may explore their data using tangible methods of sorting responses into piles or rely on a combination of statistical techniques to identify relationships among measures.

MAKING CONNECTIONS

What methods have you noticed investigators in your field using to standardize their tools? Do they differentiate qualitative and quantitative change? Have you seen both types of change measured in the same study? Are investigators selecting the right tools for their work?

MAKING GENERALIZATIONS

Strong evidence for theories of human functioning has been generated by including age as one dimension in the outcomes of development. Most developmentalists have abandoned the notion that knowledge can be acquired only through the experimental manipulation of variables or by labeling differential outcomes from individuals in various age groups. Currently, investigators rely on statistical tools that test the fit of growth curves and age is assumed to be isomorphically related to structural differences in human functioning. When such assumptions are verified and theoretical models fit the available data, generalizations about the nature of development are supported. Controversies over the role of age in developmental research continue to permeate developmental discourse, but when age differences can be accounted for, generalizations are easily accepted.

To make generalizations, investigators benefit from revisiting the purpose of their research and questioning how far to take their conclusions. Conclusions differ depending on whether inferences about change are qualitative or quantitative.

Indicators of Integration

Generalizations about *qualitative differences* typically correspond to conclusions about the integration of structure and functioning. Such generalizations require no information about the rate of development, but still involve descriptions of differences that emerge over time. Investigators consider whether data best reflect the development of groups, individuals, or both organizational levels.

Group-Level Inferences.   Relying on aggregate information about how often change occurs across individuals, investigators can draw inferences about groups but cannot support generalizations about intrapersonal change. Patterns may be apparent in how a relatively large number of individuals are classified into groups. Members of each group, in such models, would be expected to integrate structure and functioning in a similar manner, but groups would differ in how key concepts are integrated.

Intrapersonal Inferences.   Studying whether a person becomes different over time and the characteristics of those differences, investigators may also draw inferences about qualitative changes within a person. Generalizations about intrapersonal change usually emerge from tools that permit respondents to surprise researchers with evidence that may not be detectable in evaluating group dynamics. Investigators may look at the frequency of anticipated indicants and add interesting or novel indicants that spontaneously arise when performance is measured over time.

Labeling Patterns.   Regardless of whether investigators explore qualitative change in groups or individuals, they endeavor to find patterns in indicants across time, labeling the qualitative features of those patterns. They assess whether development follows continuous or discontinuous trends and the characteristics of each step in the growth process. They also look for changes in the characteristics of each pattern, recording changes in the presence or absence of particular dilemmas. At all levels of analysis, investigators explore which indicants remain stable over time and which emerge or disappear. In studies of *representational differences,* it may be enough to compare variation across individuals and groups. In studies of *representational change,* at least one temporal variable is typically factored into the analysis.

Quantitative Change

Generalizing about quantitative change, investigators may evaluate the stability of individuals' scores. Evaluating the slope and magnitude of a distribution, they can also determine if the average growth curve in a group of individuals is flat or shows a detectable rate of change. There may also be opportunities for evaluating whether the distribution of scores remains the same over time.

Cautions.   Generalizations about quantitative changes may seem easier to imagine by extrapolating from what you know about the use of psychometric tools, yet the parallels are a little too easily accepted. Developmentalists have found that differences between pretest and posttest scores can offer spurious impressions of growth because this figure offers little in the way of information about structural changes. Similarly, they have learned to question the comparability of responses across time when aggregate scores are used to support inferences.

Evidence of Plasticity.   Developmentalists may accept experimental evidence to explore the *magnitude of change* within a defined time period using tools that have interval or ratio scales. Measures of qualitative change are not replaced because quantitative tools offer no sense of the shape of a distribution of individual scores. Magnitude does support conclusions about *plasticity* because it acknowledges a specific parameter of temporal change.

Investigators can also explore plasticity by drawing generalizations about the *rate of change*. In doing so, they are careful to focus only on how fast or slow the change occurs. Developmentalists would not draw inferences about structural variation or different forms of functioning if rates of time were the only available evidence, but there are occasions when this information is helpful.

Changes in Time.   Developmentalists commonly can ask if individuals change, if group means change, and if there is evidence for individual differences in the rate of change when using quantitative measures of time. Each of these questions requires a different treatment of the indicants that might be measured by a particular tool, but the nature of the indicants need not differ from one set of concerns to the next.

■ ■ ■ ■ ■

MAKING CONNECTIONS

What generalizations were evident in the study of change you selected? How did the investigators support their generalizations? Was there enough measurement information?

VERIFYING DEVELOPMENT

The measurement of change is highly sensitive to the type of variation being considered. Using research on representational differences, developmentalists may identify which temporal variables are most important for their theoretical agendas, and determine the simplest way to accurately measure each dimension. After measuring each variable, most developmentalists use either qualitative or quantitative methods to calibrate and standardize scores for use in more complex analyses. Combinations of calibration and standardization techniques become necessary for evaluating temporal change. These goals involve careful thought about how far findings can be generalized, and whether conclusions reflect changes in structures, functioning, or both aspects of human functioning. Early in a research program, some studies may emphasize qualitative change and others the magnitude, rate, or duration of change. Later, all available approaches are used to identify change mechanisms.

A brief sense of the complexity in how investigators represent their work is evident in a sample of the designs used in existing studies. Some investigators, for example, have been primarily interested in how stable contexts are disrupted into change (see, for example, Patterson, 1995). Others have studied the comparison of different latent growth curve models to determine which models best predict change (Stoolmiller & Bank, 1995). Using cohort sequential designs, other developmentalists have untangled the effects of personal history and more general developmental concerns (Anderson, 1995), while another research team focused on verifying order effects using hierarchical linear modeling techniques (Raudenbush, 1995). For periods in development that involve a short, reactive duration, investigators have also designed discrete-time survival analysis techniques (Willet & Singer, 1995). Each of these methods addresses different aspects of a developmental system. They were constructed to explore different practical dilemmas that affect human functioning.

SUGGESTED READINGS

Allison, P. D. (2001). *Logistic regression using SAS system: Theory and application.* New York: Wiley.

Fleiss, J. L., Levin, B., & Paik, M. C. (2003). *Statistical methods of rates and proportions* (3rd ed.). New York: Wiley.

Gottman, J. M. (Ed.). (1995). *The analysis of change.* Mahwah, NJ: Erlbaum.

Hand, D., & Crowder, M. (1996). *Practical longitudinal data analysis.* London: Chapman & Hall.

Kede, M. B., & Fokianos, K. (2002). *Regression models for time-series analysis.* New York: Wiley.

Little, T. D., Schnabel, K. U., & Baumert, J. (Eds.). (2000). *Modeling longitudinal and multilevel data: Practical issues, applied approaches, and specific examples.* Mahwah, NJ: Erlbaum.

Magnusson, D., Bergman, L. R., Rudinger, G., & Torestad, B. (1994). *Problems and methods in longitudinal research: Stability and change.* New York: Cambridge University Press.

Magnusson, D., & Casaer, P. (1993). *Longitudinal research on individual development: Present status and future perspectives.* New York: Cambridge University Press.

von Eye, A., & Niedermeier, K. E. (1999). *Statistical analysis of longitudinal categorical data in the social and behavioral sciences: An introduction with computer illustrations.* Mahwah, NJ: Erlbaum.

ENDNOTES

1. Gottman (1995) and Wohlwill (1973) outline these steps and go into greater detail on how particular investigators use them.

2. These points are also introduced in Gottman (1995), Hartmann (1992), and Wohlwill (1973) with additional examples. Baltes & Goulet (1971) make this argument using theoretical evidence.

3. Hartmann (1992) and Lerner (1996) also make these assertions, using this definition to set parameters around appropriate themes for developmental research.

4. Fiske (1971) outlined another version of this logic in a critique of using difference scores.

5. Campbell (1957) and Cronbach & Furby (1970) introduce some of these themes, which were then widely critiqued. See also Nesselroade, Stigler, & Baltex (1980).

6. When the relationship is negative, the *law of initial values* predicts such outcomes (Lacey & Lacey, 1962; Wilder, 1957), and is also associated with "ceiling effects"

when the initial level is high and room for change is small. When the relationship is 0, the *overlap hypothesis* would be confirmed by such a result (Anderson, 1939). When the relationship is positive, a *fanspread* is obtained in which variance increases over time (Rogosa, 1995).

7. Furby (1973) raises some of these concerns using developmental evidence. Others raise the issue without considering development.

8. Wohlwill (1973) uses findings from behaviorism to make this point.

9. Hand & Crowder (1996) offer examples of how such analyses are conducted.

10. Chapter 5 contains common techniques for computing kappa (κ), but investigators have designed other methods of weighting raters and indicants as well.

11. Chapter 8 offers more detail on how cross-tabulations can be used to explore forms of disagreement among raters.

■ ■ ■ ■ ■

CHAPTER TWELVE

MEASURING DIVERSITY IN HUMAN FUNCTIONING

To move beyond description toward explanation, developmentalists invariably account for individual differences in human functioning. Many of the findings from personality, attitude, and cognitive research, as well as those obtained using behavioral measures, can facilitate the understanding of ontological differences among people. Developmentalists simply adjust these measurement procedures to explore individual differences in various levels of an organizational system. Questions of gender differences, for example, may be explored at the microsystemic, mesosystemic, or exosystemic levels. Developmentalists might try to explain when and why males and females differ whereas other kinds of researchers may treat these differences as systematic error variance.

The purpose of developmental studies is to explain how individual differences emerge. Some theories, such as those associated with how parent–child interaction influences attachment, focus on contextual explanations. Other theories, such as those used to explain adolescents' risk-taking behavior, look for temperamental or physiological causes. Comparisons of interpersonal and intrapersonal findings reflect two levels at which conclusions are drawn. Descriptions of *individual differences* will be subdivided to reflect these two levels of generalization. Measuring *individual variation* includes techniques for exploring how people differ and *diversity* will refer to generalizations about the range of differences in identifiable groups. In a later chapter on interpretive measurement, a third level of specificity will focus on measuring the *life cycles of particular individuals* with little or no attempt to aggregate information across persons. Comparing findings from all three levels offers the opportunity to determine how far to generalize research conclusions.

Because most developmentalists are trying to explain human variation, they integrate knowledge from experimental and descriptive research rather than simply classify individuals. It is easy to see why descriptive research would be valued, but experimental findings require extra thoughtful interpretations. Experimental researchers rarely explain individual variation, but they have designed psychometric measurement tools and other useful techniques for measuring diversity. Methods of factor and cluster analysis, many of which were introduced in earlier chapters, facilitate the classification of indicants as well as individual scores into vectors that can then be labeled and compared.

Moving beyond the study of individuals as isolated persons, developmentalists decide what kinds of structures and functioning are theoretically interesting and how to align indicants with each construct. Descriptive comparisons among indicants permit the identification of salient dimensions in a group of responses. Comparisons among scale scores offer richer definition to key constructs. Salient concepts in a particular sample are identifiable when investigators use experimental designs to compare constructs and manipulate the contexts in which they are expressed. As developmentalists notice patterns in individual variation, they construct theories of *developmental contextualism* to explain the dynamic nature of individuals' structures and functioning within and among contexts.

When measuring diversity and individual variation, investigators remember that change can occur in a set of variables or at one point in time without necessarily becoming predictable. The juxtaposition of settings, history, relationships, and personal characteristics converging at one moment may not match those of another. Nevertheless, investigators ask which characteristics of individuality match, are congruent with, or fit into a context. They commonly assume that differences within and across organizational levels offer a sign of plasticity or the potential for change. Comparing measures of individual variation and diversity can illuminate how various purposes for collecting data affect measurement.

INDIVIDUAL VARIATION

In the earliest investigations of individual differences, standardized tests were used for diagnostic purposes (Tyler, 1995). Clinicians still use such results to help individuals find ways of fitting into society, and selection committees use such information to make placement decisions. These choices reflect common assessment procedures used when practitioners are sure of the common standards to which they compare the performance of individuals (see Chapter 7). Not knowing exactly how development occurs, researchers typically move beyond evaluating competence to explore unanticipated variation in human functioning, life choices, and possibilities.

Theoretical Assumptions

The previously discussed *nomological methods* of exploring personality are commonly used to explore differences between people (Chapter 5). *Idiographic methods* focus on statelike characteristics, and are more commonly used to explore variation in the outcomes of particular experiences. In *idiographic* research, investigators label the dynamic content of a personality, capturing uniqueness without renouncing the search for regularities across persons. Rather than focus primarily on dispositions that remain apparent across time and situations, investigators working in this tradition explore the changing features of personality. They identify *states* that are assumed to be highly variable across different kinds of situations, but relatively predictable within repeated examples of a situation.

Moods, for example, are assumed to be subjective feeling states that take on circumplex structures which vary from one person to the next. (Figure 12.1 contains circumplex structures.) Within an individual, variations in affect, self-esteem, and sociability are likely to occur, yet the patterns apparent in these variations are not likely to coincide with patterns found in studies of interindividual differences. Within individuals, positive and negative mood states are likely to be *orthogonal* (relatively independent). Between individuals, these states are more likely to be *oblique* (overlapping to some degree). This difference creates special measurement dilemmas for theorists interested in discriminating characteristics within or across persons.

Person 1: Positive Mood States

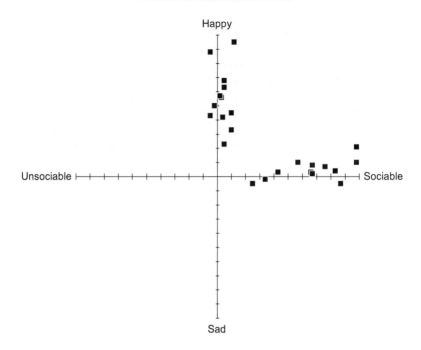

Person 2: Negative Mood States

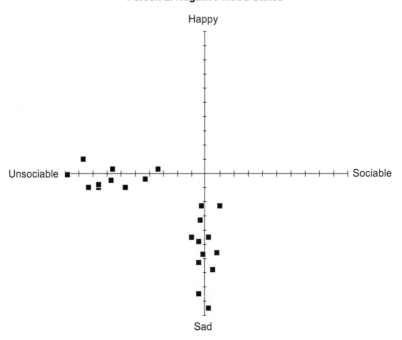

FIGURE 12.1   A Theoretical Circumplex Used to Explore the Expression of Two
Individuals' Mood States

Although developmentalists may be interested in findings from nomothetic and idiographic research, they differ from personality theorists in that they take time to explore how participants' actions and reactions are associated with their ontogeny. Collecting vectors of individual difference scores, developmentalists often verify ontologically-based theories of individuality by constructing profiles for each person in a sample, aggregating those profiles, and looking at how such profiles change over time. The dimensions included in such vectors commonly reflect different levels of organization within and outside a person.

Some studies of attachment, for example, have included measures of microsystemic dimensions of temperament, motivation, and ability. In other studies, information from both proximal and distal sources are combined by coordinating measures of individuals' sense of humanity, normative abilities, personal commitments, family experiences, and community ideologies. Theoretical reasons for studying individual differences are central to deciding what to include in a measurement plan.

Empirical Decisions

Investigators can look at intrapersonal variation by exploring their functioning in particular situations or by examining identity-related themes. In this chapter, the statelike features of such studies are introduced while identity-related themes are reserved for chapters on interpretive measurement. (Chapter 13 introduces the style; Chapter 14 focuses on individual life cycles.) Human states can be differentiated by their *valence,* whether positive and/or negative factors dominate someone's subjective experience. They can also be differentiated in terms of the *origin of psychological activation,* or the degree of arousal necessary for the onset of a state. Personality theorists studying the features of states often endeavor to nurture positive outcomes and inhibit negative outcomes. Developmentalists who study individual variation try to explain the nature and value of these entities. Both goals require an accurate recording of statelike indicants.

Developmentalists design tools to pull for comparable responses across persons, but allow for the emergence of surprising patterns. By taking into account temporal dimensions associated with finding an initial starting point or activation valence, these investigators can ensure fair comparisons across individuals. They may also choose measurement techniques that are sufficiently flexible to permit respondents to introduce unanticipated indicants.

Developmental tools are calibrated to reflect a person-centered approach to measurement rather than a variable-centered one. In some studies, tools are calibrated separately for each participant, whereas in others investigators aggregate indicants while looking for a common initiation point to begin their inquiries. Vectors of scores that are apparent across respondents are labeled, and investigators determine if the patterns reflect stable, nomological traits or more fleeting, idiographic states. Nomological findings are often translated into *typologies* that can be used to classify individuals; idiographic findings are incorporated into more elaborate theories about the *nature of change.*

DIVERSITY

Typically, investigators are most interested in understanding diversity when they hope to design programs and policies that will be responsive to individual differences in needs and expectations. Many investigators want to know how stable personal characteristics affect ontological development. Others endeavor to understand how stable contextual experiences affect development. In both cases, these investigators work with general levels of organization.

Theoretical Distinctions

Developmentalists focusing on diversity often adopt a change-oriented, multilevel, *integrated systems approach* to exploring human functioning. They may enter the system at any one of the levels described in Chapter 9, or at multiple levels simultaneously, maximizing the benefits of exploring plasticity while retaining enough control over selected variables to make sense of the findings. Using change-sensitive designs, investigators can document individual differences emerging from interactions among organizational levels, and note the differing ecologies faced by diverse groups of participants. Using tools that are sufficiently sensitive to change, investigators can find recurring patterns in how individuals differ across contexts.

Historically, investigators have been more willing to explore diversity than individual variation. They have been interested in associations between relatively stable dimensions of race, gender, ethnicity, or social class and other forms of human functioning. These researchers have been committed to understanding universal rules governing how individuals respond to internal and external pressures.

Today, developmentalists often take it for granted that individuals function in groups and are labeled according to the groups to which they belong. They design studies of functioning in different relationships (e.g., with families, friends, colleagues, or community members) and settings (e.g., home, school, communities, countries). They also consider the time at which measurements were taken, evaluating proximal and distal historical events that may play a role in causing individual differences.

Empirical Distinctions

Research on diversity is less focused on the *details of individual life cycles* and more commonly focused on *nomothetic* or *idiographic conclusions*. This distinction is of great empirical as well as theoretical importance. In the two classes of research, different emphasis is placed on *dialectical* and *normative* directions for exploring individual variation. As you will learn in Chapter 14, studies of individual life cycles are highly dialogical and measurement does not reveal consistent dimensions across persons. *Normative methods* involve techniques for aggregating data across individuals whereas *dialectical methods* do not require such techniques (see Chapters 3 through 8). Studies of individual differences focus on normative patterns found within and between groups, but may evolve from dialectical evidence. To bridge the gap between dialectical and normative assertions, investigators studying diversity use a blend of tools and look for group differences in how those tools function. They may detect patterns across descriptions of lives in progress, use those conclusions to generate predictions for more systematic inquiries, and eventually support stable conclusions about diversity in human functioning.

Consider, for example, the results of a study of gender differences in fifth graders' perceptions of classroom life (Figure 12.2; Thorkildsen & Nicholls, 1998). Before conducting this study, inferences from a wide variety of ethnographic and experimental studies were syn-

Model Obtained for Girls

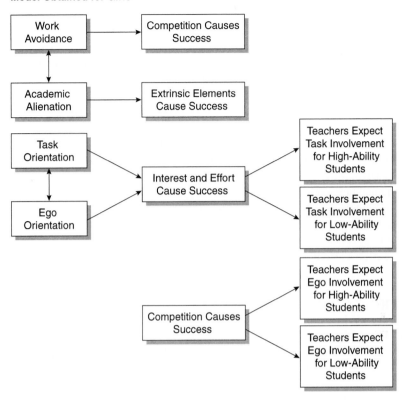

Model Obtained for Boys

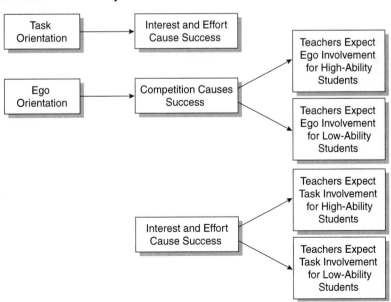

FIGURE 12.2   Gender Differences in How Fifth Graders Coordinate Beliefs about Classroom Life.

thesized. Then, children from 32 classrooms completed the same surveys under standardized conditions. After controlling for variation attributable to classroom differences, gender differences remained salient. Conclusions about gender differences at fifth grade could be supported although such differences have not been apparent among younger students (Nicholls, Cobb, Wood, Yackel, & Patashnick, 1990) and were apparent only when adolescents were asked to think about relations between schooling and future career goals.[1] With caveats, gender differences can be an important consideration in this collection of studies.

In studies of diversity, many investigators treat differences attributable to stable, group characteristics as an estimate of individual differences. Starting with complex tools, personal characteristics may offer an explanation for individual differences, or there may be as many commonalities across personal characteristics as there are differences. Investigators can test many features of a developmental system by incorporating into their research (1) multiple levels of organization, (2) cross-temporal measurements, and (3) a variety of methods for measuring each of many variables. They are also likely to use several different cohorts of participants to strengthen claims about diversity.

MAKING CONNECTIONS

Find two studies in your field, one focusing on individual variation and the other on diversity. Look at the design of each study and at the measurement tools used. Compare and contrast the measurement qualities of the two studies. What kinds of information are available in each and how do they differ?

INTERACTIVE MEASUREMENT

To fully explore individual differences, developmentalists sometimes elicit the direct involvement of participants in evaluating the research process. When investigators accept a colearner role, a variety of issues, assets, and risks that would otherwise go unnoticed can be illuminated. Investigators elicit the assistance of participants through a variety of adaptive interview techniques or by looking at item-response patterns in adaptive testing situations.

Interview Parameters

Interviews are perhaps the most commonly used interactive techniques, and there are a range of available methods. Investigators use these methods to facilitate the transfer of information in a comfortable encounter. Interviews have the potential to elicit greater depth of answers than would be possible in noninteractive methods. Investigators and respondents can acknowledge the potential for bias in their interaction and strive to control misunderstanding during the measurement process. When well executed, this method continues to be a strong means of directly discovering what respondents know, like, believe, and so forth.

Despite the best of intentions, investigators and respondents may recognize that interviews have testlike qualities. Careful planning can facilitate on-the-spot tests of predictions as investigators explore relationships among variables. Investigators also use interviews to clarify unexpected results or validate other methods. They weigh the need for courtesy against the importance of adhering to methodological rigor when determining how to organize interviews.

Before describing common interview formats, let's review typical considerations associated with all interviews.[2] Investigators typically remember that interviews are communication activities that require directors with specialized skills and respondents who have and are willing to share their abilities.

A Communication Activity.   Investigators seek to maximize communication by carefully designing questions and stimuli, using skill to elicit accurate responses. Whereas surveys and other methods of obtaining participants' reactions are easily administered once they have been designed, developmental interviews require a high degree of interpersonal sensitivity. They work best when interviewers remain acutely aware of respondents' perspectives and fail when respondents feel inhibited about expressing their ideas (see Chapter 10). Table 12.1 contains a sample of common concerns that ideally remain salient to interviewers while they are talking with each respondent; *facilitators* are likely to enhance communication whereas *inhibitors* foster misunderstandings.

Characteristics of Interviewers.   To effectively lead a communication activity, interviewers require a high degree of self-awareness as well as specialized knowledge related to the nature of the task to be accomplished (Gorden, 1975). Successful interviewers understand stereotypes about their overt characteristics such as gender, age, race or ethnicity, speech patterns, dress and grooming, and physical features. They also maintain a warm, respectful, flexible, sincere, and confident personality. Projecting positive and affirming attitudes that convey expectations of cooperation, strong interviewers also display knowledge of their intended roles.

Depending on their relationship with target respondents, investigators may or may not be aware of respondents' prevailing stereotypes about people who look, walk, and talk differently, yet these stereotypes are likely to affect the success of an interview. Communication may be more effective if respondents have characteristics similar to those of the interviewer, but differences can also be an asset. Interviews are not ordinarily a time to correct or challenge respondents' stereotypes, but investigators may use their knowledge of these biases to elicit rich responses.

As a white author working with children whose ethnicity does not match my own, for example, I find little difficulty in conveying the idea that I do not fully understand children's experience. Children offer elaborate explanations about why educational practices are fair or unfair. When conducting the same interview with white children, I am likely to hear, "you know how it is," instead of full justifications, unless I rely on another means of conveying social distance. Highlighting the ways in which I am different from the children I interview tends to elicit more complete answers than highlighting our similarities. Were I to conduct interviews of a more personal nature, the opposite might be true; respondents could feel comforted knowing about our similarities while elaborating on presumably shared associations.

It can sometimes be difficult to distinguish confidence and intimidation, but investigators have found a host of communication problems when interviewers are insecure and uncomfortable with their personality. Insecure interviewers often fail to accurately interpret

TABLE 12.1 Characteristics that Facilitate Communication during an Interview

CHARACTERISTICS	DEFINITIONS
FACILITATORS	
Fulfill everyone's expectations	Respondents and interviewers establish clear guidelines regarding the purpose of the interview and the interview itself matches everyone's understanding of the activity.
Offer recognition	Respondents are given some sort of public or private recognition for their time and energy.
Raise altruistic appeals	Respondents' sacrifices and generosity are recognized by the interviewer.
Offer sympathetic understanding	Interviewers indicate that they are listening by conveying a sympathetic understanding of the ideas put forth by respondents.
Introduce a new experience	Respondents sense a form of novelty in what they are expected to discuss or do during an interview.
Allow for catharsis	Respondents feel a sense of freedom or release when discussing ideas they have previously kept private.
Accept quests for meaning	Interviewers are aware that respondents are on a quest to make sense of their experience and use the interview to facilitate such processes.
Offer extrinsic rewards	Interviewers offer tokens of their appreciation that do not exert undue influence on a respondent's willingness to volunteer.
INHIBITORS	
Induce ego threat	Interviewers say or do something to intimidate respondents and make them feel incompetent.
Ignore etiquette	Interviewers ask respondents to do or say things that are not appropriate given cultural norms regarding manners.
Introduce trauma	Interviewers expose respondents to a traumatic event or otherwise ask them to recall trauma.
Forgetting	Interviewers forget the ideas put forth by respondents during the interview or otherwise fail to complete all aspects of the task. Respondents are made to feel ashamed of forgetting something they started to discuss.
Chronological confusion	Respondents are asked to keep track of events as they occur in time and become confused while doing so. Interviewers are discussing a sequence of events, but lose track of the position in a sequence when asking questions.
Inferential confusion	Respondents are asked to draw inferences they are not able to make and/or interviewers draw inferences that are factually inaccurate.
Unconscious behavior	Interviewers are engaged in behavior during the interview that offers unconscious judgments about respondents' ideas and/or a poor attitude about conducting the interview.

Note: Gorden (1975) offers more details on these issues.

the events of an interview and can end up so self-preoccupied that they are unable to recognize the emotional needs of respondents. These interviewers often communicate their own insecurity, empathize with respondents only when the respondents' ideas match their own, or offer insincere praise. Curbing or ignoring these tendencies, insecure interviewers can come across as cold or detached. They can also make harsh comments that unintentionally close down communication.

Interviewers also learn that attitudes are communicated in a variety of ways. When an interviewer is bored or uninterested in respondents' ideas, it can become quite transparent in their speech and gestures. Not surprisingly, any comments to the contrary come across as insincere when respondents convey these impressions. Ideally, interviewers work to communicate positive and affirming attitudes rather than those that are critical or skeptical. They learn to behave as though they expect full cooperation, even when challenges seem eminent. When conducting a large number of interviews, interviewers devise ways to treat each participant as if his or her ideas are special and fresh.

The Roles of Interviewers.   Interviewers can play different *roles in an interaction* and require specialized knowledge of the expectations associated with their roles. For some activities, interviewers are expected to help respondents *engage in role-taking.* When doing so, interviewers may dramatize different roles or play one role while respondents imagine another. These interactions can stimulate respondents' understanding of particular roles and elicit fully articulated perspectives.

Interviewers may also adopt *an auxiliary role* in which they ensure respondents understand an activity well enough to work independently. Interviewers may ask probing questions or offer directions at key points in the conversation, but their identity is not salient. They ordinarily record responses, monitor respondents' progress, and use probes to clarify ambiguities.

Most commonly, interviewers build a *conversational relationship* in which they fulfill particular roles. In some conversations, interviewers are outsiders who ask respondents to clue them in whereas, in others, interviewers are insiders who elicit privileged information. Interviewers may negotiate or simply acknowledge the hierarchical dimensions of a relationship, playing a subordinate role in some cases and a superordinate role in others.

With sensitivity to their assigned role, interviewers are expected to convey decisions about the nature of the conversation. There are times when formal instructions are necessary to help respondents understand the expectations of interviewers, but task demands may subtly convey these expectations. Telling stories, laying out problems to be solved, or asking open-ended questions communicate expectations as often as formal directions.

Interviewers' Responsibilities.   Regardless of their role, interviewers have three primary responsibilities. They are responsible for hearing a respondent, observing a respondent, and remembering each respondent's ideas for the duration of the interview.

To hear a respondent, skilled interviewers maintain rapport by attending to respondents' speech and gestures. They do their best to minimize respondents' anxiety and fatigue while maximizing interest. Interviewers constrain their own assumptions about what respondents might or should say, looking instead for communication barriers. When barriers become evident, interviewers repeat or rephrase their questions until respondents can determine what is asked. They also endeavor to minimize distractions from the task at hand.

Interviewers observe a respondent by watching nonverbal behavior such as body motions, looking for cues about respondents' attitudes. Giggles or laughter may be a sign of anxiety when evident at inappropriate moments. Similarly, distracted or bored gestures convey inattention. Interviewers who try too hard to build rapport may elicit attempts to "calm the interviewer" rather than thoughtful answers. Finding ways to maintain interest or redirect attention is an acquired skill that emerges from experience with individual differences.

Ideally, interviewers have memorized the content of an interview before interacting with respondents, relying only on cues to stimulate their memory. With complete knowledge of an interview schedule, interviewers can fully attend to the needs and answers of respondents. Likewise, practice with recording equipment or note-taking devices can minimize distractions during a conversation.

Investigators may look for ideas that are contrary to their own as often as those that confirm assumptions, and design procedures for generating and testing on-the-spot predictions. This requires full attention to participants' responses during the interview. Interviewers also devise methods for discriminating between interviews when conducting several back-to-back.

In combination, fulfilling this collection of responsibilities can elicit rich information from respondents. Self-awareness and a positive, confident attitude can go a long way toward putting respondents at sufficient ease to offer their best performance.

Characteristics of Respondents.   Developmentalists spend a great deal of energy imagining the perspectives of research participants *before* collecting data as well as during and after the process. Selecting appropriate participants involves consideration of the following questions:

- Who has the relevant information for a particular research agenda?
- Is the individual's status high or low within the target community?
- Is the individual likely to see him- or herself as an active or passive agent?
- Is the individual likely to have insider or outsider status within the community?
- Is the person a mobile or stable community member?
- How accessible is the individual? Will it be difficult to contact him or her?
- Is the individual willing to participate or are there constraints associated with time, ego threat, trauma, or etiquette?
- Which individuals are most able to be helpful? Will particular individuals succumb to forgetting or unconscious forms of confusion?
- Will selected individuals feel undue pressure to participate or are they free to volunteer?

When participants are selected to match the constraints of a particular set of interview activities, many of the challenges associated with maintaining rapport and interest during an interview are alleviated. Respondents are generally excited, flattered, or at least willing to comply with an interviewer's request because they can see the purpose of the investigation and have agreed to participate.

The Importance of Advanced Planning.   Careful planning and the pilot-testing of activities cannot be emphasized enough. Regardless of the type of interview, stronger data is likely when investigators imagine and arrange topics and subtopics in a structure that can be evaluated and altered when necessary. When interviewers work from a guide, it becomes easier to track the full range of desirable information, and ensure that all respondents have an opportunity to respond to the same questions. Guides ordinarily contain topics to be introduced, predicted sequences for introducing themes, and at least some diagram for how an interview ought to flow. To clarify this and other procedures for designing interviews, let's first distinguish common interview styles that are evident in developmental research.

MAKING CONNECTIONS

Consider your qualifications as an interviewer. What skills can you bring to the situation? What roles are you best suited for? Where would you benefit from more training or experience? Which of the key responsibilities would you find most challenging? Question someone who knows you well to learn more about how others see your skills and personality.

Interview Styles

Five interview styles, some of which were alluded to earlier, are used in developmental research.[3] Developmentalists often conduct formal, semistructured, informal, nondirective, or group interviews. Each style offers valuable information, but comparing them illuminates different measurement assumptions.

Formal Interviews. *Formal interviews* work like verbal surveys in that investigators rely on a standard set of questions and typically offer respondents a fixed set of answers. Respondents are encouraged to think of such interviews as "closed situations" in which only the investigators' questions are answered by following explicit directions. Investigators may use scaled items, similar to those found in psychometric measures. They may also ask for respondents' opinions, but score those opinions using a standard scale.

Phone interviews commonly have formal structures and are typically conducted by adapting questions to match the characteristics of respondents (Dillman, 2000). Matching questions to respondents allows investigators to minimize *sampling* and *coverage errors* because everyone answers questions tailored to their expertise. Rules for writing questions are similar to those associated with writing surveys. Investigators typically use simple words, focus on clear ideas, and keep items short. Respecting respondents' abilities, they avoid ambiguity, bias, objectionable content, and may avoid requests for conjecture.

Because respondents answer very pointed questions, data are easily coded. Uniformity in responses can also be apparent across persons because everyone hears the same questions and is given the same collection of response options. A major disadvantage is that verbal surveys contain much of the same superficiality as written surveys. Respondents may ask for and receive clarification on the meaning of an item, but are not offered an opportunity to explain their answers, raise related questions that emerge from their direct experience, or question the structure of the measure. This disadvantage becomes salient when respondents are annoyed at the limited number of alternatives or feel forced to offer an inaccurate response.

Semistructured Interviews.   *Semistructured interviews* are used to identify respondents' subjective responses to a previously analyzed situation. Interviewers often begin with a stimulus and a set of questions, but may change the wording of questions to ensure that participants fully understand the investigator's perspective. The purpose of such interviews is to explore respondents' ideas about a standard problem while encouraging a full explanation of these perspectives. Respondents are encouraged to ask questions during the conversation and investigators may add probing questions to clarify ideas that are raised in respondents' answers.

Many of Piaget's interviews utilized semistructured formats, differing in the kinds of stimuli and responses called forth. Respondents were asked to solve a problem and justify their solutions. Interviewers challenged respondents' decisions and justifications by offering countersuggestions and the interview continued until respondents' logic had been fully explored.

The major advantage of semistructured interviews is the opportunity to test the limits of individuals' reasoning. The interview schedule is sufficiently flexible that investigators can probe into those answers showing a potential for misunderstanding. Cooperation and rapport are encouraged as participants stick to predefined guidelines while allowing for the generation of surprising answers. When investigators design the interview as a funnel, more general ideas are introduced first with more specific queries later. Some topics lend themselves to a pyramid structure in which a specific topic is gradually broadened during the course of an interview. Regardless of whether topics and subtopics form funnel or pyramid structures, it becomes possible to explore depth as well as breadth in individuals' reasoning.

The primary disadvantage of semistructured interviews is the degree of training and prior knowledge necessary for designing and administering these tasks. Ordinarily, an interviewer has a great deal of background knowledge about the types of problems to be investigated and common responses to particular tasks. It is difficult to formulate predictions when a topic is largely unknown. Furthermore, this method is not always practical because interviewers require quite a bit of skill to maintain a conversational style of interaction while extracting compatible answers across participants.

Informal Interviews.   *Informal interviews* are largely unstructured and seem more like conversations. These may be referred to as open situations in which respondents as well as investigators ask and answer questions. During the conversation, participants are free to probe deeply into reasoning about particular ideas and to revise the initial plans for the interview. Unlike multifaceted discussions that tend to arise in everyday conversations, these interviews ideally focus on one topic, yet the tone and style of interaction reflect those common in friendly negotiations.

Informal interviews often serve as pilot work for more elaborate investigations. When trying to discover how young children visualize fair contests, for example, I played games with children and questioned them about the events taking place. A four-year-old's agreement that his father had cheated to win a game determined by luck revealed clues about his confusion regarding the difference between luck and skill tasks. When similar language and levels of disappointment at losing were evident in a six-year-old, a more articulate version of the same confusion became apparent. Comparing rules of the games children selected for these activities offered insight into the activities they valued. Combining the findings from such informal experiences with available research evidence, I could later design a semi-structured interview to explore why children in early elementary school are so fascinated by luck-driven contests. Older children do not share this passion and can even find contests based on luck to be unfair. With some background knowledge of how children responded to informal questioning, reasonable predictions could be generated about how larger samples of children might respond to a more structured task.

A major advantage of informal interviews is the degree of give-and-take between interviewers and respondents; respondents tend to offer much richer answers when they feel they are asking as well as answering questions. Although there may be a planned interview schedule, these interviews contain much greater flexibility than formal or semistructured interviews and can be especially useful if investigators have insufficient evidence for making predictions. Disadvantages arise if investigators want to make formal comparisons across people; no two interviews are likely to be the same. Respondents may discuss the same topic, but not necessarily explore the same questions.

Nondirective Interviews.   *Nondirective interviews* are the least goal-directed in that respondents are expected to raise issues and the interviewer serves as an active listener. This is most commonly used in therapeutic or psychiatric situations, but is also a helpful way to learn about the uniqueness of individual lives or build relationships with individuals who might later participate in more structured activities. In these interviews, the investigator may elucidate doubtful points, rephrase respondents' answers, or probe for clarification, but the respondent serves as the primary leader of the conversation (see Chapter 14).

To discover the effects of desegregation on the individuals involved, for example, Robert Coles conducted numerous nondirective interviews as he shadowed individuals through a very traumatic period in U.S. history (Coles, 2000). In this process, children and their families were asked to draw pictures or write stories and talk about the meaning of their experiences. Talking about these activities with an experienced clinician may have enriched if not helped those engaged in the resulting moral, spiritual, and social conflicts, but the net effect was a valuable data set that has been explored in several different ways.

The advantages of nondirective interviews are clearest when investigators are interested in how specific individuals view the world and can explore unusual experiences as they unfold. Because respondents are encouraged to formulate both questions and responses, investigators are able to tap into their stream of consciousness. The noninvasive line of inquiry permits investigators to encourage rather than direct the conversation. Situating an interview at key points in time allows investigators to see how individuals interpret their experience while events are unfolding. Unfortunately, comparison across individuals is highly problematic because there is nothing in the interview structure to ensure that respondents will discuss the same topic let alone the same questions.

Group Interviews.   Investigators also plan *group interviews* in which more than one respondent is included in the conversation. These interviews are used to explore teamwork or how respondents share information. Respondents are able to compare their opinions to those of others, build on others' ideas, make collaborative decisions, and disagree with others in the group. Respondents' personal interests are less likely to emerge, but it is possible to see collective interests.[4]

Early studies of children's reasoning about distributive justice contained group interviews (Damon, 1977). Children were asked to complete work and then distribute rewards for that work. Their initial decisions were recorded along with responses to investigators' probes and challenges. The nature of the interactions as well as the content of each respondent's actions and reactions proved instructive.

Group interviews can elicit many perspectives on the same topic and critique ideas in a normatively nonthreatening manner. Some respondents are even more comfortable talking in a small group than one-on-one with an investigator. The collective body of acquired information may be much richer than that obtained for a single individual because no one individual is likely to spontaneously think up or understand all the positions that come forth in a group conversation. If the goal is to understand communities, such richness can reveal patterns in how creativity and other complex processes flourish in a group.

This richness can be as much of a disadvantage as an advantage if investigators want to know whether each individual in the group understands all the ideas that were discussed. The potential for rich discussions is limited by the willingness of all group members to respond to one another. Adults as well as children tend to be relatively poor at listening to others' ideas, especially when the ideas are novel or do not match their own. Each group member is unlikely to understand all ideas put forth, and even a speaker may not fully understand the implication of particular streams of a discussion.

Choosing a Style.   Despite beliefs to the contrary, all interviews tend to intrude on the lives of respondents. When selecting a style, investigators are most successful if they articulate clear goals for the interview and choose the format that best reveals the information they would like to acquire.

MAKING CONNECTIONS

Find a sample of interview studies in your field. Which interview formats were used? How do you know? Did investigators report formal guidelines? Were the interviews informative?

Designing Interviews

When choosing an interview technique, investigators consider a wide range of dilemmas. They consider the nature and effects of social encounters on participants and the degree to which such encounters are helpful or a hindrance to theory building. These issues have been translated into the following measurement concerns.

Identifying Interview Content.   In designing interviews, investigators often begin by defining their theoretical framework and the aims of a particular line of inquiry. They anticipate desirable information by analyzing their problem and making predictions about relevant perspectives. Most investigators select stimuli, question formats, and response styles that facilitate the exploration of theoretically relevant ideas without distracting respondents. They also imagine how to respond to spontaneous ideas that might emerge during the interview. Developmentalists may anticipate verbal ideas as well as apparent symbolic or functional silences, distortions, avoidances, or blockings. Planning probes, investigators also anticipate devices for facilitating the exploration of individual responses.

In addition to carefully designing activities, investigators also plan the order of presentation. Sometimes a standard order may be logically suitable, but when the sequence of questioning could add bias, questions may be introduced in counterbalanced orders across participants. These decisions are made with respondents' perspectives in mind, minimizing confusion while maximizing the extraction of information.

Anticipating Respondents' Perspectives.   Investigators recognize variation in the degree of mutual trust assumed by participants. They anticipate the social distance between interviewers and respondents, and the effects of having interviewers control the conversation. As with most conversations, both interviewers and respondents may withhold information. Participants invariably size one another up and make judgments about the quality of the interaction. Even if everyone is committed to open communication, the degree of clarity often differs across interviews; not everyone is equally able to articulate justifications for their answers. Most investigators learn that there is no way to fully record or control every aspect of an encounter, and carefully consider the most effective means for tracking essential information.

Question Formats.   Investigators rely on questioning styles that match their theoretical goals. They decide whether to ask direct questions in which respondents' answers are taken literally, or indirect questions in which respondents' answers are taken figuratively. Selected topics may be general or specific, and questions would be formulated differently depending on how direct interviewers want to be when focusing respondents' attention. Depending on their theoretical interests, interviewers can ask respondents for factual information, opinions, or analytical reasoning.

Investigators typically construct interview guides to ensure that all necessary questions are addressed and keep track of respondents' answers. Guides are most helpful if they include a fact sheet with details such as respondents' identification number and demographic information and a schematic outline of the interview. Questions may be fully outlined or noted in codes that cue interviewers' memories. Ideally, writing during an interview is kept to a minimum. Circling indicants of each decision can be helpful for keeping track of the flow of questions while using recording devices for more elaborate responses.

Some interviews involve a series of *contingency decisions.* Guidelines serve as decision trees that reflect these contingencies. *Filter questions* can be used to select or sort respondents into clusters. *Pivotal questions* are central to the interview and form the core of the topic at hand. *Probes or conditional questions* help interviewers clarify the ideas they are hearing.

Despite myths to the contrary, *leading questions* can be valuable for confirming a context or clarifying an answer, but ideally would not appear intimidating to respondents. Leading questions are most commonly used to clarify chronological or inferential confusions, but may also help interviewers catch or retrieve an answer that would otherwise remain incomplete. Such questions are appropriate primarily when questions pose no etiquette barriers or ego threats, and if they help respondents offer a complete answer.

With children, for example, investigators may ask a series of directive questions. Ordinarily, children's responses will remain unaffected if they do not understand the implication of the leads. If they do understand a set of leads, this insight may facilitate more complete justifications. Communication is enhanced if children understand why investigators are interested in the interview topics.

Response Modes.   Responses can differ depending on whether investigators are pulling for information or allowing respondents to reveal their thoughts. Just as there are different questioning styles, there are many response modes. In formal interviews, investigators consider whether they want to rely on scaled responses, ranked responses, checklists, or categorical responses similar to those used in psychometric surveys. Respondents can also be asked to fill in missing blanks, sort cards, or otherwise critique stimuli offered by the investigator. In some cases, respondents determine the nature of the response whereas in others the investigator elicits information by indicating an outline of acceptable answers. Decisions about response modes are most commonly made in reference to theoretical and practical knowledge.

For some levels of informality, the nature of the topic dictates response modes. Interviewers may ensure they understand respondents' answers by asking them to point to stimuli or use response cards to represent their decisions. Eliciting a clear decision can direct attention to generating quality justifications. For respondent-guided interviews, interviewers may simply check to ensure they correctly hear and understand the purpose and flow of responses.

Probes.   Going beyond the etiquette of normal conversational behavior, interviewers typically work with participants until they can maximize clarity in the information acquired. The structure of an interview constrains the amount of control over a topic and the amount of detail to be elicited. Nevertheless, a major benefit of interviews is the opportunity to challenge, clarify, or otherwise probe respondents' answers, determining the full breadth and depth of emerging logic.

Table 12.2 contains definitions of common probes. Silent probes, encouragement, and immediate probes are important for clarifying ideas at the time they occur. Retrospective probes are especially helpful when interviewers seek detail while allowing for unanticipated information. Going back to an earlier point in an interview is helpful when topics and subtopics are highly interrelated and interviewers are looking for detail on all aspects of the problem at hand. When respondents are willing to talk broadly about questions, interviewers can return to ideas and explore more specific facets. Silent and retrospective probes are also helpful when interruptions would inhibit the spontaneous flow of responses.

Before using probes, it is helpful to learn a few rules of interviewing etiquette. Interviewers learn not to introduce a probe by interrupting respondents. Habitually, it is often wise to use or imagine a silent probe before introducing an immediate probe. Encouragement and other forms of active listening convey an interest in respondents' ideas and let them know that interviewers are not daydreaming or otherwise distracted. If investigators use the same vocabulary as respondents, they can avoid introducing measurement distortion. Respondents are encouraged to elaborate on their own points rather than become dis-

TABLE 12.2   Common Styles of Interview Probes

PROBE	DEFINITION
Silent probe	Say nothing to offer respondents an opportunity to think or rethink a response.
Encouragement	Offer positive reactions, often in the form of praise or affirming grunts and smiles.
Immediate elaboration	Ask respondents to offer a more complete answer.
Immediate clarification	Ask respondents to supply information that would clear up an ambiguous answer.
Retrospective elaboration	Return to an earlier point in an interview to elicit a more complete answer.
Retrospective clarification	Return to an earlier point in an interview to untangle an ambiguous answer.
Reflective probe	Offer an echo, interpretation, or summary of respondents' ideas to elicit more information.
Mutation	Introduce a new topic.

Note: Gorden (1975) offers more details on these issues.

tracted by researchers' opinions or language use. Using respondents' language to construct probes also requires interviewers to listen carefully to each set of answers.

Coordinate an Ideal Plan with Environmental Constraints.   Investigators also try to anticipate the conditions in which an interview will be conducted, developing a plan for recruiting participants and extracting necessary information. Anticipating dilemmas associated with helping all respondents feel comfortable is important for eliciting high-quality information. Anticipating data analysis can save an inordinate amount of time and frustration if researchers generate reasonable predictions that include the effects of environmental conditions.

Such anticipation may involve visiting performance sites to understand the conditions respondents take for granted, allowing investigators to learn about typical vocabularies and situations. Respondent's comfort with an interview can be enhanced when investigators find ways to assimilate. Making positive references to environmental features can also put respondents at ease, even if references involve requests for more information.

MAKING CONNECTIONS

Design an interview for work in your field. What format did you select? What activities have you planned? Does the sequence of questions form a pyramid or a funnel? How will respondents indicate their answers? How will responses be recorded? What probes would you use?

Conducting Interviews

After an interview is constructed and interviewers are trained in the subtle nuances of communication, investigators are ready to initiate conversations. To do so requires decisions about *sampling respondents* and *strategies for introducing the interview.* Investigators also determine appropriate *techniques for interviewing* and select appropriate *tactics for ensuring the flow of information* (Gorden, 1975).

Strategies for Starting.   Before interviewing, investigators' sampling strategies have usually undergone critical review from at least one human subjects protection committee (see Chapter 2). Investigators seek to minimize sampling bias while recruiting participants. They also carefully assign interviewers to respondents. Sometimes it is helpful to match interviewers and respondents along common characteristics, and other times it is more useful to randomly assign interviewers to respondents. The content of the interview as well as the results of pilot investigations are typically used to make these decisions, but any potential for miscommunication is ultimately minimized.

Several introductory steps have been used to put respondents at ease. Trust is facilitated when interviewers introduce themselves, mention research sponsors, and explain the purpose of the interview. More personal descriptions of why participants were selected, how data will be used and confidentiality preserved, and how responses will be recorded is also helpful. These details help respondents imagine what is expected of them and whether they will be treated with respect.

Techniques for Leading an Interview.   Interviewers learn that there are two communication levels to every interview. At the *verbal level,* interviewers are aware of how questions are communicated, framing the context for eliciting responses. Interviewers also select appropriate vocabulary so as not to intimidate or patronize respondents. Imagining the scope of the questions, interviewers think about whether the content is broad or narrow, and whether respondents might need help structuring an answer. Interviewers also ask themselves when leading questions or probes are appropriate while remaining careful not to interrupt respondents.

At the *nonverbal level,* interviewers also set the context for an interview. They may use silence to convey a request for elaboration or offer respondents time to think about their answers. Interviewers' nonverbal behavior also conveys their attitudes about the conversation. Attitudes are conveyed in nonverbal gestures, demeanor toward the research tasks, responses to each answer, and reactions to the respondent as a person. When interviewers cannot be positive and affirming, even while testing different predictions, it is best to find someone else to collect this kind of data.

Tactics of Exploring Answers.   During their first interview, new investigators learn about the politics of maintaining control over a topic. Respondents almost always introduce surprises and sensitive interviewers are able to detect these events. All the planning and guides in the world cannot substitute for *remaining flexible* during an interview, *facilitating a flow of ideas* as readily as adhering to a set of guidelines.

Ordinarily *probes* can help maintain a focus on one topic before turning to another. When a conversation is going well, interviewers may follow respondents' sense of which topics and subtopics are important. Probes can allow interviewers to actively listen to the flow of ideas and challenge different points by raising alternative possibilities.

Regardless of the format, interviewers are wise to recognize their *position of control* during an interview. Those asking the questions are most successful when they think carefully about when and how to use their leadership position. When probes are overly assertive, interviewers are likely to notice *symptoms of resistance* during the interview. Respondents may experience *ego threat* or feel compelled to *falsify their answers*. Resistance may be caused by the violation of etiquette norms, such as asking one person to tattle on another or otherwise asking questions that make a respondent feel uncomfortable or unqualified in answering. Overly personal or judgmental questions may also elicit ego threat or falsification.

Successful interviewers resist the temptation to directly challenge these symptoms and generally find ways of working backward to discover the source. When particular questions may elicit ego threat, investigators sometimes place them later in an interview, well after rapport has been established and respondents understand the point of the investigation. When respondents obviously falsify answers, interviewers look for ways to elicit a voluntary admission of such falsification and may reveal the known contradiction in a nonjudgmental way. To accomplish these aims, interviewers remain highly sensitive to the perspectives of the respondent.

Finding Useful Data.   It is quite challenging to simultaneously balance theoretical concerns, respondents' needs, and practical environmental considerations. Investigators find useful data by planning carefully and pilot-testing their interviews, realizing that without planning it is easy to make fatal errors. Investigators are most likely to use interview methods when studying variation, but they may also find ways to standardize answers and draw inferences about diversity.

Adaptive Testing

Adaptive testing, such as that described earlier, serves at least two purposes in developmental research.[5] One purpose involves distinguishing *individual variation* from *age-related differences* in how individuals coordinate structures and functioning. A second purpose is to *reduce the amount of error* attributable to sampling, coverage, and participants' energy and abilities in studies of individual differences.

Differentiating Development and Individual Differences.   When development progresses from simplicity to complexity to simplicity, it is natural for constructs to change in definition (see Chapter 10). Investigators may add constructs to a preexisting collection or totally revise a definition to theorize about entirely new concepts. Structural conclusions of this nature gain support only when investigators can explain individual variation and diversity well enough to remove such variation from a design, focusing only on ontological relations between structures and functioning. Adaptive testing facilitates this by ensuring that all respondents answer only personally relevant questions associated with the concepts being measured. Asking respondents to answer developmentally inappropriate questions can introduce measurement error that may be further compounded by the respondent's fatigue.

Studies of risk taking, for example, are much more complex in adolescence than in childhood or adulthood. The definitions of risk and the abilities associated with such risks would ideally match this movement from simplicity to complexity to simplicity. When the definitions of dimensions, constructs, or concepts differ across periods of development, investigators often use the same procedures for matching indicants to dimensions, but rely on different dimensions across subsamples. In a sense, they create different tools that are combined in an adaptive item bank. These tools are programmed to be administered in a hierarchical manner, reflecting participants' earlier responses.

Receiving questions about complex definitions of a construct may occur after respondents offer an ambiguous answer to a simpler question. If, for example, a participant answered "sometimes" to the question of whether they engage in risky behavior, this ambiguous response could be evidence that a respondent adheres to a more complex definition of *risk*. Subsequent questions may be generated to offer more elaborate dimensions of risky behavior. Follow-up questions would elicit respondents' working definitions of *risk* before further exploring the nature of their risky behavior. Absolute answers to the same question might indicate simpler concepts, and when respondents declare absolutely "yes," interviewers would elicit more information about the nature of such behavior. The topic might change for negative answers. Patterns in responses across related topics are helpful when investigators compare different definitions of particular constructs and explore the possibility of individual differences in conceptual understanding.

Minimizing Measurement Error.   As was mentioned earlier, there are times in developmental research when respondents show evidence of the same concepts, but are limited in their ability to communicate. Adaptive testing can be used to ensure that indicants are representative of the constructs being measured, clearly understood by each respondent, and responsive to irrelevant differences in respondents' communication abilities.

In our studies of task, ego, and work-avoidant orientations, younger children were not able to respond to the same survey items designed for adolescents. Children's difficulty was relevant to limitations in their language abilities as well as their understanding of concepts that adolescents take for granted. Adapting items to match the language of each age group, individual differences in the complexity of respondents' logic, and the point at which they experience fatigue could be controlled. Evidence of task orientation was found in all age groups, even though the indicants to measure this dimension contained more and less complex syntax. Ego orientation was also apparent, taking different forms largely because most young children do not fully differentiate ability and effort, and have difficulty understanding the discontents associated with competition. Children may feel ashamed or proud when seeing someone show off, but they do not fully understand that individuals who win are deemed superior in some way to those who lose. (These children often argue that only contests in which everyone can win are fair.) The indicants used to measure each construct differed across age groups, but all three constructs were sufficiently evident that investigators could draw general conclusions about such key motivational concepts.

Review of Adaptive Testing Procedures.   You may remember that *adaptive testing* allows investigators to explore functioning at the individual level (see Chapter 7). This is easiest to track when computers can be used to present items and record responses. The adaptive nature of the measure then becomes invisible to respondents while ensuring that the indicants they see are tailored to their interests.

To design such tests, investigators typically begin with items that have been well-calibrated on independent groups of respondents. Next, they design procedures for item selection, methods for scoring each item, and criteria for terminating the test. On some ability tests, for example, individuals may be given a series of three easy items. If they score correctly on all three, they would be given progressively more difficult items until they make sequential errors or offer unsystematic answers. Respondents may be given a mixture of items when making one or two mistakes before responding correctly, but the test is terminated when three items of similar difficulty are sequentially answered incorrectly.

If investigators want to explore individual differences using items that do not have a correct answer, participants may be given a series of screening items for identifying an initial starting point. Responses to those start items would be used to direct respondents to a particular group and the selection of subsequent items would reflect their placement within that group.

Using *item-response theory* or *Rasch techniques,* investigators have learned to fit item responses to probabilistic estimates of how an item should perform given theoretical predictions. With some or all of the item parameters, these techniques allow investigators to compare the distribution of responses for one person against predicted responses that are generated using one of a variety of probability models. This comparison removes the need for a norm group because responses are compared to a predetermined standard and decisions are made on the basis of standard probabilistic distributions. These techniques also allow investigators to determine which items or persons are outliers in a sample. From this, investigators can make generalizations about individual differences in how particular persons responded to the test.

Knowing patterns attributable to individual variation permits investigators to calibrate tools for drawing conclusions about diversity. Investigators can minimize individual variation by deleting items or persons that serve as outliers. To do so typically requires more than an empirical justification. Deleting participants from a research study is not recommended, but, when pilot-testing a tool, knowing how many people deviate from predicted probabilities can prove helpful for the calibration process.

Lessons from Interactive Methods

Interactive methods are likely to yield a high response rate; when appropriately selected most people are willing to participate. Respondents need not have strong literacy skills to be able to complete well-constructed tasks and may be willing to share their ideas if asked in a clear and polite manner. When respondents interact with researchers, it is possible to clarify the purpose of a study and any misunderstandings that might arise in the data-collection process. Many respondents are also more willing to talk than write answers, so interactive methods are likely to yield greater complexity of thought.

Paper-and-pencil measures can be used to study individual differences. When investigators are looking for honest answers to sensitive questions, paper-and-pencil measures may be ideal for preserving anonymity. Because such measures are minimally interactive, they may also be more economical and reliable for some purposes. With careful planning, adaptive formats can be introduced in which respondents who give certain answers may skip to later items.

Adaptive testing, when generated using computers, alleviates some problems associated with paper-and-pencil measures. Computers can minimize confusion by presenting appropriately selected items that essentially guide respondents through adaptive logic. Allowing computers to select appropriate items can also ensure that respondents have access to relevant items, and only those items. When administered well, investigators learn about respondents' answers to predetermined questions, but, as with most tools, there is little information on whether the right questions have been asked.

Interviews, in contrast, are very useful for learning how individuals understand particular questions and whether questions should be modified. Cooperative respondents consider the purpose of the interview and interviewers' perspectives, targeting their views to maximize communication. Interviewers can probe when they are confused and ask the occasional open-ended question to determine if they are learning all that they could. When individuals' vocabulary does not match that of investigators, conversations can continue until a mutual understanding is achieved. Interview methods may offer clues about the underlying structures that guide thoughts, feelings, and actions more readily than methods governed completely by the researchers' assumptions.

More generally, when interactive methods are used to invite participants to coconstruct meaningful interpretations of experience, information from one agent can transform the understanding of another. Participants may learn from investigator-generated activities, and investigators may learn from participants' critiques of their experiences. In the short run, interactive methods present investigators with a host of challenges in the calibration and standardization phases of research, but in the long run the findings can prove very helpful and may save years of research otherwise driven by guessing.

MAKING CONNECTIONS

Find a research report that relies on interactive research methods. Did the investigators rely on interviews? If so, what format did they use? Was that format appropriate for addressing the research question? What kinds of information were extracted? What kinds of information did the investigator predict? What methods might have been better for this type of project?

NORMATIVE MEASUREMENT

Normative aspects of human functioning are most commonly measured using psychometric tools, yet these tools can be modified for exploring individual differences in development. You may remember that investigators study behavior using naturalistic observations, laboratory elicitation techniques, experimentally induced events in naturalistic settings, and rating scales. They use a variety of methods for measuring cognitive abilities including written responses, reaction times, rating scales, and sorting tasks. Emotions are often measured with projective tests, physiological tools, or direct requests for information. Investigators may design experiments related to abstract, artificial problems; experimental analogues to actual life events; or descriptions of functioning in everyday settings. Selecting appropriate measurement tools hinges on an understanding of a theoretical framework.

The Role of Inferences

Investigators place different weight on inferences. Some prefer to eliminate inferences altogether and others may use probability distributions when forming them.[6] High levels of inference are common for *introspective ethology,* in which investigators reflect on their experiences and project those reflections into the prediction of others' experience. *Motor empathy* is another technique: Movements are recorded without labels and investigators later try to imagine respondents' perspectives on the action states that must have produced such movements. Inferences are present, but less so, in *direct observations* and in the content analysis of *interviews*; investigators can see behavior or make judgments about ideas represented in speech, but it is not always easy to use that information to imagine the experiences of participants.

Investigators who find inference-dependent methods to be of limited scientific value often make literal comparisons of the responses. These investigators are likely to equate structure and functioning, and do not evaluate how changes in functioning can occur without a requisite change in structure. For example, investigators studying applied behavioral analysis focus exclusively on changes in behavior and try to design environments to stimulate desired behavior. They avoid exploring the internal structures, looking only at the contextual features that elicit behavior.

The Effects of Context

Most investigators who use normative tools, regardless of their beliefs on whether structures and functioning can be differentiated, acknowledge the importance of context in research. Even when it appears as though tasks involve few inferences, developmental theorists acknowledge that performance may be affected by the context in which tasks are administered. They recognize that the "context in which an item is presented alters the very nature of the item by virtue of necessitated situational constraints or facilitators" (Sigel, 1974, p. 206). Part of theory construction involves predictions about whether performance will show plasticity or stability in different contexts.

When theorizing about the effects of contexts, investigators recognize that levels of organization central to understanding a developmental system are likely to elicit more and less contextual variation. The mechanics of vision, for example, are not as likely to differ across contexts as someone's motivation. Although all indicants hold contextual meaning, the outcomes of normative comparisons may be appropriate for some or all contexts. Respondents' performance can be maximized if the task is meaningful, task demands are appropriately challenging, and the social definition of situations supports functioning.

Participants' Comfort

On standardized tasks, studies of diversity have revealed patterns indicative of individual variation rather than development. New research on stereotype threat, for example, has confirmed that individuals have lower levels of performance in situations that elicit common stereotypes. This is especially marked when stereotypes are introduced as part of the instructions: Everyone, not just the members of a targeted racial or ethnic group, tends to score lower on normative tests.[7]

In another set of findings, high scorers tended to maintain eye contact, smile, and make obvious gestures toward correct answers (Mehan, 1979). They looked at materials and verbalized their thought processes more readily than lower scorers, but typically showed less tactile manipulation of stimulus materials. It is as if high-scoring respondents instinctively understood the task and had extra mental energy to consider the environment around them. If everyone performs at their best, normative comparisons like these are likely to be theoretically useful, even if they do not always lead to accurate predictions about diversity.

Lessons from Normative Methods

Investigators labeling group norms can be diversity-sensitive without having adequate information on individual variation. Ideally, studies of individual differences focus on both diversity and individual variation. Complete reliance on measures of central tendency or on correlations can be misleading. Measures of central tendency show error variance around the index and these are rarely considered for correlation coefficients, but both scores offer only a sense of how groups of participants have responded. More commonly, normative studies of individual differences facilitate inferences about latent variables. If normative tools are calibrated well, investigators can measure general patterns related to gender, ethnicity, social class, or other differences in human characteristics to determine how they are related to functioning. Such information is helpful for distinguishing ontological cycles of simplicity to complexity to simplicity and patterns attributed to more stable person characteristics.

■ ■ ■ ■ ■ ▬

MAKING CONNECTIONS

Examine common beliefs in your field about how human characteristics affect functioning. Is there evidence for such beliefs? Find a study that might be used as evidence and critique the measurement plan.

CALIBRATING TOOLS

To calibrate tools, investigators keep in mind the differing agendas associated with measuring development and individual differences. Variance may be attributable to history, cohort effects, or the time of assessment. Recognizing the limits of a tool, investigators try to maximize opportunities for finding and exploring those and other sources of variability.

Interactive Tools

Remembering that calibration involves the verification of relationships between respondents' ideas and the stimuli they are considering, investigators who interpret the findings from interactive tools learn to distinguish productive and unproductive responses. To bring out value-laden implications intended by respondents, investigators coordinate respondents' ideas with task demands such as the amount of direction given and the requested specificity of functioning. They evaluate the range of stimuli and responses available for analysis, the depth of the interview, and the quality of personal contact. These constrain the indicants, and the nature of the indicants dictates the calibration techniques for translating responses into numbers.

Psychometric Calibration.   In adaptive testing and formal interviews, investigators use scale scores, rankings, or other predetermined number systems to record answers. These methods are dependent on psychometric assumptions and are the easiest to calibrate because most of the mathematical tools developed for use with paper-and-pencil measures can be applied to such data. Item-response theory can be applied to computer adaptive test data as well. Investigators can compare responses using nonparametric statistical tools or by transforming indicants into interval scales for use in parametric analysis.

Content Analysis.   Findings from semistructured interviews may involve some scale scoring of respondents' decisions, but their justifications will inevitably have to undergo content analysis before being interpreted. Similarly, unstructured and nondirective interviews typically undergo content analysis before investigators make comparisons across respondents. *Content analysis* involves the translation of speech and/or gestures into numbers that represent categories of responses. Investigators design a *coding scheme* that consists of dictionaries or indicant categories into which respondents' ideas are classified. The numbers used to represent ideas may correspond to nominal categories or response frequencies. Answers are sometimes translated into codes on the spot, after the entire interview is transcribed, or while examining recordings.

Planning a Coding Scheme.   As with other forms of coding, most investigators maximize accuracy by minimizing bias. Nevertheless, coding schemes can be highly complex as investigators determine whether to use existing rating scales, count responses, or rank the qualities of particular ideas. These schemes are intended to minimize coding errors attributable to misclassifications, inattention, fatigue, or recording errors. Investigators typically design codes to reflect the amount of precision necessary for achieving their measurement goal. They calibrate categories finely enough to have sufficient information, but not so fine that the information is difficult to interpret. Investigators also try to use the highest possible level of measurement, doing their best to translate nominal information into ordinal or interval data.

The most literal form of content analysis is typically conducted using computer programs designed for text analysis (see Neuendorf, 2002). Computers match interview responses with the vocabulary found in a range of dictionaries. Some dictionaries are standard and others are customized to match particular theoretical arguments. Investigators can also construct their own dictionaries using information that emerges from collected data or establish word-based strings that are not treated as dictionary outcomes.

Human coding involves more interpretive kinds of content analysis and may be required for making sense of speech in individuals who may not use standard language for expressing their opinions (Mishler, 1986). In such work, investigators make the *codebook* or definition of each coding category so complete that variation among raters would be rare. In the codebook itself, investigators add sufficient detail and examples from individual responses to ensure that raters will understand the definition of the category. Shorthand labels can then be used by raters coding actual protocols.

Tools for Coding.   Currently available computer programs like those listed on the suggested Web sites are designed to measure manifest variables and estimate relations between particular scores and latent variables. Outputs often contain information on the *number of cases,* the *frequency of each dictionary term,* and an *alphabetical list of words* found in the protocol. They also contain a *measure of concordance* or key words in context, and any *message units* or *word strings* that might have been programmed into the software. Some programs can conduct specialty analysis in which the computer finds co-occurring patterns of key words in multidimensional space; a text-based procedure that works like factor analysis identifies patterns in indicants. Typically, machines rather than people score each transcript, but investigators can offer some structure to the scoring plan.

The process of human coding is quite complex. The main idea to remember is that investigators frequently revise their coding schemes in the training and pilot phases of coding. Raters usually require training to ensure they use only information from the units being coded, drawing no other inferences about the underlying meaning in an answer. Programs like *Atlas-ti* and *NVivo* assist raters in tracking their evaluations and are very helpful when investigators endeavor to establish a repeatedly reliable codebook. Like items on a psychometric measure, coding categories are usually exhaustive and mutually independent so that raters can easily decide where to place each coded unit.

The easiest way to ensure that background knowledge does not interfere with coding is to elicit the help of *blind coders*—raters who do not know the specific hypotheses of the study, information about the characteristics of participants, or anything about the desired outcomes. It is not always practical to keep coders ignorant about the purposes of an investigation, but this should not be a liability when a codebook is well-developed. It is of central importance that raters make *independent judgments* and receive no direct input from the researchers when doing the final coding. Category definitions are effectively calibrated if everyone who rates a set of protocols can see the same things. Ideally, the descriptions of each category are clear enough that investigators from other research groups can look for evidence of the same ideas in their research.

In a well-designed interview, investigators often work with more than one example of the same concept and the indicants from each example may be mathematically combined into a total score for representing each dimension. Codebooks can contain keywords or phrases that may later be combined into categories with a single meaning.

After counting each reference and exploring the proportion in each protocol, investigators can explore internal consistency. They would look at how each example of a concept performs in relation to other examples or how different raters evaluate the same protocol. If a study involves parallel examples from school and sport contexts, for example, investigators can compare responses for each context to calibrate measurement tools (Thorkildsen, 1989b). Measures of internal consistency are not always practical, but thinking creatively about how indicants are translated into numbers can elicit opportunities for such exploration.

Structural Analysis. A third kind of holistic analysis can also be conducted, one in which investigators combine information on respondents' decisions and justifications to make one global classification for each interview protocol (see Piaget, 1951; Thorkildsen, 1989a). This structural analysis involves treating each answer as a symptom or indicator of a more general system of thought. Investigators look for trends in these indicators for each set of indicants. This kind of analysis is most easily done by hand, placing protocols with similar structures in the same pile and those with different structures in another pile. After all protocols are sorted, a search for uniformity in the content of each pile can be conducted before investigators assume that protocols in the same pile are similar in structure. After investigators match protocols, they name and describe the characteristics of each pile, focusing on the trends that were used to establish each category. Formal instructions for this process would then be written and given to other raters who independently evaluate the protocols.

Testing the Calibration. Inter-rater reliability techniques introduced in earlier chapters are also appropriate for use in verifying that tools are well calibrated (Chapter 5). In addition to evaluating the success of a coding scheme, investigators consider the quality of the evaluated units and of the raters who are making judgments. Ideally, raters evaluate all the protocols in a study, but for more elaborate schemes it is acceptable to select a sample. Typically, at least two raters translate individuals' responses into numbers. When a sample of protocols is coded, investigators randomly select them while ensuring representativeness. Comparing raters' judgments to determine the extent of agreement facilitates conclusions of whether they agree on the precise values of the codes.

Investigators use inter-rater agreement to determine if a coding scheme is poor, if raters are poorly trained, if raters are fatigued, and if they are working with an untrainable rater. When agreement is low, investigators can add training or revise the coding scheme while looking for consistent forms of disagreement. In revising a coding scheme, they may find it necessary to split or merge variables. In working with different raters, investigators may also find the rare situation in which raters just cannot or will not accept the parameters of a coding scheme and may have to be replaced.

Calculating Inter-Rater Reliability. In the calibration phase, investigators ensure that findings are not the result of idiosyncratic judgments before combining indicants into scale scores.[8] These steps are consistent with the *item analysis* and *accuracy* phases of psychometric research. *Cohen's kappa* (κ) continues to be the most commonly used method of computing inter-rater agreement when investigators have nominal scales, but multiple raters. To account for multiple raters, the *kappa formula* changes as follows:

KAPPA FOR MULTIPLE RATERS

$$\kappa = \frac{\displaystyle\sum_{i=1}^{N}\sum_{j=1}^{i} n_{ij^2} - Nn\left[1 + (n-1)\sum_{j=1}^{k} p_j^2\right]}{Nn(n-1)\left(1 - \displaystyle\sum_{j=1}^{k} p_j^2\right)}$$

In this formula, p_j is the proportion of all assignments to the jth category. N represents the total number of participants in the study, n is the number of ratings per participant, and k is the number of categories to which assignments are made.

Investigators have also designed modifications of the straight percentage agreement formula when investigators have nominal scales, but only two raters. Distinguishing the raw *percentage of agreement* from estimates of *agreement controlling for chance,* they compare frequency distributions rather than scores for each respondent. You may recall that raw agreement can be calculated by dividing the total number of agreements by the total number of indicants being rated. That technique is appropriate when raters identify the same number of units, but some forms of content analysis may lead raters to end up with a *different number of units.* To correct for such differences and still rely on the percentage agreement, Holsti (1969) came up with the following:

HOLSTI'S INTER-RATER AGREEMENT

$$PA_O = \frac{2A}{(n_A + n_B)}$$

In this, PA_O reflects the percentage of observed agreement, A is the number of agreements, n_A and n_B are the number of indicants coded by each rater.

Investigators, who control for the possibility of *chance agreement,* especially when there are a relatively *small number of codes,* are likely to use one of a range of techniques. *Scott's pi* (π) relies on comparisons of how categories are used by raters, evaluating the joint distributions across raters (Scott, 1955). This is one of the simplest ways of exploring nominal data and relies on additive rather than multiplicative measurement properties. To compute Scott's *pi,* investigators use the following formula:

SCOTT'S PI

$$\pi = \frac{PA_O - \sum p_i^2}{1 - \sum p_i^2}$$

Here, p_i reflects the marginal proportions for the sum of both raters' decisions for each category in the coding scheme. The resulting number can range from 0 to 1, with 0 indicating agreement at the chance level and 1 indicating perfect agreement. Notice how the categories are not treated separately, but are aggregated in this index. Information on how codes are distributed across categories is ignored.

Pi differs from *Cohen's kappa* (κ) in that pi uses an additive distribution to represent scores across categories and kappa relies on a multiplicative function (Cohen, 1968). The multiplicative function acknowledges that categories may be weighted differently in the evaluation of an interview protocol. The weighted formula has also been used for the evaluation of ordinal data (Chapter 5).

Krippendorff's alpha (α) was also designed to control for *chance agreement* as well as the *magnitude of misses* while adjusting for the degree to which investigators have nominal, ordinal, interval, or ratio data (Krippendorff, 1980). Below are the conceptual formula and the computational formula for use with nominal data.

KRIPPENDORFF'S ALPHA

$$\alpha = 1 - \frac{D_O}{D_E} \qquad\qquad \alpha = 1 - \frac{nm-1}{m-1}\left(\frac{\sum pfu}{\sum pmt}\right)$$

In the conceptual formula, D_O reflects the observed disagreements and D_E reflects expected disagreements. In the computational formula, *pfu* is the product of frequencies for a unit showing disagreement, *pmt* is each product of total marginals for all coding categories, n is the number of units coded in common by all raters, and m is the number of raters. Krippendorff's formula may be the most flexible because it accommodates multiple raters and complex coding schemes, but it is also the most difficult to calculate.

Adjusting for Poor Calibration. When investigators find low reliability, they have a few options. Calibration can be so inaccurate that investigators assume they have made idiosyncratic judgments and drop the variable entirely. Codes can sometimes be too general to support clear coding criteria and investigators may want to form simpler categories that can be described more literally. At the opposite extreme, investigators sometimes start with definitions that are too precise and may want to create one category with a broad definition to replace many narrowly focused categories. When poorly calibrated variables are too important to drop from a study, investigators sometimes construct a short survey to remeasure dimensions corresponding to emergent definitions.

Ideally, convergence is evident in how decisions, justifications, and structural analysis are calibrated. For example, justification patterns ought to support claims generated in more holistic analyses of existing trends of thought. Similarly, the content of a decision would not contradict claims made in respondents' justifications. In many interview situations, investigators do not have information from all three types of data, but, when they do, accuracy can more easily be evaluated. The most general structural analysis would be used to test relations among variables while justification codes and decision indicants would be used to corroborate the patterns.

Normative Tools

Normative studies are not as concerned with individual variation as is common for interactive measurement. Calibration techniques are selected to improve the accuracy of patterns emerging across groups of people. Investigators begin by translating responses into numbers, much as they do in psychometric research. Treating each number as an indicant, they then conduct factor analysis to determine how indicants fall into patterns of latent variables. If there are human characteristics predicted to be a source of diversity, investigators typically collect information using samples large enough to conduct independent factor analyses for each group and compare the results.

Results of factor analysis are evaluated by identifying the structure of individual factors in each group being assessed. Time can also substitute for personal characteristics in studies of the metamorphoses of structures over time (Coan, 1966, 1972). Developmentalists are interested in the emergence, disintegration, and component interchanges as indicants are recombined over time. When groups differ in how indicants are combined, investigators speculate on whether they hold common structures. Investigators verify their assumptions by minimizing error variance and finding the same results with a second sample. They repeat this factor-analytic strategy using variables instead of indicants to draw conclusions about parallel developmental systems.

Not surprisingly, it is also helpful to compute *Cronbach's alpha* and corresponding item-analysis procedures (Cronbach, 1951). This step facilitates conclusions about the degree to which indicants form an internally consistent collection and if any indicants in the collection are undermining the measurement process. Investigators may also use the results from item-response theory or Rasch analysis to determine whether indicants are interchangeable on the same latent factor and if the factors are appropriately homogeneous and ready to name.

Coordinating Interactive and Normative Tools

Conclusions may be stronger if investigators can compare the results obtained with interactive and normative methods. Whereas some calibration techniques for measuring diversity would lead investigators to delete outliers, in many respects this would be a loss of important information. Learning more about why some individuals are significantly different from others in their age group may lead investigators to essential information for improving a tool. Knowledge of when a particular developmental cycle begins or of the asymptote for groups of individuals may be easier to acquire using interactive as well as normative data. The study of diversity can be enhanced by calibrating tools using information on individual variation and the combination offers stronger measurement of individual differences.

MAKING CONNECTIONS

Find an article measuring individual differences. Does the article focus on individual variation or diversity? What information is available on how investigators calibrated their tools? Did they rely on interactive data, normative data, or both?

STANDARDIZING TOOLS

Those developmentalists studying individual differences hope to find the same outcomes on repeated use of a tool. Such *repeatability* is possible if the conceptual definition of each variable matches the measurement definition because investigators can assume the tool will perform with a high degree of dependability. Investigators standardize tools by evaluating whether indicants of the same dimension are adequately correlated or are interchangeable.

They may also determine if indicants of different dimensions are sufficiently independent to warrant evaluating profiles of scores. Standardization also involves determining if individuals are classified in the same way when using the same measure twice, or how they are classified on more than one version of the same measure. Although the goals are the same for interactive and normative tools, the procedures for attaining these goals differ.

Interactive Tools

After verifying that raters accurately assigned numbers to units, investigators also verify that coding schemes are replicable. *Replicability* involves the quest for stability in how raters use a tool, ensuring that scores do not migrate from particular standards. Some stability indices are close to those associated with calibrating tools and involve studies of co-variation between the ratings of two or more raters.

Standardization in Interviewing.   Before calculating indices of how well the questions and coding schemes are operating, investigators look for evidence of stability in how interviews were executed. Standardizing interactive tools invariably involves controlling for bias in how interviewers and respondents function. When answers to one question can lead to inferences about subsequent answers, scoring errors may deviate from a standard in the same direction across interviews. It becomes easy to overstate or understate claims about the presence or absence of particular attributes because such migration is difficult to detect.

During the interview, investigators try to maintain a comfortable feeling and ensure that interviewers are not overly calculating, detached, or rational, but activities are planned to ensure repeatability. Interviewers can also distort their perceptions to find support for preconceived notions, and misperceive the intended meaning in respondents' speech. Minimizing bias is especially difficult when interviewers are unaware of their own attitudes and opinions and the degree to which they assume that respondents share their values and characteristics.

Interviewers who expect systematic answers may unconsciously distort particular questions to elicit patterns. Counterbalancing the order in which questions are presented offers one means by which investigators can minimize this bias. Asking for contradictory arguments can also serve this purpose. When responses are translated into a standard template, a tool may be sufficiently standardized if patterns in how questions were asked become undetectable.

Respondents can also introduce bias into the measurement process. They may exhibit a strong tendency to give socially desirable answers or try to guess what the investigators hope to discover (see Fiske, 1967; Fiske & Butler, 1963). Sometimes respondents are asked to give answers that they do not or cannot know and will offer guesses. The extent to which respondents "read between the lines" can be minimized by being direct about the purpose of an investigation and participants' role in the process. Comparisons in how easy or difficult it is to code particular interviews can illuminate such distortion. Similarly, comparing scores across interviews is also helpful.

Evaluating Multiple Tools.   Investigators may compare responses on more than one tool to verify that theoretical patterns of indicants hold up to empirical scrutiny. When scores can only be ranked, as is the case with ordinal data, investigators compute *Spearman's rho* (*ρ*) (Spearman, 1904; see Chapter 3). Methods for exploring stability in data with interval or ratio scales are typically analyzed using Pearson correlation coefficients (*r*) (Pearson, 1909; see Chapter 3). These coefficients can range from –1 (when scores are inversely related) to 0 (when there is no relationship) to 1 (when scores are perfectly aligned).

Another method of exploring covariation that accounts for systematic coding errors is Lin's concordance correlation coefficient (*r~c~*) (Lin, 1989). This technique assumes that the regression line passing between two sets of metric scores is linear and has a slope of 1. As with other methods for evaluating covariation, scores can range from –1 to 1. The formula reads as follows:

LIN'S CONCORDANCE CORRELATION COEFFICIENT

$$r_c = \frac{2\left(\dfrac{\sum ab}{n}\right)}{\dfrac{\sum a^2}{n} + \dfrac{\sum b^2}{n} + (\text{Mean}_A - \text{Mean}_B)^2}$$

In this formula, *a* is the deviation score for rater *A, b* is the deviation score for rater *B,* and *n* is the number of units coded in common by both raters. Whereas Pearson's *r* does not account for systematic differences such as those in which one coder consistently rates something higher than another, Lin's *r~c~* accounts for the imperfect correspondence between two raters.

Investigators use concordance information to determine if the distribution of scores remains the same, but cannot verify if each participant would receive the same score. To compare scores for individual participants, investigators may calculate χ^2 or other nonparametric tests to verify that the relative position of individuals in a distribution remains constant across raters (Chapter 3).

Comparing Multiple Raters.   Investigators also found ways to draw inferences about the repeatability of a coding scheme by comparing indices of agreement. Cohen's *kappa* (κ) has been adapted for use with multiple raters (Fleiss, 1971), and Krippendorff's *alpha* (α) also contains this feature. Unfortunately, neither coefficient offers information on pairwise disagreements among raters. Therefore, investigators have devised a number of ways to treat pairwise agreement indices like indicants on a psychometric measure.[9]

Some investigators graph the distribution of reliability coefficients to see the overall shape and identify outliers. They also compute pairwise matrices and look for evidence of repeatability. It is also possible to use Cronbach's *alpha* and corresponding item-analysis techniques to compare the internal consistency of multiple ratings of the same category, treating reliability coefficients for each rater as indicants (see Chapter 4). The *Spearman-Brown prophecy formula* has also been adapted for calculating effective reliability scores (Rosenthal, 1987). With these techniques, investigators look for evidence of repeatability by generalizing from a sample of raters to a theoretical population of raters.

Summary. In the standardization process, investigators compare interviewer characteristics, respondent characteristics, and the content of questions, looking for stability in how the three sources of information come together. Bias is problematic when it creates distortion in a set of responses, but the presence of patterns need not be considered distortion. If, in the dialectical process of interactive methods, investigators learn of systematic thoughts they had not anticipated, the comparison standard may require revision. If respondents learn something from the way a question is framed or answers are received, they should feel free to share such knowledge with the person asking questions. If these sources of information are not evident in the units to be coded, no amount of statistical manipulation is likely to replace the missing information.

Normative Tools

In exploring the *repeatability of normative tools,* investigators typically rely on psychometric approaches that help them determine whether items on a measure lead to a stable classification of individuals. Most of these methods have already been introduced. Investigators may use psychometric methods to differentiate individual and group performance, but when studying individual differences, they tend to standardize their tools by subdividing a sample to reflect the individual characteristics under investigation.

Norming Subsamples. Let's explore this by considering possible gender differences. Investigators would collect data using a sample of males and a sample of females. To calibrate and standardize tools, they would conduct all analyses separately for the two groups and compare the results. If there are apparent structural differences between the two groups, indicants are likely to form significantly different patterns when investigators complete factor analysis for the two subsamples. Looking carefully at any items that are outliers in a distribution, investigators would rule out the possibility that the item is poorly designed before assuming that there are structural differences in reasoning.

It is possible that such obvious human differences foster differential treatment in the world. Gender differences in treatment as well as ontogeny might lead to individual variation in how people organize their experiences. Such evidence would lead investigators to use various tools for representing each gender and to consistently describe gender differences in the dimensions of related theoretical constructs. Norms, in other words, would be established separately for each gender.

If there are individual differences in functioning, but not in structures, the resulting factor structures should remain the same for both genders. Males and females would show similar patterns in how they respond to different indicants, but such structures would be organized differently. If indicants reliably fall into the same latent factors, investigators can use a common set of tools for measuring, but systematically explore differences in functioning. Investigators could evaluate functional variation by comparing results from multiple tools designed to measure similar outcomes. Parallel analyses of associations among variables, conducted separately for males and females, could then be compared to draw inferences about gender differences in functioning while assuming structural similarities.

Classification of Individuals.   If investigators can assume that tools are calibrated the same for males and females, they may also conduct a cluster analysis to determine if groups of individuals can be sorted into different categories. Cluster analysis is a variation of factor analysis in which individuals, rather than items, are sorted into groups. Once individuals are sorted, it is possible to determine the common characteristics apparent in their responses and to theorize about the nature of those differences. Investigators who know the characteristics that reflect individual differences (e.g., gender) can use another form of discriminant analysis to evaluate differences in how particular variables function across groups.

Summary.   To standardize normative assumptions, investigators often use multiple measures of the same variables and determine the repeatability of their findings. This is not always practical, so investigators may rely on conclusions from more than one study to support their predictions. Finding stable evidence for diversity can be difficult if individual variation remains unacknowledged, but, when tools are calibrated and standardized appropriately, studies of individual differences and developmental change can be compared with greater certainty.

MAKING CONNECTIONS

In the articles you found, how were tools standardized? Are there inferences about missing information that are easy to accept without seeing results from all steps in an analysis plan? What are those inferences? Would you say that the measures were appropriately standardized? What evidence would you use?

SUPPORTING GENERALIZATIONS

In the chapters on psychometric measurement, you were introduced to traditional notions of validity that are often applied to the study of individual differences. Expanding those views to introduce more current perspectives, it is important to remember that all studies, no matter what their content, serve as validation studies as well as tests of theoretical predictions. As Cronbach pointed out, it is important to realize that all research is essentially part and parcel of a validity argument.[10] Most investigators understand that all validity arguments can address only some essential questions and findings are valid primarily for the contexts in which they were generated.

By treating questions of validity as a kind of debate, conversations focus on the supportive and contradictory conclusions that are evident in a set of findings. In this view, validity involves generating a strong argument for particular assertions. As is the case for other kinds of research, concepts, evidence, social and personal consequences, and values are all coordinated when making generalizations about development. In putting forth an interpretation, investigators endeavor to confirm, falsify, and revise their assumptions. Measurement involves clarifying possibilities, anomalies, and boundary conditions. When all these decisions are clearly executed, the resulting evidence can support descriptions, predictions, and recommended decisions, but not "prove" them.

Broad Validity Concerns

Five different validity concerns, especially important when drawing conclusions about diversity and individual variation, have been imagined. Each of these concerns is much broader than those associated with how well indicants are related to the dimensions of constructs. Playing devil's advocate with their data, labeling alternative interpretations as well as those they predicted, most investigators consider political, functional, economic, operationist, and explanatory critiques.

Sociocultural Perspectives. *Political perspectives* focus on whether findings can persuade individuals and communities of the value of particular conclusions. Investigators may consider prevailing beliefs, raise complaints to eventually nurture sound beliefs, and offer sound evidence for particular perspectives. *Functional perspectives* emphasize the value of findings rather than simply the truth of particular claims. Investigators commonly consider the consequences for people and institutions of using a measure, validating only those that further the betterment of society. *Economic perspectives* address the utility of criteria for interpreting data, evaluating the costs and benefits of such decisions. Investigators try to stay critical of any criterion used to compare scores, considering the potential for unanticipated interactions when making classifications while extrapolating from empirical evidence to make well-supported judgments. *Operationist perspectives* involve the evaluation of whether indicants match the concepts being measured. At this level, investigators evaluate how well variables are measured, but also realize that the avoidance of inferences can eventually lead them to avoid essential questions of truth and worth.

Explanatory Perspectives. *Explanatory perspectives* are those most strongly emphasized in this book. Explanations hinge on the idea that an instructive construct validation program allows investigators to move beyond an insistence on labeling "correct" theories. Instead, explanations require consideration of the long- and short-term value of any new ideas. Investigators usually reject the belief that a trait or state can ever match a test score.

Testing Perspectives. Investigators have learned that looking for "correct theories" by challenging the work of others invariably leads to personal rivalries rather than constructive research. Instead, most investigators identify *plausible rival hypotheses* in their own work and look for methods of testing disparate predictions. In a weak research program, investigators may be happy to find statistically significant patterns, but in a strong research program they make theoretical ideas as explicit as possible and devise deliberate challenges to those ideas.

Explanations generated out of this multifaceted approach to validity may not be of immediate practical value, but in the long run they can be incorporated into progressively more elegant explanations of human functioning. In doing so, investigators ask if findings can be extrapolated to other settings, times, and groups. They evaluate whether each construct is adequately measured and whether the constructs measured are sufficiently comprehensive. In determining whether findings are replicable, investigators compare the assumptions of individual differences with those of developmental change to determine which aspects of a developmental system are being measured.

Constraints on Generalizations

When exploring how far to generalize a particular set of findings, investigators consider all the issues raised by Cronbach as well as more specific issues related to the theoretical questions posed.[11] They may evaluate whether their *theories are reductionistic or emergent,* looking for evidence that later-appearing structures are part of earlier-occurring structures, and identifying emergent structures. Investigators can also ask if their theories reflect *elementaristic or holistic assumptions,* determining if findings address a small part of a developmental system or a more global structure. Investigators also label the degree to which they have *supported inferences* or merely *listed a set of observations.* The former involves conclusions supported with evidence whereas the latter avoids the synthesis of indicants. Out of these deliberations, investigators learn whether *relations among dimensions are bidirectional or unidirectional.* Early personality theories, for example, created a forced-choice definition of feeling or thinking, but the more current "Big Five" theory now classifies individuals on the degree of agreeableness in their personalities. Moving to unidirectional choices has generated richer conclusions.

Purposes of Generalizations

In studies of individual variation, investigators look for patterns across people to highlight the lessons learned from collections of agents. Findings from studies of individual variation are often used to generate predictions about diversity. In studies of diversity, investigators typically compare results from multiple measures to find patterns across groups of persons using aggregated data. Adopting a multivariate approach to studying ontogenetic change, investigators look for *interfactor relationships* and how those relationships *change over time.*[12] Patterns in two variables can be parallel, convergent, or divergent and each offers different kinds of information for the theory-building process. Combining knowledge of individual variation and diversity, investigators are able to make stronger claims about individual differences in human functioning.

■ ■ ■ ■ ■

MAKING CONNECTIONS

In the articles you have read, identify the methods by which investigators have demonstrated validity. What evidence indicated that researchers were critical of their findings? What validity questions were anticipated and answered? How did validity differ in a study of individual variation and of diversity?

COORDINATING INDIVIDUAL
VARIATION AND DIVERSITY

When investigators explore individual variation, they are primarily interested in depictions of how people function and the underlying structures that guide their reasoning, emotions, and behavior. They may explore changes within one person over time and construct a profile of outcomes; such work is usually completed to identify a person's uniqueness and how that affects his or her adjustment in society. Investigators may also explore outcomes in a relatively small number of people to determine if individuals show similar or different characteristics; these studies usually reflect an intensive investigation of characteristics that are difficult to measure, and attempt to find reasonable initial positions and asymptotes for use in more elaborate investigations. Findings from studies of individual variation can be used to make predictions about diversity or developmental change by ruling in or out pressures for more elaborate studies of individual differences.

When investigators explore diversity, predictable patterns can offer direction to policymakers and practitioners interested in establishing effective and fair practices while minimizing the potential for harm. Studies of diversity are likely to yield more valid conclusions when they incorporate information from studies of individual variation. Relying on aggregate indices can obfuscate important forms of variation and place limits on investigators' understanding of people who do not share their values or characteristics.

Studies of individual variation and diversity, when consolidated, can offer a much richer picture of individual differences than is possible when taken in isolation. It is too easy to invent inaccurate stereotypes about groups with different human characteristics using only aggregate information. Individual differences, if left unacknowledged, can also obfuscate important facts of developmental change. Despite the tedium involved in exploring all facets of individual differences, studies of developmental systems are greatly enhanced by such efforts.

SUGGESTED READINGS

Coan, R. W. (1966). Child personality and developmental psychology. In R. B. Cattell (Ed.), *Handbook of multivariate experimental psychology* (pp. 732–752). Chicago: Rand McNally.

Krippendorff, K. (1980). *Content analysis: An introduction to its methodology.* Beverly Hills, CA: Sage.

Lamiell, J. T. (1987). *The psychology of personality: An epistemological inquiry.* New York: Columbia University Press.

Lamiell, J. T. (1997). Individuals and the differences between them. In R. Hogan, J. Johnson, & S. Briggs (Eds.), *Handbook of personality psychology* (pp. 117–141). San Diego, CA: Academic Press.

Mishler, E. G. (1986). *Research interviewing: Context and narrative.* Cambridge, MA: Harvard University Press.

Neuendorf, K. A. (2002). *The content analysis guidebook.* Thousand Oaks, CA: Sage.

Popping, R. (2000). *Computer-assisted text analysis.* Thousand Oaks, CA: Sage.

Sijtsma, K., & Molenaar, I. M. (2002). *Introduction to nonparametric item-response theory.* Thousand Oaks, CA: Sage.

SUGGESTED WEB SITES

CL Research for *DIMAP-4*: http://www.clres.com/DIMAP.html
Content Analysis Guidebook Online: http://academic.csuohio.edu/kneuendorf/content
GB Software for *PCAD 2000*: http://www.gb-software.com/pcad2000.htm
German Social Sciences Infrastructure Services for *TEXTPACK*: http://www.social-science-gesis.de/en/
    software/textpack/
Harald Klein for *TextQuest*: http://www.textquest.de/tqe.htm
Language Analysis Lab for *SALT*: http://www.waisman.wisc.edu/salt/index.htm
Lawrence Erlbaum Associates for *LIWC*:
    http://www.simstat.com/wordstat.htm?http://www.simstat.com/LIWC.htm
Megaputer Intelligence, Inc. for *TextAnalyst*: http://www.megaputer.com/products/ta/index.php3
Provalis Research for *WordStat:* http://www.simstat.com/wordstat.htm
Sage Publications Software for *NVivo*: http://www.scolari.co.uk
Sage Publications Software for *Diction 5.0*:
    http://www.scolari.co.uk/frame.html?http://www.scolari.co.uk/diction/diction.htm
Scientific software for *Atlas-ti*: http://www.atlasti.com
Skymeg Software for *PRAM*: http://www.geocities.com/skymegsoftware/pram.html
Statistical Packages for the Social Sciences for *TextSmart*: http://www.spss.com/spssbi/textsmart/

ENDNOTES

1. Findings from Chapter 4 were obtained from studies in which adolescents were asked to think about the purposes of school and work.

2. Gorden (1975) still provides the most cogent summary of these many facets of interviewing.

3. Chapter 10, on measuring the integration of structure and functioning, introduced Piagetian-style interviews. To offer other perspectives on interviewing, language from Cohen & Manion (1989b) and Gorden (1975) is used here. There is some overlap between these definitions of interviews and those used to explore representational differences, but the latter are much more explicit and require more extensive training for effective use.

4. Long (1992) offers details on the method and Damon (1977) offers examples of group interviews with children.

5. Chapter 7 outlines many of the measurement parameters for such techniques, although new techniques for using adaptive testing with scale scores are being developed.

6. Sigel (1974) offers a reminder that now seems dated, but could be revisited as investigators place less value on scientific approaches to the study of human functioning.

7. Aronson, Lustina, Good, Keough, Steele, & Brown (1999) review several studies on this issue.

8. *PRAM* is a computer program that can assist investigators in computing these scores.

9. Neuendorf (2002, pp. 162–163) reviews a range of advanced and special concerns with inter-rater reliability, most of which treat raters' evaluations as one might treat indicants on a survey.

10. To make his point, Cronbach (1988) outlines the five questions associated with exploring validity introduced here and illustrates how they differ in empirical and interpretive qualities. The Joint Committee on Standards for Educational and Psychological Testing (1999) also adopted this approach, treating validity as a unitary construct that requires multiple sources of evidence to substantiate.

11. Looft (1973) summarized many of these questions, although they have also emerged from the findings generated in many different kinds of research.

12. Buss & Royce (1975) describe some of the procedures for making these comparisons in studies of individual differences.

CHAPTER THIRTEEN

ASSUMPTIONS ABOUT INTERPRETIVE MEASUREMENT

Most researchers who study human functioning find validity to be a discursive process, but ethnographers and others who rely on interpretive research make this discourse visible in their reports. Psychometricians, developmentalists, and interpretive researchers generally agree that validity involves the integration of texts, actions, statements, and societal practices. Meaning and truth cannot be fully differentiated from political contexts because discourse is shaped by beliefs and commitments, explicit ideologies, tacit worldviews, linguistic and cultural systems, politics and economics, and the distribution of power.[1] Discourse generated from different research disciplines offers material for use in more general conversations about what is worthwhile to know and experience. Resources include participants' tacit and explicit knowledge as well as conclusions generated by social scientists.

Rather than adopt the relativistic position that all ideas are equally valuable, most researchers assume everyone's contributions should be subject to criticism and that meaning can be traced through language, action, and social practices as well as isolated for independent scrutiny. Translated into measurement terms, construct validity is a discursive means of representing events. Interpretive theorists extend these assumptions and emphasize how decisions about human functioning are ethical, political, and aesthetic as well as scientific. Interpretive theorists distinguish *first-order interpretations* by participants and *second-order interpretations* by investigators, documenting each dimension and using first-order evidence in second-order analysis.

Levels of Interpretation

Interpretive work is often conducted at one of three levels of specificity. Investigators may conduct:

- *case studies* to learn how particular individuals negotiate their lives and the meaning embedded in their everyday choices;
- *ethnographies* to explore local circumstances that illuminate the strengths of a community and areas of dysfunction;
- *ethnologies* to make cross-cultural comparisons that facilitate future conversations about how communities are situated in the larger world.

At the measurement level, these three very different approaches to theory building contain more commonalities than differences. Rather than treat them as independent entities, similarities in measurement will be highlighted in this chapter and differences will be illustrated in the final three chapters of the book. Commonalities can be obfuscated by the different labels used for each type of analysis, yet first-order evidence can look quite similar for the study of communities, and the narrower study of individuals or the broader comparison of cultures.

A Broader Notion of Validity

To validate interpretive measurement, most investigators consider issues of privilege in who defines constructs, terms, metaphors, models, and explanations. Constructs are validated by examining the social and material effects of relevant dimensions in cultural contexts. Measurement tools facilitate persuasive theories if they offer pragmatically convincing evidence that also acknowledges how people in positions of authority communicate with subordinates who may not offer generalizations about their experience. Investigators justify their theoretical constructs by asking what communities should be built, how findings contribute to new or changed communities, and what strengths are already apparent in existing communities.

APPROACHES TO INTERPRETATION

Ethnography reflects the most common forms of interpretive measurement, but attempts to define it invariably reveal many different approaches, each directing attention to different levels of the macrosystem in which human functioning occurs. In one review, *ethnography* is the study of how people who are not like us function in their communities.[2] Studies of communities can involve:

- a *comprehensive approach* that describes the general system in which groups of people function, labeling all the features of a system and making generalizations about cultures;
- a *topic-oriented approach* in which investigators compare and contrast thematic insights, collect systematic information about particular contexts, and formulate historical and evolutionary interpretations of their findings;
- a *hypothesis-oriented approach* in which investigators begin with a targeted set of assumptions and strive to disconfirm as well as confirm those assumptions.

These three levels of analysis may require different measurement techniques, but need not be treated like isolated disciplines. Information from one kind of research is typically used to inform conclusions about another when investigators design a rich interpretation of a particular system.

Interpretive Measurement Assumptions

Ethnography is definitely not a simple description of behavior, yet many first drafts have led readers to assume otherwise. This confusion has not metamorphosed from thin air. Early definitions of construct validity, those that supported behaviorism, introduced the ideas that *to validate is to investigate* and that validation is an ongoing process. Such researchers assumed that *nomological networks,* lawlike statements that outline how constructs and their corresponding dimensions correspond to one another, have explanatory power that could be improved over time.[3]

Most interpretive theorists agree with the idea that investigation is central to validation, but reject the assumption that behavior can be systematically described such that findings from one context could be easily generalized to another. They challenge the idea that systematic improvements will invariably lead to robust constructs offering meaningful information across people, points in time, and settings. Instead, interpretive theorists commonly assume that constructs and dimensions are difficult to identify, record, and confirm in each situation, let alone across settings.

Indicants and Inferences. Ethnographers refute behaviorists' assumption that indicants can ever be so closely matched with a construct as to achieve identity, disagreeing with the tendency to equate content and construct validity. They are also critical of *process* → *product* or *outcomes-focused ideologies* that assume research is valuable only if it leads to stable improvements in behavior. Outcomes-oriented research, in this view, offers insufficient information on the settings in which events take place, the cultural antecedents and consequences of behavior, and the macrocontexts required for interpreting experimental findings. Similarly, change does not always lead to improvements, and programmatic recommendations are as likely to be premature and misinformed as beneficial.

Developmentalists and psychometricians often ask questions about the purposes for identifying a sample of indicants and the principles investigators use to define research tasks. They ask where measurement rules originate when investigators link indicants to constructs and create scores. They also ask about the interests that are reflected in measurement rules and question the exclusion of alternative rules. Interpretive theorists add new questions to this list.

Interpretive theorists question who is authorized to speak, who listens, what ideas can be put forth, and what ideas remain unspoken. They also ask how individuals become authorized to speak, and what utterances are rewarded or penalized. These theorists label the categories, metaphors, explanations, and assertions that are praised and those that are excluded and silenced. Examining levels of organization, such investigators also ask about the social and political arrangements that are rewarded and penalized. The ideas advanced by investigators are seen as foundational to a particular discourse community, but those ideas are grounded in the perspectives of persons from particular cultures.

Self-Corrective Calibration. Ideally, the measurement process is subject to self-correction as investigators interact with participants to determine the most accurate representation of experience. It is a myth that interpretive theorists who are naïve and/or ignorant about the cultures with which they interact offer the most valuable insights. The more knowledgeable researchers are about relevant contexts, participants, and theoretical ideas, the more likely they are to find subsequent information for developing an even richer understanding of a social system.

Considering All the Evidence.   In addition to relying on information from case studies, ethnographies, and ethnologies, information from psychometric and developmental tools is welcomed, but scrutinized in interpretive research. The process of scrutiny differs, depending on which of several interpretive discourse communities an investigator chooses to join.

Conclusions in Interpretive Research

Interpretive analysis involves the generation of conclusions intended for particular purposes and investigators realize that findings collected for one set of agendas may or may not be useful for understanding another situation or set of constraints. The research process is invariably dialectical and the initial questions that were formulated at the beginning of a study may change as a result of the information acquired during an investigation. Conclusions may reveal the process itself or only the final outcomes of such deliberations. To determine if conclusions are supported by evidence, these investigators often rely on assumptions emerging from the interpretive research found in their discourse community.

TYPES OF INTERPRETIVE RESEARCH

Four different discourse communities that rely on ethnographic data will be introduced here: phenomenology, critical theory, interpretive analytics, and deconstructionism.[4] They rely on interpretive measurement, but apply different discourse rules to offer vastly different interpretations of the same events. Different research groups have been known to place themselves in competition, yet the conjunction of findings from all four traditions can yield an elaborate description of human functioning.

Phenomenology

Phenomenological discourse treats the object of study as a basis for generating constructs.[5] Grounded in field research and ethnographic methods, phenomenologists are likely to treat people as subjects and determine how they interpret objects under investigation. Participants offer information and investigators' interpret the resulting discourse to identify patterns in individuals' subjective experience. *First-order interpretation,* generated from participants, focuses on the phenomenon and *second-order interpretations,* generated by researchers, explain how individuals view the phenomenon under investigation. Investigators avoid designing coding schemes and categories a priori and identify participants' styles or strategies for making meaning out of an object of inquiry. In such work, levels of organization consist of *conversational floors* or perspectives that are necessary for interpreting an object. Investigators spend their time perceiving rather than judging how participants co-construct reality.

An Example of Comprehensive Phenomenology.   To understand what happened to individuals in the midst of social change, Robert Coles studied how children and their families coped with forced school desegregation in the South.[6] He explored how people relinquished old habits and took up new ones, focusing primarily on how individuals managed the stress and exertion of change. As a psychiatrist, Dr. Coles's work permeated the boundaries of medicine, psychiatry, anthropology, history, and political science. Taking a comprehensive approach, he noted the words, foods, stories, methods of worship, and social and economic systems of the South by comparing evidence from a number of regions around the United States. Dr. Coles found that local differences in history, geography, climate, language, and literature influenced the qualities of exploitation and pain that emerged among individuals and within communities once desegregation was introduced. Without placing too much emphasis on local variations in community responses, Dr. Coles looked at how variability in human functioning reflected differences in political and economic power. His study of resistance and acceptance became a study of fear and courage with so many layers that multiple books were necessary for summarizing and defending the emergent conclusions.

Walking a tightrope between being an impartial observer and an active participant, Dr. Coles collected many kinds of first-order evidence. For eight years he conversed with black and white children as well as the family members, teachers, and community members who supported or impeded the children's growth. Conversations occurred at home, in school, traveling between home and school, and at basketball games. They also occurred in restaurants, during demonstrations, in jails, in parks, and in offices. The nature and duration of each conversation differed considerably as some were interrupted by events and others could run their natural course. Some conversations were audiotaped whereas details from others were recorded as field notes or later impressions. In both obvious and discrete ways, Dr. Coles also observed carefully the behavior of individuals in different communities to support comparisons among people who faced different versions of a similar phenomenon.

Participants were asked to inform Dr. Coles about themselves and other people in the same social network who were experiencing similar changes. White children and teachers talked about the welfare of black children in school. Similarly, black children and their families discussed their observations of white children, teachers, and families. Everyone was asked to consider questions of their own self-regard, how the children were coping in school, how students viewed their teachers, and how teachers viewed the children. They also explored salient communal topics of the personal and collective understanding of skin color, getting along with individuals of other races, how mobs form, and the purposes served by protests. Some voices came across as shrill and resentful whereas others were passive sufferers or silent warriors for a hopeless cause.

Dr. Coles was trained as a psychiatrist and found the technique of asking individuals to represent their experiences using paint and crayons to be the most beneficial conversation starter. This allowed everyone to express fantasies and dreams as well as concrete depictions of everyday life. Listening carefully to the themes in each illustration and the resulting talk that was generated, sentiments were revealed about the nature of segregation and how people handle stress. Discovering no link between formal mental illness and rioters' reactions to desegregation, conclusions about how individuals respond to unusual amounts of stress were supported, and the inappropriateness of relying on clinical language to label individuals' responses became evident.

Slipping in and out of roles as passive observer or active participant, Dr. Coles fulfilled the responsibilities of doctor, psychiatrist, child development expert, and community member. He was able to accomplish these transitions with the cooperation of some community members and resistance from others. While changing roles, Dr. Coles remained committed to the belief that each individual has a unique destiny to fulfill and that most people meet life's plan relentlessly in an affirming and all-consuming manner. Becoming fully embedded in one community and visiting many others, Dr. Coles drew conclusions about how private lives were affected by world events.

The final products contain only fragments of the total quantity and style of first-order evidence. Dr. Coles identified second-order themes and used fragments to support his conclusions. Many interesting monologues and dialogues were left out of the final analyses, not because they lacked interest, but because they reflected individual agendas that were too far removed from the agendas evident in second-order interpretations. Choosing the best example of each set of ideas also invariably resulted in the elimination of other equally worthy conversations. In generating conclusions, Dr. Coles found ways to preserve the dignity of individuals while classifying drawings and interpretations, and still supported theoretical assumptions. Remaining careful not to claim too much about the accumulated evidence, Dr. Coles was able to offer vivid portraits of the internal struggles faced by individuals who were engrossed in social change.

Strengths of Phenomenology.   In *phenomenological research,* participants as well as researchers are included in validity conversations. Investigators derive secondary constructs from participants' analysis of daily events. They offer a liberal use of metaphor in conjunction with minimal reliance on argument to make their point. Openly acknowledging the role of institutions, investigators make explicit the details of interactions. They also see the importance of labeling rather than controlling for structural constraints in the measurement process. Put another way, phenomenologists avoid depending on preconceived measurement rules and place greater emphasis on lived experience than is common in developmental or psychometric approaches.

Limitations of Phenomenology.   One of the most noteworthy limitations in this line of work is its heavy reliance on the knowledge of participants. Investigators notice shortcomings in their conclusions if they ask themselves whether participants are sufficiently knowledgeable about events to offer cogent interpretations of particular objects. Nevertheless, failing to consider participants' analysis of their experience reveals an almost equally incomplete representation of the object under investigation. Conclusions may be more convincing if community members review second-order inferences as well as offer first-order evidence.

Critical Theory

In *critical theory,* investigators question the assumption phenomenologists make regarding the competence of participants as informants (Morrow & Brown, 1994). To draw conclusions, critical theorists use *first-order interpretation* to define an analytical framework rather than emergent patterns in respondents' beliefs and actions. *Second-order inferences* involve the application of the analytical framework to a phenomenon. Critical theorists assume that research is always constrained by the historical period in which it is generated. They challenge the belief that knowledge can be separated from the context in which it was generated; in any culture, the existing social order privileges only some human displays and those displays have context-specific meaning.[7] Existing power and subjective understanding determine the constructs incorporated into a theory and the presence or absence of perspectives can distort, bias, or oppress speakers as well as listeners within the discourse community.

Issues of communicative competence, externally generated evidence, and comprehensive representations of rationality are coordinated in the critical analysis of events (Habermas, 1990). Investigators and their participants use an analytical framework to co-construct consensus-based notions of local truths. They look for missing as well as salient ideas in their community and draw conclusions about possibilities as often as actualities. Critical theorists operate under the assumption that consensus in interpretations of everyday life can be attained if everyone strives to eliminate bias. Validity is established through critical discourse as researchers and participants label their assumptions and compare them against those of a more balanced framework. These investigators watch for distortions that are attributable to differences in power, interest, ideology, commitments, and values.

Accepting that everyone's perspectives are likely to contain error, these investigators reject rationalist notions that consensus can be achieved by adhering to common measurement practices. Instead, they look for normative and material constraints in critical discourse, striving to organize symmetrical conversations in which everyone is permitted to participate.

A Topical Example of Critical Theory.   In one example of critical theory, Dwight Boyd and Mary Louise Arnold (2000) explored teachers' beliefs about the aims of education and used those beliefs to construct an analytical framework. Next, Drs. Boyd and Arnold compared the resulting three ethical dimensions of the framework to assumptions embedded in education programs for teaching antiracism. In doing so, they generated conclusions about reasonable expectations for interventions.

More specifically, two groups of teachers articulated their most basic assumptions about the aims of education and their understanding of particular policy initiatives for addressing individual differences in race and ethnicity. The first-order evidence consisted of responses from a graduate seminar focusing on educational philosophy and policy, and from teachers' responses in formal interviews and surveys. The resulting three perspectives focused on personal well-being, social welfare, and relationships among social groups. Investigators then matched this triarchic framework to the beliefs embedded in programs for promoting antiracist education. Second-order inferences focus on the similarities and differences between these two sets of beliefs, pointing to areas in need of reconciliation.

Strength of Critical Theory.   Although they may select controversial topics, critical theorists avoid conflict-laden, competitive, or debatelike conversations, eschewing adversarial dialogues. They are highly sensitive to moral concerns with dominance and monopoly, and leave every aspect of a conversation open to moral scrutiny. Critical theorists identify who is free to initiate comments, challenge assertions, or question theoretical, metatheoretical, and meta-ethical frameworks. Conversations are valid when anyone may speak; researchers, observers (e.g., readers, reviewers), and participants are all free to offer their analysis of events and persons. Although critical theorists usually write abstract, philosophical papers, they may use situationally valid scores to generate conclusions. Their systematic analysis of persons in context involves a quest for patterns of rational social choice. Rather than situating discourse in an analysis of persons or settings, critical theorists embed their research operations in social theory, criticisms of societal expectations, and the imagination of social alternatives.

Limitations of Critical Theory.   A limitation of this type of analysis is the fact that conclusions are invariably embedded in historical contexts that may not be as enduring as critical theorists would like them to be. The highly abstract nature of second-order analysis can leave out details that might offer readers an opportunity to fully imagine authors' perspectives and evaluate their conclusions. Research papers can sometimes read like lists of propositions that lack support because writers tell readers their conclusions about first-order evidence rather than show them how the conclusions were derived. Meaning becomes less well-grounded the further readers are led away from the first-order discourse and, if the analysis becomes too far removed, it becomes difficult to follow.

Interpretive Analytics

Investigators working in the *interpretive analytic* tradition are primarily concerned with themes that seem to be missing in critical theory. Like others, these investigators also assume that forces of history and current power dynamics play an important role in human functioning (see, for example, Foucault, 1980a, 1980b). They are more likely than other interpretive theorists to assume that individuals cannot control the historical constraints they inherit because those constraints are part of an individual's very being, embedded in how they act, and central to any available social discourse or practices. Interpretive analysts are interested in describing why researchers and the persons they study use particular words, gestures, metaphors, analogies, models and other forms of communication when making statements, arguments, inferences, or other assertions about what they believe. *First-order interpretations* consist of observable entities and *second-order inferences* focus on the meaning of the identifiable indicants. There is causal language in this discourse community, and, like others who rely on interpretive methods, these investigators build causal networks by looking at how individuals make meaning out of their experience.

A Hypothesis-Testing Example of Interpretive Analytics.   In his *Manwatching Project,* Desmond Morris (1977) generated a range of hypotheses about commonalities in human behavior. He conducted cross-cultural investigations of everyday behavior to test these predictions, and document how individuals inherit historical constraints that become embedded in their actions and gestures. Dr. Morris documented how actions become gestures and how gestures transmit messages.

First-order interpretations contained the extensive recording of how humans are physically active, especially in situations where individuals are unaware of their actions. Behavior could be classified as inborn, discovered, absorbed, trained, or mixed in nature. Comparable gestures were also evident and classifiable across cultures. Second-order inferences were then generated to highlight just how postures and expressions tell their own story. Collections of unconscious actions and gestures, for example, were judged to offer signals to those who observe them. By assuming that people are animals who behave in predictable ways, Dr. Morris generated causal assertions about the social meaning of gestures and actions to draw conclusions about cross-cultural similarities in human functioning.

Strengths of Interpretive Analytics.   Rather than eliminate asymmetries or differences in how people are rewarded and indulged or penalized and deprived, interpretive analysts accept that differences are inevitable. They define power as involving more than questions of censorship, exclusion, blockage, and repression. When used effectively, power can produce improvements in everyone's knowledge, desires, and human comforts. Because everything is embedded in historical contexts, it is difficult to find the origin or authors of commonly accepted ideas. Interpretive analysis offers a kind of pessimistic activism in which discourse is assumed to be part of history and an artifact of current power distributions that reveals how individuals and institutional representatives choose to exercise their power.

This conservatism is also apparent in how interpretive analysts approach questions of validity. Like other interpretive theorists, these analysts assume it is impossible to achieve identity between indicants and constructs, but even the labeling of constructs is assumed to be dangerous. In this view, validity involves an exploration of the dangers posed by invented constructs. Analysts challenge claims regarding conceptual order or systematic answers to life's dilemmas. In this analytical perspective, all individuals are assumed to make ethical and political choices as they pass through each day, and those choices may or may not form clear patterns. Interpretive analysis also involves questions about which choices are hidden, how they became hidden, and why this absence was historically and politically necessary.

Limitations of Interpretive Analytics.   A major limitation of interpretive analytics is the propensity to encourage social reproduction. Investigators tend to conform to existing standards and discourse norms while finding methods for interpreting them. Beliefs in the deterministic qualities of history and power can lead to a natural reluctance to challenge the status quo. Interpretive analysts endeavor to understand society, not to change it.

Deconstructionism

Change agents may be most commonly found among investigators interested in *deconstructionism* because they believe there is no foundational place for starting or terminating the search for meaning.[8] These investigators assume that any logical foundation for theoretical positions is at best temporally valid. They see all ideas as embedded in those established at an earlier point in time, but the understanding of these ideas takes different forms as individuals and societies evolve. Meaning in text, for example, is apparent at many levels. Some ideas are clear on a literal reading of the text, but other ideas are peppered throughout in subtle traces that may be overlooked on first reading. Newly discussed ideas are likely to have been embedded in older texts, but ignored. The resulting concepts, constructs, and dimensions that emerge in discourse are assumed to be a reflection of how individuals view the world; they are not seen as tangible indicants that can correspond to things.

A Topical Example of Deconstructionism.   In her studies of classroom discourse, Courtney Cazden deconstructed the conversations taking place in a number of common educational settings.[9] Looking at how students talk with teachers and peers, Dr. Cazden drew more general inferences about how children consider the perspectives of their target audience.

More specifically, Dr. Cazden recorded and deconstructed the conversations between students and teachers during sharing time and teacher-directed lessons. She also explored differential treatment in how teachers talk to students and in how students respond to discourse. Similarly, Dr. Cazden compared discourse between children to explore obvious cognitive processes, and how context influences the quality of conversations. *First-order interpretations* consisted of a wide range of conversations that included student narratives, teacher responses, and dialogues between peers. *Second-order interpretations* focused on the purposes of talk, speaking rights, and cycles of consequences. Generalizations about how teachers use conversations to scaffold lessons for students or otherwise help students reconceptualize their existing knowledge followed from studies of student–teacher discourse. Conversations between peers were less hierarchical and resulted in inferences about how discourse builds relationships, serves an exploratory function, and is embedded in cultural contexts. Dr. Cazden focused on how discourse inevitably fosters changes within and between persons, but did not assert a stable foundation from which meaning-making was expected to evolve.

Strengths of Deconstructionism.   Members of a deconstructionist discourse community assume that there is no fixed, immutable grounding on which to begin building constructs. Meaning-making evolves from investigators' theories and observations. As time passes, different individuals add their evaluations, and a greater awareness of existing ideas becomes salient. Deconstructionists assume that categorical distinctions are inherently vague and may be contradictory. Validity involves the recognition of instability in current constructs and measurement techniques. Instability, in this view, is not caused by an investigator's viewpoint or methods. It emerges from the text, observations, or other material used as evidence because such material is constrained by language or other means of human communication.

Limitations of Deconstructionism.   One limitation of this approach, for anyone interested in social change, is the assumption that all constructs can be deconstructed. When deconstruction occurs, existing social problems are as likely to be reproduced as resolved. Change agents can also become lost in reductionistic detail to such an extent that they are unable to offer sufficient responses to existing dilemmas; the proverbial forest can become lost when focusing only on the trees. Validity remains intransigent because of the dynamic nature of meaning, populations, treatments, and confounding effects; no standard, unmediated version of the world exists for use in comparing observations and interpretations.

PURPOSES FOR INTERPRETIVE RESEARCH

It should be clear that each of these interpretive approaches offers a different perspective on human functioning, theory building, and the process of research. Nevertheless, they share a relatively common purpose of meaning-making. This is most apparent in how interpretive theorists consider behavior. Rather than treat behavior as a unidimensional construct, most investigators who engage in interpretive inquiry distinguish behavior from action and acts

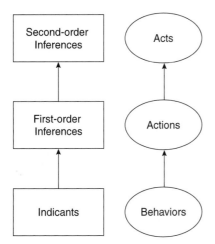

FIGURE 13.1   Theoretical and Measurement Levels of Interpretation

(Figure 13.1).[10] Using a narrower definition than might be used in psychometric or developmental research, interpretive theorists define *behavior* as emotional, physical, or mental indicants that can be recorded using research instruments. *Action* involves both the behavior and the meaning of that behavior to the agents, and *acts* are labeled by looking at the second-order inferences generated by investigators. Indicants of behavior may not be salient in research focusing on the relations between actions and acts.

Rule-Governed Interpretations

You may remember my earlier point that all forms of measurement involve some type of rule-governed logic. Interpretive researchers may use more general rules than psychometric or developmental researchers, but rules can still be identified. Five obvious rules are described in this chapter and others are generated in relation to the topic and style of inquiry.

Measuring the Dynamic Features of the World.   Interpretive theorists typically question the idea that behavioral uniformity may be used to support theoretical claims because such uniformity can be simply an illusion. Individuals may engage in unconscious, habitual behaviors that lack even first-order meaning, rendering any second-order interpretations fallacious. Furthermore, behavior is typically elicited in a dynamic system and that system is likely to lead individuals to offer different interpretations of their experience over time, across settings, and in different historical periods. Because different interpretations of the same behavior can occur in first or second-order analyses, the purposes for conducting interpretive research play an important role in what evidence is collected and how that evidence is used to support theoretical claims.

Challenging Assumptions.   Most commonly, investigators conduct interpretive research when they want to learn about the structure of particular events and step away from current or restrictive assumptions about the general character or overall distribution of events. Interpretive theorists may be solely interested in the perspectives of the agents in each event and in the meaning individuals make out of their experience. Such information can enable practitioners, for example, to better meet the needs of persons facing similar predicaments. Measurement techniques can also help caregivers discover how to glean information from individuals and settings in which they live.

Finding Contrasting Evidence.   Investigators also consider interpretive frameworks when they want to identify naturally occurring points of contrast in the world, assuming that differences as well as similarities can be highly informative. To determine how families in different cultural contexts meet the common needs of children, for example, ethnographic data can offer multiple perspectives on similar events. Drawing inferences about divergent meaning-making processes need not foster a slow progression toward homogeneity; the resulting information may simply help with more accurate explanations for particular circumstances.

Clarifying Dimensions of a Construct.   Interpretive theorists who work most closely with developmental and psychometric tools may also be interested in exploring causal relationships that are too unclear in experimental research to be explained by systematic means. Unable to rely only on current knowledge, these investigators may use ethnographic data to help them label common dimensions associated with particular concepts and constructs. In these cases, investigators may use ethnographic data to make predictions that would be tested in later experimental research. They could design more formal tools to align with noticeable dimensions and compare the resulting data with theoretical predictions.

Avoiding Reification.   Regardless of when investigators use interpretive techniques, they generally address issues of bias, dependability, credibility, and confirmability in measurement. The measurement concerns may hold different meaning, depending on the form of interpretive research being conducted. For this reason, many theorists are hesitant to offer measurement guidelines and caution new scholars against reifying such ideas when doing so.

MAKING CONNECTIONS

Find an ethnographic account of something in your area of interest. How did you know you found an ethnography? Why do you suppose the authors took an ethnographic approach to measurement? Which of the four interpretive positions did they seem to adopt when constructing a theoretical framework?

MINIMIZING BIAS

There are many dilemmas associated with minimizing bias. In interpretive measurement, investigators strive for accuracy when documenting first-order evidence, using techniques similar to those for creating balanced, representative, theoretically grounded tools for psychometric or developmental purposes. Acknowledging the inevitability of bias, investigators often begin interpretive research from one of two directions.[11] Taking an *emic* approach, they acknowledge their personal biases, but explore actual cultures and systems before constructing a theoretical framework. Taking an *etic* approach, investigators begin with a general framework and look for evidence to confirm and disconfirm aspects of that framework. When investigators discern how fieldwork influences their thinking, they may think of $etic_1$ as the framework constructed before collecting ethnographic data and $etic_2$ as the framework that emerges from the coordination of predictions and evidence.

Although strategies for beginning the measurement process may differ, definitions of valuable knowledge often remain the same. Labeling what one knows and corresponding assumptions about the target community is important for minimizing bias. The more aware investigators become of their own perspectives, the more easily they can disconfirm as well as confirm useful indicants. Over time and with experience, investigators learn that unintentional misunderstandings are a feature of interpretive research. Representations of the meaning, terms, or worldviews of another community may inevitably be distorted.

Nature of Bias

Bias is inevitable because interpretive research hinges on the awareness that not all individuals hold the same definitions of activities. Cultural variation is more likely for some kinds of activities than for others, but investigators can minimize bias only by learning how individuals communicate within a particular community. By becoming directly involved in the field, investigators discover community members' meaning-making enterprise.

When teaching a course on the characteristics of early adolescence, for example, I have asked students to coordinate information from existing normative research, media representations of adolescents, and lives in progress. If these future practitioners were to rely only on their personal memories of those years, they would not be able to understand, much less accurately represent, the diverse perspectives encountered over the course of the semester. Were I to ask these practitioners to elicit only self-reported views from actual teens, another kind of distortion would emerge because it would be difficult to situate those views within a more general context. Similarly, media representations offer distorted views intended to entertain as well as inform, and normative research involves only the analysis of group norms. The coordination of multiple forms of evidence, albeit only some that reflects local knowledge, seems to help most course members come away with a rich sense of the varied perspectives they are likely to encounter and a method for exploring those perspectives over time.

Ethnographers conduct similar investigations for research purposes, paying close attention to the nature of personal and collective bias in each source of information. They also document indicants of their first-order interpretations and generate second-order interpretations that may be useful to people in other contexts.

Addressing Bias

Bias is evaluated as investigators define where a particular ethnography is situated in time and place. They label the focal points of each set of observations, how often particular events occur, and disconfirming evidence. Investigators also avoid forming premature conclusions or collecting only evidence that confirms their conclusions. They balance the consideration of recurring and rare events, labeling the two rather than eliminating one or another.

Investigator Bias.   Researchers have conducted studies to explore how observer bias and informant reactivity can be endemic to any ethnography (see Johnson & Bolstad, 1973, for a review of such studies). Observers have created distortion by offering informants subtle information about how they should behave through gestures, speech, or the timing of observations. Informants may be conscious or unconscious of these subtle messages, but alter their behavior and conform to implicit expectations. Investigators ask participants to interpret their experiences, in part, to reveal reactivity effects and allow self-correcting participant-observation mechanisms to call attention to these perceptions. If both parties remain committed to generating accurate first-order evidence, labeling agreements or disagreements become possible.

Participant Bias.   Despite the best intentions, participant biases are also possible. Participants may simply respond to a set of uncharacteristic demands introduced by investigators. They may also offer habitual, preformed response sets or fake changes in behavior over time. Some studies, in which investigators look for improvement, may contain subtle pressure to show positive change, give desired responses, or pretend rather than behave naturally.

Detecting Bias.   Investigators who conducted reactivity studies asked four questions that are helpful for all interpretive theorists to consider. Even if the answers and their implications differ across discourse communities, it is helpful to ask:

- How conspicuous is the observer in the setting?
- Are there individual differences in participants' tendency to react to situational constraints?
- Do observers' personal attributes have an effect on participants' responses?
- What are participants' assumptions about the purposes of the investigation?

Improving Social Exchanges.   Many forms of bias can be alleviated by generating socially sensitive devices for facilitating communication. Ethnographers consider methods of helping participants find the project rewarding, constraining personal costs, and building trust. Table 13.1 outlines common practices for facilitating such exchanges, although the cultural context for interactions is central to the effectiveness of these devices.

Misconceptions

Two common misconceptions can lead investigators astray when conducting strong ethnographies. One common misconception is that investigators must somehow like or be like the participants in their research. Experienced ethnographers challenge this assumption, even claiming that valid research cannot be conducted if investigators identify too closely

TABLE 13.1   Devices for Facilitating Social Exchange

REWARDS FOR PARTICIPANTS	COSTS TO PARTICIPANTS	TRUST ENHANCERS
Convey positive regard	Minimize feelings of subordination	Thank participants before beginning
Thank participants	Avoid embarrassment	Find credible sponsorship for research
Ask for advice	Avoid inconvenience	
Support group values	Make tasks seem easy	Choose important tasks
Ask interesting questions	Make time commitment seem short	Maximize clarity in the exchange
Offer social validation	Minimize requests for personal information	Set reasonable boundaries for the project
Convey privileged status		
Offer tangible rewards	Make requests parallel to other familiar tasks	

with their participants. The study of how cultural norms, ideologies, and pressures constrain human functioning hinges on intensive involvement in local settings and would not be informative if investigators considered only impersonal, contrived, simplified, or decontextualized evidence. Investigators might work closely with local informants who can facilitate an elaborate understanding of a research site, but they are obligated to retain a mixture of detachment and involvement in such settings (see, for example, Huberman & Miles, 1985).

A second misconception is that bias is always problematic. When investigators compare human functioning to an externally generated standard, tools that are not calibrated against the standard introduce problematic forms of measurement error. In contrast, investigators who identify idiosyncratic forms of meaning-making may find it necessary to openly accept and discuss the nature of investigator, informant, and interpretive biases. Comparing the three levels of information can enhance communication by revealing commonalities and differences in the meaning-making enterprise.

Respectable Bias

Investigators use measurement tools to facilitate an understanding of initial social settings and establish rapport while maintaining a critical stance. They try to maximize accuracy when collecting first-order data before beginning second-order interpretations. Working with people who can help them reflect on the determinants of events, interpretive theorists may selectively choose events that offer the best means of testing assumptions. They highlight how knowledge is contaminated by issues of power and ideology, and modify their research practices to reveal these issues while fulfilling situational expectations.

Investigators compromise the integrity of their work if they cannot offer critical analysis of the perspectives they explore. Therefore, they sometimes instigate contradictory challenges to determine the consistency of emerging patterns. When bracketing segments of time, for example, most investigators are careful to acknowledge the limitations of their observations, but find bracketing helpful for facilitating comparisons. Ethnographers remain self-conscious about biases in their data, realizing that all methods, even when used appropriately, will yield some level of interpretive disagreement.

MAKING CONNECTIONS

Imagine how you might conduct ethnographic research in your field. What assumptions would you make about the culture you are investigating? What steps would you take to ensure that you did not offer a biased account? How would you disconfirm your assumptions?

DEPENDABILITY AND CREDIBILITY

Dependability and credibility are central features of second-order analysis in which investigators draw inferences about patterns in the participant-observation process. Most investigators learn to expect diversity in perspectives and search for uniformity in the meaning-making enterprise. They write accounts of immediate experience with an integrity that involves formal and informal reasoning. To preserve integrity, investigators and participants label patterns without falling into an infinite regress of idiosyncrasies associated with a constant questioning of assumptions or one another's evaluations.

Because investigators become the primary measurement instrument, their dependability and credibility are central to the calibration and standardization process. They and those with whom they communicate evaluate the quality of their relationships with participants and the credibility of any observations and analyses. While collecting first-order evidence, most investigators record the perspectives of their informants as they are habitually expressed. They represent this evidence as coherent responses to life events while minimizing distortion in the recording process. The dependability and credibility of second-order evidence involves a stepping back process in which investigators explore particular hunches, constructs, propositions, questions, or relationships that seem to be apparent in first-order events (Huberman & Miles, 1985). These processes are likely to be concurrent as investigators analyze *while* they investigate.

Dependability

While translating emic evidence for use in etic studies, researchers often vacillate between trusting and mistrusting their informants and benefit from remaining dependable during this process. Investigators and participants question one another's judgments and observations to disconfirm assumptions. Informants become *partners* when investigators are confirming evidence, but *suspects* during the disconfirmation process.

Investigators also question their own judgments at some points and accept them at others. Investigators and participants may not assume deception or dismiss one another, but together they can explore how different perspectives seem to be coordinated. Each perspective is operationalized so that investigators can later construct causal claims using evidence grounded in first-order experiences.

Establishing Dependability.   In establishing dependability, most investigators endeavor to maintain a mutually beneficial relationship with their informants. They openly discuss issues as they arise, listening for missing perspectives as well as those immediately apparent. Ethnographers often recognize that the representativeness of observed behavior in comparison to unobserved behavior may be faulty because participants react to observers as often as the reverse. Three devices are helpful in facilitating richer levels of communication in first-order contexts. Investigators can look for similar events across time, compare different degrees of obtrusiveness in researcher–participant interactions, and label similar events in different contexts.

Credibility

Credibility involves the strength with which second-order inferences are defended. As is common when psychometricians compare reliability and validity, there is a symbiotic relationship between dependability and credibility. When data lack dependability, credibility is absent, but dependability alone is also insufficient for building a convincing story. Techniques for enhancing dependability also enhance the credibility of inferences made at the second-order level because they help investigators determine how common or rare particular events and reactions can be.

Enhancing Credibility.   Investigators enhance credibility by verifying the match between participants' interpretations of events and other accounts of how behaviors and institutions are understood. This verification is not simply a matter of honesty in representing ideas that emerge in a conversation; the meaning of terms, events, persons, and institutional norms are dynamic and can be critiqued in this phase of analysis. Some differences in the convergence across data sources will invariably result in a revision of the accounting of events, but other differences in interpretation will be intractable. Reconciliation need not occur, but investigators learn how to incorporate different perspectives in their writing to offer the most truthful account of events and perceptions.

Grounded Interpretations

The research process itself as well as the interpretation of events invariably involves reinterpretations and reconstruction of an evolving story. For this reason, it is important to keep careful track of evidence used to ground interpretations. Credibility is not undermined by such revisions if investigators establish dependable levels of rapport and permit self-correction processes to unfold over the course of a study.

Many investigators place a premium on knowledge acquired through participant-observation, but each community member need not have complete knowledge of all emerging models or be able to articulate a comprehensive evaluation.[12] Investigators who offer critical analysis or deconstruct first-order evidence often assume that participants will not be able to see broader societal implications and that it is the researchers' job to do so.

It might be interesting to know why, for example, parents, teachers, and children sometimes offer three different recollections of the same event. Reconciliation of these differences might be necessary for determining a course of action, but irrelevant when investigators want to explore issues of power, development, or historical perspectives. Drawing associations between first-order representations of each perspective and second-order interpretations to explore relations among these persons could be less insightful if investigators recorded only those dimensions along which everyone agreed. Grounding claims about similarities and differences in direct quotes or examples from first-order interpretations offers strength to more general claims about the interaction.

Verifying Dependability and Credibility

Regardless of a point of entry, accounts are dependable if everyone involved agrees on the events that transpired and can offer his or her evaluation of those events. The analysis is credible if implicit or explicit levels of meaning are gradually discerned in connections among apparent dimensions. For findings to be both dependable and credible, inferences are ideally grounded in evidence.[13]

MAKING CONNECTIONS

Imagine the process of conducting ethnographic research. What would you do to maximize the dependability of your evidence? What procedures will you use to establish rapport and maintain comfortable levels of communication with participants? How will you evaluate second-order inferences for credibility? How would these measurement practices change if you asked a completely different research question?

CONFIRMABILITY

Regardless of whether investigators are interested in direct interpretation, criticism, or deconstruction, there are no superior methods for validating interpretive techniques. Validity in interpretive research is not inherent in measurement techniques or research designs. Community members and their experiences impose validity conditions, and valid knowledge is the accurate description of such experiences. There are disputes about the foundation of new knowledge, but investigators often obtain valid first-order knowledge using the language of description. If they collect information with perceptiveness and imagination, that knowledge is available for second-order critique and later theorizing. At best, investigators build a strong argument that seems plausible to those reading it and offers an accurate representation of the more tangible forms of evidence brought to bear on the problem.

Balancing Internal and External Validity

In developmental and psychometric measurement, investigators evaluate the internal validity of a study by asking if causality can be inferred and labeling the directions of such causality. They also determine if findings can be generalized across types of persons, settings, and times, looking for those situations in which conclusions are seen as reasonable, warranted, or plausible. In interpretive research, investigators move beyond matching indicants to theoretical constructs and exploring relations among constructs. They assume that ideology and normative assumptions about power are central to how indicants are interpreted in different contexts. Many interpretive theorists eschew all claims about the external validity of a study and focus more intently on internal validity. These investigators are self-conscious about their role as interpreters and limit claims about how "most people" function or global assertions about how acts are elicited.

Interpretive theorists may explore movement from past to present in ways that prohibit simple diagrams of their results. New forms of privilege would be created if researchers decided on the nature of instability and structures of communal boundaries. Because interpretive theorists try to reveal the logic of their evaluations, valid measurement is typically inferred in written accounts.

Levels of the Validation Process

Validity in interpretive research is not established using a standard set of methods, but investigators can differentiate five levels of validity.[14] Investigators often explore *descriptive, interpretive,* and *theoretical* validity. They also evaluate the *generalizability* of their studies and consider *evaluative* validity.

Many of these levels have parallel concepts in psychometric research. Although they take a somewhat different form, descriptive and interpretive validity show parallels to content and criterion validity explored for psychometric research. Theoretical validity is explored in the same way for both kinds of tools. Generalizability and evaluative validity are not commonly associated with psychometric measurement, but emerge when evaluating most research designs. These latter two levels of validity are important to interpretive measurement because they offer information related to the self-correcting calibration of first-order interpretations.

Descriptive Validity. In interpretive research, *descriptive validity* is defined as the factual accuracy of the account. As is the case when establishing content validity for a standardized tool, investigators look for evidence that data are not fabricated or distorted and that indicants offer a representative account of the constructs or phenomena under investigation.

In interpretive research, verification can involve *etic* or *emic* approaches to theory building, but differs for first-order and second-order levels of inference. For *first-order data,* investigators determine if behavior is adequately recorded and minimize inferences about actions. *Second-order analysis* involves the coordination of indicants that can be directly observed or inferred from looking at other collections of indicants.

Ordinarily, descriptive validity involves representing experience as literally as possible. For example, looking at whether indicants of an interview reflect the full range of ideas would be considered a form of descriptive validity. Inferences involve verifying representations of how events are sampled, the dimensions of a construct, or the typicality of a particular set of indicants.

Interpretive Validity. *Interpretive validity* is unique to this type of research, but might be seen as parallel to criterion validity. It involves participants' analysis of the meaning of their experiences and can reflect second-order interpretations. Most investigators adopt an *emic* approach, assuming they cannot know how participants perceive and evaluate their world. Indicants take the form of participants' language and their conscious or unconscious gestures, speech, or reactions. To evaluate the relationship between *first-order and second-order inferences,* investigators typically design criteria for verifying participants' accounts and comparing those accounts with other forms of available evidence. Participants' *second-order inferences* are assumed to be part of measurement and those inferences could later be used in a third *theory-building phase.*

Threats to interpretive validity are difficult to identify from simply looking at the indicants in a data set. Investigators usually rely on information from other types of data to confirm their inferences. In Dr. Coles's research, for example, he asked black and white children to report on one another as well as themselves. Everyone's judgment was subject to scrutiny by other participants and this was continued for many years. Later, in writing three books about the moral, spiritual, and political lives of these children, Dr. Coles added a third, theory-building layer to these interpretations.

Theoretical Validity. Investigators typically look beyond the concrete representations of data when evaluating *theoretical validity.* They label the features of their theoretical framework and explore how available interpretations correspond to theoretical assumptions. As is common in developmental measurement, investigators coordinate information about structure and function while offering explanations for these relationships. Interpretive theorists often establish dimensions, constructs, and concepts, although these levels of analysis might be called something different. Relations among constructs may also be labeled in ways that correspond to psychometric assumptions about internal or causal validity. Interpretive theorists often draw inferences that are more remote from first-order experience than is the case for exploring descriptive or interpretive validity, yet the logic is often difficult to distinguish from that used in earlier phases of a study.

Theoretical validity is sometimes thought of as a form of critical validity because it is here that the different interpretive research questions diverge. When investigators are adopting a comprehensive approach, they commonly construct thick descriptions of particular cultures or contexts and align events with a framework for organizing the narrative. When a topical approach is used, investigators defend the dimensions and constructs that comprise key concepts. When hypothesis-testing approaches are used, investigators draw associations between the predictions tested and their placement in a more general theoretical framework. These levels of interpretation will also differ for phenomenological, critical theoretical, interpretive analytic, or deconstructionist research.

Generalizability. After establishing theoretical validity, interpretive theorists are ready to explore *generalizability.* Some theorists skip this level, assuming that only theoretical relations within a study can be supported. More commonly, they ask whether conclusions from one account can be extended to the interpretation of other populations, settings, or points in time. Interpretive theorists may determine if a theory is useful for showing how the same processes in different situations can lead to different outcomes or consequences. They may also highlight how different processes and contexts can elicit the same outcomes or consequences.

Generalizability involves questions of sampling, representativeness, and generalizability that are similar to those found with developmental and psychometric techniques. In interpretive research, however, investigators accept that sampling is purposeful rather than random. Interpretive theorists endeavor to understand variation in the objects of interest and test ideas about relations of environmental pressures and human functioning. They often control the sampling of events, persons, and time periods to permit explicit comparisons in how particular phenomena influence actions. Rather than reflect probabilities of future occurrence, generalizations are invariably laden with contextual detail.

Like psychometricians who explore internal or statistical conclusion validity, interpretive theorists consider whether findings from one set of persons, settings, or time periods can be generalized to other situations or persons within a community, group, or institution. Parallel to evaluations of external validity, interpretive theorists also consider whether findings can be generalized to persons and situations in other communities. Whereas psychometricians place a premium on external validity, interpretive theorists find internal validity to be crucial and external validity superfluous. Knowing how well a particular community or culture is represented is more important in interpretive research than knowing how similar one community is to another.

The emphasis placed on generalizability differs, depending on what kinds of interpretive research investigators are conducting. Phenomenologists, for example, are likely to be most interested in how converging evidence from multiple persons, settings, or time periods offers consistent knowledge about the same phenomena. Investigators interested in critical theory, interpretive analytics, or deconstructionism may seek only enough generalizability to permit reasonable support for more abstract conclusions.

Evaluative Validity.   Theorists who focus primarily on second- or third-order inferences are most likely to be concerned with *evaluative validity* or the degree to which an evaluative framework can be applied to particular objects. They look for evidence that critical generalizations made about a phenomenon are sufficiently grounded in first-order evidence and that the evaluation of evidence is coherent.

Thinking again about the antiracist programs, Drs. Boyd and Arnold used criteria generated from participants to build a framework for evaluating existing programs. If participants were unaware of the topic of inquiry, their answers might not have offered a sufficiently valid framework for the later evaluations. To use the results of such interviews to then critique the comprehensiveness of moral development programs could lead to oversights or exaggerated claims about the significance of findings. Investigators often try to avoid such shortcomings by comparing each framework to evaluative standards before proceeding to other analytical steps.

Evaluative validity is not necessarily central to the work of investigators who rely on psychometric and developmental research traditions, but is essential for determining the validity of abstract criticisms regarding power and ideology in human and societal functioning. To offer fair and balanced critiques of general phenomena, social structures, or personal habits, most interpretive theorists evaluate the qualities of their informants, and of the second-order inferences generated from their data. They typically do not rely on random samples of participants or predetermined definitions of constructs and concepts to calibrate, standardize, or validate their measurements.

Confirmation Processes

Interpretive theorists ask a wide range of questions when confirming their conclusions. Like developmentalists, they distinguish *structural differences,* the underlying representations of experience, from *presentation differences,* or how information is conveyed, shared, and recorded. Sometimes this analysis involves comparing first-order evidence and second-order analysis to determine if there are disputes in how accurately the descriptive information is represented. More often, the second-order analyses of findings are contentious. Interpretive theorists use a number of different techniques for confirming their conclusions, using first-order interpretations.

Label Key Ideas Systematically.   A concrete device for confirming conclusions is to use different methods of highlighting ideas in a narrative. By choosing different colors for moral and political themes in conversations about desegregation, for example, investigators might find patterns across conversations that would otherwise remain undetected.[15]

This method is not foolproof. In some cases, investigators may label points of disagreement in a narrative that later serve as confirming evidence for another set of unnoticed patterns. Precision in structural accounts can illuminate potentially conflicting views. Reconciliation is possible when central findings are sufficiently grounded in first-order evidence to support general claims. Additional themes may also exist in the remaining text, but become apparent only after central themes are labeled. Concrete highlighting can also allow investigators to discuss emerging themes with persons in different situations, contexts, and cultures.

Compare Descriptions with Events.   Interpretive theorists commonly confirm the match between descriptive information and particular events. They may determine if their analysis offers information that is continuous with ordinary life and whether inferences correspond with existing knowledge of others in the community. This may involve the comparison of different narrative accounts of everyday events generated to establish interpretive validity, or the search for common structural patterns in first-order data at the descriptive phase. If there is a marked difference between structural or interpretive claims and those evident in the descriptive information, investigators explore the nature of those discrepancies to determine if these are theoretically useful, or if they reflect incomplete fieldwork or inaccurate interpretations.

Critique Researchers' Performance.   Because interpretive theorists are a factor in every inquiry, their personal characteristics are considered in the confirmation phase of an investigation. Often characterized as the measurement instrument, these researchers ask if the same findings would be apparent for different investigators. They also determine if investigators' age, gender, race, or talents influenced the accessibility of information. When such differences are apparent, interpretive theorists take note rather than disregard these descriptions. Whereas an observer is expected to be impartial in some forms of research, interpretive research incorporates the characteristics and careful analysis of this role in theoretical and practical accounts.

Evaluate Interpersonal Relationships.   Interpretive research could not be completed without a high degree of trust and confidence between participants and observers, and that invariably involves a degree of partiality. Partiality is usually incorporated into second-order analyses, where investigators and community members reveal their personal perspectives, offering a narrative accounting of the ongoing relationship and how well issues of trust and confidence were maintained. In that accounting, investigators consider patterns in the roles played by each agent and various status differentials. They consider individual rights and duties, the differential command of resources, how values are transmitted, and other environmental constraints. This type of narrative serves to locate situations in time and space, and assists investigators in finding a center of gravity for more elaborate forms of analysis.

Evaluate Persuasiveness.   Most investigators working in the interpretive traditions realize that the definition of persuasive research differs along three dimensions. They see differences attributable to investigator's theoretical discourse community, the community in which an investigator lives, and the communities with which investigators strive to communicate. Too much or too little information about each level can undermine the believability of an account.

Investigators' contributions to a research community hinge on their standing in relation to a nonhuman notion of reality. Persuasiveness is inevitably affected by the amount of first-order material, which, in turn, is constrained by the selection of measurement techniques. Nevertheless, the primary theoretical material to be considered emerges in the form of second-order discourse. Most interpretive theorists assume that any attempt to describe objectivity invariably results in a description of communal rather than personal norms.

MAKING CONNECTIONS

Imagine procedures for confirming evidence in an ethnographic study. Which of the five validity questions would be most central to achieving your goals? How would the different validity concerns change in meaning if you tried to do phenomenology, critical theory, interpretive analysis, or deconstructionist work?

PURPOSES FOR INTERPRETIVE MEASUREMENT

Investigators conduct interpretive studies when they want to offer a thick description of events and cultures or to fully understand how individuals function within a particular community. Most comprehensive approaches are eventually subdivided into topically oriented or hypothesis oriented inquiries as investigators learn more about their own questions and/or the complexity of cultures under investigation. Second-order interpretations and theory building involve processes that differ, depending on researchers' chosen discourse community. This choice leads investigators to raise different questions about bias, dependability, credibility, and the confirmation of conclusions. Most interpretive theorists coordinate information about beliefs and commitments, explicit ideologies, tacit world-views, linguistic and cultural systems, and politics and economics. They also explore the distribution of power apparent in first-order evidence and second-order interpretations to place cultural and communal norms in high relief.

SUGGESTED READINGS

Agar, M. (1980). *The professional stranger: An informal introduction to ethnography.* New York: Academic Press.

Bruner, J. (1990). *Acts of meaning.* Cambridge, MA: Harvard University Press.

Carspecken, P. F., & Walford, G. (Eds.). (2001). *Critical ethnography and education.* New York: JAI Press.

Creswell, J. W. (1998). *Qualitative inquiry and research design: Choosing among five traditions.* Thousand Oaks: Sage.

Denzin, N. K., & Lincoln, Y. S. (Eds.). (2003b). *The landscape of qualitative research: Theories and issues* (2nd ed.). Thousand Oaks, CA: Sage.

Geertz, C. (1973). *The interpretation of cultures.* New York: Basic Books.

Geertz, C. (1983). *Local knowledge: Further essays in interpretive anthropology.* New York: Basic Books.

Glaser, B. G., & Strauss, A. L. (1967). *The discovery of grounded theory: Strategies for qualitative research.* New York: Aldine De Gruyter.

Howell, M., & Prevenier, W. (2001). *From reliable sources: An introduction to historical methods.* Ithaca, NY: Cornell University Press.

ENDNOTES

1. Cherryholmes (1988) offers a rich contrast between the nomothetic assumptions of Cronbach & Meehl (1955) and those of interpretive researchers. Those contrasts are only briefly summarized here.

2. Hymes (1982) reports on the findings of a commissioned report by the National Institute of Education in which he outlines some of the points raised here.

3. Cronbach & Meehl (1955) offered the groundbreaking claims, and this has been expanded, critiqued, and revised over time.

4. The definitions used here were obtained from Cherryholmes (1988). Creswell (1998) places ethnography as a fifth category of interpretive research, but does not offer sufficient insight into obtaining evidence from the other four traditions. On careful scrutiny, it seems as though ethnographic measurement techniques are used by all these researchers, but they use the techniques to obtain very different kinds of evidence. I see Geertz's (1973, 1983) analysis of interpretive research as supportive of the measurement assertions I make here.

5. Husserl (1931) is often credited with founding this movement.

6. These methods were extracted from Coles (2003), originally published in 1964.

7. McDermott & Hood (1982) offer a critical evaluation of schooling using this approach.

8. Derrida (1982) is the founding philosopher, and Culler (1984) and Norris (1982) have offered suggestions on measurement and methods.

9. Cazden (1988) offers an early version of what became a more elaborate area of inquiry.

10. Bruner (1990) highlights the importance of such distinctions. Erickson (1986) offers a detailed account of how educators make distinctions between behavior and actions, but many critics of behaviorism offer similar definitions.

11. Pike (1965) outlines the definitions I have used here although this language is widely available.

12. Hymes (1982) introduces this idea, but Johnson & Bolstad (1973) offer several examples of how these concerns are salient in naturalistic observation studies.

13. Glaser & Strauss (1967) offer the most comprehensive description of this process.

14. Maxwell (1992) offers this structure to the exploration of validity. There are many others currently available, but this one helps readers imagine each phase of the analysis in a highly elaborate sense.

15. Computer programs like *Atlas-ti* offer a means of keeping track of these, but concrete examples are used here for clarity.

CHAPTER FOURTEEN

MEASURING CYCLES OF A LIFE'S COURSE

To fully understand the structural cycles of a person's life, some investigators measure the idiosyncrasies of particular individuals. Measuring development reveals general trends in the lives of many individuals, and allows investigators to determine if life cycles show discontinuity, no growth, or a progression toward greater levels of unity and wisdom. Identifying common personality structures, attitudes, and abilities facilitates the establishment of norms or standards to which individuals can be compared. These findings help researchers determine if cycles are triggered by events or if they are age-related. Missing from these approaches are the details of cycles within a particular life, whether particular individuals show greater coherence even if general trends do not, or if coherence is apparent only in general structures. Bearing in mind the advantages of comparing individuals' performance to a standard or to that of other individuals, it can also be beneficial to understand the unique ways in which a person's life takes shape and unfolds over time. The richest understanding of an individual's life includes information gleaned from psychometric, developmental, and interpretive techniques because each addresses a different set of measurement dilemmas.

STUDYING LIVES IN PROGRESS

Adding to the information previously introduced, this chapter emphasizes interpretive approaches to measuring life cycles, with one caveat. To help readers distinguish issues of identity from other structural approaches to personality, four methods (nomothetic, idiographic, idiothetic, and interpretive) are contrasted here, with the understanding that they serve different theoretical purposes. This comparison illustrates why investigators often assume that life structures may evolve even when personality does not. Three central questions for studying life cycles are parallel to interpretive theorists' interest in individual, interpersonal, and transpersonal levels of organization (Levinson, Darrow, Klein, Levinson, & McKee, 1978).

- How do individuals understand their identities and concepts of self?
- How does a person participate in the larger world?
- What are the components of an individual's sociocultural world?

Purposes for Exploring Individual Lives

As with all research, the historical times in which we live play a central role in the value placed on particular topics and approaches.[1] Investigators' imaginations are juxtaposed with salient dilemmas in particular contexts to raise and address key concepts that can facilitate solutions to real-world problems. Questions about individual lives have emerged and waned along with everything else. The lives of saints and moral exemplars have been studied to determine how they balance life's challenges with commitments to moral principles. The life cycles of tyrannical rulers have been explored to imagine why and how they came to be so evil. Experiences of victims have been mined for secrets that might explain their courage and resilience in the face of harm. And, the lives of individuals who are representative of a family, era, or specific set of circumstances are explored to offer a richer sense of how individuals function in a particular time and place.

Lives are also studied because they are of theoretical interest. Thick descriptions of how someone interacts with others have been used to explore the structure of discourse and general conventions associated with communication.[2] Multiple case studies have been compared to determine the structure of social networks, cultural norms, constraints, and the unfolding of events in time.[3] Conclusions about the benefits and harm of particular social institutions have been generated from looking at the effects of organizational structures on the lives of particular individuals (Cosslett, Lury, & Summerfield, 2000). In some of these projects, individuals' lives are intrinsically interesting in their own right, whereas in others they are a means to the end of drawing more elaborate generalizations.

Dimensions of a Life Course

A life course has many dimensions. At the individual level, investigators tend to focus primarily on issues of *identity.* An interpersonal level focuses heavily on information from *case studies* or the insights of *discourse analysis.* Transpersonal interpretations are commonly associated with research on *framing* and *sociopolitical implications* of how individuals are situated within a culture. As with most interpretive work, investigators typically rely on text that records actions, beliefs, and knowledge about someone's functioning, yet the means of generating text differ, depending on the interpretations individuals hope to make.

MAKING CONNECTIONS

How often do you see the study of lives in progress? What kinds of people have been included in such studies? Are target individuals representative of a group? Are they pivotal leaders or information carriers for a set of events? Do they offer negative or extreme examples of human functioning? What kinds of information have been gleaned from such research?

MEASURING IDENTITY

Generally speaking, *identity* reflects how individuals define themselves and affects how they approach particular tasks. Asking individuals for a straightforward autobiographical account of their life is a direct means of discerning their sense of identity. Investigators can also ask respondents to complete standardized tasks, engage in interviews, participate in focus groups, or complete surveys. Identity theorists may extract beliefs and reactions to questions about the self-system, or ask for responses to hypothetical events. To clarify how individuals can look at identity from a range of perspectives, let's briefly compare *nomothetic, idiographic, idiothetic,* and *interpretive* goals for exploring personality.

Nomothetic Approaches

As you may remember, *nomothetic* measurement coordinates indicants of *surface traits* to draw inferences about *source traits* (see Chapter 5). Theorists who rely on this theoretical approach identify general processes through which personalities emerge, change, and function over time. Relying on deductive logic, respondents typically answer questions posed by researchers rather than questions they might otherwise pose to themselves. Stability is an important feature of nomothetic measurement because investigators are looking for source traits that will endure across situations, over time, and across persons.

Limitations. The purpose of nomothetic theories is to draw conclusions about the general structure of personality. Investigators are not particularly interested in describing the functioning of one person or in documenting the cycles of a life. Individual differences in the structure of personality are assumed to reflect measurement error. Nevertheless, researchers can use tools designed for such structural evaluations to add detail to representations of a particular life cycle. Normative tools facilitate evaluations of how an individual's traits compare with those commonly found for populations of which the target person is a member.

Idiographic Approaches

Idiographic research involves a quest for *source states* that are conceptually similar, but theoretically distinct from source traits. As components of a dynamic drive, source states are factors that account for a variety of mood fluctuations. States like fatigue, exhilaration, depression, and contentment are highly correlated with general motivational drives as well as more specific emotional fluctuations, all of which could be measured.

Surface states are the concrete representations of thoughts, emotions, and actions from which investigators draw inferences about more general source states. Surface states are typically represented by clusters of indicants within a measure whereas source states encompass the entire factor structure. Surface states, in other words, are combinations of indicants used to reflect the dimensions of a source state. With evidence from surface states, inferences about source states are consolidated in theories of how drives or volition influence behavior.

Structure of States. As is the case for traits, states may be unidimensional or multidimensional and investigators try to identify the structure of how dimensions are associated. Traits may gradually shift over time, but states reflect significantly higher and lower *magnitudes of change.* Profiles of states change *in direct response to external stimuli,* and, when averaged over time, are likely to result in a flat distribution. Profiles of traits, in contrast, show fairly stable variation across time. As is the case for traits, a state is valid when there is factorial unity across indicants of each dimension.

Despite their dynamic qualities, simply finding variation in item functioning over time is insufficient for verifying the existence of states. To identify the structure of a state, investigators commonly ask if states form opposite poles of the same continuum or represent distinct entities, under what conditions states are activated, and how states are induced and manipulated.

Detecting States.   Investigators identify states by exploring *state-response patterns* or sets of reactions and behaviors that contain multiple dimensions arising from a single internal response. Generally, methods of experimentation and calculation facilitate the recognition and isolation of such response patterns. To begin the recognition process, investigators look for repeated patterns in the indicants used to represent a concept. Next, they verify whether responses are replicable psychophysiological processes by identifying *stimuli* within a given culture that *trigger the state*. Researchers typically label the *origin of psychological activation* and *valence* apparent in different situations and conditions. Knowing the triggers or points of activation and the intensity of valence offers secondary information about the features of a state. Distinctions between stable and malleable features of personality are facilitated by comparing information about (1) the modulating stimuli for a given state, (2) process successions in indicants of the state, and (3) knowledge of related traits.

Limitations.   Research on general states offers somewhat limited information on a person's identity. As is the case for nomothetic research, investigators are primarily interested in the structure and functioning of states across people. They typically do not make elaborate inferences about development or about how states function within one person. Investigators may use tools for measuring states as a stimulus for more elaborate conversations on respondents' awareness of their states and how states affect daily functioning.

Idiothetic Approaches

Some theorists have disagreed with the separation of nomothetic and idiographic theoretical assumptions. They advocate an *idiothetic* approach to personality theory in which nomothetic and idiographic concerns are synthesized in the study of a person's ontogeny.[4] Idiothetic research emerged from a respect for uniqueness and individuality such that individual differences are accommodated without making those differences the object of inquiry. Investigators have measured surface states and traits to draw inferences about how source traits and states are coordinated across individuals. The assumption in this work is that traits influence individuals' interpretation of events to such a degree that external stimuli alone cannot elicit a state. Investigators document response patterns induced by external stimuli and more enduring features of how individuals imagine the world. Personality structures, in this view, reflect a synthesis of states and traits, all of which are features of someone's ontogeny.

The Unpredictable Coordination of States and Traits.   When investigators are exploring structural and functional integration, they may use idiothetic methods to explore multiple levels of organization. Personal characteristics such as age, physical features, and reactions to and from others are likely to elicit different pressures across individuals. Individuals differ in the details of their biological, psychological, relational, sociocultural, and ecological experiences, which in turn are likely to influence the experiences available to them. Their life choices and historically grounded possibilities also constrain how they coordinate internal and external pressures. All these considerations are coordinated in studies of individual variation.

The original conceptions of the competence orientations discussed in earlier chapters fits with an idiothetic approach to personality theory.[5] The traitlike features of someone's orientation profile involves a balance between task, ego, and work-avoidant *orientations*. While the orientations have been assumed to reflect traits, evidence also exists for parallel source states of task-involvement, ego-involvement, and work avoidance. Situations can pull for particular types of *involvement*, but individuals are more and less susceptible to such environmental pressures. In experimental research, it has been relatively easy to induce ego-involvement by infusing situations with competition (Thorkildsen & Nicholls, 1998). Some individuals become ego-involved whenever they confront an opportunity for competition. For other people, a task orientation can be sufficiently strong that they withstand competitive pressure. These source traits and states have similar structures, but are likely to be combined differently within individuals.

Because idiothetic research accommodates individual variation but does not make it the focus of investigations, differences are treated as a means to the end of finding theoretical information about structures, change mechanisms, or functioning that would otherwise remain undetected. Investigators are interested in patterns that emerge across different studies of lives in progress, but details of individual lives are not necessary for validating idiothetic research.

Limitations. Given the malleability of states, information about someone's orientations is not likely to offer reliable predictions about his or her behavior when confronted with situational demands. It is difficult to determine when a particular set of environmental pressures will override someone's natural proclivities toward a particular disposition. Investigators may also behave in accordance with environmental expectations, but fail to hold the requisite beliefs and values assumed to correspond to such behavior. To study an individual's life cycle, investigators may use their knowledge of how states and traits are commonly synthesized to draw conclusions about how particular individuals compare to population norms.

Interpretive Approaches

You may remember that interpretive research is highly dependent on the generation and analysis of textual representations of human functioning. Text is typically selected using convenience sampling methods that invariably reflect the expertise of the person whose life course is under examination. The content of textual representations differs, depending on the information researchers would like to obtain.

Interpret What? At the individual level, investigators mine details of respondents' personal stories looking for clues about their identities. In this work, *self* is often represented as someone's self-concept, social roles, intimate relationships, body image, self ideal, abilities, dispositions, and other characteristics associated with the question, "Who am I?" Most investigators distinguish the malleable features of a person from those features that are indicative of a slowly evolving ontological structure.[6] Individuals' behaviors, habits, attitudes, opinions, social roles, and interpersonal relationships are most easily changed. Depending on a respondent's age, his or her identity and beliefs about the self are also highly malleable. Features that are more deeply rooted in someone's ontogeny include his or her overall psychological adjustment, personal projects, careers, and, sometimes, their marriage and divorce patterns. Individuals may offer a life narrative or investigators may include other sources of information to construct a more complete psychobiography of the target individual.

Why Use Interpretive Methods?   Some investigators rely on interpretive methods because they reject the assumption that valid theories require comparisons among individuals. They find individuals' reports of their own experience to be much more informative than others' judgments about them. These investigators explore particular lives and the direction of personal interests to understand how internal needs and external pressures converge to guide daily functioning. In such work, investigators draw comparisons between who a person is, who he or she is not, and who he or she would like to be. Ordinarily, these judgments are framed dialectically rather than normatively.

Autobiographies.   Autobiographies reflect a special genre of interpretive research that focuses exclusively on participants' interpretations of their own lives; investigators play a minor role in how the evidence is generated even if they might help the target person put together a full story. To extract an autobiographical account of someone's life, investigators may collect evidence in a number of ways.

Information from any of the tools described in previous chapters is useful as long as participants can offer input into the meaning of those measures. Investigators can, for example, make videotaped records of an individual's behavior in a particular setting and then ask that individual to explain what was going on and why she or he did the things she or he did. Similarly, conversations between researchers and participants can be facilitated using standardized tests, surveys, formal interviews, and other tools ordinarily evaluated in relation to a set of standards. *Standardized tools* are selected to offer the participant a forum in which to fully expound on his or her life.

More commonly, investigators rely on a range of *personal interviews* to elicit someone's autobiography. Such interviews can take different forms. Clinical interviews, for example, typically request diagnostic information whereas a therapeutic interview involves thinking through a particular problem. When personal interviews are conducted for research purposes, investigators seek an understanding of respondents' representations of their self-system.

When asked to offer a *life narrative,* respondents convey a sense of how they see themselves in relation to others, whether they like themselves, whether they feel in control of their life, and whether they identify with particular groups. Personal narratives also reveal information about important relationships, social roles, and patterns of thought. When directed to discuss particular issues, investigators can also learn about respondents' values, concerns, and interests from the stories they tell about themselves and their social position.

During interviews, investigators can learn a lot by considering respondents' body language alongside what is actually said. Respondents are free to challenge or explore investigators' questions, talking back to the interviewer rather than passively responding to agendas they had no role in forming. In a well-conducted conversation, investigators can also explore inconsistencies in someone's narrative or ask for elaborations on points that would otherwise be misunderstood.

Documents, such as diaries, letters, or other forms of writing, and *artifacts,* such as the products owned or produced by an individual, are also common sources of autobiographical information. These data sources are valued, in large part, because the focal person is free to structure his or her views. With participants' help, investigators may also be able to situate particular artifacts or documents within the person's life cycle to offer evidence for other narrative assertions.

Limitations. The primary limitations of autobiographical accounts are also their strength. When investigators take time to carefully explore individual lives, they presumably have good reasons for selecting individuals. Often, the result is a rather idiosyncratic representation of a life cycle, rich with historical details that are unlikely to be replicated and ripe with personal interpretations that are difficult to extract from aggregated data. The idiosyncratic nature of these accounts makes it difficult to draw comparisons among them, even if each account can be instructive in its own right.

Another limitation emerges when investigators become preoccupied with questions of "what *really* happened?" Human judgments are highly fallible and are regularly influenced by subtle forms of priming. Clinicians with extensive training on pathological forms of functioning, for example, may see pathology wherever they look. Preoccupations with social injustice can set people up for a life of anger and resentment. Investigators may relish the revealing ways in which individuals talk about their experience, but distortion is likely when the perspectives of one individual are compared with those of others. Similarly, any conversation is likely to be of normatively short duration and may not convey enough detail for the holistic judgments investigators sometimes make. For this reason, life cycles are more commonly documented by using interactive data and exploring each life from more than one perspective.

MAKING CONNECTIONS

Imagine a person whose life you find fascinating. What would you do to learn more about that life? Which individualistic approaches to studying life cycles would be most helpful? Would you want to combine measurement techniques? How? Why? What would your final report contain?

MEASURING INTERACTIONS

Functioning at the interpersonal level is most commonly explored by looking at how individuals interact with others. Participants may play a central or tangential role in selecting interactions to explore, but investigators often look at the structure of those interactions as well as at their manifest purpose and content. As will be apparent in the next chapter, there are many ways to explore the nature of interaction itself, but this chapter will focus on how investigators extract information about a person.

Relying solely on indicants in text, *discourse analysis* helps investigators identify the means by which individuals communicate. Combining evidence from many different sources, *case studies* help investigators see how an individual functions in the world and how others evaluate that functioning. *Biographies* are represented here as a special type of case study in which a target individual may or may not be available to offer new information or evaluate an investigators' conclusions.

Discourse Analysis

Discourse analysis is a set of techniques for discovering regularities in text.[7] This approach to evaluating interactions is commonly found in the fields of history, literary criticism, and cultural studies, but variants are evident in other fields.

What Is Analyzed?   Typically, discourse analysts find whatever forms of text are available, using sources such as interviews, focus group transcripts, informal conversations, observational summaries, written accounts of daily lives, or formal documents. They look for different types of discourse taking place within a text. Comparing *syntax, semantics,* and *pragmatics,* discourse analysts have distinguished four kinds of evaluation. Using the sentence as an object and text as a product, syntax can be evaluated. Semantics involves the process of discourse and pragmatics reflects the utility of words and gestures.

Discourse analysts typically explore relations between speakers and their utterances, asking questions about the occasion in which an utterance was used and what speakers and listeners were doing when the text was generated. Within a particular setting or course of events, for example, participants rarely show unanimous agreement on what took place or the meaning of events that transpired. Discourse analysts study the textures of these different understandings.

Qualities of Discourse Analysis.   Discourse analysts often contrast their assumptions with those of grammarians, who focus on how the structures of sentences or utterances affect the linguistic properties of communication. Researchers evaluating discourse focus on six socially constructed components of language that enhance or undermine individuals' ability to communicate:

- socially constructed productions such as discursive, rhetorical, or dialogic speech that emerges in particular contexts;
- what is said or written rather than the context in which text is generated;
- changes in the content and texture of the discourse itself;
- macrolevel conclusions from patterns in *discursive turns* within the text as a whole;
- microlevel conclusions from patterns in *linguistic turns* in segments of text;
- how many levels of discourse (individual, interpersonal, transpersonal) are evident in a particular text.

These six questions reflect assertions about *reference,* or the relation of words to things, *presuppositions,* or the underlying assumptions made by speakers, *implicature,* or the implied features of a text, and *inference,* or the interpretations made about utterances and the connections between them.

Text as a Context.   Rather than explore how a text is situated in the world, discourse analysts emphasize the context of what is talked about. *Contextual features* include those related to the speaker, listener, and audience for a text. *Codes* are the language used to represent ideas, the events transpiring, and topics raised and aborted within an interaction. Discourse analysts may also describe the setting in which text is generated, the medium through which individuals are communicating, the messages being sent, and evaluations that occur. All of these features are affected by the text's general purpose, and investigators often start their analysis by determining if a particular text is sufficiently representative to warrant meaningful generalizations.

Guiding Questions.   Once a text is selected, discourse analysts evaluate where language changes within a text and how it is arranged in relation to other symbolic elements. They devote most of their energy to answering *how* questions. Accepting the *principle of logical interpretation,* which indicates that listeners will not construct a context larger than necessary for interpreting a transaction, and the *principle of analogy,* which acknowledges that past and parallel experiences constrain participants' interpretations of events, discourse analysts often raise a number of text-relevant questions:

- How are ideas expressed?
- How is the progression of events portrayed in the text?
- How are cultural symbols used?
- How do individuals or groups develop discursive repertoires to reflect their interests?
- How is discourse within a community changed by economic and political contexts?
- How are frames and ideologies mixed within a text?

Limitations.   Discourse analysts take a relatively informal stance on where text production occurs and how text is generated. These researchers spend most of their energy trying to align indicants with meaningful dimensions, constructs, or concepts. Without scrutinizing the circumstances in which text is generated, it becomes difficult to compare the products of discourse analysis across settings and situations. Discourse analysis, therefore, is most useful in combination with framing or other assessments of the context in which text is generated.

Case Studies

Discourse analysis may reflect a story in its own right, but the results are also combined in larger case studies. Formally, *case studies* involve the investigation and analysis of social phenomena bounded in time and place. Although the focus of this chapter is on the study of individual lives, case studies can also be conducted for events, organizations, institutions, or any other bounded social entity. Most case studies include three components: (1) a bounded social phenomenon, (2) rich detail about the phenomenon, and (3) multiple methods to support conclusions via triangulation.[8]

Selecting Lives to Study.   Before conducting a person-focused case study, investigators typically select a target person by considering a series of guiding questions. They decide why they want to select a target person, if the person represents an instance of a more generally interesting phenomenon, and what roles the person represents. They also ask if there are particular theoretical concepts to be explored and if the target person is adequately representative of the population to be understood.

Choosing Sources of Evidence.   Researchers also ask a series of questions about the evidence to be gathered:

- What facets of the life will be emphasized?
- What interrelated activities and routines were experienced by the target person? How are findings likely to overlap? Where are they likely to differ?
- In what contexts will the target person's functioning be explored? How representative are the selected contexts of those in the target person's everyday experience? What contextual parameters constrain the investigation? How are activities bounded?
- What methods will be used? How can depth be added to the data corpus? How does the evidence contain adequate breadth? How can multilayered, nuanced information be generated? Can information be extracted from interviews, informal conversations, focus groups, formal documents, archives, or products generated by the participant (e.g., diaries, homework, artwork)?
- Which tasks can be standardized? How would data sources complement one another to supplement the limitations of each technique?
- Will the target person be shadowed using participant-observation techniques for gathering data? How will those experiences be recorded?

A Study of Lives in Progress.   Consider, for example, a study of how boys with learning disabilities tend to fracture their intellectual lives by ignoring their own needs, others' expectations, or a combination of the two (Thorkildsen & Nicholls, 2002). Individual variation was explored to illuminate different motivational concerns. Each of the four boys completed similar activities related to a common second-grade curriculum. The boys had been shadowed at home, in school, and in peer groups to explore how they functioned in those contexts. Several structured activities were also used to explore how the boys organized their experiences. The tasks were implemented by different people and were modified to account for variation in how the boys were functioning and the challenges they faced. Existing theoretical and empirical evidence obtained from other research programs was also used to direct attention to particular patterns in the observed behavior, to design appropriate activities, and to guide the details of interactions with the boys and their caregivers. The resulting details of the boys' lives showed dialectical reasoning and the value of including an interactive measurement component in case study research.[9]

Biographies.   *Biographies* are a particular genre of case studies, offering a rich depiction of the life cycle for one particular individual. Nevertheless, they are different from the case studies described so far in several respects. First, most biographies focus on the lives of eminent individuals who are sufficiently well known that readers may want to know more about them. Second, biographers often go to great lengths to portray the historical era in which a life occurred, cross-checking each claim with evidence from sources outside the target person's normal social circles. Third, only some biographers are fortunate enough to be able to talk with the target of their research. Most biographers are dependent on letters, diaries, or other testimonies to learn of the feelings and thoughts of their subject. Despite these differences, biographers and other researchers who construct case studies typically use many of the same procedures for obtaining and synthesizing evidence.

Procedural Guidelines.   When designing a case study, investigators sometimes distinguish procedural and analytical guidelines for gathering and making sense of evidence. Procedurally speaking, investigators often attempt to:

- design open-ended, flexible plans;
- seek multiple perspectives;
- use different measurement techniques;
- adopt a longitudinal perspective in which the target person is shadowed over time or narratives include a relatively broad conception of time;
- look for surprising evidence-gathering opportunities;
- include multiple investigators.

Analytical Guidelines.   After investigators have combined indicants within each measure and discerned relations between dimensions, constructs, and concepts, they spend time revisiting some of their initial decisions and determining if they have gathered enough evidence. This analytic phase includes a second questioning of how a selected case compares to other, related cases or to the phenomenon under investigation. Researchers ask *what kind of case* has been constructed, comparing this with their initial intentions. With a product in hand, investigators are better able to evaluate the case they have. They can determine if it is representative of a larger population or unique to a particular set of circumstances. Investigators can see if the case is crucial for more general theoretical or social understanding, and whether it offers mundane or repetitive information. Investigators can also determine if they have found a person who offers a negative example of the phenomenon under consideration or otherwise represents an extreme case.

A second set of analytical questions involves the degree to which the information gathered contains *sufficient depth*. Investigators ask whether they are reporting the details of a *single case* or of *multiple cases* related to a specific set of circumstances. They may also find they have an unusual, *revelatory case* that highlights new perspectives. A case may also be *synecdochic* in that it is a part of a larger whole or *particularistic* in that it is like no others. Reevaluating the case in light of gathered evidence helps investigators report realistic levels of generality and may lead to suggestions about how to improve the project.

Limitations.   A major limitation of case studies concerns the difficulty of comparing findings across individuals to draw generalizations. When investigators are aware of possible theoretical yields from a particular case, they are likely to select helpful people and measure things that will offer such return. If investigators plan to compare cases, they commonly broaden their designs and use a wide range of measurement techniques. Unfortunately, such awareness is not always possible.

Comparisons between individuals are unnecessary for finding interpretable outcomes, yet investigators can strengthen their conclusions by considering divergent theoretical predictions and observing the correspondence between such predictions and life stories of target persons. Case studies are particularly useful if investigators want to find meaningful patterns that are not detectable using computer-generated models.

MAKING CONNECTIONS

When might you want to understand how a particular individual interacts with the world? What kind of data would you collect? What interactions would be helpful to understand? Would discourse analysis yield theoretically useful information? Would a full case study be helpful for making theoretical discoveries, extensions, or refinements?

MEASURING LIVES IN SOCIOCULTURAL CONTEXTS

Many forms of interpretive research focus heavily on transpersonal levels of analysis and inferences about the structure of cultures. Studies of individuals become a means to the end of understanding how social conditions affect human functioning. Two approaches to transpersonal analysis are introduced here, but there are others. Research on *framing* explores how discourse is situated in cultural contexts. In *action research,* participants study their own lives to offer transpersonal generalizations about the social conditions they experience.

Framing

Investigators who take a cultural approach to exploring discourse may be especially interested in *framing.* Frame analysts try to discern what is going on within a community by identifying layers of interaction and their constituent conventions. The products of such investigations typically direct readers' attention to the perspectives inherent in a particular person, interaction, and context.

Assumptions in frame analysis.   Frame analysts are interested in the *texture of collective action* and the *role of particular persons* in the unfolding of events. Five basic assumptions are commonly considered in this research.

- Most people orient current expectations by considering past experiences.
- People rely on internal schema for making sense of their world.
- Meaning-making is simultaneously individual and social.
- Frames consist of fixed structures and emergent processes.
- Framing relies on written and spoken language for drawing inferences about what people say and do.

Like discourse analysts, frame analysts collect convenience samples of textual data consisting of documents, case studies, biographical information, testimonies, and so forth. Unlike discourse theorists, frame analysts are interested in why discourse takes the shape and form it does. Frame analysts, in other words, are looking for *decision-making algorithms* to explain why people do what they do in particular situations. Most commonly, general algorithms are used to explain specific behaviors or patterns of discourse.

Key Questions.   Frame analysts often rely on human interpretations of text and compare such interpretations with computer-generated analysis of standard codes. They commonly address four major questions that can be explored from different levels of organization.

- What are key issues in a particular frame?
- What responsibilities and solutions drive the action? Is it reasonable to think in terms of diagnosis and prognosis?
- What symbols are apparent in the text? Are there detectable visual images, metaphors, historical examples, stereotypes, and/or catch phrases?
- What are the historical roots of supporting arguments?

Central skills.   Several *key skills,* relevant to framing, are brought forth in an iterative fashion. Investigators are interested in detecting consistent algorithms to support transpersonal generalizations. They do so by documenting their processes for making diagnostic evaluations, frames of action sequences, and connections between details of their own reading of a text and computer-generated analyses. Over time they also record expanding and contracting goals of the investigation that match emergent evidence, details of collective identities, cultural outcomes, and new challenges faced by a culture.

Frame analysts often rely on case study information to extract general algorithms for explaining how institutional forces and sociocultural structures shape specific kinds of action in particular fields. Because framing is concerned with algorithms rather than the simple amplification of text, investigators sometimes construct *story-grammars* to convert complex text into *nodes* that can later be compared. Story-grammars typically specify the *function* of an interaction by using codes to reflect particular *actions, subjects, objects,* and *modifiers* (Figure 14.1). Researchers can then predict *bridges, amplifications,* and *master outlines* for an interaction and test the viability of these judgments against computer-generated probabilities. Various specialized programs have been developed to match the common content and grammatical structures of particular topics.

Limitations.   Framing is heavily dependent on the quality and representativeness of the interpreted text. It is sometimes difficult to fully capture the contexts in which text is generated, yet framing involves generalizations about such contexts.

Another concern emerges when investigators use patterns within a text to identify general decision-making algorithms. Although most humans are creatures of habit, the contexts in which they live may elicit a wide range of interactions that do not conform to general algorithms. Distortion in how investigators label frames can be compounded if investigators too readily assume that patterns in one type of text will be evident in all or most related texts.

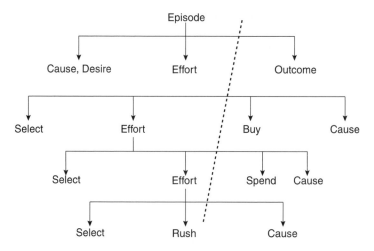

FIGURE 14.1   Sample Story-Grammar

Action Research

Rather than study decision-making algorithms, individuals who engage in *action research* are typically the object and subject of inquiry.[10] Action researchers engage in recurring cycles progressing from *action,* to *reflection,* to *practical theorizing* to *the generation of new ideas,* and back to *action.* Most agents study their circumstances to make improvements in their daily functioning. Educators, clinicians, and other professionals are the most likely candidates for this type of research because they simultaneously try to achieve two goals. They are looking for thoughtful, practical ways to improve their own work, and sharing their personal discoveries with other professionals.

Defining Features.   Action research typically has six *defining features* that can lead agents through the participant-observation process.

- Investigators are the agents in situations being researched.
- Research starts with a practical problem and questions that emerge from a particular setting.
- Actions are compatible with the values upheld in a setting.
- Decisions are made by considering a cost-to-benefit ratio in which investigators maximize practical benefits without diminishing preexisting results.
- Action and reflection are closely linked mechanisms by which investigators develop their own actions and knowledge.
- The nature of the problem rather than standardized procedures shapes the process and the results.

Procedures for Action Research.   Procedures in action research are similar to other interpretive research practices. Missing is the requirement that investigators seek outside advice or somehow collect evidence using a team of researchers. When teachers studied their teaching, for example, they were encouraged to:

- pose a question and find a starting place for inquiry;
- write a diary in which daily reflections are recorded, but one that can include additional information helpful for identifying key features of a situation or for goal setting;
- use reflections and practical theorizing to further clarify and refine the question to be investigated;
- collect interpretive data while engaging in ethical practice, considering alternative perspectives, and testing assumptions through practical action;
- analyze data to identify the features of practice that improved situations along with those features that require further improvement;
- develop action strategies and include them in practice while documenting the outcomes and reflecting on the results;
- formulate a representation of the findings and share new knowledge with other practitioners (Altrichter, Posch, & Somekh, 1993).

Evaluating Action.   As with discourse analysis and framing, action researchers typically look for patterns in the text generated from their experiences. They often identify topics in a larger data corpus to *chunk segments* of interactions. They may focus on *sentential topics* in which particular comments are linked to a theme. Action researchers may also identify *discourse topics* in which propositions are linked to more general ideas. A *topical framework* typically consists of activated features of a context for following a train of thought or particular ideas in a text. *Presupposition pools* contain general knowledge for situating a particular discourse.

Many action researchers stop after finding the *relevance of ideas* for improving praxis. They may be well-placed to distinguish *conversational topics* for generating text and personal *topics as the speaker* within a context. Teachers, for example, recognize that they have goals that differ from those of other learners. They can look at a videotape of the discourse from a lesson and evaluate their own intentions as well as the effect of those intentions on their students.

The details of *how events were staged* in a situation also prove interesting alongside *emergent themes.* Tinkering with how events are organized and evaluating the results is parallel to designing interventions in experimental research. New ideas about how to stage events in a profession bring an investigator back to the action phase of their research. This action allows investigators to repeat the cyclical patterns of reflection, practical theorizing, and generating new ideas.

Transpersonal conclusions are generated when investigators imagine other contexts and extract new possibilities for praxis. Action researchers draw inferences about their own and others' roles in the profession, and look for generalizations that might be useful in similar contexts. Practical theorizing of this type differs from other forms of theory development because action researchers retain only the ideas that work well, discard ideas that failed, and do not always take time to understand why particular decisions are disconfirmed.

Limitations.   Action research is heavily dependent on the logical skills and commitments of investigators. When investigators have institutional responsibilities, it may be difficult to engage in the high levels of reflection and theorizing necessary for generating useful

transpersonal contributions. Methods of action research are quite useful for practitioners interested in improving their skills and sustaining high levels of professional involvement, but
original conclusions are likely to be rare when direct action is used as the primary source of
information. Despite this limitation, action researchers often experience a great sense of
fulfillment from sharing their professional talents with like-minded professionals and improvements in practice are a likely result.

MAKING CONNECTIONS

Find a study in your area that includes framing or reflects action research. What types of evidence were included in that study? What transpersonal conclusions were drawn? Did the evidence support the conclusions or simply illustrate particular points? How could the study have
been improved?

MEANS OF TEXT PRODUCTION

Research on individual life cycles is commonly dependent on textual representations of
human experiences, but there are various ways in which text can be produced. Investigators
may rely on existing documents or standardized tests, analyze the content of interviews,
transcribe observations into verbal form, or construct story-grammars to reflect the structure of events. The same text can be analyzed in different ways, but procedures for gathering first-order evidence remain consistent regardless of whether investigators are interested
in individual, interpersonal, or transpersonal levels of analysis.

Self-Report Approaches

When investigators rely on interview and survey data, they seek lifelikeness rather than theoretical truth (Caprara & Cervone, 2000). They accept that people make meaning from their
knowledge of the historical circumstances shaping existing cultures and events.[11] Self-reported views reveal individuals' sense of self when investigators identify commitment
themes. Accepting that someone's life story is a feature of his or her self-concept, self-report data reveal how individuals think about themselves as subjects.[12] Expanding the analysis to draw inferences about individuals' daily functioning or the contexts in which they live
is facilitated by combining self-reported information and other types of evidence. Six approaches for generating self-report data are sampled here.

Personal Narratives.   Individuals' *personal narratives* are probably the most common
forms of text, but there are several methods for collecting such evidence. Investigators can
simply ask people to *tell their life story, answer more pointed questions* to elicit shorter stories, or *describe their inner, polyphonic speech.* Such conversations commonly begin with
a series of open-ended questions followed by probes to elicit more information on emerging themes. Table 14.1 contains guidelines for formulating interview questions. Respondents are encouraged to structure the narratives and investigators monitor the process to

TABLE 14.1   Suggested Guidelines for Developing Personal Interview Questions

GUIDELINES

Does the question require an answer?

Are respondents likely to have a ready-made answer? Will they have thought about the topic?

Can past behaviors be recalled and reported accurately?

Is the respondent likely to want to share the requested information?

Will the respondent feel motivated to give a full answer?

Is the respondent expected to have special expertise or background knowledge related to the questions?

What other data collection techniques are being used? Is there a way to align questions with other tasks to improve the triangulation of information?

Is the interviewer free to alter the questions to match the interests of respondents?

ensure clarity and comprehensiveness. Investigators may ask difficult or challenging questions, but take their lead from the respondent's willingness to address sensitive themes.

Pointed Narratives.   Once investigators have identified a central theme, they may ask respondents to offer more *pointed narratives* or respond to other self-directed measures. Respondents may generate sentences about an assigned topic, list phrases or adjectives, or respond to "true" projective tests that require them to define a question as well as the answer. Ideally, chains of responses become evident when such personal reflections are compared across time in each person or across persons. When sources of variance and covariance are brought together, it becomes possible to identify source traits, source states, stimuli that trigger such states, and the unique features of a particular life.

Self-Directed Interviews.   Using *self-directed measures,* participants can reflect on personal themes that emerge from designated activities. Respondents offer direct critiques of possible traits, states, and impressions about their identity. In one such activity, individuals have been asked to list personal attributes they possess, would like to possess, and think they should possess (Higgins, Bond, Klein, & Strauman, 1986). Comparing the three lists allows individuals to identify and reflect on patterns in their thinking. Respondents can evaluate the degree to which their responses are realistic, artistic, inquisitive, conventional, enterprising, and so forth. Investigators can accept such judgments at face value or incorporate them into more comprehensive assessment plans.

Experience-Sampling Methods.   Related to the self-directed measures, *experience-sampling methods* offer individuals the opportunity to label their emotions at a particular point in time. When a beeper or some other indicator is activated, respondents generate a short narrative or summary of their current activities, emotions, and thoughts. When measures are constructed using open-ended questions, respondents can structure their own responses. If individuals respond to standardized items, the results are more consistent with standardized tasks. Experience-sampling techniques offer one means for exploring self-reported reactions at the time they occur.

Talk-a-Loud Procedures.   Narratives that reflect an individual's *inner speech* are probably the most difficult to extract. Ideally, individuals would offer cues about emergent characters as they engage in, rehearse, or replay events in their imagination. Most individuals can engage such in polyphonic speech, hearing the voices of the others in the situation, but translating images into speech eliminates these different transitions between agents. Attempting to translate a story or dream into language that can be shared is often difficult for individuals who usually keep such thoughts private. Despite this difficulty, the effort can be worthwhile because information about inner speech can offer insightful clues regarding the valence of states, point of activation, and self-evaluations.

Diaries and Letters.   Diaries and letters offer unstructured reflections on the peaks and valleys of life. Diaries are commonly written without the intention to share the resulting reflections. Letters are typically written to someone else and reflect the author's attempt to imagine a recipient's perspective. Although diaries and letters are not written for research purposes, they may offer useful information when the text is compared with other findings.

Observational Records

Observational data offer a means of comparing individuals' self-reports with their actions or of extracting information when individuals lack enough self-awareness to be able to accurately represent all their thoughts, emotions, or actions. Using transcripts of videotapes or written field notes, investigators often identify those characteristics that are immediately recognizable.

Observing Intangible States.   Although source states remain relatively constant across people, they can be observable. Happiness, for example, looks relatively similar even though some individuals may experience this state while receiving a gift and others may find it when walking in the woods or succeeding on an onerous task. In all cases, it may be possible to detect interest, excitement, and cheerfulness.

Public Conversations and Focus Groups.   Investigators sometimes blend narrative inquiry and observational techniques by analyzing public conversations. In public settings or focus group discussions, people often monitor their actions to advance personal goals. By watching patterns in their speech and actions, it becomes possible to draw inferences about life events that may elicit such activities. Exploring combinations of behavior directs attention away from the study of isolated mental entities toward an analysis of social conditions in which action is noted and evaluated.

Standardized Tests and Personal Documents

On occasion, it is helpful to administer standardized tests or look at formal documents that record the details of life events. Investigators who are reasonably certain that some states or traits are important may use standardized tools to verify their impressions. Systematic forms of experimentation may also be helpful for determining activation points, valence, and social purposes served by particular states. Standardized tools can also be used as a stimulus for more elaborate conversations about a person's life.

Standardized Tests.   Investigators may use interest inventories, personal-style measures, and sorting tasks to elicit controlled reflections. Less standardized measures include the systematic interpretation of essays and structured think-a-loud protocols by comparing text to population-specific norms.

With standardized tools, investigators can compare respondents' self-reports with their evaluations of others. This comparison can reveal the extent to which self-interest dominates someone's thinking. In one such measure, individuals were asked to define the characteristics of particular social roles and indicate how pairs of roles are similar or different. In a second activity, respondents were also asked to describe their own social roles. Comparing the two sets of responses supported inferences about the respondents' commitments or attitudes about such social roles.[13]

Projective Measures.   *Projective measures* are ideally useful in combination with other measures for exploring interests and values. Inferences about relatively stable features of someone's personality are easily supported with respondents' reactions to the tasks as well as their answers to investigators' questions. Some researchers go so far as to suggest that nonprojective items are unsuitable for measuring someone's strength of interest or dynamic states because standardized tools place restrictions on how individuals can define their beliefs (Cattell, 1973). Needless to say, these decisions are usually derived from theoretical concerns and procedural measurement rules follow.

Personal Documents.   Investigators sometimes turn to formal legal or other institutional records to augment claims about someone's life. These records are standardized across persons within an era or region of the world, but may not be standardized across populations. Nevertheless, they offer external validation of when particular events took place, which agencies were involved, and possibly how some forms of functioning have changed over time. Common documents such as medical records, grades, and standardized test scores may be transferred from more than one source. Other legal documents such as marriage, divorce, and death certificates may require knowledge of where the events took place.

Summary

When investigators study individual lives, they look for methods for capturing the uniqueness of persons without undermining possible regularities. Investigators can use multiple sources of information to identify stimuli that trigger states, the process of succession for a particular state (activation and valence), and the relationship between states and traits. They can also write an autobiography, biography, or case study of a particular life. Transpersonal conclusions, such as those generated using phenomenology, critical theory, interpretive analytics, or deconstructionism, can also be supported using multiple kinds of text.

MAKING CONNECTIONS

Can you find examples of innovative methods for generating text? Are there common taxonomies used to classify the content of such text? What evidence can you find that such categories are valid, useful, and ethical? Were multiple methods used in that research?

CALIBRATING MEASURES

Procedures for calibrating interpretive evaluations of persons are highly flexible and match investigators' theoretical questions. This differs from developmental or psychometric approaches in that the same first-order evidence can be treated differently depending on whether investigators are concerned only with the individuals' perspective, interpersonal interactions, or transpersonal inferences. They also differ depending on the discourse community for which the research is being generated. Let's look at examples of such variability.

Describing Individuals

At the individual level, nomothetic, idiographic, and idiothetic approaches are quite similar, but differ from interpretive calibration techniques. A comparison of calibration approaches for evaluating states and life cycles can be exemplified at this point.

Calibrating Measures of States.   As with traits, investigators are likely to use tools when evaluating states. If an individual's experience is represented with a variety of indicants and repeated measures, factor analysis can be used to identify latent variables. The resulting factor structures can be compared across persons or treated independently.

More commonly, investigators have used *generalizability theory* rather than the more restricted classical measurement assumptions to explore reliability and the functioning of indicants. Using analysis of variance or regression techniques, investigators can partial out sources of variance rather than attribute all unexplained variability to error. This leads investigators to speculate on the sources of variance that may be operating for a set of indicants and estimate that variance.

Consider a self-report measure in which respondents participate in a series of activities. Their judgments during these activities may fluctuate such that they reveal *intrajudge variance.* When more than one person completes the same task, they may show different levels of commitment and introduce *interjudge variance.* There may also be variance in how indicants perform within a measure, leading researchers to explore possible *internal inconsistency.* And, when different raters evaluate the same text resulting from these activities, evidence of *inter-rater variance* might be found. With states, investigators may also be interested in the *point of activation* and *valence.*

To explore which types of variance might be evident in a particular outcome, investigators often calibrate tools while keeping each parameter in mind. Looking at the same text, they may create different codes to represent theoretically relevant dimensions.

When comparing sources of variance, investigators may label *factor-homogeneous* indicants. After representing each response with an indicant, investigators conduct factor analysis of standard scores (e.g., *z*-scores) extracted from repeated administrations of multiple measures. If homogeneity is attained, all indicants should be related to one another. In addition, regression or analysis of variance techniques could be used to understand *factor-heterogeneous* dimensions or constructs.

If indicants within a single measure are predicted to be *test-homogeneous,* it may also be worthwhile to look at measures of internal consistency within a single tool. If indicants are predicted to be *test-heterogeneous,* it may be worthwhile to explore graphic representations to verify the representativeness of items in the *relational circumplex*. Over multiple occasions, differences in *valence* could be evident if the placement of items changes in the circumplex while the angles between items (θ) remain constant.

Giving up the idea that each investigator is unique, calibration can also involve the evaluation of *person clusters*. Source states or common factor structures may correspond to primary drives or motivational forces. Ideally, a representative sample of persons would have responded to the same measures of a particular state on at least two occasions. The two administrations are usually spaced sufficiently apart so that fluctuations in the state can be identified, but not so far apart that intervening variables could account for differences in responses. If both sets of responses are factored independently, investigators can see if the same dimensions occur for each administration.

Investigators try to anticipate which of these possibilities are theoretically relevant and which sources of variance can be conveniently lumped into an error term. Researchers evaluate many ways in which indicants, dimensions, or constructs should not be associated as well as those in which they theoretically could.

Calibrating Interpretive Measures. The primary challenge in calibrating interpretive measures involves defining and applying an appropriate coding scheme to the generated text. Each source of variance related to states may also be apparent when interpreting text, but interpretive theorists are also likely to focus on broader possibilities. Like developmentalists, who are exploring changes in structures and functioning, interpretive theorists may evaluate at least three dimensions in individualistic data. They might look for patterns in an individual's *decisions,* complete a *content analysis* of the justifications, and/or conduct a *holistic analysis* of an entire protocol. Codes for the latter two kinds of evidence are highly dependent on theoretical claims to be tested, but coding is ordinarily systematic and verified by at least one additional rater. Table 14.2 offers suggestions for designing a coding scheme that, if added to ideas introduced in previous chapters, can facilitate replicability

TABLE 14.2   Sample Guidelines for Calibrating Evaluations of Text

GUIDELINES
Look for balanced comparisons.
Distinguish answers that reflect uncertainty from those reflecting a neutral stance.
Distinguish the expression of positive and negative attitudes.
Reduce primacy effects.
Keep codes mutually exclusive.
Note memory cues for facilitating recall.
Assume references to time were provided.
Recheck questions for technical accuracy.
Match the wording of a question to existing evidence.
Avoid double negatives when developing codes.
Classify one idea per code.

should two raters evaluate the same text when studying a single life cycle (see Chapters 10 and 12 for additional ideas).

Describing Interactions

Two approaches to evaluating how individuals interact with the world have been introduced, but both tend to rely on one style of calibration. Guidelines for discourse analysis are also useful for case studies. Case studies, of course, are likely to contain more than one type of data, but the calibration process is completed separately for each measure.

Calibrating Discourse.   Calibration is easier for discourse if investigators have specified the criteria for selecting texts and label how the text was produced. The coding process is also easier if investigators adopt a systematic means of presenting ideas. Table 14.3 contains formal guidelines used for evaluating various forms of text.

There are different computer programs designed to explore patterns in text, but these mechanical scoring techniques assume that vocabulary holds the same meaning to all individuals and that the structure and/or content of the conversation is rather well known. Therefore, investigators often use a combination of human judgment and mechanical scoring techniques to evaluate an interaction. In both approaches, investigators rely on simple coding categories and construct clear definitions of each category. There may be fewer ambiguities if the framing of the text being evaluated is known to the raters along with the context in which it was generated.

Describing Transpersonal Relations

Framing and action research, two approaches to exploring transpersonal relations in a life cycle, are quite different and often require different approaches to calibrating tools. Two possibilities are discussed here, but investigators may find other theoretically driven approaches for generating transpersonal conclusions.

TABLE 14.3   Guidelines for Discourse Analysis of Text

GUIDELINES

- What is the shared understanding of the speech situation at the time the text was produced? Does the definition change over the course of the interaction?
- What constitutes the whole of the text? What are the different parts of connected discourse (e.g., subjects, objects, story lines, themes, goals)? How do parts of the discourse relate to the whole?
- What roles are apparent in the interaction? Are respondents seen as experts, friends, subordinates, short-term community members, long-term members?
- What are the purposes for the interaction? What goals are respondents bringing to the conversation? How do goals change? What is the pragmatic intent of each speaker?
- What nonverbal information is apparent? How does that information convey role status, speech situations, or discursive styles?

Calibration in Framing. When engaged in *framing,* many investigators translate text into the conventions associated with story-grammars. This translation is one means of calibrating transpersonal evidence because the content of the text is removed so that investigators can make direct comparisons of each schematic representation. Frame analysts' interest in identifying the algorithms used in decision making renders the content of a text less important than the relations between subjects, objects, modifiers, actions, and so forth. At the point of calibration, more than one rater might construct a story-grammar for each text and the two renditions are then evaluated for accuracy. This is most easily accomplished if investigators create a standard frame for comparing text and anticipate the structure of that frame when documenting their interpretations.

Calibration in Action Research. Calibration in action research is a difficult concept to even imagine. The iterative nature of the action → reflection → theorizing → generating new ideas → action cycle creates fleeting standards in a highly dynamic system. Investigators determine what entities in a particular sequence of events are relevant to the questions they are trying to explore and which events or entities are irrelevant. They also look for multiple causes that might explain responses to the implementation of new ideas. Problems that are normatively easy to address are likely to be too transient for revealing stable patterns. Those with enduring qualities may not foster new action cycles. Many action researchers have learned to overlook the calibration process, but second-guess their decisions. Calibration entails the quality of particular reflections on what is taking place in a particular situation.

MAKING CONNECTIONS

Find a study of persons. What techniques were used to calibrate tools in that study? What does that information tell you about the nature of the inquiry? What would you have done differently if this were your study?

DEPENDABLE AND CREDIBLE EVIDENCE

As with calibration, definitions of *dependability* and *credibility* are likely to be altered to reflect theoretical goals. Investigators may want to rely on logically consistent decisions to ensure stability over time. However, they may also want to be responsive to the strengths and limitations of different kinds of text. It would be overly simplistic to assume that everything can be accounted for using one set of procedures. Indicants may reflect unique dimensions or constructs that are highly idiosyncratic. Patterns may be apparent *between* texts that are not evident *within* a text.

When indicants are assumed to reflect *fixed* variables, it becomes important to establish their stability. When indicants are expected to be *random,* generalizability theory can help investigators distinguish forms of measurement error. In interpretive research, neither of these conditions is particularly interesting, but investigators look for *meaningful* patterns that coincide with someone's values, expertise, or other personality characteristics.

Dependable and Credible Fixed Variables

By definition, a fixed variable should show no change across persons or across time, depending on the nature of the variable. Someone's sex, for example, is a stable feature of her or his ontogeny, but gender may reflect identity-related beliefs that can change and are likely to do so quite slowly. Variability also occurs across persons. Some people are males and others are females, but such fixed variables are measured with dependability and credibility if there is no intrapersonal variance among scores. When theoretical assumptions of where variables are fixed can be verified, measurement is likely to be dependable and claims about the corresponding indicants are likely to be credible.

Dependable and Credible Random Variables

The tenets of *generalizability theory* lead investigators to imagine sources of variance in how each variable is measured and emphasize the importance of verifying reliability within each testing context.[14] To attribute variability only to the content of indicants, investigators look for stability in dimensions other than content. For many theoretical purposes, dependability and credibility involve the following:

- *Intrajudge reliability*—no variance in how an observer or rater performs over time
- *Inter-rater reliability*—no variance in how a group of observers or raters evaluate the same set of text
- *Internal consistency*—no variance in the patterns of relations among indicants of a single dimensions
- *Response variance*—variability in how an individual responds to different tasks
- *Response heterogeneity*—stability in how individuals function across related tasks constructed using different methods

Again, investigators can use factor-analytic tasks to verify some of these assumptions, but are more likely to use analysis of variance (ANOVA) or regression techniques for comparing persons and dimensions. When using factor analysis, the same comparisons of factor loadings and internal consistency common to *psychometric theory* can be used to verify the stability of a state's structure and the accuracy with which each dimension is measured. *Controlling for the time* at which each set of responses is obtained, separate analyses can control for the likelihood that *valence* may change across repeated exposure to similar experiences. Time can be a variable in regression or ANOVA models to test stability.

One advantage of including several respondents in such an analysis is that investigators can target a narrower range of dimensions and explore commonalities across persons. Exploring a relational circumplex to determine whether data are *factor-homogeneous, test-homogeneous,* or *test-heterogeneous* can reveal the possible shortcomings of starting with a small number of indicants; not all dimensions of a state may be adequately represented. However, this is helpful only when investigators want to learn about structures across persons.

Because the measurement of states assumes dynamic valence, investigators may pay more attention to the stability of a construct's structure than is common in the measurement of traits. Traits and states are assumed to have relatively stable structures, but the dynamic nature of other state characteristics makes it imperative that structures be verified each time a tool is used. Should both structure and valence change simultaneously, investigators would have a difficult time calibrating their tools.

Dependable and Credible Interpretations

Evaluating the measurement of interpretations is multifaceted and can involve many different steps. Investigators may consider all of the sources of variance assumed with random variables, but are unlikely to expect the variability to be random. In this respect, they borrow many of the same techniques while violating the assumption that indicants are randomly distributed in a population. Invariably, statistical tools sometimes fail as readily as human judgments. Combining the two kinds of thought enhances the meaning-making process.

Inter-Rater Reliability.   The process of establishing inter-rater reliability has been introduced on several occasions, but is included here as a reminder that interpretive research is best conducted using multiple evaluators.[15] You probably remember that at least two people would be asked to evaluate the same material and their judgments are compared. Statistical techniques for evaluating these decisions have also been introduced, but not all comparisons are so easily evaluated.

Interpretive theorists are sometimes dependent on finding two witnesses to the same event, recording that event with the same level of detail from each perspective. Perspectives need not match, and spending time making direct statistical comparisons can undermine the parsimony rule of good research. Dependable judgments in the selection and recording of perspectives improve the credibility of inferences about those judgments.

Computer-Generated Analysis.   Some kinds of analysis are not highly dependent on humans' ability to engage in symbolic, metaphorical, or other forms of abstract thought. Mechanical procedures for comparing nodes in a network, grammatical structures of utterances, or key words in a text are highly useful for generating dependable coding. Having two individuals complete the same coding procedures can also facilitate high levels of inter-rater agreement and ensure that coding instructions are written clearly. Credibility in such analysis is highly dependent on the content of coding instructions and the alignment of those instructions with theoretical goals.

Comparing Human and Computer Judgments.   Some investigators replace inter-rater reliability with comparisons between human evaluations and those generated by computers. This is most realistic when researchers can write programs for analyzing text with their own schemes or use available programs with scoring procedures that align with their theoretical goals. Because mechanical and human scoring can serve two different purposes, it may be problematic to assume that the two kinds of analysis must be coordinated in credible evidence. Most investigators rely heavily on their own judgment when using technical approaches to verifying the dependability of their evidence.

Credibility calls attention to questions of a text's *representativeness* regardless if it is analyzed using human judgment, computer evaluations, or some combination. Once a decision-rule is established for comparing the evidence, it is generally applied to all text within a given sample. Failure to remain systematic raises issues of credibility because it introduces uncontrolled distortion that is often difficult to justify.

Triangulation.   Most interpretive research is highly dependent on comparisons among different sources of evidence. To establish the dependability of coding schemes and procedures, researchers often adopt more than one method of exploring stability and accuracy. *Triangulation,* in this work, is the process of comparing results obtained from different kinds of text analysis. Investigators determine how well various methods yield the same findings or add depth to stories about a life cycle. Errors at one level of coding or evaluation are only compounded in later stages if investigators do not cross-check their evaluations.

Summary.   *Dependable measurements* contain meaningful patterns of indicants and dimensions that are evident to anyone looking at a particular text. *Credibility* continues to reflect how dimensions correspond to constructs and concepts. Ideally, investigators maintain a commitment to individual, interpersonal, and transpersonal analyses when verifying these features of measurement, even though they may later generalize to more than one of these levels.

MAKING CONNECTIONS

In the research you are reading, what assumptions are used to measure the life cycle of a person? Are there fixed, random, or interpretive variables in the design? What methods have investigators used to explore dependability in the study of persons? Is the evidence credible? How do you know?

CONFIRMING GENERALIZATIONS

Staying with the comparison of statistical approaches to confirming generalizations and interpretive approaches, it should not be surprising to learn that many interpretive theorists use a combination of validation techniques. Any approach that adds convincing evidence while allowing investigators to achieve their theoretical goals is permissible. Details of how investigators have used generalizability theory and triangulation when studying a life cycle will be contrasted to illustrate this point.

Comparing Scores across Methods

Investigators relying on generalizability theory have asked questions of whether scores related to particular dimensions, constructs, and concepts remain the same regardless of the methods used by investigators. Using statistical tools, investigators evaluate content, criterion, and construct validity to determine if all related measures are associated (Kane, 1982). Each score is assumed to be an indicator of the universe of possible scores for the focal person across measurement conditions. Investigators may explore *factor-homogeneity* to determine if scores are stable across maximally dissimilar measures of the same theoretical constructs or concepts. They may use ANOVA or regression techniques to determine sources of disagreement when multiple measures are assumed to be *factor-heterogeneous.* The general agenda can be summarized as follows:

MULTI-METHOD EXPLORATION OF VALIDITY

$$E\rho^2 = \frac{\sigma_s^2}{(\sigma_s^2 + \sigma_m^2 + \sigma_e^2)}$$

Here, σ_s^2 represents the true variance in a set of scores, σ_m^2 represents the main effect variance associated with the different methods of measurement, and σ_e^2 represents the sum of all other variance components. Investigators use this formula when they want to determine if scores are invariant across methods. Methods can also be treated as fixed variables and scores can be evaluated across measurement conditions.

To fully explore validity using generalizability theory, investigators deliberately attempt to vary facets of the situation that can potentially influence the observed scores. They often distinguish *G-studies,* which focus on variance associated with the facets of measurement from *D-studies,* which strive to identify the optimal design of a tool by changing facets to minimize error and maximize information about theoretical constructs and concepts. Researchers may alter how, when, and where the data are collected. They may also alter the topics respondents consider and whether respondents are expected to reveal their typical beliefs or immediate reactions. Investigators then estimate the effects of these variations by identifying the percentage of variance accounted for in each step. Over time, intraclass correlations can be computed to estimate relationships among subsamples.

Triangulation

Interpretive theorists are more likely to rely on triangulation when comparing information across methods. The goal of interpretive research is to offer the thickest possible description of an individual life while maintaining theoretical goals. Stability in findings is not necessarily a major goal when offering a rich account of particular life cycles.

Identify Redundancies. Investigators are not particularly interested in generating tediously repetitious narratives. They may aggregate a number of details extracted from various sources to find consistent patterns. In doing so, interpretive theorists often look for the best examples of ideas they hope to convey in their analysis and may take stock of how often the concepts are apparent in their evidence. Generalizations are rarely supported with an aggregate index of all the examples of a particular construct or concept.

Find Exemplary Illustrations. To write an engaging account of a life cycle that illustrates the uniqueness of the focal person, investigators spend a great deal of energy identifying details from text that offer the best example of ideas emerging in a story. In the study of boys with learning disabilities, for example, a second grader who had great difficulty producing any ideas in an interview about his interests later named himself "Quiet Bird" during a lesson on Native Americans (Thorkildsen & Nicholls, 2002). This bit of evidence conveyed the point that this boy found his voice silenced in school more powerfully than all the empty "ums" and "ahs" of interviews about his beliefs. The triangulation process facilitates labeling such opportunities for conveying rich ideas in a simple manner.

Coordinate Multiple Sources of Evidence.   Most studies of a life cycle are highly dependent on multiple methods, regardless of how investigators synthesize their findings. Interpretive researchers are less likely than personality theorists (who look for general structures) to combine methods. Instead, interpretive theorists commonly highlight different types of information offered by each tool and illuminate the strengths of each approach. Stability in broad concepts may be helpful, but variability in how those concepts are conveyed is also essential for a strong measurement plan.

Explore Multiple Contexts.   Before making assertions about the stability of an individual's functioning, investigators generally look for evidence within and across contexts. Quiet Bird, for example, was relatively silent in school, but had a host of interesting personal projects and agendas at home. Parents and teachers hardly saw the same boy. Part of the challenge of helping this young man become engaged in school involved helping teachers see the lively boy that parents saw everyday and parents see the quiet, avoidant boy who was functioning in school. Only by finding evidence from multiple contexts was it possible to offer an accurate description of Quiet Bird's interests.

Validity in Reference to Sociopolitical Contexts

Representations of any life cycle are stronger when embedded in the sociopolitical contexts in which the life is unfolding. Identifying these contexts can be inordinately difficult, validating them while they are unfolding in time is nearly impossible. This leads most investigators to be very careful about the conclusions they formulate about a life. Wise researchers also learn to discriminate information that might be construed as gossip from information that could offer meaningful insights over time.

MAKING CONNECTIONS

When looking at how a life cycle is represented, what evidence do you see that validates investigators' assumptions? Are investigators relying solely on statistical approaches to exploring relations? What interpretations are evident? What kind of evidence is available to support any interpretations you find? In what sociopolitical context is the focal person's life unfolding?

THE STORY OF A LIFE

The primary operative word in research on a person's life is *dignity.* Investigators who offer distorted or politically skewed representations of a person's life cycle are taken less seriously than those who offer a balanced representation, even if both representations are somewhat critical. Starting with clear goals that distinguish the exploration of general personality structures from thick descriptions of an individual life is essential to designing a useful measurement plan. Reliance on multiple methods, with careful attention to the strengths and limitations of those methods, can best facilitate anyone's theoretical agendas.

SUGGESTED READINGS

Boje, D. M. (2001). *Narrative methods for organizational and communication research.* Thousand Oaks, CA: Sage.

Brown, G., & Yule, G. (1983). *Discourse analysis.* New York: Cambridge University Press.

Cosslett, T., Lury, C., & Summerfield, P. (2000). *Feminism and autobiography: Texts, theories, methods.* London: Routledge.

Gumperz, J. J. (1982). *Discourse strategies.* Cambridge, MA: Cambridge University Press.

Hersen, M., & Van Hasselt, V. B. (Ed.). (1998). *Basic interviewing: A practical guide for counselors and clinicians.* Mahwah, NJ: Erlbaum.

Klandermans, B., & Staggenborg, S. (Eds.). (2002). *Methods of social movement research.* Minneapolis: University of Minnesota Press.

Phillips, N., & Hardy, C. (2002). *Discourse analysis.* Thousand Oaks, CA: Sage.

Roberts, C. (Ed.). (1997). *Text analysis for the social sciences: Methods for drawing statistical inferences from texts and transcripts.* Hillsdale, NJ: Erlbaum.

Wodak, R., & Meyer, M. (Eds.). (2002). *Methods of critical discourse analysis.* Thousand Oaks, CA: Sage.

Wodak, R., Titscher, S., Meyer, M., & Vetter, E. (2000). *Methods of text and discourse analysis.* Thousand Oaks, CA: Sage.

SUGGESTED WEB SITES

Computer Assisted Qualitative Data Analysis Software for *CAQDAS*: http://caqdas.soc.surrey.ac.uk/

Qualis Research Associates for *The Ethnograph*: http://www.qualisresearch.com/

The Qualitative Report: http://www.nova.edu/ssss/QR/web.html

ENDNOTES

1. Cosslett, Lury, & Summerfield (2000) offer autobiographical evidence for this assertion.

2. Sperber & Wilson (1995) draw a host of conclusions about how individuals communicate with one another.

3. Tannen (1993) has edited a book on framing with several examples of these benefits.

4. Lamiell (1987, 1997) offers a theoretical basis for this argument, with measurement examples as evidence.

5. Nicholls (1989) summarizes this in a form that is easiest to read although he formulated this approach earlier in time.

6. McCrae & Costa (1990) do an elegant job of contrasting details of a life course with more general personality structures and states.

7. Johnston (2002) offers a clear sense of how discourse analysis differs from framing in research on social movements. Brown and Yule (1983) offer an important linguistics text on the topic.

8. Snow and Trom (2002) outline the structure of case studies for use in social movement research.

9. Sigel (1974) and White (1975) offer early examples of how important this kind of work can be.

10. Altrichter, Posch, & Somekh (1993) offer a guide to such work in teaching.

11. Bruner (1990) offers one argument to this effect, but the idea has become widely accepted.

12. William James's (1983) concept of "me" is once again entering the conversation of idiographic theorists.

13. Kelly (1955) used this and other similar methods in the construction of a cognitive-phenomenological theory of personality.

14. Cronbach, Gleser, Nanda, & Rajaratnam (1972) introduced these ideas. Suen (1990) offers a strong comparison between generalizability theory, the psychometric version of classical measurement theory, and item-response theory.

15. Chapters 5, 8, 10, and 12 introduce different approaches to this kind of evaluation.

CHAPTER FIFTEEN

MEASURING GROUP STRUCTURES AND FUNCTIONING

One area of research that remains dependent on ethnographic, developmental, and psychometric tools is the measurement of groups and individuals' placement within them. Knowledge of the formation and maintenance of groups is helpful for learning how group structures influence an individual's daily functioning and for identifying salient levels of organization within a culture. Information on how individuals evaluate or avoid groups can illuminate participants' understanding of their relationships with particular persons and of general relations among various social roles. Groups can be freestanding entities with collectivist agendas that have the power to dramatically alter the behavior of individuals.[1] These agendas have led investigators to distinguish the measurement of intact groups using developmental and psychometric approaches from the measurement of evolving groups or group processes using ethnographic approaches. Intact groups are usually measured by determining individuals' *social status* or as *social networks.* Evolving groups and group dynamics are usually measured using a variety of *ethnographic approaches.*

Four different purposes for measuring groups become readily apparent when looking at how and why investigators have explored this topic.

- Investigators working within psychometric measurement traditions have used sociometric measures to label individuals' social status and corresponding skills.
- Researchers studying development have explored the dynamic nature of an individual's social status, his or her evolving social skills, and environmental constraints on an individual's ontogeny.
- Group psychologists see groups as having self-contained structures that function independently within society, but may be influenced by outside pressures.
- Ethnographers study groups within a larger culture to gain insight into social norms and individuals' acceptance or rejection of such norms. They try to measure the structure of groups while retaining the local meaning of those structures, and explain individual differences in functioning from a cultural perspective.

ASSUMPTIONS ABOUT GROUPS

Because groups are more than the mere aggregate of individuals, mixing measurement traditions is common when representing groups. For example, investigators often begin interpretive research by conducting at least a rough form of social network analysis, even if they do not plan to conduct formal studies of how groups function.[2] Like other forms of interpretive research, groups can be studied from one or a combination of organizational levels.

Although individual, interpersonal, and transpersonal levels may be studied in combination or in isolation, theories differ in the degree to which analysis requires all three perspectives. At the *individual level* studies focus on how individuals' performance on a range of measures is correlated with their membership in a group. At the *interpersonal level,* participants' social competence is less important than which individuals are members of the same groups, how such affiliations affect daily functioning, and why such affiliations are important. For both of these organizational levels, direct comparisons between groups are difficult to support because even groups with surface similarities can have marked structural differences. It is at the *transpersonal level* that groups are the unit of analysis. Investigators verify that different groups share the same structure or use local norms to compare the behaviors, thoughts, and actions of collections of individuals. In psychometric or developmental research, investigators may delineate group boundaries using common external standards. Groups, for example, may include all members of a class of students, those who attend a particular church, or other easily identifiable criteria. Such stable, external standards are usually unavailable in interpretive research, rendering cross-group comparisons difficult or impossible.

PURPOSES FOR MEASURING GROUPS

Regardless of an investigators' theoretical orientation, the analysis of group behavior can offer insight into social processes that would otherwise be overlooked. Individuals' attempts to get by, degrade others, or shine with intelligence may be more recognizable in group contexts than by studying individuals alone. It may even take a group to notice these behaviors, appreciate the effects, and organize events to preserve or eliminate such actions.

Measuring groups can lead to comparative studies across communities or to the study of human functioning within a community. The study of social functioning within groups will receive closer scrutiny in the next chapter, but we will focus here on how investigators verify a group's existence. Approaches to measuring how people work together or share beliefs will be classified according to the emphasis placed on one of three methods commonly used to measure the structure of groups. Coordinating individual, interpersonal, and transpersonal levels of organization, investigators can measure *individuals' social status, collective social networks,* or *patterns among a range of human groups.*

Social Status

Studying individual and interpersonal levels of analysis, investigators who measure *social status* have done so for diagnostic and descriptive purposes (Moreno, 1953, 1960). Diagnostic agendas have involved classifying individuals into status categories and labeling the corresponding social skills exhibited by persons in each class. Social status is measured in descriptive studies to facilitate richer accounts of group structures. Regardless of these differences, investigators have used theoretical and empirical criteria to define social status.

Possible Uses.   Two common theoretical structures have been identified by measuring liking or disliking among and between group members. Many investigators differentiate the measurement of *social preference,* how much an individual is liked or disliked, from *social visibility,* the overall recognition received by each group member (Peery, 1979). These constructs are measured either by asking for nominations or by rating all individuals in a predetermined group. Estimates of social preference compare the relationship between nominations or ratings to determine if someone is liked more than disliked. Social visibility is calculated by looking at the total number of nominations or positive and negative ratings an individual receives.

Social preference and social visibility have been represented as orthogonal and investigators have labeled categories by comparing ratings along these dimensions (Figure 15.1). In early studies, for example, *accepted* children were classified as those who receive high performance and visibility ratings, *rejected* children were seen as low on preference, but high on visibility, *amiable* children were those high in preference and low in visibility, and *isolated* children were low on both visibility and preference. Most of the measurement controversies involve the use of these dimensions and validity in how unidimensional measurements are combined into multidimensional indices.[3]

Four theoretical constructs, each with several dimensions, have been identified, but only some dimensions seem to be measured in current studies.[4] Dimensions that are commonly measured focus on *social status of target individuals,* and include ratings of whether a target person is attractive, rejected, or isolated within a group. Dimensions that are often overlooked involve the *social dispositions of each rater*; investigators could measure whether raters like or are attracted to at least one person in the group, whether they typically find members attractive, and whether they tend to reject group members. Two additional di-

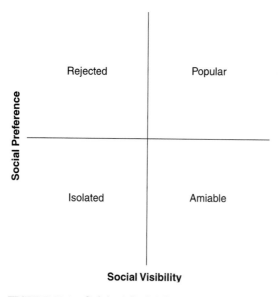

FIGURE 15.1   Original Social Status Categories

mensions reflect *raters' preference for their own or other groups*; raters are seen as extraverted when they are more attracted to outgroup members than to ingroup members, and are more introverted when they are more attracted to members of their own rather than other groups. Raters can also show *indifference* when there is little or no reciprocity between being recognized and recognizing others.

This framework is more and less easy to measure at given points in time, and there are different theoretical reasons for assuming that stability or change should be apparent in such sociometrics (Cillessen & Bukowski, 2000). Clinicians, for example, use status information to determine how well individuals are adjusting to the environments in which they live. Intervention research may focus on changing individuals or environments.

Measurement Guidelines.   Psychometric rules for designing survey questions often apply to social status measures, yet investigators have refined them for use identifying groups. Existing *sociometric tools* reflect five guidelines.[5]

- Sociometrics involve the measurement of two-way relations between persons.
- Persons are from intact groups drawn together in response to one or more criteria.
- Spontaneous responses are generated quickly to minimize reflection time, restricting socially desirable or otherwise calculated responses.
- Participants who are sincere about responding are recruited for their willingness to offer meaningful decisions.
- Strong conclusions are facilitated by interpreting responses in light of criteria that are enduring across time, settings, and historical periods.

Instrument Development.   When designing social status tools, decisions often fall into four general categories. Two categories focus on how indicants are generated. As is the case for other interviews or surveys, investigators decide *what stimuli to use* when directing respondents' attention to the parameters of rating social status. Common stimuli have included the consideration of friendship, acquaintance, direct preferences (like or dislike most), and indirect or task preferences (e.g., who to play with, sit by). Investigators also decide on *response parameters.* They have considered the strengths and limitations of peer nominations, rankings, rating scales, and paired-comparisons. Because no approach seems ideal for all purposes, a range of stimulus-and-response parameters are still common.

Investigators also define *scaling techniques* by determining whether to transform indicants into categories or continuous scales. They decide how to combine unidimensional indicants to represent multidimensional constructs. In individual-directed techniques, investigators explore each person's relationship to a group and may be most comfortable with continuous representations of individual variation. Categorical data continue to be easier to manage in later phases of analysis, so such transformations are also quite common.

Determining the *meaning of particular scores* poses the fourth measurement problem that is not easily addressed. Investigators may simply use social preference and visibility as primary dimensions, or existing knowledge about a group to identify salient, measurable themes. In a classroom, for example, investigators may ask students to consider ability or sense of humor as prompts for evaluating social status. Relying on themes relevant to a more general group identity can help investigators determine if comparisons are reasonable and complete.

Critiques of Social Status Tools.   Social status measures are commonly used to verify individuals' status and interpersonal relationships. Critics have assumed that by asking individuals to report their preferences, investigators may be somehow "creating" stereotypes, but studies have disconfirmed these assumptions (Foster, Bell-Dolan, & Berler, 1986; Foster & Ritchey, 1979; Frederickson & Furnham, 1998; Hayvren & Hymel, 1984). Investigators who use sociometrics are careful to minimize risk and distress while preserving confidentiality. They have done quite a bit of work exploring the social status of target individuals, but less work on raters' social dispositions, preferences for their own and other groups, or tendencies to remain indifferent to groups. It should be clear that these perspectives focus primarily on the beliefs of individuals, but that will be more apparent when comparing status concerns with those related to social networks.

Social Networks

Social networks are constructed to offer descriptions of group structures, their effects on groups' functioning, and the evolution of groups over time. More formally, *social networks* are a collection of actors or elements and relations among them, measured at a transpersonal level.[6] Theoretically, networks are comprised of interdependent *social entities* grounded in actions (persons, corporations, schools), and *relational ties* among such entities. Relational ties are channels for sharing material or nonmaterial resources and have included things such as affective evaluations, kinship, the flow of resources, or behavioral interactions. The parts of a social network are defined in formal rather than personal terms although the resulting models may represent different perspectives on environmental opportunities or constraints. Individuals' lived experience may not be measured, but aspects of their identity such as their gender, ethnicity, or social class may be incorporated into formal definitions.

Until now, we have primarily concerned ourselves with theoretical *levels of organization* associated with measuring the ontogeny of persons and culture. Working with social networks, investigators typically distinguish this from *levels of operation* associated with measuring sets of social entities and their relations. As you may remember, considering multiple levels of organization becomes important when comparing social networks to offer a comprehensive account of how groups function in different contexts. Considering multiple levels of operation is helpful for defining the functioning of a group and ensuring that all relevant dimensions of a social network are considered. Network analysts often focus on one level of organization (e.g., peer groups) but look at the social networks from multiple levels of operation (e.g., prominence, balance, transitivity). Available mathematical concepts facilitate analysis of consistency in multiple levels of operation that might otherwise remain hidden in the details of lived experience.

Possible Uses.   Networks that have been identified include enduring patterns of relations among entities in social, economic, political, and other societal structures. Not surprisingly, social networks have been commonly studied in political science, business, sociology, and anthropology, but are also beginning to find their way into psychological and educational research (see Cairns, Cairns, Neckerman, Gest, & Geriépy, 1988; Cairns, Leung, Buchanan, & Cairns, 1995; Iacobucci, 1990). Investigators study social networks to determine the effects of such networks on relations among social entities (e.g., people or institutions) and identify patterns of relations among interacting units.

Investigators concerned with relation among churches in a district, for example, may look at mobility rates among parishioners and how that affects the flow of information, resources, and other cultural rituals. They could label observable transactions such as the sharing of bulletins, scripture, music, or other material resources to determine if regularities are ideological, spiritual, or material. Networks could involve patterns in worship rituals, affiliation networks among church members, or more specific behaviors. To compare denominations, investigators might label each type of social network and look for formal relations among them, treating networks rather than people as the unit of analysis.

Guidelines for Defining Networks. Whereas social status focuses on individuals, social networks offer statistical analyses of multirelational systems. Because network analysts rely on formal definitions, measures, and descriptions of relationally defined theoretical concepts, they do not often concern themselves with the characteristics of individuals or elements within a social network. Instead, they evaluate all types of interactions between pairs of social entities.

Social networks are commonly represented using *sociograms* or interpersonal structures in which people or social units are represented as points in two-dimensional space and lines depict relations among them (Figure 15.2).[7] Network analysts may use *inductive logic* and begin with an elaborate theory to be tested. They may also use *deductive logic,* collecting data and testing relations among the points before constructing formal definitions of roles and relations. Regardless of their approach, these investigators evaluate models and theories containing assumptions about the relational processes and structural patterns of a group. They begin by developing a formal definition of the group's structure and retain that definition for the duration of the research program.

Network Structures. Social networks are fixed in that new entities cannot be added over time and only entities that reflect similar levels of organization are included in analysis. The resulting networks consist of social entities, relational ties, relations, and groups.

Social entities are configurations of actors to be linked with one another, even if those actors may not show movement on their own. For example, investigators have included individuals, classrooms, corporations, and a host of other entities in different social networks, but ensure that all social entities in a single network are of the same type. Comparing students and classes in one network would be problematic because they represent different levels of organization even though one group might be a member of the other.

Relational ties or specific links between social entities are documented, and *relations* reflect the total collection of relational ties in a social network. Investigators have focused on evaluations of one person by another, how material resources are transferred, patterns of affiliations among individuals, and other types of interactions to identify the formal relations reflected in a group's structure. The patterns among social entities and relational ties are integrated into formal, informal, or material definitions of group boundaries, activities,

Directional Dyad

Nondirectional Triad

Network Chain

A Study of Centrality in a Subgroup

FIGURE 15.2 Sample Social Network Structures

and other parameters that make up the social network. The enduring properties of a structure are then labeled in a representation of the group.

Representations of social networks commonly take one of three forms; dyads, triads, and larger subsets of entities. Looking at *dyads,* investigators identify all the various ties between two entities. They commonly do this when they want to explore cohesiveness themes such as reciprocity in relational ties or mutuality in affect. Using *triads,* subsets of three entities, investigators explore issues of balance in a structure and transitivity in levels of operation. *Transitivity* involves information about social roles, social status, and the social position of entities within a network. When *larger subsets of entities* are treated as a whole, investigators can explore issues like actors' centrality or prestige within a group or the centralization and prestige of one group in relation to others. Investigators can also label subsets within a group by looking for evidence of clusterability in which positive relations are consistent among members who show negative relations with social entities outside the cluster.

The resulting *groups,* in this approach, are defined as relations among systems of social entities rather than specific persons. All the social entities for which ties are measured are incorporated into a *set of social entities* that is treated like a freestanding entity in other types of analysis. It should not be surprising, therefore, to learn that network theorists focus on *fixed* sets of entities while they explore the characteristics of a group. It would not be possible to label sets if groups had permeable boundaries.

Measuring a Social Network. Some measurement approaches for social network analysis are descriptive, whereas others are based on probabilistic assumptions. Investigators generally make predictions between social entities and relational ties, looking for evidence that these structures exist. In *descriptive work,* investigators have identified structural models that are then compared to obtained observations and theoretical frameworks. When the proposed relations between social entities and relational ties correspond to predicted models such that there is a good fit between the two, the model reflects a solid description of the group structure and internal functioning. *Probabilistic approaches* begin with stochastic assumptions about actors. Investigators look for probabilities that explain patterns in obtained data and represent these findings using graph theories, deterministic or stochastic statistical theories, or algebraic models to compare multirelational networks.

Comparing findings from descriptive and probabilistic techniques has strengthened theories of group density, span, connectedness, and clusterability. Such comparisons highlight relations between obtained information and mathematically verifiable standards.

Social networks as indicants. Starting with social networks in which all entities are of the same type, networks reflecting different levels of organization can be compared with one another. One social network may serve as an environment for other networks, so investigators may look for structural hierarchies as well as parallel structures in a particular culture. This is easiest to explain by distinguishing *relationships,* connections between particular persons and their current environment, from *relations,* or links between abstract roles and general contexts. Investigators may measure *relationships* between individuals to draw inferences about abstract *relations* like roles, responsibilities, and agendas, and then explore the placement of different social networks within a system.

Critiques of Network Analysis. Critiques of social networks are most commonly found among humanists who prefer generalizations about individuals' lives. Causal inferences about relations among social networks start with the assumption that human behavior and group structures do not change over time. If considered at all, individuals are pawns in a larger chess game of causal relations. Supporters emphasize that lives are enmeshed in historical and structural relations that have preceded individuals in time and will outlast them. Nevertheless, they are cautious about drawing conclusions concerning the life course of particular individuals.

Structures in Ethnography and Ethnology

Ethnographic accounts of group structures emphasize the emergent properties of groups as systems. Systems, in this view, are intercorrelated collections of objects, relations, and corresponding dimensions.[8] Elements are related to one another such that changes in one part of the system affect all other parts despite internal boundaries and indirect connections. Unlike social network analysts, ethnographers and ethnologists do not assume that systems are fixed. These interpretive theorists look for the origin of group properties assuming that groups are more than the aggregate of individuals or their interactions, and that *individual* and *interpersonal* forms of analysis are as important as *transpersonal* levels. Constructs like cohesion and schism, for example, are characteristics of a group rather than individuals, yet they can be studied from three different perspectives.

Measuring first-order indicants of all three levels, ethnographers and ethnologists are not looking for a standard, unmediated view of the world. They find the measurement of boundaries to be of central importance because studying parts within a larger system requires a clear distinction of those parts. These researchers treat groups like cases to be studied and use many different methods to identify patterns across groups and details of how each system is unique. First-order indicants reveal the internal form or structure of a system, and investigators draw second-order inferences about the meaning of internal relations within and between groups. At the second- or third-order levels, they employ theoretical concepts to explain groups from vantage points outside those systems. Interpretive theorists may begin with formal models, with anticipated norms for verifying causes, structures, and functioning, but their final cultural representations reflect conclusions based on known information about actual events or consequences.

Possible Uses.   Ethnographers and ethnologists are likely to take a *topical* or *hypothesis-oriented approach* to measuring groups rather than a comprehensive approach to explaining how groups are embedded in a culture. The measurement of group structures is inherently challenging and requires some a priori assumptions if measurement is to be accurate. To explore the permeability of group boundaries, for example, these investigators generally assume the existence of such boundaries. This assumption coincides with cultural and cross-cultural analyses because entities for comparison can be used later.

Investigators offering thick descriptions of one or more cultures often construct causal explanations of change in transpersonal and interpersonal concepts. Their explanations typically emerge from more than one measurement technique and multiple levels of organization. In labeling groups, these ethnographers focus on the qualities of interpersonal interactions as they pertain to the permeability of group boundaries. Interpretive theorists are likely to make generalizations about communication patterns and relations between individuals and group structures.

When drawing comparisons among cultures, ethnologists focus primarily on transpersonal concepts, treating the group as a whole in which the patterning of individuals' behavior and interactions reflect metalevel concepts about group boundaries, norms, and agendas (Long, 1992). Ethnologists and ethnographers differ from researchers interested in psychometric or developmental measurement in that they are not particularly interested in individuals' ontogeny and do not assume changes in groups typically reflect signs of growth. Nevertheless, they may take such information into account when describing individuals' roles within a culture and drawing second-order inferences by comparing groups.

In one analysis, for example, investigators identified three unconscious collusions of beliefs that could be used to differentiate groups (Bion, 1961). *Dependency groups* were assumed to be those in which members expect to be led by a powerful, dependable leader. *Fight-or-flight groups* seemed to battle with enemies or flee from danger. *Pairing groups* represented the impulse to change existing groups or start new groups by finding their own new leader.

Other researchers treat groups like developmental systems with an ontogeny of their own (Slater, 1966). They may identify a group occupation or reason for coming together and look at how such functions are embodied in the group. In such systems, investigators have found that the central person within a group is not always the authority figure assigned to be the leader. Central persons may serve as ringleaders who can first express the forbidden desires of other group members or as exemplars best embodying group norms. To identify these possibilities in a specific culture, investigators look at boundaries within individuals, between individuals, and around the group as a whole (see, for example, Long, 1992).

Measurement Guidelines.   When collecting information about how individuals and groups are interdependent, investigators can consider several different theoretical dimensions. Interpretive theorists have considered psychological, membership, and operative levels.

At the *psychological level,* individuals are treated as independent systems that have strong links with one another. Group psychologists operating at this level question the idea that individuals are ever independent of groups, and assume individuals' perceptions of independence reflect the internalization of group conflicts as readily as dimensions of personal functioning.

At the *membership level,* the identity of an individual can be distinguished from the roles an individual fulfills as a member of a group. One individual may be a member of many different groups or fulfill more than one role within a single group. Looking at how individuals integrate their various roles offers information on the strength and permeability of group boundaries as often as about personal agency.

Levels of operation within a group can involve both conscious and unconscious dimensions of daily functioning. In one study, operational levels included a (1) *manifest level* of how a group represented community, public opinion, and leadership styles, (2) *transference level* of the group as a family with the conductor serving a parental role and members as siblings, (3) a *mental image level,* in which group dynamics reflected psychologically grounded object relations that mirrored rejected parts of individuals' selves, and (4) the *primordial level,* in which primitive cultural and collectivist images predominated (Foulkes, 1964). Collecting enough first-order evidence to offer a balanced representation of such group structures and functioning, while considering all meaningful levels of operation, requires a priori consideration of at least some theoretical dimensions.

Matching Tools to Goals.   Ethnographers studying groups find deterministic theories to be problematic and may not spend energy labeling antecedent causes of group structures or functioning. First-order evidence may involve information gathered through observations and surveys, or interviews about salient dimensions. Investigators have also collected evidence of contexts that are difficult to observe by planting surveillance equipment or using experience-sampling methods in which informants are signaled to offer responses.

Selected measurement techniques serve different purposes, but investigators often collect information about the quality of social interactions, especially when information collected from narratives would be too difficult to interpret. The following list illustrates common solutions to measurement problems.

- Using observational tools, investigators may rely on an explicit template, use event-recording techniques, or simply record all the activities that occur in a specified setting.[9]
- Self-report evidence may be gathered by asking group members to describe and evaluate their behavior with peers and the corresponding thoughts and emotions associated with such discoveries. Reasoning about others and personal goals or strategies as well as feelings of affection, loneliness, and relationship quality are only some examples of things that are best measured using self-report instruments (Coles, 2003).
- Respondents may describe particular group structures and their positions within such structures. Using social status measures, each individual usually responds privately (Bukowski, et al., 2000).
- Group dialogue involves a combined analysis of abstract acts and accounts of daily activities; participants serve as theorists who critique their experiences alongside researchers (Nicholls & Hazzard, 1993).
- Gathering reports from others in the environment, be they fellow group members, members of other groups, or individuals who are not part of the groups being assessed serves as corroborating evidence for second-order inferences. In research with children, for example, investigators frequently ask parents, teachers, or peers to complete a range of standardized instruments that are then compared to other, more direct forms of evidence.[10]
- Improvements in technology continue to enhance investigators' ability to record events that have previously been difficult to observe. As individuals interact with computers, for example, the machines can record details of Web sites visited, E-mail exchanges, spam received, or a host of other methods for conveying group structures and functioning.

Tools designed for psychometric or developmental purposes may be used in ethnographic research, but if used alone would not sufficiently document the dynamic features of group life. The ethnographic study of groups often involves the integration of structural, personal, interpersonal, and linguistic boundaries. Investigators use a variety of tools and techniques to gather first-order evidence for all these dimensions.

Levels of Analysis.   Cultural dimensions can be measured as symbolic, imaginary, or concrete systems that may not involve normative standards (Lacan, 1979). There is a great deal of resistance to formulating measurement guidelines among interpretive theorists (Long, 1992). These researchers emphasize dynamic patterns within and between different operational levels and assume the dimensions of a group are not static entities. The cultural norms and daily events to be measured are unlikely to conform to formal rules.

Other interpretive theorists have found common questions useful for evaluating first-order evidence. One question involves determining if groups are *open or closed systems.* This question reflects the permeability of group boundaries and, for particular groups, there may be no absolute answers; a closed system may open up as easily as open systems become closed. Information on individuals' beliefs and commitments as well as collective linguistic and cultural systems offers evidence for the permeability of such systems. Open groups have a greater quantity of and more avenues for boundary transactions than do closed groups. Decisions about the relative degree of openness are rarely final. If systems are malleable, boundaries may be open and closed at different points in time. Documenting those events that trigger changes in permeability and labeling the distribution of power within a group is essential for retaining a focus on the group as well as labeling its structure and functioning.

Investigators can also ask direct questions about the *structure and functioning of groups*. They label structures by measuring the personal identity of particular members and the group's collective identity. Ethnographers and ethnologists can also explore intergroup identities. Describing the transpersonal processes that occur within a group can also be measured by asking what common tasks brought the group together. This allows investigators to label relations among group members and relationships among individuals without relying exclusively on formal definitions of roles or responsibilities.

Within each level of operation, investigators can explore questions about *leadership and authority*. They can ask if a group is institutionally legitimate and whether members have a conscious acceptance of norms and authority. Investigators can also explore whether designated leaders have a desire to be led and whether there are unacknowledged norms or ideals deemed to be preferable over those manifest in daily behavior. For example, to evaluate whether group members identify with the manifest leader and/or with a symbolic leader who gains authority by group accolade, judgments about whether leadership was accorded consciously or unconsciously could be supported. This detailed exploration of leadership roles directs attention to meaning apparent in first-order evidence regardless of whether that evidence is gathered using psychometrically defined tools or less formal measurement approaches.

In addition to treating groups as a phenomenon, investigators explore levels of *meaning from participants' perspective*. They can ask participants to think like critical theorists, evaluating their lived experience to determine what human displays are valued and what forms of bias should be evaluated. Investigators may also ask group members to think like interpretive analysts, considering how the forces of history and power dynamics affect the structure and functioning of a group. Missing as well as salient features in such descriptions could illuminate the quality of group life. Informants may also be asked to deconstruct their experience, describing temporal changes in the meaning-making enterprise without focusing on the group structure.

Listening to these evaluations, interpretive theorists would look for evidence of who is authorized to speak and who listens. They would also look for information on how individuals become validated as group members and on the human characteristics that are rewarded or penalized. Such interpretations require information on who is excluded and included in a group and the reasons for such dynamics.

Critiques of Ethnographic Approaches. Ethnographers often accept that group-related concepts may be best understood in terms of their functioning within a dynamic system of concepts. Firm boundaries are assumed to be largely nonexistent, and indicants represent only a sample of information necessary for representing cultural norms. A "true" representation of culture cannot be measured, but cultures can be represented metaphorically.

Critics argue that this agenda is too intangible and offers no clear way to validate inferences. These interpretive theorists assume that concepts and their indicants offer such essential definition to a group structure that measurement can reflect only the immediate experiences recorded. All accounts are metaphorical because investigators extract interesting stories about the dynamic nature of human functioning. Theory-driven guidelines may be used to organize and interpret evidence, but all causal assertions are grounded in the present meaning of evidence. These interpretive theorists find it problematic to draw inferences about future relations, and assume that explanations of present and past events can be inherently beneficial.

MAKING CONNECTIONS

Find a study that involves groups. How were the group structures and processes measured? Did investigators classify each participant's social status? Did they explore social networks by labeling the social entities and the abstract roles, responsibilities, and agendas that guide relations? Did the investigators create ethnologies or ethnographies out of multiple kinds of evidence? What levels of organization were measured? What levels of operation were measured?

MINIMIZING BIAS IN DESCRIBING GROUPS

Techniques for measuring the structure and functioning of groups differ in precision, and therefore, in the nature and form of bias. Social status approaches tend to be highly empirical and bias looks more like that found for psychometric tools. At the opposite extreme, ethnographic studies of group dynamics tend to include many different measures and bias can be inherent in first-order recording of experience as well as second-order inferences. Lessons from existing studies reveal forms of bias for social status, social network, and ethnographic measurements of groups. If these approaches are combined, the various types of bias are compounded.

Social Status

Perhaps because of the prolific quantity of research on social status, the most detailed accounts of measurement bias are available for sociometric tools. Limitations will be classified here according to their focus on the *qualities of stimuli, response contingencies,* and the *interaction of both constraints* when determining social status.

Qualities of Stimuli.   Investigators have used a wide range of stimuli and questioning formats to elicit information about social preference without reaching consensus about which approaches are most accurate. Measures of direct preference of liking and disliking are problematic in that they can be insufficiently anchored to a common criterion; as with psychometric tools, reliance on probability theory is important for calibrating preferences, but setting parameters for such estimates can be tricky. Asking respondents to nominate or rate their friends, enemies, or acquaintances, for example, can allow for too much variation in how these terms are defined. Some individuals will define anyone with whom they have exchanged favors as a friend whereas others will assume that close bonds of trust and intimacy are necessary.

Choosing stimuli that are both age-appropriate and that maximize comparisons in long-term studies is challenging and, as with other measures, requires the acknowledgment of at least some bias. In studies with children, for example, investigators have sometimes preferred indirect measures that focus on specific movements for eliciting preferences because those stimuli are sufficiently concrete that children can visualize action. Asking "Who do you like to sit by in school?" may offer more consistent answers than "Who do you like?" because the criterion is embedded in the prompt.

Older respondents are able to imagine many different reasons for each action, so the concreteness of the prompt may not show the desired effect. Shaking hands, for example, can have many different meanings, depending on whether the gesture indicates a greeting, the closing of a business deal, or an acknowledgment. Such interpretations may or may not be associated with social status.

Response Contingencies. For each question, investigators have also used different *response contingencies.* Most commonly, they have used nominations, ratings, rankings, and paired-comparisons.

Peer nomination in which respondents are asked to list persons who meet particular criteria (e.g., liked or disliked) are probably used most frequently. Debates continue over whether nominations should reflect a specified number or remain unlimited, and resolutions depend on the agendas of researchers. Asking respondents to limit their nominations to a specified number can make the measures easier to administer; a specified threshold also facilitates the transition from one type of nomination to the next and clarity in parameter estimates for establishing dependability. Unlimited nominations allow respondents to reveal their *social expansiveness* or the tendency to choose many individuals, and minimize error in the estimates of *social isolation* or the tendency to remain unselected by everyone. Unlimited procedures are also ideal when investigators assume that acceptance and rejection fall along a continuum, using continuous rather than discrete measurement scales (Terry 2000). There are few differences in social preference classifications as investigators transform limited and unlimited responses into categorical forms, but the two approaches offer different ancillary information (Bukowski, Sippola, Hoza, & Newcomb, 2000).

The second most commonly used method involves the construction of *rating scales.* Respondents are often asked to evaluate how much they like or dislike each person in the group and these ratings can provide more detailed information on each group member than is possible with nominations. Those sociometric measures operate in the same way as social distance scales in that they reveal more subtle distinctions between accepted and rejected status. Nevertheless, investigators cannot consistently distinguish persons with identical scores or who predominantly receive moderate ratings. Controversies over whether nominations or ratings offer the best evidence remain unresolved, but different measurement purposes invariably support one contingency over another.[11]

Several problems with rating scales limit their use for exploring social status. Completing such measures is time-consuming when groups are relatively large and respondents may not know each member well enough to offer a rating. The mere presentation of names can minimize spontaneity in responses because participants may naturally look for patterns in the presentation of names or in their emerging ratings. Participants may also show a propensity to use response sets, but those tendencies will remain unpredictable across individuals. In addition, social isolates will be difficult to identify if respondents are encouraged to rate everyone.

Some investigators have also used *rank-order procedures* in which respondents are asked to list names in order of preference or rank those on a list. This is more commonly used for assessing direct or task-focused preferences. As with ratings, investigators obtain more information on individual differences than is possible with nomination methods.

Many of the same limitations for ratings are apparent for rankings. When a group is relatively large or if participants do not know all the members, the process of ranking may be inordinately complex. Rankings in the middle of a distribution are difficult to interpret because they are often unstable or reflect inconsistent evaluation criteria. Investigators have minimized these problems by offering partial rank-order tasks in which investigators retain rankings at the end of the distribution while assigning all middle range tasks the same number. They have also reduced the complexity by asking respondents to complete paired comparisons; names are presented two at a time and respondents choose the best fit of each dyad for all possible dyads.

Computing Status Ratings.   Combining stimuli-and-response contingencies to compute social status ratings is quite complex. Results from each of these measures are translated into social status categories using several different transformations. In some cases, investigators convert raw totals into standardized scores to control for the size of the nomination pool or reference group. They do this to create a common metric for comparing variance so cutoff scores can be established for each status. When investigators have used ratings or rankings, they may standardize mean ratings across peers or the number of times a person receives the highest or lowest possible score. *Social preference scores* are computed by subtracting standardized rejection scores from standardized acceptance scores for each person. Next, this difference score is standardized.[12]

Social visibility or impact is calculated by adding standardized acceptance and rejection scores and then standardizing the sum. Much like the assigning of grades, investigators set criteria for high and low social visibility by using this impact score. Standardizing the frequency of positive or negative nominations, average ratings, or average rankings allows investigators to use common criteria for accepted and rejected status. Ratings at extreme ends of the distribution are classified as popular or rejected. Scores for socially neglected or isolated status are usually 0 or near 0 because individuals would receive no nominations. Scores in the middle ranges between 0 and extreme rejected or popular status would indicate average social status.

The use of standard scores obfuscates someone's controversial social status or tendency to receive as many strong liked preferences as disliked preferences. Positive and negative scores would cancel one another out, leaving scores for controversial status similar to those scores otherwise obtained by individuals with neglected or isolated status. For this and other related reasons, some investigators have compared individuals' scores to an overall probability distribution to determine the likelihood of obtaining particular combinations of scores by chance alone. This method allows investigators to isolate different probability distributions for each status category and compare distributions across seemingly average scores.

Understanding Bias.   Sociometric approaches to exploring social status have combined theoretical and empirical information to minimize bias in measurement. As is the case for all measurement tools, bias is still endemic. Missing from these studies is information on the criteria used by respondents when making their judgments. As you may remember, measuring the reciprocity in a relationship is theoretically relevant to understanding the nature of groups, but simple levels of agreement between persons does not convey whether respondents use the same criteria when making their determinations. One person's criteria could involve a preference for anyone in physical proximity whereas others may prefer levels of intimacy or common interests. Comparing findings from different approaches can offer insight into the dependability and credibility of classifications, but first it might be helpful to see how the measurement of social status differs from the measurement of social networks and ethnographic accounts of group structures.

Social Networks

Measures of social networks also involve combinations of theoretical and empirical information to minimize bias in measurement. In fact, social network analysts may use the same sociometric tools designed to evaluate social status. Rather than simply classify individuals, social analysts use such tools to identify the placement of particular social entities in a group, exploring relational ties to draw generalizations about particular roles and links between such roles.[13] Network analysts may measure the attributes of particular social entities, but do so primarily to understand the subtle forces operating within a network.

Label the Population.   The first step in measuring social networks while minimizing bias involves labeling the population to be studied. Ordinarily social network analysts begin with a known, fixed collection of social entities such as the members of a class, participants at a party, or employees in a company. Definitions that are external to a set of social entities can make it seem easy to label group boundaries. However, there may be other occasions in which boundaries cannot be so easily identified. Investigators may rely on indices such as the intensity of particular relational ties or the frequency of interaction to draw distinctions between members and nonmembers of a set.

Some investigators have also distinguished realist and nominalist approaches to labeling a population. *Realist approaches* involve asking those people who are social entities or who represent them to label group membership or boundaries. *Nominalist approaches* rely on boundaries established by considering theoretical interests (Laumann, Marsden, & Prensky, 1989).

Represent Members with Indicants.   Ordinarily, social network analysts take measurements on all members of a population, but this is sometimes impossible or impractical. Three readily identifiable sampling methods are apparent in existing research: casting random nets, using snowball sampling, and considering ego-centered sampling.

When *casting random nets,* investigators sample informants and label relational ties among them, much like researchers would sample participants of a larger population. *Snowball sampling* involves the identification of social entities to form a first zone for the network, and asking each person or representative of the social entity to nominate other participants for inclusion in a second zone. This process is repeated for as many cycles as is necessary for testing theoretical assumptions. *Ego-centered sampling* may identify individuals' personal networks in which a social entity is asked to report on her or his own relational ties and the possible ties among a targeted group.

Identify Dimensions of Social Entities.   In addition to labeling a population or designing an appropriate sampling technique, investigators determine the *structural variables* to be measured for the collection of social entities. They use whatever tools or measurement techniques best capture their theoretical interests. Researchers studying social networks may use the same tools as researchers working within psychometric, developmental, or ethnographic traditions, but they have developed an approach to transforming their first-order evidence into second-order inferences about social networks. Building a social network involves specifying units of observation, modeling units, and procedures for quantifying relations.

Units of observation are the social entities on which measurements are taken (e.g., persons, events, dyads). *Modeling units* involve the kinds of groupings that are considered; investigators may focus on individual, interpersonal, or transpersonal levels at the first-order phase of measurement. They might also focus on the details of a social entity, dyads, triads, subgroups, sets of actors, or the total network.

The *quantification of relations* involves decisions about the qualities of relational ties. Investigators determine if ties are directional, reflecting origins and destinations between social entities, or nondirectional, such that there is no ordering to the tie. They also determine if relational ties are represented using dichotomous data, recording only the presence or absence of information, or if ties are valued in ways that reflect issues like strength, intensity, or frequency.

Identify Network Dimensions.   To make decisions about each of these types of data, investigators differentiate two dimensions of a social network. Network analysts explore the *structural features* of a network by taking measurements on the relational ties among all pairs of social entities and ensuring that they have considered the full range of ties. They also measure the *composition of a group* by labeling the essential attributes of each social entity. Both sources of information are coordinated when investigators generate second-order inferences about the network.

Select a Network Type.   Investigators also label networks according to the number and types of modes under consideration. Common network structures found in research include one-mode, two-mode, or multimode networks. They may also reflect affiliation or ego-centered networks and contain dyadic or triadic relations.

The type of network that can be generated from social status data reflects a *one-mode network* because all social entities and their actions form a single unit for analysis. Social entities, relational ties, and relations are combined to draw inferences about group structures and the composition of a social network in which all social entities come from the same level of organization and are of the same type. You may remember that *social entities* may be people, subgroups, organizations, or other collectives such as nations or cultures. Many of the psychometric measurement approaches are useful for measuring the attributes of these social entities. *Relations* in a one-mode network can take many forms, depending on the type of information necessary for supporting theoretical claims. Examples from available research include measures of sentiment, material transfers, kinship, communication, daily behavior, and physical or social movements. *Relational ties* may be directional such that one social entity can be labeled a *point of origin* and the other a *destination.* They can also be bidirectional, such that causal inferences are not supported.

A *two-mode network* typically involves either comparisons among two sets of social entities or two dimensions of a single set. For *dyadic, two-mode networks,* comparisons are made between each social entity of one set and every social entity of a second set to explore relational ties among them. Sets may include different types of social entities (e.g., persons and corporations), the relations among social entities within a set (e.g., friends or acquaintances), or the attributes of actors (e.g., males, females). Investigators may also look for relations between sets, labeling features that are unlike those within a single set while remaining careful to note any directionality in relations.

A second type of two-mode network is known as an *affiliation network.* This involves one set of social entities and one set of affiliation variables (e.g., memberships, events, or activities). In addition to measuring relational ties between all the social entities, investigators measure relational ties between social entities and affiliation variables. They may also measure the attributes of both social entities and the designated affiliation variables. Although it becomes highly challenging to do so, *multiple-mode networks* may also be measured by extending the same techniques for measuring two-mode networks to all desirable modes. This does not happen often, primarily because it becomes difficult to interpret the results, but computer technologies are making this much easier to accomplish.

Less commonly measured networks have been labeled by treating social entities, dyads, or triads as freestanding entities. Investigators measure such *ego-centered networks* by treating each social entity independently and looking at the nodes labeled by that entity. A person may label his or her social supports or a corporate CEO may label the various departments within a company, but the core of the social network is a social entity and much of the rest of the network is constructed from inferences made by that entity.

Investigators also treat dyads or triads as social entities in *dyadic or triadic networks.* Assuming a married couple is a unit, for example, investigators may represent them either as independent pairs not in the same set, or as members of a larger set of dyads. Similarly, triads of law partners or doctors may be explored independently of all other lawyers and doctors or as members of larger set of triads in their profession. Investigators rely on theoretical interests to support their decisions, but bias is introduced if these decisions are not enforced throughout the study.

Find Necessary Indicants. Once investigators make decisions about each network parameter, they determine what evidence would be most helpful for exploring each dimension. Investigators have measured different aspects of a social network using questionnaires, interviews, observations, archival records, and a host of other tools. These tools typically involve a top-down approach to measurement in that their design is determined by the theoretical needs of the investigator rather than by members of the community being evaluated. Error is introduced for each new tool, but hopefully that error is randomly distributed.

Estimating Bias.   Investigators have considered people's perceptions of networks, conducted experimental studies in which levels of operation are systematically manipulated, and completed partial analyses of relations. Small-world studies have been conducted by beginning with a target person and determining how many degrees of separation are apparent in a chain of social entities. In these studies, precision in measurement was determined using most of the techniques that have been addressed in previous chapters, but the tasks asked of respondents are kept as simple and concrete as possible. Methods for evaluating measurement error are considered at each level of operation rather than by exploring the fully coordinated second-order inferences.[14]

Ethnographic Structures

Ethnographic approaches to measuring groups hinge on the assumption that group boundaries may be open as often as they are closed, making it difficult to label the dimensions of a group. Using information from social status and social network theories, it becomes easier to talk about the various levels of operation considered simultaneously. Many ethnographers measure the characteristics of a group member, both within and outside a group context, to determine how that individual fits into a group structure. They remember that classes of members have a structure and function that is more than the aggregate of individuals' characteristics; groups have independent properties that are also measured. As is the case for social network theories, members and classes of members represent different levels of abstraction. Both levels of organization are measured by collecting a balanced repertoire of first-order evidence before drawing second-order inferences. Issues of bias are explored by treating evidence on members and classes as though they contain independent properties.

Evaluate First-Order Evidence.   Determining the accuracy of first-order evidence involves evaluating how well information about particular group members corresponds to their identities and roles within a group. It also involves determining how well information about particular groups corresponds to the identities and roles within the broader cultural context. Investigators look for information on whether individuals identify with a group, whether the group acknowledges them, individuals' leadership and authority roles, and personal assumptions about how power is distributed within the group. They also label how a group's identity fits within a larger cultural context and how issues of leadership, authority, and power are distributed among groups in a cultural system. Looking for evidence of group cohesion, for example, involves knowledge about the occupation of the group and the range of tasks that brought individuals together. Measurement is accurate when investigators or informants can label how individuals are related to group tasks.

Start with an Emic Approach.   To accomplish this matching of roles, responsibilities, and life experiences to a group structure, ethnographers usually begin using an *emic ap-*

proach that places restrictions on theoretical predictions until personal assumptions about cultural norms become transparent. Investigators also try to understand what knowledge is available to their informants and to imagine who knows what within a group. They look at *how individuals communicate* within a group before assuming that structures across groups are sufficiently parallel to warrant inclusion in a comparative analysis. When differences among groups are idiosyncratic, investigators may not draw intergroup comparisons, focusing instead on thick descriptions of one group's structure within a broader context.

Identify Levels of Operation. Once investigators have accurately represented individuals' communication patterns, they may begin labeling essential *levels of operation* within a group and boundaries between groups. The systems to be measured begin to seem clearer as investigators label attributes of the system and plan a more balanced approach to measuring each attribute. The group structure is measured when investigators label relations, but the relations reflect different aspects of a group's history. Levels of operation occur within and between several dimensions. Investigators have evaluated contextual antecedents of the group, consequential information about the group, and leadership and authority norms. They also document changes in a group's identity, and the location of a group in broader cultural contexts.

It is during the group formation process that investigators look for the *contextual antecedents and consequential information* leading to the convergence of persons. Such information may be gleaned from the imaginations of individuals, in illusion, fantasy, or myth. It may also be apparent in overt speech and gestures as individuals invite one another to participate in activities. Decisions about whether individuals are joining or reproducing an existing group raise different measurement considerations from those associated with forming a new group. Questions of what people expect to do in a group and what opportunities were available prior to the formation of a group are as important as establishing particular roles and responsibilities. As individuals join a group, boundaries and roles as well as inclusion and exclusion rules inevitably change and ethnographers try to offer a balanced account of that change.

The initial reasons for group formation can change. Therefore, many ethnographers try to document details and changes in *a group's identity* as different individuals identify and disidentify with the group. They may measure identity from outside the group or by considering the beliefs of particular group members. At the group level, individuals may be tied to one another through direct or indirect commitments. Group members are sometimes bound together because of common habits that find expression in group ideals and activities. General affect patterns or common resolutions to conflicts may also facilitate a group identity even if individuals do not directly interact with one another. Groups differ in the complexity of their identity and these are just a sample of the possibilities unearthed by ethnographers.

Ethnologists and ethnographers alike may consider the accurate measurement of *how groups are situated in a broader cultural context,* but would have different reasons for doing so. An ethnologist may be searching for evidence to support a sufficiently pancultural theoretical framework to allow for cross-cultural comparisons. An ethnographer may be satisfied with measuring intergroup relations within a particular culture to offer a more accurate representation. To measure intergroup relations, these interpretive theorists try to accurately construct a matrix of groups and explore each group's function in that matrix. Ethnographers may also label the identities of particular group members and determine how members view their own and other groups. The precision of this kind of matrix hinges on the accurate representation of group boundaries, cohesion, and the clarity with which community members are able to represent their social position. Investigators also determine if there are external sources that impose identities on particular groups by labeling features that would otherwise have remained unnoticed.

Structural relations associated with *leadership and authority* involve distinctions between *relations* or the parameters of particular structural positions and *relationships* or the details of interactions between persons. In one account, for example, investigators identified four relations common in a collection of groups even though their expression in relationships differed (Long, 1992). *Symbolic leadership* was associated with predefined roles such as that of the tyrannical parent who tried to control everyone's behavior through reward-and-punishment contingencies. Harsh and uncompromising, *interdictory authority* was associated with responsibilities and prohibitions emerging from moral imperatives. *Remissive authority* emerged only in the face of wrongdoing to restore balance among the wayward. *Transgressive authority* emerged once it was clear that neither interdictory nor remissive authority patterns remained intact and members introduced new values to challenge an old order.

Consider Multiple Dimensions for each Level of Operation.   Investigators have labeled these and other aspects of group structures and functioning by recording changes in behavioral, symbolic, and imaginary dimensions. Interpretive theorists involved in action research find such aspects by engaging in systematic observation while in collaboration with an organization to determine cultural entities, changes in the dimensions of each entity, and the effects of their own systematic manipulation of events at the time they occur (Clark, 1972). Using multiple data sources, investigators try to situate groups in time and place, label focal points for their observations, and look for opportunities to obtain information from community members about their lived experience.

Challenge Assumptions.   To determine if they have enough evidence, investigators look for information that disconfirms as well as confirms their understanding of a group. They also try to minimize any tendency to form premature conclusions by determining the nature and frequency of events apparent in informants' accounts. While collecting information in their fieldwork, most investigators articulate differences in how groups are related to one another by asking if a group is evolving within an environment or if environmental changes are antecedents to group changes. Investigators look at the behavior of informants for habitual responses, signs of deception, or a preoccupation with pleasing investigators. To anchor their evaluations, many investigators also analyze their personal gestures, speech, and timing to explore biases they might introduce when interacting with a culture. Ethnographers also question everyone's tendency to formulate unfounded interpretations by remaining skeptical of the information they acquire and striving to identify missing behaviors and first-order meaning-making on the part of community members.

Differentiating Informative and Uninformative Bias

Investigators measuring social status and social networks can offer mathematical estimates of bias that are derived from the assumption that obtained information can be compared to absolute or probabilistic standards. Such comparisons are possible when investigators control for or overlook some of the dynamic features of groups. Standardized estimates are important for generating policies and practices that are likely to affect individual lives, but may not offer the most accurate representation of lived experience. For this reason, ethnographers and ethnologists rely on measurement techniques that eschew formal standards and offer thick descriptions of how individuals and groups function within a particular community.

Measuring the ebb and flow of individuals in and out of groups requires a level of trust and communication that need not be apparent for less intrusive questions. Investigators introduce informative bias by becoming a participant as well as an observer in the community under investigation. Concerns with sustaining communication and trust invariably lead to a level of helpful bias in the measurement process; investigators and informants engage in loosely structured activities that are altered by the perspectives each brings to the interaction. For these reasons, researchers who study groups are comfortable distinguishing informative bias that allows for tests of contextual predictions from that which causes unhelpful distortion.

- - - - -

MAKING CONNECTIONS

Looking at an account of groups in your area of interest, did investigators rely on mathematical algorithms to represent bias? Did they acknowledge the existence of informative types of bias? What kinds of evidence did investigators offer to convey that they considered issues of bias in the measurement process?

DEPENDABILITY AND CREDIBILITY IN INFERENCES

Procedures for exploring the *dependability* of information and the *credibility* of inferences differ, depending on whether groups are treated as open or closed systems. *Dependability* continues to reflect questions of stability in first-order inferences, but the meaning of stability differs, depending on whether group boundaries are known. Measures of social status and social networks reflect the assumption that boundaries are not permeable, making it easier to determine if the dynamics within a group remain stable over time. Ethnographic approaches involve the assumption that the groups themselves as well as activities within groups change over time; stability, in this view, is measured by looking for repeated occurrences of acts as often as actions.

Credibility for both kinds of research involves the match between second-order inferences and first-order evidence, but mathematical algorithms are easier to use when groups are assumed to be closed rather than open systems. These differences should be apparent in the following, more detailed descriptions of how investigators verify the dependability of their evidence and credibility of second-order inferences.

Social Status

Sociometric techniques contain a number of challenges to traditional estimates of reliability and validity. While it may be possible to explore some forms of accuracy, there are no logical reasons why nominations, ratings, or rankings should be internally consistent; informants need not agree on a person's social preference; second-order inferences are used to determine social visibility, and coordination of the two dimensions in the calculation of social status is inconsistent. Investigators have tried to estimate stability in individuals' social status, but test-retest evaluations do not account for the permeability of group boundaries or the dynamic nature of relationships within a group. Establishing the dependability and credibility of sociometric tools is especially challenging because groups are statistically generated rather than formed using a predetermined criterion.

Limitations of Statistical Classifications.   Statistical classification works well enough when evaluation criteria are unilateral in that decisions reflect one criterion. Given that current formulations are, at best, the bilateral coordination of social preference and social visibility and that these criteria are not consistently applied in the classification of persons, investigators cannot rely simply on psychometric approaches to evaluating reliability. Distortion can be compounded when investigators start with continuous data, created by asking respondents to generate ordinal or interval indicants, and then transforming such information into nominal categories; such transformations reflect movement away from rather than toward the ratio scales ideal for use in calculating inferential statistics. Distortion is less problematic when investigators are describing general patterns, or using status categories as independent variables in their research designs, but such transformations undermine statistical power if social preference, visibility, or status are used as outcome variables.

Restrictions on Difference Scores.   Social preference is another name for a difference score that can be problematic if it is simply equated with indices of acceptance and rejection (Bukowski, Sippola, Hoza, & Newcomb, 2000). A graph of the relationship between acceptance and rejection scores, for example, is likely to look quite different from the distribution of social preference scores. When acceptance and rejection scores are compared by placing one parameter on the x-axis and the other on the y-axis, variation is likely at the tails of the distribution, but not in the middle. Group members who are regarded in a neutral manner are likely to be evaluated more consistently than those who are either rejected or popular. Social preference scores are likely to be homogeneous at either end of the distribution, but show a great deal of variability in the middle. Subtracting dislikeability ratings or ranks from evaluations of likeability to obtain social preference scores should be relatively homogeneous if everyone agrees on a person's social preference, but not if there is disagreement. Because social preference scores involve information from acceptance and rejection ratings, the three types of scores are not completely synonymous or independent of one another.

Selecting an Appropriate Score.   Choosing an appropriate score is essential for verifying credibility, even if all the indices are somehow dependable. Investigators who treat accepted status, rejected status, and social preference as three distinct measures without equating them are likely to find that using nomination and rating scales results in equivalent social preference scores, but that accepted and rejected status classifications are likely to differ for the two response contingencies. Similar challenges are apparent in the comparison of social visibility scores with those obtained for accepted and rejected social status. Some investigators keep estimates of acceptance, rejection, social preference, and social visibility separate in their analysis. Those who do so are likely to assess dependability and credibility using more than one approach to measuring each construct, comparing findings across various measurement techniques. They are not likely to treat acceptance and rejection as opposite poles on a continuum.

Explore Balance.   Other investigators introduced the concept of *balance* into conversations of the measurement process (Terry, 2000). They look for balanced logic in the social meaning of each construct as well as in the empirical representations of such logic. Using *item-response theory* (IRT), these investigators incorporate three types of information into their evaluations of a measure.[15] They look at the *dimensionality* of a construct, the degree to which *optimal scaling methods* were used, and *models for testing representativeness*. It is important, in this approach, to separately measure each dimension of a construct, but that is difficult to do when respondents hold different interpretations of each dimension.

Dimensionality evaluations of a construct involve the analysis of whether the range of measured dimensions reflects those that are most meaningful. Identifying *optimal scaling* involves a comparison of different weighting procedures to determine if the weighting of data offers a more precise measurement than simple means or sums. *Representativeness* with IRT compares simple and complex schemes to determine if one works better or if the two work equally well in generating dependable classifications, supporting parsimony whenever possible.

Applying IRT to the evaluation of sociometrics, the general question of how one person regards another in a group context is translated into a comparison of individuals' reasoning against a probabilistic standard. More often, investigators try to map *latent-trait concepts* onto psychologically meaningful variables (Figure 15.3). This comparison should ideally include information on the *level of an attribute* in the target person being evaluated (e.g., her or his likeability), the *social sensitivity of each rater,* and a *social threshold of raters' understanding of the criterion.* If the measured attribute is unidimensional, the likelihood of finding a common definition of the attribute increases. If all raters reach consensus in their definition, it should be possible to reliably discriminate the presence or absence of that attribute. The *slope* of a distribution of scores should be flat if all respondents were equally able to distinguish individual differences in the presence or absence of the attribute. More realistically, there is variability in all three parameters that influences their coordination (see Chapter 7).

Identify Patterns in Outliers.   Investigators can compute independent and collective analyses of ratings to compare individual and group ratings. If investigators learn that ratings

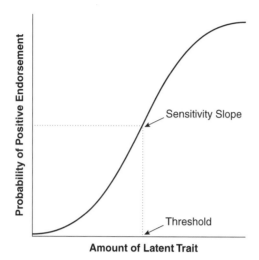

FIGURE 15.3   Schematic of Latent-Trait Estimates

of the latent trait or measured attributes are inconsistent across a distribution of persons, they may look for *patterns in the outliers* to determine where their tools lack dependability. The greater the degree of social consensus, the more dependable and credible the evaluations of social status become. Using estimates of social sensitivity as a guide, investigators may choose to weight scores to obtain optimal measurements of each dimension. This is most likely when respondents offer direct preferences. Friendship ratings, for example, have not been sufficiently unidimensional or stable for inclusion in latent-trait models. Nevertheless, such methods can offer precise comparisons when investigators want to empirically distinguish friendship and acceptance ratings, evaluate socially acceptable and unacceptable behavior, and consider the perspectives of perceivers and those they evaluate. This approach treats all preferences as independent of one another while accepting their association with a common latent trait or theoretical dimension.

Statistical Verification.   Although investigators have not been able to rely on psychometric estimates of accuracy and stability to evaluate their tools, they have found ways to determine dependability in how social status is determined. IRT is currently being refined and methods for making programs more accessible are underway. These methods involve the transformation of indicants into scale scores or latent-trait estimates and the exploration of how well each approach works in relation to others.

Social Networks

Latent-trait models used to evaluate social status data are similar to the *structural models* used to verify social networks. Social network theorists assume that it is not possible to explore functioning within and between networks until the structure of a network is measured in a credible manner. Investigators measuring social networks and social status start with different theoretical assumptions, but they both look for mathematical verification that their obtained patterns correspond to those predicted in theoretical frameworks. Starting with formal definitions and descriptions of the structural properties of social entities, subgroups, or groups, social network analysts *translate core concepts into relational terms* (Wasserman & Faust, 1994). Details about the attributes may be included in social network models or used as a parameter for constructing more than one social network. *Dependability* typically involves first-order interpretations whereas *credibility* involves second-order interpretations.

Dependability as the Verification of Relations. Even the simplest network undergoes complex analysis for determining whether measured relations are dependable. At the social network level, investigators explore first-order interpretations by translating the construct of social visibility or *prominence* into two theoretical dimensions. *Centrality* involves the location of a social entity within nondirectional relations. *Prestige* involves the labeling of relational ties directed toward a particular social entity. Social entities can be evaluated using a number of prominence criteria, and the presence or absence of directional ties affects the definitions of these criteria. Measurement is dependable when these relations are recorded with consistency.

Explore Centrality. When relations are nondirectional, the *degree of centrality* reflects the number of ties each social entity has with other social entities and offers an index of the activity level of each social entity. Five dimensions are commonly evaluated: closeness, betweenness, information flow, differential status, and indices of prominence.

The first four of these dimensions are commonly evaluated for symmetry before looking for asymmetrical or directional patterns. *Closeness* reflects the social distance between entities and may be assessed using ratings rather than dichotomous indices or by comparing the position of entities within a chain. *Betweenness* is a measurement of interactions between nonadjacent social entities and how such interactions are affected by a third entity placed between them. *Information flow* is evaluated by comparing all the various social ties associated with a particular social entity. Including information on the attributes of social entities, evidence of *differential status* is recorded.

These criteria for evaluating centrality can be evaluated for credibility by looking exclusively at how social entities are involved with one another. They can also be evaluated in terms of the symmetry of each social pattern. When relational ties are not symmetrical, investigators can reevaluate their model to determine if relational ties are better represented as directional, considering *indices of prominence.*

Dependability Comparing Groups. Criteria for labeling the locational properties of individuals within a group can also be applied to groups within a collection of groups. Network analysts construct a social network of groups rather than individuals. They sometimes compare relational ties between the social entities of each group with those of other groups to explore group centrality and/or prestige. Analysis of groups is easier to theorize about when groups reflect the same levels of organization, but investigators may also use this approach to compare the structure and locational properties of different levels.

Given that levels of operation focus on relations among entities of the same type and levels of organization focus on relations among different types of entities, complex networks may involve second-order inferences about first-order interpretations, which are again evaluated in a third-order analysis. Comparisons among apples and oranges can offer interesting information, but must be distinguished from comparisons of apples and apples if the resulting inferences are to be interpretable. These distinctions could undergo a third level of analysis comparing fruits and vegetables.

Evaluating Group Structures.   Another set of considerations when exploring dependability and credibility involves the assessment of groups' structures. In doing so, investigators have isolated balance, clusterability, and transitivity. *Balance* is determined by evaluating whether informants for two social entities share equivalent relations between one another and with other social entities. *Clusterability* involves the degree to which social entities can be grouped into a finite number of subsets such that positive relations are apparent within a subset and negative or no relations are apparent between subsets. *Transitivity* works just like the mathematical theorem: In a triad of actors *i, j,* and *k,* if there is a positive relation between *i* and *j,* and a positive relation between *j* and *k,* there should also be a positive relation between *i* and *k.* A *vacuously transitive* triad is possible when at least one of the two conditions cannot be explored, and *intransitivity* is evident when conditions are contradicted in the triad.

Cohesiveness in Parallel Groups.   Investigators also explore the *cohesiveness of subgroups* within a social network to determine the relative strength, directness, intensity, frequency, and/or value of particular ties. At the one-mode level, investigators use pairwise comparisons to look at the directionality and strength or intensity of ties. They may begin by exploring *connectedness* or whether social entities can be joined. Defining a *geodesic* as the shortest pathway between two nodes in a graph of social entities and their relations, investigators use this unit to estimate social distance. Measuring how many geodesics are between pairs of entities, for example, they can compute the *geodesic distance* and verify the *reachability* between social entities. Cohesiveness is assumed if groups contain many reachable ties, evident by looking at whether the *diameter,* or the distance between nodes, falls within an acceptable geodesic distance. Acceptable distances differ, depending on whether investigators are defining cliques or placing subgroups into more restrictive clans or clubs.[16]

Connectedness alone offers an insufficient measure of cohesiveness, leading investigators to also explore *mutuality.* In mutual ties, members of each pair represent their relation in the same way. Ties with identical relations are classified as adjacent and reflect the strongest indication of cohesiveness.

Investigators may also look at the number of relational ties between social entities with more cohesive subgroups containing a higher *density of relational ties* than less cohesive subgroups. They can also compare *in-group and out-group ties* by looking at the relative frequency of ties between group members and one another, relative to members and nonmembers. Each of these measurements can be explored at the individual, interpersonal, and transpersonal levels to draw conclusions about the dependability of first-order data and the credibility of claims about cohesiveness.

Cohesiveness in Complex Networks.   When investigators find two or more levels of organization, they most often consider parameters of *affiliation networks* and/or *overlapping* *groups.* Treating social entities as one mode and events as a second mode, they move beyond relations between pairs of social entities to determine how social entities are linked through subsets of events and other entities. Typically, comparisons between social entities (e.g., persons) evaluate how each social entity is linked with the same set of events (e.g., corporations). In exploring the duality between social entities and events, investigators can consider whether social entities are linked by events or events are linked by social entities.

Such seemingly straightforward comparisons become significantly more complex as investigators combine entities and events that serve multiple purposes. Looking at ties between social entities, investigators can explore *comembership* or *coattendance* in one-mode analysis. Looking at ties between events, they can determine if events are *overlapping* or *interlocking,* also using one-mode techniques. Eventually, many investigators find themselves exploring *co-occurrence* in relations between social entities and events. Co-occurrence can be documented by constructing an *affiliation matrix,* a table in which actors are classified by events or vice versa. They can also construct *bipartite graphs* or *hypergraphs* to illustrate subsets of entities. (See Figure 15.4.) Problems with dependability become apparent when investigators have difficulty graphing the relations they detect.

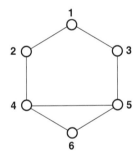

Cliques: (2, 3, 4, 5, 6) and (1, 2, 3, 4, 5)
Clan: (1, 2, 3, 4, 5)
Clubs: (1, 2, 3, 4, 5), (2, 4, 5, 6), (3, 4, 5, 6)

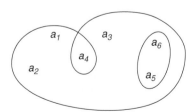

Sample Hypergraph

FIGURE 15.4   Representations of Cliques

Coordinating Dependability Themes.   Despite the complexity of establishing dependability, investigators use the same logic regardless of whether they are evaluating a single group or multiple groups. They evaluate issues of centrality, structure, and cohesiveness. In doing so, network analysts invariably answer questions about prestige or prominence, determining the social visibility of each entity in a network and the directionality of relations.

Credibility.   Returning to credibility, investigators determine if their measurement parameters offer a solid account of the information they are trying to summarize. They may document the *rate of participation* by determining how many events are tied to each social entity. They may also determine the *size of events* by looking at the number of social entities classified as having been involved in each event. These data can support generalizations about *span, density, reachability, connectedness,* and *diameter* in single-mode analysis of either social entities or events.

Single-mode analysis does not account for the theoretical assumption that all connections between social entities are through their links with events. Therefore, investigators exploring the duality of affiliation or overlapping networks are most likely to explore issues of reachability for *pairs of actors* with events as a mediating variable. Network analysts may also rely on *correspondence analysis,* complex statistical procedures that permit the simultaneous comparison of social entities and events.[17]

Coordinating Dependability and Credibility.   Complex procedures verify the dependability of first-order or second-order evidence and the credibility of second-order or third-order inferences about social networks. Most social network analysts rely on common mathematical principles to compare social entities and relations. They often use graphs to represent the resulting networks and have developed a wide range of graphic procedures to reflect different theoretical assumptions. Network analysts who find relations they cannot graph sometimes collect new first-order evidence or revise their assumptions about an emerging social network. When social networks account for all the first-order evidence and are aligned with participants' perspectives and/or theoretical assumptions, the resulting networks are assumed to be credible.

Ethnographic Structures

Establishing the dependability and credibility for ethnographic evidence is inevitably dialogical. Investigators explore their hunches, questions, and relationships while collecting first-order evidence, but look for how the information is integrated when making second-order inferences. Some investigators assume that information is integrated into a group structure in much the same way as it is in individuals. As individuals acquire new knowledge within a preexisting context, they use that context as a reference point to engage in the conceptual integration of old and new information. Similarly, groups form within a preexisting context and members may rely on the features of that context when first integrating roles, responsibilities, and functions into a newly emerging structure. The parts of a group, or the roles fulfilled, cohere as a group carries out the tasks that brought individuals together. Assumptions like these are likely to play a role in how investigators go about establishing the dependability and credibility of their first-order data and second-order inferences.

Participants as Informants.   Regardless of investigators' assumptions about the dynamic qualities of group structures and functioning, they often converse with group members to determine what events are noteworthy and where to draw boundaries in their interpretations. Investigators may make decisions about when in a group's history to begin their investigations and the roles of researchers and group members, but these decisions cannot be implemented without the cooperation of participants. Dependability and credibility hinge on thoughtful decisions about what segments of group life to include in analysis, what processes are noted and by whom, and what processes are ignored.

Dependability in Ethnography.   Investigators can look at the *dependability* of their first-order evidence by exploring the frequency of occurrence for recorded events. They also look for missing information and, after determining the reasons for such absences, investigators engage in reparations either by collecting more first-order evidence or drafting a clearer explanation of the group structure and functioning. This process invariably involves movement from fully trusting informants and recording techniques to mistrusting them. Informants' accounts and information gleaned from various measurement tools are taken at face value when investigators confirm their assumptions, but are treated with skepticism when they engage in the critical reflection necessary for understanding disconfirming evidence. Investigators organize first-order information to facilitate the generation of causal claims in second-order analyses. They endeavor to retain mutually beneficial relationships with informants to gain insight into the balance among observed and unobserved aspects of group functioning.

Credibility in Ethnography.   To establish the credibility of second-order inferences, investigators ask whether events are common or rare and look for overlap in the interpretations of multiple informants. The dynamic nature of groups makes it unlikely that all important events will occur frequently or that informants will agree with one another. Investigators do not try to reconcile such information, but try to explain the resulting patterns. If second-order inferences are sufficiently credible, changes are apparent as group activities and structures are tracked over time. It may not be necessary for each informant to understand all the inferences drawn by investigators, but informants' perspectives are usually represented in final ethnographic accounts of group structures.

Dependability and Credibility in Ethnology.   Because ethnologists are interested in how group structures and functioning compare with one another, they may eliminate much of the detail of individuals' lives when making second-order and third-order inferences. Comparing groups inevitably involves reflection on commonalities and differences in relations, not relationships. Ethnologists may benefit from the methods used by network analysts, but compare such approaches to findings generated using emic styles of inference.

Dependability can be estimated by exploring the independent entities operating in the same environment. Ethnologists generally ask if groups are of a similar logical type or if they represent different levels of a system. They can explore the credibility of second-order inferences by looking for *nonhierarchical patterns*. Ethnologists may also explore whether groups can be *hierarchically ordered* to illuminate differences among them. Credibility, in this analysis, verifies whether group members are peers.

At a more specific level, investigators explore dependability by determining if entities that appear to be similar actually share the same dimensions or if they share similar dimensions that serve different functions within the group. Consider, for example, a system of friendship groups within a middle school. Students would all be classmates, but they may also fulfill other roles. Some students might be members of extracurricular clubs or sports teams, whereas others may form spontaneous friendship groups. Individuals may be members of multiple groups or of one or no groups. These relations sometimes contain hidden hierarchical features even if, from another cultural perspective, individuals would be seen as peers. Ethnologies are dependable when all these possibilities have been considered, even if only some are relevant to the final conceptual framework.

Ethnologists also ask if relations between groups are of a different *logical type.* In comparing groups, they can determine if one group is a *subsystem* of another. Two groups, for example, may be interdependent in functioning such that both are working on different levels of the same agenda. These groups may also be parallel or seem equivalent, but serve different functions. When groups are of different logical types, one group may be superordinate to another in ways that might be obfuscated in direct comparisons within a single system or culture. The state of the economy, for example, can affect the availability of cultural events within a community in ways that would be overlooked if investigators simply evaluated the quantity and range of cultural events.

Another form of logical analysis involves the degree to which *reciprocal relations* are evident between groups. It is possible that the parts and whole of two different groups are completely dependent on one another such that a larger system could not function if one group deconstructed. For example, the amount of schooling evident within a group is likely to affect the kinds of jobs available to members, yet the nature of available work also affects the range of jobs for which preparation might be beneficial.

Coordinating Dependability and Credibility.   Determining the dependability of first-order or second-order evidence and credibility of second-order or third-order inferences invariably involves comparisons in the accounts of individuals as well as the information gathered about group structures and functioning. The more actively informants interpret evidence and offer feedback about inferences, the more believable the final account of group structures and functioning is likely to become. Although it may not be practical or even desirable for all informants to agree with every inference generated about group experiences, their perspective can save a great deal of time when investigators coordinate their evidence with theoretical frameworks to draw conclusions.

Verifying Second-Order or Third-Order Inferences

The three approaches to measuring groups introduce different measurement dilemmas to be solved. The reliance on intact groups when measuring social status or social networks facilitates mathematical comparisons of obtained evidence with theoretically generated standards or probability assumptions. The permeability assumptions of ethnographic and ethnological research require more concrete comparisons or the avoidance of group comparisons. Investigators use second-order inferences to support generalizations about direct experience, but comparing groups may add an extra level of interpretation.

Measurement techniques for one type of data may be used in conjunction with evidence from another, but the level of organization associated with evidence constrains procedures for verifying second-order or third-order inferences. Regardless of the techniques used, investigators work to ensure their inferences are sufficiently connected with actual entities and settings. They also recognize that the theory-building process will be undermined if first-order evidence is gathered poorly or overlooked.

MAKING CONNECTIONS

What inferences did authors make in the report you found on groups? How can you tell these are inferences? What first-order evidence was introduced to support the inferences? How was dependability established? What information was included to verify the credibility of second-order or third-order inferences? Did you notice any unacknowledged levels of distortion in this report?

CONFIRMING CLASSIFICATIONS, NETWORKS, AND STRUCTURES

Procedures for confirming conclusions about social status, social networks, and cultural representations of groups are influenced by the different levels of organization in a measurement plan. Investigators do not always use the term *validity* to represent this evaluation, primarily to distinguish the confirmation process from a ritualistic use of rules. Techniques for measuring social status and social networks can involve mathematical comparisons of obtained evidence to probabilistic standards, but only if those standards are sufficiently grounded in theoretical assertions about how individuals function in groups or how groups function in comparison to one another. Similarly, investigators who simultaneously explore group boundaries and group dynamics invariably rely on validity criteria generated using information gathered in local contexts. As you may notice, this resistance to deterministic thinking should not be taken as a sign that validity is unimportant for the measurement of groups; the process is significantly more complex than for other types of measurement, but it is significant.

Social Status

To confirm sociometric findings, investigators often begin by determining if status classifications are stable along three dimensions. They look for stability over time, across measurement styles, and in relation to other attributes of the target person.

Stability Over Time. Longitudinal studies do not support the long-term stability of sociometric classifications, but the popular and rejected groups tend to be more stable than isolated, neglected, or controversial groups (Cillessen, Bukowski, Haselager, 2000). Individuals at extreme ends of the distribution seem to have other attributes that help them retain their status, whereas those in the middle may be more responsive to status-related life experiences.

Stability Across Measurement Styles.   Comparisons among different classifications also yield somewhat unstable findings. Using standard scores to compare methods, investigators often designate preference scores greater than 1 as indicative of popular status and of less than –1 as indicative of rejected status. They tend to use 0 as the cutoff for interpreting direct standard scores of who is liked most or least; scores greater than 0 would indicate high acceptance and less than 0 would indicate rejection.

With probability methods of interpreting scores, investigators tend to look at deviations from the group mean. They assign accepted status to those with liked scores that are significantly higher than the mean, and disliked scores that are at or below the mean. Rejected status is assigned to persons with disliked scores falling significantly above the mean and liked scores falling at or below the mean.

When investigators use multidimensional classification methods to compare preference and visibility scores, they may combine the total number of nominations and ratings into a single standard score, standardizing each score separately and averaging the two. With such variability in scoring techniques, it may not be surprising that there is so little stability across studies. Nevertheless, these different sources of information are useful for different purposes.

Comparisons with Other Attributes.   Investigators may not expect high degrees of stability in classifications, but, when they do, exploring personal attributes can help strengthen particular tools. High levels of aggression, for example, may elicit rejected social status. Social status may also reflect the qualities of interpersonal relationships and/or a person's ability to hear and respond to feedback. Investigators can evaluate whether enduring personality characteristics have the strongest influence on social status, revising their theory accordingly.

Groups of persons may also construct stereotypes or prejudicial views that become resistant to change and create powerful expectancy effects. Such biased perceptions may not be generated by group members; they can be generated using the self-perceptions of the target person. Investigators identify convergence among these possibilities by comparing status classifications with other measures of personality and ecological settings.

Changing Social Status.   In some confirmation studies, social status is used as an outcome variable and investigators may try to predict adjustment or maladjustment in particular individuals. In other studies, social status is a predictor variable and investigators label those individuals whose status is stable or unstable. Looking for the attributes associated with stable social status, investigators may also identify valuable or problematic social skills. Exploring associations between unstable classifications and other attributes may reveal information about problematic measurement or new patterns that were not previously understood. Investigators would generate predictions about whether changes in particular behaviors could lead to changes in status. They might rule out measurement error when changes in group experiences, personal behavior, social self-perceptions, or peer perceptions do not lead to a corresponding change in status.

Coordinating Evidence.   Patterns in individuals' assignment to status categories need not be common for measures to be valid. When investigators explore the dynamic qualities of social status, they may look for associations among different measurements. Looking at whether rejected social status is associated with aggressive behavior, for example, the status classification could be verified even if children with initially high levels of aggression changed their behavior and became less disliked as a result. The consistent pairing of related concepts rather than the placement of individuals within a status system would be sufficient for validating the system itself.

Social Networks

To confirm the structure of a network, investigators typically explore the equivalence of the roles and positions of social entities. *Position* is used to indicate those social entities within a network that have similar activities, ties, or interactions (White, Boorman, & Breiger, 1976). Social entities with the same positions need not be in direct or indirect contact with one another, but their identities are equivalent. *Role* refers to comparisons among collections of relational ties and associations among relations (Boorman & White, 1976). Roles can only be determined if investigators have a clear definition of the various positions within a network. Verifying roles involves looking at how relations are linked with all the social entities in a network and their respective positions. Confirming the structure of a network involves comparing obtained relations with those of similar networks or subgroups within networks.

Identify Roles and Positions.   When investigators have collected a multirelational data set, they can identify roles and positions through one of three routes. They can use multirelational data to explore group relations, evaluate social entities, or simultaneously coordinate information.

Group relations are explored by labeling typical or local roles, which are then compared with groups of social entities to identify positions. *Social entities* can be the starting point by first identifying typical or local positions and then using that information to find roles in groups of relations. A more direct approach is difficult to do with accuracy, but investigators may *simultaneously coordinate information* on social entities and group relations to label roles and positions. To confirm conclusions, some investigators analyze multirelational data using all three approaches to determine if the results remain the same. When they do, the findings are assumed to be more robust.

Select a Definition of Equivalence.   Investigators confirm conclusions about positions by exploring the equivalence apparent between collections of social entities. They look for equivalence in the entire model of positions and roles. Network analysts typically begin by establishing a formal *definition of equivalence* and currently can choose from one of six types. They can evaluate structural or regular equivalence and isomorphic or automorphic equivalence. They can also consider equivalence in local roles or ego algebras.

Groups with *structural equivalence* are defined as those with identical relational ties. Equal ties are expected between the social entities themselves or dyads, triads, or subgroups of social entities, and between those entities. They are also expected between each entity and all other entities in the network.[18] For this to be accomplished, investigators also consider whether the relations are dichotomous (present or absent) or valued (often compared using standard scores). They also consider whether relations are directional or nondirectional and if the relative meaning of reflexive self-ties (e.g., $i \leftrightarrow i, j \leftrightarrow j$) is such that the diagonals in a matrix may be meaningful.

Other approaches to establishing equivalence are less restrictive (Wasserman & Faust, 1994). *Regular equivalence* is defined as similar to structural equivalence, with the exception that social entities need not have identical ties with entities that are not related to a subgroup. That is, all ties need not be structurally indistinguishable, but social entities should have identical relational ties between the various positions in a network or cluster. *Isomorphic equivalence* involves a one-to-one correspondence between two groups. Social entities may show this correspondence without necessarily restricting the types of relations. Relations may show this correspondence without restricting the types of social entities. *Automorphic equivalence* is a special case of isomorphic equivalence applied to a single network. Automorphic equivalence is evident if equivalent social entities occupy indistinguishable structural locations. Although the definitions of isomorphic and automorphic equivalence need not focus exclusively on positions of social entities, these definitions are typically used for such comparisons.

Two additional types of equivalence focus more on the types of relational ties than on the position of social entities within a group. *Equivalence in local roles* involves the verification of identical role sets such that roles are assumed to be stable, but social entities may move in and out of such roles. *Ego algebras* are calculated by simultaneously mapping roles for each social entity and roles for the group structure, using relational algebra to accomplish this challenging goal.

Match Obtained Patterns to Equivalence Definitions.   Once a definition of equivalence is established, investigators may evaluate the degree to which subsets of social entities match the definitions to be tested. These questions have been addressed earlier, but it is helpful to remember that even at the confirmation phase of a study, investigators consider whether they have adequately recorded all the necessary first-order evidence for drawing conclusions.

With definitions and measurements in hand, investigators begin the complex task of determining how to *represent equivalences* found in the first-order data and explaining the predictions that were not supported. It may be easiest to begin by illustrating how position analysis is accomplished, while bearing in mind that the same logic can be applied to roles analysis. You may remember that equivalence can take on *parallel, spatial,* or *hierarchical* forms and investigators establish positions by assigning social entities to equivalent classes. Relations are restated within and between classes, depending on the degree to which predictions are upheld. Position definitions are used to represent the evidence by following guidelines apparent in definitions of equivalence and statements of relations between positions.

Reporting Confirmations.   Investigators report their representations using at least one of four different forms. They use density tables, image matrices, reduced graphs, and/or blockmodels. A *density table* may summarize all ties between positions. An *image matrix* reduces the rows and columns of a sociomatrix by collapsing those cells that contain equivalent social entities to describe only ties between positions. A *reduced graph* represents positions and relations rather than social entities and relational ties.

Blockmodels are hypotheses about how social entities are located in discrete subsets or positions, and statements of the presence or absence of relational ties among positions. Such models facilitate confirmation of how well obtained evidence corresponds to predictions. Blockmodels can be either theoretical image matrices or reduced graphs that serve as a standard for comparison.

Evaluate the Representations.   Investigators confirm the *adequacy of representations* by determining if an image matrix or graph of a single relation matches that predicted by a blockmodel. They may also make similar comparisons for collections of image matrices or graphs that represent the entire multirelational network. Network analysts often evaluate the goodness-of-fit apparent when matrices and graphs are compared with blockmodels. When using modifications of *latent-trait models,* they may also compare representations to a range of probability models to determine the most parsimonious set of findings. Investigators can compare the Euclidean distances among various subgroups or networks, or simply correlate indicants from one network with those in another potentially equivalent network. Once confirmed, these social networks may be incorporated into more complex relational algebras to coordinate positions with roles.

In confirming their conclusions about the structure of social networks, investigators distinguish issues of *social status, position,* and *roles* (Goodenough, 1969). Many network analysts work with at least two of three kinds of data. Using somewhat different language, the individual level is sometimes referred to as the ego level, the interpersonal level is the local level, and the transpersonal level indicates the whole network. As has been done here, investigators may start by grouping indicants representing social entities and their attributes to determine local positions. They may also start by grouping relational ties and corresponding relations to determine local roles. Once local positions and roles are verified, most investigators are ready to begin analysis that explores how global roles and positions are associated across networks.

Ethnographic Structures

Confirming the structure and functioning of groups in ethnographic work is invariably complex and heavily grounded in theoretical assumptions about why the study of groups is important. Neither ethnographers nor ethnologists approach validity with the assumption that patterns should recur, show equivalence to other patterns, or otherwise be rule-governed. While looking at themes of ideology and power, ethnologists and ethnographers rely on goal-specific criteria for verifying descriptive, interpretive, and theoretical validity. Ethnologists are more interested than ethnographers in generalizability and evaluative validity, but external confirmation is necessary for both. Differences in the purposes for exploring cultures have led ethnographers and ethnologists to assume that validity is highly conditional. Most interpretive theorists avoid proposing general procedures for confirming their conclusions. Despite the necessity of different techniques, ethnographers and ethnologists keep a few definitions in mind when evaluating their work with groups.

Confirming Patterns in Obtained Data.   Three types of validity apply to the verification and comparison of groups within a cultural context. *Descriptive validity* is established by comparing first- and second-order inferences to determine the factual accuracy of how groups are represented. Working much like content validity in other paradigms, investigators verify the balance and representativeness of their evidence about individual memberships, group structures, and functioning. *Interpretive validity* involves comparisons between the inferences drawn by community members and researchers. Investigators look for congruence in these representations of group life and try to explain points of agreement as well as disagreement. Investigators may also explore the congruence between second-order inferences and theoretical constructs or perspectives when establishing *theoretical validity.* The parameters for such verification differ considerably, depending on whether investigators adopt phenomenological, critical theoretical, interpretive analytic, or deconstructionist perspectives because each discourse community calls attention to different facets of community life.

Confirming Second-Order or Third-Order Interpretations.   The remaining two types of validity are more frequently considered by ethnologists, but ethnographers may respond to implicit concerns when justifying why their account of groups is more cogent than other accounts. When exploring *generalizability,* investigators ask whether their conclusions can be extended to other settings, historical periods, and populations. Ethnographers may be more concerned with verifying consistency across settings and in time whereas ethnologists may be more interested in generalizing their conclusions to other populations, but determining how conclusions can be extended enhances future planning for topical and hypothesis-oriented research. When investigators compare their accounts to others in a discourse community, the resulting *evaluative validity* offers information on the relative usefulness of the conclusions.

The Iterative Nature of Validity.   Although validity is an iterative process that may not be completed after investigators collect first-order information and draw second-order inferences, there are a few common steps that can be identified. Investigators can *reevaluate* how they determined *group membership* and the structure of groups, verifying the accuracy of first- and second-order comparisons and looking again at relationships between second-order inferences and theoretical generalizations. They would label *criteria for organizing evidence* and strive to *balance generalizations* with particular details.

Looking at first-order information, investigators also look again at the *qualifications of the researcher.* In one study, for example, a male ethnographer worked with boys who had learning disabilities. The ethnographer was able to establish a level of rapport with these boys that would not have been possible if he had been another female educator who was probing into the boys' feelings of competence (Thorkildsen & Nicholls, 2002). Investigators' skills and social sensitivities also play a central role in high-quality measurement.

Most investigators also evaluate and *reevaluate the levels of trust* between ethnographers and informants, offering a final analysis only when validating their conclusions. Claims about the "objectivity" of a study simply reflect an investigator's assumptions about the norms operating within ethnographic discourse communities. Therefore, evaluative validity may be established only once a final account leaves an investigator's desk.

Metasystemic Evaluation Criteria.   Ethnographers and ethnologists usually avoid generating procedural rules for confirming their findings, but generate culturally sensitive criteria for the contexts in which they work. These criteria can be best characterized as metasystemic concepts used to explain the system of groups. Such concepts offer language that is sufficiently detached from lived experience to offer explanations of group dynamics.

In one quest, for example, the investigator identified five theoretical criteria for confirming the validity of her conclusions (Long, 1992). These observed states formed a hierarchy that could be used when making comparisons across groups. In the *nonintegrated state,* group members were involved in making introductions, labeling roles, and otherwise looking for common ground on which to base decisions. Later, groups entered a *mirror state* in which they studied the norms, agendas, and parameters of other groups, labeled their identities, and drew comparisons that offered information for the formulation of their own group identity. Next, groups entered a *state of internal focus and division* in which they formed an identity, created factions among themselves, and later became reintegrated. Throughout this exploration, groups retained a public identity that was readily apparent to observers, but overtly negotiated positions within that identity. A *state of symbiosis* occurred once leadership structures were in place, a group identity was achieved, and individuals were all willing or able to identify with group norms and agendas. Group structures inevitably changed when members entered a *state of created autonomy* in which some members tried to leave and create their own groups. In such a state, the group inevitably splits and may be reformulated or disappear. This hierarchy of group dynamics emerged from evidence of movements and actions among several different groups and involves an outsider's judgment of functioning within a group.

Differentiate Acts from Actions and Behavior.   Using relevant criteria, investigators can draw comparisons across groups to determine the validity of their concepts. In doing so, they differentiate abstract acts from actions that are grounded in local knowledge and movements that are recorded in first-order analysis. Investigators may confirm their conclusions by building a hierarchy of social interpretations and articulating each level of organization within an environment. Considering different levels of operation, they draw generalizations about meaning by looking for redundancies in actual movement and in accounts of those movements, actions, and acts. The level of meaning-making varies according to the assumptions embedded in different theoretical discourse communities, and it is those controversies that lead investigators to propose alternative theories.

Choosing an Approach to Validity

Investigators who study groups may mix evidence gathered from measures of social status, social networks, and ethnographic accounts of group experience. When interested in exploring intact groups, it is easiest to rely on measures that assume groups reflect closed systems, despite the fact that some details of individual lives may be overlooked. When exploring the dynamic process of group formation and maintenance, groups are treated as open systems and investigators may have multiple measures of group boundaries to ensure they accurately represent permeability in how each group is defined. These decisions affect how investigators prioritize different types of validity and the criteria they establish for confirming their conclusions.

■ ■ ■ ■ ■ ▬▬▬

MAKING CONNECTIONS

How did investigators validate their conclusions in the study you found? Did they generate their own criteria for organizing evidence and inferences, or did they rely on criteria generated from other research programs? Were the findings typical and easy to summarize or more complex and challenging to represent? What types of validity were apparent in the account you read? Did you find the argument compelling?

GROUPS AS LEVELS OF ORGANIZATION

In this chapter, techniques for measuring and defining groups were outlined. The idea of levels of organization, introduced in chapters on measuring development, were revisited when comparing techniques for exploring the systems of an environment in which individuals develop and function. Measures of social status and social networks differ appreciably in their design, but both rely heavily on empirical accounts of intact groups. Ethnographic measures are intended to explore the malleability of group boundaries, formation and maintenance processes, and other less tangible features of groups.

As you will see in the next chapter, investigators can also measure the functioning of individuals within a group. In such analyses, humans are represented as active agents who create their own social environments. Many of these agents realize that they are embedded within a social nexus wherein they establish both personal and collective or socially derived identities, and look for ways of making meaning out of this process. In determining which kinds of measurement to emphasize, investigators consider whether they want to know how people are embedded within or are subordinate to groups, or if they want to know how groups are embedded within or are subordinate to individuals. Ethnographers assume that, through processes of integration, personalization, and realization, groups become embodied within individuals, but also understand this process requires more than one style of investigation.

SUGGESTED READINGS

Barbour, R. S., & Kitzinger, J. (1999). *Developing focus group research.* Newbury Park, CA: Sage.

Cillessen, A. H. N., & Bukowski, W. M. (2000). *Recent advances in the measurement of acceptance and rejection in the peer system.* New York: Jossey-Bass.

Freeman, L. C., White, D. R., & Romney, A. K. (Eds.). (1992). *Research methods in social network analysis.* New Brunswick, NJ: Transaction.

Greenbaum, T. L. (1997). *The handbook for focus group research.* Newbury Park, CA: Sage.

Hoyle, R. H., Harris, M. J., & Judd, C. M. (2001). *Research methods in social relations* (7th ed.). Stamford, CT: Wadsworth.

Long, S. (1992). *A structural analysis of small groups.* New York: Routledge.

Moreno, J. L. (1934). *Who shall survive? A new approach to the problem of human interrelations.* Washington, DC: Nervous and Mental Disease Publishing.

Morgan, D. L. (1998). *The focus group guidebook.* Thousand Oaks, CA: Sage.

Wasserman, S., & Faust, K. (1994). *Social network analysis: Methods and applications.* New York: Cambridge University Press.

ENDNOTES

1. Hogg, Terry, & White (1995) offer one theoretical comparison of social identity theory and group identification theory.

2. Wasserman & Faust (1994) and Freeman, White, & Romney (1992) offer many examples of such research.

3. Asher & Dodge (1986), Coie, Dodge, & Coppotelli (1982), and Newcomb & Bukowski (1983) offer different systems and measurement approaches.

4. Moreno (1943, 1951) was systematic in offering these dimensions, but did not measure them all himself.

5. Moreno (1934) is credited with the initial presentation of these rules, but, as is apparent from a close reading of the research, this information is selectively attended to in different research programs.

6. Wasserman & Faust (1994) offer an elaborate review of the methods that have been used in the study of social networks.

7. Moreno (1953) offered the earliest sociograms, but investigators have developed significantly more elaborate ways of representing such networks since then.

8. Hall & Fagen (1955) offer this definition, but many other ethnographers work from variants on this theme.

9. Parten (1932) is often credited as offering the first reliable system for recording children's group behavior.

10. To explore gender-based ratings see Frederickson & Furnham (1998). The Child Behavior Checklist (Achenbach & Edelbrock, 1986), Social Skills Rating System (Gresham & Elliott, 1990), Revised Class Play (Masten, Morrison, & Pellegrini, 1985) have been used to evaluate children's behavior in relation to their social position.

11. Maassen, van der Linden, Goossens, & Bokhorst (2000) conclude that rating scales may be preferable over nomination methods, but Cillessen, Bukowski, & Haselager (2000) offer a more elaborate picture of how the methods for classifying responses result in different levels of stability. Generalizations remain problematic.

12. Standardized scores are usually left in z-score terms for this analysis, but linear transformations are sometimes used to enhance readability.

13. Harré (1979) offered an early account of the theoretical implications of such comparisons.

14. Holland & Leinhardt (1973) are frequently cited as offering the best accounting of measurement error for social network analysis, but new tools are likely to lead to new studies.

15. Embretson (1983) offers a clear sense of how this type of analysis operates and Terry (2000) compares this approach to evaluating sociometric data with recommendations of Rasch (1966). Chapter 7 outlines the parameters used in such analysis and the fundamental assumptions about their relations.

16. Mokken (1979) offered an early version of these definitions that has been retained in social network theories. *Cliques* are defined as three or more social entities, represented as nodes on a graph, that each have relational ties with one another. Cliques can be adjacent, but one cannot subsume another (Wasserman & Faust, 1994). Clans and clubs have more restrictive definitions that reflect the details of relational ties.

17. Wasserman & Faust (1994) offer a very detailed sense of each of these kinds of analysis.

18. Lorrain & White (1971) are credited with this approach although Guttman (1977) offered a definition of *graph equivalence* that also works for this type of analysis. Graph equivalence is appropriate for a single reflexive set of relations such that if $(i \leftrightarrow i)$ and $(j \leftrightarrow j)$, for all i and j, then $x_{ij} = x_{ij}$.

CHAPTER SIXTEEN

MEASURING MICRO- AND MACROCULTURES

The study of cultures entails movement beyond the analysis of individuals' skills and behaviors to identify the intricacies of societal institutions and their meaning in everyday life. Cultural theorists explain how human functioning is grounded in particular norms and often realize that responsibility for institutional success and failure is not solely in persons. These researchers draw inferences about how contexts provide a structure for interpreting human functioning. They measure individuals' responses to life's dilemmas, cultural norms, and changes in the resulting organizational structures. The resulting ethnographies or ethnologies often increase our interest in familiar events by making them seem strange.[1] In making the familiar seem strange, investigators study meaning-in-action to describe the vagaries of everyday life and learn that even minor organizational changes can initiate a wide variety of human responses.

PURPOSES FOR CULTURAL THEORY

Cultural theorists usually appreciate the flexibility of ethnographic methods for exploring the process and structure of social ecologies. With ethnographic tools, they describe conditions that shape the trajectories of human functioning, and evaluate when and how participants can adopt an overly narrow perspective.[2] Some investigators study only part of a social ecology, but many compare information about persons, settings, and actions to generate a comparative understanding of communities. Cultural theorists place practices in sufficiently high relief that the local meaning of events can be analyzed, and participants can learn about the strengths and limitations of their communities without necessarily engaging in social comparisons. Members of other cultures can find new languages for representing human functioning by comparing descriptions of particular settings with their own experience. Ethnologists take such comparisons a step further and compare contextual details with patterns in a more global social system.

Common Research Paradoxes

At the onset of this journey, it was pointed out that the distinctive features of measurement do not reflect paradigmatic differences. Investigators may formulate rival theories and research programs to determine which ideas are more helpful for understanding human functioning, but they do not usually replace one paradigm with another. Paradigms are noncompetitive metaphysical ontologies such that old and new paradigms inevitably coexist; investigators simply become more and less interested in different parts of such ontologies. This coexistence occurs even if one set of theoretical propositions may be replaced by another. Theoretical propositions, rather than paradigms, play a central role in which measurement techniques are used and when.

Not surprisingly, the agendas of each investigator profoundly influence her or his choice of measurement techniques. All research, regardless of the theoretical traditions from which it emanates, is laden with the values and interests of investigators who design and conduct each study. In addition to being theory-driven, values that affect measurement are found in individuals' daily functioning, position in the life cycle, and historical context.

Discussions about what is worthwhile to know are invariably affected by the *social distance* investigators uphold between themselves and the participants in their research.[3] The most common form of ethnography is *participant-observation research* in which investigators acknowledge that social distance is a phenomenon to be explored. Some investigators want to understand how every participant sees the world, whereas others endeavor to identify principles for generating context-sensitive inferences about human functioning. Ethnologists typically focus on cross-cultural generalizations and spend little time imagining individual lives. These various goals play a central role in how investigators design particular tools, combine evidence in a study, and combine studies to support more general theoretical claims.

In one sociological course, for example, students and their teacher discovered that they spent relatively little time evaluating particular hypotheses by considering the quality of presented evidence (Kurzman, 1991). They also seemed to ignore the theoretical traditions from which their values emanated. Instead, these scholars spent most of their time discussing issues of how human subjects should be treated in social science research. They discovered contradictory and often mutually exclusive assumptions that were inconsistently brought forth to credit or discredit ideas.

One set of contradictions, found both in the class and in other discourse communities, involves (1) the desire to listen carefully to participants' own analysis of their experiences, and (2) the assumption that social forces prohibit participants from ever being able to understand their situation. A second set of contradictions involves (1) the social deterministic claim that participants' actions are caused by broad social forces, and (2) the belief that self-determination and free will permit individuals to overcome social forces. In both cases, the role of participants is questioned, but the same might be said for investigators. Some investigators assume that (1) they should be like participants to fully understand them, whereas others assume that (2) social distance facilitates a necessary sense of objectivity that would be absent if investigators are also community members. Admitting these contradictions, many investigators accept the paradox associated with their roles and label obvious influences. They see their roles as (1) *political activists* who formulate questions intended to elicit social change and self-reflection, and (2) *academics* who put forth enduring ideas that can help individuals transcend dehumanizing conditions. This tension is particularly obvious when considering how investigators theorize about and measure micro- and macrocultures.

THE LOGIC OF CULTURAL THEORIES

Because most ethnographers are interested in situations and how persons are embedded within them, they study how individuals negotiate their lives in communities, how institutions are organized, and how to improve cultural practices. In studying educational settings, for example, investigators may move away from evaluating individuals' competence and explore the dominant means by which individuals can display competence (see Erickson, 1986, and Turner, 1980). They look at how some displays are more highly valued than others and how values embedded in the social order are associated with behavior. Looking for patterns in the display behavior of individuals can also offer clues about expectations inherent in a particular culture. Investigators coordinate individual and cultural perspectives by replacing the *if → then* logic of prediction and control with the *what and how* logic of description and explanation.

You may remember that some investigators limit their inquiries to *case studies,* exploring how particular individuals negotiate their lives and the meaning embedded in everyday choices. Investigators conduct *ethnographies* to extend the study of individuals and explore local circumstances. They illuminate the strengths of a community and areas of dysfunction. Investigators who conduct *ethnologies* make cross-cultural comparisons to facilitate future conversations about how communities are situated in the larger world. To accomplish any of these goals, investigators give up the simple notion that culture is a uniformly owned property of a discrete society. Instead, they recognize that *culture is a collection of interpretation principles and the products of that system.* All conversations, observations, and artifacts are inextricably cultured, and cultural theorists typically extract meaning from the sequential analysis of these entities.

Hopefully, as you have read through the different approaches to measurement, you have been able to imagine your own uses for particular tools and techniques that were not necessarily highlighted. In this way, you may have been able to see just how the toolbox metaphor works in practice: tools designed for one purpose may be modified and recalibrated for other purposes. If so, you have thought like cultural theorists, who generally rely on all measurement approaches that yield culturally useful information. The study of cultures inevitably involves a combination of many methods because interpretation principles raise a wide range of measurement dilemmas.

To investigate how social processes operate within a given culture, most researchers document human variability and suppress the tendency to make comparative judgments about individuals' functioning within groups. Tools that offer the richest evidence about micro- and macrocultures can be classified into one of three categories; the analysis of text, participant-observations of cultural rituals, and the analysis of cultural artifacts. Cultural theorists often bracket their investigation by conducting small-scale studies of one or more levels of organization. They may rely on a single source of information in each study, but combine studies to justify interpretation principles. Theorists may also collect ethnographic data along with other, more standardized forms of evidence while embarking on an elaborate study of a particular culture.

Generalizations about a specific culture or comparisons across cultures are usually situated in reference to multiple kinds of evidence, but most investigators are careful about how they coordinate such information. Cultural theorists realize that mistakes in perspective-taking can occur when investigators try to integrate assumptions from psychology, sociology, and anthropology without considering the amount of social distance embedded in each discipline. To explore cultures, psychological conclusions are kept to a minimum, whereas anthropological and sociological conclusions become most salient. The remainder of this chapter introduces examples of how these goals are accomplished while retaining respect for the perspectives of all community members.

MAKING CONNECTIONS

Find an ethnography in your field and label the evidence used in that work. Do the authors analyze text? How are cultural rituals explored? What do investigators do to verify participants' interpretation of events? What kinds of cultural artifacts are evident in this work?

ANALYSIS OF TEXT

Investigators often begin ethnographic work with interviews or storytelling and analyze the resulting text. The study of cultures is heavily dependent on conversations, what one native says to another or to anyone collecting first-order evidence.[4] Cultural theorists may observe meetings, conduct interviews, or engage in casual conversation. While doing so, they extract and record the things said and the sequence of reactions and events associated with such talk. Investigators also recognize that occasions and their social meaning elicit particular kinds of talk and responses. Ethnographers accept responsibility for determining the meaning associated with questioning, telling, arguing, and so forth. They also explore how the organization of talk influences what people say. *Text analysis* is the measurement process commonly associated with the search for cultural meaning in documented conversations.

Building Relationships

Most directly, talk allows investigators to learn something about the perspectives of informants and establish a strong working relationship with each one. When ethnographers rely on new data rather than existing evidence, the quality of their relationships with participants affects the quality of the research. Through tactful negotiations, investigators can let participants know of emerging research agendas and establish comfortable boundaries for future conversations and observations. Establishing such parameters at the outset of a study and maintaining a collaborative spirit throughout can facilitate accurate descriptions because comfortable interactions serve as a reasonable basis for trust.

Centrality of Text in Analyzing Interactions

It is difficult to explore meaning-making in cultures without getting involved in some sort of text analysis. Investigators may ask informants to describe their autobiographies, others' life histories, or stories about the communities in which they live. They may also analyze the content of informants' written accounts of their experience. To explore more pointed topics or predictions, investigators may also conduct a wide range of interviews (see Chapters 5, 10, 12, and 14). Text analysis is also conducted on historical documents to extract information about stability and change. Over the course of a project, investigators may use empirical reports, analytic narratives, quotes from key informants, and interpretive commentaries to construct written accounts of a culture. Text, in other words, is commonly used to generate and test assertions about participants' perspectives because these perspectives are difficult to identify by other means.

Rely on Literal Interpretations

When looking for patterns in linguistic representations, most investigators focus on concrete events and literal interpretations rather than abstract universals and figurative or metaphorical implications. They are careful not to read too much into first-order evidence when making second-order inferences, realizing that their inferences must be evident to other observers. Such concreteness also facilitates the preservation of the *structures of interactions,* offering clues about the meaning of speech, turn-taking, and sequential patterns. At the time data are collected, for example, interview participants can see how researchers try to understand their frame of mind. Participants can also see that researchers are suspending judgment during these interactions. In addition, historians find such literal records to be more insightful if first-order representations are accurately documented, and second-order inferences are treated as entities that require validation in their own right.

Investigators have a wide range of methods for analyzing text, many of which have already been reviewed, but cultural theorists are preoccupied with identifying cultural principles and norms from their first-order data.[5] These ethnographers use the details of interactions to find a comfortable language for representing how mental activities are constituent parts of a larger communication stream and how that stream is profoundly affected by the organization of particular social situations.

Multiple Questions, Multiple Approaches

Investigators have offered many different kinds of outlines for conducting text analysis (see Edwards & Lampert, 1993; Ericsson & Simon, 1993; Mishler, 1986). In one hermeneutic approach, for example, investigators created reading guides for evaluating each narrative at multiple levels (see Brown, Tappan, Gilligan, Miller, & Argyris, 1989; Dilthey, 1976). The readers guide called attention to particular theoretical dimensions and differed from coding manuals that focus only on key words.[6]

In establishing how participants understand the world, text is often treated like a piece of literature that can be both deconstructed and analyzed holistically. Such cultural theorists could ask:

- How do informants define the topic of conversation?
- What are the parameters placed on the conversation?
- What is the literal content of the conversation?
- What is the content or drama of the text?

- Where is the speaker positioned in the account?
- Which theoretical features are and are not apparent?

Looking for points of agreement in the interpretations of different readers, investigators can establish dependability while avoiding mechanical scoring techniques. You may remember how investigators have distinguished the structures of an entire protocol from the microlevel content analysis of themes in each justification. Finding convergence in these two levels of analysis lends strength to second-order inferences.

Limitations of Text Analysis

Moving away from reverence for text, investigators recognize that there are shortcomings to text analysis.[7] When text is deconstructed, the analysis can remove meaning as often as clarify the linguistic structure of verbal accounts. It becomes difficult to preserve confidentiality when writing elaborate narratives and investigators can find themselves creating composites that are so far removed from the first-order data they might as well have fabricated their evidence. Investigators involved in *interpretive analytic discourse,* for example, sometimes look only at text, but their emphasis on second- and third-order inferences obfuscates details of the historical context in which text is situated. Invariably text analysis offers only a selective interpretation of a culture, even though that interpretation may be highly valuable.

MAKING CONNECTIONS

How many different levels of analysis are evident in the ethnography you are reading? Do investigators include analysis of the text? How is text represented? Do investigators locate the informant in the analysis? Are narrative vignettes analyzed? What levels of inference are apparent? What theoretical dimensions are investigated? Do investigators critique their own perspectives as readily as they critique the perspectives of their informants? What does this balance tell you about the target audience for this work?

MEASURING CULTURAL RITUALS

Participant-observation research involves the measurement of settings and the rituals that take place within them. In exploring *cultural rituals,* investigators become preoccupied with the measurement of actions without making judgments of whether those actions reflect skills or competencies. The focus of such work is on how and why such actions and acts occur. Investigators are not particularly interested in predicting or controlling such rituals; they want to describe the features of each ritual and explain its purpose.

Formally, *cultural rituals* are regularly followed procedures within a particular culture or subculture. They often fall into one of two categories, *everyday events* or *special displays, ceremonies,* and *enactments.* In everyday life, individuals have *habits of action* that are full of meaning although that meaning is taken for granted by the agents. Community members may place greater value on *rarely occurring ceremonies* or performances because they serve as reminders of special occasions or historical events. Customary observances of ordinary and extraordinary experience may be undertaken without reflection as often as with deliberate thought, but serve as the metaphorical glue that affirms cultural norms and group membership. Knowing the structure and function of particular rituals can reveal more general patterns of human functioning or may be interesting in their own right.

The Importance of Participant-Observation

Cultural rituals are most easily measured using methods in which investigators remember that observations alone do not constitute ethnography. To translate behavior into actions and acts, cultural theorists typically look for guidance from community members on what to observe, record, and interpret. Investigators' fieldwork involves movement beyond simply recording consistencies and inconsistencies in behavior and includes the documentation of how people make meaning out of their experience. Observers explore everyday social interactions by coordinating the details of individuals' experience with situational information to describe how informants construe life in their communities.[8]

Parallels to drama may help clarify this process (Turner, 1980). Knowing that life consists of a series of social dramas, investigators can record these dramas by recording events much like playwrights construct scripts. The script with all its detail of both staging and character development constitutes first-order evidence. Investigators use second-order techniques to identify the implicit rhetorical structure of such drama, using details of their own reactions and those of different informants.

Communication as Negotiation

When communication is well established, participants are likely to welcome observers and avoid staging a drama that misrepresents their experience. If there are sufficient levels of trust, informants may also offer insightful critiques of second-order inferences when investigators' ideas are translated into comprehensible language. If investigators avoid jargon and converse in short clear sentences, participants' reactions can sometimes strengthen the ecological validity of second-order inferences or at least offer another kind of first-order evidence.

When communication is not well established, participants might stage a drama at the first-order level. Most investigators who are actively involved in fieldwork can detect deception or attempts to offer socially desirable responses because staged events ring phony and informants are unable to fully justify their reactions. Furthermore, mistrustful participants are rarely able to sustain the falsehood, especially if investigators are prepared to remain open-minded and curious rather than become harshly punitive.

Deception is most likely to succeed when investigators are not directly involved in fieldwork. If investigators rely too much on mechanical recording techniques or testimonial reports of a particular setting, they may not be able to detect staged events and could easily draw inaccurate inferences. The implicit social processes that led to the staging of events may become apparent, but it would be too late to gain insight into why events were staged.

Procedures for Fieldwork

There are two popular perspectives on how new investigators learn to conduct fieldwork, only one of which is accepted by researchers. The mistaken notion has been fostered by the romantic belief that ethnographic procedures cannot be taught. When that assumption was commonly accepted, ethnographers were offered solid grounding in the substance of their discipline and expected to use that information to guide their instinctive reactions to new cultural experiences. Today, *formal training* has made it possible to preserve human dignity and obtain more accurate representations of a community. Such training:

- fosters an essential stereoscopic social vision in which observers learn how to balance theoretical and concrete information in a deliberative approach;
- helps observers, early in their fieldwork, learn to propose contextually derived interpretations, grounded in theory;
- teaches observers to engage in a progressive critique of the ideas they label.

The Cyclical Nature of Measurement

Data collection becomes a cyclical problem-solving process of sampling events, generating hypotheses about the meaning of those events, and testing hypotheses about how individuals' experience the settings in which they live. Fieldwork involves sensitivity to intuitive reactions as investigators make deliberate decisions about which events to explore, how to explore those events, and how to *collect information that might disconfirm as well as confirm* their assumptions. Not surprisingly, intensive firsthand experience is essential for this iterative measurement process.

Guiding Questions

Ideally, perceptions are gathered at the time events occur, but events may also be critiqued later. Investigators look for social hierarchies within particular levels of organization as well as in how individuals are embedded within various organizational levels. Information from these different kinds of inquiry is coordinated when investigators ask how everyday life is similar or different across settings. To accomplish these goals, investigators may be guided by the following questions (Turner, 1980):

> What is happening in the social action of a given setting?
> What do particular actions mean to the agents?
> How are events organized?
> How do participants learn of the organization?
> Are organizational themes apparent in meaningful actions?
> How do events in one setting relate to events in other settings?

Summarizing Evidence

Evidence of cultural rituals is commonly summarized in four ways. Investigators write synoptic data reports containing frequencies or tallies, interpretive commentaries about particular events, interpretive commentaries about general events, and/or historical accounts of how studies unfold in time. In writing such summaries, investigators basically look for information in their database to support assertions about particular events. These assertions may vary in scope and level of inference, but investigators typically look for confirming and disconfirming evidence by connecting fragments from a larger corpus.

Describing Rituals

The study of cultural rituals involves the study of *moments in relation to persons* rather than persons in relation to moments (McDermott & Hood, 1982). Investigators look for behavioral displays that are evoked by or place constraints on the development of social situations. They explore what individuals did to arrange particular events, tasks, or settings and the roles and display rules used for structuring and accomplishing common agendas.

MAKING CONNECTIONS

Identify a sample of cultural rituals in your daily experience. How would you represent those rituals? Do they reflect habits of action or rarely occurring performances? What makes such rituals valuable? What features would you find essential to writing about such experiences? What features are optional? Next, label some of the rituals apparent in the ethnography you read. How do they compare to the rituals evident in your life?

COLLECTING ARTIFACTS

Although researchers engaged in *participant-observation research* may find artifacts helpful for making meaning out of events, artifacts are most commonly associated with *historical research*. Investigators who focus on artifactual evidence rely on preexisting information and face the burden of connecting such relics, documents, and testimonials to theoretical claims. Generally speaking, *cultural artifacts* are concrete entities that can represent a person's effort, the setting in which events take place, existing organizations, tools available for accomplishing particular goals, and circumstantial outcomes. Such artifacts can facilitate a richer understanding of parts to the whole of cultural experience.

Looking for meaning even in seemingly trivial objects can lead investigators to important forms of evidence that might not otherwise be considered for inclusion in a study. Evaluating artifacts involves careful consideration of the politics, practices, and events of the time in which the entities were generated. Entities that seem commonplace today may have been rare earlier in time. Entities that seem rare today may have been typical at the time artifacts were generated.

Purposes for Artifacts

Historians are primarily interested in artifacts that have been left by the past, but their methods may be used to compare past and present information. Artifacts may offer historical knowledge about religious ideologies, social and economic factors, biological or racial issues, environmental contingencies, science, technology, inventions, and information apparent in the mass media.

To draw inferences, cultural theorists look for *relics, documents,* or *testimonies* to discover interpretation principles of preexisting cultures. *Relics and remains* offer clues about the very existence of cultures, and comparing such artifacts from different settings can reveal commercial and intellectual relations. *Documents* typically record details of individual lives, organizational structures, events, and outcomes. *Testimonies* are oral or written reports that describe events. Combining these information sources, investigators can learn what happened, how, in what circumstances, and why things occurred.

In the present, artifacts continue to be products of human workmanship that offer physical evidence of intangible ideas, the direction toward which effort has been applied, or symbols used to remind individuals of particular rituals or experiences. Living archives are those where the source is still growing. New information can be combined with historical archives to offer a richer sense of how people, events, or institutions may have changed. Such artifacts can conjure up emotion, fulfill ceremonial roles, or serve as tools for achieving ordinary goals. They can also reveal the existence of social networks that might otherwise remain unnoticed (Burt & Lin, 1977).

Relics and Remains.   As a trip to most museums will indicate, investigators sometimes compare objects or the physical remains of available individuals to draw inferences about daily functioning. Some relics reflect unusual events or activities, whereas others are used everyday. Relics can also reveal common symbols of solidarity within a community or serve as memorabilia for past events. In combination with skeletal remains and so forth, it is possible to date the objects and place them along an historical time line.

You may remember an era in which individuals were encouraged to wear small golden angels on their collar or shoulder as a symbolic representation of their guardian angel. The symbolic meaning of this gesture was known to community members and may not have been detected by noncommunity members at the time. Individuals who wore these angels were members of a group without firm boundaries and the relics that are now in many jewelry boxes offer a tangible reminder of those days.

Documents.   Written artifacts such as documents, diaries, letters, newspapers, or scientific reports can be treated like text, but are more often classified into one of three types: literary artifacts, diplomatic or judicial artifacts, or social documents (Howell & Prevenier, 2001). *Literary artifacts* offer chronicles or narratives that impart a particular message. Investigators evaluate the coherence of the message as well as the author's intentions when determining how to classify such entities. *Diplomatic/judicial* artifacts are those generated in legal situations, or that create legal situations for proof of transactions or events. The fixed nature of these documents facilitates interpretation and comparisons that reveal traditions common within a particular historical period. Structurally, such documents often open with rules of protocol that declare the intent and the parties involved in a transaction, followed by the content or recitation of the case, and a closing or authentication formula that may include seals and witnesses. *Social documents* are associated with record keeping by bureaucracies and usually contain information of economic, social, political, or judicial importance. Studies of social records can offer clues about the structure of various social institutions or family contexts. Comparisons across time can clarify changes in policies and life events.

Testimonies.   You may remember that diaries, newspaper accounts, medical records, autobiographies, and biographies often contain useful testimonies about a sequence of events and corresponding outcomes (see Chapter 14). These differ from the documents described earlier in that they reflect someone's account of events rather than direct indicators of organizational structures, settings, or personal actions.

Culture as Principles of Interpretation

Investigators sensitive to the value of artifacts learn how to read the signs they offer and draw inferences about connections between signifiers and the values signified.[9] They learn to identify symbols of power inherent in who acquires a particular artifact, how artifacts are displayed, and the use of these indicants. Artifacts can have personal meaning only to those who collect them or collective meaning to any community member who observes them. Investigators learn to make such classifications as part of their training and while becoming familiar with new cultural expectations. Living and historical artifacts can offer information about societal institutions and practical life as easily as ancient rituals and ceremonies.

Guiding Questions

When using artifacts, investigators consider several issues that can be equated with measurement issues in other fields.[10] They evaluate the credibility of an artifact and the genre represented as well as the authenticity and representativeness of each one. As with evaluating the content of survey items, these questions reflect the appropriateness of an artifact for a particular theoretical framework.

Credibility.   To evaluate credibility, cultural theorists typically situate an artifact in time and place such that it is possible to evaluate its accuracy. They have asked:

- Where was the artifact constructed?
- When was the artifact constructed?
- In what setting was the artifact used?
- Who used the artifact and for what purpose?
- Is the information contained within the artifact accurate?

Genre.   Evaluating the genre of an artifact speaks more elaborately to its purpose. Using comprehensible language representing an artifact's content, investigators typically evaluate the artifact in relation to easily understood, modern norms. This representation includes details on an artifact's use, intended audience, and adherence to the communication conventions of its day. For ancient artifacts, it becomes easy to adopt the language of the era in which it was generated, but cultural theorists endeavor to communicate with people living in the present.

Authentication. The *authentication process* involves a wide range of disciplines, and the nature and purpose of each artifact plays a key role in which type of expertise is called for. Investigators may authenticate artifacts using guidelines from:

- *Archaeology,* the physical evidence from lost civilizations
- *Chronology,* how people mark time
- *Diplomatics,* the formal properties of each source
- *Paleography,* studies of handwriting
- *Epigraphy,* the study of text written on hard materials
- *Codicology,* the study of handwritten books as documents
- *Papyrology,* the study of writing on papyrus
- *Sigillography,* the meaning of seals on documents
- *Heraldry,* when studying coats of arms
- *Numismatics,* when studying coins
- *Linguistics,* when exploring grammars and vocabularies
- *Genealogy,* or family relationships
- *Prosopagraphy,* or the use of biographical material in the construction of group portraits

Representativeness. Cultural theorists evaluate representativeness by considering the typicality of an artifact within a particular culture. To thoroughly explore this issue, artifacts are often considered in relation to one another. This comparison strengthens the accuracy of conclusions about the culture under investigation as well as the similarities and differences of the social ecologies operating across cultures.

To understand daily life, for example, investigators might collect pictures, household objects, toys, jewelry, clothing, and equipment. Other patterns reveal less global expressions, as is apparent when investigators look carefully at the artwork, cartoons, music, films, and architecture to detect the expression of human emotions. Settings can be documented when investigators or their informants draw maps, take photographs, make diagrams, or otherwise document the artifacts in their immediate environment. Reports, products available for sale, receipts, memos, and computer equipment are common artifacts reflecting work in some communities, whereas boots, toolboxes, automotive parts, and safety equipment may reflect work in others.

These examples suggest that artifacts alone do not always tell revealing stories, but combinations of artifacts are likely to reveal quite a bit of information about cultures. Cultural theorists can find challenges when determining the typicality of particular artifacts at the time of their use. From such information they can draw stronger inferences about particular identities, networks, careers, events, institutions, and repertoires. Investigators can also evaluate how well particular organizations are represented and the adequacy of available resources. Inferences about particular attributes and outcomes are likely to be more accurate if investigators have first-order information about how well initial conditions, event structures, temporal sequences, and catalysts for change are documented. Ethnographies and ethnologies are also strengthened by detecting the absence as well as the presence of artifacts.

The Value of Artifacts

Investigators collect and evaluate artifacts in ways similar to those used to collect and evaluate narratives; looking at how objects are used and what they mean to individuals can tell tangible stories. To identify historical documents, there are preservation rules in place that help investigators place reasonable parameters around what to collect and how to authenticate first-order evidence, yet those rules have been inconsistently applied to artifacts from the past. Many historians today are working to reconstruct missing details of cultures or parts of cultures that were once ignored by revising preservation rules to accommodate new sources of evidence.

Limitations of Artifacts

One limitation of artifacts is that, like observations of behavior, they serve as representations of experience, but cannot convey the actual experience itself. Artifacts are best used as signs of meaning that can be incorporated into more general analyses to draw inferences about the whole of a community or culture. Artifacts can be used to tell stories in themselves or as parts of a story, but stories are richer if there is a narrator. Investigators can draw inferences without the benefit of informants, but the resulting description is much more accurate if informants can convey the meaning of artifacts to their observers. As with most research, conclusions are constrained by the availability of evidence. For events from the past, it is not possible to construct new evidence, but with training historians learn to detect more and less plausible versions of cultural norms and interpretation principles.

MAKING CONNECTIONS

Imagine that you will be making a time capsule. What artifacts would you include to convey the realities of your daily life? What artifacts would you include to identify your various reference groups (e.g., gender, religion, ethnicity, friendship groups)? Identify artifacts that could represent your local and national communities. How do these artifacts differ from one another? How would you convey the meaning of each artifact to a stranger? Next, consider the ethnography you read and identify artifacts in that account. What are the characteristics of these artifacts?

COMBINING SOURCES OF EVIDENCE

Although cultural theorists may report some findings in short journal articles, most write books to reveal ethnographic or ethnological accounts of cultures. Books facilitate the combination of evidence extracted from multiple kinds of data. As investigators look at relations between different sources of information, they can reveal evidence for conclusions about local and nonlocal forms of social organization. They may identify narrative accounts, images, enactments, and points of reflexivity to find information on what experience means to the individuals involved (Turner & Bruner, 1986). Analysis that considers either individual or group functioning invariably offers incompatible sources of information if investigators do not try to reconcile their evidence around a common thesis or theoretical frame. Looking at relations between individual choices and collective social action, for example, investigators can identify the features of a culture and how those features are associated with specific people and activities. Invariably, cultural theorists revisit questions about the purpose of their project in light of new evidence.

As you might recall, the information about text, rituals, and artifacts can be combined to construct case studies, ethnographies, or ethnologies. Decisions about how to coordinate findings differ, depending on which of these purposes are accepted. Investigators who want to understand the life of an individual or compare the lives of several individuals will differ in whether they adopt an emic or an etic approach to recording first-order evidence. Those researchers interested in offering a thick description of one particular culture usually start with an *emic approach,* striving for balance and fairness in the representation of a specific culture. Cross-cultural studies invariably rely on an *etic approach* because cultural representations are compared directly and common parameters are essential for generating balanced and fair comparisons.

Procedural Advice

There are no simple guides for constructing strong case studies, ethnographies, or ethnologies, but investigators have begun to offer some procedural advice for combining sources of evidence.[11] New researchers need practice and guidance in learning to talk a little, listen a lot, record events accurately, and begin writing early.

In the process of writing, cultural theorists learn to write so that readers can see first-order evidence for themselves, accurate links between first- and second-order evidence, and a full report of the findings. Writing is part of fieldwork and is as central to the measurement process as to the reporting of conclusions. Analysis requires candor about how evidence was collected, the availability of representative indicants, and the complexity associated with obtaining evidence. Most accounts contain gaps that can be equated with measurement error found in other research traditions. Such gaps may be filled by seeking new evidence, but this is not always possible.

Cultural theorists also seek feedback from everyone who might be interested in a project and try to achieve balance in the reporting of different perspectives. They may coordinate information extracted from multiple sources by first evaluating each source independently and later comparing the integration. As in other forms of research, cultural theorists endeavor to minimize bias, establish the dependable evidence, establish credible evidence, and confirm conclusions by coordinating evidence.

MAKING CONNECTIONS

Choose one of the regular events that occur in your life and imagine what evidence could be used to document that event. Would you analyze text, record rituals, and/or collect artifacts? How would you organize the collected evidence to support conclusions about the event?

MINIMIZING BIAS

When comparing evidence, investigators do not rely on radically inductive methods. They typically minimize bias separately for each type of evidence by considering the strengths and limitations of each measurement approach and following guidelines that match assumptions valued by their discourse community. Although investigators may eventually generate categories for organizing information, categories may be identified before, during, or after evidence is collected. Useful techniques for text analysis, measuring rituals, and comparing artifacts are introduced here, but investigators also learn new ways of minimizing bias from their informants or from the contextual parameters under consideration.

Text Analysis

Three common approaches to text analysis differ, depending on the nature of the text. Investigators may evaluate the details of individuals' lives, use the constant-comparative methods, or interpret a more general phenomenon.

Exploring Individual Lives.   In the analysis of individuals' lives, investigators rely on biographical, autobiographical, or case study methods that differ in the degree of involvement by the target individual (see Chapter 14). *Biographical accounts* may involve the study of a person's life course, achievements, chronologies, and the historical context in which these events occurred. *Autobiographical accounts* are likely to contain similar details of someone's life course, but include personal stories, epiphanies, and oral histories of the lives that influenced the target person. *Case studies* are often seen as ethnographies of a person rather than a community. The life in question is treated as a bounded system, and investigators collect multiple sources of evidence, only some of which involve text.

　　　Cultural theorists collect different kinds of text for each method of studying individuals' lives, but invariably compare segments of a text with one another. They look at the literal ideas embedded in a text, identify themes, make inferences, and offer details of the context of the case being studied. These researchers minimize bias by looking for multiple indicants of the same idea, comparing their inferences to other time-bound information, and details of a target person's life.

Constant-Comparative Methods.   The *constant-comparative method* involves weighing information using a mixture of deductive and inductive logic to draw abstract inferences about apparent themes (see Glaser & Strauss, 1967). The specific use of this approach varies from project to project, depending on the amount of prior information available and the philosophical commitment of an investigator. Critical theorists and deconstructionists may have different reasons for using this approach.

　　　Researchers may minimize bias by distinguishing *opening coding* from other types of analysis. In open coding, the text is segmented to create categories. After identifying codes, investigators may construct memos to explain each category and how they cluster, anchoring such ideas to the text. As a first step in moving from description to inference, these interim summaries contain the properties or dimensions of each category and examples from available text. Raters use these descriptions to label all aspects of a text that reflect each code. Bias is minimized if investigators offer concrete links to the text when noting trends and tentative coding families.

Interpreting Phenomena.   Investigators interested in phenomenology are looking for evidence that supports the interpretation of a phenomenon. They often ask informants to write or talk about lived experience and may include the analysis of documents along with testimonies. While looking at text, these investigators may suspend or bracket their own judgments and look for *intentionality in the consciousness of participants.* Some investigators adopt a transpersonal approach while others look at the psychology of individuals, but both try to describe the texture and structure of experience. Maintaining *epoche,* or the suspension of judgment, investigators can segment the vertical structure of a text into statements that can be arranged horizontally. Placing statements on strips of paper that can be sorted can help learners see clusters of meanings and describe the texture and structure of the language individuals use to represent experience. This involves an ability to think abstractly and ignore the order in which ideas were introduced in a text, and may take mental training before using computers to replace manual scoring.

Document Procedures.   Regardless of which discourse community investigators work with, they often write scoring manuals to document the means by which coding and classification were accomplished. Using those guides, other raters can find the same information such that inter-rater agreement can be calculated. Investigators may evaluate levels of agreement by looking at different units of a text; ratings of literal phrases, summaries, or interpretations are common. Not surprisingly, kappa (κ) or other common methods of establishing inter-rater reliability are used to verify the accuracy of coding. Scoring guides may have a relatively long shelf-life if investigators are more interested in comparisons among individuals or ethnologies, but a relatively short one if the focus is on idiosyncratic details of one individual's life or ethnographies.

Cultural Rituals

It is much more difficult to minimize bias in evaluating cultural rituals than text. Fieldwork is necessarily intensive and involves the collection of many different kinds of evidence. Investigators may arrange for a period of *long-term involvement in the setting* they hope to understand and carefully record the things they see, hear, and experience. They may also *identify* persons who serve as *gatekeepers, key informants,* and *secondary informants* as well as different methods of sharing information in the community. Each of these decisions involves some level of bias, and it may be impractical to expect all events to be documented by two raters. In addition, some forms of bias may enrich researchers' understanding of a culture.

Negotiate a Point of Entry.   Most cultural theorists take time to carefully *negotiate points of entry and boundaries* for access before collecting data. Ideally, they gain broad access to the environments they hope to explore and identify methods for protecting privileged information that is invariably gathered over the course of a study. Although investigators endeavor to fully inform participants about research procedures and practices, it is not always easy to anticipate risks and benefits at the onset of a study. Nevertheless, if investigators are honest about these limitations and vigilant in responding to issues as they occur, they are less likely to find participants faking or engaging in deception, and informants would be less likely to be passively resistant to researchers' presence in their community.

Develop Collaborative Relationships.   Another means by which investigators minimize bias is to maintain a collaborative relationship throughout the research enterprise. Informants commonly critique investigators' work while it is in progress and may alter the course of evaluations. Strong relationships are maintained if investigators and participants resist judging one another and informants remain as fully aware of developing inferences as is practical. Making evaluative comments while in the field is one good way to undermine a collaborative spirit because such comments can restrict participants' sense that they are qualified informants. By encouraging participants to strategize about how ideas and events are distinguished or clustered, subtleties that might otherwise remain undetected could become apparent.

Record Events Carefully.   Another device for minimizing bias is inherent in the method of recording events. Although ethnographers do not rely exclusively on machine recordings (e.g., audio, video, or digital equipment), it is helpful to do so for some kinds of events. Machine recordings, if done well, can maximize the completeness with which events are remembered and minimize an observer's tendency to make primitive analytic judgments at the time the events occur. These techniques can facilitate a greater balance in the events sampled because it is easier to see less salient features of a situation when one is not immediately reacting to the drama of unfolding events. Investigators are less likely to notice only frequently occurring incidents or the most dramatic events if they have time to revisit a sequence. Their analysis is less primitive if they can look for subtle details in recordings and create categories to incorporate the full range of occurrences.

Equipment limitations inevitably bracket the kind of information that is collected and offer little information about a larger system in which recorded events are situated. Recordings can serve as one means of obtaining information on cultural rituals, but would not offer sufficient information if used as the only means of data collection. Recordings are limited in that investigators can vicariously interact with the details of a recorded event, but they cannot adequately fulfill a participant-observer role. As observers, researchers should be free to test their emergent theories while events are underway and cannot do so if they are only watching recordings. The medium in which events are recorded also constrains the documented information and important contextual details may be obfuscated if investigators rely on recordings alone.

Look for Helpful Bias.   It is also helpful to remember that bias is sometimes the topic of inquiry in participant-observation studies. Investigators endeavor to understand and explain rather than minimize the influence of their presence. In labeling bias, investigators construct social hierarchies by looking for a range of variation in the *formality or informality of relationships* with participants. They are careful not to become therapists, but cultivate a wide range of relationships with people in different roles. Analyzing the different types of relationships that informants are willing or able to establish can facilitate clearer labels for naturally occurring distortion. This variability offers alternative sources of information that can later be incorporated into second-order interpretations. Bias, in these cases, would be accepted rather than challenged.

Cultural Artifacts

Attempts to minimize bias in the use of cultural artifacts is highly dependent on the artifacts collected, purposes for collecting such items, and relations of artifacts to other forms of evidence. Generally speaking, investigators try to avoid isolating items from the contexts in which they are found. In accounts involving different evidence, artifacts can serve as *concrete symbols* for ideas that might otherwise be difficult to convey. In such cases, bias would be a benefit rather than a liability because the artifact would be carefully chosen to confirm rather than disconfirm ideas.

In situations where artifacts are studied to *generate a story* or *set of conclusions,* cultural theorists often seek a representative sample of such items, treating those items in much the same way as investigators would treat coding categories or accounts of particular rituals. Investigators would look for themes in how individuals select, store, and share items and evaluate the meaning of items to different kinds of informants. They might also use information on the frequency with which items are found to draw inferences about their relative importance or use within a community.

Evaluate Each Artifact.   Cultural theorists who work with artifacts evaluate each one for bias. Artifacts have been classified into five common classes of information and these classifications may be weighed when determining how seriously to consider an artifact (see Howell & Prevenier, 2001). On the positive side, information can be accurate and genuine or useful copies of an original. It can also be intellectually false, deliberately faked, or simply altered in an overzealous restoration.

More specifically, artifacts confirmed as *accurate and genuine* may be incorporated into analysis with little critique. To preserve the original, investigators may also use *copies of artifacts* and openly acknowledge this in their analysis. Artifacts declared *intellectually false* may have been altered to mislead contemporaries or to make illegitimate claims about rights and privileges. Such artifacts are studied to determine why individuals would make such claims. Other artifacts may also be *deliberately faked* to reflect pseudo-originals that are intended as false evidence. Investigators do little with these artifacts, although collectors may enjoy them.

Overzealous *attempts at restoration* may combine original artifactual material with new material intended to mimic or offer a more complete sense of the original. Sometimes such composites are created by synthesizing information from multiple sources, but they may also be generated from the imaginations of investigators. Mentally taking apart such composites, cultural theorists may focus only on original details or retain the composite until new, primary source information becomes apparent.

Acceptable Distortion.   The falsification apparent in some of these classes is not always inherent in the material qualities of an artifact. The meaning of an artifact can also be distorted. To understand the words of the *Declaration of Independence,* for example, investigators need not work with the original parchment on which it was written. Working with a copy would not be problematic unless the actual wording was altered to change the meaning of the text.

Similarly, authenticating the use of an artifact is tricky, partly because some material artifacts may not offer clear clues about the use of that artifact. Attempts to mislead or distort usage information cannot always be rectified by studying the objects themselves with more rigor. On such occasions, cultural theorists commonly compare different information sources to extract meaning.

Organizing Artifacts. Artifacts may be counted, clustered, and labeled for later use when generating inferences about their form, function, and value to informants. Cultural theorists look at the concrete features of artifacts and the representativeness of selected items before generating credible tactics for telling a story about their meaning. When classifying items, they may look for inter-rater agreement to ensure that their own idiosyncratic judgments are not the basis for category assignments. Cultural theorists also label procedures for selecting artifacts, sharpening their judgment about each one, devising plans for sorting them, and considering the role of each artifact in a larger organizational structure. Ideally, each of these decisions is evaluated by informants and/or other experts in the field.

MAKING CONNECTIONS

Find an ethnology, ethnography, or case study in your field and identify the types of evidence included. Was the evidence primarily from text, participant-observations, or patterns in cultural artifacts? Did investigators use a combination of methods? What did the investigators do to minimize bias?

DEPENDABILITY AND CREDIBILITY

When establishing *dependability and credibility,* investigators begin to make inferences. They start to construct deterministic plots of relationships and link those relationships with evidence from informants or about the settings and historical period in which the research is situated.

Data Reduction. Investigators participate in *data reduction* to select important indicants, focus attention, simplify representations, or otherwise abstract and transform the information they have gathered. They become involved in partitioning and clustering information, looking for replicable patterns that seem plausible to others. Logic for analyzing text, rituals, and artifacts is often similar but the indicants to be evaluated vary. Through the process of *triangulation,* investigators also compare different types of evidence to evaluate the credibility of more general conclusions, but do so with caution.

Text Analysis

Methods for verifying text analysis typically involve the *generation* and *comparison of causal fragments.* Investigators translate segments of speech, details of events, or classifications of artifacts into variables. They rate the resulting variables for importance or salience, and begin to make associations among them, or look for latent variables that explain patterns. Some variables are likely to overlap, whereas others can be ordered temporally or hierarchically.

Cultural theorists look for three common possibilities when defining a causal network and theoretical assertions (Figure 16.1). You may recall from the developmental chapters that *temporal precedence* involves a study of the historical progressions or sequential ordering in which meaning is situated. *Concomitant variation* involves associational logic for noting relations between theoretical dimensions. *Directional influence* involves the degree to which meaning originates in one place and ends in another.

Notice that in the first diagram of Figure 16.1 that information presented on the left occurs at an earlier point in time than information on the right. Information linked with lines

Sample Multirelational Representation

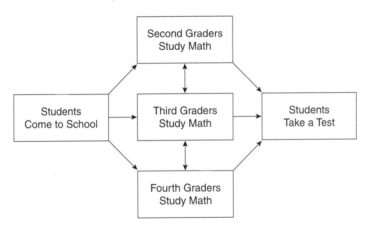

Sample Hierarchical Representation

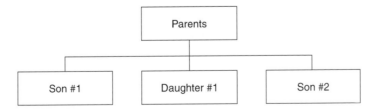

FIGURE 16.1   Sample Representations of Second-Order Inferences

containing two-way arrows represents concomitant variation and information with one-way arrows represents directional assumptions. Hierarchies are typically represented by presenting superordinate information at the top and subordinate information at the bottom of such diagrams.

Coding Techniques.   Investigators using constant comparative methods have labels for different steps in this process. They start with *axial coding* by assembling the categories established during the open coding phase into more theoretically grounded codes, outlining a *logical diagram* in which a central phenomenon is identified and causal conditions are anticipated. As part of this process, investigators draw inferences about the resulting strategies, contextual constraints, and intervening conditions necessary for finding particular consequences.

Cultural theorists may also develop a story line and engage in selective coding to integrate features of a logical diagram. *Selective coding* involves the formulation of propositions, usually about the order of dimensions or theoretical relationships among them, and the search for evidence to confirm or disconfirm those propositions. A *conditional matrix* may be used to outline the broader conditions associated with a central phenomenon. Together these steps work to ground inferences in specific acts of text.

Investigators analyzing text for use in phenomenological, critical theoretical, or case study analysis tend to follow similar logic even if they do not label each step so systematically. They note patterns, plausible associations, and methods for splitting or combining variables. These researchers may count the appearance of particular ideas or structures and write metaphors or narrative accounts of the relations they see and how those relations are associated with more general theoretical claims. Cultural theorists may also complete inductive exercises of factoring, correlating, or chaining text-related variables to identify points of theoretical or conceptual coherence.

Cultural Rituals

To ensure the dependability and credibility of evidence about cultural rituals, investigators are careful to *stay close to the setting* in which research takes place. They define variables in contextually meaningful ways and label how agents define particular experiences. In this phase of the study, it is essential that investigators avoid stripping contextual details from their analysis because those details are part of the story.

Dependability.   The most common means of establishing dependability in first-order data is to *record recurring instances* of common events. Cultural theorists may look for the same indicants of an event across settings or over time. They may also look for different indicants in a single setting or within a bracketed time period. By constructing tables or other systematic means of recording observations, predictions can be generated about the relative typicality of an occurrence. Looking at the same event using the perspectives of different kinds of informants, details of the levels of organization that dominate a particular social system become apparent.

Ideally, cultural theorists look for information about *all levels of a system* and from a *wide range of informants,* but recognize that the structure of any system is too complex to apprehend all at once. The inevitable *bounded rationality* may be addressed by spending a lengthy period of time in the field.[12] Documenting a system is usually accomplished by starting at the broadest level and recording as much information as is available on the normative frequency of particular practices, roles, and persons. It becomes possible to target specific events or topics for more in-depth analysis. Even while looking at narrower fields within a culture, investigators periodically revisit the broader social context to determine where particular events are situated in a more general system. This process of working between the search for simplicity and complexity in how events fit within the larger social structure offers information essential to verifying dependability in the quest for information and the credibility of inferences.

Cultural theorists also engage in *analytic reflection* on the records they acquire as events occur, immediately after a period of involvement, and later in the theory-building process. They may write narrative vignettes, rhetorical, analytic, evidentiary stories designed to persuade readers that the settings, events, and perspectives are represented accurately. Investigators may also quote directly from spontaneous conversations or those that emerge from formal interviews. Cultural theorists also construct analytic charts, write summary tables, or compute descriptive statistics to help them organize their thoughts.

Conclusions about the dependability of evidence are often represented in an abstract, analytical summary that includes only relevant detail and leaves other aspects of the situation to readers' imagination. In these summaries, writers alter the density and texture of their descriptions, calling attention to more and less important features of a situation. They also choose more and less dramatic words to make their point, peppering the narrative with direct quotes to add clarity or variety.

Credibility.   To verify the credibility of written accounts, cultural theorists look at the *immediate and local implications* of particular actions from the *perspective of participants.* They move beyond the rich descriptions of individuals' functioning commonly associated with studies that rely on psychometric and developmental measurement techniques. Cultural theorists also remain dissatisfied with sociological descriptions of communal norms and patterns of functioning. Grounded in local knowledge, these researchers acknowledge that past rituals are determined in ways that can be explained, but future rituals are dynamic and unpredictable.

Cultural Artifacts

Exploring the dependability and credibility of inferences about cultural artifacts often requires the involvement of agents who are willing to help investigators make meaning of each artifact. Investigators may count, classify, or otherwise arrange artifacts into common categories, but meaning-making comes from community members. To keep from forming faulty heuristics, cultural theorists often *ask informants* to verify the empirical connections they make. They may also seek advice on the representativeness of particular artifacts, their various uses and purposes, and the value of each item.

Dependability.   Cultural theorists explore the *dependability* of artifacts by labeling the intended meaning of the source. They often consider four dimensions when evaluating dependability: genealogy, genesis, significance, and originality. Looking at the *genealogy* of an artifact, cultural theorists may determine if the artifact is an original, a copy of an original, or a copy of a copy. They determine if copies contain faults that are not apparent in the original and if necessary information can be extracted from copies. Investigators may also look at the *genesis* of an artifact to determine who produced it, when, where, and the significance of this information for making meaningful inferences. They can also determine if the *significance* of an artifact is embedded within or if such an assessment can only be extracted by comparing related sources. The *originality* of a document is determined by considering traditions that were common when artifacts were generated and how well artifacts represent particular traditions.

Credibility.   To explore *credibility* in second-order inferences, cultural theorists may address five dimensions: accuracy of interpretations, authority of any authors, competence of informants, the era in which the analysis was conducted, and overall trustworthiness. Deciphering the intended meaning of a document, investigators determine if it was *interpreted* appropriately. They also evaluate the *authority of the author* to determine if the creator of an artifact or author of a document is a credible source and why such persons would be credible.

When artifacts are evaluated by informants, investigators consider two additional dimensions. They consider the *competence* of the informant and the *era* in which the analysis was conducted. Considering informants' competence, cultural theorists may evaluate their psychological states, the degree of selectivity in their account, the prejudices that inform the account, and any pressures or undue influence that might alter an informant's account. When evaluating the era in which informants' knowledge was shared, investigators may consider whether informants showed a critical awareness of the information they were sharing, and if informants could understand the artifacts or events they witness. Investigators may also determine if the informant was technically and socially qualified to evaluate artifacts and able to believe their own interpretations of experience. Cultural theorists may want to know what aspects of their experience informants are consciously aware of and what aspects remain unconscious or habitual responses to cultural norms.

Coordinating evaluations of the informant with the times in which inferences were generated improves the credibility of such analyses, but only if the fifth credibility criterion of *trustworthiness* is considered. Most informants offer distorted accounts of their experience, but cultural theorists determine if the resulting distortions are conscious or unconscious. For example, individuals making political commentaries intentionally distort their representations of evidence to draw attention to a call for change or agreement with any positions being offered. Discerning informants may also deliberately withhold details of their experience to mislead investigators or achieve a more general goal. The natural vanity of observers also places them at center stage in any narrative and investigators determine the implicit or explicit accuracy of this representation.

Artifacts may not be credible if they are improperly selected, classified, or evaluated. Cultural theorists look for evidence of deception or distortion in how artifacts are placed temporally, socially, and in relation to other artifacts. The logic underlying this process is much like that associated with establishing content validity; artifacts can serve a function similar to indicants on a measure, or evaluations of a particular artifact are completed using a predetermined coding scheme.

Triangulation

Ordinarily the process of *triangulation* is defined as the comparison of data collected using two or more measurement techniques.[13] Because each measurement tool and corresponding method is bounded, restrictions are placed on the conclusions that can be supported by each type of evidence. Triangulation may involve comparison of evidence generated using normative and interpretive measurement techniques. When contrasting methods yield the same conclusions, investigators can make strong generalizations that are not constrained by a *mono-method bias.* Nevertheless, cultural theorists also realize that evidence may not converge to support a single set of conclusions and this *lack of convergence* can also offer valuable insights. These researchers are critical of the idea that constructs inevitably undergo a cycle of birth, critique, and reification because they respect the dynamic nature of local cultures.

Outcomes of Triangulation.   When comparing sources, triangulation has resulted in at least seven possible outcomes. There may be situations in which findings in *all sources agree* and investigators are likely to assume that conclusions are supported. When there is convergence in some sources, but not all sources, investigators may *reconcile the disagreements* rather than simply defer to the most frequently found conclusion. Investigators may also look to sources outside their first- and second-order analyses for external confirmation or convergence with *evidence from other authorities.* They can also *prioritize sources in terms of authority* and accept those findings from the most authoritative position. Sometimes, researchers also *prefer testimonies from eyewitnesses* rather than second-hand informants, but this may not always be an option. Cultural theorists are also more likely to agree with findings that involve the *independent corroboration of multiple informants.* Finally, when there is disagreement between parallel sources, cultural theorists are not afraid to rely on their own *common sense.*

Distinguish Surface Characteristics and Intended Meaning.   Regardless of how evidence is coordinated, cultural theorists are careful not to confuse *surface characteristics* with the *intended meaning* of text, rituals, and artifacts. Meaning among different sources of evidence can be compared to reveal information that might otherwise remain hidden. Surface characteristics may be compared to determine if convergence in meaning is even plausible. The process of selecting measurement techniques, making decisions about which findings to consider, comparing and contrasting particular findings, and recognizing the limitations of particular methods has a profound impact on the conclusions of a study. When cultural theorists establish categories that offer sufficient clarity, they do not reduce valuable information into simple *if→then* or *process→product* kinds of statements. These investigators are usually careful to avoid overly reductionistic views of the methods for drawing inferences and strive to maintain an adequately broad definition of the theory-building process.

Coordinate Multiple Roles.   When comparing evidence, cultural theorists fill a *didactic role* by showing the particulars of everyday meaning and a *rhetorical role* by offering sufficient support for conclusions about how participants interpret their experience. Charts and graphs may be used to inform readers about the typicality of events, but investigators may also rely on key narrative vignettes to represent a wide range of concerns. Rather than offering a literal recording of events, the triangulation process invariably involves contrasts between events that vary in density and in the use of vocabulary for describing action. Investigators may collect as much first-order evidence as possible, but consider the epistemological status of this evidence when coordinating it. Decisions about which vocabulary to use often hinge on which discourse community authors hope to inform; the farther away from first-order evidence an investigator tries to work, the less richness is apparent in descriptions of everyday events and the broader the generalizations.

Multiple Kinds of Coordination.   There are many ways in which evidence can be compared in the triangulation process.[14] Cultural theorists often make comparisons based on time, space, or levels of organization within and between persons. Treating the ordinary as extraordinary, there are times when levels of organization considered in conjunction with psychometric and developmental work are also useful for consideration here; investigators may compare findings within and between individuals, groups, institutional practices, institutional purposes, ecological location, and cultures. They may try to situate a subculture within a larger culture, maintain a local focus, or adopt a pan-cultural perspective in which sociological trends are explored. Investigators can also use theoretical constructs as the basis for comparison or compare the findings from different investigators, methods, or measurement techniques.

Multidimensional Theories.   Decisions about what specific evidence to consider and what to ignore are also multidimensional and theory-bound. There are times when cultural theorists find it most beneficial to privilege recurring evidence, but they may miss important insights if this decision rule is always used. These investigators may also privilege specific events and all the evidence related to those events. In doing so, they inevitably ignore or suppress other kinds of events or data. There are also times when evidence is so scarce that investigators privilege all available sources.

Summary.   Triangulation is used for many different reasons. Cultural theorists compare findings when conducting case studies, adjusting for distortions in the data-collection process, and exploring controversies. They also use triangulation when evaluating different methods, elucidating complex phenomena, and verifying holistic outcomes. Some investigators also refer to the process of verifying dependability and credibility in each type of data as a form of triangulation, drawing comparisons within rather than across methods. Although these different purposes are relevant to determining if findings are dependable and credible, you may also see comparisons used in the confirmation phase.

■ ■ ■ ■ ■

MAKING CONNECTIONS

Looking at the ethnology, ethnography, or case study you selected earlier, identify the means by which authors determined the dependability and credibility of their findings. Did they evaluate text, rituals, artifacts, or more than one of these cultural indicators? Did they use comparative methods for each type of data? Did they triangulate evidence from more than one measurement technique? How?

CONFIRMING CONCLUSIONS

Cultural theorists rely on interpretive techniques rather than specific procedures to look for *discontinuities* and *continuities* in how individuals coordinate their lives within communities and how subgroups of individuals are related to one another. However, coordinating information that hinges on the use of disparate methods and orientations is usually done with caution. When combining inferences, cultural theorists often remember the limitations of each measurement technique, but not all investigators are knowledgeable enough about measurement to accomplish such fine-grained analysis with precision. This is one advantage of working with a team in which each member has a range of different skills. Each investigator can focus on a different level of analysis, looking for discrepancies and inaccuracies.

Guiding Questions

Regardless of the type of investigation, inferences are often coordinated by considering three guiding questions:

- What levels of organization are represented in each study?
- What are the limitations of each method and measurement technique?
- What kinds of conclusions are important to share?

The exploration of cultures invariably involves descriptions of how institutions are socially and culturally organized within the community being studied, the role of each actor within the community, and the perspectives of all focal agents. Invariably some features of community life are included and others are left out. Case studies might involve the same cultural contexts, but focus on different levels of organization. Cultural theorists often use practical guidelines for making such decisions, but only those conclusions that can be sufficiently supported are usually incorporated into the final analysis.

Choose an Exemplary Vignette

To draw conclusions, cultural theorists continue to collect first-order evidence and draw second-order inferences until they are satisfied with the convergence of evidence from multiple sources, a topic is adequately covered, or a hypothesis is examined. In writing about their work, these investigators often start with a central *narrative vignette* generated from careful scrutiny of available evidence. They often note regularities, relationships, co-variation, and other configurations, analyzing why the selected event was most salient in their minds. Cultural theorists often ask and answer questions about the density of the narrative and explore the theoretical loading of evidence by contrasting selected terms with alternative vocabularies. In the writing and confirmation process, they sometimes learn that an event they initially selected was not as central as they initially thought, but this exercise helps investigators identify their own analytic distinctions as they produce each narrative.

Write a General Description

Cultural theorists often write and critique *general descriptions* that serve as evidence of the trends they are noticing. Linking the details of this description to the fragments of available evidence, they can determine if their fieldwork is complete. They can also determine if findings can be reported in one easily digested pattern and may use inferential statistics to confirm such a pattern. The goal in analysis is to avoid creating holistic fantasies by grounding any general conclusions in evidence.

Evaluate Interpretive Commentaries

Cultural theorists may also treat their more specific *interpretive commentaries,* completed at the time data were collected, as a form of evidence. These commentaries sometimes precede or follow a particular sequence of events and are attempts to associate particular actions with theoretical claims. To avoid imposing their own biases, investigators note general patterns in their findings and any changes that occur in their perspectives over time. They also conduct a *member check* to verify that participants did not feel co-opted into behaving in particular ways and if informants agree with particular inferences (Guba, 1981). In such analysis, informants analyze the commentaries generated earlier and look for evidence of faulty heuristics in an investigator's account of events, perspectives, and values. Some commentaries, in other words, serve as self-interviews in which investigators ask and answer questions about their observations. Cultural theorists may also share their evaluations with informants to generate another level of confirmation. All reviewers commonly mark frequently occurring biases and establish procedures for correcting them.

Evaluate Causal Networks

Another step involves *drawing and evaluating a causal network* for representing evidence (Huberman & Miles, 1985). Cultural theorists often look for conceptual clusters by constructing matrices of common effects, describing the dynamics of the investigation site, and relating observables to consequences. This process is completed after investigators generate a final variable list in which they document goals, outcomes, events, and patterns. Most cultural theorists are careful to link variables to specific indicants and avoid redundancies. The processes of sorting cases, using a stratification plan or randomly sampling events from a larger data file, occurs in research using psychometric and developmental tools, but in ethnography these steps occur near the end of an investigation rather than near the beginning.

Construct an Historical Record

Generating an *historical account of the study* serves as yet another kind of interpretation. Cultural theorists may look at the representativeness of their evidence and any researcher effects that might be apparent. Assuming that the study is distorted or unbalanced until they have confirmed otherwise, investigators compare the process by which evidence was collected. Although this is the easiest step to leave out of the confirmation process, it is helpful to verify how individuals' thinking has changed over the course of the project. These are done well if investigators remain open to perceiving, recording, and reflecting on evidence that would otherwise disconfirm their beliefs. Starting with the question of how change occurred, cultural theorists may try to imagine the various perspectives of their informants, the various situational constraints, and the timing of events.

Compare the Typical and Unusual

Cultural theorists often triangulate evidence by looking at how sources, methods, levels of organization, and researchers influence the outcomes. To draw second-order inferences, they weigh evidence by looking for similarities and differences across levels of influence. A third level of inference may be possible when investigators compare second-order inferences to an emerging theoretical framework.

At all levels of inference, outliers are identified, evaluated, and compared against more typical events. Rather than overlook extreme or unusual points of evidence, as is common in developmental or psychometric traditions, cultural theorists look for a range of rival explanations. They may decide to rule out such information if it conveys spurious relations or try to replicate an unusual finding. Investigators may also recognize that an atypical action or setting falls within a more general pattern that would otherwise go undetected. The confirmation process serves to audit conclusions for negative evidence and outliers may serve this purpose. Before writing the final narrative of a causal network, cultural theorists usually seek feedback on their representations from informants, maximizing the possibility that they have offered a fair and balanced treatment of evidence.

Limitations of Ethnographic Evidence

Cultural theorists often find several sources of inadequacy with ethnographic methods as they attempt to validate their findings (see Erickson, 1986, for a summary of such problems). Whereas investigators using psychometric or developmental tools try to link indicants to particular constructs, theories of cultures are inevitably too broadly construed to be designed and tested this way. Inadequacy can come about when there is insufficient evidence for supporting particular ideas or essential evidence is missing from the records.

There can also be insufficient variability in the evidence collected. If investigators fail to look for disconfirming evidence, for example, they may construct only distorted interpretations of a particular community or setting. It becomes impossible to conduct the discrepant case analyses necessary for generating a balanced account of communal life.

Without a comparison of disconfirming and confirming evidence, cultural theorists may offer a faulty interpretation of events that is only compounded in later stages of theory building and confirmation. These limitations do not outweigh the benefits of conducting thick descriptions of lives in progress, dynamic cultures, and global commonalities across cultures.

MAKING CONNECTIONS

In the case study, ethnography, or ethnology you are reading, how did investigators confirm their conclusions? Do they offer an account of the confirmation process? Is there an historical representation of how the study was conducted? What levels of analysis can you detect from reading the account itself? Is it necessary to have a separate section on methods and measurement that outlines procedures used in the study?

STUDYING CULTURES AS SOCIAL ORGANIZATIONS

Investigators who spend most of their energy studying cultures ask about the ethics of treating individual differences in performance as indicators of competence. Adopting an intermediate position between cultural realism and cultural idealism, they may look for problems in the social organization when performance is particularly low or strengths of such structures when performance is high. Individual differences in daily functioning may be as much a virtue as a problem in a culture.

Ethnographers and ethnologists recognize that not all levels of organization are immediately apparent and look for subtle norms and display rules that seem to be guiding human functioning. They use display rituals and artifacts to illuminate the factors affecting individuals' functioning; if individuals consistently demonstrate competence or incompetence, for example, investigators may identify the parameters of situations that affect individuals' fitness. Cultural theorists often become involved in labeling rules that individuals use to organize their behavior, the structures in which informants must function, and how institutional structures are used to create disorganization as well as coherence.

Evaluations of persons, settings, and values are periodically unbundled and reassembled as cultural theorists strive for agreement on what constitutes local events. Outliers in a culture may be assumed to lack fitness rather than incompetence. Mismatches can be documented by evaluating whether individuals are unaware of social constraints used to organize persons and events and/or deliberately ignore pressures for normative order and the preservation of their good standing in such order. Cultural theorists may look for explanations of why and how particular conditions, thoughts, and behaviors are elicited, but rely on a wide variety of local explanations to develop these generalizations. Ethnographers and ethnologists are less interested in a science of prediction and control than in a science of description and explanation. Validity in the study of cultures inevitably depends on the unpredictable, dynamic nature of lives, institutions, and environments.

SUGGESTED READINGS

Clubb, J. M., & Scheuch, E. K. (Eds.). (1980). *Historical social research: Use of historical and process-product data.* Stuttgart, Germany: Kett-Cotta.

Denzin, N. K., & Lincoln, Y. S. (Eds.). (2003c). *The strategies of qualitative inquiry* (2nd ed.). Thousand Oaks, CA: Sage.

Denzin, N. K., & Lincoln, Y. S. (Eds.). (2003a). *Collecting and interpreting qualitative materials* (2nd ed.). Thousand Oaks, CA: Sage.

Dobbert, M. L. (1982). *Ethnographic research: Theory and application for modern schools and societies.* New York: Praeger.

Donaldson, S. I., & Scriven, M. (Eds.). (2002). *Evaluating social programs and problems: Visions for the new millennium.* Mahwah, NJ: Erlbaum.

Howell, M., & Prevenier, W. (2001). *From reliable sources: An introduction to historical methods.* Ithaca, NY: Cornell University Press.

Levine, H. G., Gallimore, R., Weisner, T., & Turner, J. L. (1980). Teaching participant-observational methods: A skills-building approach. *Anthropology and Education Quarterly, 11,* 38–54.

Pelto, P., & Pelto, G. (1977). *Anthropological research: The structure of inquiry.* New York: Harcourt Brace.

Wax, R. H. (1971). *Doing fieldwork: Warnings and advice.* Chicago: University of Chicago Press.

ENDNOTES

1. Erickson (1986) offers some of this language for making clear the agendas of cultural theorists.

2. McDermott & Hood (1982) offer an early example of this kind of work applied to a critique of schooling and the process of sorting students into ability groups.

3. Kurzman (1991) offered one example of how social distance played a role in sociological discussions about the nature of participant-observation research.

4. Moerman (1988) makes this case by laying out first-order data and second-order inferences about Thai culture.

5. There are many different ways to analyze text. Such analysis was introduced in Chapters 4 and 5 and elaborated in Chapters 10 and 12, but ethnographic uses are often seen as more personal and sometimes more flexible than other methods. Text analysis of linguistic differences was introduced in Chapter 14, but work cited here focuses on how inferences about culture are generated.

6. Contrasting the approaches in Packer & Addison (1989) with those in Edwards & Lampert (1993) and Ericsson & Simon (1993) can illustrate this difference.

7. Gilbert & Gubar (1991) offer more details on the shortcomings of this approach to research.

8. Erickson (1986) offers a vivid description of how this might be accomplished in educational settings.

9. Boon (1986) offers a vivid description of the symbolism inherent in artifacts, but Babcock (1986) offers a delightful example of how artifacts can tell stories in their own right.

10. This representation was offered by Clemens & Hughes (2002) when exploring historical research on social movements.

11. Wolcott (1990) offers the most straightforward set of guidelines although, as you can see, there is a great deal of room for interpretation in these suggestions.

12. Simon (1957) offers more information on the importance of establishing some boundaries for such inquiries.

13. Cohen & Manion (1989a) offer a clear summary of the technique of triangulation, but imply that investigators can use this technique to offer a progressively more truthful account of reality. The positivist assumptions embedded in this paper contradict the views of many ethnographers, who see the importance of understanding multiple perspectives on the same set of parameters.

14. Denzin (1970) and Smith (1975) outline some of these parameters and offer examples of their use.

■ ■ ■ ■ ■

TABLE A.1 Probabilities and Y-ordinates Associated with z-Scores under the Normal Curve

ABSOLUTE VALUE OF z	PR. ≤ −z	PR. ≤ +z	Y-ORDINATE	ABSOLUTE VALUE OF z	PR. ≤ −z	PR. ≤ +z	Y-ORDINATE
3.00	.001	.999	.0044	1.50	.067	.933	.1295
2.95	.002	.998	.0051	1.45	.074	.926	.1394
2.90	.002	.998	.0060	1.40	.081	.919	.1497
2.85	.002	.998	.0069	1.35	.089	.911	.1604
2.80	.003	.997	.0079	1.30	.097	.903	.1714
2.75	.003	.997	.0091	1.25	.106	.894	.1827
2.70	.003	.997	.0104	1.20	.115	.885	.1942
2.65	.004	.996	.0120	1.15	.125	.875	.2059
2.60	.005	.995	.0136	1.10	.136	.864	.2179
2.55	.005	.995	.0155	1.05	.147	.853	.2299
2.50	.006	.994	.0175	1.00	.159	.841	.2420
2.45	.007	.993	.0198	.95	.171	.829	.2541
2.40	.008	.992	.0224	.90	.184	.816	.2661
2.35	.009	.991	.0252	.85	.198	.802	.2780
2.30	.011	.989	.0283	.80	.212	.788	.2897
2.25	.012	.988	.0317	.75	.227	.773	.3011
2.20	.014	.986	.0355	.70	.242	.758	.3123
2.15	.016	.984	.0396	.65	.258	.742	.3230
2.10	.018	.982	.0440	.60	.274	.726	.3332
2.05	.020	.980	.0488	.55	.291	.709	.3429
2.00	.023	.977	.0540	.50	.309	.691	.3521
1.95	.026	.974	.0596	.45	.326	.674	.3605
1.90	.029	.971	.0656	.40	.344	.656	.3683
1.85	.032	.968	.0721	.35	.363	.637	.3752
1.80	.036	.964	.0790	.30	.382	.618	.3814
1.75	.040	.960	.0863	.25	.401	.599	.3867
1.70	.045	.955	.0941	.20	.421	.579	.3910
1.65	.049	.951	.1023	.15	.440	.560	.3945
1.60	.055	.945	.1109	.10	.460	.540	.3970
1.55	.061	.939	.1200	.05	.480	.520	.3984

TABLE A.2   Chi Square (χ^2) Distribution Values

	ONE TAILED PROBABILITY						
DF	0.001	0.005	0.010	0.025	0.050	0.100	0.250
1	10.83	7.88	6.63	5.02	3.84	2.71	1.32
2	13.82	10.60	9.21	7.38	5.99	4.61	2.77
3	16.27	12.84	11.34	9.35	7.81	6.25	4.11
4	18.47	14.86	13.28	11.14	9.49	7.78	5.39
5	20.52	16.75	15.09	12.83	11.07	9.24	6.63
6	22.46	18.55	16.81	14.45	12.59	10.64	7.84
7	24.32	20.28	18.48	16.01	14.07	12.02	9.04
8	26.13	21.96	20.09	17.53	15.51	13.36	10.22
9	27.88	23.59	21.67	19.02	16.92	14.68	11.39
10	29.59	25.19	23.21	20.48	18.31	15.99	12.55
11	31.26	26.76	24.73	21.92	19.68	17.28	13.70
12	32.91	28.30	26.22	23.34	21.03	18.55	14.85
13	34.53	29.82	27.69	24.74	22.36	19.81	15.98
14	36.12	31.32	29.14	26.12	23.68	21.06	17.12
15	37.70	32.80	30.58	27.49	25.00	22.31	18.25
16	39.25	34.27	32.00	28.85	26.30	23.54	19.37
17	40.79	35.72	33.41	30.19	27.59	24.77	20.49
18	42.31	37.16	34.81	31.53	28.87	25.99	21.60
19	43.82	38.58	36.19	32.85	30.14	27.20	22.72
20	45.32	40.00	37.57	34.17	31.41	28.41	23.83
21	46.80	41.40	38.93	35.48	32.67	29.62	24.93
22	48.27	42.80	40.29	36.78	33.92	30.81	26.04
23	49.73	44.18	41.64	38.08	35.17	32.01	27.14
24	51.18	45.56	42.98	39.36	36.42	33.20	28.24
25	52.62	46.93	44.31	40.65	37.65	34.38	29.34
26	54.05	48.29	45.64	41.92	38.89	35.56	30.44
27	55.48	49.65	46.96	43.19	40.11	36.74	31.53
28	56.89	50.99	48.28	44.46	41.34	37.92	32.62
29	58.30	52.34	49.59	45.72	42.56	39.09	33.71
30	59.70	53.67	50.89	46.98	43.77	40.26	34.80
40	73.40	66.77	63.69	59.34	55.76	51.81	45.62
50	86.66	79.49	76.15	71.42	67.50	63.17	56.33
60	99.61	91.95	88.38	83.30	79.08	74.40	66.98
70	112.32	104.22	100.43	95.02	90.53	85.53	77.58
80	124.84	116.32	112.33	106.63	101.88	96.58	88.13
90	137.21	128.30	124.12	118.14	113.15	107.57	98.65
100	140.45	140.17	135.81	129.56	124.34	118.50	109.14

Achenbach, T. M., & Edelbrock, C. S. (1986). *Child behavior checklist and youth self-report.* Burlington, VT: University of Vermont, Department of Psychiatry.

Agar, M. (1980). *The professional stranger: An informal introduction to ethnography.* New York: Academic Press.

Agresti, A. (2002). *Categorical data analysis* (2nd ed.). New York: Wiley.

Allen, M. J., & Yen, W. M. (2001). *Introduction to measurement theory.* Long Grove, IL: Waveland.

Allison, P. D. (2001). *Logistic regression using SAS system: Theory and application.* New York: Wiley.

Altrichter, H., Posch, P., & Somekh, B. (1993). *Teachers investigate their work: An introduction to the methods of action research.* New York: Routledge.

American Bar Association. (1990). *Model code of professional responsibility and code of judicial conduct.* Chicago: Author.

American Psychological Association. (2001). *Publication manual of the American Psychological Association* (5th ed.). Washington, DC: Author.

American Psychological Association. (2002). Ethical principles of psychologists and code of conduct. *American Psychologist, 57,* 1060–1073.

Anderson, E. R. (1995). Accelerating and maximizing information from short-term longitudinal research. In J. M. Gottman (Ed.), *The analysis of change* (pp. 139–164). Mahwah, NJ: Erlbaum.

Anderson, J. E. (1939). The limitations of infant and preschool tests in the measurement of intelligence. *Journal of Psychology, 8,* 351–379.

Angoff, W. H. (1971). Scales, norms, and equivalent scores. In R. L. Thorndike (Ed.), *Educational measurement* (2nd ed., pp. 508–600). Washington, DC: American Council on Education.

Angoff, W. H. (1984). *Scales, norms, and equivalent scores.* Princeton, NJ: Educational Testing Service.

Arkin, R. M., Appelman, A. J., & Burger, J. M. (1980). Social anxiety, self-preservation, and the self-serving bias in causal attribution. *Journal of Personality and Social Psychology, 38,* 23–35.

Arkin, R. M., & Lake, E. A. (1983). Plumbing the depths of the bogus pipeline: A reprise. *Journal of Research in Personality, 17,* 81–88.

Aronson, J., Lustina, M. J., Good, C., Keough, K., Steele, C. M., & Brown, J. (1999). When White men can't do math: Necessary and sufficient factors in stereotype threat. *Journal of Experimental Social Psychology, 35,* 29–46.

Asendorpf, J. B., & Valsiner, J. (1992). *Stability and change in development: A study of methodological reasoning.* Newbury Park, CA: Sage.

Asher, S. J., & Dodge, K. A. (1986). Identifying children who are rejected by their peers. *Developmental Psychology, 22,* 444–449.

Babcock, B. A. (1986). Modeled selves: Helen Cordero's 'little people' In V. W. Turner & E. M. Bruner (Eds.), *The anthropology of experience* (pp. 316–343). Urbana: University of Illinois Press.

Bain, A. (1981). Presenting problems in social consultancy. *Human Relations, 34,* 643–657.

Bakeman, R., & Gottman, J. M. (1997). *Observing interaction: An introduction to sequential analysis* (2nd ed.). New York: Cambridge University Press.

Baltes, P. B., & Goulet, L. R. (1971). Exploration of developmental variables by manipulation and simulation of age differences in behavior. *Human Development, 14,* 149–170.

Baltes, P. B., Reese, H. W., & Nesselroade, J. R. (1977). *Life-span developmental psychology: Introduction to research methods.* Monterey, CA: Brooks/Cole.

Barbour, R. S., & Kitsinger, J. (1999). *Developing focus group research.* Newbury Park, CA: Sage.

Barrett, G. V., & Depinet, R. L. (1991). A reconsideration of testing for competence rather than for intelligence. *American Psychologist, 46,* 1012–1024

Baumrind, D. (1964). Some thoughts on ethics of research: After reading Milgram's 'Behavioral study of obedience.' *American Psychologist, 19,* 421–423.

Baumrind, D. (1985). Research using intentional deception: Ethical issues revisited. *American Psychologist, 40,* 165–174.

Bennett, E. M., Alpert, R., & Goldstein, A. C. (1954). Communications through limited response questioning. *Public Opinion Quarterly, 18,* 303–308.

Best, J. W., & Kahn, J. V. (2003). *Research in education* (9th ed.). Boston: Allyn & Bacon.

Binet, A., & Simon, T. (1948). The development of the Binet-Simon scale. In W. Dennis (Ed.), *Readings in the history of psychology* (pp. 412–424). New York: Appleton-Century-Crofts.

Bion, W. R. (1961). *Experiences in groups.* London: Tavistock.

Bishop, G. F. (1990). Issue involvement and response effects in public opinion surveys. *Public Opinion Quarterly, 54,* 209–218.

Bjorklund, D. F. (2000). *Children's thinking: Developmental function and individual differences* (3rd ed.). Belmont, CA: Wadsworth.

Blanck, P. D., Bellack, A. S., Rosnow, R. L., Rotheram-Borus, M. J., & Schooler, N. R. (1992). Scientific rewards and conflicts of ethical choices in human subjects research. *American Psychologist, 47,* 959–965.

Bloom, B. S., Engelhart, M. D., Furst, E. J., Hill, W. H., & Krathwohl, D. R. (1956). *Taxonomy of educational objectives: Handbook I. Cognitive domain.* New York: David McKay.

Bobko, P. (2001). *Correlation and regression: Applications for industrial/organizational psychology and management* (2nd ed.). Thousand Oaks, CA: Sage.

Boje, D. M. (2001). *Narrative methods for organizational and communication research.* Thousand Oaks, CA: Sage.

Bond, T. G., & Fox, C. M. (2001). *Applying the Rasch model: Fundamental measurement in the human sciences.* Mahwah, NJ: Erlbaum.

Boon, J. A. (1986). Symbols, sylphs, and siwa: Allegorical machineries in the text of Balinese culture. In V. W. Turner & E. M. Bruner (Eds.), *The anthropology of experience* (pp. 239–260). Urbana: University of Illinois Press.

Boorman, S. A., & White, H. C. (1976). Social structure from multiple networks II. Role structures. *American Journal of Sociology, 81,* 1384–1446.

Bornstein, M., Lamb, M. E., & Pierson, H. (1999). *Developmental psychology: An introduction* (4th ed.). Hillsdale, NJ: Erlbaum.

Boyd, D., & Arnold, M. L. (2000). Teachers' beliefs, antiracism, and moral education: Problems of intersection. *Journal of Moral Education, 29,* 23–45.

Brainerd, C. J. (1974). Postmortem on judgments, explanations, and Piagetian cognitive structures. *Psychological Bulletin, 81,* 70–71.

Brainerd, C. J. (1978). The stage question in cognitive-developmental theory. *Behavioral and Brain Sciences, 2,* 173–213.

Braun, H. I., Jackson, D. N., & Wiley, D. E. (2002). *The role of constructs in psychological and educational measurement.* Mahwah, NJ: Erlbaum.

Brennan, R. L. (1972). A generalized upper-lower item discrimination index. *Educational and Psychological Measurement, 32,* 289–303.

Bronfenbrenner, U. (1979). *The ecology of human development: Experiments by nature and design.* Cambridge, MA: Harvard University Press.

Bronson, W. C. (1981). Toddlers' behaviors with age-mates: Issues of interaction, cognition, and affect. *Monographs on Infancy, 1,* 127.

Brown, G., & Yule, G. (1983). *Discourse analysis.* New York: Cambridge University Press.

Brown, L. M., Tappan, M. B., Gilligan, C., Miller, B. A., & Argyris (1989). Reading for self and moral voice: A method for interpreting narratives of real-life moral conflict and choice. In M. J. Packer & R. B. Addison (Eds.), *Entering the circle: Hermeneutic investigation in psychology* (pp. 141–164). New York: State University of New York Press.

Brownell, C. A., & Brown, E. (1992). Peers and play in infants and toddlers. In V. B. Van Hasselt & M. Hersen (Eds.), *Handbook of social development: A lifespan perspective* (pp. 183–200). New York: Plenum.

Bruner, J. (1990). *Acts of meaning.* Cambridge, MA: Harvard University Press.

Bukowski, W. M., Sippola, L., Hoza, B., & Newcomb, A. F. (2000). Pages from a sociometric notebook: An analysis of nomination and rating scale measures of acceptance, rejection, and social preference. In A. H. N. Cillessen & W. M. Bukowski (Eds.), *Recent advances in the measurement of acceptance and rejection in the peer system* (pp. 11–26). San Francisco, CA: Jossey-Bass.

Burisch, M. (1984). Approaches to personality inventory construction: A comparison of merits. *American Psychologist, 39,* 214–227.

Burman, E. (1997). Minding the gap: Positivism, psychology, and the politics of qualitative methods. *Journal of Social Issues, 53,* 785–801.

Burt, R. S., & Lin, N. (1977). Network time series from archival records. In D. R. Heise (Ed.), *Sociological methodology* (pp. 224–254). San Francisco, CA: Jossey-Bass.

Buss, A. R., & Royce, J. R. (1975). Ontogenetic changes in cognitive structure from a multivariate perspective. *Developmental Psychology, 11,* 87–101.

Butcher, J. N. (Ed.). (1996). *International adaptations of the MMPI-2: Research and clinical applications.* Minneapolis: University of Minnesota Press.

Byrne, B. M. (2001). *Structural equation modeling with AMOS: Basic concepts, applications, and programming.* Mahwah, NJ: Erlbaum.

Cairns, R. B., Cairns, B. D., Neckerman, H. J., Gest, S. D., & Gariépy, J-L. (1988). Social networks and aggressive behavior: Peer support or peer rejection? *Developmental Psychology, 24,* 815–823.

Cairns, R. B., Leung, M-C., Buchanan, L., & Cairns, B. D. (1995). Friendships and social networks in childhood and adolescence: Fluidity, reliability, and interrelations. *Child Development, 66,* 1330–1345.

Campbell, D. (1957). Factors relevant to the validity of experiments in social settings. *Psychological Bulletin, 54,* 297–312.

Campbell, D. T., & Fiske, D. W. (1959). Convergent and discriminant validation by the multitrait-multimethod matrix. *Psychological Bulletin, 56,* 81–105.

Campbell, D. T., & Russo, M. J. (2001). *Social measurement.* Thousand Oaks, CA: Sage.

Campbell, D. T., & Stanley, J. C. (1963). *Experimental and quasi-experimental designs for research.* Chicago, IL: Rand McNally.

Canter, M., Bennett, B., Jones, S., & Nagy, T. (1994). *Ethics for psychologists: A commentary on the APA ethical code.* Washington, DC: APA.

Caprara, G. V., & Cervone, D. (2000). *Personality: Determinants, dynamics, and potentials.* New York: Cambridge University Press.

Carroll, J. B. (1989). Factor analysis since Spearman: Where do we stand? What do we know? In R. Kanfer, P. L. Ackerman, & R. Cudeck (Eds.), *Abilities, motivation, and methodology: The Minnesota symposium on learning and individual differences* (pp. 43–67). Hillsdale, NJ: Erlbaum.

Carspecken, P. F., & Walford, G. (Eds.). (2001). *Critical ethnography and education.* New York: JAI Press.

Case, R., & Okamoto, Y. (2000). *The role of central conceptual structures in the development of children's thought.* London: Blackwell.

Cattell, R. B. (1963). Theory of fluid and crystallized intelligence: A critical experiment. *Journal of Educational Psychology, 54,* 1–22.

Cattell, R. B. (1973). *Personality and mood by questionnaire.* San Francisco: Jossey-Bass.

Cazden, C. B. (1988). *Classroom discourse: The language of teaching and learning.* Portsmouth, NH: Heinemann.

Chatterjee, S., Hadi, A. S., & Price, B. (1999). *Regression analysis by example* (3rd ed.). New York: Wiley.

Cherryholmes, C. H. (1988). Construct validity and the discourses of research. *American Journal of Education, 96,* 421–457.

Cillessen, A. H. N., & Bukowski, W. M. (Eds.). (2000). *Recent advances in the measurement of acceptance and rejection in the peer system.* San Francisco, CA: Jossey-Bass.

Cillessen, A. H. N., Bukowski, W. M., & Haselager, G. J. T. (2000). Stability of sociometric categories. In A. H. N. Cillessen & W. M. Bukowski (Eds.), *Recent advances in the measurement of acceptance and rejection in the peer system* (pp. 75–93). San Francisco, CA: Jossey-Bass.

Cizek, G. J. (2001). *Setting performance standards: Concepts, methods, and perspectives.* Mahwah, NJ: Erlbaum.

Clark, P. A. (1972). *Action research and organizational change.* London: Harper & Row.

Clemens, E. S., & Hughes, M. D. (2002). Recovering past protest: Historical research on social movements. In B. Klandermans & S. Staggenborg (Eds.), *Methods of social movement research* (pp. 201–230). Minneapolis: University of Minnesota Press.

Clifford, J. (1988). *The predicament of culture.* Cambridge, MA: Harvard University Press.

Clubb, J. M., & Scheuch, E. K. (Eds.). (1980). *Historical social research: Use of historical and process-product data.* Stuttgart, Germany: Kett-Cotta.

Coan, R. W. (1966). Child personality and developmental psychology. In R. B. Cattell (Ed.), *Handbook of multivariate experimental psychology* (pp. 732–752). Chicago: Rand McNally.

Coan, R. W. (1972). The changing personality. In R. M. Dreger (Ed.), *Multivariate personality research: Contributions to the understanding of personality in honor of Raymond B. Cattell.* Baton Rouge, LA: Claitor.

Cohen, J. (1968). Weighted kappa: Nominal scale agreement with provision for scaled disagreement or partial credit. *Psychological Bulletin, 70,* 213–220.

Cohen, L., & Manion, L. (1989a). Triangulation. In L. Cohen & L. Manion, *Research methods in education* (pp. 269–286). New York: Routledge.

Cohen, L., & Manion, L. (1989b). The interview. In L. Cohen & L. Manion, *Research methods in education* (pp. 307–333). New York: Routledge.

Coie, J. D., Dodge, K. A., & Coppotelli, H. (1982). Dimensions and types of social status: A cross-age perspective. *Developmental Psychology, 18,* 557–570.

Coles, R. (2003). *Children of crisis.* New York: Back Bay Books.

Cosslett, T., Lury, C., & Summerfield, P. (2000). *Feminism and autobiography: Texts, theories, methods.* London: Routledge.

Cox, R. C., & Vargas, J. S. (1966). *A comparison of item-selection techniques for norm-referenced and criterion-referenced tests.* Paper presented at the annual meeting of the National Council on Measurement in Education.

Creswell, J. W. (1998). *Qualitative inquiry and research design: Choosing among five traditions.* Thousand Oaks, CA: Sage.

Creswell, J. W. (2002). *Educational research: Planning, conducting, and evaluating qualitative and quantitative research.* Upper Saddle River, NJ: Merrill-Prentice-Hall.

Crocker, L., & Algina, J. (1986). *Introduction to classical and modern test theory.* New York: Holt, Rinehart, & Winston.

Cronbach, L. J. (1946). Response sets and test validity. *Educational and Psychological Measurement, 6,* 475–494.

Cronbach, L. J. (1950). Further evidence on response sets and test design. *Educational and Psychological Measurement, 10,* 3–31.

Cronbach, L. J. (1951). Coefficient alpha and the internal structure of tests. *Psychometrika, 16,* 297–334.

Cronbach, L. J. (1988). Five perspectives on validity argument. In H. Wainer & H. I. Braun (Eds.), *Test validity* (pp. 3–18). Hillsdale, NJ: Erlbaum.

Cronbach, L., & Furby, L. (1970). How should we measure 'change'—or should we? *Psychological Bulletin, 74,* 68–80.

Cronbach, L. J., Gleser, G. C., Nanda, H., & Rajaratnam, N. (1972). *The dependability of behavioral measurements: Theory of generalizability for scores and profiles.* New York: Wiley.

Cronbach, L. J., & Meehl, P. E. (1955). Construct validity in psychology tests. *Psychological Bulletin, 52,* 281–301.

Culler, J. (1984). *On deconstruction: Theory and criticism after structuralism.* Ithaca, NY: Cornell University Press.

Damasio, A. (1999). *The feeling of what happens: Body and emotion in the making of consciousness.* San Diego, CA: Harcourt.

Damon, W. (1977). *The social world of the child.* San Francisco: Jossey-Bass.

Damon, W. (Series Ed.), Eisenberg, N. (Vol. Ed.). (1998). *Handbook of child psychology: Vol. 3. Social, emotional, and personality development* (5th ed.). New York: Wiley.

Damon, W. (Series Ed.), Kuhn, D., & Siegler, R. S. (Vol. Eds.). (1998). *Handbook of child psychology: Vol. 2. Cognition, perception, and language* (5th ed.). New York: Wiley.

Damon, W. (Series Ed.), & Lerner, R. M. (Vol. Ed.). (1998). *Handbook of child psychology: Vol. 1. Theoretical models* (5th ed.). New York: Wiley.

Damon, W. (Series Ed.), Sigel, I. E., & Renninger, K. A. (Vol. Ed.). (1998). *Handbook of child psychology: Vol. 4. Practice* (5th ed.). New York: Wiley.

Dana, R. H. (Ed.). (2000). *Handbook of cross-cultural and multicultural personality assessment.* Mahwah, NJ: Erlbaum.

Dawes, R. M. (1972). *Fundamentals of attitude measurement.* New York: Wiley.

Dawes, R. M., Faust, D., & Meehl, P. E. (1989). Clinical versus actuarial judgment. *Science, 243,* 1668–1674.

Dawes, R. M., & Smith, T. L. (1985). Attitude and opinion measurement. In G. Lindzey & E. Aronson (Eds.), *Handbook of social psychology* (3rd ed., Vol. 1, pp. 509–566). New York: Random House.

Dawson, W. E. (1982). On the parallel between direct ratio scaling of social opinion and of sensory magnitude. In B. Wegener (Ed.), *Social attitudes and psychophysical measurement* (pp. 151–176). Hillsdale, NJ: Erlbaum.

Denison, D. G. T., Holmes, C., Mallick, B. K., & Smith, A. F. M. (2002). *Bayesian methods for nonlinear classification and regression.* New York: Wiley.

Denzin, N. K. (1970). *The research act in sociology: A theoretical introduction to sociological methods.* London: Butterworth.

Denzin, N. K., & Lincoln, Y. S. (Eds.). (2003a). *Collecting and interpreting qualitative materials* (2nd ed.). Thousand Oaks, CA: Sage.

Denzin, N. K., & Lincoln, Y. S. (Eds.). (2003b). *The landscape of qualitative research: Theories and issues* (2nd ed.). Thousand Oaks, CA: Sage.

Denzin, N. K., & Lincoln, Y. S. (Eds.). (2003c). *The strategies of qualitative inquiry* (2nd ed.). Thousand Oaks, CA: Sage.

Derrida, J. (1982). *Of grammatology.* Baltimore: Johns Hopkins University Press.

DeVellis, R. F. (2003). *Scale development: Theory and applications* (2nd ed.). Thousand Oaks, CA: Sage.

Dillman, D. A. (2000). *Mail and Internet surveys: The tailored design method* (2nd ed.). New York: Wiley.

Dilthey, W. (1976). The development of hermeneutics. In W. Dilthey, *Selected writings* (H. Rickman, Ed. & Trans.). Cambridge, UK: Cambridge University Press. (Originally published in 1900.)

Dixon, J. A. (1998). Developmental ordering, scale types, and strong inference. *Developmental Psychology, 34,* 131–145.

Dobbert, M. L. (1982). *Ethnographic research: Theory and application for modern schools and societies.* New York: Praeger.

Donaldson, S. I., & Scriven, M. (Eds.). (2002). *Evaluating social programs and problems: Visions for the new millennium.* Mahwah, NJ: Erlbaum.

Dorans, N. J. (2000). Scaling and equating. In H. Wainer (Ed.), *Computerized adaptive testing: A primer* (2nd ed., pp. 135–158.) Mahwah, NJ: Erlbaum.

Duda, J. L., & Nicholls, J. G. (1992). Dimensions of achievement motivation in schoolwork and sport: Situational specificity or general traits. *Journal of Educational Psychology, 84,* 290–299.

Eagly, A., & Chaiken, S. (1993). *The psychology of attitudes.* New York: Harcourt Brace.

Ebel, R. L. (1965). *Measuring educational achievement.* Englewood Cliffs, NJ: Prentice-Hall.

Edelman, G. M. (1992). *Bright air, brilliant fire: On the matter of the mind.* New York: Basic Books.

Edwards, J. A., & Lampert, M. D. (Eds.). (1993). *Talking data: Transcription and coding in discourse research.* Hillsdale, NJ: Erlbaum.

Eisner, E. W. (1992). Are all causal claims positivistic? A reply to Francis Schrag. *Educational Researcher, 21,* 8–9.

Eisner, E. W. (1997). The promise and perils of alternative forms of data representation. *Educational Researcher, 26,* 4–10.

Ellickson, P. L., & Hawes, J. A. (1989). An assessment of active versus passive methods for obtaining parental consent. *Evaluation Review, 13,* 45–55.

Embretson, S. (1983). Construct validity: Construct representation versus nomothetic span. *Psychological Bulletin, 93,* 179–197.

Embretson, S. E., & Reise, S. P. (2000). *Item-response theory for psychologists.* Mahwah, NJ: Erlbaum.

Erickson, F. (1986). Qualitative methods in research on teaching. In M. C. Wittrock (Ed.), *Handbook of research on teaching* (3rd ed., pp. 119–161). New York: Macmillan.

Erickson, F. (1992). Why the clinical trial doesn't work as a metaphor for educational research: A response to Schrag. *Educational Researcher, 21,* 9–10.

Ericsson, K. A., & Simon, H. A. (1993). *Protocol analysis: Verbal reports as data* (2nd ed.). Cambridge, MA: MIT Press.

Ethical principles of psychologists and code of conduct. (1992). *American Psychologist, 47,* 1597–1611.

Ethical Standards of the American Educational Research Association. (1992). *Educational Researcher, 21,* 23–26.

Everston, C. M., & Green, J. L. (1986). Observation as inquiry and method. In M. C. Wittrock (Ed.), *Handbook of research on teaching* (3rd ed., pp. 162–213). New York: Macmillan.

Eysenck, H. J. (1982). *A model for intelligence.* New York: Springer-Verlag.

Fassnacht, G. (1982). *Theory and practice of observing behavior.* London: Academic Press.

Feldman, J. M., & Lynch, J. G., Jr. (1988). Self-generated validity and other effects of measurement on belief, attitude, intention, and behavior. *Journal of Applied Psychology, 73,* 421–435.

Feldt, L. S., & Brennan, R. L. (1993). Reliability. In R. L. Linn (Ed.), *Educational measurement* (pp. 105–146). Phoenix, AZ: Oryx.

Fine, M. A., & Kurdek, L. A. (1993). Reflections on determining authorship credit and authorship order on faculty—students' collaborations. *American Psychologist, 48,* 1141–1147.

Fisher, C. B., Hoagwood, K., Boyce, C., Duster, T., Frank, D. A., Grisso, T., Levine, R. J., Macklin, R., Spencer, M. B., Takanishi, R., Trimble, J. E., & Zayas, L. H. (2002). Research ethics for mental health science involving ethnic minority children and youths. *American Psychologist, 57,* 1024–1040.

Fiske, D. W. (1967). The subject reacts to tests. *American Psychologist, 22,* 287–296.

Fiske, D. W. (1971). *Measuring the concepts of personality.* Chicago: Aldine.

Fiske, D. W. (1978). *Strategies for personality research.* San Francisco, CA: Jossey-Bass.

Fiske, D. W., & Butler, J. M. (1963). The experimental conditions for measuring individual differences. *Educational and Psychological Measurement, 23,* 249–266.

Flaugher, R. (2000). Item pools. In H. Wainer (Ed.), *Computer adaptive testing: A primer* (2nd ed., pp. 37–60). Mahwah, NJ: Erlbaum.

Flavell, J. H. (1963). *The developmental psychology of Jean Piaget.* Princeton, NJ: van Nostrand.

Fleiss, J. L. (1971). Measuring nominal scale agreement among many raters. *Psychological Bulletin, 76,* 378–382.

Fleiss, J. L. (1986). *The design and analysis of clinical experiments.* New York: Wiley.

Fleiss, J. L., Levin, B., & Paik, M. C. (2003). *Statistical methods of rates and proportions* (3rd ed.). New York: Wiley.

Fletcher, G. J. O. (1984). Psychology and common sense. *American Psychologist, 39,* 203–213.

Foster, S. L., Bell-Dolan, D., & Berler, E. S. (1986). Methodological issues in the use of sociometrics for selecting children for social skills training. *Advances in the Behavioural Assessment of Children and Families, 2,* 227–248.

Foster, S. L., & Ritchey, W. (1979). Issues in the assessment of social competence in children. *Journal of Applied Behaviour Analysis, 12,* 625–638.

Foucault, M. (1980a). *Power/knowledge.* New York: Pantheon.

Foucault, M. (1980b). *Language, counter-memory, practice.* Ithaca, NY: Cornell University Press.

Foulkes, S. H. (1964). *Therapeutic group analysis.* New York: International University Press.

Frederiksen, N. (1984). The real test bias: Influences of testing on teaching and learning. *American Psychologist, 39,* 193–202.

Frederiksen, N., & Furnham, A. F. (1998). Sociometric classification methods in the school peer groups: A comparative investigation. *Journal of Child Psychology and Psychiatry and Allied Disciplines, 39,* 921–933.

Freeman, L. C., White, D. R., & Romney, A. K. (Eds.). (1992). *Research methods in social network analysis.* New Brunswick, NJ: Transaction.

Furby, L. (1973). Interpreting regression toward the mean in developmental research. *Developmental Psychology, 8,* 172–179.

Gardner, H. (1983). *Frames of mind: The theory of multiple intelligences.* New York: Basic Books.

Gardner, W. (1995). On the reliability of sequential data: Measurement, meaning, and correction. In J. M. Gottman (Ed.), *The analysis of change* (pp. 339–360). Mahwah, NJ: Erlbaum.

Geertz, C. (1973). *The interpretation of cultures.* New York: Basic Books.

Geertz, C. (1983). *Local knowledge: Further essays in interpretive anthropology.* New York: Basic Books.

Ghiselli, E. E., Campbell, J. P., & Zedeck, S. (1981). *Measurement theory for the behavioral sciences.* New York: Freeman.

Gilbert, S. M., & Gubar, S. (1991). Masterpiece theatre: An academic melodrama. *Critical Inquiry, 17,* 693–717.

Glaser, B., & Strauss, A. (1967). *The discovery of grounded theory.* Chicago: Aldine.

Glaser, R. (1963). Instructional technology and the measurement of learning outcomes: Some questions. *American Psychologist, 18,* 519–521.

Goodenough, W. H. (1969). Rethinking 'status' and 'role': Toward a general model of the cultural organization of social relationships. In S. A. Tyler (Ed.), *Cognitive anthropology* (pp. 311–330). New York: Holt, Rinehart, & Winston.

Gorden, R. L. (1975). *Interviewing: Strategy, techniques, and tactics* (2nd ed.). Homewood, IL: Dorsey.

Gottman, J. M. (Ed.). (1995). *The analysis of change.* Mahwah, NJ: Erlbaum.

Gould, S. J. (1981). *The mismeasure of man.* New York: Norton.

Graham, S., & Hudley, C. (1994). Attributions of aggressive and nonaggressive African-American male early adolescents: A study of construct accessibility. *Developmental Psychology, 30,* 365–373.

Green, B. F. (1981). A primer of testing. *American Psychologist, 36,* 1001–1011.

Green, B. F. (2000). System design and operation. In H. Wainer (Ed.), *Computerized adaptive testing: A primer* (2nd ed., pp. 23–36.) Mahwah, NJ: Erlbaum.

Green, B. F., Bock, R. D., Humphreys, L. G., Linn, R. L., & Reckase, M. D. (1984). Technical guidelines for assessing computerized adaptive tests. *Journal of Educational Measurement, 21,* 347–360.

Green, R. G. (1997). Psychophysical approaches to personality. In R. Hogan, J. Johnson, & S. Briggs (Eds.), *Handbook of personality psychology* (pp. 387–414). New York: Academic Press.

Greenbaum, T. L. (1997). *The handbook for focus group research.* Newbury Park, CA: Sage.

Gresham, F. M., & Elliott, S. N. (1990). *The social skills rating system.* Circle Pines, MN: American Guidance Service.

Grimmett, G., & Stirzaker, D. (2002). *Probability and random processes* (3rd ed.). New York: Oxford University Press.

Gronlund, N. E. (1998). *Assessment of student achievement* (6th ed.). Boston: Allyn & Bacon.

Guba, E. (1981). Criteria for assessing the trustworthiness of naturalistic inquiries. *Educational Communication and Technology Journal, 29,* 75–91.

Guilford, J. P. (1954). *Psychometric methods* (2nd ed.). New York: McGraw-Hill.

Guilford, J. P. (1967). *The nature of human intelligence.* New York: McGraw-Hill.

Guilford, J. P. (1988). Some changes in the structure-of-the-intellect model. *Educational and Psychological Measurement, 48,* 1–4.

Gulliksen, H. (1987). *Theory of mental tests.* Hillsdale, NJ: Erlbaum.

Gumperz, J. J. (1982). *Discourse strategies.* Cambridge, MA: Cambridge University Press.

Guttman, L. (1941). The quantification of a class of attributes: A theory and method of scale construction. In P. Horst, *The prediction of personal adjustment* (Bulletin No. 48, pp. 319–348). New York: Social Science Research Council.

Guttman, L. (1944). A basis for scaling qualitative data. *American Sociological Review, 9,* 139–150.

Guttman, L. (1947). The Cornell technique for scale and intensity analysis. *Educational and Psychological Measurement, 7,* 247–280.

Guttman, L. (1959). A structural theory for intergroup beliefs and actions. *American Sociological Review, 24,* 318–328.

Guttman, L. (1968). A general nonmetric technique for finding the smallest coordinate space for a configuration of points. *Psychometrika, 33,* 469–506.

Guttman, L. (1977). A definition of dimensionality and distance for graphs. In J. C. Lingoes (Eds.), *Geometric representations of relational data* (pp. 713–723). Ann Arbor, MI: Mathesis.

Habermas, J. (1990). *Moral consciousness and communicative action.* Cambridge, MA: MIT Press.

Haladyna, T. M., & Downing, S. M. (1989). A taxonomy of multiple-choice item-writing rules. *Applied Measurement in Education, 2,* 37–50.

Hall, A. D., & Fagen, R. E. (1955). Definition of a system. *Systems Engineering.* New York: Bell Telephone Laboratories.

Hand, D., & Crowder, M. (1996). *Practical longitudinal data analysis.* Boundary Row, London: Chapman & Hall.

Harré, R. (1979). *Social being: A theory for social psychology.* Totowa, NJ: Rowman & Littlefield.

Harris, C. W., & Pearlman, A. P. (1977). Conventional significance tests and indices of agreement or association. In C. W. Harris, A. P. Pearlman, & R. R. Wilcox (Eds.), *Achievement test items—Methods of study.* (CSE monograph series in evaluation, No. 6). Los Angeles: Center for the Study of Evaluation, University of California.

Hartmann, D. P. (1982). Assessing the dependability of observational data. In D. P. Hartmann (Ed.), *Using observers to study behavior: New directions for methodology of social and behavioral science* (No. 14, pp. 51–65). San Francisco: Jossey-Bass.

Hartmann, D. P. (1992). Design, measurement, and analysis: Technical issues in developmental research. In M. H. Bornstein & M. E. Lamb (Eds.), *Developmental psychology: An advanced textbook* (3rd ed., pp. 59–151). Hillsdale, NJ: Erlbaum.

Hayvren, M., & Hymel, S. (1984). Ethical issues in sociometric testing: Impact of sociometric measures on interaction behavior. *Developmental Psychology, 20,* 844–849.

Hersen, M., & Van Hasselt, V. B. (Ed.). (1998). *Basic interviewing: A practical guide for counselors and clinicians.* Mahwah, NJ: Erlbaum.

Higgins, E. T., Bond, R. N., Klein, R., Strauman, T. (1986). Self-discrepancies and emotional vulnerability: How magnitude, accessibility, and type of discrepancy influence affect. *Journal of Personality and Social Psychology, 51,* 5–15.

Himmelfarb, S. (1993). The measurement of attitudes. In A. H. Eagly & S. Chaiken, *The psychology of attitudes* (pp. 23–87). Fort Worth, TX: Harcourt Brace.

Hoagwood, K., Jensen, P. S., & Fisher, C. B. (Eds.). (1996). *Ethical issues in mental health research with children and adolescents.* Hillsdale, NJ: Erlbaum.

Hogan, R., Johnson, J., & Briggs, S. (Eds.). (1997). *Handbook of personality psychology.* San Diego: Academic Press.

Hogg, M. A., Terry, D. J., & White, K. M. (1995). A tale of two theories: A critical comparison of identity theory with social identity theory. *Social Psychology Quarterly, 58,* 255–269.

Holland, P. W., & Leinhardt, S. (1973). The structural implications of measurement error in sociometry. *Journal of Mathematical Sociology, 3,* 85–111.

Hollnagel, E., & Dobson, D. L. (2003). *Handbook of cognitive task design: Human factors and ergonomics.* Mahwah, NJ: Erlbaum.

Holsti, O. R. (1969). *Content analysis for the social sciences and humanities.* Reading, MA: Addison-Wesley.

Hopkins, K. D. (1997). *Educational and psychological measurement and evaluation* (8th ed.). Boston: Allyn & Bacon.

Horn, J. L., & Cattell, R. B. (1966). Refinement and test of the theory of fluid and crystallized general intelligence. *Journal of Educational Psychology, 51,* 253–270.

Hosmer, D. W., Jr., & Lemeshow, S. (2000). *Applied logistic regression* (2nd ed.). New York: Wiley.

Howe, D. (2002). *Interpreting probability: Controversies and developments in the early twentieth century.* New York: Cambridge University Press.

Howell, M., & Prevenier, W. (2001). *From reliable sources: An introduction to historical methods.* Ithaca, NY: Cornell University Press.

Hoyle, R. H., Harris, M. J., & Judd, C. M. (2002). *Research methods in social relations* (7th ed.). Stamford, CT: Wadsworth.

Huberman, A. M., & Miles, M. B. (1985). Assessing local causality in qualitative research. In D. N. Berg & K. K. Smith (Eds.), *Clinical methods for social research* (pp. 351–381). Beverly Hills, CA: Sage.

Hull, C. L. (1922). The conversion of test scores into series which shall have any assigned mean and degree of dispersion. *Journal of Applied Psychology, 6,* 298–300.

Husserl, E. (1931). *Ideas: General introduction to pure phenomenology.* Evanston, IL: Northwestern University Press.

Hymes, D. (1982). What is ethnography? In P. Gilmore & A. A. Glatthorn (Eds.), *Children in and out of school: Ethnography and education* (pp. 21–32). Washington, DC: Center for Applied Linguistics.

Iacobucci, D. (1990). Derivation of subgroups from dyadic interactions. *Psychological Bulletin, 107,* 114–132.

Jackson, D. N. (1984). *Personality Research Form manual* (3rd ed.). Port Huron, MI: Research Psychologists Press.

Jagacinski, C. M., & Nicholls, J. G. (1990). Reducing effort to protect perceived ability: "They'd do it but I wouldn't." *Journal of Educational Psychology, 82,* 15–21.

James, W. (1983). *The principles of psychology.* Cambridge, MA: Harvard University Press.

Jensen, A. R. (1984). Test validity: g versus the specificity doctrine. *Journal of Social and Biological Structures, 7,* 93–118.

Johnson, S. M., & Bolstad, O. D. (1973). Methodological issues in naturalistic observation: Some problems and solutions for field research. In L. A. Hamerlynck, L. C. Handy, & E. J. Marsh (Eds.), *Behavioural change: Methodology, concepts, practice* (pp. 7–67). Champaign, IL: Research Press.

Johnston, H. (2002). Verification and proof in frame and discourse analysis. In B. Klandermans & S. Staggenborg (Eds.), *Methods of social movement research* (pp. 62–91). Minneapolis: University of Minnesota Press.

Joint Committee on Standards for Educational and Psychological Testing. (1999). *Standards for educational and psychological testing.* Washington, DC: American Educational Research Association.

Jonassen, D. H., Tessmer, M., & Hannum, W. H. (1999). *Task analysis methods for instructional design.* Mahwah, NJ: Erlbaum.

Juvonen, J., & Graham, S. (2001). *Peer harassment in school: The plight of the vulnerable and victimized.* New York: Guilford.

Kalton, G., Collins, M., & Brook, L. (1978). Experiments in wording opinion questions. *Journal of the Royal Statistical Society Series C, 27,* 149–161.

Kalton, G., Roberts, J., & Holt, D. (1980). The effects of offering a middle response option with opinion questions. *Statistician, 29,* 11–24.

Kane, M. T. (1982). A sampling model for validity. *Applied Psychological Measurement, 6,* 125–160.

Kede, M. B., & Fokianos, K. (2002). *Regression models for time-series analysis.* New York: Wiley.

Kelley, D. L. (1999). *Measurement made accessible: A research approach using qualitative, quantitative, and quality improvement methods.* Thousand Oaks, CA: Sage.

Kelly, G. (1955). *The psychology of personal constructs.* New York: Norton.

Kerlinger, F. N., & Lee, H. B. (2000). *Foundations of behavioral research* (4th ed.). Stamford, CT: Wadsworth.

Kingston, N. M., & Dorans, N.J. (1985). The analysis of item-ability regressions: An exploratory IRT model fit tool. *Applied Psychological Measurement, 9,* 281–288.

Klandermans, B., & Staggenborg, S. (Eds.). (2002). *Methods of social movement research.* Minneapolis: University of Minnesota Press.

Kohlberg, L. (1969). Stage and sequence: The cognitive developmental approach to socialization. In D. A. Goslin (Ed.), *Handbook of socialization theory and research* (pp. 347–480). Chicago: Rand McNally.

Krantz, D. H., Luce, R. D., Suppes, P., & Tversky, A. (1971). *Foundations of measurement* (Vol. 1). San Diego, CA: Academic Press.

Krippendorff, K. (1980). *Content analysis: An introduction to its methodology.* Beverly Hills, CA: Sage.

Krosnick, J. A., & Schuman, H. (1988). Attitude intensity, importance, and certainty and susceptibility to response effects. *Journal of Personality and Social Psychology, 54,* 940–952.

Kubiszyn, T., & Borich, G. D. (2002). *Educational testing and measurement* (7th ed.). New York: Wiley.

Kuhn, D. (1992). Thinking as argument. *Harvard Educational Review, 62,* 155–178.

Kuhn, T. S. (1968). A function for thought experiments. *Ontario Journal of Educational Research, 10,* 211–231.

Kuhn, T. S. (1970). *The structure of scientific revolutions* (2nd ed.). Chicago: University of Chicago Press.

Kurzman, C. (1991). Convincing sociologists: Values and interests in the sociology of knowledge. In M. Burawoy, A. Burton, A. A. Ferguson, K. J. Fox, J. Gamson, N. Gartrell, L. Hurst, C. Kursman, L. Salzinger, J. Schiffman, & S. Ui (Eds.), *Ethnography unbound: Power and resistance in the modern metropolis* (pp. 250–268). Berkeley, CA: University of California Press.

Lacan, J. (1979). *Four fundamental concepts of psychoanalysis.* Harmondsworth: Penguin.

Lacey, J. I., & Lacey, B. C. (1962). The law of initial value in the longitudinal study of autonomic constitution: Reproducibility of autonomic responses and response patterns over a four-year interval. In W. M. Wolf (Ed.), *Rhythmic functions in the living system. Annals of the New York Academy of Science, 98,* 1257–1290.

Lamiell, J. T. (1987). *The psychology of personality: An epistemological inquiry.* New York: Columbia University Press.

Lamiell, J. T. (1997). Individuals and the differences between them. In R. Hogan, J. Johnson, & S. Briggs (Eds.), *Handbook of personality psychology* (pp. 117–141). San Diego, CA: Academic Press.

Larsen, G. Y. (1977). Methodology in developmental psychology: An examination of research on Piagetian theory. *Child Development, 48,* 1160–1166.

Lau, S., Nicholls, J. G., Thorkildsen, T. A., & Patashnick, M. (2000). Chinese and American adolescents' perceptions of the purposes of education and beliefs about the world of work. *Social Behavior and Personality, 28,* 73–90.

Laumann, E. O., Marsden, P. V., & Prensky, D. (1989). The boundary specification problem in network analysis. In L. C. Freeman, D. R. White, & A. K. Romney (Eds.), *Research methods in social network analysis* (pp. 61–87). Fairfax, VA: George Mason University Press.

Lerner, R. M. (1996). Relative plasticity, integration, temporality, and diversity in human development: A developmental-contextual perspective about theory, process, and method. *Developmental Psychology, 32,* 781–786.

Levine, H. G., Gallimore, R., Weisner, T., & Turner, J. L. (1980). Teaching participant-observational methods: A skills-building approach. *Anthropology and Education Quarterly, 11,* 38–54.

Levinson, D. J., Darrow, C. N., Klein, E. B., Levinson, M. H., & McKee, B. (1978). *The seasons of a man's life.* New York: Random House.

Likert, R. (1932). A technique for the measurement of attitudes. *Archives of Psychology, 140,* 5–53.

Likert, R., Roslow, S., & Murphy, G. (1934). A simple and reliable method of scoring the Thurstone attitude scales. *Journal of Social Psychology, 5,* 228–238.

Lin, L. I-K. (1989). A concordance correlation coefficient to evaluate reproducibility. *Biometrics, 45,* 255–268.

Little, T. D., Schnabel, K. U., & Baumert, J. (Eds.). (2000). *Modeling longitudinal and multilevel data: Practical issues, applied approaches, and specific examples.* Mahwah, NJ: Erlbaum.

Long, S. (1992). *A structural analysis of small groups.* New York: Routledge.

Looft, W. R. (1973). Socialization and personality throughout the lifespan: An examination of contemporary psychological approaches. In P. B. Baltes & K. W. Schaie (Eds.), *Life-span developmental psychology: Personality and socialization* (pp. 25–52). New York: Academic Press.

Lord, F. M. (1952). The relationship of the reliability of multiple-choice items to the distribution of item difficulties. *Psychometrika, 18,* 181–194.

Lord, F. M. (1980). *Applications of item-response theory to practical testing problems.* Hillsdale, NJ: Erlbaum.

Lord, F. M., & Novick, M. (1968). *The statistical theory of mental test scores.* Reading, MA: Addison-Wesley.

Lorrain, F., & White, H. C. (1971). Structural equivalence of individuals in social networks. *Journal of Mathematical Sociology, 1,* 49–80.

Lowman, R. L. (1985). What is clinical method? In D. N. Berg & K. K. Smith (Eds.), *Exploring clinical methods for social research* (pp. 173–187). Beverly Hills, CA: Sage.

Luciana, M., & Nelson, C. A. (2002). Assessment of neuropsychological function through use of the Cambridge Neuropsychological Testing Automated Battery: Performance in 4- to 12-year-old children. *Developmental Neuropsychology, 22,* 595–624.

Maassen, G. H., van der Linden, J. L., Goossens, F. A., & Bokhorst, J. (2000). A ratings-based approach to two-dimensional sociometric status determination. In A. H. N. Cillessen & W. M. Bukowski (Eds.), *Recent advances in the measurement of acceptance and rejection in the peer system* (pp. 55–73). San Francisco, CA: Jossey-Bass.

Madigan, R., Johnson, S., & Linton, P. (1995). The language of psychology: APA style as epistemology. *American Psychologist, 50,* 428–436.

Magnusson, D., Bergman, L. R., Rudinger, G., & Torestad, B. (1994). *Problems and methods in longitudinal research: Stability and change.* New York: Cambridge University Press.

Magnusson, D., & Cesaer, P., (1993). *Longitudinal research on individual development: Present status and future perspectives.* New York: Cambridge University Press.

Malinowski, B. (1922). *Argonauts of the Western Pacific.* New York: E. P. Dutton.

Marcoulides, G. A., & Moustaki, I. (Eds.). (2002). *Latent variable and latent structure models.* Mahwah, NJ: Erlbaum.

Marecek, J., Fine, M., & Kidder, L. (1997). Working between worlds: Qualitative methods and social psychology. *Journal of Social Issues, 53,* 631–644.

Masten, A. S., Morrison, P., & Pellegrini, D. S. (1985). A revised class play method of peer assessment. *Developmental Psychology, 21,* 523–533.

Maxwell, J. A. (1992). Understanding validity in qualitative research. *Harvard Educational Review, 62,* 279–300.

McCall, W. A. (1939). *Measurement.* New York: Macmillan.

McCrae, R. R. (2002). NEO-PI-R data from 36 cultures: Further intercultural comparisons. In R. R. McCrae & J. Allik (Eds.), *The five-factor model of personality across cultures* (pp. 105–126). New York: Kluwer Academic.

McCrae, R. R., & Allik, J. (Eds.). (2002). *The five-factor model of personality across cultures.* New York: Kluwer Academic.

McCrae, R. R., & Costa, P. T., Jr. (1988). Recalled parent-child relations and adult personality. *Journal of Personality, 56,* 417–434.

McCrae, R. R., & Costa, P. T., Jr. (1990). *Personality in adulthood.* New York: Guilford.

McDermott, R. P., & Hood, L. (1982). Institutionalized psychology and the ethnography of schooling. In P. Gilmore & A. A. Glatthorn (Eds.), *Children in and out of school: Ethnography and education* (pp. 232–249). Washington, DC: Center for Applied Linguistics.

McDonald, R. P. (1999). *Test theory: A unified treatment.* Hillsdale, NJ: Erlbaum.

McGhee, P. E. (1974). Cognitive mastery and children's humor. *Psychological Bulletin, 81,* 721–730.

McIver, J. P., & Carmines, E. G. (1981). *Unidimensional scaling.* Beverly Hills, CA: Sage.

McMillan, J. H., & Schumacher, S. (2001). *Research in education: A conceptual introduction* (5th ed.). Boston: Allyn & Bacon.

Meehl, P. E. (1986). Causes and effects of my disturbing little book. *Journal of Personality Assessment, 50,* 370–375.

Mehan, H. (1979). *Learning lessons: Social organization in the classroom.* Cambridge, MA: Harvard University Press.

Mertens, D. M. (1998). *Research methods in education and psychology: Integrating diversity with quantitative and qualitative approaches.* Thousand Oaks, CA: Sage.

Messick, S. (1979). Potential uses of noncognitive measurement in education. *Journal of Educational Psychology, 71,* 281–292.

Messick, S. (1983). Assessment of children. In P. Mussen (Ed.), *Handbook of child psychology: Vol. 1. History, theory, and methods* (4th ed., pp. 477–526). New York: Wiley.

Messick, S. (1993). Validity. In R. L. Linn (Ed.), *Educational measurement* (pp. 13–203). Phoenix, AZ: Oryx.

Miller, S. A. (1998). *Developmental research methods* (2nd ed.). Upper Saddle River, NJ: Prentice-Hall.

Millman, J., & Popham, W. J. (1974). The issue of item and test variance for criterion-referenced tests: A reply. *Journal of Educational Measurement, 11,* 137–138.

Mills, C. N., Potenza, M. T., Fremer, J. J., & Ward, W. C. (Eds.). (2002). *Computer-based testing: Building the foundation for future assessments.* Mahwah, NJ: Erlbaum.

Mishler, E. G. (1986). *Research interviewing: Context and narrative.* Cambridge, MA: Harvard University Press.

Moerman, M. (1988). *Talking culture: Ethnography and conversation analysis.* Philadelphia: University of Pennsylvania Press.

Mokken, R. J. (1979). Cliques, clubs, and clans. *Quality and Quantity, 13,* 161–173.

Montgomery, D.C., Peck, E. A., & Vining, G. G. (2001). *Introduction to linear regression analysis* (3rd ed.). New York: Wiley.

Moreland, K. L., Eyde, L. D., Robertson, G. J., Primoff, E. S., & Most, R. B. (1995). Assessment of test-user qualifications: A research-based measurement procedure. *American Psychologist, 50,* 14–23.

Moreno, J. L. (1934). *Who shall survive? A new approach to the problem of human interrelations.* Washington, DC: Nervous and Mental Disease Publishing.

Moreno, J. L. (1943). Sociometry and the cultural order. *Sociometry, 8,* 268–272.

Moreno, J. L. (1951). *Sociometry, experimental method, and the science of society.* Beacon, NY: Beacon House.

Moreno, J. L. (1953). *Who shall survive? Foundations of sociometry, group psychotherapy, and sociodrama.* Beacon, NY: Beacon House.

Moreno, J. L. (Ed.). (1960). *The sociometry reader.* Glencoe, IL: Free Press.

Morgan, D. L. (1998). *The focus group guidebook.* Thousand Oaks, CA: Sage.

Morris, D. (1977). *Manwatching: A field guide to human behavior.* New York: Abrams.

Morrow, R. A., & Brown, D. D. (1994). *Critical theory and methodology.* Thousand Oaks, CA: Sage.

Mosteller, F. (1951). Remarks on the method of paired comparisons: III. A test of significance for paired comparisons when equal standard deviations and equal correlations are assumed. *Psychometrika, 16,* 207–218.

Myers, I. B., & McCaulley, M. H. (1985). *Manual: A guide to the development and use of the Myers-Briggs Type Indicator.* Palo Alto, CA: Consulting Psychologists Press.

National Commission for the Protection of Human Subjects of Biomedical and Behavioral Research (1979, April) *The belmont report: Ethical principles and guidelines for the protection of human subjects of research.* Retrieved May 16, 2004 from the Office for Human Research Protections website: http://ohrp.osophs.dhhs.gov/humansubjects/guidance/belmont.htm.

Nelson, C. A., Monk, C. S., Lin, J., Carver, L. J., Thomas, K. M., & Truwit, C. L. (2000). Functional neuroanatomy of spatial working memory in children. *Developmental Psychology, 36,* 109–116.

Nesselroade, J., Stigler, S., & Baltex, P. (1980). Regression toward the mean and the study of change. *Psychological Bulletin, 88,* 622–637.

Netemeyer, R. G., Bearsen, W. O., & Sharma, S. (2003). *Scaling procedures: Issues and applications.* Thousand Oaks, CA: Sage.

Neuendorf, K. A. (2002). *The content analysis guidebook.* Thousand Oaks, CA: Sage.

Newcomb, A. F., & Bukowski, W. M. (1983). Social impact and social preference as determinants of children's group status. *Developmental Psychology, 19,* 856–867.

Nicholls, J. G. (1978). The development of the concepts of effort and ability, perception of own attainment, and the understanding that difficult tasks require more ability. *Child Development, 49,* 800–814.

Nicholls, J. G. (1989). *The competitive ethos and democratic education.* Cambridge, MA: Harvard University Press.

Nicholls, J. G. (1990). What is ability and why are we mindful of it? A developmental perspective. In R. J. Sternberg & J. Kolligian, Jr. (Eds.), *Competence considered* (pp. 11–40). New Haven, CT: Yale University Press.

Nicholls, J. G., Cobb, P., Wood, T., Yackel, E., & Patashnick, M. (1990). Assessing students' theories about success in mathematics: Individual and class differences. *Journal for Research in Mathematics Education, 21,* 109–122.

Nicholls, J. G., & Hazzard, S. P. (1993). *Education as adventure: Lessons from the second grade.* New York: Teachers College Press.

Nicholls, J. G., Licht, B. G., & Pearl, R. A. (1982). Some dangers to using personality questionnaires to study personality. *Psychological Bulletin, 92,* 572–580.

Nicholls, J. G., McKenzie, M., & Shufro, J. (1994). Schoolwork, homework, life's work: The experience of students with and without learning disabilities. *Journal of Learning Disabilities, 27,* 562–569.

Nicholls, J. G., Patashnick, M., & Nolen, S. B. (1985). Adolescents' theories of education. *Journal of Educational Psychology, 77,* 683–692.

Nicol, A. M., & Pexman, P. M. (2003). *Displaying your findings: A practical guide for creating figures, posters, and presentations.* Washington, DC: American Psychological Association.

Nolen, S. B. (1988). Reasons for studying: Motivational orientations and study strategies. *Cognition and Instruction, 5,* 269–287.

Nolen, S. B. (2003). Learning environment, motivation, and achievement in high school science. *Journal of Research in Science Teaching, 40,* 347–368

Norris, C. (1982). *Deconstruction: Theory and practice.* New York: Methuen.

Nunnally, J. C., & Bernstein, I. H. (1994). *Psychometric theory* (3rd ed.). New York: McGraw-Hill.

O'Donohue, W., & Mangold, R. (1996). A critical examination of the Ethical Principles of Psychologists and

Code of Conduct. In W. O'Donohue & R. F. Kitchener (Eds.), *The philosophy of psychology* (pp. 371–380). Thousand Oaks, CA: Sage.

Osgood, C. E., Suci, G. J., & Tannenbaum, P. H. (1957). *The measurement of meaning.* Urbana: University of Illinois Press.

Overton, W. F. (1998). Developmental psychology: Philosophy, concepts, and methodology. In W. Damon (Series Ed.) & R. M. Lerner (Vol. Ed.), *Handbook of child psychology: Vol 1. Theoretical models* (5th ed., pp. 107–188). New York: Wiley.

Ozer, D. J. (1985). Correlation and the coefficient of determination. *Psychological Bulletin, 97,* 307–315.

Packer, M. J., & Addison, R. B. (Eds.). (1989). *Entering the circle: Hermeneutic investigation in psychology.* New York: State University of New York Press.

Parten, M. B. (1932). Social participation among preschool children. *Journal of Abnormal Psychology, 27,* 243–269.

Patterson, G. R. (1995). Orderly change in a stable world: The antisocial trait as a chimera. In J. M. Gottman (Ed.), *The analysis of change* (pp. 83–102). Mahwah, NJ: Erlbaum.

Patz, R. J., & Junker, B. W. (1999a). A straightforward approach to Markov Chain Monte Carlo Methods for item-response models. *Journal of Educational and Behavioral Statistics, 24,* 146–178.

Patz, R. J., & Junker, B. W. (1999b). Applications and extensions of MCMC in IRT: Multiple item types, missing data, and rated responses. *Journal of Educational and Behavioral Statistics, 24,* 342–366.

Pearson, K. (1909). On a new method of determining a correlation between a measured character of A and a character of B, of which only the percentage of cases wherein B exceeds (or falls short of) intensity is recorded for each grade of A. *Biometrika, 7,* 96–105.

Pedhazur, E. J. (1982). *Multiple regression in behavioral research: Explanation and prediction.* New York: Holt, Rinehart, & Winston.

Peery, J. (1979). Popular, amiable, isolated, rejected: A reconceptualization of sociometric status in preschool children. *Child Development, 50,* 1231–1234.

Pellegrini, A. D. (1996). *Observing children in their natural worlds: A methodological primer.* Mahwah, NJ: Erlbaum.

Pelto, P., & Pelto, G. (1977). *Anthropological research: The structure of inquiry.* New York: Harcourt Brace.

Pett, M. A., Lackey, N. R., & Sullivan, J. J. (2003). *Making sense of factor analysis: The use of factor analysis for instrument development in health care research.* Thousand Oaks, CA: Sage.

Phillips, N., & Hardy, C. (2002). *Discourse analysis.* Thousand Oaks, CA: Sage.

Piaget, J. (1951). Problems and methods. In J. Piaget, *The child's conception of the world* (pp. 1–32). Savage, MD: Littlefield Adams.

Pike, K. L. (1965). *Language in relation to a unified theory of the structure of human behavior.* The Hague: Mouton.

Popham, W. J. (1999). *Modern educational measurement: Practical guidelines for educational leaders* (3rd ed.). Boston: Allyn & Bacon.

Popham, W. J., & Husek, T. R. (1969). Implications of criterion-referenced measurement. *Journal of Educational Measurement, 6,* 1–9.

Popkewitz, T. S. (1992). Cartesian anxiety, linguistic communism, and reading texts. *Educational Researcher, 21,* 11–15.

Popper, K. (1999). *The logic of scientific discovery.* New York: Routledge.

Popping, R. (2000). *Computer-assisted text analysis.* Thousand Oaks, CA: Sage.

Pritchard, I. A. (1993). Integrity versus misconduct: Learning the difference between right and wrong. *Academic Medicine, 68,* S67-S71.

Pritchard, I. A. (2002). Travelers and trolls: Practitioner research and institutional review boards. *Educational Researcher, 31,* 3–13.

Quigley-Fernandez, B., & Tedeschi, J. T. (1978). The bogus pipeline as lie detector: Two validity studies. *Journal of Personality and Social Psychology, 36,* 247–256.

Rabinowitz, V. C., & Weseen, S. (1997). Elu(ci)d(at)ing epistemological impasses: Reviewing the qualitative/quantitative debates in psychology. *Journal of Social Issues, 53,* 605–630.

Rasch, G. (1966). An item analysis which takes individual differences into account. *British Journal of Mathematical and Statistical Psychology, 19,* 49–57.

Raudenbush, S. W. (1995). Hierarchical linear models to study the effects of social context on development. In J. M. Gottman (Ed.), *The analysis of change* (pp. 165–202). Mahwah, NJ: Erlbaum.

Rawls, J. (1972). *A theory of justice.* Cambridge, MA: Harvard University Press.

Raykov, T., & Marcoulides, G. A. (2000). *A first course in structural equation modeling.* Mahwah, NJ: Erlbaum.

Roberts, C. (Ed.). (1997). *Text analysis for the social sciences: Methods for drawing statistical inferences from texts and transcripts.* Hillsdale, NJ: Erlbaum.

Rogosa, D. (1995). Myths and methods: 'Myths about longitudinal research' plus supplemental questions. In J. M. Gottman (Ed.), *The analysis of change* (pp. 3–66). Mahwah, NJ: Erlbaum.

Rosenbaum, B. L. (1973). Attitude toward invasion of privacy in the personnel selection process and job applicant demographic and personality correlates. *Journal of Applied Psychology, 58,* 333–338.

Rosenblum, L. (1978). The creation of a behavioral taxonomy. In G. P. Sackett (Ed.), *Observing behavior: Vol. 2. Data collection and analysis methods* (pp. 15–24). Baltimore: University Park Press.

Rosenthal, R. (1987). *Judgment studies: Design, analysis, and meta-analysis.* Cambridge, NJ: Cambridge University Press.

Rubin, D. B. (1980). Using empirical Bayes techniques in the law school validity studies. *Journal of the American Statistical Association, 75,* 801–816.

Sackett, G. (1978). *Observing behavior.* Baltimore: University Park Press.

Saffir, M. A. (1937). A comparative study of scales constructed by three psychophysical methods. *Psychometrika, 2,* 179–198.

Sales, B. D., & Folkman, S. (Eds.). (2000). *Ethics in research with human subjects.* Washington, DC: American Psychological Association.

Sands, W. A., Waters, B. K., & McBride, J. R. (Eds.). (1997). *Computerized adaptive testing: From inquiry to operation.* Washington, DC: American Psychological Association.

Sattler, J. M. (2001). *Assessment of children: Behavioral and clinical applications* (4th ed.). San Diego, CA: J. M. Sattler.

Sattler, J. M. (2001). *Assessment of children: Cognitive applications* (4th ed.). San Diego, CA: J. M. Sattler.

Schraagen, J. M., Chipman, S. F., Shalin, V. J. (2000). *Cognitive task analysis.* Mahwah, NJ: Erlbaum.

Schrag, F. (1992a). In defense of positivist research paradigms. *Educational Researcher, 21,* 5–8.

Schrag, F. (1992b). Is there light at the end of this tunnel? *Educational Researcher, 21,* 16–17.

Schuman, H., & Ludwig, J. (1983). The norm of even-handedness in surveys as in life. *American Sociological Review, 48,* 112–120.

Schuman, H., & Presser, S. (1981). *Questions and answers in attitude survey: Experiments on question form, wording, and context.* San Diego, CA: Academic Press.

Schwartz, N., & Strack, F. (1991). Context effects in attitude surveys: Applying cognitive theory to social research. In W. Stroebe & M. Hewstone (Eds.), *European review of social psychology* (Vol. 2, pp. 31–50). Chichester, England: Wiley.

Scott, W. A. (1955). Reliability of content analysis: The case of nominal scale coding. *Public Opinion Quarterly, 19,* 321–325.

Seber, G. A. F., & Wild, C. J. (2003). *Nonlinear regression.* New York: Wiley.

Shepard, L. A. (1982). Definitions of bias. In R. A. Berk (Ed.), *Handbook of methods for detecting item bias* (pp. 9–30). Baltimore: Johns Hopkins University Press.

Shepherd, A. (2000). *Hierarchical task analysis.* New York: Taylor & Francis.

Shweder, R. A. (1991). *Thinking through cultures: Expeditions in cultural psychology.* Cambridge, MA: Harvard University Press.

Sieber, J. E. (1992). *Planning ethically responsible research: A guide for students and internal review boards. Applied social research methods series: Vol. 31.* Thousand Oaks, CA: Sage.

Sigel, I. E. (1974). When do we know what a child knows? *Human Development, 17,* 201–217.

Sijtsma, K., & Molenaar, I. W. (2002). *Introduction to nonparametric item response theory.* Thousand Oaks, CA: Sage.

Simon, H. A. (1957). *Models of man.* New York: Wiley.

Slater, P. E. (1966). *Microcosm: Structural, psychological and religious evolution in groups.* New York: Wiley.

Smith, H. W. (1975). *Strategies of social research: The methodological imagination.* London: Prentice-Hall.

Snow, D. A. & Trom, D. (2002). The case study and the study of social movements. In B. Klandermans & S. Staggenborg (Eds.), *Methods of social movement research* (pp. 146–172). Minneapolis: University of Minnesota Press.

Society for Research in Child Development. (1990). SRCD ethical standards for research with children. *SRCD Newsletter,* 5–6.

Spearman, C. (1904). The proof and measurement of association between two things. *American Journal of Psychology, 15,* 72–101.

Spearman, C. (1923). *The nature of "intelligence" and the principles of cognition.* London: Macmillan.

Sperber, D., & Wilson, D. (1995). *Relevance: Communication and cognition* (2nd ed.). Malden, MA: Blackwell.

Steiger, J. H. (1980). Tests for comparing elements of a correlation matrix. *Psychological Bulletin, 87,* 245–251.

Steinberg, L., Thissen, D., & Wainer, H. (2000). Validity. In H. Wainer (Ed.), *Computerized adaptive testing: A primer* (2nd ed., pp. 185–230). Mahwah, NJ: Erlbaum.

Sternberg, R. J. (1985). *Beyond IQ: A triarchic theory of human intelligence.* New York: Cambridge University Press.

Sternberg, R. J. (1990). Prototypes of competence and incompetence. In R. J. Sternberg & J. Kolligian, Jr. (Eds.), *Competence considered* (pp. 117–145). New Haven, CT: Yale University Press.

Sternberg, R. J., & Berg, C. A. (Eds.). (1992). *Intellectual development.* New York: Cambridge University Press.

Stevens, J. (2001). *Applied multivariate statistics for the social sciences* (4th ed.). Hillsdale, NJ: Erlbaum.

Stevens, S. S. (1956). The direct estimation of sensory magnitudes—loudness. *American Journal of Psychology, 69,* 1–25.

Stevens, S. S., & Galanter, E. H. (1957). Ratio scales and category scales for a dozen perceptual continua. *Journal of Experimental Psychology, 54,* 377–411.

Stoolmiller, M., & Bank, L. (1995). Autoregressive effects in structural equation models: We see some problems. In J. M. Gottman (Ed.), *The analysis of change* (pp. 261–278). Mahwah, NJ: Erlbaum.

Strike, K. A., Anderson, M. S., Curren, R., van Geel, T., Pritchard, I., & Robertson, E. (2002). *Ethical standards of the American Educational Research Association: Cases and commentary.* Washington, DC: AERA.

Subkoviak, M. J. (1984). Estimating reliability of mastery-nonmastery classifications. In R. A. Berk (Ed.), *A guide to criterion-referenced test construction* (pp. 267–291). Baltimore: Johns Hopkins University Press.

Suchman, E. A. (1950). The intensity component in attitude and opinion research. In S. A. Stouffer, L. Guttman, E. A. Suchman, P. F. Lazarsfeld, S. A. Star, & J. A. Clausen (Eds.), *Measurement and prediction* (pp. 213–276). Princeton, NJ: Princeton University Press.

Suen, H. K. (1988). Agreement, reliability, accuracy, and validity: Toward a clarification. *Behavioral Assessment, 10,* 343–366.

Suen, H. K. (1990). *Principles of test theories.* Hillsdale, NJ: Erlbaum.

Suppes, P., & Zinnes, J. L. (1963). Basic measurement theory. In R. D. Luce, R. R. Bush, & E. Galanter (Eds.), *Handbook of mathematical psychology* (Vol. 1, pp. 1–76). New York: Wiley.

Swann, W. B., Jr. (1983). Self-verification: Bringing social reality into harmony with the self. In J. Suls & A. G. Greenwald (Eds.), *Psychological perspectives on the self* (Vol. 2, pp. 33–66). Hillsdale, NJ: Erlbaum.

Tannen, D. (Ed.). (1993). *Framing discourse.* New York: Oxford University Press.

Taplin, P. S., & Reid, J. B. (1973). Effects of instructional set and experimenter influence on observer reliability. *Child Development, 44,* 547–554.

Taylor, C., & Nolen, S. B. (2005). *Classroom assessment: Supporting teaching and learning in real classrooms.* Upper Saddle River, NJ: Pearson Education.

Terry, R. (2000). Recent advances in measurement theory and the use of sociometric techniques. In A. H. N. Cillessen & W. M. Bukowski (Eds.), *Recent advances in the measurement of acceptance and rejection in the peer system* (pp. 27–53). San Francisco, CA: Jossey-Bass.

Thelen, E., & Smith, L. B. (1998). Dynamic systems theories. In W. Damon & R. M. Lerner (Eds.), *Handbook of child psychology: Vol. 1. Theoretical models of human development* (5th ed., pp. 563–634). New York: Wiley.

Thissen, D. (2000). Reliability and measurement precision. In H. Wainer (Ed.), *Computerized adaptive testing: A primer* (2nd ed., pp. 159–184). Mahwah, NJ: Erlbaum.

Thissen, D., & Mislevy, R. J. (2000). Testing algorithms. In H. Wainer (Ed.), *Computerized adaptive testing: A primer* (2nd ed., pp. 101–134). Mahwah, NJ: Erlbaum.

Thompson, B. (2002). *Score reliability: Contemporary thinking on reliability issues.* Thousand Oaks, CA: Sage.

Thorkildsen, T. A. (1988). Theories of education among academically able adolescents. *Contemporary Educational Psychology, 13,* 323–330.

Thorkildsen, T. A. (1989a). Justice in the classroom: The student's view. *Child Development, 60,* 323–334.

Thorkildsen, T. A. (1989b). Pluralism in children's reasoning about social justice. *Child Development, 60,* 965–972.

Thorkildsen, T. A. (1991). Defining social goods and distributing them fairly: The development of conceptions of fair testing practices. *Child Development, 62,* 852–862.

Thorkildsen, T. A. (1993). Those who can, tutor: High ability students' conceptions of fair ways to organize learning. *Journal of Educational Psychology, 85,* 182–190.

Thorkildsen, T. A. (2000). The way tests teach: Children's theories of how much testing is fair in school. In M. Leicester, C. Modgil, & S. Modgil (Eds.), *Education, culture, and values: Vol. III. Classroom issues: Practice, pedagogy, and curriculum* (pp. 61–79). London: Falmer.

Thorkildsen, T. A., & Nicholls, J. G. (1998). Fifth graders' achievement orientations and beliefs: Individual and classroom difference. *Journal of Educational Psychology, 90,* 179–201.

Thorkildsen, T. A., & Nicholls, J. G. (with Bates, A., Brankis, N., & DeBolt, T.). (2002). *Motivation and the struggle to learn: Responding to fractured experience.* Boston: Allyn & Bacon.

Thorkildsen, T. A., Nolen, S. B., & Fournier, J. (1994). What is fair? Children's critiques of practices that influence motivation. *Journal of Educational Psychology, 86,* 475–486.

Thorkildsen, T. A., & Schmahl, C. (1997). Conceptions of fair learning practices among low-income African American and Latin American Children: Acknowledging diversity. *Journal of Educational Psychology, 89,* 719–727.

Thorkildsen, T. A., & White-McNulty, L. (2002). Developing conceptions of fair contest procedures and the differentiation of skill and luck. *Journal of Educational Psychology, 94,* 316–326.

Thorndike, E. L. (1925). *The measurement of intelligence.* New York: Teachers College, Columbia University.

Thorndike, R. M. (1997). *Measurement and evaluation in psychology and education* (6th ed.). Columbus, OH: Merrill.

Thurstone, L. L. (1927a). A law of comparative judgment. *Psychological Review, 34,* 273–286.

Thurstone, L. L. (1927b). Psychophysical analysis. *American Journal of Psychology, 38,* 368–389.

Thurstone, L. L. (1928). Attitudes can be measured. *American Journal of Sociology, 33,* 529–554.

Thurstone, L. L. (1938). *Primary mental abilities.* Chicago: University of Chicago Press.

Thurstone, L. L. (1947). *Multiple factor analysis.* Chicago: University of Chicago Press.

Thurstone, L. L., & Chave, E. J. (1929). *The measurement of attitude.* Chicago: University of Chicago Press.

Tracey, W. R., Flynn, E. B., & Legere, C. L. (1966). *The development of instructional systems.* Fort Devens, MA: U.S. Army Security Agency Training Center.

Turner, V. (1980). Social dramas and stories about them. *Critical Inquiry, 7,* 141–168.

Turner, V. W., & Bruner, E. M. (Eds.). (1986). *The anthropology of experience.* Urbana: University of Illinois Press.

Tyler, L. E. (1995). The challenge of diversity. In D. Lubinski & R. V. Dawis (Eds.), *Assessing individual differences in human behavior: New concepts, methods, and findings.* Palo Alto, CA: Davies-Black.

Vasta, R. (Ed.). (1982). *Strategies and techniques for child study.* New York: Academic Press.

von Eye, A., & Niedermeier, K. E. (1999). *Statistical analysis of longitudinal categorical data in the social and behavioral sciences: An introduction with computer illustrations.* Mahwah, NJ: Erlbaum.

Wainer, H. (with Dorans, N.J., Eignor, D., Flaugher, R., Green, B. F., Mislevy, R. J., Steinberg, L., & Thissen, D.). (2000). *Computerized adaptive testing: A primer* (2nd ed.). Mahwah, NJ: Erlbaum.

Wainer, H., & Mislevy, R. J. (2000). Item-response theory, item calibration, and proficiency estimation. In H. Wainer (Ed.), *Computerized adaptive testing: A primer* (2nd ed., pp. 61–100.) Mahwah, NJ: Erlbaum.

Walzer, M. (1983). *Spheres of justice: A defense of pluralism and equality.* New York: Basic Books.

Wasserman, S., & Faust, K. (1994). *Social network analysis: Methods and applications.* New York: Cambridge University Press.

Watson, M. W., & Fischer, K. W. (1980). Development of social roles in elicited and spontaneous behavior during the preschool years. *Developmental Psychology, 16,* 483–494.

Wax, R. H. (1971). *Doing fieldwork: Warnings and advice.* Chicago: University of Chicago Press.

Wechsler, D. (1939). *The measurement of adult intelligence.* Baltimore: Williams and Wilkins.

West, S. G., & Finch, J. F. (1997). Personality measurement: Reliability and validity issues. In R. Hogan, J. Johnson, & S. Briggs (Eds.), *Handbook of personality psychology* (pp. 143–195). San Diego, CA: Academic Press.

White, H. C., Boorman, S. A., & Breiger, R. L. (1976). Social structure from multiple networks: I. Blockmodels of roles and positions. *American Journal of Sociology, 81,* 730–779.

White, R. W. (1975). *Lives in progress* (3rd ed.). New York: Holt, Rinehart, & Winston.

White-McNulty, L. (2002). *An examination of adolescents' motivation for homework.* Doctoral dissertation, University of Illinois at Chicago.

Wilder, J. (1957). The law of initial value in neurology and psychiatry. *Journal of Nervous and Mental Disease, 125,* 73–86.

Willett, J. B., & Singer, J. D. (1995). Investigating onset, cessation, relapse, and recovery: Using discrete-time survival analysis to examine the occurrence and timing of critical events. In J. M. Gottman (Ed.), *The analysis of change* (pp. 203–260). Mahwah, NJ: Erlbaum.

Wodak, R., & Meyer, M. (Eds.). (2002). *Methods of critical discourse analysis.* Thousand Oaks, CA: Sage.

Wodak, R., Titscher, S., Meyer, M., & Vetter, E. (2000). *Methods of text and discourse analysis.* Thousand Oaks, CA: Sage.

Wohlwill, J. F. (1973). *The study of behavioral development.* New York: Academic Press.

Wolcott, H. F. (1990). On seeking—and rejecting—validity in qualitative research. In E. W. Eisner & A. Peshkin (Eds.), *Qualitative inquiry in education: The continuing debate* (pp. 121–152). New York: Teachers College Press.

Wright, B. D. (1999). Fundamental measurement for psychology. In S. E. Embretson & S. L. Hershberger (Eds.), *The new rules of measurement: What every psychologist and educator should know* (pp. 65–104). Mahwah, NJ: Erlbaum.

Youden, W. J. (1998). *Experimentation and measurement.* Mineola, NY: Dover.

Zeiler, R. A., & Caraines, E. G. (1980). *Measurement in the social sciences.* Cambridge, MA: Cambridge University Press.

Zigler, E., Levine, J., & Gould, L. (1967). Cognitive challenge as a factor in children's humor appreciation. *Journal of Personality and Social Psychology, 6,* 332–336.

Zwick, R. (1988). Another look at inter-rater agreement. *Psychological Bulletin, 103,* 374–378.

INDEX